CONSTITUTIONALISING THE EU JUDICIAL SYSTEM

These essays, written in honour of retired ECJ judge Pernilla Lindh, reflect on the development of courts and judging in the EU since the founding of the Union. In particular they focus on recent reforms and proposals aimed at further increasing public confidence and democratic accountability throughout the EU judicial system.

Judge Pernilla Lindh

Constitutionalising the EU Judicial System

Essays in Honour of Pernilla Lindh

Edited by

Pascal Cardonnel
Allan Rosas
and
Nils Wahl

·HART·
PUBLISHING

OXFORD AND PORTLAND, OREGON
2012

Published in the United Kingdom by Hart Publishing Ltd
16C Worcester Place, Oxford, OX1 2JW
Telephone: +44 (0)1865 517530
Fax: +44 (0)1865 510710
E-mail: mail@hartpub.co.uk
Website: http://www.hartpub.co.uk

Published in North America (US and Canada) by
Hart Publishing
c/o International Specialized Book Services
920 NE 58th Avenue, Suite 300
Portland, OR 97213-3786
USA
Tel: +1 503 287 3093 or toll-free: (1) 800 944 6190
Fax: +1 503 280 8832
E-mail: orders@isbs.com
Website: http://www.isbs.com

British Library Cataloguing in Publication Data
Data Available

ISBN: 978-1-84946-336-2

Typeset by Hope Services, Abingdon
Printed and bound in Great Britain by
MPG Books Group Ltd

Preface

This collection of essays commemorates the career of Pernilla Lindh who in October 2011 retired from the Court of Justice after over sixteen years of service in Luxembourg. To the Union Courts, Pernilla brought her *personnalité hors du commun* – to borrow the phrase so aptly coined by President Skouris in his farewell speech – and all the qualities required of a judge: independence, rigour and an acute ability to move from one substantive area of the law to the next with procedural fairness as a guiding compass. For Pernilla is first and foremost a judge. After her studies in Lund, she joined the Swedish judiciary in 1971 where she held a variety of posts from Trollhättan to Stockholm where she worked at the Court of Appeals. In 1982, her career took a different turn as she joined the Ministry for Foreign Affairs as a legal advisor and eventually became Director and then Director General for Legal Affairs. During this time, she was responsible for legal and institutional issues regarding the relationship between Sweden and 'Europe', in particular the launch of the European Economic Area Agreement and subsequently, the accession of Sweden to the European Union. These efforts culminated on 1 January 1995, when Sweden became a Member of the EU, harnessing itself to the rest of the continent and, on the same occasion, sent Pernilla to Luxembourg to serve as the first Swedish judge of the Court of First Instance. After over a decade in the world of diplomacy, she was thus back at the bench. In 2006, she became a judge of the Court of Justice.

During these sixteen years, the European Union has undergone profound changes and the process of constitutionalisation has reached new heights, in particular with the entry into force of the Lisbon Treaty and the Charter of Fundamental Rights. This book addresses the federative nature of the EU judicial system. It explores the role of the Union courts and their dialogue with the national courts of the Member States and other international courts. The authors, largely current or former members or legal secretaries of the Court of Justice and the General Court, with additional contributions from well-known academic experts, focus on three themes which have dominated discussions about the constitutional nature of the EU judicial system: its architecture, the notions of Union citizenship and fundamental rights, and procedure and due process; themes which are dear to Pernilla's heart.

Allan Rosas
Judge, Court of Justice
Nils Wahl
Judge, General Court
Pascal Cardonnel
Legal Secretary, Court of Justice

Table of Contents

List of Contributors

Alexander Arabadjiev, Judge of the Court of Justice.

Carl Baudenbacher, President of the EFTA Court, Director of the Institute of European and International Economic Law at the University of St Gallen HSG.

Lars Bay Larsen, Judge of the Court of Justice.

Ulf Bernitz, Professor of European Law, Stockholm University, Jur Dr, Dr jur h c (Copenhagen), MA (Oxon), Senior Associate Fellow, St Hilda's College, University of Oxford.

Jean-Claude Bonichot, Judge of the Court of Justice.

José Narciso Da Cunha Rodrigues, Judge of the Court of Justice.

Gianni De Stefano, Associate, Latham & Watkins (Brussels).

David Edward, Professor Emeritus, University of Edinburgh. Judge of the Court of First Instance (1989–92) and Judge of the Court of Justice (1992–2004).

Anna Falk, Director at the Swedish Ministry for Foreign Affairs, Legal Secretariat, Acting Agent before the Court of Justice of the European Union.

Christer H:son Fallenius, Chairman, Swedish Market Court.

Jörgen Hettne, Senior Researcher and Deputy Head of Agency at the Swedish Institute for European Policy Studies, SIEPS.

Marc Jaeger, President of the General Court.

Martin Johansson, Advokat, Partner, Advokatfirman Vinge, Brussels. Formerly, inter alia, Legal Secretary at the Court of Justice, the General Court and the EFTA Court.

Heidi Kaila, Legal Secretary, Court of Justice.

Koen Lenaerts, Judge and President of Chamber at the Court of Justice, and Professor of European Union Law, Leuven University. Formerly Judge of the Court of First Instance (1989–2003).

Hans Henrik Lidgard, Professor, University of Lund.

Fidelma Macken, Judge of the Supreme Court of Ireland. Judge of the Court of Justice (1999–2004).

Paolo Mengozzi, Advocate General of the Court of Justice, Professor of International Law and Union Law, University of Bologna. Judge of the Court of First Instance (1998–2006).

Sven Norberg, Jur Dr h c Formerly Judge of the EFTA Court; Director of the EU Commission (1995–2005) and Director Legal Affairs, EFTA (1982–93).

Aindrias Ó Caoimh, Judge of the Court of Justice.

Síofra O'Leary, Legal Secretary, Court of Justice and Visiting Professor, College of Europe (Bruges).

Jörg Pirrung, Bonn, Judge of the Court of First Instance of the European Communities (1997–2007), honorary professor at the University of Trier.

Allan Rosas, Judge of the Court of Justice.

Javier Ruiz Calzado, Partner, Latham & Watkins (Brussels), and former Legal Secretary of the Court of First Instance.

Eleanor Sharpston, Advocate General of the Court of Justice.

Vassilios Skouris, President of the Court of Justice.

Olivier Speltdoorn, Legal Secretary, General Court.

Virpi Tiili, Judge of the General Court (1995–2009).

Christiaan Timmermans, Professor of Law, University of Rotterdam. Judge of the Court of Justice (2000–10).

Thomas Von Danwitz, Prof Dr Dr hc, Judge of the Court of Justice.

Table of Cases

EUROPEAN UNION COURTS

Alphabetical

Court of Justice

General Court

Chronological

Court of Justice

General Court

EFTA Court

European Court of Human Rights

List of Abbreviations

CFI	Court of First Instance of the European Communities
EC	European Community
ECHR	Convention for the Protection of Human Rights and Fundamental Freedoms
ECJ	European Court of Justice (Court of Justice of the European Union)
ECR	European Court Reports
ECtHR	European Court of Human Rights
EEA	European Economic Area
EEC	European Economic Community
EFTA	European Free Trade Agreement
EU	European Union
GC	General Court of the European Union
OJ	Official Journal of the European Union
TEC	Treaty establishing the European Community
TEU	Treaty on European Union
TFEU	Treaty on the Functioning of the European Union

Part I

The European Judicial System

1

The Court of Justice of the European Union: A Judiciary in a Constant State of Transformation

VASSILIOS SKOURIS*

INTRODUCTION

PERNILLA LINDH HAS served the administration of justice of the European Union in an exemplary way for more than 16 years. As a member both of the General Court and the Court of Justice (ECJ), she contributed significantly to the development of their jurisprudence. Indeed, it would not be an exaggeration to claim that judgments covering almost the whole range of EU law bear her hallmark. For this reason, in order to contribute to this collective work dedicated to her impressive career, I have chosen to share some considerations of a more general nature on the recent past, the present and the near future of the EU judicial system.

Since it was established in 1952, the ECJ has been able to adapt to the circumstances arising from every step taken towards further European integration. Indeed, it could be argued that historically the Court has become accustomed to changes and reforms. Nevertheless, from this point of view, the last decade was unprecedented since – during this period – the Court was in a constant state of transformation. In the following pages, I will, on the one hand, try to run through this period briefly in order to carry out a preliminary evaluation and, on the other hand, attempt to assess how the Court could meet any foreseeable future challenges.

THE TREATY OF NICE

This period of transformation begins with the adoption and the entry into force of the Treaty of Nice. This Treaty introduced a number of changes into the judicial architecture of the Union as well as several reforms in the organisation

* President of the Court of Justice of the European Union.

and functioning of the ECJ.[1] The former consist in the possibility, on the one hand, of creating specialised courts having jurisdiction to hear and determine at first instance certain classes of action[2] and, on the other hand, to derogate from the 'one judge per Member State' rule as regards the appointment of judges to the Court of First Instance,[3] renamed the 'General Court' by the Treaty of Lisbon in 2009.[4] The latter, concerning the ECJ itself, are summarised in the creation of the Grand Chamber[5] which requires the participation of the presidents of the five-judge chambers,[6] the election of these presidents for a period of 3 years[7] and the possibility of rendering judgments without an opinion of the Advocate General where the Court considers that the case raises no new points of law.[8]

The reforms introduced by the Treaty of Nice had a double objective: to maintain the consistency of the jurisprudence in view of the enlargement, which at that time was imminent, and to improve the efficiency of the European judiciary.[9] Today, there is no doubt that these objectives have been met.

ENLARGEMENTS

The evolution of the ECJ in the post-Nice era has been characterised by two successive enlargements of the European Union, in 2004[10] and 2007[11] respectively, and by the organisational changes that those enlargements entailed for the Court. The arrival of 24 new judges with their Cabinets (12 judges at the ECJ and 12 judges at the General Court), along with the significant increase in the number of staff of the institution, illustrates that, after 2004, the Court changed in a radical way.

At an organisational level, the arrival of the new judges made it necessary to increase the number of judicial panels. There thus exist at the ECJ four chambers of five judges and four chambers of three judges. The General Court, on the other hand, is composed of eight chambers of three judges. At an administrative level,

[1] *cf* G Vandersanden, 'Le système juridictionnel communautaire après Nice' (2003) *Cahiers de droit européen* 3 ff.

[2] See ex-Art 220(2) EC and ex-Art 225a EC, now Art 257 TFEU.

[3] For reasons of coherence and clarity, it is hereinafter referred to as the General Court.

[4] See ex-Art 224(1) EC, now Art 19(2), second sub-para TEU and Art 254(1) TFEU.

[5] See ex-Art 221(2) EC, now Art 251(1) TFEU.

[6] See Art 16(2) of the Statute of the Court of Justice of the European Union.

[7] ibid, Art 16(1).

[8] ibid, Art 20(5).

[9] V Skouris, 'De nouveaux défis pour la Cour de justice dans une Europe élargie' (2008) *ERA Forum* 101.

[10] See Documents concerning the accession of the Czech Republic, the Republic of Estonia, the Republic of Cyprus, the Republic of Latvia, the Republic of Lithuania, the Republic of Hungary, the Republic of Malta, the Republic of Poland, the Republic of Slovenia and the Slovak Republic to the European Union and especially Art 13 of the Act concerning the conditions of accession, [2003] OJ L236/1, 37 and [2003] OJ C227E/1.

[11] See Documents concerning the accession of the Republic of Bulgaria and Romania to the European Union and especially Art 10 of the Protocol concerning the conditions and arrangements for admission, [2005] OJ L157/1, 32.

the staff of the Court currently exceeds 2000 employees[12] and its organisational chart is structured into five directorates-general, ten directorates and 48 units.[13]

Finally, the greatest challenge these enlargements represented for the ECJ was the increase in the number of the official languages of the EU and consequently of potential languages of the procedure. From 110 in the EU-15, the number of language combinations had risen to 462 in 2007. This number will increase to 506 when the derogation measures concerning the Irish language[14] come to an end.[15] Nevertheless, through the adoption of measures both innovative and courageous, the Court managed not only to maintain the translation deadlines, but also to shorten them.

TRANSFER OF COMPETENCES – EUROPEAN UNION CIVIL SERVICE TRIBUNAL

In addition to the changes in the organisation and operation of the Court of Justice introduced by the Treaty of Nice and the aforementioned enlargements, it is worth noting that two reforms in the judicial structure of the European Union have been carried out through the modification of the Statute of the Court of Justice and acts of secondary legislation.

First, in 2004, some of the ECJ's competences were transferred to the General Court. It has thus acquired jurisdiction over certain direct actions for annulment and for failure to act brought by the Member States.[16] It is worth mentioning that the Treaty of Nice has also provided the possibility of transferring to the General Court the competence to hear preliminary references.[17] Since no provisions have been introduced into the Statute in that regard yet, the Court of Justice still has exclusive jurisdiction to render preliminary rulings.

Second, a new judicial panel was established at the ECJ in October 2005. The European legislator made use, for the first time, of the possibility of creating a specialised court introduced by the Treaty of Nice.[18] The European Union Civil Service Tribunal is henceforth given jurisdiction of first instance in any dispute between the Union and its servants.[19] Its decisions are subject to appeal before the General Court. Consequently, the European Union disposes of two courts of

[12] From 2003 to 2011, the number of posts (including the contingency reserve) has increased from 1182 to 2056; see the General Budget of the European Union for the Financial Year 2003, [2003] OJ L54/139 and the General Budget of the European Union for the Financial Year 2011, [2011] OJ L68/I/301.

[13] See the Abridged Organisational Chart of December 2010 in Court of Justice of the European Union, *Annual Report 2010*, 248.

[14] See Art 2(1) of Council Regulation (EC) No 920/2005 of 13 June 2005, [2005] OJ L156/3; Art 1 of Council Regulation (EU) No 1257/2010 of 20 December 2010, [2010] OJ L343/5.

[15] MA Gaudissart, 'Le régime et la pratique linguistiques de la Cour de justice des Communautés européennes' in D Hanf, K Malacek and E Muir (eds), *Langues et construction européenne* (Brussels, PIE Peter Lang, 2010) 147; n 24.

[16] See Art 51(a) of the Statute of the Court of Justice of the European Union.

[17] See ex-Art 225(3) EC, now Art 256(3) TFEU.

[18] See ex-Art 225a EC, now Art 257 TFEU.

[19] See Annex I of the Statute of the Court of Justice of the European Union.

appellate review. Of course, it rests with the Court to ensure the preservation of the unity and consistency of Union law through the extraordinary review procedure.[20] Nevertheless, it is necessary to underline that this procedure does not represent a third degree of jurisdiction, but an exceptional procedure set up following the proposal of the First Advocate General.

WORKING METHODS

Along with the above reforms and changes, the Court has adopted a series of internal measures with regard to its working methods in order to make them more efficient and to reverse the trend of increasing procedural delays. The most important of those measures consists of setting up a more rigorous monitoring system concerning the Court's judicial work as well as the adoption of a stricter approach with regard to the extensions of time limits for submitting pleadings in the context of direct actions and appeals. The considerable effects of these measures are clearly visible in the judicial statistics of the Court which are in continuous improvement.

Finally, reference should be made to the adoption of a more selective policy concerning the publication of decisions in the European Court Reports according to their importance for the development of European law. However, the text of those decisions not published in the Reports will still be accessible to the public via the Court's website in the available languages.

THE TREATY OF LISBON

The above-mentioned observations concern the recent past of the Court of Justice. The present is characterised mainly by the entry into force of the Treaty of Lisbon on 1 December 2009. The judicial system of the European Union was not disrupted by this development since its essential features have remained those defined by the Treaty of Nice.[21] Nonetheless, this does not imply that the entry into force of the Treaty of Lisbon does not constitute a significant challenge for the Court of Justice.

It has to be noted that its jurisdiction now extends to the law of the EU in its entirety, unless the Treaties provide otherwise.[22] Thus, the ECJ is conferred with general jurisdiction to give preliminary rulings in the area of freedom, security and justice, as a result of the disappearance of the pillars, and the repeal by the Treaty of Lisbon of Articles 35 EU and 68 EC which imposed restrictions on its jurisdiction.[23]

[20] ibid, Art 62.

[21] M Dougan, 'The Treaty of Lisbon 2007: Winning Minds, not Hearts' (2008) *CML Rev* 673.

[22] See Art 19 (1) TEU; *cf* K Lenaerts, 'Challenges Facing the European Court of Justice after the Treaty of Lisbon' (2010) *Revista Român de Drept European* 20.

[23] ibid, 25–26.

On the one hand, as regards police and judicial cooperation in criminal matters, the jurisdiction of the ECJ to give preliminary rulings has become obligatory and is no longer subject to a declaration by each Member State recognising that jurisdiction and specifying the national courts that may request a preliminary ruling.[24] Transitional provisions nevertheless provide that such full jurisdiction will not apply until five years after the entry into force of the Treaty of Lisbon.[25]

On the other hand, concerning visas, asylum, immigration and the other policies related to free movement of persons (in particular, judicial cooperation in civil matters as well as recognition and enforcement of judgments), any national court or tribunal – and not just the higher courts – can henceforth request preliminary rulings.[26] Additionally, the Court has jurisdiction to rule on measures taken on grounds of public policy in connection with cross-border controls.[27]

Further, it has to be underlined that the Charter of Fundamental Rights of the European Union becomes a binding legal act with the same legal value as the Treaties.[28] This conversion of the Charter is the logical consequence of the constant evolution of the jurisprudence and the legislation and contributes to the visibility and better protection of fundamental rights within the European Union.

The introduction of a legally binding Bill of Rights for the Union is certainly a very important step forward in the process of EU integration which confirms, deepens and improves its democratic legitimacy. Apart from reaffirming an already existing system of protection of fundamental rights, it contributes to the achievement of a level of transparency, clarity and legal certainty which is of paramount importance in the field of fundamental rights.

Indeed, the Court has already examined the first cases involving a direct application of the provisions of the Charter[29] and its classic legal reasoning in the field of protection of fundamental rights has changed. From now on the Court uses as a starting point the Charter itself[30] and no longer the common constitutional

[24] Repeal of Art 35 EU, except for para 5 of this Art, which is now Art 276 TFEU.

[25] See Art 10 of Protocol No 36 on transitional provisions; *cf* M Dougan, n 21, 682.

[26] Repeal of Art 68(1) EC.

[27] Repeal of Art 68(2) EC.

[28] See Art 6(1) TEU.

[29] For a first analysis of the cases involving a direct application of the provisions of the Charter, see A Rosas and H Kaila, 'L'application de la Charte des droits fondamentaux de l'Union européenne par la Cour de justice: un premier bilan' (2011) *Il diritto dell'Unione Europea* 1.

[30] See, eg Case C-403/09 PPU *Detiček* [2009] ECR I-12193, paras 53 ff; Case C-555/07 *Kücükdeveci* [2010] ECR I-365, para 22; Case C-578/08 *Chakroun* [2010] ECR I-1839, paras 44, 63–65; Joined Cases C-317/08 to C-320/08 *Alassini* [2010] ECR I-2213, para 61, in which the Court invokes not only common constitutional traditions of the Member States and the ECHR but also provisions of the Charter; Joined Cases C-570/07 and C-571/07 *Blanco Pérez and Chao Gómez*, [2010] ECR I-4629, paras 65 –66; Case C-407/08 P *Knauf Gips v Commission*, [2010] ECR I-6375, paras 91 –92; Case C-271/08 *Commission v Germany*, [2010] ECR I-7091, para 37; Case C-409/06 *Winner Wetten*, judgment of 8 September 2010 nyr, para 58; Case C-550/07 P *Akzo Nobel Chemicals and Akcros Chemicals v Commission*, judgment of 14 September 2010 nyr, paras 54, 92; Case C-149/10 *Chatzi*, judgment of 16 September 2010 nyr, paras 38, 39, 45, 63; Case C-400/10 PPU *McB*, judgment of 5 October 2010 nyr, paras 50 ff; Case C-162/09 *Lassal*, judgment of 7 October 2010 nyr, para 29; Case C-243/09 *Fuß*, judgment of 14 October 2010 nyr, para 66; Joined Cases C-92/09 and C-93/09 *Volker and Markus Schecke*, judgment of 9 November 2010 nyr, paras 45 ff, 76, 80, 86; Case C-232/09 *Danosa*, judgment of 11 November 2010 nyr, para 71; Case

traditions and the European Convention on Human Rights (ECHR).[31] According to this new approach, the Court first analyses the rights guaranteed by the Charter, applies them based on its own jurisprudence as well as the relevant jurisprudence of the European Court of Human Rights (ECtHR),[32] and refers lastly, and only if necessary, to the provisions of the Convention,[33] which until now constituted the primary source of reference.[34]

However, the conversion of the Charter into a binding legal text does not resolve all problems relating to the effective protection of fundamental rights. A multitude of sources of law with overlapping fields of application (national Constitutions, the Charter of Fundamental Rights, the ECHR) can be the source of confusion for private individuals, lawyers and judges. The range of protected rights and the level of protection can be different from one text to another and the risk of conflicting case law between the ECJ on the one hand and national supreme courts and the ECtHR on the other is always present.

Nevertheless, it must be underlined that these problems are rare and they are certainly not the result of the transformation of the Charter's legal character. The evolution of fundamental rights protection in the European Union has clearly demonstrated that such difficulties are not insurmountable.[35] The harmonisation of systems of protection of those rights and sustained convergence efforts contribute to the reduction and the elimination of conflicting solutions. The cooperation between the Courts responsible for the protection of fundamental rights and, in particular, between the ECJ and the ECtHR will fill many of these gaps.

In any event, the Treaty of Lisbon expressly provides that the Union accedes to the ECHR.[36] The first stage of this process has already been achieved and the Council of the European Union agreed on giving a negotiation mandate to the

C-145/09 *Tsakouridis*, judgment of 23 November 2010 nyr, para 52; Case C-279/09 *DEB Deutsche Energiehandels- und Beratungsgesellschaft mbH*, judgment of 22 December 2010 nyr, para 30; Joined Cases C-444/09 and C-456/09 *Gavieiro Gavieiro and Iglesias Torres*, judgment of 22 December 2010 nyr, para 75; Case C-491/10 PPU *Aguirre Zarraga*, judgment of 22 December 2010 nyr, paras 60 ff; Case C-236/09 *Association Belge des Consommateurs Test-Achats e a*, judgment of 1 March 2011 nyr, paras 17, 30 ff; Case C-221/09 *AJD Tuna*, judgment of 17 March 2011 nyr, paras 48 ff; Case C-372/09 *Penarroja*, judgment of 17 March 2011 nyr, para 62; Case C-352/09 P *ThyssenKrupp Nirosta*, judgment of 29 March 2011 nyr, para 80; Case C-434/09 *McCarthy*, judgment of 5 May 2011 nyr, para 27; Case C-543/09 *Deutsche Telekom*, judgment of 5 May 2011 nyr, paras 49 ff; Case C-391/09 *Runevič-Vardyn and Wardyn*, judgment of 12 May 2011 nyr, paras 66 ff, 86 ff.

[31] See, eg Case C-144/04 *Mangold* [2005] ECR I-9981, para 74.

[32] See, eg *Alassini*, n 30 above, para 63; *McB*, n 30 above, paras 53 ff; *Volker and Markus Schecke*, n 30 above, paras 52, 59, 72, 87; *Tsakouridis*, n 30 above, para 52.

[33] See, eg *Chakroun*, n 30 above, paras 44, 58, 62, 65; *Alassini*, n 30 above, paras 31, 61; *McB*, n 30 above, para 53; *Volker and Markus Schecke*, n 30 above, paras 44, 51, 52, 59; *Runevič-Vardyn and Wardyn*, n 30 above, paras 66, 89.

[34] J Kokott and C Sobotta, 'The Charter of Fundamental Rights of the European Union after Lisbon' (2010) 6 *EUI Working Paper AEL* 2.

[35] V Skouris, 'Introducing a Binding Bill of Rights for the European Union – Can Three Parallel Systems of Protection of Fundamental Rights Coexist Harmoniously?' in A Blankenagel, I Pernice and H Schulze-Fielitz (eds), *Verfassung im Diskurs der Welt – Liber Amicorum für Peter Häberle zum siebzigsten Geburtstag* (Tübingen, Mohr Siebeck, 2004) 273.

[36] See Art 6 (2) TEU.

European Commission.[37] Meanwhile, the negotiations within the Council of Europe came to an end with ad hoc terms of reference concerning the accession of the EU to the ECHR given to the Steering Committee for Human Rights (CCDH) by the Ministers' Deputies.[38] The official talks on the European Union's accession to the ECHR started on 7 July 2010[39] and are expected to conclude shortly.

As the ECJ points out in its discussion document on certain aspects of the accession of the European Union to the ECHR, published on 5 May 2010, the accession of the Union, as a regional integration organisation, is subject to specific conditions which are different from those laid down for the accession of a State. In accordance with Article 6 TEU, the accession 'shall not affect the Union's competences as defined in the Treaties', and, as stated in Protocol No 8 annexed to the Treaties, the agreement on the accession 'shall make provision for preserving the specific characteristics of the Union and Union law'.

Finally, I would like to briefly point out that in the sensitive area of common foreign and security policy (CFSP), the Court, by way of exception, has jurisdiction, on the one hand, to monitor the delimitation of the Union's competences and the CFSP, the implementation of which must not affect the exercise of the Union's competences or the powers of the institutions in respect of the exercise of the exclusive and shared competences of the Union,[40] and, on the other hand, over actions for annulment brought against decisions providing restrictive measures against natural or legal persons adopted by the Council in connection, for example, with the freezing of assets of terrorism suspects.[41] It should be noted that the number of those particular cases, which are brought at first instance before the General Court, has increased significantly in the last months due to the recent events in the Arab world.

This extension of jurisdiction of the Court can only entail the increase in the number of cases brought before it. In this regard, some recent statistics are particularly telling. In 2010, the number of references for a preliminary ruling submitted has increased, compared to 2009, by about 30 per cent.[42] A first analysis of the type of preliminary rulings requested shows that this increase is not yet due to the entry into force of the Treaty of Lisbon but rather due to the two successive enlargements. However, taking into account the effect of the entry into force of the Treaty of Lisbon, it cannot be excluded that, in the near future, more than 500 requests for a preliminary ruling will be submitted to the Court each year.

Moreover, the possibility of a significant increase in the number of cases brought before the courts of the EU is also related to the important procedural reforms introduced by the Treaty of Lisbon. The most important of these consist, first, in easing the conditions for the admissibility of actions brought by individuals against

[37] See Press Release of the Council of the European Union of 3/4 June 2010, 10630/1/10 Rev 1.
[38] See Document of the Council of Europe of 3 June 2010, CDDH(2010)008.
[39] See Press Release of the European Commission of 7 July 2010, IP/10/906.
[40] See Art 24(1), second sub-para TEU, Art 40 TEU and Art 275 TFEU.
[41] See Art 275(2) TFEU.
[42] See Court of Justice of the European Union, *Annual Report 2010* 102.

regulatory acts of the institutions, bodies, offices and agencies of the EU. In particular, natural or legal persons may henceforth bring proceedings against a regulatory act if they are directly affected by it and if it does not entail implementing measures.[43] Consequently, they no longer have to demonstrate that they are individually concerned.

Second, the Treaty of Lisbon strengthens the system of pecuniary sanctions (lump sum and/or periodic penalty payment) in the event of non-compliance with a judgment establishing a failure of a Member State to fulfill obligations.[44] In particular, where a Member State fails to notify national measures transposing a directive to the Commission, it is henceforth possible for the Court to impose pecuniary sanctions in the initial judgment establishing a failure to fulfill obligations.[45]

Apart from the above, I would also like to refer to the element of urgency characterising certain cases arising within the context of the area of liberty, security and justice. It is well known that a new procedure, called the urgent preliminary ruling procedure, was introduced in the texts governing the proceedings before the Court,[46] with the aim of expediting the handling of those cases.[47]

The principal features of the urgent preliminary ruling procedure are apparent from its differences with the ordinary and accelerated preliminary ruling procedures. First, the written procedure is limited to the parties to the main proceedings, the Member State from which the reference is made, the European Commission and other institutions if a measure of theirs is at issue.[48] The parties and all the interested persons referred to in Article 23 of the Statute will be able to participate in an oral procedure where they can express a view on the written observations that have been lodged.[49] Second, cases subject to the urgent preliminary ruling procedure will, as soon as they arrive at the Court, be assigned to a chamber of five judges that is specially designated for this purpose.[50] Finally, the procedure in these cases will, for the most part, be conducted electronically, since the new provisions of the Rules of Procedure allow procedural documents to be lodged and served by fax or e-mail.[51]

In practice, the application of the urgent preliminary ruling procedure was requested in more than twenty cases and the designated chamber considered that the conditions under Article 104b of the Rules of Procedure were met in fifteen of them. In another case, the application of this procedure was decided by the Court on its own motion. So far the mechanism has been particularly effective since it

[43] See Art 263(4) TFEU.

[44] See Art 260 TFEU.

[45] See Art 260(3) TFEU.

[46] See Art 23a of the Statute of the Court of Justice of the European Union and Art 104b of the Rules of Procedure of the Court of Justice.

[47] A Tizzano and B Gencarelli, 'La procédure préjudicielle d'urgence devant la Cour de justice de l'Union européenne' in G Cohen-Jonathan, V Constantinesco, V Michel, JC Piris and P Wachsmann (eds), *Chemins d'Europe, Mélanges en l'honneur de Jean Paul Jacqué* (Paris, Dalloz, 2010) 639.

[48] See Art 104b(2) of the Rules of Procedure of the Court of Justice and Art 23 of its Statute.

[49] *cf* A Tizzano and B Gencarelli, n 47 above, 648.

[50] See Art 9(1), second sub-para of the Rules of Procedure of the Court of Justice.

[51] See Art 104b(6) of the Rules of Procedure of the Court of Justice.

has enabled the Court to deliver judgments in an average period of less than two and a half months.[52] Nevertheless, the cumulative effect of an increase in requests for urgent preliminary rulings, combined with a general rise in the number of cases, is difficult to predict. Thus, in order to maintain its efficiency, the Court must remain vigilant over the next few years so as to be able to adopt internally appropriate practical solutions and propose the necessary amendments to its Statute and its Rules of Procedure to the competent legislative authorities.

THE FUTURE: THE PROPOSALS TO AMEND THE STATUTE OF THE COURT

Apart from the particular context of the urgent preliminary ruling procedure, the Courts of the Union constantly face the requirement for an effective handling of cases in a reasonable period of time. As far as the ECJ is concerned, this challenge is particularly important in the context of preliminary rulings, since the procedure before the Court entails the suspension of the proceedings before the national courts. With regard to the General Court, the rights and interests of individuals are almost always directly in question.

The measures adopted by the ECJ and the General Court during the last 10 years have borne fruit to the extent possible. Nevertheless, the General Court is now in a critical situation with an unprecedented increase in the number of new cases, which exceeded 600 in 2010.[53] As regards the ECJ, although the current situation is still satisfactory, it is necessary to take into account the prospects of a constant increase in the number of cases brought, following, in particular, the enlargements of 2004 and 2007 and the entry into force of the Treaty of Lisbon. It is in this context that the Court has recently submitted to the legislative authorities of the Union[54] a series of proposals to amend its Statute[55] and to recast its Rules of Procedure.[56]

Regarding the proposed amendments of the Statute, the most important is the increase in the number of judges of the General Court by 12.[57] Following a lengthy internal consultation procedure, the Court concluded that the sole adoption of internal measures would not suffice to resolve the efficiency problems related to the raised caseload of the General Court. An increase in staff was deemed essential.

This consideration led the Court to opt for the increase of the number of the judges of the General Court instead of establishing a new specialised court, namely a court with jurisdiction to hear and determine direct actions in the area of trade

[52] For the statistics concerning the urgent preliminary ruling procedure, see Court of Justice of the European Union, *Annual Reports* from 2008 on.

[53] See Court of Justice of the European Union, *Annual Report 2010* 175.

[54] According to Art 281(2) TFEU concerning the Statute and to Art 253(6) TFEU regarding the Rules of Procedure.

[55] Interinstitutional file 2011/0901 (COD), document of 7 April 2011.

[56] Draft Rules of Procedure of the Court of Justice, attached to the letter of the President of the Court of Justice to the President of the Council of 25 May 2011, Council document 11147/11.

[57] See Interinstitutional file 2011/0901 (COD), document of 7 April 2011.

marks. In particular, the Court considered that the cases representing the highest workload for the General Court consist of economic disputes relating to competition law and state aid, etc. Trade marks cases, on the other hand, are treated by the General Court in a simplified way within a relatively reasonable period of time.

The Court is aware of the difficulties this proposal may present for the legislative authorities of the Union. On the one hand, the procedure for the appointment of 12 additional judges according to their country of origin is a complex issue. On the other hand, in a context of financial austerity, it is difficult not to consider the budgetary impact of this proposal. Nonetheless, we believe that these difficulties are not insurmountable and we are confident that the legislator of the Union will support the Court in its overall effort to maintain and improve its efficiency for the benefit of the citizens of the Union.

Our confidence is strengthened by the fact that it is the EU legislative authorities that are leading the negotiations for the accession of the European Union to the ECHR. Consequently, they have to take all the measures necessary to avoid a situation where the EU Courts will be unable to deliberate and rule on the cases brought before them in a reasonable time frame. In this case, there would be the risk of a condemnation of the Union by the European Court of Human Rights due to the violation of Article 6 of the ECHR. Nevertheless, the Court of Justice is going to make all possible efforts in order to avoid such a scenario.

Apart from the increase in the number of the judges of the General Court, the Court also proposes to increase the number of judges constituting the Grand Chamber from 13 to 15, to end the automatic participation of all the presidents of chambers of five judges in the composition of the Grand Chamber and to establish the office of the Vice President of the Court.[58] Following a constant and sustained examination of its internal functioning, the Court considers that those measures will bring improvements without jeopardising the consistency of its case law.

Finally, as mentioned above, the Court has recently proposed a general recast of its Rules of Procedure.[59] This initiative aims to simplify the procedure, to adapt the Rules of Procedure to the case law and the current practices and to improve its structure and its legibility.

CONCLUSION

With these thoughts on the evolution of the ECJ during the last decade, I wanted to highlight the fact that while the European Union is constantly changing, its judicial system can only follow the same path. Throughout this period, our institution has proved to be vigilant and ready to adapt to new circumstances. However, the advancement of the European integration process and especially the

[58] ibid.

[59] Draft Rules of Procedure of the Court of Justice, attached to the Letter of the President of the Court of Justice to the President of the Council of 25 May 2011, Council document 11147/11.

enhancement of judicial protection at the European level compel the Court to be both responsive to changes of circumstances and proactive in order to avoid a possible decline in quality and effectiveness of the system for the administration of justice. In this difficult task, the Court has always found staunch allies in the political and legislative authorities of the EU as well as in the academic world and amongst practitioners.

2

Multilevel Judicial Co-operation

CHRISTIAAN TIMMERMANS*

THE PLURALIST, MULTILEVEL/MULTILAYER APPROACH AND THE PRIMACY PRINCIPLE

IT HAS BECOME fashionable to characterise the relationship between Union law and national (sometimes also international) law not in terms of a legal hierarchy but to speak of constitutional pluralism, of multilayered or multilevel legal systems, a construct not so much based on hierarchy as on co-operation.[1] It is hard to find any article published nowadays on the relationship between Union and national law which does not refer to 'multilevel/multilayered'. In fact, these terms seem somewhat ambiguous; they still express some kind of hierarchy (higher levels/layers, and lower ones), contrary to what is meant. Therefore, I would personally prefer to speak of constitutional pluralism.

Apart from this terminological point of lesser importance, what do we think about this approach, and more particularly, how do we reconcile it with the principle of primacy of EU law over national law? It is certainly true that the ECJ is not hierarchically superior to Member States' Supreme Courts. It cannot quash or annul their judgments. It can answer questions for a preliminary ruling, but the final say in applying the answers received belongs to the national court. However, if a national court does not respect Union law, the EU legal system is not entirely empty handed: in exceptional circumstances (the conditions are very strict) the State can be held liable for damage caused, but again, only by a national court.[2]

* Professor of Law, University of Rotterdam and former Judge of the Court of Justice of the European Union.

[1] See M Poiares Maduro, 'Contrapunctual Law: Europe's Constitutional Pluralism in Action' in Walker (ed), *Sovereignty in Transition* (Oxford, Hart Publishing, 2003) 501; E Cloots, 'Germs of Pluralist Judicial Adjudication: Advocaten voor de wereld and other references from the Belgian Constitutional Court' (2010) 47 *CML Rev* 645; R Barents, 'De voorrang van unierecht in het perspectief van constitutioneel pluralisme' (2009) *SEW* 44; LFM Besselink, *Een samengestelde Europese constitutie* (Groningen, Europa Law Publishing, 2007); A Meij, 'Kringen van coherentie, Over eenheid van rechtspraak in de context van globalisering' (Inaugural Address, University of Utrecht, 2009); W Van Gerven and S Lierman, *Veertig jaar later. Algemeen deel, Privaat- en publiekrecht in een meergelaagd kader van regelgeving, rechtsvorming en regeltoepassing* (Mechelen, Kluwer, 2010) 21, 564.

[2] Case C-224/01 *Köbler* [2003] ECR I-10239; Case C-173/03 *Traghetti del Mediterraneo* [2006] ECR I-5177.

Some kind of hierarchy may be enforced through the infringement procedure of Articles 258 to 260 TFEU. The Commission could indeed sue a Member State when a supreme court of that State has infringed Union law and even ask the ECJ to impose financial sanctions. Until now, as far as I know, the Commission has never brought such a case.[3] And, indeed, it might not be very wise to do so. Bringing such a case before the ECJ might risk prejudicing conditions for enforcement of Union law instead of improving them. This would put the relationship between national courts and the ECJ under severe strain, not to mention the fact that the independence of the national judiciary, depending on the case at issue, could make it difficult for the national legislator to redress the situation.

Of course the ECJ insists in its case law on the fundamental principle of the primacy of Union law over national law. That primacy is absolute and unconditional; Union law even overrides national constitutional law.[4] However, in practice the ECJ does not really have the power to enforce this principle for the reason I have just mentioned: it is not hierarchically superior to national courts. This means that in reality the enforcement of Union law in and by Member States largely depends on the willingness of national courts to give full effect to primacy, and not on coercion. That is, I understand, the main idea the experts of the multilayer approach intend to express. I should add that in practice most national courts appear to have no difficulty in accepting the primacy of Union law. In the Netherlands the Hoge Raad and the Council of State have never queried this primacy.

However, national courts function within a specific constitutional context which must be taken into account. Union law might sometimes require them to depart from that context, to step out of it. For constitutional courts particularly, whose primary responsibility is to protect and uphold the Constitution, this is asking a lot. A constitutional court could consider that to be too much. I have always felt an understanding for the dilemma a constitutional court faces and that sometimes it might express a *non possumus*, if enforcing primacy would force it to derogate from what it regards as core principles of the Constitution, more particularly where fundamental rights are concerned. It is fascinating to see how national supreme courts and the ECJ have handled this dilemma. Over the past 50 years they have largely succeeded in neutralising it thanks to the co-operation that has developed between them through the European judicial dialogue. This dialogue takes place both on a formal and an informal level.

FORMAL JUDICIAL DIALOGUE

The formal dialogue occurs through the preliminary ruling procedure, a procedure characterised, as the Court recently put it, by a dialogue from court to court,

[3] Case C-129/00 *Commission v Italy* [2003] ECR I-14637 finally concerned the legislator because the national rule had allowed an interpretation by the Italian courts contrary to Union law.

[4] Case 11/70 *Internationale Handelsgesellschaft* [1970] ECR 1125; Case C-409/06 *Winner Wetten* [2010] ECR I-8015.

'*un dialogue de juge à juge*'.[5] To this day, the clearest example of how this formal dialogue has allowed serious tensions to be overcome between the principle of primacy and the need for a national court to respect national constitutional constraints is probably the *Internationale Handelsgesellschaft* case.[6]

In its referring decision the German Verwaltungsgericht opined that the EEC agricultural regulation to be applied in the main case was incompatible with various fundamental rights protected by the German Constitution, and could therefore not be applied. In a strongly worded statement the ECJ rejected this conclusion: national courts must ensure the uniform application of EC law, even if to do so they have to derogate from the Constitution. However, the Court then added, of course, that the protection of fundamental rights is also an essential part of the EEC legal order (albeit in the absence of any written source).

This judgment is a good example of judicial co-operation because it is the national court which indirectly gives the impetus for the development of the ECJ case law on fundamental rights. On the other hand, the ECJ offered the national court a solution for this conflict with the German Constitution, a solution that finally also convinced the Bundesverfassungsgericht to accept the *Solange II* approach.[7]

INFORMAL DIALOGUE

This judicial dialogue, this co-operation between European courts also takes place on an informal level and quite extensively so. As it might be less well known, let me illustrate how this informal co-operation takes place. For more than 50 years, the ECJ has been organising twice a year an informal meeting with national judges with the aim of acquainting them with the functioning of the ECJ and, more generally, with the importance – and consequences – of Union law for national judicial practice. But this is not a one-way street. These regular meetings with national judges allow the ECJ to hear about their experiences, problems, and criticisms, for instance with regard to the functioning of the preliminary rulings procedure.

Moreover, the ECJ regularly receives delegations from national supreme and constitutional courts. These visits normally take the form of round table discussions during which, after short introductory briefings by members of each court, developments in their respective caseloads are discussed. For instance, in recent years the ECJ held such meetings with delegations from the supreme courts of the new Member States to hear about their approach to the relationship between domestic law and Union law, in other words primacy. These discussions are generally open and frank, but can occasionally become fraught with criticism, as for instance during a visit of a delegation of the Bundesverfassungsgericht with regard

[5] See eg, Case C-210/06 *Cartesio* [2008] ECR I-9641, para 91.

[6] *Internationale Handelsgesellschaft*, n 4 above.

[7] Bundesverfassungsgericht, judgment of 22 October 1986, BVerfGE 73,339.

to the judgment of that court on the Lisbon Treaty. Sometimes, but much less frequently, a delegation of the ECJ pays a visit to a national supreme court.

Informal contacts, particularly, between the presidents and sometimes also senior members of national supreme courts and their homologues of the ECJ are also fairly frequent. Judges come to know each other quite well; these contacts are normally easy and open. There is also another reason for that. Judicial co-operation within the EU has not been initiated by the ECJ only, far from it. The process of European integration has prompted an ever more intensive exchange between national judiciaries and not only at the level of the supreme courts. An impressive number of networks and associations of judges has over the years spread over Europe, channelling and fostering judicial co-operation.

There is first of all the network of the presidents of EU supreme courts; then the very active and well-organised association of Councils of State and supreme administrative courts of the EU. Networks and groupings have also been set up among judges who specialise in specific fields of the law, such as environmental law, competition law, consumer protection law, commercial law and administrative law. Representatives of the ECJ are normally invited to the activities organised by these groups. The ECJ has a seat on the board of the association of Councils of State. Moreover, there are bilateral contacts between the supreme courts and there exist still other multilateral fora, like the Sechser Treffen, bringing together delegations of the German speaking supreme courts in Europe (Austria, Germany, Liechtenstein, Switzerland and both the ECJ and the ECtHR).

All these networks and groups function as laboratories of comparative law. Judges from all over Europe meet to discuss legal issues of common interest and developments in their case law; sometimes special databases have been set up, for instance by the association of Councils of State, allowing access to recent case law of mutual interest. Union law development and the experience of national judges with Union law are often on the agenda of international judicial conferences. The ECJ is also actively involved in facilitating these exchanges. The research department of the Court produces a bulletin signalling and giving a short analysis of important judgments from national and international courts. This bulletin (called 'Reflets') is available in French on the website of the Court, with an English translation on the website of the association of Councils of State.

All this demonstrates a fascinating process of judicial integration, not top-down as ordained by Brussels or Luxembourg, but bottom-up. Legal frontiers are being opened. From personal experience, these contacts left me with the impression that judges are generally interested in legal developments in other Member States and in learning from the experience of foreign courts.

I have sometimes wondered whether this open-mindedness from judges, their openness towards the experiences of foreign courts could be explained, at least in part, by professional *habitus* or attitude. Normally, judges have to function in a system of collegiate decision-making; there is no hierarchy, at least not formally, in a judicial college. One must convince one's colleagues and be convinced by them. That might contribute to an attitude facilitating co-operation and exchange with fellow judges from foreign jurisdictions. In that respect judges might differ from politicians who always have to defend their national turfs. But, I admit, one has to be careful with such generalisations.

In the United States of America there is an ongoing discussion, stimulated by a difference of opinion between Justices of the Supreme Court, Justices Breyer and Scalia particularly, as to whether references to decisions of foreign courts can ever be considered as legitimate or whether they must be regarded as encroaching upon national sovereignty or even worse, as unconstitutional. I have never been confronted with such reactions in Europe.

A final element may be added to this list of informal contacts. The contacts of the ECJ with foreign jurisdictions are not limited to the national courts within the EU. First of all there are contacts with international courts, particularly intensive ones with the ECtHR, the EFTA Court, its homologue within the European Economic Area, with the International Court of Justice in The Hague, the Appellate Body of the World Trade Organization in Geneva, as well as with regional international courts in Africa and South and Central America. The ECJ has had regular encounters with delegations from the US Supreme Court both in Washington and Luxembourg. It has also paid a visit to the Supreme Court in Beijing and to various regional courts in China, and it has hosted visits of delegations from Chinese courts.

JUDICIAL CO-OPERATION IN PRACTICE: SOME EXAMPLES

My personal impression after 10 years at the Court and having participated in a number of the informal judicial contacts just mentioned is that judicial co-operation at the EU level functions rather well, and also that this co-operation has intensified over the years. In 2007, the ECJ, on the fiftieth anniversary of its foundation, organised a conference to which it invited the presidents of all supreme and constitutional courts of the Member States. The theme of the conference was the influence of national law and legal principles on the evolution of Union law. Speakers during that conference were solely presidents of supreme courts.

A further example of this process of intensifying judicial co-operation is the conference the ECJ organised on the occasion of the opening of its new building in 2009. The subject of this conference was a report produced at the initiative of the Dutch Council of State by a joint working group set up by the Association of Councils of State in co-operation with the Network of Presidents of the Supreme Courts. This report examines the functioning of the preliminary ruling procedure, signals weaknesses, shortcomings, and problems as seen from the perspective of national courts and proposes solutions and reforms.[8] All this was discussed between members of the ECJ and presidents of national supreme courts. One strong impression I gained from this conference was how much the preliminary

[8] The report was published in Newsletter no 20 of the association (www.juradmin.eu).

ruling procedure was considered as a common asset by both national judges and the ECJ.

What might also be regarded as an illustration of the close linkages between the ECJ and national supreme courts is the new Article 255 TFEU committee. This committee has to produce an opinion on the qualifications of candidates proposed by governments of Member States for appointment as a judge or Advocate General of the ECJ and the General Court. This committee is of the highest importance for surveying the quality of nominees at the Union courts, and ultimately, the quality of the case law of these courts. Even if the opinions of the committee are only of a consultative nature, it is obvious, a nomination requiring unanimity, that a negative opinion will not be overruled. The composition of the committee in itself provides sufficient guarantees in that regard. The majority of its members are judges of national supreme courts. Among its seven members, two are former judges of the Union courts, one is designated by the European Parliament, and the other four members are presidents or members of national supreme courts (currently: the Vice President of the French Conseil d'Etat who presides over the committee, a member of the UK Supreme Court, the President of the Czech Constitutional Court and the President of the Danish Supreme Court who was, at the time of his nomination, the President of the afore-mentioned network of presidents of EU supreme courts).

CO-OPERATION IN THE CASE LAW

Apart from these manifestations of judicial co-operation of a more institutional or sociological nature, the results of this co-operation may also be detected in the evolution of the case law of both national supreme courts and the ECJ, the evolution with regard to the way in which these courts approach the relationship between national law and Union law or, to put it more bluntly, the way in which they handle the primacy principle.

It is in the nature of things that national supreme courts and the ECJ might occasionally have different views – even marked ones – as to how Union law should be interpreted. Yet, they will be aware that not much can be gained from entering into a conflict. The price to be paid, constitutionally and politically, would be too high. Such a clash could disrupt the functioning of the EU. Fortunately, at least this is my impression, both the ECJ and national supreme courts are definitely trying to prevent such a conflict from emerging.

For its part, the ECJ should of course do its utmost to prevent its judgments from being perceived as encroaching upon fundamental principles of a Member State's constitutional law. To some extent this could even be viewed as an obligation under the EU Treaty. Indeed, according to Article 4 TEU 'the Union shall respect . . . [Member States'] national identities, inherent in their fundamental structures, political and constitutional . . .'. Moreover, this Article also provides that the Union shall respect the essential functions of the State, including ensuring its territorial integrity, maintaining law and order and safeguarding national security. This enumeration of state functions – not exhaustive – together with the reference to the fundamental constitutional and political structures, thus indirectly defines the hard core of national sovereignty, which the Union may not affect.

The ECJ has been respectful of national constitutional identity in its case law on fundamental rights. Further examples can be found in recent case law explicitly allowing a Member State to justify national measures restricting trade in goods or services for reasons relating to the protection of a fundamental right, leaving in that regard a considerable margin of discretion to that Member State, taking into account values that are specific to its constitution. Consequently, no uniform solution is being imposed on Member States.[9] Another example is provided by recent judgments on lotteries and gambling issues where the ECJ also accepted that Member States may follow different approaches provided that the measures adopted remain proportionate and coherent.[10] In recent case law the Court has made explicit reference to Article 4 TEU.[11]

National supreme and constitutional courts have also over the years demonstrated an attitude of co-operation and conflict avoidance, even when in some cases loud warning shots have alternated with moderate, soothing statements. The French and Spanish constitutional courts have developed fairly sophisticated, sometimes somewhat intricate, interpretations to reconcile the primacy principle with national sovereignty. The Bundesverfassungsgericht has of course the most developed doctrinal position: the EU is a union of sovereign states, Member States remaining Herren der Verträge; the Union cannot interfere with the essence of the national state, and the exercise of Union competences remains subject to ultra vires control by the Bundesverfassungsgericht. Democratic legitimacy can only be assured on the national level, the role of the European Parliament being no more than a complement.

In spite of all this – fortunately – no real conflict has occurred. On the contrary we see a process of accommodation and co-operation, as the following examples will illustrate. I have already referred to the special difficulties national constitutional courts may encounter in accepting the primacy of Union law. As an illustration of such difficulties, various constitutional courts like the Italian and the German ones, have refused in the past to use the preliminary ruling procedure considering that their responsibility exclusively regarded the protection of the Constitution. They left to the other courts the responsibility of using that procedure. However, this position is changing. The Italian Constitutional Court submitted preliminary questions to the ECJ for the first time in 2008.[12] The German Constitutional Court, and this is a very interesting development, has now

[9] Case C-36/02 *Omega* [2004] ECR I-9609. This was already apparent in Case 41/74 *Van Duyn* [1974] ECR 1337.

[10] See, eg Case C-42/07 *Liga Portuguesa* [2009] ECR I-7633.

[11] Case C-208/09 *Sayn Wittgenstein*, judgment of 22 December 2010 nyr; Case C-391/09 *Runevič-Vardyn and Wardyn*, judgment of 12 May 2011 nyr.

[12] Case C-169/08 *Presidente del Consiglio dei Ministri* [2009] ECR I-10821.

announced in its recent *Honeywell* judgment that, if in a future case, it considers that an EU act might be ultra vires, it will first ask a preliminary question on that issue before deciding the case.[13] Finally, the Spanish Constitutional Court, on 9 June 2011, sent its first preliminary reference to the ECJ.[14]

Another example is the evolution of the position of the French Conseil d'Etat from first openly resisting the full consequences of the primacy of Union law, for instance with regard to directives, to having now fully aligned its case law in that regard.[15] This much more EU-friendly approach is perhaps best illustrated by the position of the Conseil d'Etat during the preparatory works of the new regime of ex post control of the constitutionality of acts of Parliament through the so-called 'priority question of constitutionality', the procedure allowing the Cour de cassation and the Conseil d'Etat to submit such a question to the Conseil Constitutionnel. Despite their obligation to give priority to this procedure, both the Cour de cassation and the Conseil d'Etat have firmly upheld their autonomous competence under the Treaties to refer preliminary questions to the ECJ where the problem in question also raises issues of Union law.[16]

Finally, even the Bundesverfassungsgericht, in the above-mentioned *Honeywell* judgment, has now considerably softened the threatening language of its judgment on the Lisbon Treaty.[17] It not only announced its willingness to refer preliminary questions to the ECJ before judging an EU act contrary to the German Constitution, but it also clarified that it will declare such an act ultra vires only when it is confronted with a manifest transgression of the limits of EU competences implying a structural change of considerable importance in the division of competences to the detriment of the Member States. One might think that such a case should remain a hypothetical one.

CONCLUSION

How do we explain this willingness to co-operate? One of the reasons might be the capability of Union law to address citizens directly and to grant them rights. Normally, protecting and enforcing those rights would require citizens to petition national courts, direct access to the Union courts being only exceptionally available. National courts are by nature receptive to this task. They take citizens' rights seriously, including when these rights are not conferred by national but by Union

[13] Bundesverfassungsgericht, judgment of 6 July 2010, 2 BvR 2661/06. See also Payandeh, 'Constitutional Review of EU law after Honeywell: Contextualizing the Relationship between the German Constitutional Court and the EU Court of Justice' (2011) 48 *CML Rev* 9.

[14] Bundesverfassungsgericht, judgment of 9 June 2011 in *Stefano Melloni* (nr 6922-2008).

[15] See R Mehdi, 'French Supreme Courts and European Union Law: Between Historical Compromise and Accepted Loyalty' (2011) 48 *CML Rev* 439.

[16] Ibid, 456; *cf* with regard to Belgium where a similar procedure has been introduced: P Gerard, 'De hoeder van de meerlagige Europese Constitutie tussen unierecht en grondwet in Frankrijk en Belgie' (2011) *SEW* 152.

[17] See n 13 above.

law. To dispel any doubts on this point, one should read for instance the grounds of preliminary references in cases regarding Union citizenship.

In my view the tensions between respect by national courts of the principle of primacy and their natural loyalty to their national Constitution can only be mastered by judicial co-operation. Both the ECJ and national supreme and constitutional courts have demonstrated their willingness to participate actively in this co-operation. In a recent interview when asked about the profile of a good European judge, the Vice President of the French Conseil d'Etat, Jean-Marc Sauvé, declared:

> This judge, whether a national or an international one, should not forget either that he forms part of an increasingly wider network that largely exceeds his legal specialism and even his internal legal system. Nowadays, one of the main responsibilities of a judge is to contribute to the equilibrium and the harmony of this network by, as far as possible, looking after the coherence and the articulation between the national legal system, notably on a constitutional level, and the European legal systems. We could at any moment oppose these systems by making them contradict each other and even cause major blockades. However, that would be contrary to our mission which is to ensure legal security and to maintain the rule of law.[18]

Judicial dialogue is, in my view, a better and more promising solution than trying on a dogmatic level to nuance or accommodate the primacy principle. The qualification by Pierre Pescatore of that principle as an existential requirement of Union law remains today as pertinent as when it was written 30 years ago.[19] The language of the ECJ in upholding the primacy principle is as categorical today as it was 40 years ago in *Internationale Handelsgesellschaft*.[20]

The national judges are of course the main players in the process of reconciling the principle of the primacy of Union law with national constitutional constraints when articulating the relationship between national and Union law. In that regard, to qualify the national judge explicitly as Union judge and in doing so fully integrate him into the Union legal system, stressing his direct responsibility for the effective enforcement of Union law may be considered in hindsight a strategic and psychological stroke of genius to facilitate and foster respect of the primacy principle in the national legal systems.

[18] Translated by the author from *Recueil Dalloz* of 19 May 2011, 1336.

[19] P Pescatore 'Aspects judiciaires de l'acquis communautaire' (1981) *Revue trimestrielle de droit européen* 631.

[20] *Winner Wetten*, n 4 above.

3

Private Parties' Access to the Courts of Regional Economic Integration Organisations: A Comparative Analysis

MARC JAEGER*

INTRODUCTION

IN THE SECOND half of the last century, sovereign States have established regional or sub-regional economic integration organisations (REIOs). This evolution of the international community led to broader economic and political jurisdictional regimes, where sovereign States have made room for supranational entities.[1] In this handover of powers, private parties have gained in importance, in particular where they are the addressees of REIO treaty provisions. Obviously, in most developed REIOs, the acknowledgment of rights and duties of private parties has required the establishment of jurisdictional bodies where they could bring their grievances.

The aim of this article is to examine, in the field of private parties' direct and indirect access to the other regional courts, whether the European model has also been followed. This contribution analyses, from a comparative point of view, private parties' access to the courts of REIOs both directly and indirectly through the preliminary reference procedure, which constitutes a remedial bedrock for private applicants. Legal literature recognises that the judicial architecture and the case law of the ECJ have been models for all the other courts of REIOs.[2] First, it is

* President of the General Court of the European Union since 17 September 2007.

[1] See A Del Vecchio, 'Globalization and Its Effects on International Courts and Tribunals' in *New International Tribunals and New International Proceedings* (Milano, Giuffré, 2006) 3; A von Bogdandy, 'Globalization and Europe: How to Square Democracy, Globalization and International Law' (2004) *European Journal of International Law* (2004) 885; F Orrego Vicuña, *International Dispute Settlement in an Evolving Global Society* (Cambridge, Cambridge University Press, 2004); I Shihata, 'The Changing Role of the State and Some Related Governance Issues' (1999) *Revue européenne de droit public* 1462; B Simma, 'From Bilateralism to Community Interest in International Law' (1994) *Recueil des Cours* 233.

[2] L Burgorgue-Larsen, 'Prendre les droits communautaires au sérieux ou la force d'attraction de l'expérience européenne an Afrique et en Amérique latine' in Collectif, *Les dynamiques du droit européenne en début du siècle. Etudes en l'honneur de JC Gautron* (Paris, Éditions Pédone, 2004) 563; H Weiland, 'The European Union and Southern Africa. Interregionalism between Vision and Reality' in H Hanggi, R Roloff and J Ruland (eds) *Interregionalism and International Relations. A Stepping Stone*

necessary to specify which types of legal actions are taken into account for the purpose of this comparative analysis. Concerning private parties' direct access to the courts of REIOs, the following procedures on the basis of the European model will be analysed: action for annulment; action for failure to act; disputes between organisations and servants, and actions seeking compensation for damages.[3] The issue of human rights protection will be analysed taking into account that the European experience of the European Court of Human Rights (ECtHR) has not been totally transferred to other economic integration organisations. Private parties' indirect access to the courts will be examined to understand if the preliminary ruling procedure of Article 267 TFEU inspired other REIOs.

This contribution analyses the EFTA Court,[4] the Benelux Court of Justice,[5] the Court of Justice of the Andean Community (CJAC),[6] the Court of Justice of the Central American Integration System (CJCAIS),[7] the Court of Justice of the Caribbean Community (CJCC),[8] the Tribunal of Southern African Development Community (TSADC),[9] the Common Court of Justice and Arbitration (CCJA) of

to Global Governance (New York, 2006) 185; T Marauhn, 'Re-considering Regional Integration in Africa' (2003) *Recht in Afrika* 187; G Ortiz de Zevallos, 'Common Market Law and its Influence in the Latin American Andean Region' in *Du droit international au droit de l'intégration. Liber Amicorum Pierre Pescatore* (Baden-Baden, Nomos Verlagsgesellschaft, 1987) 843 at 859.

[3] The other actions that can be brought by natural or legal persons under EU Law and their respective legal bases are: actions against fines and penalties provided for in EC regulations (Art 261 TFEU), actions based on an arbitration clause (Art 272 TFEU), actions against the applicability of EC regulations (Art 277 TFEU) and actions relating to Community Trade Marks (Regulation 207/2009, [2009] OJ L78/1).

[4] D Gallo, 'From Autonomy to Full Deference in the Relationship between the EFTA Court and the CJEU: The Case of International Exhaustion of Trademark Rights' in (2010) *EUI Working Papers* 78; C Baudenbacher, 'The EFTA Court Ten Years On', in C Baudenbacher, P Tresselt, T Örlygsson (eds), *The EFTA Court – Ten Years On* (Oxford, Hart Publishing, 2005) 13; V Kronemberger, 'Does the EFTA Court Interpret the EEA Agreement as if it were the EC Treaty? Some Questions Raised by the Restamark Judgment' (1996) *International & Comparative Law Quarterly* 198.

[5] A Braun, E Cornu, *Précis des marques: la Convention Benelux, le droit communautaire, les lois pénales et de compétence civile belges, les conventions internationales* (Bruxelles, Larcier, 2009).

[6] LR Helfer, KJ Alter, MF Guerzovich, 'Islands of Effective International Adjudication: Constructing an Intellectual Property Rule of Law in the Andean Community' (2009) *American Journal of International Law* 11 at 12; LR Helfer and KJ Alter, 'The Andean Tribunal of Justice and Its Interlocutors: Understanding Preliminary Reference Patterns in the Andean Community' (2009) *New York University Journal of International Law & Policy* 883 at 886; N De Pierola, 'The Andean Court of Justice' (1987) *Emory Journal of International Dispute Resolution* 11; EB Keener, 'The Andean Common Market Court of Justice: Its Purpose, Structure, and Future', ivi, 39.

[7] R Virzo, 'Central American Court of Justice (CACJ)' in Wolfrum (ed), *The Max Planck Encyclopedia of Public International Law*, online edition available at www.mpepil.com; MA Cano Linares, 'La Corte Centroamericana de Justicia: un órgano único con diversidad de competencias' in Fernadéz Liesa (ed), *Tribunales internacionales y espacio iberoamericano* (Madrid, Civitas, 2009) 111.

[8] L Birdsong, 'The Formation of the Caribbean Court of Justice: The Sunset of British Colonial Rule in the English Speaking Caribbean' (2004–2005) *University of Miami Inter-American Law Review* 197; EE Pollard, *The Caribbean Court of Justice: Who Stands to Gain*, available at www.caribbeancourtofjustice.org.

[9] W Scholtz, G Ferreira, 'Much Ado About Nothing? The SADC Tribunal's Quest for the Rule of Law Pursuant to Regional Integration' (2011) *Zeitschrift für ausländisches öffentliches Recht und Völkerrecht* 331; OC Ruppel, FX Bangamawabo, 'The SADC Tribunal: A Legal Analysis of its Mandate and Role in Regional Integration' in A Bösl and T Hartzenberg, *Monitoring Regional Integration in Southern Africa* (2008), available at www.kas.de; OC Ruppel, 'The Southern African Development Community (SADC)

the Organization for the Harmonization of Business Law in Africa (OHADA),[10] the Court of Justice of the Common Market for Eastern and Southern Africa (CJCOMESA),[11] the Court of Justice of the Common Market of West African States (CJECOWAS),[12] the Court of Justice of the East African Community (CJEAC)[13] and the Court of Justice of Economic and Monetary Community of Central Africa (CJCEMAC).[14]

PRIVATE PARTIES' DIRECT ACCESS TO THE COURTS

Action for Annulment

In the EU, the action for annulment could have been the main channel of judicial review open to private parties. However it has been limited by the restrictions on standing imposed by the Treaties and by the notion of 'individual concern', as interpreted in *Plaumann.*[15] As is well-known, scholars have criticised the strict interpretation given by the ECJ of the notion of 'individual concern' in the *Jégo-Quéré* judgment following an attempt by the Court of First Instance (now the General Court, GC)[16] to redefine the rules governing private parties' access to community courts, in the aftermath of the opinion delivered by Advocate General Jacobs in the *Union de Pequenos Agricultores* (*UPA*) case. Although *Jégo-Quéré* was indirectly and, later on, directly overturned on appeal,[17] the ECJ recognised the possibility of envisaging a new system of review of EU acts by means of a revision of the treaties according to Article 48 TEU.[18] The outcome of this process is

and its Tribunal: Reflexions on Regional Economic Communities' Potential Impact in Human Rights Protection' (2009) *Verfassung und Recht in Übersee* 173; 'The SADC Tribunal, Regional Integration and Human Rights: Major Challenges, Legal Dimensions and Some Comparative Aspects From the European Legal Order' (2009) *Recht in Afrika* 213.

[10] D Ndoye, *La Cour commune de justice et d'arbitrage des pays de l'OHADA: organisation, procédure et jurisprudence* (Dakar, Editions juridiques africaines, 2009).

[11] PK Kiplagat, 'Dispute Recognition and Dispute Settlement in Integration Processes: The COMESA Experience' (1995) *Northwestern Journal of International Law and Business* 445.

[12] A Banjo, 'The ECOWAS Court and the Politics of Access to Justice in West Africa' (2007) *Africa Development* 69.

[13] TO Ojienda, 'The East African Court of Justice in the Re-established East African Community: Institutional Structure and Function in the Integration Process' (2005) *East African Journal of Peace and Human Right* 220; '"Alice's Adventures in Wonderland": Preliminary Reflections on the Jurisdiction of the East African Court of Justice' (2004) *The East African Journal of Human Rights and Democracy* 94.

[14] See J-M Ntoutoume, 'Présentation de la Cour de justice de la CEMAC' in *Agence Intergouvernementale de la Francophonie, Actes du séminaire sous-régional sur le droit communautaire de la CEMAC* (Paris, Giraf, 2003) 36; M Kamto, 'Les Cours de justice des communautés et des organisations d'intégration économique africaines' (1998) *Annuaire africain de droit international* 107.

[15] Case 25/62 *Plaumann v Commission* [1963] ECR 95.

[16] Case T-177/01 *Jégo-Quéré v Commission* [2002] ECR II-2365.

[17] Case C-263/02 P *Commission v Jégo-Quéré* [2004] ECR I-3425.

[18] V Kronenberger, P Dejmek, 'Locus Standi of Individuals before Community Courts under Article 230(4)EC: Illusions and Disillusions After the Jégo-Quéré (T-177/01) and Unión de Pequeños Agricultores (C-50/00 P) judgments' (2002) *The European Legal Forum = Forum iuris communis europae* 257; R Mehdi, 'La recevabilité des recours formés par les personnes physiques et morales à l'encontre

the new formulation of Article 263(4) TFEU according to which, besides proceedings against an act addressed to a person which is of direct and individual concern to him, any natural or legal person may institute proceedings against a regulatory act which is of direct concern to them and does not entail implementing measures.[19] To this end, it must be pointed out that of late the GC has ruled on the *Inuit* case, the first case regarding the interpretation of the meaning of regulatory act.[20]

Regarding actions for annulment in other REIOs, it is possible to distinguish four different situations: no equivalent procedure;[21] substantially identical procedure to the EU;[22] an equivalent procedure with some differences concerning the conditions of access to justice for private parties; and procedures where private parties' access to the Courts is guaranteed, but the aim is different from the action for annulment.

Only the EFTA system contains a procedure substantially identical to the EU's. Indeed, Article 36(2) of the Agreement between the EFTA States on the Establishment of a Surveillance Authority and a Court of Justice (SCA) provides that

> [a]ny natural or legal person may, under the same conditions, institute proceedings before the EFTA Court against a decision of the EFTA Surveillance Authority addressed to that person or against a decision addressed to another person, if it is of direct and individual concern to the former.

Regarding the third hypothesis, the conditions of access to justice are more restrictive to private parties in some cases, more favourable in others. In the Caribbean Court of Justice, we find a more restrictive approach to the access of private parties because Article 222 of the Treaty establishing the Caribbean

d'un acte de portée générale: l'aggiornamento n'aura pas eu lieu' in (2003) *Revue triumestrielle de droit européen* 22, 50; J Schwarze, 'The Legal Protection of the Individual Against Regulations in European Union Law: Remarks on the CJEU Judgment in the UPA case of 25 July 2002 in View of the European Constitutional Reform' (2004) *European Public Law* 285; N Fennelly, 'The Role of the National Judge in Ensuring Access to Community Justice Reflections on the Case Law of the Community Courts Four Years on from Jégo-Quéré/UPA' (2006) *ERA Forum* 463. See, for the analysis of the new Art 48 TEU, MF Orzan, 'Art 48' in Curti Gialdino (ed), *Codice dell'Unione Europea Operativo*, forthcoming.

[19] S Balthasar, 'Locus Standi Rules for Challenges to Regulatory Acts by Private Applicants: The New Article 263(4) TFEU' (2010) *European Law Review* 542; D Chalmers, G Davies and G Monti, *European Union Law*, 2nd edn (Cambridge, Cambridge University Press, 2010) 414 at 415.

[20] See Case T-18/10 *Inuit Tapiriit Kanatami ea v Parliament and Council*, order of 6 September 2011 nyr, in which the GC has established that 'it must be held that the meaning of "regulatory act" for the purposes of the fourth paragraph of Art 263 TFEU must be understood as covering all acts of general application apart from legislative acts. Consequently, a legislative act may form the subjectmatter of an action for annulment brought by a natural or legal person only if it is of direct and individual concern to them' (para 56).

[21] Regarding the first hypothesis, for instance, the Benelux Court of Justice has no jurisdiction on actions for annulment by private parties.

[22] As regards the issue of private parties' access to the action for annulment, in this article we will adopt the numbering before the entry into force of the Lisbon Treaty, because Art 230(4) EC has been the model for the other REIOs.

Community makes private parties' access depend on four conditions.[23] By contrast, in five other REIOs, private parties' access conditions to justice are more favourable. In the Andean Community (AC), the Protocol of Modification of the Treaty Establishing the Court of Justice of Andean Community (PMTAC) establishes that '[n]atural or artificial persons may bring a nullity action against the Decisions . . . that affect their subjective rights or their legitimate interests'.[24] Moreover, the CJAC in Case 14-AN-2001 has ruled that

> [e]n el caso concreto de la acción de nulidad la reforma para consagrar esta concepción amplia de participación de los particulares, sustituyó el requisito existente en el Tratado originario de que el titular de la acción de nulidad debía ser, en el caso de los particulares, quien demostrara que la norma demandada le era aplicable y le causaba perjuicio, por el requisito mucho más amplio y genérico de que las normas acusadas afecten sus derechos subjetivos o sus intereses legítimos.[25]

In the COMESA and in the EAC, private parties can bring an action not only against an act of an institution but of a Member State too.

In the EAC, the right is extended to private parties of a third country who are resident in a Member State.[26] The CEMAC Court of Justice has jurisdiction over actions for annulment of private parties that have a 'legitimate interest'.[27] Finally, in the CAIS, Article 22 of the Statute of the Court of Justice establishes that 'cualquier afectado por los acuerdos del Organo u Organismo del Sistema de la Integracion Centroamericana'[28] can bring an action before the CJCAIS.

In three other REIOs, direct access of private parties to justice is guaranteed by procedures different from the action for annulment. In the ECOWAS, the Supplementary Protocol[29] permits persons to bring an action against acts of community servants, on condition that the act constitutes a breach of their rights. In the

[23] According to Art 222 of the Revised Treaty of Chaguaramas Establishing the Caribbean Community Including the CARICOM Single Market and Economy: '[p]ersons, natural or juridical, of a Contracting Party may, with the special leave of the Court, be allowed to appear as parties in proceedings before the Court where: (a) the Court has determined in any particular case that this Treaty intended that a right or benefit conferred by or under this Treaty on a Contracting Party shall ensure to the benefit of such persons directly; and (b) the persons concerned have established that such persons have been prejudiced in respect of the enjoyment of the right or benefit mentioned in paragraph (a) of this Article; and (c) the Contracting Party entitled to espouse the claim in proceedings before the Court has: (i) omitted or declined to espouse the claim, or (ii) expressly agreed that the persons concerned may espouse the claim instead of the Contracting Party so entitled; and (d) the Court has found that the interest of justice requires that the persons be allowed'. Regarding these conditions see D Perrot, 'La Cour de Justice de la Caraïbe, une nouvelle Cour de justice communautaire' (2007) *Revue trimestrielle de droit européen* 451.

[24] See Art 19 of the Treaty Establishing the Court of Justice of the Andean Community, (1999) *Gaceta Oficial del Acuerdo de Cartagena* 483/5.

[25] See Proceso 14-AN-01 *Bonilla c Comision*, in *Gaceta Oficial del Acuerdo de Cartagena* (18 de marzo de 2002) no 773, 10.

[26] See Art 26 of the Treaty Establishing the Common Market for Eastern and Southern Africa, available at www.comesa.int; Art 30 of the Treaty for the Establishment of the East African Community, available at www.eac.int.

[27] See Art 14 of the Treaty Establishing the Court of Justice of CEMAC, available at www.cemac.int.

[28] See Art 22 of the Statute of the Central American Court of Justice, available at www.ccj.org.ni.

[29] See 2005 Supplementary Protocol (A/SP.1/01/05), available at www.ecowas.int.

OHADA, according to Article 14(3) of the Treaty on the Harmonisation of Business Law in Africa, the CCJA rules as above with regard to non-appellable decisions delivered by any national court of the contracting States which pertains to those matters raising questions concerning the application of uniform acts and to the regulations provided in the treaty establishing the organisation.[30] The SADC Tribunal has exclusive jurisdiction over all disputes between natural or legal persons and the Community, on condition of the exhaustion of domestic remedies.[31]

On the whole, it seems that the action for annulment as laid down in Article 230 EC has been taken as a model in the other REIOs, but in every organisation it has been revised, taking into account the needs of each system of integration. However, it must be pointed out that in other REIOs, in particular in Africa, 'the Community lawmaker' has paid little attention to the establishment of the standing requirements that private parties must satisfy in order to bring an action. In some cases, the access to the courts has been extended to citizens and enterprises of third country residents in one of the Member States or the expression 'individual concern' has been given a less restrictive meaning. Evidently, the lawmaker in these REIOs has been less inclined towards an *actio popularis*. At present, in the absence of much case law, the importance of this judicial policy cannot be assessed. Nevertheless, this situation is somehow perplexing. The establishment of conditions of access to private parties to justice pursues the aim of 'docket control'. Such a policy is not likely to strike a proper balance between the private parties' right to access to justice and the sound administration of justice in due time.

Action for Failure to Act

The action for failure to act complements the action for annulment, targeting, respectively, the illegal inaction and illegal action of EU institutions. They have been described by the ECJ as prescribing 'one and the same method of recourse',[32] because they can be pleaded in the alternative but both cannot be applied to the same circumstance. This might suggest that in every REIO in which the action for annulment is provided, there should be an action for failure to act. However, in most REIOs, the action for failure to act is not a known species. The EFTA, the AC and the ECOWAS are the only three organisations where private parties can bring a claim against the illegal inaction of the institutions.

In the EFTA, Article 37(3) of the SCA provides that '[a]ny natural or legal person may, under the conditions laid down in the preceding paragraphs, complain to the EFTA Court that the EFTA Surveillance Authority has failed to address to that person any decision'.

[30] See Art 14 of the Treaty on the Harmonisation of Business Law in Africa, available at www.ohada.com.

[31] See Art 18 of the Agreement Amending Protocol on Tribunal, available at www.sadc-tribunal.org.

[32] Case 15/70 *Chevalley v Commission* [1970] ECR 975, para 6; Case T-2/04 *Kormaz ea v Commission* [2006] ECR II-32, para 62.

In the AC, Article 37 of the PMTAC establishes that when institutions abstain from carrying out an activity for which they are expressly responsible under the legal system of the AC, private parties whose subjective rights and legitimate interests are affected may demand the fulfilment of those obligations. Compared to the action for failure to act provided in the EU, there are differences. First of all, it seems that the expressions 'subjective rights' and 'legitimate interests' are less restrictive than the 'individual and direct concern' required by the EU system. Moreover, from a procedural point of view there are two important differences: if the request fails to be acted upon within 30 days, the petitioner may appeal to the CJAC, which must rule within 30 days. In the EU, private parties must wait 60 days before bringing an action before the GC and the court cannot issue an injunction to the institution.

ECOWAS' supplementary protocol has introduced a new article concerning private parties' *locus standi*. Article 10(c) establishes that private parties can bring a claim against an omission of a servant of an institution which affects their subjective rights. Unlike in the EU, the claim is not directed against an institution but an official of the organisation.

The most important element of this comparative analysis is the absence in most REIOs of an action for failure to act. This absence shows that in these organisations the system of protection of rights can be completed in order to give private parties the right to act against illegal inactions of institutions. On the other hand, the comparison proves that, despite criticisms directed at the severe interpretation of the expression 'direct and individual' concern, the EU guarantees private parties a complete system of protection of their rights, balanced by the need for a sound administration of justice.

Action for Damages

In the EU, Articles 268 and 340 TFEU establish the jurisdiction of the ECJ in disputes relating to the non-contractual liability of the Union which shall make good any damage caused by its institutions or by its servants in the performance of their duties, in accordance with the general principles common to the laws of the Member States.[33] The comparative analysis concerning the action for damages by private parties shows that this action is absent from most REIOs. A similar procedure only exists in the EFTA, COMESA, ECOWAS and CEMAC. In particular, Articles 36 and 46(2) of the SCA establish the jurisdiction of the EFTA Court in actions against the EFTA Surveillance Authority relating to compensation for damage caused by it, or by its servants, in the performance of its duties, in the case of non-contractual liability.[34]

[33] C Von Bar, *Non-Contractual Liability Arising out of Damage Caused to Another Principles of European Law* (Bern, Stämpfli, 2009).

[34] Unlike Art 340 TFEU, the EFTA Agreement addresses general principles of law and not general principles of law of the Member States. In the three African Courts which have jurisdiction for non-contractual liability of the organisation the dispositions are similar to the EU one. For instance, see Art 20 of the Treaty Establishing the Court of Justice of CEMAC, available at www.cemac.int, according to

Staff Disputes

In the field of disputes between organisations and their staff, the presence of specialised courts is an additional factor which must be taken into account for the purpose of this comparative analysis. Within the EU's judicial institutions, the European Union Civil Service Tribunal (CST) has jurisdiction over disputes relating to the EU civil service.[35] Jurisdiction in this field was previously exercised by the ECJ and subsequently by the Court of First Instance. The creation of the CST can be attributed to the growth in litigation due to the enlargement of competences and membership of the Union, the inflation of EU legislation and the creation of new agencies. Decisions of the CST can be appealed on points of law only to the GC with, in exceptional circumstances, further review by the ECJ. This framework guarantees several sets of proceedings to the servants for pursuing their claims before the EU Courts.

Most REIOs recognise the right of their servants to bring a claim against the organisation.[36] However, no other REIOs have a specialised court[37] to hear staff cases. No other system offers a two-tier system of judicial oversight.

Human Rights Protection before the Courts of REIOs

Human rights in Europe have been regulated by two distinct institutional regimes. The ECtHR interprets the European Convention on Human Rights (ECHR), and the ECJ regards human rights as general principles of EU Law. Though the two regimes were distinct and independent from each other, they have not acted in isolation: since 1973, the ECJ has made references to the ECHR. After thirty years of discussion concerning the accession of the EU to the ECHR, Article 6(2) TUE puts the EU under a legal obligation to conclude an accession treaty, which nego-

which '[l]a Chambre Judiciaire connaît, en dernier ressort, des litiges relatifs à la réparation des dommages causés par les Organes et Institutions de la Communauté ou par les agents de celle-ci dans l'exercice de leurs fonctions. Elle statue en tenant compte des principes généraux de droit qui sont communs aux droits des Etats membres'.

[35] See *Le Tribunal de la fonction publique de l'Union européenne (TFP) = The European Union Civil Service Tribunal (CST)* (Luxembourg 2011); S Van Raepenbusch, 'Le contentieux de la fonction publique de l'Union européenne' (2008) *La fonction publique européenne* 145; C Hazel, 'Establishment of the European Union Civil Service Tribunal' (2006) *The Law and Practice of International Courts and Tribunals* 273.

[36] The EFTA Court has no jurisdiction on disputes with its servants but it assures their right to bring a claim against the organisation because it has recognised the jurisdiction of the Administrative Tribunal of the International Labour Organisation. The Tribunal hears complaints from serving and former officials of the International Labour Office and of the other international organisations that recognise its jurisdiction.

[37] In the Benelux Court of Justice, the Protocol of 29 April 1969 has established a Special Chamber within the Court to judge disputes between the organisation and its servants. The protocol is available at www.courbeneluxhof.be/fr/basisdocumenten.asp.

tiation is in progress.[38] Thanks to the accession to the ECHR, human rights will have a protection both internal, guaranteed by the ECJ,[39] and external, guaranteed by the ECHR, just like the other Member States of the Convention. This further evolution will render the European system of protection of human rights the most advanced and effective regional human rights regime in the world.

The situation in America and Africa is rather different. There are two regional human rights courts: the Inter-American Court of Human Rights (IACHR)[40] and the African Court on Human and Peoples' Rights (ACHPR).[41] However, the two courts have not had a similar place in the evolution of the protection of human rights. Especially in Africa, the establishment of a regional judicial body to ensure the implementation of fundamental rights is an afterthought, unlike the European and Inter-American systems, where the ECHR and the IACHPR were originally cardinal instruments of the system.

From a comparative perspective, it is worthwhile examining whether the courts of REIOs assure human rights protection like the ECJ and if in America and Africa there is a dialogue between the courts of REIOs and regional human rights courts.

Concerning human rights protection before the courts of the American REIOs, the AC experience has been very interesting. The Andean Charter for the Promotion and Protection of Human Rights signed at Guayaquil[42] does not contain any provisions concerning human rights remedies. It reaffirms the important role of the administration of justice in each Andean Community Member State for the protection of human rights through the application of national laws and international instruments and there are no provisions regarding the role of the CJAC. Moreover, unlike the ECJ, the CJAC has not developed a case law on human rights protection. In the *Guayasamín Villacís* case, the only one in which the CJCA could have heard a claim of that nature, the court declined jurisdiction.

[38] A Tizzano, 'Les Cours européennes et l'adhésion de l'Union à la CEDH' in (2011) *Il Diritto dell'Unione europea* 29.

[39] A Rosas, H Kaila, 'L'application de la Charte des droits fondamentaux de l'Union européenne par la Cour de justice: un premier bilan' (2011) *Il Diritto dell'Unione europea* 1; J Dutheil de la Rochère, 'Droits fondamentaux: quelle place dans l'architecture de l'Union' in *Chemins d'Europe: mélanges en l'honneur de Jean-Paul Jacqué* (Paris, Dalloz, 2010) 263; HJ Blanke, 'Protection of Fundamental Rights Afforded by the European Court of Justice in Luxembourg, Governing Europe under a Constitution' (Springer Berlin Heidelberg, 2006) 265.

[40] See L Burgorgue-Larsen, *The Inter-American Court of Human Rights: Case Law and Commentary* (Oxford, Oxford University Press, 2011); JL Cavallaro, S Brewer, 'Reevaluating Regional Human Rights Litigation in the Twenty-First Century: The Case of the Inter-American Court' (2008) *American Journal of International Law* 768, 827; H Fix-Zamudio, 'Judicial Protection of Human Rights in Latin America and the Inter-American Court of Human Rights' (1991) *Judicial Protection of Human Rights at the National and International Level* 387, 466.

[41] See CM Peter, 'The African Court on Human and Peoples' Rights: Ready to Take Off?' (2007) *Recht in Afrika* 199, 230.

[42] See E Salmón Gárate, 'La Carta Andina para la Promoción de los Derechos Humanos: un paso hacia la humanización del proceso de integración andino' in (2003) *Derecho Comunitario Andino* 449; JM Casal, *Los derechos humanos y su protección: estudios sobre derechos humanos y derechos fundamentales* (Caracas, 2008) 223.

Legal commentators have explained this approach on different grounds.[43] Although the charter is not a binding instrument, the CJCA could have taken an active part in the development of human rights protection in the AC, referring to the principles enshrined in the charter.[44] Indeed, the implementation of the charter could be the first step in the evolution of human rights protection, taking into account that in the EU system, the Charter of Fundamental Rights was a non-binding instrument when it was proclaimed in Nice.[45]

Concerning the protection of human rights in Africa, the trend is rather different: the courts of some REIOs have extended their jurisdiction to human rights.[46] Despite the lack of provisions in the treaty establishing the SADC and its protocols giving the TSADC jurisdiction in the field of human rights, in the *Campbell* and *Tembani* cases, the Tribunal approved a broader interpretation of Articles 4 and 6 of the treaty, establishing that the two articles oblige Member States to respect human rights and to refrain from taking any measure likely to jeopardise their sustenance.[47] The Tribunal ruled that Member States are under a legal obligation to respect, protect and promote human rights. However, the judgments are facing difficulties at the enforcement stage as the Member States are reluctant to see a loss of their sovereignty. Nevertheless, the importance of such a development in the SADC must be underlined with a view to fostering an African culture of protection of human rights.

In the EAC, although the treaty does not give jurisdiction in the field of human rights to the Court of Justice, in the *Katazabi* case, the Court ruled that even if it does not 'assume jurisdiction' on human right disputes, it does not 'abdicate from exercising its jurisdiction' on human rights disputes.[48] As a consequence, under a broad interpretation of Articles 6 and 8 of the treaty, the court exercised its jurisdiction on human rights grounds when reviewing the legality of the act of the organisation. However, as in the SADC, the execution of this judgment is resisted by the Member States.

In the ECOWAS, the system of human rights protection differs from the other two REIOs. First, in the field of human rights, the jurisdiction of the court stems

[43] See W Hummer, M Frischhut, 'Diferentes Concepciones de la Protección de los Derechos Humanos en la Integración Europea y Latinoamericana. La Carta Andina para la Promoción y Protección de los Derechos Humanos' (2004) *Anuario Argentino de derecho Internacional* 47.

[44] The President of the CJCA during an interview has declared that 'los derechos fondamentales forman parte, a título de principio general del derecho comunitario, del orden comunitario de la Comunidad. . . . Los derechos fundamentales son parte en el contexto del Artículo 1 del Acuerdo de Cartagena'.

[45] See especially U Villani, 'I diritti fondamentali tra Carta di Nizza, Convenzione europea dei diritti dell'uomo e progetto di Costituzione europea' (2004) *Il Diritto dell'Unione europea* 73, 116.

[46] See AR Lamin, 'African Sub-Regional Human Rights Courts: The ECOWAS Court of Justice, the SADC Tribunal and the EAC Court of Justice in Comparative Perspective' in J Akokpari, DS Zimbler (eds), *Africa's Human Right Architecture* (Cape Town, Jacana Media, 2008) 232.

[47] See Case 03/2009 *Campbell v Zimbabwe* and Case 07/2008 *Tembani v Zimbabwe* available at www.sadc-tribunal.org. See M Beukes, 'Zimbabwe in the Dock. The Southern African Development Community (SADC) Tribunal's First Decision' in (2008) *South African Yearbook of International Law* 228.

[48] See Ref 01/2007 *James Katabazi and 21 ors v The Secretary General of the EAC and anor*, available at www.eacj.org.

from Article 4 of the supplementary Protocol. Access to the court is opened to individuals on application for relief for violation of their human rights in the Member States. Second, in the *Mani* case, the court ruled that the condition of exhaustion of national remedies does not apply before it and there is no reason to consider this absence as a lacuna that the practice of the Court must address.[49] Third, in the *Keita* case, recalling Article 4(g) of the ECOWAS Treaty, according to which the Community recognises the promotion and protection of human and peoples' rights in accordance with the provisions of the African Charter on Human and Peoples' Rights (ACHPR), the court exercised its jurisdiction over a case of breach of human rights by a Member State.[50] CJECOWAS seems to be a 'hybrid' Court: a court of an economic integration organisation but, on the other hand, a regional human rights court. This development in Africa can be explained in light of the weakness of the ACHPR. While the ECtHR enjoys exclusive jurisdiction on the interpretation of the ECHR, the ACHPR does not.

PRIVATE PARTIES' INDIRECT ACCESS TO THE COURTS: PRELIMINARY RULING PROCEDURES

In the EU, the preliminary ruling procedure has played a major role in shaping EU law as well as deciding on the relationship between EU Law and national legal orders. Article 267 TFEU has ensured access to the ECJ for the protection of private parties' rights and the ECJ has repeatedly pointed to it as a substitute for Article 263(4) TFEU, because it provides an alternative means for individuals to challenge the legality of Community acts. As a consequence, for our comparative analysis, we need to examine whether other REIOs have procedures equivalent to Article 267 TFEU. In most of the treaties establishing regional systems of economic integration there are procedures for judicial co-operation comparable to the preliminary ruling procedures. Legal literature has classified these judicial co-operation procedures in broad categories: advisory, advisory and annulment, optional and compulsory.[51]

An advisory procedure is provided for in the EFTA Agreement. According to Article 34 SCA, national courts can request the EFTA Court to give an opinion if they consider it necessary to enable them to give judgment.[52] In the OHADA,[53] the

[49] See Case *Hadijatou Mani Koraou v Republic of Niger* ECW/CCJ/JUD/06/08. On the judgment see J Allain, 'Hadijatou Mani Koraou v Republic of Niger' in (2009) *American Journal of International Law* 311; Y Hamuli Kabumba, 'Discrimination, arrestation et détention arbitraires selon la Cour de justice de la CEDEAO dans *Hadijatou Mani Koraou c Niger* (27 October 2008)' (2009) *Revue de Droit International de Sciences Diplomatiques et Politiques* 291.

[50] See Case *Léo Keita v Mali*, ECW/CCJ/APP/03/07, para 32.

[51] See especially R Virzo, 'The Preliminary Ruling Procedures at International Regional Courts and Tribunals' (2011) *The Law and Practice of International Courts and Tribunals* 1.

[52] See M Broberg, N Fenger, *Preliminary References to the European Court of Justice* (Oxford, Oxford University Press, 2010) 16, 17.

[53] See H Tchantchou, *La supranationalité judiciaire dans le cadre de l'OHADA* (Paris, L'Harmattan, 2009).

CCJA must be seized by a national supreme court of a Member State if a question of interpretation or application of OHADA law is raised before it. If the CCJA declines jurisdiction, the case is decided by the national supreme court but, should the CCJA declare that it has jurisdiction, the CCJA takes the entire proceedings for annulment and the national supreme court loses its jurisdiction over the case. In ECOWAS[54] and CAIS,[55] the preliminary ruling procedure is optional in nature because national courts may decide to exercise this option before the community court of justice. In six other REIOs, the preliminary ruling procedure is compulsory, but it is worth making a further distinction depending on whether infringement proceedings can be initiated in the event of a breach of the obligation to refer for a preliminary ruling. In CARICOM and SADC, there is no provision for effective remedial action in the event of a breach of the obligation to refer for a preliminary ruling. Otherwise, in EAC, COMESA,[56] CEMAC[57] and AC[58] a failure to comply with the obligation to refer to the community court for a preliminary ruling envisages sanctions for breach of the obligation.

Clearly, the EU preliminary reference procedure has been a model for other REIOs. Indeed, the dialogue and co-operation between community courts and national ones is a prerequisite for integration.[59] As a consequence, REIOs have established this procedure to guarantee the evolution of their systems. Obviously, the transposition of the EU procedure has not been automatic. Except for the last four REIOs referred to above, in the other REIOs the preliminary reference rulings have different features.

[54] See AO Enabulele, 'Reflections on the ECOWAS Community Court Protocol and the Constitutions of Member States' (2010) *International Community Law Review* 111.

[55] See R Chamorro Mora, *La corte de justicia de la Comunidad Centroamericana* (Managua, Imprimátur Artes Gráficas, 2000); K Nyman-Metcalf, I Papageorgiou, *Regional Integration and Courts of Justice* (Antwerp, Intersentia, 2005); MA Cano Linares, n 7 above, 111; R Virzo, n 7 above; S Maldonado Jordison, 'The Central American Court of Justice: Yesterday, Today and Tomorrow?' (2009) *Connecticut Journal of International Law* 183.

[56] Art 29 of the EAC Treaty and Art 25 of the COMESA Treaty, whose terms are almost identical, provide that infringement proceedings are to be instituted respectively by the EAC Secretary General or the COMESA Secretary General and that each of the latter individuals – after an administrative or pre-litigation phase attempting to resolve the dispute on infringement directly with the Member State concerned – may refer the matter respectively to the EAC Council or the COMESA Council as the case may be.

[57] See Art 19 of the Treaty of Libreville regarding the CEMAC Court of Justice.

[58] In some recent judgments, the TJCA held that a failure by a domestic court to seek a preliminary ruling is a breach by its Member State that can lead to infringement proceedings pursuant to Art 23 of the Treaty Creating the Court of Justice of the Cartagena Agreement. See TJCA judgments in Case 106-IP-2009 *Pfizer v Instituto Nacional de Defensa de la Competencia y de la Protección de la Propiedad Intelectual – INDECOPI – de la República del Perú* (21 April 2010), [2010] *Gazeta Oficial del Acuerdo de Cartagena 1853/4*; Case 103-IP-2009 *Ebel International Limited v Instituto Nacional de Defensa de la Competencia y de la Protección de la Propiedad Intelectual – INDECOPI – de la República del Perú* (29 April 2010), [2010] *Gazeta Oficial del Acuerdo de Cartagena 1853/27.* See especially MF Orzan, 'I diritti di proprietà industriale nella Comunità andina: il ruolo delle agenzie nazionali della proprietà intellettuale e quello del Tribunale di giustizia' in (2011) *Diritto comunitario e degli scambi internazionali* 155.

[59] See Art 23 of the Treaty Creating the Court of Justice of the Cartagena Agreement.

CONCLUSION

This comparative analysis shows that the EU system has been a model for private parties' access to the courts. REIOs have essentially adapted the EU procedures to their regional features. The action for annulment is quite different in each organisation; the actions for failure to act and the action seeking compensation for damages are absent from most REIOs; only the EU guarantees a well-developed system of judicial protection to its servants.

Besides, the African and American courts for the protection of human rights have not played the same role in the evolution of the protection of human rights as the ECtHR and ECJ have in Europe. In Europe, the courts have furthered the development of the protection of human rights through two regimes that were distinct and independent from each other, but they have not acted in isolation. Especially in Africa, the establishment of a regional judicial body to ensure the implementation of human rights is an afterthought. The effect of this situation is peculiar. Following the case law of the ECJ, the courts of some REIOs have extended their jurisdiction over human rights. Despite the efforts of some African REIOs to improve the protection of human rights, the European system of protection seems to be the most advanced and effective regional human rights regime in the world.

Also the comparative analysis of private parties' indirect access to the Courts of REIOs comes to a similar conclusion. The preliminary ruling procedure has been followed in most other REIOs. To reach the aim of integration it is necessary to have a mechanism of judicial co-operation which ensures the uniform interpretation and application of the law of the organisation. However, this analysis shows that each organisation has transposed this procedure of co-operation between national and community courts in a different manner, according to regional features.

4

From Diplomacy to Judicialisation? – Some Thoughts on EU–Swiss Relations

CARL BAUDENBACHER*

INTRODUCTION

ALTHOUGH BOTH OPTIONS are open, Switzerland is neither a Member State of the European Union nor of the European Economic Area. The country has so far acted according to the maxim of Groucho Marx, 'Why belong to any club that will accept one as a member'? Its relationship with the EU is regulated by way of bilateral agreements and through the means of diplomacy. Switzerland is thus the only country in the EU and EFTA which opposes the judicialisation of the law linking it to the EU to date.

The EU and Switzerland have concluded some 120 bilateral agreements, 20 of which have special significance. Conflicts are to be settled by diplomatic means. They are understood as intergovernmental affairs, even if they involve private parties. The perspective in Switzerland is always 'them against us' or 'us against them'. Still, provisions in bilateral agreements can possibly be invoked before the courts of either Contracting Party; that is, before the ECJ and the Swiss Supreme Court. Experience shows, however, that there are limitations. A common court is missing. In the European Union, the Commission may bring an infringement action against a Member State for violation of a bilateral agreement. It has done so on rare occasions upon repeated complaints from Switzerland.[1] On the Swiss side, there is no such surveillance mechanism. Most conflicts are dealt with by joint committees. Such bodies are not permanent. They will be convened on an ad hoc basis, that is, after a problem has occurred. The committees meet behind closed doors, there are no time limits, they are not obliged to make a decision and if they do make a decision they are not obliged to give reasons. Political and economic power can be very relevant.

* President of the EFTA Court, Director of the Institute of European and International Economic Law at the University of St Gallen HSG.

[1] www.nzz.ch/nachrichten/wirtschaft/aktuell/eu_schaltet_sich_in_schweizerisch-italienischen_streit_ueber_diskriminierung_von_firmen_ein_1.9936891.html.

For Switzerland, the 'bilateral path' until recently was the lowest common denominator of European policy. At least since the second half of 2010 it has, however, become clear that, in the EU's view, bilateralism as we know it has reached its limits. At different levels the Union has put four institutional demands on the table. It calls for: (1) the dynamic adjustment of bilateral law to the new EU *acquis*, (2) a mechanism ensuring uniform interpretation of bilateral law, (3) a mechanism for monitoring compliance with the bilateral treaties, and (4) a judicial mechanism.

The following considerations will trace the development of Swiss–EU bilateralism over the past 40 years. They will also discuss whether bilateralism could be judicialised. I am delighted to write this contribution for my good friend Pernilla Lindh. Judge Lindh was the Swedish negotiator on institutional issues in the EEA negotiations. These proceedings led to the establishment of the EFTA Surveillance Authority and the EFTA Court. It must have been painful for her to see the Swiss reject the EEA Agreement not least because of their fear of a central enforcement mechanism. Now, it seems that Switzerland is getting caught up by the institutional question. I am therefore confident that my thoughts will be of interest to Pernilla.

PRE-EEA BILATERALISM: DIPLOMACY WITHOUT HARMONISATION

The heart of pre-EEA bilateralism was, and is, the 1972 Free Trade Agreement (FTA).[2] The conclusion of the FTA was a consequence of the accession of the leading EFTA State, the United Kingdom, to the EEC. It essentially replicates the main free trade and competition law provisions of the Treaty. Harmonisation, however, is not provided for. With the conclusion of the FTA, Switzerland found itself in the good company of eight like-minded States. Efforts to deny individuals and economic operators access to the courts under the FTA were in line with the policy of those other EFTA States. The dualistic Nordic countries reached this result by avoiding incorporation of the relevant FTA into their national legal orders. In the monistic countries, Switzerland and Austria, the Supreme Courts decided in the years 1978 and 1979 that private operators could not invoke the provisions of the respective FTAs.[3] This narrow-minded approach of the EFTA side did not prevent the ECJ from recognising the possibility of direct effect of the EEC–Portugal FTA in its 1982 *Kupferberg* judgment. The fact that the EFTA States did not grant reciprocity was deemed not to be an obstacle.[4]

[2] Free Trade Agreement, [1972] OJ L300/189.

[3] U Bernitz, *European Law in Sweden* (Stockholm, Skriftserien/Juridiska Faculteten, 2002) 25; see also from the same author, 'The EEC–EFTA Free Trade Agreements with Special Reference to the Position of Sweden and the other Scandinavian EFTA Countries' [1986] *CML Rev* 567; judgments of the Swiss Federal Supreme Court in Cases ATF 104 IV 1975 *Stanley Adams* and ATF 105 II 49 *Bosshard Partners Intertrading AG*, in which direct effect of the FTA EEC–Switzerland provisions concerning competition and free movement of goods was denied; the Austrian Supreme Court came to the same result with regard to the free movement of goods in OGH *Austro-Mechana* [1980] GRUR Int 185, but used more cautious language.

[4] Case 104/81 *Kupferberg* [1982] ECR 3641.

Still, conflict resolution is largely based on the diplomatic model. According to Articles 29 and 30 FTA, a joint committee consisting of representatives of the EU and of Switzerland is established which is in charge of administering the proper implementation of the FTA. The joint committee acts by consensus. Its decisions must be put into effect by the Contracting Parties in accordance with their own rules. Under Article 31(2) FTA, the joint committee must meet at least once a year to review the general functioning of the FTA. It must also, at the request of either party, meet as often as necessary. If the joint committee cannot find a solution to a problem the injured party may impose trade sanctions under Article 22(2) FTA.

POST-EEA BILATERALISM: DIPLOMACY WITH HARMONISATION

General

Had Switzerland ratified the EEA Agreement, its relations with the other EFTA States, as well as with the EU, would have been judicialised to a large extent. The EEA Agreement is based on a two pillar approach. The EFTA Surveillance Authority (ESA) and the EFTA Court have similar competences in the EFTA pillar of the EEA to the European Commission and the ECJ in the EU pillar. Individuals and economic operators from all 30 EEA countries may lodge a complaint with the ESA if they feel that their rights flowing from the EEA Agreement have been violated. Moreover, they may, if a dispute has its origin in an EU country, bring the matter before a national court of a Member State and ask this court to request a preliminary ruling from the ECJ. If the dispute originates in the EFTA pillar, they may resort to a national court of an EEA/EFTA country and request a reference to the EFTA Court. Whether EEA law is of a supranational nature is a matter of definition. In any case, it is much closer to supranational Union law than to general international law. According to the jurisprudence of the EFTA Court the EEA Agreement is an international treaty sui generis, 'which contains a distinct legal order of its own'.[5] EEA law has a far-reaching effect in the legal orders of the EEA/EFTA States.[6] Hence, the EFTA Court does not follow the conservative interpretation rules of the Vienna Convention but, rather, applies the same principles as the ECJ.[7]

[5] Case E-9/97 *Sveinbjörnsdóttir* [1998] EFTA Court Rep 95, para 39.

[6] See Case E-1/94 *Restamark* [1994-1995] EFTA Court Rep 15; Case T-115/94 *Opel Austria v Council* [1997] ECR II-39, paras 107–08; Case E-1/01 *Einarsson* [2002] EFTA Court Rep 1; *Sveinbjörnsdóttir*, n 5 above, para 59; Case C-140/97 *Rechberger* [1999] ECR I-3499, para 39.

[7] See C Baudenbacher, 'Zur Auslegung des EWR-Rechts durch den EFTA-Gerichtshof' in G Müller, E Osterloh, and T Stein (eds), *Festschrift für Günter Hirsch zum 65 Geburtstag* (München, Beck, 2008), 27.

EU Law as the Basis

Under the EEA Agreement, the EFTA States take over EU internal market legislation across the board. Second generation bilateralism advances step by step, but the basis is always EU law. Already the Commission's Communication of 1 October 1993 on 'Future relations with Switzerland' stated that '[a]ny agreement would need to deal satisfactorily with the implementation of the Community acquis and the need for Switzerland to accept the discipline involved'.[8] By requesting the conclusion of a Free Movement of Persons Agreement (FMPA) and an Agreement on Land Transport, the Union also made it clear from the beginning that there would be no EEA à la carte. Seven bilateral agreements were signed on 21 June 1999 and entered into force on 1 June 2002. This first package further encompassed treaties relating to the areas of air transport, land transport, agricultural trade, mutual recognition of conformity assessment, public procurement and scientific and technological co-operation. In light of the EEA experience, the EU insisted on linking the treaties of the first package together by way of a so-called 'guillotine clause'. The clause states that in the case of termination or non-renewal of an agreement, the other six agreements would also lapse. A second set of nine bilateral agreements was signed on 26 October 2004 and entered into force between 2005 and 2009. The second package includes, in particular, agreements on the taxation of savings income and on the accession of Switzerland to the Schengen and Dublin systems.

The contractual terms of the post-EEA bilateral agreements are taken from primary and secondary EU law. On transitional periods and other minor points, Switzerland could score some partial victories, but only where the EU allowed it. An academic commentator stated aptly: 'Where the EU sought an approximation based on the *acquis*, namely in the sectors of the free movement of persons, air and land transport, taxation, security (Schengen), and asylum (Dublin), it obtained it.'[9]

Preservation of Switzerland's Sovereignty?

The Swiss Government does not tire of emphasising that the bilateral agreements are by definition static and that adaptations to the recent developments of the EU *acquis* require the consent of Switzerland. According to official language, the bilateral agreements therefore do not affect Switzerland's sovereignty. Despite all the sovereignty rhetoric, one must not overlook the fact that joint committees

[8] So were the apt remarks of the first president of the EFTA Surveillance Authority, K Almestad, at the sitting marking the inauguration of the EFTA Court on 4 January 1994, EFTA Court Rep [1994–1995] 177.

[9] F Maiani, 'Legal Europeanization as Legal Transformation: Some Insights from Swiss "Outer Europe"', (2008) 32 *MWP* 6, cadmus.eui.eu/bitstream/handle/1814/9017/MWP_2008_32.pdf;jsessionid=F33FDE1371D95BA764189AF3FE1463D0?sequence=1.

may have the competence to amend an agreement. Article 18 FMPA states that amendments to Annexes II and III shall be adopted by a decision of the Joint Committee and may enter into force immediately after that decision. Annex II contains the provisions on the co-ordination of social security systems whereas Annex III deals with the mutual recognition of professional qualifications. At the same time Switzerland is, unlike the EEA/EFTA States, excluded from any creative involvement in the development of new EU law.[10]

Securing Judicial Homogeneity

Homogeneity through Behavioural Rules

Unlike the FTA, the FMPA obliges the Swiss courts to follow ECJ case law rendered prior to the date of signature. Article 16 FMP states under the heading 'Reference to Community law':

> 1. In order to attain the objectives pursued by this Agreement, the Contracting Parties shall take all measures necessary to ensure that rights and obligations equivalent to those contained in the legal acts of the European Community to which reference is made are applied in relations between them.
>
> 2. Insofar as the application of this Agreement involves concepts of Community law, account shall be taken of the relevant case-law of the Court of Justice of the European Communities prior to the date of its signature. Case-law after that date shall be brought to Switzerland's attention. To ensure that the Agreement works properly, the Joint Committee shall, at the request of either Contracting Party, determine the implications of such case-law.

The Air Transport Agreement contains a similar provision.[11]

On paper, these homogeneity rules do not go as far as those of EEA law. Article 6 EEA and Article 3(2) SCA subject the EFTA Court to an obligation to follow relevant ECJ case law rendered before the signature of the agreement (2 May 1992) and to take into due account case law rendered after that date. The differentiation between old and new case law is politically important. The EFTA Court has, however, never relied on it in order to refuse to follow new case law of the ECJ. Applications made by the EEA/EFTA States to that effect were rejected.[12]

[10] There are two exceptions to that rule: under Art 6 of the Schengen Agreement and Art 2 of the Dublin Agreement with Switzerland, Swiss experts have a right to participate in the decision-shaping in the same way as EU experts; see Swiss Federal Office of Justice, *Schengen/Dublin: The Development of Provisions, September 2008*, www.ejpd.admin.ch/content/dam/data/sicherheit/polizeizusammenarbeit/schengen_weiterentwicklungbj-ibe.pdf. The same holds true according to Art 22 of the Agreement on Customs Facilitation and Security. See with regard to the comprehensive participation of the EEA/EFTA States in the decision shaping EFTA Bulletin, Decision Shaping in the European Economic Area, 1 March 2009, www.efta.int/~/media/Files/Publications/Bulletins/eeadecisionshaping-bulletin.pdf.

[11] Art 1(2) Air Transport Agreement.

[12] See Baudenbacher, 'Governments Before the EFTA Court' in *Festskrift Til Claus Gulmann* (København, Thomson, 2006) 23.

In practice, the differences between the rules of the Free Movement of Persons Agreement and the EEA Agreement are, however, minor. The Swiss Supreme Court basically understands the duty to take account of old ECJ case law laid down in Article 16(2)(1) FMPA as a contractually agreed obligation. The judgments of the ECJ are being referred to as 'massgebend' (authoritative). In a landmark ruling which was rendered in Italian, the Supreme Court even used the term 'vincolante' (binding). To be sure, the Supreme Court maintains that the agreement constitutes a treaty under public international law, but this amounts largely to paying lip service. It has been said that the homogeneity rule in Article 16(2)(1) FMPA encompasses the ECJ's *effet utile* jurisprudence.[13] For the sake of completeness, it should also be noted that in the Air Transport Agreement Switzerland has accepted the exclusive competence of the European Commission, the General Court and the ECJ to apply the antitrust rules which were taken from the TFEU (Articles 8, 9 and 11 of the Agreement). The fact that Switzerland is the only country in Europe which has subjected itself to the jurisdiction of a foreign court is somewhat ironic in the light of the almost irrational Swiss fear of foreign judges.

The provision concerning new ECJ case law is interpreted according to the general rules of international law that have been codified in the Vienna Convention on the Law of Treaties. The Supreme Court considers itself not to be bound by new ECJ case law. It is, however, prepared to make use of new jurisprudence on a case by case basis, even without a decision of the Joint Committee.[14] This is done in the first instance where the new case-law clarifies old case-law. In the interest of creating a parallel legal situation and a uniform free movement area to the largest extent possible, the Supreme Court has also followed new ECJ case-law in other instances. It has, for example, decided that the foreign children of the third country spouse of a French national enjoy a right to join their family under Article 3(2)(a) FMP.[15] As a result, it is considered that the provision which provides that post-signature ECJ case-law will be brought to Switzerland's attention is understood as amounting to a de facto duty to take due account of such case law. The Supreme Court would only deviate from it if there were valid reasons and, in any case, not lightly. The differences from the EEA legal situation are therefore only minimal. Academic literature speaks of the relativity of the deadline for the takeover of ECJ case law.[16] The point is, however, that there is no legal certainty. In particular in politically sensitive cases, it is conceivable that the Supreme Court refuses to follow new ECJ case law. An important example concerns the issue of exportability of the helplessness allowance. In a ruling dated 24 July 2006, the Supreme Court took the view that the case law of the ECJ on European Union law, which assumes an export duty in this area, dates from the period after the signing of the FMP. An adoption of this case law was unwarranted.[17] Two things should be noted in

[13] A Epiney, 'Zur Bedeutung der Rechtsprechung des EuGH für die Anwendung und Auslegung des Personenfreizügigkeitsabkommmens' (2005) 151 *ZBJV* 1, 6.

[14] See, eg ATF 113 II 1, 10 f.

[15] Judgment 2c 269/2009 of 5 January 2010, consideration 4.

[16] Epiney, n 13 above, 30.

[17] ATF 132 V 423.

this respect: first, there were good arguments in this specific case to conclude that the new case law was based on the (binding) old case law. Second, the EFTA Court ruled shortly after, in a case concerning Liechtenstein, that under the substantially identical EEA law the helplessness allowance had to be exported to other EFTA and EU States parties to the EEA.[18]

Decisions of the Joint Committee to amend Annexes II and III under Article 18 FMPA are deemed to be binding on the Supreme Court.[19] On the other hand, the scope of the third sentence of Article 16, paragraph 2 FMPA is controversial. That provision states that in order to ensure that the Agreement works properly, the Joint Committee shall at the request of either Contracting Party determine the implications of new case law. Professor Astrid Epiney has taken the view that such a decision makes the case law in question binding for the Supreme Court.[20] It should be noted in this context that the EFTA Court held in *CIBA* that a decision of the EEA Joint Committee, which is, mutatis mutandis, composed in the same way as the Joint Committee under the FMP, constitutes a simplified form of an international agreement between the Community and its Member States on the one hand and the EFTA side on the other.[21] This finding may also be relevant for the interpretation of Article 18 FMPA.

The ECJ maintains no judicial dialogue with the Swiss Supreme Court as it does with the EFTA Court. It can therefore be argued that the loss of sovereignty of Switzerland is more significant than that of the EEA/EFTA countries, Norway, Iceland and Liechtenstein, under the EEA Agreement. Through the EFTA Court these countries dispose of a forum to shape the development of the case law in the whole of the EEA. Finally, it should not be overlooked that national high courts such as the England and Wales Court of Appeal, the German Supreme Court, the German Supreme Fiscal Court and the Austrian Supreme Court have referred to EFTA Court case law.[22]

In view of the integration-friendly approach of the Supreme Court, some may have hoped that the ECJ would refrain from applying its *Polydor* case law to the FMPA. According to *Polydor*, the similarity of the wording is not a sufficient reason to transfer the interpretation given to rules of EU law to the parallel provisions of the FTA. This was justified, in particular, with the different objectives and activities of the TEC (today TFEU) on the one hand and the FTA on the other and the lack of instruments to ensure uniform application of the law under the FTA.[23] In *Grimme*, *Focus Invest AG* and *Hengartner and Gasser*, the Fourth Chamber of

[18] Case E-5/06 *EFTA Surveillance Authority v Liechtenstein* [2007] EFTA Court Rep 296.

[19] ATF 132 V 423 consideration 9.2.

[20] ibid, 22 f.

[21] Case E-6/01 *CIBA* [2002] EFTA Court Rep 281, para 33.

[22] See, eg judgment of the German Supreme Court of 19 September 2005 – II ZR 372/03, 6; judgment of 14 June 2007 – I ZR 173/04 – *STILNOX*, para 23; judgment of 24 April 2008 – I ZR 89/05 *Micardis*, Rdnr 17; judgment of 24 April 2008 I ZR 30/05 – *Lefax/Lefaxin*, para 22; judgment of 29 April 2010 – I ZR 66/08 *Holzhocker*; judgment of the Supreme Fiscal Court of 9 August 2006 – I R 31/01; decision of the German Supreme Financial Court of 9 May 2007 to request a preliminary ruling from the ECJ I R 56/05.

[23] Case 270/80 *Polydor et RSO Records* [1982] ECR 329 paras 15–20.

the ECJ has disappointed such expectations. It referred to the Swiss 'No' to the EEA and transposed *Polydor* to the FMPA. Certain discriminations are therefore possible under that agreement which would be unlawful under the TFEU and under the EEA Agreement.[24] Of course one can criticise the ECJ for that, and the legal representatives of the two defeated Swiss citizens in the case *Hengartner and Gasser* did that.[25] It just does not help. The explicit statement that Switzerland rejected the EEA Agreement, which would have been given the same interpretation, indicates that the EU Court took offence at the fact that there is no surveillance and court mechanism under the FMPA.[26]

Homogeneity through Threat to Terminate the Agreements

A different solution was found in the Schengen and Dublin Agreements. According to Article 2(3) of the Schengen Agreement and Article 1(3) of the Dublin Agreement, Switzerland also adopts future changes or amendments of EU law. In return, Switzerland has a co-determination right. Contrariwise, there is no provision requiring the Supreme Court to take account of the jurisprudence of the ECJ. To conclude from this that the sovereignty of Switzerland has been spared, would, however, be premature. According to its Article 10, the Schengen Agreement will be deemed as terminated if a significant difference between the case law of the ECJ and that of the Swiss courts cannot be settled within the framework of proceedings of the Joint Committee within certain time limits. The same applies under Article 7 of the Dublin Convention. No distinction is made between old and new ECJ case law.

THE EMERGENCE OF A 'SWISS EUROPEAN LAW'

The Autonomous Implementation Programme

In addition to the contractual rapprochement, Switzerland after the rejection of the EEA in 1992 has intensified its policy to implement EU law unilaterally. The first autonomous implementation programme was launched in 1988.[27] To be sure, this does not produce reciprocal rights and therefore no access to the EU's internal market for Swiss citizens and economic actors. The goal was rather to

[24] Case C-351/08 *Grimme* [2009] ECR I-10777, paras 27–29; Case C-541/08 *Fokus Invest AG* [2010] ECR I-1025, paras 26–32; Case C-70/09 *Hengartner and Gasser*, judgment of 15 July 2010 nyr, paras 41–43; similar remarks can be found in Case C-476/10 *projektart* order of 24 June 2011 nyr, para 37 although this case was dealt with under the EEA Agreement and had no implications for Switzerland.

[25] V Turnher and A Wittwer, 'Warum dürfen Schweizer Jäger in Vorarlberg diskriminiert werden?' www.jagdportal.ch/jagdampnatur/jagd-umwelt/jagd-umwelt-einzelansicht/browse/3/article/8/warum-duerfe-101679.html.

[26] L Baudenbacher, 'Das Personenfreizügigkeitsabkommen EU-Schweiz ist doch kein Integrationsvertrag' (2010) *EL Rev* 34; 'Gar lustig ist die Jägerei – aber für Schweizer ist sie teurer als für andere' (2010) *EL Rev* 280.

[27] See C Baudenbacher, 'Zum Nachvollzug europäischen Rechts in der Schweiz' (1992) *Europarecht* 309.

keep open the possibility of eventual EU or EEA membership and to guarantee a level playing field for Swiss operators. Furthermore, certain goodwill with the EU should be created. In 2002, this technique became a permanent element of federal legislation. Article 141 of the Federal Assembly Act of 13 December 2002 states, inter alia, that the Federal Council (Government) when reasoning and annotating draft legislation, has to give comments on 'the compatibility with higher-ranking law and the relationship to European law'.[28] Parliament is not obliged to take over European law. But it does so in most cases. The systematic adoption of Union law amounts to a significant giving up on State sovereignty. Switzerland has no right whatsoever to participate in the formulation of EU law.

Inconsistencies in Legislation

On closer inspection one discovers, moreover, that autonomous implementation is a somewhat chaotic undertaking. First, there is no guarantee that EU legislation will result in a reaction of the Swiss legislature at all. Second, there is no surveillance mechanism which ensures that the implementation is done in a correct way as far as substance is concerned and Swiss courts cannot seize the ECJ or the EFTA Court for a preliminary ruling. It may therefore happen that an EU directive is wrongfully implemented without there being any consequences. The State liability case law of the ECJ and the EFTA Court does not apply. If special interest groups in the Parliament are able to build up enough resistance in a particular case, implementation will be blocked or diluted. Thus, the adoption of EU product safety standards has been prevented for many years. That is possible because the taking over of EU law is hardly an issue in the political debate. There is a simple reason for this: which Member of Parliament is prepared to tell his voters that his role consists, in an ever increasing number of cases, of nodding through laws of the EU (possibly in a slightly different form)? Third, there is no guarantee that the implemented Swiss law will be adapted to amendments of the EU *acquis* in a timely manner. University of Lausanne law professor Francesco Maiani has aptly remarked: 'It is . . . often the case that originally euro-compatible Swiss rules become over time euro-incompatible, due to the evolution of EU legislation and case law.'[29] In other words, the clash of the Swiss leisurely pace of politics and the dynamic policy approach of the EU leads to disparities.

Inconsistencies in Interpretation

But that's not all. The Swiss legislature does not oblige the courts to construe autonomously implemented EU law in a euro-compatible way. The Supreme Court uses the same rules as when it interprets autochthonous Swiss law. That means that it

[28] SR 171.10.
[29] Maiani, n 9 above, 13.

proceeds according to the principle of method pluralism. Depending on the circumstances, the text, the history, the scheme or the purpose of the norm may be decisive. This is in clear contrast to the methodological approach of the courts in the EU and the EEA. Both in EU law and in EEA law dynamic interpretation and interpretation according to the *effet utile* or principle of effectiveness play an important role.[30] Academic authors have called upon the Supreme Court to interpret Swiss law in the sense of normative compliance with EU law, unless the legislature has clearly taken a decision to do the opposite.[31] The Court is, however, hesitant and sticks to its traditional approach. There is, in particular, no *unité de doctrine.*

The First Civil Division, in a celebrated ruling on issues of transfer of undertaking, held that the approximation of the Swiss legal order to European harmonisation must also aim at the interpretation and application of the law. In such cases, the court should not merely orient itself towards the European legal situation which existed at the time of the implementation in Switzerland. It rather has to keep track of the further developments in European law. At any rate, this must apply as far as Swiss methodology allows.[32] When sitting in a different composition, the same Division has, however, taken another stand. In a judgment on the Copyright Act, it found that even if harmonisation with European law was a concern of the Swiss legislature, it was not possible to introduce, by way of Europe-friendly interpretation, a rule which was not provided for in the law.[33]

One will also remember that the First Civil Division has shown great restraint in the interpretation of the Cartel Act with regard to euro-compatible interpretation although that Act was designed in 1995 as far as possible according to the European model.[34] In a product liability judgment of 18 March 2011 the First Civil Division summarised its jurisprudence concerning the significance of the case law of the ECJ for the interpretation of autonomously implemented EU law. It stated that the Swiss Product Liability Act had largely been inspired by Council Directive 85/374/EEC. Other than when applying the Lugano Convention on jurisdiction and the enforcement of judgments in civil and commercial matters,

> il n'existe toutefois aucune obligation pour les tribunaux suisses, lors de l'interprétation de la LRFP (sc. loi fédérale sur la responsabilité du fait des produits), de tenir compte de

[30] See generally, with regard to the *effet utile* principle in EU law, C Baudenbacher and A Bergmann, 'Der EuGH ausser Kontrolle?' in U Haltern und A Bergmann, *Der EuGH in der Kritik* (Tübingen, Mohr Siebeck, 2011) forthcoming; concerning the situation in EEA law; JT Lang, 'The Duty of National Courts to Provide Access to Justice in the EEA', paper presented at the EFTA Court Conference 'Judicial Protection in the European Economic Area' on 17 June 2011, on file with the author. See also Case E-4/-4 *Pedicel* [2005] EFTA Court Rep 4, para 28, where the EFTA Court stated that the objective of creating a dynamic and homogeneous EEA 'may make a dynamic interpretation of EEA law necessary'. See with regard to *effet utile* in EEA law Case E-4/11 *Arnulf Clauder*, judgment of 26 July 2011 nyr, para 34.

[31] See especially M Amstutz, 'Evolutorische Rechtsmethodik im europäischen Privatrecht – Zur richtlinienkonformen Auslegung und ihren Folgen für den autonomen Nachvollzug des Gemeinschaftsprivatrechts in der Schweiz' in F Werro and T Probst (eds), *Le droit privé suisse face au droit communautaire européen* (Berne, StaempFli, 2004) 105.

[32] ATF 129 III 335, Consideration 6.

[33] ATF 133 III 568, Consideration 4.6.

[34] ATF 124 III 495, Consideration 2(a); of late see also the *Swisscom* judgment of 11 April 2011 from the Second Public Law Division, 2C_343/2010, 2C_344/2010, Consideration 4(3).

> la jurisprudence européenne en matière de responsabilité du fait des produits. Cela étant, l'intention du législateur d'adapter le droit suisse au droit européen de manière autonome doit être prise en compte et il convient donc d'éviter de contrecarrer l'harmonisation voulue sans qu'il y ait pour cela un bon motif.[35]

The Second Public Law Division of the Supreme Court seems to understand EU law only as a source of inspiration.[36] The Federal Administrative Court found in a decision dated 5 December 2007 that the Federal Law on Pharmaceutical and Medicinal Products must be construed autonomously, although the legislature had aimed at euro-compatibility. The reference of the complainant to EU law was called a 'comparative remark'.[37] In another context, the Federal Administrative Court also expressed what pundits had suspected all along: that a main feature of European methodology, the interpretation according to the principle of effectiveness, is unknown to Swiss methodology.[38]

It is fair to say that from an economic point of view, post-EEA bilateralism and autonomous implementation have been quite a success story for Swiss industry and Swiss banks. Industry obtained almost full access to the EU single market whereas the banks managed to avoid the conclusion of a bilateral free movement of services agreement. In the first ten years after the rejection of the EEA Agreement, Switzerland had one of the lowest growth rates in Western Europe. After the conclusion of the bilateral agreements, this changed fundamentally.[39]

Nevertheless, the government's claim that sovereignty has been preserved appears to be an exaggeration. The most important bilateral agreement, the FMPA, can be updated by the Joint Committee. Parliament and the people have no say on that. Moreover, the Supreme Court follows in most cases not only old, but also new, ECJ case law. Unlike the EEA/EFTA States, Switzerland is, as a rule, excluded from any participation in the preparation of new EU legislation and the case law of the Supreme Court is not being taken into account by the ECJ. Most importantly, the lack of judicial enforcement is at the expense of individual rights and of legal certainty. Individuals and economic operators can hardly take their case to court; their only possibility is to petition the government. Diplomatic conflict resolution is associated with the ancient concept of state sovereignty. The main focus is on the legislature's autonomy whereas the sovereignty of citizens and businesses is blanked out. A Swiss entrepreneur facing difficulties in performing services in an EU Member State must normally rely on diplomatic protection.[40]

35 4A 16/2011, Consideration 2(2).

36 ATF 124 II 193, Consideration 6.

37 C-2092/2006, Consideration 3(5).

38 Judgment of 21 January 2010, A-7789/2009, Consideration 3(5)(2).

39 See Federal Department of Economic Affairs, 'Growth Report of 2 April 2002', www.google.lu/#hl=fr&sa=X&ei=tEwwTtCzOsfOsga_x9gV&ved=0CBUQBSgA&q=Seco+Wachstums+Bericht+2002&spell=1&bav=on.2,or.r_gc.r_pw.&fp=77cede195e67401b&biw=1280&bih=583.

40 See 'Integrationsbüro EDA/EVD, Umfrage zur Anwendung der bilateralen Abkommen zwischen der Schweiz und der EU – Auswertender Bericht und Analyse der Problemfälle' (Bern 2010), www.google.lu/#hl=fr&source=hp&biw=1277&bih=580&q=Vgl.+Integrationsb%C3%BCro+EDA%2C+Umfrage+zur+Anwendung+der+bilateralen+Abkommen+zwischen+der+Schweiz+und+der+EU+%E2%80%93+Auswertender+Bericht+und+Analyse+der+Problemf%C3%A4lle%2C+Bern+2010%2C+6.+&btnG=Recherche+Google&aq=f&aqi=&aql=&oq=&fp=c1eb3b723979dd64.

The flaws of autonomous implementation and of interpretation of the autonomously implemented European law call into question the use of this legislative technique itself. The result is not a (partial) recovery of state sovereignty, but rather a loss of legal certainty and predictability. A level playing field is lacking. It must finally not be overlooked that the emergence of a 'Swiss European law' may have negative consequences for academic teaching and doctrine.

THIRD GENERATION BILATERALISM: JUDICIALISATION?

Preliminary Remarks

For a number of years Switzerland sought to conclude further bilateral agreements with the EU primarily in the areas of trade in electricity, chemical safety (REACH), food and product safety and free trade in agricultural goods. The EU, however, made it clear that it was not prepared to continue with post-EEA bilateralism. In fact, there seems to be a clash of two concepts of integration of Switzerland in Europe. According to the view of the Swiss government, Switzerland and the EU are two sovereign entities which meet as equals. Consequently, their relations are governed by public international law. The EU sees Switzerland primarily as a participant in its internal market. Since Switzerland enjoys the advantages of participation in the internal market, it must abide by its rules. From the perspective of the EU this means that there must be a level playing field for individuals and economic operators in Switzerland and in the EU. When it comes to the adoption of the new EU *acquis*, the taking over of the new ECJ case law, the surveillance and judicial review, the same conditions must apply. What counts is not a formalistic legal approach which operates with the concepts of classical international law but a functional view.

There are probably three reasons that led the EU to rethink its policy vis-à-vis Switzerland. Firstly, as long as the bilateral agreements, in contrast to the EEA Agreement, had only sectoral character, and thus Swiss players only had punctual access to the EU internal market, the EU was ready to accept Swiss wishes for the renunciation of dynamisation of the adoption and the interpretation of bilateral law and to leave conflict resolution to the diplomats. With the increase in the number of bilateral agreements, Switzerland resembles the EEA/EFTA States more and more. Secondly, with the enlargement round of 2004/2007 the number of Member States has almost doubled and through the Lisbon Treaty, the EU has deepened its own integration. The Union seems to be less willing to accept Swiss special requests. The fact that the Swiss were so successful with their bilateral path has led to the emergence of a bilateralism movement in Norway. In Austria, voices can be heard pointing out the alleged advantages of Swiss bilateralism over EU membership. The EU is obviously not amused by such developments. Thirdly, it has been largely forgotten in Switzerland that in the early 1990s the bilateral agreements were considered by both sides as a transitional model until Switzerland made a second attempt to join the EEA or envisaged EU membership. In its Communication of 1 October 1993 on the future relations with Switzerland, the Commission explicitly stated that '[i]n the meantime, Switzerland has requested the opening of negotiations with a view to the conclusion of new bilateral agreements in a wide range of areas'.[41] In a way, the EU seems to think that the interim period is now exhausted.

The EU Council's December 2008 Paper

It became evident for the first time that the future of post-EEA bilateralism would not be as bright as Swiss industry and the Government wanted people to believe, when the EU Council issued its December 2008 report on relations with EFTA countries. The Council recalled that participation in the internal market requires the simultaneous and uniform application and interpretation of the evolving EU *acquis*. This indispensable condition for the functioning of the internal market must, like in the EEA, be reflected in all agreements currently being negotiated. Moreover, the Council made it clear that it wishes to dynamise also the existing bilateral agreements and ensure their uniform interpretation. The inconsistent application of bilateral agreements by Switzerland was considered to be particularly worrying because of the lack of a judicial mechanism in the bilateral treaties along the lines of the EEA.[42]

The new policy of the Council was not least prompted by the Swiss–EU tax dispute which has been smouldering since 2007. The European Commission, by a decision dated 13 February 2007, unilaterally stated that certain cantonal tax arrangements were incompatible with the State aid provision in Article 23(1) of the 1972 Free Trade Agreement. Discussions in the Joint Committee had remained fruitless.[43] On 14 May 2007, the Council gave the Commission a mandate for negotiations with Switzerland. Switzerland denied the existence of a violation of the FTA and first took the view that there was nothing to negotiate, but subsequently agreed to hold a 'tax dialogue' with the EU.[44] Since there is no judicial mechanism under the FTA, the conflict is not resolved to this day. The EU complains further about alleged violations of the FMPA by Switzerland.[45] Again, only diplomatic solutions are possible.

[41] Com(93) 486 final, para 4.

[42] register.consilium.europa.eu/pdf/de/08/st16/st16651-re01.en08.pdf; BGE 124 III 495 para 2a.

[43] europa.eu/rapid/pressReleasesAction.do?reference=IP/07/176.

[44] www.efd.admin.ch/dokumentation/medieninformationen/00467/index.html?lang=en&msg-id=16933; www.nzz.ch/2007/02/14/wi/articleEX7OD.html.

[45] See, eg www.tagesanzeiger.ch/schweiz/standard/EUBotschafter-Reiterer-nimmt-Protestbrief-entgegen/story/10179430.

2010: Change of Thinking

The Council's December 2008 report did not prompt any significant reactions in Switzerland. One had the impression that the Government was trying to sit the problems out. But some observers began to wonder about the fact that the new bilateral negotiations were not leading anywhere. In a study presented to the public on 15 July 2010, the liberal think tank Avenir Suisse called the EEA superior to bilateralism.[46] This was the first time after years of silence that some kind of a debate on Europe was launched.

In the run-up to the 19 July 2010 visit of Swiss President Doris Leuthard in Brussels, EU Council President Herman van Rompuy stated that Switzerland's bilateral approach vis-à-vis the European Union had seemed to reach its limits.[47] Commission President José Manuel Barroso agreed with Leuthard to set up a working group to find new solutions by the end of 2010. In a resolution of 7 September 2010 the European Parliament urged the Commission and Switzerland to promote the dynamisation of the bilateral agreements and to find horizontal solutions for specific institutional issues at short notice.[48] It was already clear in the spring of 2010 that such a resolution would be adopted.

The response of Switzerland to these advances was a cautious one. On 18 August 2010, the Federal Council of Europe met *in corpore* and heard three experts from the federal administration and one external expert.[49] The day after, President Leuthard and Foreign Minister Calmy-Rey announced the decision of the Federal Council to hold on to the bilateral approach. However, they admitted that modifications would be inevitable in the short term. In his report on the evaluation of European policy of 17 September 2010, the Federal Council declared its readiness to consider a new bilateralism, based on the demands of the EU.[50]

In its conclusion on EU relations with the EFTA countries of 14 December 2010 the EU Council noted the intention of the Federal Council to adhere to the sectoral approach, but reiterated its criticism of Switzerland's position as regards free movement of persons and cantonal tax regimes. The four institutional demands of the EU were reiterated.[51]

[46] C Baudenbacher, 'Rechtsprechung: Rechtssicherheit als Standortfaktor' in K Gentinetta and G Kohler (eds), *Souveränität im Härtetest* (Zurich, Neve Zürcher Zeitung, 2010) 247.

[47] bazonline.ch/schweiz/standard/Grenze-erreicht/story/19898576.

[48] European Parliament Resolution of 7 September 2010 on EEA–Switzerland: Obstacles with regard to the full implementation of the internal market (2009/2176(INI)), www.europarl.europa.eu/sides/getDoc.do?pubRef=-//EP//TEXT+TA+P7-TA-2010-0300+0+DOC+XML+V0//EN.

[49] The external expert was the author.

[50] www.ssn.ethz.ch/var/ssn/storage/original/application/a976a1db23cdce44a60778c8d16ab5b6.pdf, 70 ff.

[51] www.consilium.europa.eu/uedocs/cms_data/docs/pressdata/EN/foraff/118458.pdf, para 42.

2011: 'Drôle de Negotiations'

During the 8 February 2011 visit of the new President of the Confederation Micheline Calmy-Rey to the Presidents of the European Parliament, the Council and the Commission, it became clear that the working group which was established in the autumn of 2010 had not reached any tangible results. The Federal Council is trying to buy time in view of the federal election to be held in October 2011. One is afraid that a Europe debate would play into the hands of the anti-European Swiss People's Party. The fact that since the negative EEA referendum in 1992, little or nothing has been done to put the people in the picture on European integration, is now taking its toll. Officially, Switzerland and the EU are at present negotiating, but in reality nothing noteworthy is happening.

WHAT COULD A JUDICIAL MECHANISM LOOK LIKE?

General

In my view, a judicialisation of its relationship with the EU would also be in the interest of Switzerland. The aim of the network of bilateral agreements is to secure Swiss players' access to the EU single market. The protagonists of a market are entrepreneurs, workers, traders, consumers and investors. It is strange, to say the least, that they can hardly defend their rights flowing from the bilateral agreements in court. Adherence to the traditional concept of State sovereignty with diplomatic protection in cases of conflict is out of date in twenty-first-century Europe. For citizens and economic operators to beg for diplomatic help has something paternalistic about it, a whiff of the *ancien régime.* Actually, a country with as proud a democratic tradition as Switzerland should realise that judicialisation is in the interest of individuals and businesses. It is an expression of people's sovereignty, for the benefit of which State sovereignty has to step back.

Proposed Models

The Commission is trying to persuade Switzerland to accept the competence of the EFTA Surveillance Authority and the jurisdiction of the EFTA Court. The evaluation report of the Federal Council of September 2010 mentions, under the title of a possible surveillance and court mechanism under the sectoral approach, three models: (1) the establishment of a bilateral arbitration tribunal, (2) the establishment of a common court of Switzerland and the EU and (3) the use of the surveillance authorities and interpretation instances of the EEA, that is, the EFTA Surveillance Authority and the EFTA Court.[52] It appears that in the

[52] ibid, 70 ff.

working group Switzerland also proposed a fourth model under which each side would monitor its own loyalty. This would amount to a two pillar structure. As far as judicial review is concerned, it would mean that the ECJ will be competent to decide cases originating from the EU, and the Swiss Supreme Court will adjudicate cases stemming from Switzerland.

Assessment

As regards the latter proposal, one may assume that, according to EU understanding, compliance with internal market rules by definition cannot be controlled by the supreme court of the country concerned. The Swiss Supreme Court cannot be compared to the EFTA Court with its three judges from three different EFTA States. Other models favoured by Switzerland, the establishment of a bilateral arbitration tribunal or of a common (bilateral) court of the European Union and of Switzerland are, in my view, unrealistic.

In the past, the EU has been reluctant to accept the establishment of arbitration tribunals. Such instances were only approved provided their sole competence was to assess the proportionality of safeguarding and rebalancing measures which the EU intends to impose for failure to adopt relevant EU legislation. An example is Article 111 paragraph 4 EEA. According to that provision, safeguarding measures taken in accordance with Article 111(3) or Article 112 EEA, or the proportionality of rebalancing measures taken in accordance with Article 114, may be referred to arbitration. However, no question of interpretation of the provisions of the EEA Agreement, which are identical with EU law in substance, may be dealt with in such procedures. Article 29(3) of the bilateral Agreement on Customs Facilitation and Security is modelled on this provision, but here the EU must even agree to the establishment of the tribunal. That the Union would accept the establishment of an arbitration tribunal with full powers of dispute resolution is therefore difficult to imagine. The same applies to the proposal to establish a common court of Switzerland and the EU. Above all, the ECJ which enjoys an interpretation monopoly in EU law would hardly agree to such a solution. A bilateral court would be competent to interpret norms that are identical in substance with Union law. The EU would be represented in such a court with one judge. The decisions would be binding on Switzerland and on the EU. That could hardly be reconciled with the reading of the ECJ's interpretation monopoly in that Court's first EEA Opinion 1/91.[53] The EU negotiators probably envisage a multilateral court in which the Union itself would not be represented.

That leads to the question whether the institutions of the EFTA pillar, which were created under the EEA Agreement, could be entrusted with the surveillance and the interpretation of the bilateral agreements. I believe that such a solution

[53] Opinion 1/91 *Draft Agreement Relating to the Creation of the European Economic Area* [1991] ECR I-6079.

could be feasible provided that both the Swiss side and the three actual EEA/EFTA countries would show some flexibility in the negotiations. ESA and the EFTA Court would then consist of four or five permanent members who would be competent to decide on EEA law cases as well as on bilateral law cases. From a technical perspective, such an arrangement would be relatively easy to formulate. It could also bring benefits for the actual EEA/EFTA States. One should not forget in this context that for five decades Liechtenstein, Iceland, Norway and Switzerland have been linked through the EFTA Convention. The best solution for Switzerland would be, however, to become a full-fledged Member State of the EEA on the EFTA side. Switzerland could thereby play a leadership role in a small, but fine, club. That makes much more sense than the current isolation it has confined itself to.

5

20 Years On: Some Reflections on the European Economic Area Judicial Mechanism

SVEN NORBERG*

I AM VERY grateful to have been asked to contribute to this celebration of my old friend Pernilla Lindh's long and dedicated service as a European judge, first in the Court of First Instance and then in the Court of Justice. After having first met in the Swedish judiciary in the early 1970s, we worked very much together during the 1980s and early 1990s, on the creation of what finally became the European Economic Area (EEA), she as a delegate for Sweden and I in the EFTA Secretariat. It has always been a very great pleasure to work with Pernilla, and her wise and always very pertinent arguments considerably strengthened the EFTA negotiating positions as well as the quality of the final result. It is with this in mind that I decided to devote these few pages to a subject the creation of which Pernilla made crucial contributions, the EEA judicial mechanism.

INTRODUCTION

When, on 2 May 1992, seven EFTA States together with the European Community and its 12 Member States in Oporto concluded the Agreement on the European Economic Area (EEA), a new legal order, EEA law, was created in parallel with EC law, which for the areas covered by the EEA Agreement should be able to deliver the same results as EC law gives as far as the four freedoms of the Internal Market are concerned. The EEA Agreement aims to fulfil the quite ambitious objective of, in practice, extending the EC Internal Market to encompass the EFTA States, thus creating a dynamic and homogeneous EEA, that with the entry into force of the Agreement on 1 January 1994, covered 12 EC and 5 EFTA States. Today,

* Jur Dr h c Formerly Judge of the EFTA Court; Director of the EU Commission (1995–2005) and Director of Legal Affairs, EFTA (1982–93).

18 years later, the EEA comprises in total 27 EU Member States and three EFTA States[1] with a population of around 500 million inhabitants.

The principle of homogeneity is the single most important legal principle of the EEA Agreement. It explains the genesis of the EEA Agreement and guarantees its continued existence. It is of fundamental importance for the application and interpretation of the EEA Agreement to understand this principle correctly and the relevance thereof for the sustainability of the EEA Agreement. Therefore, initially a summary background[2] will be given from the perspective of what has turned out to be essential to the EEA judicial mechanism. Thereafter I will address how the EFTA Court and the European Courts in some early judgments approached the new EEA law, and the matter of homogeneity, and give some examples of how the dialogue between these courts has developed. Finally, a few words will be said on the future challenges facing the EFTA Court.

BACKGROUND

When Denmark and the United Kingdom left EFTA for the European Communities (EC) on 1 January 1973, the remaining EFTA countries concluded the EC bilateral Free Trade Agreements (FTAs) for industrial goods. To celebrate the abolition of the last duties and quotas under these FTAs a first Ministerial meeting was held between the two groupings in Luxembourg on 9 April 1984. In the declaration adopted at the end of that meeting, EC and EFTA Ministers and the EC Commission[3] expressed their conviction of the importance of further actions to consolidate and strengthen co-operation, with the aim of creating a dynamic European economic space (EES) of benefit to their countries.

Particularly important for the development of the so-called Luxembourg follow-up was the 1985 EC Commission White Paper on 'Completing the Internal Market'. The subsequent adoption of the 'Single European Act', implying a radically simplified and improved decision-making procedure for the EC internal market, suddenly made the White Paper, with its close to 300 specific measures, quite a realistic possibility. Numerous EFTA analyses showed that the White Paper project represented a major threat with considerable risks of discrimination against the EFTA States, their economies and their citizens, if this development could not be met by guarantees for their equal treatment in the EC Internal Market. The work on the follow-up of the Luxembourg declaration on the EES thus took on quite new dimensions. A first expression of this was the decision in June 1986 in Reykjavík by the EFTA Ministers and the EC Commissioner in

[1] Iceland, Liechtenstein and Norway. Austria, Finland and Sweden acceded on 1 January 1995 to the EU. Switzerland also signed the EEA Agreement but failed to ratify it following a negative referendum in 1992.

[2] For a more comprehensive presentation of the historical background, see S Norberg, 'Justice in the European Economic Area – The Role of the EFTA Court' in C Baudenbacher (ed) *Judicial Protection in the European Economic Area*, forthcoming.

[3] *Twenty-fourth Annual Report of the European Free Trade Association* (Geneva, EFTA, 1985).

charge of external relations, Willy De Clercq, to characterise the EES not only as dynamic but also as homogeneous.

Both sides worked intensively during the following two and a half years on the setting up of the EES. Although there were several areas in which substantial progress was made, it became clear towards the end of 1988 that the creation of the dynamic and homogenous EES required a completely new approach regarding the legal issues and the institutional framework. While the Commission had repeatedly raised the issue of how international agreements were treated in the EC, where after the 1982 judgment of the ECJ in *Kupferberg*[4] it was clear that an EFTA citizen could have access to that Court to defend his or her rights under the FTAs, none of the legal orders of the EFTA States had given individuals the possibility of invoking individual provisions of these agreements. Such a legal imbalance was a problem for a more developed co-operation in the future. On the EFTA side, Ministers finally agreed to create a special Group of Legal Experts (GLE) with the task of examining legal questions arising in the co-operation between the EFTA countries and the EC. The GLE, with Pernilla Lindh as a member from the very first meeting, started its work by studying:

(a) differences in the application and interpretation of the FTAs and other agreements between the EFTA countries and the EC;
(b) the settlement of disputes under the FTAs and other agreements between the EFTA countries and the EC; and
(c) the legal aspects of models for co-operation between the EC and the EFTA countries in areas covered by mandates from the High-Level Contact Group.

From the outset, the experts were confronted with national differences on the treatment of international agreements in the domestic legal order. While Austria and Switzerland[5] more or less followed a monist tradition, the four Nordic EFTA countries in this respect were dualists. The GLE spent considerable time analysing this issue and the critical questions of primacy and direct effect.[6] In June 1989, when exploratory talks with the EC with a view to possibly opening formal negotiations on the EEA had been initiated, EFTA Ministers welcomed the GLE report 'on such legal matters as the direct applicability and direct effect of treaty provisions between the EFTA countries and the EC . . .'. They endorsed the GLE conclusions and agreed that a good basis had been established for the exploratory talks with the EC on these issues.[7]

In September 1988 a Diplomatic Conference in Lugano between all the then 18 EC and EFTA Member States concluded a Convention that was parallel to the

[4] Case 104/81 *Hauptzollamt Mainz v Kupferberg & Cie KG a A* [1982] ECR 3641.

[5] This was also the case for Liechtenstein which only joined EFTA on 1 September 1991.

[6] See also N Wahl, 'The Free Trade Agreements between the EC and EFTA Countries, Their Implementation and Interpretation', A Case Study, Institute for Intellectual Property and Market Law at Stockholm University, Stockholm, 1988. Wahl had, as a trainee in EFTA Legal Affairs, been the main draftsman of the EFTA Secretariat background document for the Group, GLE 1/87.

[7] Declaration of Ministerial Meeting of the EFTA Council meeting in Kristiansand on 13 and 14 June 1989, Twenty-ninth Annual Report of EFTA, Geneva 1990.

1968 EC Convention on the jurisdiction and enforcement of judgments in civil and commercial matters, the 'Brussels Convention'. One of the main challenges for the negotiators had been to secure a uniform interpretation between the Brussels Convention, where ultimately the ECJ was competent to provide preliminary rulings, and the Lugano Convention for which there was neither any such judicial mechanism nor one for the settlement of disputes. The solution that was finally found is laid down in Protocol No 2 to the Lugano Convention on the uniform interpretation of the Convention.[8] This experience would later prove to be of crucial importance for the successful conclusion of the EEA negotiations.

On 17 January 1989 the President of the EC Commission, Jacques Delors, in an address to the European Parliament, raised the question of how the relationship between the Community and the EFTA countries should be developed. He put the question whether the EFTA States really were prepared to go as far in their co-operation with the Community as they sometimes seemed to indicate. Were they prepared to harmonise their legislation to ensure free circulation of goods, to accept judicial control by the ECJ and to accept the same discipline on State aid and rules of competition as the Community Member States? If they were ready for this and to strengthen the EFTA structures, Delors saw possibilities on the basis of one EC pillar and an EFTA pillar to develop a far-reaching joint co-operation.

EFTA Heads of Government delivered an unequivocally positive reply on 12 March 1989 in Oslo,[9] and stated that negotiations should lead to the fullest possible realisation of free movement of goods, services, capital and persons, with the aim of creating a dynamic and homogeneous EES. They would explore ways and means to strengthen the institutional links between the EFTA States and the EC and would not exclude any option.

The EC and its Member States and the Member States of EFTA then met in Brussels on 20 March 1989. The Declaration clearly reflects the important progress made by the EC in completing its internal market, and in noting that important results had also been achieved in the process of creating the single EES. Ministers discussed the scope for broadening and deepening their co-operation in the areas linked to the internal market – free movement of goods, services, capital and persons – and in other areas such as research, technology, education, environment, social policy aspects and transport. The Commission considered this and how to achieve a more structured partnership along the lines of the ideas outlined earlier by Delors and by the EFTA Heads of Government.[10] The most important difference when such high level fact-finding talks were initiated a month later was that the EFTA countries could no longer choose the areas for co-operation. They had now, in principle, agreed to take over into the EEA every

[8] For a commentary on the Convention and in particular Protocol 2 thereof, reference is made to the 'Jennard-Möller Report' finalised at the end of the Lugano Conference, published by the Swiss Institute of Comparative Law (Zürich Schulthess Polygraphischer Verlag, 1991).

[9] Declaration of EFTA Heads of Government, Oslo, 14 and 15 March 1989, *Twenty-ninth Annual Report of EFTA* (Geneva, EFTA, 1990).

[10] ibid; Joint Declaration adopted at Informal Ministerial Meeting between the EC and its Member States and the Member States of EFTA, Brussels, 20 March 1989.

single piece of what could be qualified as being part of 'EEA relevant *acquis communautaire*'.

An EC–EFTA Ministerial meeting on 19 December 1989 welcomed a report on the exploratory talks and decided to commence and conclude formal negotiations as soon as possible. The negotiations should permit provisions for 'appropriate formulae to ensure the direct effect of common legislation, surveillance of its implementation as well as judicial monitoring and the good functioning, in general, of the agreement.'[11]

As can be seen from these developments, the work concerning the future EES advanced considerably during 1989, this fateful year in European history. Already six months after the Brussels meeting, the formal EC–EFTA negotiations commenced on 20 June 1990[12] between the EC represented by the Commission and the seven EFTA countries speaking with one voice under Swedish chairmanship.

THE EEA NEGOTIATIONS AND THE JUDICIAL MECHANISM

Political Agreement on an EEA Court

After 10 months of negotiations, only two major issues remained to be settled; the judicial mechanism and trade in fish. The EFTA side had immediately been attracted by what Delors had called 'possibilities for a new form of association, more structured institutionally with common organs for decisions and administration, with common decision-making' in his address to the European Parliament. They had expected to be more directly involved together with the EC Member States in real joint decision-making. At this stage, however, they understood that they would only be able to have input during the decision-shaping phase, while the EC took a decision that they would later have to approve for the EEA as well. In view of the considerable disappointment this caused in many EFTA capitals, it became even more important for the EFTA to find a judicial mechanism where all parties to the agreement would be on an equal footing.

At the Joint Ministerial Meeting in Brussels on 13 May 1991 agreement was reached on the creation of a Joint EEA Court,[13] functionally integrated with the ECJ, which would function with a composition of five judges from the ECJ and three judges from the EFTA States. The EEA Court was to give rulings concerning: dispute settlement (including interpretation of EEA rules) at the request of the

[11] ibid; Joint Declaration from the Meeting between EFTA and EC Ministers and the Commission in Brussels, 19 December 1989.

[12] At the opening of the negotiations the EC side suggested that the term so far used in English 'the European Economic Space' should be changed to 'European Economic Area' for linguistic reasons. No substantive change was intended but the UK Prime Minister, Mrs Thatcher, had expressed a preference for a more down to earth expression. The EFTA side accepted the proposal.

[13] Declaration from the Ministerial Meeting between the European Community, its Member States and the EFTA Countries of the European Free Trade Association, Thirty-first Annual Report of the European Free Trade Association (Geneva, EFTA, June 1992).

Joint Body or the Contracting Parties; disputes between the EFTA Surveillance Body and an EFTA country; cases brought by enterprises or States against decisions of the EFTA Surveillance Body in the field of competition (including State aid). This agreement was generally welcomed as a major breakthrough in the EEA negotiations and in October 1991 the negotiators also found an agreement regarding trade in fish.[14] In parallel, the EC Commission submitted the draft agreement to the ECJ for an opinion under Article 228 EC (now Article 264 [11] TFEU).

Opinion 1/91[15]

The ECJ then, in Opinion 1/91, firmly rejected the idea of a Joint EEA Court by concluding that '[T]he system of judicial supervision which the agreement proposes to set up is incompatible with the Treaty establishing the European Economic Community'. I refrain here from commenting upon this opinion or on some erroneous findings of the Court relating to its dismissal of the feasibility to achieve 'the objective of homogeneity in the interpretation and application of the law in the EEA'.[16]

Renegotiations

Many sceptics welcomed the ECJ Opinion as the mortal blow to the whole idea of the EEA. However, if anyone had ever believed that an end had been put to the plans of creating a dynamic and homogeneous EEA, they had profoundly underestimated the considerable political ambitions behind the project which encouraged the negotiators to find solutions to overcome the criticism of the Court without delay. On 14 February 1992 the EC and EFTA chief negotiators signed a declaration to the effect that the negotiations on the EEA Agreement had been concluded.

The new solution implied that the idea of a joint judicial mechanism through an EEA Court had been abolished. Instead, the EEA judicial mechanism would follow the general two pillar structure of the EEA with the ECJ for the Community pillar and a new EFTA Court for the EFTA pillar. Disputes between the two pillars would have to be settled by the EEA Joint Committee. The EFTA Court would be created with corresponding competences for the EFTA countries to those of the ECJ with regard to the EC. In addition, considerable efforts were spent reinforcing the provisions on homogeneity, surveillance and dispute settlement in the

[14] Detailed provisions were elaborated into Part VII Institutional provisions, s 3 of the draft Agreement. They consisted of 11 articles and a separate Protocol 34, under which the EFTA States might allow a court or tribunal to ask the ECJ to express itself on the interpretation of EEA rules corresponding to EC rules; see further my contribution mentioned in n 2 above.

[15] Opinion 1/91 para 29, Draft Agreement Relating to the Creation of the European Economic Area ECR [1991] I-6079.

[16] For such comments, see my contribution in n 2 above.

Agreement. Modifications were also made regarding Article 56 in the Agreement, dealing with the sharing of competences between the Commission and the EFTA Surveillance Authority in the field of competition.[17] The Commission submitted the new text to the ECJ for a new opinion on the compatibility with the EEC Treaty of the renegotiated version of the Agreement and more specifically of the new Articles regarding the distribution of competences in the field of competition between the EC Commission and the EFTA Surveillance Authority and the dispute settlement mechanism of the Agreement.

In Opinion 1/92[18] the ECJ did not raise any objections and declared the following compatible with the EEC Treaty:

(1) the provisions of the Agreement which deal with the settlement of disputes, as long as the principle that decisions taken by the Joint Committee are not to affect the case law of the Court of Justice is laid down in a form binding on the Contracting Parties;[19]
(2) Article 56 of the Agreement, dealing with the sharing of competences in the field of competition.

When the EEA Agreement was signed in Oporto on 2 May 1992, the EFTA States also signed several agreements between themselves called for by their participation in the EEA. Particularly important is the Agreement on the Establishment of a Surveillance Authority and a Court of Justice (ESA/EFTA Court Agreement), by which the new and independent EFTA Surveillance Authority and the EFTA Court were set up.

THE EEA PRINCIPLE OF HOMOGENEITY

When it was clear that the concept of an EEA court would have to be replaced by a full two pillar structure with an EFTA Court, the negotiators also realised that they would have to make other amendments to the Agreement. It had previously been assumed on both sides that an EEA court with a majority of judges from the ECJ would, without too detailed written instructions, be able to guarantee the preservation of homogeneity. The matter came into an entirely different light after the heavy criticism from the ECJ regarding the feasibility of achieving this objective. With the new perspective that interpretation on the EFTA side would be entrusted to a newly set up EFTA court, it was evident that special efforts were made in renegotiating this part of the Agreement.

[17] A persistent rumour was that the ECJ, if asked a second time, would focus upon the question whether the EC Commission through the EEA could cede competence to the EFTA pillar. It was thus agreed to limit the duties for the EFTA Surveillance Authority in comparison to what had first been agreed.

[18] Opinion 1/92, Draft Agreement between the Community, on the one hand, and the countries of the European Free Trade Agreement, on the other, relating to the Creation of the European Economic Area [1992] ECR I-2821 delivered on 10 April 1992.

[19] Such a provision was transferred from an Agreed Minute to become Protocol 48. In order to avoid any conclusion *a contrario*, the Final Act states that the Agreed Minutes have a binding character.

A homogeneous EEA implies that in the areas covered by the EEA Agreement, individuals and economic operators are to be given the same treatment within the whole EEA Area, irrespective of whether it is a matter of applying EU rules or EEA rules. The word homogeneity refers thus not only to homogeneity regarding the application of the EEA rules as such and the relations between the EFTA- and EU-States, but also to homogeneity between these EEA rules and corresponding EU rules. In addition, homogeneity will not only apply at the entry into force of the EEA Agreement but also as the agreement develops in pace with the development of EU law in corresponding fields. It must also be 'dynamic'. To secure this in a treaty, guaranteeing the independence of the Contracting Parties, obviously poses major difficulties. The Contracting Parties have also made this objective very clear in the Agreement itself. This is expressed most clearly in the fifteenth recital of the preamble that was added during the renegotiations:

> Whereas, in full deference to the independence of the courts, the objective of the Contracting Parties is to arrive at, and maintain, a uniform interpretation and application of this Agreement and those provisions of Community legislation which are substantially reproduced in this Agreement and to arrive at an equal treatment of individuals and economic operators as regards the four freedoms and the conditions for competition.

This recital is an expression of the principle that in spite of the fact that, formally speaking, two separate legal orders will exist, EU law and EEA law, these in practice together form a common European legal system. In addition, the parties added to the EEA Agreement in Part VII Institutional Provisions in Chapter 3 a new Section 1 on Homogeneity, consisting of Articles 105–07 EEA, before the sections on the surveillance procedure and on settlement of disputes.

Particular efforts were also made as to the formulation of the provisions regarding the taking over and the taking into account of the case law of the ECJ, for the period up to signature of the Agreement and thereafter. Article 6 of the EEA Agreement expressed this already, as far as case law until the date of signature was concerned. As to later case law, the EFTA States laid down in Article 3(2) of the ESA/EFTA Court Agreement an obligation to 'pay due account to the principles laid down by the relevant rulings by the Court of Justice of the European Communities given after the date of signature' of the EEA Agreement and

> which concern the interpretation of that Agreement or of such rules of the Treaty establishing the European Economic Community and the Treaty establishing the European Coal and Steel Community in so far as they are identical in substance to the provisions of the EEA Agreement.[20][21]

As mentioned above, the principle of homogeneity is the single most important principle of the EEA Agreement. As follows from the above, 'it' is not just a prin-

[20] The wording is modelled on the language in Protocol 2 to the 1988 Lugano Convention mentioned above.

[21] The ESA/EFTA Court Agreement contains in its Preamble a recital corresponding to the fifteenth recital of the Preamble to the EEA Agreement.

ciple of law. It is to the fullest possible extent a political principle, expressing the parties' overarching political objectives. This was also demonstrated at the final simultaneous examination by EC–EFTA lawyer-linguists in April 1992 of all EEA texts of the EEA Agreement in the 13 authentic languages. Some Nordic delegations claimed that the 'foreign' word 'homogeneous' should be replaced by an indigenous word, 'enhetligt' in Swedish or 'ensartet' in Norwegian and Danish. The agreed conclusion was, however, that such a change would not express the same 'value'. Due to the major political importance of this adjective, it was decided that each language that knew 'homogeneous' should use this word. This was followed in the Swedish text but not in the Norwegian one.[22]

The EEA Judicial Mechanism, EEA Law and the Principle of Homogeneity

Here follows a brief overview of some steps in the development of the case law regarding the interpretation of the EEA Agreement, as handled by the Courts forming the EEA judicial mechanism, with the EFTA Court on the EFTA side, and the Court of Justice and the General Court (previously the Court of First Instance – CFI) on the EU side.

The EFTA Court – Restamark[23]

In its first judgment, *Restamark*, which concerned the Finnish import monopoly for wine and spirits, the Court dealt extensively with the question of the principles for interpretation of the EEA Agreement. The Court first pronounced in general on the application of the principles for interpretation. It thus initially recalled under 'Remarks on the interpretation of the EEA Agreement'[24] the objective of the Contracting Parties to create a dynamic and homogeneous EEA. Thereafter it quoted in full the fourth and fifteenth recitals of the Preamble to the EEA Agreement.

Further, the Court referred to Article 6 EEA, according to which, without prejudice to future developments of case law, the provisions of the EEA Agreement, in so far as they are identical in substance to corresponding rules of the EEC Treaty, must in their implementation and application be interpreted in conformity with the relevant rulings of the ECJ given prior to the date of signature of the EEA Agreement.[25] Then the Court also recalled Article 3(2) of the Surveillance and Court Agreement, according to which the EFTA Court and the EFTA Surveillance Authority, in the interpretation and application of the EEA Agreement are to pay due account of the principles laid down by the relevant rulings of the ECJ given

[22] See, eg, in the Norwegian language version: the fourth recital of the Preamble, Art 1(1), the headings of ch 3 and its s 1, as well as Arts 105(2) and (3) EEA.

[23] Case E-1/94, *Ravintoloitsijain Liiton Kustannus Oy Restamark* [1994–1995] EFTA Court Rep 15.

[24] ibid, para 32.

[25] ibid, para 33.

after the date of the signing of the EEA Agreement and which concern the interpretation of that Agreement or of such rules of the EEC Treaty in so far as they are identical in substance to the provisions of the EEA Agreement.[26] Finally, the Court recalled that the EEA Agreement also contains in other places a number of elements aimed at achieving the homogeneity objective.[27] The EFTA Court then expressed itself more specifically with regard to the interpretation of each of the individual rules of law that were relevant in the case.[28]

Another matter of great importance that the Court decided on in *Restamark* concerned the admissibility of the reference from the Appeals Committee at the Finnish Board of Customs.[29] The Court first recalled that it was not bound in its interpretation of Article 34 of the ESA/Court Agreement laying down the procedure under which courts or tribunals of EFTA States might refer questions of interpretation of EEA rules to the EFTA Court for advisory opinions. As to the expression 'court or tribunal' it found nevertheless the reasoning that had led the ECJ to its interpretations of the same expression in Article 177 EC (now Article 267 TFEU) relevant. The purpose of Article 34 was to establish co-operation between the Court and the national courts and tribunals intended as a means of ensuring a uniform interpretation of the EEA Agreement and to provide assistance to these courts and tribunals when applying EEA provisions. That purpose had to be taken into account in the interpretation of 'court or tribunal'.

Of the relevant criteria enumerated by the ECJ in a recent case,[30] the Court particularly addressed the one regarding adversarial procedure. The Court recalled that the procedure before the Tullilautakunta is the same as before the administrative courts. In the present case only one party appeared before the Tullilautakunta. That happened, however, frequently in Finland as well as in Sweden in proceedings before administrative courts, including the Supreme Administrative Court. If the right to make a reference would be subject to the procedure before the national court being adversarial, this would result in the administrative courts in Finland (and also in Sweden) being largely unable to refer a question to the EFTA Court. In most cases these are the very courts that are the competent judicial bodies for the application of EEA rules (paragraph 27). The Court then concluded that the request for an advisory opinion was admissible. As can be understood from the Court's reasoning, this conclusion was particularly important for administrative courts in Finland and Sweden, two countries sharing a common legal heritage.[31]

The *Restamark* case was no doubt very important for the Court, which has often referred to it. This is not the place for a more detailed presentation of how the EFTA Court, during the following 17 years, has continued on the road laid out in *Restamark* to fulfil its task to ensure homogeneity in the EEA and thereby

[26] ibid, para 34.
[27] ibid, para 35.
[28] ibid, paras 46, 52, 64, 80.
[29] ibid, paras 7–31.
[30] Case C-393/92 *Municipality of Almelo and ors* [1994] ECR I-1477, para 21.
[31] Case C-498/97 *Abrahamsson and ors* [2000] ECR I-5539. The ECJ found a request by a Swedish Universities Appeals Board admissible, in spite of an opinion to the contrary of AG Saggio.

secure the continued credibility of the EEA Agreement. It deserves, however, to be underlined that the EFTA Court in its application and interpretation of EEA law applies the same methods as the ECJ when it interprets EU law. This is not surprising, taking into account how strongly the Contracting Parties have emphasised the principle of a homogeneous EEA and expressed the objective of achieving within the whole EEA the same results, irrespective of whether EU rules or corresponding EEA rules are applied. This is furthermore entirely in line with the principles laid down in the Vienna Convention on the Law on Treaties.[32] It is also clear that any other way of handling this would have resulted very easily in obvious divergences in the application of the common rules with an imminent risk for the collapse of the EEA, with all the consequences this would have led to, not only for citizens and economic operators in the three EFTA States but also for EU citizens and economic operators and their relations with the former.

Finally, it may be noted that in addition to the Finnish Government, two other Nordic EFTA Governments holding alcohol monopolies, Norway and Sweden, expressed observations at the oral hearing in *Restamark*. All three were represented by a former member of the EFTA GLE, with Ambassador Pernilla Lindh, Under-Secretary for Legal Affairs, representing Sweden.[33]

The CFI – Opel Austria[34]

This was the first case in which one of the EU Courts had to give outright interpretations of provisions of the EEA Agreement. The dispute before the Court concerned a Council Regulation adopted on 20 December 1993 but coming into force only in January 1994 after the entry into force of the EEA Agreement. Thereby a customs duty for certain gearboxes produced by Opel Austria and exported to the Community was reintroduced to counter distortive effects of Austrian State aid to the company. The applicant claimed that the measure violated Article 10 EEA prohibiting customs duties and measures of equivalent effect. The Council referring to Opinion 1/91 claimed that there were major differences between the EC Treaty and the EEA Agreement which required Article 10 EEA to be interpreted differently. The Commission also argued that Article 10 EEA and the corresponding provisions of the EC Treaty were not identical in substance and that therefore Article 6 EEA was not applicable.

The Court first concluded that, since Article 10 EEA was unconditional and precise, it had had direct effect ever since the entry into force of the EEA Agreement. It then stated that it could not accept the Council's contention that major differences between the EEA Agreement and the EC Treaty meant that, notwithstanding the wording of Article 6 EEA, Article 10 should not be interpreted in the same way as corresponding provisions of the EC Treaty. The Court then at some length (paragraphs 106 to 108) elaborated on the main characteristics of the EEA Agreement,

[32] untreaty.unorg/ilc/texts/instruments/english/conventions/1_11969.pdf.
[33] N Jääskinen, now Advocate General at the Court of Justice, represented Finland.
[34] Case T-115/94 *Opel Austria v Council* [1997] ECR II-39.

which 'involves a high degree of integration, with objectives which exceed those of a mere free-trade agreement' (paragraph 107). The Court also referred to the case law of the EFTA Court, inter alia in *Restamark* (paragraph 108). As to the Council's arguments based upon the ECJ Opinion 1/91 (paragraph 109), the Court stated:

> Contrary to the Council's contention, the significance in regard to the interpretation and application of the Agreement of the Contracting Parties' objective of establishing a dynamic and homogeneous EEA has not been diminished by the Court of Justice in Opinion 1/91, cited above. When the Court held that the divergences existing between the aims and context of the Agreement, on the one hand, and the aims and context of Community law on the other, stood in the way of the achievement of the objective of homogeneity in the interpretation and application of the law in the EEA, it was considering the judicial system contemplated by the EEA Agreement for the purposes of ascertaining whether that system might jeopardize the autonomy of the Community legal order in pursuing its own objectives; and not a specific case in which it is necessary to determine whether a provision of the EEA Agreement identical in substance to a provision of Community law must be interpreted in conformity with the rulings of the Court of Justice and the Court of First Instance.

The CFI concluded that Article 10 EEA is identical in substance to Articles 12, 13, 16 and 17 of the EC Treaty and must be interpreted in conformity with the relevant rulings of the ECJ and the CFI (paragraph 112). The Court, which also addressed a number of other issues regarding the obligations of the Council when it adopted the Regulation and had it published, for the rest rejected the Council's and the Commission's arguments and annulled the Council Regulation. The judgment was never challenged before the ECJ.

The CFI in *Opel Austria* elaborated thoroughly on the special characteristics of the dynamic and homogeneous EEA and the considerable efforts of the Contracting Parties to ensure that both the Agreement itself and the institutions in charge of its implementation and interpretation would be able to live up to the explicitly expressed objectives of the EEA. By so clearly dismissing both the Council's and the Commission's efforts to play down the qualities and the credibility of the EEA Agreement,[35] the Court, also in this the very first judgment where one of the EU Courts in the EEA judicial mechanism interpreted the EEA Agreement, did the whole EEA venture an immense service. The EFTA Court had until then been the only Court in this judicial mechanism that had pronounced on the interpretation of the EEA Agreement. In this judgment the EFTA Court was no longer alone in defending the EEA, but was by now also strongly supported by the CFI.

As a last observation, it may be noted that Pernilla Lindh as one of the three CFI judges that delivered this important judgment was judge-rapporteur.

[35] It is nothing less than a scandal that these two institutions, immediately following the entry into force of the EEA Agreement, in order to save their own skin after a too late adoption of a very minor customs regulation, did not hesitate to use arguments that, if accepted by the Court, would have threatened seriously to undermine the credibility of the whole EEA.

The EFTA Court – Sveinbjörnsdottir[36]

In this case the EFTA Court had to address the question of State liability for the incorrect implementation of a directive incorporated into the EEA Agreement for the first time. The directive in question was the one that had been the subject of the ECJ judgment in *Francovich*[37] (Council Directive 80/987/EEC of 20 October 1980 relating to the protection of employees in the event of insolvency of the employer). The Governments of Iceland, Norway and Sweden had argued that the EEA Agreement differed from the EC Treaty so much that the EC case law on State liability was not transferable to the EEA. The EFTA Court, however, concluded

> that the provisions of the EEA Agreement are, to a great extent, intended for the benefit of individuals and economic operators throughout the European Economic Area. Therefore the proper functioning of the EEA Agreement is dependent on those individuals and economic operators being able to rely on the rights thus intended for their benefit [paragraph 58];
>
> that the EEA Agreement is an international treaty sui generis which contains a distinct legal order of its own . . . The depth of integration . . . is less far-reaching than under the EC Treaty, but the scope and the objective goes beyond what is usual for an agreement under public international law [paragraph 59];
>
> that the homogeneity objective and the objective of establishing the right of individuals and economic operators to equal treatment and equal opportunities are so strongly expressed in the EEA Agreement that the EFTA States must be obliged to provide for compensation for loss and damage caused to an individual by incorrect implementation of a directive [paragraph 60];
>
> the principle of State liability must be seen as an integral part of the EEA Agreement as such [paragraph 63].

In this landmark judgment, the EFTA Court thus first established that the EEA Agreement is an international treaty *sui generis* which contains a distinct legal order of its own, and then without taking over the case law of the EC independently interpreted the EEA Agreement and established a principle of State liability. The principle of State liability was later confirmed by the Court in *Karlsson*.[38]

The ECJ – Rechberger[39] *and* Andersson[40]

The questions of interest in these two cases arose due to the EFTA States having cut off the jurisdiction of the EFTA Court for those States that acceded to the EU on 1 January 1995, which was to be terminated only six months after the accession, that is, on 30 June 1995.

[36] Case E-9/97 *Sveinbjörnsdottir* [1998] EFTA Court Rep 95.
[37] Joined Cases C-6/90 and C-9/90 *Francovich and ors* [1991] ECR I-5357.
[38] Case E-4/01 *Karlsson* [2002] EFTA Court Rep 240.
[39] Case C-140/97 *Rechberger* [1999] ECR I-3499.
[40] Case C-321/97 *Andersson* [1999] ECR I-3551.

Rechberger concerned State liability for Austria due to an incorrectly implemented directive. The issue was also how to treat this during the period before the accession of Austria to the EU, while that country was an EFTA member of the EEA. The ECJ first, with reference to paragraphs 28 to 31 in another judgment delivered the same day, *Andersson*[41], pointed out that it did not have jurisdiction either under Article 177 EC or under the EEA Agreement to rule on the interpretation of the EEA Agreement as regards its application by Austria during the period prior to its accession to the EU (paragraph 38). The Court, however, continued:

> Moreover, in view of the objective of uniform interpretation and application which informs the EEA Agreement, it should be pointed out that the principles governing the liability of an EFTA State for infringement of a directive referred to in the EEA Agreement were the subject of the EFTA Court's judgment of 10 December 1998 in Sveinbjörnsdottir.

The ECJ conclusions in paragraph 38 of the judgment in *Rechberger* need no comment. The Court's statement in paragraph 39 is, however, remarkable. By making such an explicit reference to the EFTA Court's judgment in *Sveinbjörnsdottir*, the Court implicitly gives recognition to it. Thereby the Court also gives very clear directions to the Landesgericht in Linz that in its reference had raised the question about where to get the reply to its question regarding State liability under the EEA Agreement.

The *Andersson* case concerned the question of State liability for Sweden for not having correctly implemented a directive referred to in the EEA Agreement. It was different from *Rechberger*, however, in that the claim pertained exclusively to the period while Sweden as an EFTA State was bound by the EEA Agreement. Here the ECJ dismissed the question referred by the Stockholms Tingsrätt stating, as mentioned above, that it had no jurisdiction either under Article 177 EC or under the EEA Agreement to answer the referred questions. Unlike in *Rechberger*, however, the Court did not mention the EFTA Court's judgment in *Sveinbjörnsdottir* at all.

In comparing these two judgments delivered on the same day in plenary compositions of nine and 11 judges respectively, the obvious question is of course why clear guidance was given to the Austrian court but nothing was said to the Swedish court. Since the ECJ in *Rechberger* so clearly refers to its judgment of the same day in *Andersson* and seven of the eleven judges in that case also participated in *Rechberger*, the explanation could hardly be that the judges participating in *Andersson*[42] were unaware of *Sveinbjörnsdottir*.

[41] Case C-321/97 *Andersson* [1999] ECR I-3551.

[42] While AG Saggio in *Rechberger* neither mentioned the EEA Agreement nor the EFTA Court, AG Cosmas in *Andersson* criticised the CFI in *Opel Austria* and its characterisation of the EEA Agreement.

The EFTA Court Goes First

A major challenge for the EFTA Court that the negotiators were well aware of even 20 years ago, was the fact that due to EFTA having in general much faster judicial proceedings both at a national and at an international level than the EU, it was very likely that issues regarding the interpretation of a new EEA relevant EU act would arise for decision much sooner before the EFTA Court than before the ECJ. It was not long after the entry into force of the EEA Agreement before this proved to be true. Already in its third judgment, the EFTA Court in *Mattel and Lego*[43] had to pronounce on the interpretation of *EC Directive 89/552*,[44] also called the '"*Television without frontiers*" *Directive*' in relation to a Norwegian prohibition on TV advertising aimed at children. In two parallel Swedish cases, *De Agostini* and *TV-shop i Sverige*,[45] which had both first been referred to the EFTA Court but then withdrawn upon Sweden's EU accession, the ECJ reached similar conclusions to the EFTA Court. The ECJ also made a reference to a conclusion in the form of obiter dicta in the EFTA Court judgment regarding the relevance of the Council Directive on misleading advertising.[46] This was the first time any of the EU Courts referred to a judgment of the EFTA Court.

There have since been numerous examples of the EFTA Court being the first European court to be addressed in such situations, and it has to be said that the Court has achieved a very impressive track record in handling such issues. Of the many examples there are, let me mention two. The first one is *Kellogg's*,[47] the fortified cornflakes case. The Commission in a case with very similar facts later brought an action against Denmark, in which the ECJ closely followed the reasoning of the EFTA Court, that the Commission had characterised 'as an element in the development of the law'[48] which reflected the considerable changes in methods used to determine health risks in the past 20 years. Thereby, the ECJ clarified its earlier case law.[49] Another EFTA Court judgment that deserves particular mention is *Paranova*[50] which dealt with the conditions for repackaging of parallel-traded pharmaceutical products. Here too the ECJ, in a request for a preliminary ruling by the Court of Appeal for England and Wales,[51] followed the approach taken by the EFTA Court.

It is evident, however, that there may also be a situation where a Court that is the first one to adjudicate an issue, in the light of a judgment with different

[43] Joined Cases E-8/94 *Forbrukerombudet v Mattel Scandinavia A/S* and E-9/94 *Forbrukerombudet v Lego Norge A/S* [1994–1995] EFTA Court Rep 113.

[44] Council Directive 89/552/EEC of 3 October 1989 on the coordination of certain provisions laid down by Law, Regulation or Administrative Action in Member States concerning the pursuit of television broadcasting activities, [1989] OJ L298/23.

[45] Joined Cases C-34/95 *Konsumentombudsmannen (KO) v De Agostini (Svenska) Förlag AB* and C-35/95 and C-36/95 *KO v TV-shop i Sverige AB* [1997] ECR I-3843.

[46] Para 37. In his Opinion AG Jacobs had disagreed with the EFTA Court's statement.

[47] Case E-3/00 *EFTA Surveillance Authority v Norway* [2000-2001] EFTA Court Rep 73.

[48] Case C-192/01 *Commission v Denmark* [2003] ECR I-693, para 79.

[49] Case 174/82 *Sandoz* [1983] ECR 2445.

[50] Case E-3/02 *Paranova v Merck* [2003] EFTA Court Rep 101.

[51] Case C-348/04 *Boeringer Ingelheim KG and ors v Swingward and ors* [2007] ECR I-3991.

conclusions from one of the other courts and taking into account further developments, decides to overrule its earlier case law. This is illustrated by three cases: *Maglite*,[52] *Silhouette*[53] and *L'Oréal*.[54] All three cases concerned the scope of the exhaustion of trade mark rights under the EC 'Trade Mark Directive'.[55] In *Maglite* the EFTA Court found that EEA law did not permit a trade mark proprietor to use his rights to prevent imports from a country outside the EEA, thus allowing EFTA States to have in their legislation provisions on 'international exhaustion'. This conclusion was partly based on interpretation of the 'Trade Mark Directive', which had not yet come before the ECJ. The conclusion was also based upon the fact that the EEA, as opposed to the EU, is a free trade area and not a customs union with a Common Trade Policy. Later the ECJ in *Silhouette* concluded differently, that since there was an EEA-wide exhaustion of trade marks, the Member States were not allowed in their legislation to provide for international exhaustion. This unique example of differences in the case law between the EFTA Court and the ECJ came to an end 10 years later with the EFTA Court's judgment in *L'Oréal*. There the Court first noted, in general terms, that the consequences of not following later case law of the ECJ would have the same result for the internal market within the EEA as in a case of not following the case law of the ECJ where that Court had ruled first. This, according to the Court, called for an interpretation of EEA law in line with new case law of the ECJ regardless of whether the EFTA Court had previously ruled on the question (paragraph 29). Notwithstanding this statement of principle, the Court then carefully examined all arguments for and against changing its case law, until it finally came to the conclusion that this should be done.

Judicial Dialogue

The dialogue between these three courts constituting the EEA judicial mechanism, which by its very nature has to be quite subtle and is mainly seen through one court's reference to the reasoning of another court in a parallel case, had a somewhat late start mainly due to the slower procedure in the EU Courts. The first judgment where such a reference was made, was as mentioned above in *Opel Austria*[56] where the CFI both referred to case law of the EFTA Court and made very important statements regarding the true nature of the EEA Agreement. The ECJ through *Rechberger*[57] and the recognition there of the EFTA Court's judgment in *Sveinbjörnsdottir*[58] also contributed to the development of this dialogue.

[52] Case E-2/97 *Maglite* [1997] EFTA Court Rep 129.

[53] Case C-355/96 *Silhouette* [1998] I-4799.

[54] Joined Cases E-9/07 and E-10/07 *L'Oréal* [2008] EFTA Court Rep 258.

[55] First Council Directive 89/104/EEC of 21 December 1988 to approximate the laws of the Member States relating to trade marks [1989] OJ L40/1.

[56] *Opel Austria v Council*, n 34 above.

[57] *Rechberger*, n 39 above.

[58] *Sveinbjörnsdottir*, n 36 above.

The *Maglite*,[59] *Silhouette*[60] and *L'Oréal*[61] 'trilogy' referred to above should also be mentioned as an example of how this dialogue can work in practice.

On this subject Vassilios Skouris, President of the ECJ, has stated:

> As far as the ECJ is concerned . . . it does not have a statutory obligation to follow or pay due account to case-law of the EFTA Court. Nevertheless, ignoring EFTA Court precedents would simply be incompatible with the overriding objective of the EEA Agreement which is homogeneity. Conscious of that fact, the ECJ has contributed to the fulfilment of that objective by taking under consideration the EFTA Court case-law although, in most cases it has not done so expressly.[62]

As can be seen from many more judgments than those mentioned above, the judicial dialogue has developed continuously in quite an impressive way.[63] Clearly, this has been of great importance for the good functioning of the EEA judicial mechanism and not least for the continued credibility of the EFTA Court and the whole of the EEA.

CONCLUSION

In order to be able correctly to understand the EEA today, it is of key importance to place the Agreement in its right context. Twenty years after the EEA negotiations were running at full speed, it may not be so easy to realise the importance of these negotiations on the political agenda of not only the EFTA States but also the top politicians of the European Community[64]. For the EFTA States it was the opportunity, in areas of vital interest and without having to become full members of the EC, to participate in and enjoy the fruits of the EC Internal Market. Delors and others had most likely hoped that they, through offering the EEA to the EFTA States, would be able to prevent further applications for EC membership. Such hopes proved futile, at least with regard to Austria, Sweden, Finland and Norway, where instead the interest in full participation in the decision-making led to applications for full membership of the EC. For Austria, Sweden and Finland, EEA membership in the EFTA pillar became a fairly brief experience, although

59 *Maglite*, n 52 above.

60 *Silhouette*, n 53 above.

61 *L'Oréal*, n 54 above.

62 'The ECJ and the EFTA Court under the EEA Agreement' in C Baudenbacher and ors (eds), *The EFTA Court Ten Years On* (Oxford and Portland, 2005) 125.

63 In this context it may also be appropriate to quote Rosas J of the ECJ, '[F]or me the question as to whether judges should be open to the outside world and be aware of discussions taking place in other jurisdictions, is not any longer a question of opinion. It is a question of whether you are competent or incompetent. If you close your eyes, you belong to the latter category'. A Rosas, 'Methods of Interpretation – Judicial Dialogue' in C Baudenbacher and E Busek (eds), *The Role of International Courts* (Heidelberg, 2008). For a more comprehensive overview, see C Baudenbacher, 'Lecture 5' in *Dialogue with the EU Judiciary in the EFTA Court in Action, Five Lectures* (Stuttgart, German Publishers, 2010).

64 On 7 November 1989, President François Mitterrand of France, who held the EC Presidency, went to Reykjavik for the day (Iceland holding the EFTA Chair) to reassure himself of how seriously the EFTA States were regarding the EEA.

especially for Sweden the EEA remains very important due to its close integration and economic relations with Norway. There were certainly also those who thought that they were providing a model that could be used for Central and Eastern European countries that now freed themselves from Soviet domination. As we have seen, these countries were most interested in the political dimension of the EU, which is seriously lacking in the EEA.

The EEA judicial mechanism has become much more long-lived than most could ever have expected. Important steps towards the recognition of the true character of the EEA Agreement as a public international law treaty sui generis have been the EFTA Court's judgments in *Restamark*,[65] *Sveinbjörnsdottir*,[66] *Einarsson*[67] and *Karlsson*,[68] as well as the CFI judgment in *Opel Austria*[69] and the ECJ judgment in *Rechberger*.[70] The EFTA Court in its steady carrying out of the tasks entrusted to it has also become much more influential than could reasonably have been expected. It has in an excellent way, and with the good and loyal support of the EU Courts, succeeded in guaranteeing the homogeneity of the EEA and thereby not only its continuity but also its credibility. Thus the EEA judicial mechanism that replaced the Joint EEA Court has proved its viability. Actually, for the EFTA pillar there is no doubt that an independent EFTA Court instead of the Joint EEA Court foreseen in the first version of the Agreement has proved to be a much better solution. Different from the EEA Court, that as to interpretation of EEA rules mainly would have been seized by the Contracting Parties, the EFTA Court is fully equipped to assist national courts in the EFTA States with such an interpretation by the most important instrument for judicial co-operation, the advisory opinion procedure for interpretation of EEA rules. The importance of continuing in this way cannot be underlined enough, especially at a point in time when the question of an EEA with only two or even one EFTA State is raised.[71]

As can be seen from the above, the main challenges now, 20 years after the conclusion of the negotiations on the EEA Agreement and in a situation where it seems more and more likely that it will have a much longer future than anyone ever had expected, lies mainly on the EFTA side. The EU now has well consolidated case law in relation to the EEA Agreement and in particular the defence of any rights for individuals and operators created thereby, and there are no reasons to believe that this situation will change. The EFTA Court has also succeeded well in this field. However, there still exist two striking differences that especially with a long-term perspective on the EEA ought to be remedied. The first one concerns the procedure for advisory opinions for interpretation by the EFTA Court, and the other the issue of primacy and direct effect of EEA rules.

[65] *Andersson*, n 40 above.

[66] *Sveinbjörnsdottir*, n 36 above.

[67] Case E-1/01 *Einarsson* [2002] EFTA Court Rep 1.

[68] Case E-4/01 *Karlsson* [2002] EFTA Court Rep 240.

[69] *Opel Austria v Council*, n 34 above.

[70] *Rechberger*, n 39 above.

[71] Iceland is negotiating EU membership, and of the originally seven EFTA/EEA States it is only Liechtenstein that has never expressed such an ambition.

The procedure rules for requesting an 'advisory opinion'[72] of the EFTA Court on the interpretation of EEA rules are laid down in Article 34 ESA/Court Agreement. The second paragraph thereof states that 'where such a question is raised before any court or tribunal in an EFTA State, that court or tribunal may, if it considers it necessary to enable it to give judgment, requests the EFTA Court to give such an opinion.'[73] While there have been many references over the years, the fact is that in Iceland and Norway there seems to be a public policy of obstruction of this instrument. Thus in both countries the State Attorneys regularly object to such requests. The third paragraph of Article 34 is also invoked to support the idea that national EFTA courts, as opposed to their colleagues in EU States, would have no unconditional right to make such a reference.[74] It is clear that such a state of affairs is most unsatisfactory and goes against the explicit objectives of a homogeneous EEA as expressed in the Preamble to the Agreement (eg, 8th recital) and against the wording of the provision which only allows an EFTA State to decide to limit the right to make a reference. It should be corrected without delay. The best way for the EFTA States to live up to the objectives of the EEA would simply be to delete the third paragraph of Article 34.

It is still argued that the EEA rules do not have primacy and direct effect in the EFTA pillar,[75] since the Agreement does not require 'any Contracting Party to transfer legislative powers to any institution of the EEA'.[76] A characteristic of EU law for half a century is its inherent dynamic character, which through the case law of the Court of Justice over time has led to a development of EU law in big steps and far beyond what the fathers of the Treaty of Rome ever could have imagined. A legal order like EEA law, which through explicit statements in the provisions on the objectives of the EEA Agreement is not only dynamic but also homogeneous in relation to corresponding parts of EU law, can against this background obviously not be static. This has also been well demonstrated in the case law of the EFTA Court. Whatever the intentions behind Protocol 35 may have been twenty years ago, the time would now be ripe after almost 20 years of development of EEA law to reassess profoundly the question of primacy and direct effect of EEA rules. There should be no obstacle any more for the EFTA Court or a national court in an EFTA State establishing that the defence of the rights of individuals weighs heavier than the absence of legislative powers and that thus the

[72] While the term advisory opinion ought to be changed to preliminary ruling, this difference in terms would at the end of the day seem to be of minor importance compared to the subsequent effects of non-compliance.

[73] The third paragraph, that has only been applied by Austria, makes it possible to limit the rights to make such requests to courts and tribunals against whose decisions there is no legal remedy under national law.

[74] For a thorough discussion on this, see S Magnusson, 'On the Authority of Advisory Opinions, Reflections on the Functions and the Normativity of Advisory Opinions of the EFTA Court' 2010 *ERT* 528; 'Judicial Homogeneity in the European Economic Area and the Authority of the EFTA Court' in (2011) 80 *Nordic Journal of International Law* 507, 518.

[75] The CFI clarified the situation under EU law in *Opel Austria*, see n 34 above.

[76] From the preamble of Protocol 35 EEA on the Implementation of EEA rules.

provisions of EEA law take precedence and, if fulfilling the criteria, therefore have direct effect.[77]

Both of these differences between the EU and EFTA pillars are of a character that they may negatively affect the possibilities of individuals and economic operators, for the benefit of whom the EEA Agreement was negotiated, to defend their rights under the Agreement if this is to be done in an EFTA State. There can be no reason to allow such a discriminatory situation to continue.

[77] See also M Johansson and S Norberg, '*EES-RÄTTEN – DYNAMISK IPSO JURE!*' (2011) *ERT* 795.

6

A Special Relationship: The EU and The Hague Conference on Private International Law

JÖRG PIRRUNG*

INTRODUCTION

THE RELATIONSHIP BETWEEN the European Union and the Hague Conference on Private International Law (Conference) has always had a special character. When the treaties establishing the EEC and Euratom were signed in the Spring of 1957 – six years after the European Coal and Steel Community – Belgium, Germany, Luxembourg and the Netherlands had ratified the Statute of the Conference of 31 October 1951. Italy followed in June 1957; France had participated in its sessions of 1951 and 1954.[1] In addition to these six founding members of the ECSC and EEC, 11 other European States had ratified the Statute (Denmark, Finland, Greece, Ireland, Norway, Austria, Portugal, Sweden, Spain, Turkey and the United Kingdom), Switzerland in June 1957. Japan was the only non-European State to have done so in June 1957. In 1960, at a regular session of the Conference, both the USA and the EEC sent observers.[2]

Today the Conference has 71 Member States from 'all over the world',[3] including the 27 Member States of the EU. The success of the Conference is still essentially influenced by its European origin, as is generally demonstrated by the numbers of ratification of its conventions. Both the EU and the Conference have to meet organisational challenges arising from the large – not to say enormous – numbers of representatives from member and observer States participating in sessions dedicated to specific child protection matters such as child abduction and international adoption. During recent decades, the growing competence of the EU in the subject

* Formerly Judge of the Court of First Instance of the European Communities. All opinions expressed herein are personal to the author.

[1] France ratified the Statute in 1964; see generally, www.hcch.net.

[2] Conférence de La Haye de droit international privé, Actes et documents (Proceedings) de la Neuvième Session, tome I (La Haye, 1961, Bureau Permanent) 12, 15, namely representatives of the Commission (J Dieu and H Arnold).

[3] 14 European States which are not members of the EU, 13 States from the Americas, 11 from Asia, three from Africa as well as Australia and New Zealand.

matters covered by the Conference has given rise to practical problems. In 2007, after the insertion in the Statute of a new Article 3 opening up membership to any regional economic integration organisation, the EU acceded to the Conference. The developments that led to the EU accession are described by H van Loon, the Secretary General of the Conference.[4]

The following observations will, after some general remarks on the Conference and the membership of the EU, deal with certain specific problems arising from concurring provisions in EU regulations[5] and Hague conventions, especially in the context of child protection.

As a member of the ECJ Pernilla Lindh sat in four[6] of the first dozen preliminary ruling proceedings[7] concerning the Brussels IIbis Regulation. Judicial co-operation in this context does not merely refer to the mutual responsibilities of national judges and the ECJ in the framework of Article 267 TFEU. Rather, in the realm of international family protection, it is an essential characteristic of the necessary co-ordination in the interpretation of international texts including between the General Court and the ECJ, a co-operation exemplified by Pernilla Lindh's relationship with her colleagues in both Union courts.

THE HAGUE CONFERENCE AND ITS RELATIONSHIP TO THE EU IN GENERAL

The purpose of the Conference is to achieve the progressive unification of the rules of private international law by drafting international conventions at diplomatic conferences. Relations between the Conference and the EU are complex. Under Articles 67(4) and 81(2)(c) TFEU, the Union has competence for judicial co-operation in civil matters, including private international law. This means that there are partially identical working spheres in certain areas, with divergences due to the regional limitations of the EU. This situation can lead to problems, as is demonstrated by the fact that important non-European Member States of the Conference have ratified relatively few conventions. The work of the Conference focuses essentially on three main areas, namely cross-border legal assistance and recognition of foreign judgments, international family and succession law, and

[4] H Van Loon and A Schulz, 'The European Community and the Hague Conference on Private International Law' in B Martenczuk and S van Thiel (eds), *Justice, Liberty, Security: New Challenges for EU External Relations* (Brussels, BUP, 2008) 257, 259.

[5] Especially Council Regulation (EC) No 2201/2003 of 27 November 2003 concerning jurisdiction and the recognition and enforcement of judgments in matrimonial matters and the matters of parental responsibility, repealing Regulation (EC) No 1347/2000, [2003] OJ EC L338/1 (Brussels IIbis Regulation), changed by Council Regulation (EC) No 2116/2004 of 2 December 2004, [2004] OJ EC L367/1. See J von Staudinger, Kommentar zum BGB/J Pirrung, *Internationales Kindschaftsrecht 2, Vorbemerkungen C – H zu Art 19 EGBGB* (Berlin, Sellier – de Gruyter, 2009), 1 (Brussels IIbis Regulation); see also ibid, 197 (1980 Hague Abduction Convention), 455 (1996 Hague Protection of Children Convention).

[6] Case C-168/08 *Hadadi* [2009] ECR I-6871; Case C-195/08 PPU *Rinau* [2008] ECR I-5271; Case C-523/07*A* [2009] ECR I-2805; Case C-256/09 *Purrucker*, judgment of 15 July 2010 nyr.

[7] See K Lenaerts, 'Accelerated and Urgency Procedures in the Area of Freedom, Security and Justice' in T Baumé et al (eds), *Today's Multi-layered Legal Order: Current Issues and Perspectives, Liber Amicorum AWH Meij* (Zutphen, Uitgeverij Paris, 2011) 155; J Pirrung, 'Expedited Procedures Before the ECJ in Parental Responsibility Cases', ibid 265.

the international law of obligations, especially trade law. In the following overview the main subjects of the Hague conventions with at least a certain success are mentioned, as well as their importance, especially with regard to the numbers of ratifications, for EU States. A list of these conventions with the dates of entry into force for the EU States is included (p 88). The abbreviated titles of these treaties are indicated in italics in the following text.

International Civil Procedure

The Convention on Civil Procedure of 1 March 1954 (*Civ*), with 47 contracting States, among them 21 EU Member States, facilitates the service of documents and taking of evidence abroad. It has been modernised by the Convention on Service Abroad of 15 November 1965 (*Serv*), with 65 contracting States, among them 26 EU Member States, the Convention on the Taking of Evidence Abroad (*Evid*), 56 contracting States (including 24 EU Member States) and the Convention on International Access to Justice (*AcJ*), 26 States (among them 17 EU Member States). The highest number of ratifications (103 contracting States, among them all EU Member States) of all Hague conventions was achieved by the Convention Abolishing Legalisation of 5 October 1961 (*Leg*), that is, the requirement that public documents used in foreign countries must be authenticated in foreign countries. The Convention on Choice of Court Agreements of 30 June 2005 (*CAg*) seems to be a not very promising effort to achieve worldwide harmonisation; though signed by the United States and the EU, the convention has as yet been ratified by only one State (Mexico).

International Family and Succession Law

In this area the Conference focuses today on the protection of children. According to the Convention of 24 October 1956 (*M L 1956*, with 14 contracting States, including 9 EU Member States), the determination of the applicable law as to maintenance obligations depends on the habitual residence of the child. The Convention on the Recognition and Enforcement of Decisions Relating to Maintenance Obligations Towards Children of 15 April 1958 (*M E 1958*) was ratified by 20 States (among them 14 EU Member States). These conventions have been modernised and extended to adults by the Conventions of 2 October 1973 on the Law Applicable (*M L 1973*, 15 ratifications, among them 11 EU Member States) and on the Recognition and Enforcement of Decisions Relating to Maintenance Obligations (*M E 1973*, 24 ratifications, including 17 EU Member States). Recently, on 23 November 2007, the Convention on International Recovery of Child Support was adopted (*M R*) and has been signed by the United States as well as by the EU and ratified by Norway, but is not yet in force. In addition, the EU has already ratified the Protocol on the Law Applicable to

Maintenance Obligations of 23 November 2007 (*M Pr*, which also is not yet in force) introducing the possibility for maintenance debtors and creditors to designate the applicable law and replacing *M L 1956 and M L 1973*.

According to the Convention Concerning the Protection of Minors *(Infants)* of 5 October 1961 (*Min*, 14 contracting States including 11 EU Member States), the courts of the State of the child's habitual residence have jurisdiction in custody matters and apply, principally, their own law, but the child's national law is to be applied as to parental custody by operation of law. The Protection of Children Convention of 19 October 1996 (*PCh*) corrects these and other deficiencies of *Min* and institutes better co-operation between contracting States by introducing central authorities. The number of contracting States (currently 34, including 23 EU Member States) will increase, as another four EU Member States are bound to accede, according to a judicial co-operation decision (without Denmark), and the USA signed the Convention on 22 October 2010 and will certainly ratify this Convention in the near future. The Convention on the Protection of Adults of 13 January 2000 (*PAd*), already ratified by five EU Member States and Switzerland, expands the principles of *PCh* to adults.

The Convention on the Civil Aspects of International Child Abduction of 25 October 1980 (*ChA*, 87 contracting States, including all 27 EU Member States, is a worldwide success that ensures, by the operation of central authorities, the immediate return of children taken abroad in violation of parental custody rights. The Inter-Country Adoption Convention (*Ado*) of 29 May 1993, ratified by 87 States (among them all 27 EU Member States) equally establishes co-operation through central authorities for the realisation of cross-border adoptions. The Convention on the Recognition of Divorce Decisions (*Div*) of 1 June 1970 has been ratified by 19 States, among them 13 EU Member States.

The application of multiple connecting factors in the Convention on the Conflicts of Laws Relating to the Form of Testamentary Dispositions of 5 October 1961 (*F W*), with 41 contracting States (including 16 EU Member States), favours the validity of testaments. The Convention on the Law Applicable to Succession of 1 August 1989 (*Succ*), which has not yet entered into force, permits a *professio juris* by the testator; otherwise the law of the habitual residence of the deceased is applicable, if he had lived there for five years before his death. The Convention on the Law Applicable to Trusts and on their Recognition of 1 July 1985 (*Tru*) has 12 contracting States (among them five EU Member States).

International Law of Obligations

In the area of private international law concerning obligations, property and negotiable instruments, as yet only the Convention on the Law Applicable to Traffic Accidents of 4 May 1971 (*TAc*, 21 ratifications, among them 12 EU Member States) and the Convention on the Law Applicable to Products Liability of 2 October 1973 (*PLi*, 11 ratifications, 6 EU Member States) have met a certain success.

THE EU AND CONFERENCE MEMBERSHIP

Judicial Co-operation of the EC Member States in the Context of the Hague Conventions

During the last phase of the negotiations regarding the adaptation of the Brussels Convention[8] on the occasion of the adhesion of the UK, Ireland and Denmark to the EEC, Belgium asked for additional provisions concerning child abduction. As this request went far beyond the subject matter of the Convention, it was rejected. However, within the European political co-operation framework, the EEC Member States unanimously agreed, informally, in the 1980s, to ratify both the Hague Child Abduction Convention[9] and the Council of Europe Convention on Recognition and Enforcement of Custody Decisions.[10] Achieving this goal took many years and only ended on 1 May 1999, when the *ChA* entered into force in Belgium as the last State concerned.[11]

This experience may have been one of the reasons why judicial co-operation formally became, first, part of the third pillar of the EC/EU. More important for this final result, of course, was the growing necessity for the EC Member States to harmonise their positions in the framework of international negotiations, a fact that was not always really appreciated by other States in international organisations such as Unidroit or the Conference. Nowadays, this situation has been formalised in the Conference system.

EC ACCESSION TO THE CONFERENCE

Article 3 of the Statute of the Hague Conference currently states:

> (1) The Member States of the Conference may, at a meeting concerning general affairs and policy where the majority of Member States is present, by a majority of the votes cast, decide to admit also as a Member any Regional Economic Integration Organisation which has submitted an application for membership to the Secretary General. References to Members under this Statute shall include such Member Organisations, except as

[8] Convention on Jurisdiction and the Enforcement of Judgments in Civil and Commercial Matters of 27 September 1968 ('Brussels I Convention'), now replaced by Council Regulation (EC) 44/2001, [2000] OJ EC L12/1.

[9] Convention on the Civil Aspects of International Child Abduction of 25 October 1980, Hague Conference on Private International Law, *Actes et Documents of the XIVth Session 6–25 October 1980*, Tome III (The Hague: Permanent Bureau: 1982, *ChA*) 413.

[10] European Convention of 20 May 1980 on Recognition and Enforcement of Decisions concerning Custody of Children and on Restoration of Custody of Children, Bundesgesetzblatt 1990 II 206, 220.

[11] *cf* also the experience with regard to the intended common ratification by the EU States of the Hague Convention on jurisdiction, applicable law, recognition, enforcement and co-operation in respect of parental responsibility and measures for the protection of children, Hague Conference on Private International Law, *Proceedings of the XVIIIth Session 30 September to 19 October 1996* (The Hague: Permanent Bureau: 1998) 515, and Explanatory Report by P Lagarde, ibid 535 – a convention in the meantime ratified by 34 States, among them 23 EU States.

otherwise expressly provided. The admission shall become effective upon the acceptance of the Statute by the Regional Economic Integration Organisation concerned.[12]

(2) To be eligible to apply for membership of the Conference, a Regional Economic Integration Organisation must be one constituted solely by sovereign States, and to which its Member States have transferred competence over a range of matters within the purview of the Conference, including the authority to make decisions binding on its Member States in respect of those matters. . . .

(8) The Member Organisation may exercise on matters within its competence, in any meetings of the Conference in which it is entitled to participate, a number of votes equal to the number of its Member States which have transferred competence to the Member Organisation in respect of the matter in question, and which are entitled to vote in and have registered for such meetings. Whenever the Member Organisation exercises its right to vote, its Member States shall not exercise theirs, and conversely.

The Statute entered into force for the EU on 3 April 2007. In accordance with the provisions of the Statute, the EC submitted a declaration of competence specifying the matters in respect of which competence had been transferred to it by its Member States and declared:

The European Community endeavours to examine whether it is in its interest to join existing Hague Conventions in respect of which there is Community competence. Where this interest exists, the European Community, in co-operation with the HCCH, will make every effort to overcome the difficulties resulting from the absence of a clause providing for the accession of a Regional Economic Integration Organisation to those Conventions.

The European Community further endeavours to make it possible for representatives of the Permanent Bureau of the HCCH to take part in meetings of experts organised by the Commission of the European Communities where matters of interest to the HCCH are being discussed.[13]

On 29 January 2010, in a declaration of succession, the EU notified the Conference that, as from 1 December 2009, the Union replaced and succeeded the EC.

These texts demonstrate the enormous change undergone by the Conference as a consequence of the accession of the EC, especially seen from the perspective of negotiation from non-EU Member States but also for Conference participants from these Member States. As the extraordinary voting power of a regional economic integration organisation consisting of 27 – and in the future probably many more – States could, if ever, only be balanced by an enormous amount of negotiation among the non-EU members of the Conference, it is evident that in the future voting procedures will be avoided whenever possible. Solving problems will no longer be left to majority voting; consensus will prevail.[14] This was already largely the case during the final phase of the negotiations leading to the *CAg*.[15] A trend towards compromises with very restrained solutions will be the consequence.

[12] www.hcch.net/index_en.php?act=conventions.text&cid=29; see Van Loon and Schulz, n 6 above, 259.

[13] www.hcch.net/index_en.php?act=status.comment&csid=992&disp=resdn.

[14] cf van Loon and Schulz, n 4 above, 266 ff.

[15] Although at that period still without a basis in the Statute.

Thus, it is to be assumed that the future work of the Conference will become ever more administrative. It is to be feared that its legislative power will decline because of the new voting practice. Working for the success of existing conventions, which began with *Serv* and *Evid* in the late 1970s, is, in itself, not necessarily a disadvantage, as is shown by the great participation in meetings on the practical functioning of child protection conventions. But one does not see how the period during which the Conference regularly produced progressive treaties on the basis of convincing ideas could be indefinitely prolonged without facing fundamental technical difficulties. This is not to say that the past always led to successful conventions. The table on page 88 demonstrates the extent to which results in meeting past challenges were achieved. However, in those days there was always a real chance of bringing the process to a successful outcome, while one might fear that the current organisational structure of the Conference renders such a probability ever more remote.

RELATIONSHIP BETWEEN THE BRUSSELS IIBIS REGULATION AND THE HAGUE CONVENTIONS

An instructive example of how the EU sees its relationship with the Hague and other international conventions is to be found in Chapter V of the Brussels IIbis Regulation. The general principle underlying this chapter is that of nearly absolute priority of Community – and now Union – law, which was first established, in this context, in the provisions of the Brussels I Convention (Articles 55 and 56), but with important exceptions for special subject matter according to Article 57. Article 39 of Regulation 1347/2000, with the possibility offered to Member States to add to, or facilitate the application of, the provisions of Regulation 1347/2000 on a bilateral basis, has not survived in the Brussels IIbis Regulation. Therefore, EU States can no longer establish specific rules to be applied in the relations between each other in addition to the rules of the Regulation. Thus, the new Regulation has, among EU States, in principle, exclusive character, with exceptions concerning the Treaties between the Holy See and Portugal, Italy, Spain and Malta, respectively, Article 63, and in relation to the Hague Convention of 1996, Article 61.[16]

According to Articles 59(1) and 62(1), Regulation 2201/2003 supersedes all treaties between Member States relating to matters to which the regulation applies, in so far as they cover such matters. That means that the Brussels IIbis Regulation does not only have priority over such conventions, but replaces them completely and does not leave open to them any kind of subsidiarity.

As between EU States, Article 60 of the Brussels IIbis Regulation expressly takes precedence over five multilateral conventions, specifically listed, namely *Min* (1961) and *ChA* (1980). As far as they concern other matters, these conventions are not affected (Article 62(1)); that is, they are beyond the scope of application of

[16] *cf* also the general possibilities concerning the Scandinavian Convention of 6 February 1931 in the relations between Finland and Sweden, Art 60(2).

the Regulation. *ChA* (1980) on child abduction, in force for all EU States and 58 other States, tries to guarantee the prompt return of children wrongfully removed by a person that does not have sole custody to another contracting State. Articles 2(11) and 11 of the Regulation contain specific prevailing provisions regarding such a return, and Articles 40–45 contain provisions concerning access as well as the specific situation dealt with in Article 11(8). These are additions to favour an effective return of the child from one EU Member State to another.

The relationship between the Brussels IIbis Regulation and the Hague Convention of 19 October 1996 (*PCh*) merits specific attention. The Hague Convention was substantially the basis for those parts of the Regulation that deal with parental responsibility. It is now in force for 23 EU States and 11 other States, such as Australia and Switzerland; after the recent signature by the USA on 22 October 2010 it will probably soon enter into force there. All EU States have signed it, in conformity with a common decision made long ago. The substantial difference between this Convention and the Regulation lies in the fact that the Convention deals with private international law, while the Regulation does not, thus breaking the fundamental link between jurisdiction and applicable law, both based on the same grounds.

THE IDEAL OF UNIFORM INTERPRETATION OF BRUSSELS REGULATIONS AND CORRESPONDING HAGUE CONVENTIONS

In her opinion in Case C-435/06 *C*, Advocate General Kokott points out:

> Admittedly, as regards relations between the Member States, within its scope of application Regulation No 2201/2003 takes precedence over international conventions (see Articles 60 and 61 of the regulation). However, international instruments continue to apply between Member States and third countries. For that reason, the provisions of the regulation and corresponding provisions in other conventions ought, so far as possible, to be interpreted in the same way, in order to avoid different results according to whether a case concerns another Member State or a third country.[17]

In her opinion in Case C-523/07 *A*, she states:

> 23. The conventions . . . form an important part of the legislative history of the regulation. In addition, the fields of application of the various instruments must be consistently demarcated from each other. That presumes a uniform understanding of the concept of habitual residence to which the provisions of the conventions and of the regulation both relate.
>
> 24. As regards its content, Regulation No 2201/2003 is inspired in this area primarily by the Hague Child Protection Convention of 19 October 1996. Article 5(1) of the Convention, like Article 8(1) of the regulation, confers jurisdiction in the first place on the courts of the State of the habitual residence (résidence habituelle) of the child. . . .

[17] Case C-435/06 *C* [2007] ECR I-10141, para 50.

> 26. As the Finnish, German, Greek and United Kingdom Governments rightly emphasise, the concept of habitual residence must be given a uniform interpretation, in order to demarcate consistently the scope of application of the Child Protection Convention from the scope of the regulation and avoid conflicts of jurisdiction between the courts of the Member States and the courts of other Contracting States to the Child Protection Convention.[18]

These are remarkable statements in the sense that not only a common and uniform interpretation within EU law, but also, as far as possible, conformity with the corresponding provisions in EU regulations and Hague conventions should be achieved. The first point is not surprising,[19] but is nevertheless important and in substance has been achieved since the 1976 judgment of the ECJ in *LTU v Eurocontol*.[20] The opinion has been cited extensively, as the second point seems to be the important one, and the one that has not yet, expressly, been taken up by the ECJ. This may have been the result of a certain traditional restraint of the ECJ in matters where the law should, in case of doubt, not be fixed too early. Yet, the uniform interpretation of the notion of 'civil matters' in the Brussels I Convention – nowadays approved everywhere – was also a rather revolutionary conceptual idea that the ECJ accepted[21] in *LTU v Eurocontrol*[22] without this fear and relating to a subject matter that, at that time, was a completely new one for the Court. So this may be the place to express the hope that in a future decision, where this problem arises again, the ECJ will come to an express conclusion in the sense indicated, namely accepting the principle of achieving as much conformity of interpretation of the Brussels IIbis Regulation with the Hague Child Protection Convention as possible.

McB

Is an example of such an interpretation to be found – implicitly – in the judgment of the ECJ, pronounced in an urgent procedure on 5 October 2010,[23] in *McB*? The facts behind this case were as follows. An Irish/English couple had lived together for many years with their three children before the deterioration of their relationship. The mother, in July 2009, left the family home in Ireland with the children

[18] Case C-523/07 *A* [2009] ECR I-2805, paras 23, 24, 26.

[19] ibid, paras 38–40. See also Case C-292/05 *Lechouritou and ors* [2007] ECR I-1519, para 29 and the case law cited.

[20] Case C-29/76 *LTU v Eurocontrol* [1976] ECR 1541.

[21] On the basis of a statement of the federal German Government which led the EEC Commission to a fundamental change of position compared to its first (written) proposal; by the way, the ECJ accepted the admissibility of the request of a German appeal jurisdiction that asked the ECJ for a preliminary decision, although, strictly speaking it was, according to the provisions of the German Code on Civil Procedure, bound by a judgment of 26 November 1975 of the Bundesgerichtshof (VIII ZB 26/75, Entscheidungen des Bundesgerichtshofs in Zivilsachen Band 65, 291) in the same case.

[22] See n 20 above, an important decision taken against the views of the Rapporteur on the adaptation negotiations (P Schlosser).

[23] Case C-400/10 PPU *McB*, judgment of 5 October 2010 nyr; see Lenaerts n 7 above, 165; Pirrung n 7 above, 271, 278.

and set off for England. In November 2009 the father brought an action before an English court seeking the return of the children to Ireland, on the basis of the Hague Convention (*ChA* 1980) and the Brussels IIbis Regulation. The English court requested that the father, pursuant to Article 15 *ChA*, obtain a determination from the Irish authorities declaring that the removal of the children was wrongful within the meaning of Article 3 *ChA*. The father brought an action before the High Court of Ireland seeking such a declaration. The Irish courts dismissed this claim, as the father had not previously (ie, before the mother had left Ireland) initiated court proceedings with the aim of obtaining custody. Consequently, under Irish law, he had no custodial rights over the children at the time of their removal and the removal was not wrongful within the meaning of either the Hague Convention or the Regulation. The Supreme Court of Ireland considered that the definition of 'rights of custody', for the purposes of an application to obtain the return of children from one Member State to another on the basis of the Hague Convention, is now to be found in Article 2(9) of the Regulation, and so requested a preliminary decision of the ECJ.

The ECJ decided that the Brussels IIbis Regulation does not preclude a Member State from providing under national law that the acquisition of rights of custody by a father, who is not married to the mother, is dependent on the father's obtaining a judgment from a national court awarding such rights to him, on the basis of which the removal of the child by its mother or the retention of that child may be considered wrongful within the meaning of Article 2(11) of the Regulation.

There lay the problem. As the request of the English court for a determination according to Article 15 *ChA* was solely based on the Convention, there was neither a jurisdiction nor a recognition base for the application of the Brussels IIbis Regulation. In accordance with Article 60(e), this Regulation takes precedence over the *ChA* only 'in so far as (it) concern(s) matters governed by this Regulation'. According to Article 62(1) of the Regulation, once again: 'The agreements and conventions referred to in Articles 59(1), 60 and 61 shall continue to have effect in relation to matters not governed by this Regulation'. The Regulation clearly does not govern the determination requested under Article 15 *ChA*. So there was no justification for jurisdiction of the Irish courts under the Regulation, even for the claim of the father to accord him custody (now), as the mother, who according to the opinion of the Irish courts had sole custody, had changed the habitual residence of the children to England. So the request of the Irish Supreme Court for a preliminary ruling by the ECJ was, from an objective point of view and under all possible aspects of the case, strictly speaking, inadmissible. The problem had been presented to the ECJ by the German Government and the EU Commission.[24] But the Chamber did not follow this line and held, that,

> according to the Court's case-law, it is solely for the national courts before which actions are brought, and which must bear the responsibility for the subsequent judicial decision, to determine in the light of the special features of each case both the need for

[24] ibid, para 30.

a preliminary ruling in order to enable them to deliver judgment and the relevance of the questions which they submit to the Court.

– 33. Consequently, where the questions submitted by the national court concern the interpretation of European Union law, the Court of Justice is, in principle, bound to give a ruling.

– 34. It follows that the presumption that questions referred by national courts for a preliminary ruling are relevant may be rebutted only in exceptional cases, in particular where it is quite obvious that the interpretation which is sought of the provisions of European Union law referred to in those questions bears no relation to the actual facts of the main action or to its purpose.

– 35. In the present case, the referring court considers that it needs an interpretation of Regulation No 2201/2003, and in particular Article 2(11), in order to give a ruling on the application before it, which seeks from that court a decision or a determination declaring that the removal or retention of the children concerned in the dispute in the main proceedings was wrongful. It is evident moreover from the relevant national legislation, namely Section 15 of the Child Abduction and Enforcement of Custody Orders Act 1991, as amended by the European Communities (Judgments in Matrimonial Matters and Matters of Parental Responsibility) Regulations 2005, that, in cases of removal of a child to another Member State, the issue on which the national court must rule, when an applicant requests that it deliver such a decision or determination in accordance with Article 15 of the 1980 Hague Convention, is whether the removal is lawful under Article 2 of Regulation No 2201/2003.

– 36. Furthermore, it must be observed that, pursuant to Article 60 of Regulation No 2201/2003, in relations between Member States that regulation is to take precedence over the 1980 Hague Convention in so far as the latter concerns matters governed by that regulation. Subject to the primacy of that regulation, the Convention is to continue to produce effects between the Member States which are party thereto, in compliance with Article 60, pursuant to Article 62(2) of Regulation No 2201/2003, as stated in recital 17 in its preamble. Consequently, abductions of children from one Member State to another are now subject to a body of rules consisting of the provisions of the 1980 Hague Convention as complemented by those of Regulation No 2201/2003, though the latter take precedence on matters within the scope of that regulation.

– 37. In those circumstances, it is not obvious that the interpretation sought by the referring court is of no relevance to the decision which that court is called upon to make.

– 38. Consequently, the reference for a preliminary ruling must be declared to be admissible.[25]

This answer from the ECJ may satisfy the Irish Supreme Court; in an urgent procedure, one could not expect a thorough discussion of the question of admissibility. Whether in this case there really was a need for an urgent procedure remains an open question. Rather not, if one accepts, as one is obviously obliged to do, the substantial result of the ECJ. On the other hand, can one deduce from the answer of the ECJ that conformity of interpretation for the Brussels IIbis Regulation and the Convention is a value in itself? This is at least doubtful. One might hope so, but probably one will have to wait for somewhat clearer statements in this sense.

[25] ibid, paras 32–38.

Selected Hague Conventions and their ratifications by EU States[26]

*	Civ 1954	M L 1956	M E 1958	Min 1961	F W 1961	Leg 1961	Serv 1965	Div 1970	T Ac 1971	Evid 1970	P Li 1973
Austria	12. 4.57	1.1. 62	1.1. 62	11.5.75	5.1.64	13. 1.68			3.6. 75		
Belgium	23. 6.58	24. 9.70	1.1. 62		19. 12.71	9.2. 76	18. 1.71		3.6. 75		
Bulgaria						29. 4.01	1.8. 00			22.1.00	
Cyprus	1.3. 01					30. 4.73	1.6. 83	14. 3.83		14. 3.83	
Czech Republic	1.1. 93		29. 12.70			16. 3.99	1.1. 93	1.1. 93	1.1. 93	1.1.93	
Denmark	18. 6.58		1.1. 66		19. 9.76	29. 12.06	1.10.69	24. 8.75		7.10.72	
Estonia					12. 7.98	30. 9.01	1.10.96	6.1.03		2.4. 96	
E U						X					
Finland	12. 4.57		24. 8.67		23. 8.76	26. 8.85	10. 11.69	15. 8.77		6.6. 76	1.11.92
France	22. 6.59	1.7. 63	25. 7.66	10. 11.72	19. 9.67	24. 1.65	1.9. 72		3.6. 75	6.10.74	1.9. 77
Germany	1.1.60	1.1. 62	1.1. 62	17. 9.71	1.1. 66	13. 2.66	26. 6.79			26. 6.79	
Greece					2.8. 83	18. 5.85	18. 9.83			19. 3.05	
Hungary	18. 2.66		19. 12.64			18. 1.73	1.4. 05			11.9.04	
Ireland					2.10.67	9.3. 99	4.6. 94				
Italy	12. 4.57	1.1. 62	1.1. 62	23. 4.95		11. 2.78	24. 1.82	20. 4.86		21. 8.82	
Latvia	12. 9.93			25. 3.01		30. 1.96	1.11.95		15.10. 00	27. 5.95	
Lithua-nia	17. 7.03			22. 12.01		19. 7.97	1.6. 01		24. 3.02	1.10.00	
Luxem-bourg	12. 4.57	1.1. 62		4.2. 69	5.2. 79	3.6. 79	7.9. 75	14. 4.91	13. 12.80	24. 9.74	1.8. 85

[26] In the list the date of entry into force of a convention is stated in an abbreviated way: instead of the name of the month its number is indicated, and for the year only the last two numbers are given, so that, eg, '12.4.57' means: '12 April 1957'. As regards the line concerning the EU, an 'X' indicates that the convention is in force for all 27 EU Member States, but in these cases the dates of entry into force are stated for each EU State individually, because, according to the text of the respective conventions, only States can ratify them; in this line, for the last three treaties 'S' stands for 'signed', 'R' for 'ratified (but not yet in force)'. A complete simplified chart of all Hague conventions with indications as to signatures, ratifications and accessions, but without dates, is available at www.hcch.net/upload/statmtrx_e.pdf, while complete status tables for each convention can be found at www.hcch.net/index_en.php?act=conventions.status&cid=33 ff.

M E 1973	M L 1973	ChA 1980	AcJ 1980	Tru 1985	Succ 1989	Ado 1993	PCh 1996	PAd 2000	CAg 2005	M R 2007	M Pr 2007
		1.10.88				1.9. 99	1.4. 11				
		1.5. 99				1.9. 05					
		1.8. 03	1.2. 00			1.9. 02	1.2. 07				
		1.2. 95	1.10.00			1.6. 95	1.11.10				
1.1.93		1.3. 98	1.7.01			1.6. 00	1.1. 02				
1.1. 88		1.7. 91				1.11.97					
1.4. 98	1.1. 02	1.7 .01	1.5. 96			1.6. 02	1.6. 03	1.11.11			
		X				X			*S 1. 4.09*	*S 6. 4.11*	*R 8. 4.10*
1.7. 83		1.8. 94	1.9. 88			1.7. 97	1.3. 11	1.3. 11			
1.10.77	1.10.77	1.12.83	1.5. 88			1.10.98	1.2. 11	1.1. 09			
1.4. 87	1.4. 87	1.12.90				1.3. 02	1.1. 11	1.1. 09			
1.2. 04	1. 10. 03	1.6. 93				1.1. 10	1.6. 12				
		1.7. 86				1.8. 05	1.5. 06				
		1.10.91				1.11.10	1.1. 11				
1.1. 82	1.1. 82	1.5. 95		1.1. 92		1.5. 00					
		1.2. 02	1.3. 00			1.12.02	1.4. 03				
1.10.03	1.9. 01	1.9.02	1.11.00			1.8. 98	1.9. 04				
1.6. 81	1.1. 82	1.1. 87	1.5. 03	1.1. 04		1.11.02	1.12. 10				

*	Civ 1954	M L 1956	M E 1958	Min 1961	F W 1961	Leg 1961	Serv 1965	Div 1970	T Ac 1971	Evid 1970	P Li 1973
Malta						3.3. 68	1.10.11			25. 4.11	
Nether-lands	27. 6.59	14. 12.62	28. 4.64	18. 9.71	1.8. 82	8.10. 95	2.1. 76	22. 8.81	30. 12.78	7.6. 81	1.9. 79
Poland	13. 3.63			25. 7.93	2.11.69	14. 8.05	1.9. 96	24. 6.96	28. 5.02	13. 4.96	
Portugal	31. 8.67	3.2. 69	24. 2.74	4.2. 69		4.2. 69	25. 2.74	9.7. 85		11.5.75	
Romania	29. 1.72					16. 3.01	1.4. 04			20. 10.03	
Slovakia	1.1. 93		29. 11.70			18. 2.02	1.1. 93	1.1. 93	1.1. 93	1.1. 93	
Slovenia	25. 6.91				25. 6.91	25. 6.91	1.6. 01		25. 6.91	17. 11.00	25. 6.91
Spain	19. 11.61	25. 5.74	9.6. 73	21. 7.87	10. 6.88	25. 9.78	3.8. 87		21. 11.87	21. 7.87	1.2. 89
Sweden	19. 2.58		1.3. 66		7.9. 76	1.5. 99	1.10.69	24. 8.75		1.7. 75	
United Kingdom					5.1. 64	24. 1.65	10. 2.69	24. 8.75		14. 9.76	

M E 1973	M L 1973	ChA 1980	AcJ 1980	Tru 1985	Succ 1989	Ado 1993	PCh 1996	PAd 2000	CAg 2005	M R 2007	M Pr 2007
		1.1. 00	1.5. 11	1.3. 96		1.2. 05	1.1. 12				
1.3. 81	1.3. 81	1.9. 90	1.6. 92	1.2. 96	*R 27. 9.96*	1.10.98	1.5. 11				
1.7. 96	1.5. 96	1.11.92	1.11.92			1.10.95	1.11.10				
1.8. 76	1.10.77	1.12.83				1.7. 04	1.8. 11				
		1.2. 93	1.11.03			1.5. 95	1.1. 11				
1.1. 93		1.2. 01	1.6. 03			1.10.01	1.1. 02				
		1.6. 94	25. 6.91			1.5. 02	1.2. 05				
1.9. 87	1.10.86	1.9. 87	1.5. 88			1.11.95	1.1. 11				
1.5. 77		1.6. 89	1.5. 88			1.9. 97					
1.3. 80		1.8. 86		1.1. 92		1.6. 03		1.1. 09			

CONCLUSION

In *McB*, as regards admissibility of the preliminary procedure, co-operation between European and national judges has led to a substantially satisfying, though theoretically perhaps not altogether convincing, result. Is this also the case, as regards co-operation between the EU and the Conference in general? One might suppose that in the application of comparable provisions in regulations and conventions comparable interpretations should be achieved, but the factual basis for this assumption seems rather weak. Clear principles call for unambiguous answers, yet the present situation of the EU, not least because of the discussions about the current financial crisis, shows that this seems to be wishful thinking. When organisations grow too fast, they may encounter the same danger as living beings do under comparable circumstances. At this stage may the hope be expressed that the sceptic undertones of these observations will, in the end, be proved to have been too pessimistic.

7

Subsidiarity as a Legal Concept

DAVID EDWARD*

NIL NOVI SUB SOLE: THERE IS NO NEW THING UNDER THE SUN
(ECCLESIASTES 1.9)

IT IS DIFFICULT to think of something new to write in honour of Pernilla Lindh whose conversation and companionship has given us all so much pleasure over the years. A further addition to the *arcana* of Union law hardly seems a fitting tribute to a remarkable lady whose legal skills are matched by a lively sense of humour and a warm heart. But something must nevertheless be written that is suitable for this volume of essays.

The contribution that follows is a personal reflection on the significance of subsidiarity as a legal concept in the light of Article 5 of the Treaty on European Union as amended by the Treaty of Lisbon. Is subsidiarity a principle of limited (though important) application relating only to the exercise of shared competences, or should we view it as a wider principle of good governance and public morality?

WHAT IS SUBSIDIARITY?

Subsidiarity formally entered the vocabulary of Community law with the Treaty of Maastricht, but it did not spring fully armed from the heads of the Treaty makers.

The underlying idea has a long history under a variety of different labels. As a principle of governance, it goes back at least as far as the Peace of Westphalia in 1648 with its assertion of exclusive state sovereignty (or at least the exclusive sovereignty of the monarch) and freedom of religion (or at least the freedom of the monarch to choose the religion of his subjects). In this form, subsidiarity is reflected in the international law principles of state sovereignty and non-interference.

Under the label of 'federalism', subsidiarity is a basic tenet of the United States Constitution. Such powers and competences as are not given to the authorities of the Federation remain with the States which are entitled to exercise them without federal interference.

* Professor Emeritus, University of Edinburgh; Judge of the Court of First Instance of the European Communities (1989–92); Judge of the Court of Justice of the European Communities (1992–2004).

Subsidiarity can also be viewed as a common sense principle of good governance. In an essay originally composed in 1884, the Scottish constitutional thinker, James Bryce, explained how it can avoid political tensions:

> Nothing contributes more to the smooth working of a central government and to the satisfaction of the people under it, than the habit of leaving to comparatively small local communities the settlement of as many questions as possible. The practice of local government and the love for it are not a centrifugal force, but rather tend to ease off any friction that may exist by giving harmless scope for independent action, and thus producing local contentment. It is only where there exist grievances fostering disruptive sentiments that the existence of local bodies with a pretty large sphere of activity need excite disquiet.[1]

In 1931 Pope Pius XI enunciated the principle as one of public morality. This is said to be the route through which it entered modern political discourse:

> As history abundantly proves, it is true that on account of changed conditions many things which were done by small associations in former times cannot be done now save by large associations. Still, that most weighty principle, which cannot be set aside or changed, remains fixed and unshaken in social philosophy: just as it is gravely wrong to take from individuals what they can accomplish by their own initiative and industry and give it to the community, so also it is an injustice and at the same time a grave evil and disturbance of right order to assign to a greater and higher association what lesser and subordinate organizations can do. For every social activity ought of its very nature to furnish help to the members of the body social, and never destroy and absorb them.[2]

Whether one looks at it as principle of non-interference, a principle of federalism, a common sense principle of good governance or a principle of public morality, subsidiarity has now become part of the vocabulary of the EU embedded in the Treaties. How will it work as a legal concept?

SUBSIDIARITY IN THE MAASTRICHT TREATY

Subsidiarity in the Maastricht Treaty was essentially a restatement of Westphalian subsidiarity. Article 3b (later Article 5) EC stated, in a briefer form, the three principles of conferral, subsidiarity and proportionality that now appear in Article 5 TEU. Only subsidiarity was explicitly identified as a 'principle':

> In areas which do not fall within its exclusive competence, the Community shall take action, in accordance with the principle of subsidiarity, only if and in so far as the objectives of the proposed action cannot be sufficiently achieved by the Member States

[1] J Bryce, 'The Action of Centripetal and Centrifugal Forces on Political Constitutions' in *Studies in History and Jurisprudence*, vol I (Oxford, 1901) 244.

[2] Pope Pius XI, Encyclical *Quadragesimo Anno* of 15 May 1931, para 79. The approach differs markedly from that of Innocent X whose portrait by Velasquez inspired a series of paintings by Francis Bacon. He condemned the Peace of Westphalia as nulla, irrita, invalida, iniqua, injusta, damnata, reprobata, inania, viribusque et effectu vacua – Bull *Zelo Domus Dei* of 26 November 1648.

> and can therefore, by reason of the scale or effects of the proposed action, be better achieved by the Community.

According to this formulation, the sole relevant actors were the Community on the one hand and the Member States on the other. At the time it seemed that this was no more than a defiant reassertion of the rights of the Member States as *Herren der Verträge*, defining the borderline between the respective competences of the Community and the Member States in areas of shared competence. There was no reference to any level of governance below that of the Member State, although there was a curtsey towards the citizen in the Preamble to the new Treaty on European Union (TEU):

> RESOLVED to continue the process of creating an ever closer union among the peoples of Europe, in which decisions are taken as closely as possible to the citizen in accordance with the principle of subsidiarity.

The Treaty of Amsterdam added a Protocol to the EC Treaty on the Application of the Principles of Subsidiarity and Proportionality. It contained a number of provisions that foreshadow the detailed procedures established in the Lisbon Treaty, but their focus was still on the Community/Member State relationship.

In the course of the European Convention, two major deficiencies were identified by Working Group I on the Principle of Subsidiarity:

> First of all, with the notable exception of the possibility to obtain an opinion from the Court provided for in article 300 paragraph 6 EC[3], the current legal monitoring mechanisms only operate once a legal act has entered into force. Neither a preliminary ruling pursuant to article 234 EC nor a decision of annulment pursuant to article 230 EC can be obtained before a specific act causes legal effects. It is clear that the Court is less likely to overturn Community action that forms already part of the *Acquis communautaire* and is already being applied by the Courts and authorities of the Member States, than a legislative project without legal consequences at the moment of its examination. In the latter case the Court is more likely to take a detailed look at the factual evidence underlying the legislator's claim that the objective of the act cannot be achieved at the level of the Member States.
>
> Secondly, actions for annulment can only be brought by Member States, the Council, the Commission, the European Parliament (after the entry into force of the Treaty of Nice not only to protect its prerogatives), by the Court of Auditors and the ECB (both institutions only as far as the protection of their prerogatives is concerned) as well as by natural and legal persons, if the incriminated act is of direct and individual concern to them. National parliaments, the Committee of the Regions and Regions given legislative powers by the Constitutions of Member States, who are, in practice, primarily concerned by violations of the subsidiarity principle, are not entitled to institute legal action under the existing monitoring mechanisms. This is without any doubt another reason for the relative inactivity of the ECJ as far as subsidiarity questions are concerned.[4]

[3] Art 300 EC concerning proposed agreements with third countries and international organisations is replaced by Art 218 TFEU.

[4] european-convention.eu.int/docs/wd1/2140.pdf, 7–8.

SUBSIDIARITY IN THE LISBON TREATY

The Working Group's call for pre-legislative monitoring and recognition of the rights of national and regional legislatures explains the thinking behind the revised formulation of subsidiarity in Article I-11 of the Constitutional Treaty and now in Article 5 TEU, as well as the governmental machinery provided for in Protocols No 1 on the Role of National Parliaments and No 2 on the Application of the Principles of Subsidiarity and Proportionality.

The new provisions in Article 5 and the Protocols should be read in light of the statements of values and aims in Articles 2 and 3. These include references to respect for the rights of minorities, pluralism, the Union's rich cultural and linguistic diversity and Europe's cultural heritage – aspects of national life that were stressed by the Bundesverfassungsgericht in its judgment on the Lisbon Treaty.[5]

The context in which subsidiarity is to be understood is now much wider than the dialogue between the Union and the Member States and includes non-political aspects of the everyday life of citizens. If not quite a principle of public morality, it is at least the basis of sound multi-level governance.

Article 5 TEU redefines the principles of conferral, subsidiarity and proportionality. Although the formulation of the three principles remains very similar to the Maastricht version, Article 5(1), following Article 1 of the Amsterdam Protocol, defines how they are related to each other. The principle of conferral is a limit (délimitation) of competence; subsidiarity and proportionality are limits to the use (exercice) of shared competence.

The distinction between the existence of a right and its exercise is already well known to EU lawyers, notably in the field of intellectual property law. Its significance in the present context suggests the sort of question that we should be asking where subsidiarity is in issue. The principle of conferral requires us to ask 'Does the Union have competence?' If the answer is that the Union has shared competence, subsidiarity poses the question 'Does the Union need to exercise that competence?' Finally proportionality asks 'Does the Union need to exercise it in that way? Could it do so in a way that is less intrusive?'

Article 5(3) TEU adds a further important element to the definition of subsidiarity:

> Under the principle of subsidiarity, in areas which do not fall within its exclusive competence, the Union shall act if and in so far as the objectives of the proposed action cannot be sufficiently achieved by the Member States, *either at central level or at regional or local level*, but can rather, by reason of the scale or effects of the proposed action, be better achieved at Union level.

The regional or local dimension is further emphasised in Protocol No 2, Article 5 of which provides that:

[5] BVerfG, judgment of 30 June 2009, 2BvE 2/08, paras 249, 260.

> Any draft legislative act should[6] contain a detailed statement making it possible to appraise compliance with the principles of subsidiarity and proportionality. This statement should contain some assessment of the proposal's financial impact and, in the case of a directive, of its implications for the rules to be put in place by Member States, *including, where necessary, the regional legislation.* [. . .] Draft legislative acts shall take account of the need for any burden, whether financial or administrative, falling upon the Union, national governments, *regional or local authorities, economic operators and citizens*, to be minimised and commensurate with the objective to be achieved. (emphasis added)

Looking at these Treaty provisions as a whole, one can see that both the tone and the content are new. Subsidiarity is not just an assertion of the powers and prerogatives of the Member States vis-a-vis the union. There is now explicit recognition of sub-state entities as part of the constitutional order of the Union[7] and economic operators and citizens are recognised as having a legitimate interest in the scope and effects of governmental action.

Under the former Treaties, democratic participation in the process of European government was exercised indirectly through the Heads of State or Government in the European Council or ministers in the Council and directly through the European Parliament. The role of national parliaments was limited to 'scrutinis[ing] their governments in relation to the activities of the Union',[8] and regional parliaments were not recognised at all. But as the Working Group pointed out, it is national and regional parliaments that have the greatest interest in observance of the principle of subsidiarity or, to put it more bluntly, in resisting intrusion into areas of national, regional and local life that are properly their domain.

Now national parliaments must be directly informed about all Commission proposals (green and white papers and communications)[9] and legislative proposals must contain 'a detailed statement making it possible to appraise compliance with the principles of subsidiarity and proportionality'.[10] Acting together, national parliaments can place a temporary block on legislation, and an independent role is given to their separate chambers, one of which (notably in Germany) may represent the organs of regional government. They in turn are given the role of consulting regional parliaments with legislative powers, and possibly the obligation to do so.[11]

6 *Devrait* in the French text; *sollte* in the German text.

7 Discussed in D Edward & J Bengoetxea, 'The Status and Rights of Sub-state Entities in the Constitutional Order of the European Union' in A Arnull, C Barnard, M Dougan and E Spaventa (eds), *A Constitutional Order of States* (Oxford, Hart Publishing, 2011) 25–38.

8 See the preamble to Protocol No 1.

9 Protocol No 1, Art 1.

10 Protocol No 2, Art 5.

11 There is a minor but possibly significant difference between the different language texts of Art 6 of the Protocol. In English '[i]t is for [the Parliaments] to consult . . .'; in French '[i]l incombe [aux parlements] de consulter . . .'; in German '[d]abei obliegt es [die Parlamente] . . . zu konsultieren'. The German text, unlike the English or French, appears to connote a positive obligation to consult.

These and other features of the new Treaty lead one to ask three questions:

- At what stage in the legislative process does compliance with the principle of subsidiarity become subject to judicial control?
- How is the Court to go about the task of determining whether the principle has been complied with?
- In a more general way, is subsidiarity to be seen, not merely as a principle of good governance and public morality, but as a legal norm pervading all aspects of Union activity?

JUDICIAL ENFORCEMENT UNDER PROTOCOLS NOS 1 AND 2

The machinery laid down in Protocols Nos 1 and 2 is clearly susceptible of judicial scrutiny and enforcement. The Protocols set out in some detail the procedure that must be followed at various stages of the legislative process and there is no reason why failure to comply with the prescribed steps of procedure should not be open to judicial review in the normal way under Article 263 TFEU as a breach of a Treaty provision.

However, Article 8 of Protocol No 2 goes further and extends the jurisdiction of the ECJ to

> actions on grounds of infringement of the principle of subsidiarity by a legislative act, brought, in accordance with the rules laid down in Article 263 [TFEU] by Member States, or notified by them in accordance with their legal order on behalf of their national Parliament or a chamber thereof.

In addition, the Committee of the Regions may bring such an action where the act is one for which the TFEU provides that the Committee must be consulted. In this respect the Committee is placed in a position analogous to the former position of the European Parliament.

The wording of Article 8 raises a number of questions. The first, and perhaps the most important, is whether the new procedure can be invoked in the course of the legislative process or only when that process has resulted in a 'legislative act'? The answer is not obvious.

The expression 'infringement of the principle of subsidiarity by a legislative *act*' implies that the legislative process must be complete since it is only then that the act, rather than the process of its adoption, can infringe anything. Moreover, the wording of Article 8 echoes precisely the revised wording of Article 263 TFEU: 'The Court of Justice . . . shall review the legality of legislative acts . . . other than recommendations and opinions'. In principle, the right of action does not extend to acts of a preparatory character.[12]

But there are several contra-indications. The wording of Article 5(3) implies that the test of subsidiarity is to be applied to '*proposed* action' rather than a com-

[12] Case 60/81 *IBM v Commission* [1981] ECR 2639.

pleted legislative act. That would respond to the first concern of the Working Group on Subsidiarity (quoted above), that legislative projects should be open to judicial scrutiny *before* they enter into force and become part of the EU law. If Article 8 applies only when the legislative process is complete, it does nothing to meet that concern.

In addition, the right of action conferred on the Member States by Article 8 must presumably be additional to the right to challenge legislative acts which they already enjoy as privileged applicants under Article 263 TFEU. It may seem odd to allow Member States both to take part in the legislative process in Council and, at the same time, to stymie its progress by raising an action in the ECJ claiming that the proposal under consideration does not comply with the principle of subsidiarity. But this objection is less obvious in the case of national parliaments.

In essence, the question is whether the procedure laid down by Protocols Nos 1 and 2 is designed to enable disputes about subsidiarity during the pre-legislative phase to be resolved through negotiation between the political institutions (and, where appropriate, national parliaments and the Committee of the Regions) or whether, as the Working Group wanted, questions of subsidiarity can be referred to the ECJ as the legislative process proceeds. There seems to be no obvious answer.

A subordinate question of interpretation arises in relation to the words 'actions . . . notified by [the Member States] in accordance with their legal order on behalf of their national Parliament or a chamber thereof'. Nowhere in the texts is there any provision for an action to be 'notified' to the Court by one party (even a privileged applicant) on behalf of another. It is not even clear who will be the party to the action – the Member State, the national parliament or the relevant chamber of the parliament? The idea seems all the more curious if one has in mind that the government of a Member State may have cast its vote in Council in favour of the legislative act that is being impugned by its own parliament. Having 'notified' the action on behalf of its parliament, will it be possible for the government of the same Member State to intervene to argue against its parliament? Again, there seems to be no obvious answer.

HOW SHOULD THE COURT APPROACH THE ISSUE OF SUBSIDIARITY?

Assuming that the procedural conundrums can be resolved, how is the ECJ to go about judging the question whether the principle of subsidiarity has been complied with? Much may depend on whether the Court interprets its jurisdiction under Article 8 as extending to review of pre-legislative proposals or only to post-legislative scrutiny.

On any view, the Court will need to ask itself a series of questions. The first group of questions, as suggested above, will be:

– Does the Union have competence? (conferral)
– If it is a shared competence, does the Union need to use it? (subsidiarity)

- Does the Union need to use its competence in this way, or could it be used in a less intrusive way? (proportionality)

Having reached the second (subsidiarity) question, the wording of Article 5(2) TEU suggests three further questions:

- What is the 'objective' of the action?
- Can that objective be '*sufficiently* achieved by the Member States at central, regional or local level'?
- Can it 'by reason of the scale or effects [of the measure] be *better* achieved at Union level'?

It is important to note that the second and third questions deal with separate issues. Even if the objective in question can be 'sufficiently' achieved by action at national, regional or local level, it must also be considered whether it can be 'better' achieved at Union level.

If the action (or proposed action) has passed all these hurdles, the enquiry will shift to proportionality. Fortunately, the Court has already developed an effective approach to proportionality:

- What is the objective?
- Is the action (or proposed action) necessary to achieve it?
- Does the measure go further than is necessary to achieve it?

The foregoing analysis of the questions to be asked and the tests to be applied suggests that the Court will be faced with problems of a new dimension. The expressions '*sufficiently* achieved' and '*better* achieved' imply a qualitative assessment involving an element of subjective judgment based on some comparison between the quality and efficiency of the expected result of action at different levels with a view to achieving the objective in question.

The comparison cannot be confined to the situation in a few Member States. In a Union of 27 or more Member States, the larger states, their regions or local authorities may have financial and other resources 'sufficient' to achieve the objective in question. Other Member States may not be so fortunate and action at Union level may be 'better' to enable the desired objective to be achieved Union-wide. Does that justify infringing the national, regional or local autonomy of the larger states? Presumably the answer will be yes, but it is hardly a question that the Court would be well equipped to answer.

How should the Court approach these questions? It seems unlikely that it will be faced with an action claiming that the Union has not acted, or has refused to act, in circumstances where it ought to have done so. The situation is far more likely to be the reverse, that the Union is accused of acting where subsidiarity would require restraint. In such a case, the Court will be able to focus on the quality and adequacy of the reasoning in the texts where the institutions of the Union seek to justify the action taken. At the pre-legislative stage, the relevant text would be the 'detailed statement' prospectively justifying the legislative act. Once the post-legislative stage has been reached, the focus would shift to the preamble of the legislative act since this should explain why the legislation is necessary.

That approach would correspond reasonably well to what the Court does already in its scrutiny of legislative acts. A wider question is whether we should now regard subsidiarity as a legal norm permeating all aspects of Union life including, most controversially, action in the areas where the Union has exclusive competence.

DOES SUBSIDIARITY NOW PERMEATE ALL ASPECTS OF UNION LIFE?

This article is being written in the midst of the crisis in the eurozone. The outcome is not foreseeable, but one idea seems to be uppermost if the crisis is to be resolved. That is the belief that the states of the eurozone must move towards a more integrated fiscal and economic policy. If that is correct, the corollary must be that those states would be less free than they are at present to make choices between different fiscal and economic options. Put another way, effective crisis management and the requirements of long-term stability are hardly compatible with adherence to subsidiarity (at least in the field of fiscal economics).

At the same time it is argued by others that the current crisis is the consequence of overreach at Union level. It is said that the so-called 'Brussels élite' have pressed ahead with grandiose projects of integration, disregarding the legitimate interests and concerns of the citizen at national, regional and local level. Subsidiarity as a moral principle of good governance is needed to restrain such ambitions and allow decision-making to occur 'as closely as possible to the citizen'.

There is no obvious solution to the conflict between these two points of view. As the writer of Ecclesiastes said, there is nothing new under the sun. Such conflict is a perennial feature of democratic politics, as current events in the United States also show. It cannot be eliminated, but it can at least be managed. In that respect, what matters most is the attitude of mind with which the problems of the Union are approached.

It used to be said of the ECJ that its attitude was 'in dubio pro Communitate' (in doubt the interests of the Community should take precedence). Perhaps the motto should now be 'in dubio pro subsidiaritate' (when in doubt don't interfere). This approach need not be confined to areas of shared competence. It is just as important in areas of exclusive competence that the Union institutions should ask themselves whether action is necessary and, if so, whether the action proposed is proportionate.

There are several indications in the new texts following Lisbon that this is the proper approach to adopt. Consider, for example, Article 4(2) TEU with its call upon the Union to respect the 'fundamental structures [of the Member States], political and constitutional, inclusive of regional and local government'.

There is, however, a difference between adopting an attitude of mind and complying with a legal obligation. To what extent, apart from the machinery prescribed by Protocols Nos 1 and 2, are the institutions of the Union obliged by the Treaties to comply with the principle of subsidiarity?

The Treaty wording is ambivalent. On the one hand, Article 5(1) TEU states without qualification that '[t]he use of Union competences is governed by the principles of subsidiarity and proportionality'. The two principles are placed on a footing of equality, as indeed they were in Article 1 of the Amsterdam Protocol.[13] Proportionality is well established as a general principle of Community law. Why should subsidiarity not be also? This would imply that, even where the Union enjoys exclusive competence, it is bound, in the use of that competence, to observe both principles.

On the other hand, Article 5(3) begins '[u]nder the principle of subsidiarity, in areas which do not fall within its competence, the Union shall act only if . . .' and Article 3 of the Amsterdam Protocol stated that this is the context in which it should be applied. This suggests that subsidiarity applies as a legal requirement only in areas of shared competence. Indeed, the idea that an objective can be sufficiently, or better, achieved at national, regional or local level hardly makes sense if the power to act belongs exclusively to the Union.

Nevertheless, the generality of Article 5(1) is compelling, and there is at least one indication elsewhere in the Treaty to suggest that subsidiarity will be a relevant consideration even where the Union has exclusive competence. Under Article 3(1)(b) TFEU, the Union has exclusive competence in 'the establishing of the competition rules necessary for the functioning of the internal market'. Under Article 106(2) TFEU (part of the Rules on Competition):

> Undertakings entrusted with the operation of services of general economic interest . . .shall be subject to the rules contained in the Treaties, in particular to the rules on competition, in so far as the application of such rules does not obstruct the performance, in law or in fact, of the particular tasks assigned to them.

Article 14 TFEU (formerly Article 16 EC) includes the provision of services of general economic interest within the 'shared values of the Union'. This is now given more precise content by Protocol No 26 on Services of General Interest, Article 1 of which provides that:

> The shared values of the Union include in particular:
>
> the essential and the wide discretion of national, regional and local authorities in providing, commissioning and organising services of general economic interest as closely as possible to the needs of the users;
>
> the diversity between various services of general economic interest and the differences in the needs and preferences of users that may result from different geographical, social or cultural situations;
>
> a high level of quality, safety and affordability, equal treatment and the promotion of universal access and of user rights.

[13] 'In exercising the powers conferred on it, each institution shall ensure that the principle of subsidiarity is complied with. It shall also ensure compliance with the principle of proportionality . . .'.

Here we find a direct echo of the words of the Preamble and Articles 2 and 3 TEU (quoted above) forming part of the context in which Article 5 TEU is to be read. It seems reasonable to regard Protocol No 26 as an indication of the intention of the Treaty-makers to reaffirm that the Treaty is ultimately about the welfare of the people of Europe in the very diverse geographical, social and cultural situations in which they find themselves.

It is both a common sense principle of good governance and a principle of public morality that rules and policies devised for a continent should take account of where the inhabitants of that continent live, how they live and how they would like to live. Surely subsidiarity in that broad sense should be treated, like proportionality, as a general principle of law permeating all aspects of the life of the Union.

8

The National Judge as EU Judge: Opinion 1/09

ALLAN ROSAS*

INTRODUCTION

IT HAS BECOME almost trite to observe that the courts and judges of the EU Member States play an important role not only at the purely national level but also as part of the Union judicial system.[1] The EU is a highly *decentralised* system, implying that EU legal norms are in most cases applied and implemented by the authorities, including the courts, of the Member States rather than by the Union institutions which have enacted those norms.[2] This basic tenet of the EU is, in the founding Treaties, reflected above all in Article 4(3) TEU, which, inter alia, instructs the Member States to take any appropriate measure 'to ensure fulfilment of the obligations arising out of the Treaties or resulting from the acts of the institutions of the Union', and Article 291(1) TFEU, according to which Member States shall adopt all measures of national law necessary to implement legally binding Union acts.

The obligation of the authorities of the Member States to apply and implement EU law has found ample reflection in the case law of the ECJ. The Court has affirmed that the obligation to ensure observance of the rules of Union law applies not only to national courts but to 'all organs of the administration' of a Member State[3] and thus includes political and administrative authorities. In this context, it should also be recalled that the ECJ has confirmed that fundamental rights, constituting general principles of Union law, must be respected not only by the Union

* Judge of the Court of Justice of the European Union.

[1] See, eg M Claes, *The National Court's Mandate in the European Constitution* (Oxford, Hart Publishing, 2006).

[2] See, eg A Rosas and L Armati, *EU Constitutional Law: An Introduction* (Oxford, Hart Publishing, 2010) 91–96, 231–39.

[3] Case 103/88 *Fratelli Costanzo* [1989] ECR 1839, para 31. See also Case C-453/00 *Kühne & Heitz* [2004] ECR I-837, para 20. See further M Verhoeven, *The Costanzo Obligation: The Obligations of National Administrative Authorities in the Case of Incompatibility between National Law and European Law* (Antwerp, Intersentia, 2011).

institutions but also by the Member States when they act in the scope of Union law.[4]

With regard to the role of *national courts* in particular, the ECJ in *Simmenthal*, after having referred to the direct applicability of rules of Community law in the Member States and to the fact that these rules 'are therefore a direct source of rights and duties for all those affected thereby', observed that '[t]his consequence also concerns any national court whose task it is as an organ of a Member State to protect . . . the rights conferred upon individuals by Community law'.[5] It follows that every national court 'must . . . apply Community law in its entirety and protect rights which the latter confers on individuals' and must also 'set aside any provision of national law which may conflict with it, whether prior or subsequent to the Community rule'.[6] In other cases, the ECJ has added that the national court, in collaboration with the ECJ, 'fulfils a duty entrusted to them both of ensuring that in the interpretation and application of the Treaties the law is observed'.[7]

The preliminary ruling mechanism laid down in Article 234 of the Treaty establishing the European Community (TEC) and before that Article 177 of the Treaty establishing the European Economic Community (EEC Treaty) has constituted the foremost institutional expression of the role of the national courts in the EU legal order and their collaboration with the ECJ. If the application of EU law by national courts has raised problems of interpretation or validity, the right, and as the case may be, obligation[8] of national courts to request a binding preliminary ruling from the ECJ has functioned as a guarantee for the uniform application of EU law in the whole Union area.

With the entry into force of the Treaty of Lisbon on 1 December 2009, the Treaty provision corresponding to Article 234 TEC is Article 267 TFEU. The latter provision repeats the text of Article 234 TEC and adds an obligation of the ECJ to act 'with the minimum of delay' if the case pending before the national court concerns a person in custody.[9] According to the ECJ, Article 234/267 confers upon

[4] It is not possible here to analyse the precise contours of the condition that the Member States act 'in the scope of' Union law or the interpretation of Art 51(1) of the Charter of Fundamental Rights of the European Union, [2010] OJ C83/389, which provides that the provisions of the Charter are addressed to the Member States 'only when they are implementing Union law'. See, eg the Explanations relating to Art 51 of the Charter, [2007] OJ C303/17. See also Rosas and Armati, n 2 above at 148–51; A Rosas and H Kaila, 'L'application de la Charte des droits fondamentaux de l'Union européenne par la Cour de justice: Un premier bilan' (2011) 16 *Il Diritto dell'Unione Europea* 1, 19.

[5] Case 106/77 *Simmenthal* [1978] ECR 628, paras 15, 16.

[6] ibid, para 21. See also, eg *Constanzo*, n 3 above, para 33; Case C-207/05 *ITC* [2007] ECR I-181, paras 68–69; Case C-429/09 *Fuss*, judgment of 25 November 2010 nyr, para 40.

[7] Case 244/80 *Foglia* [1981] ECR 3045, para 16; Joined Cases C-442/93 to C-424/93 *Zabala Erasun and ors* [1995] ECR I-1567, para 15.

[8] Courts of last instance are, in principle, under an obligation to request a preliminary ruling on problems of interpretation, while all courts are obliged to refer a question of validity to the ECJ if they consider that an EU legal act is invalid (and probably also if they have serious doubts about the validity of the act), see, eg Rosas and Armati, n 2 above, 233–34.

[9] This obligation of the ECJ is further underlined by the possibility, introduced in 2008, of resorting to an urgent procedure in all matters relating to the area of freedom, security and justice. See, eg A Rosas, 'Justice in Haste, Justice Denied? The European Court of Justice and the Area of Freedom, Security and Justice' (2008–2009) 11 *Cambridge Yearbook of European Legal Studies* 1.

each national court an 'autonomous jurisdiction' to make a reference to the ECJ, which remains seized of a reference so long as it has not been revoked or amended by the referring national court.[10] National rules whereby courts against whose decisions there is a judicial remedy are bound on points of law by the rulings of a superior court cannot deprive the lower national court of the right provided for in Article 267 TFEU to refer questions to the ECJ.[11]

The main Treaty provision defining the role of the ECJ and the other Union Courts in Luxembourg is what is now Article 19(1) TEU (ex Article 220 TEC, ex Article 164 of the EEC Treaty). According to this provision, the Court of Justice of the European Union – an expression which refers to the institution as a whole, today encompassing the ECJ, the General Court and the Civil Service Tribunal as a specialised tribunal – shall ensure that in the interpretation and application of the Treaties[12] the law is observed. This and the other provisions of the Treaties relating to the Union Courts as well as the mechanism of preliminary rulings are supplemented by what is now Article 344 TFEU (ex Article 292 TEC, ex Article 219 of the EEC Treaty). According to this provision, Member States 'undertake not to submit a dispute concerning the interpretation or application of the Treaties[13] to any method of settlement other than those provided for therein'.

The Treaty of Lisbon not only reaffirms the preliminary ruling mechanism as well as the role of the Union Courts in general but also introduces a reference to national judicial remedies in the above-mentioned provision of the TEU relating to the EU judicial system in general. Article 19 TEU, as amended by the Treaty of Lisbon, thus lays down not only the basic rules concerning the Union judicial institution, the Court of Justice of the European Union and its three above-mentioned subcomponents, but also a provision obliging Member States to 'provide remedies sufficient to ensure effective legal protection in the fields covered by Union law'. In the same vein, Article 47 of the Charter of Fundamental Rights of the European Union,[14] which is also applicable at the national level in a situation falling under Union law,[15] provides for the right to an effective remedy and to a fair trial.

[10] Case C-210/06 *Cartesio* [2008] ECR I-9641, paras 88–98. See also *Foglia*, n 7 above, para 16, where the ECJ stressed that the relations which the national courts maintain with the ECJ in the context of the then Art 177 of the EEC Treaty (now Art 267 TFEU) 'are governed exclusively by the provisions of Community law'.

[11] Joined Cases C-188/10 and C-189/10 *Aziz Melki* (C-188/10) and *Sélim Abdeli* (C-189/10), judgment of 22 June 2010 nyr, paras 42, 45. See also Case 166/73 *Rheinmühlen-Düsseldorf* [1974] ECR 33, paras 4, 5; Case C-210/10 *Cartesio*, n 10 above, para 94; Case C-378/08 *ERG and ors*, judgment of 9 March 2010 nyr, para 32.

[12] Art 164 of the EEC Treaty and Art 220 TEC referred to 'this Treaty' in the singular. The broader formula of Art 19(1) TEU is explained by the extension, by the Treaty of Lisbon, of the jurisdiction of the Court to cover, in principle, not only the TFEU (ex TEC) but also the TEU.

[13] Art 219 of the EEC Treaty and Art 292 TEC referred to 'this Treaty' (*cf* n 12 above). On the interpretation of this provision in the context of an international agreement concluded by both the Community and its Member States (mixed agreement) see Case C-459/03 *Commission v Ireland* [2006] ECR I-4635.

[14] See n 4 above.

[15] ibid.

These provisions draw upon the case law of the ECJ relating to the principle of effective judicial protection.[16] The Court has, in this context, based itself on a holistic view of the EU judicial system, holding that it is a 'complete system' which, in case there is no direct access to the Union Courts in Luxembourg, may require the existence of national judicial remedies.[17]

So far so good. The developments outlined above are by now fairly uncontroversial and have, in any case, been largely confirmed by the developments in Union primary law, including in particular the modifications brought about by the Treaty of Lisbon. But what are the implications of these developments for the *institutional* structure of the EU judicial system, in particular for the organisation of the national judicial systems?

Union law is not silent on the functioning of the national judicial system. First of all, primary law, as explained above, contains some basic provisions, notably Article 19 TEU, Article 267 TFEU and Article 47 of the Charter of Fundamental Rights. Secondly, Union secondary law may, exceptionally, require that Member States designate one or more national courts to function, in a given context, as Union courts.[18] Thirdly, Union secondary law increasingly contains instructions on minimum requirements concerning national legal remedies and judicial procedures in areas such as asylum and refugees, public procurement, environmental protection, intellectual property rights and competition.[19]

That said, the institutional and procedural aspects of the organisation of the national judicial system are still largely left to the discretion of Member States.[20] The national systems may vary considerably, notably with regard to public law litigation, the question of general versus specialised courts and the number of judicial instances.[21] But what are the limits, if any, which EU constitutional law imposes on the organisation of national judicial systems in areas where there are no specific Union rules of direct relevance for this question, apart from the very general provisions of primary law mentioned above?

[16] Case 33/76 *Rewe-Zentralfinanz* [1976] ECR 1989; Case 222/84 *Johnston* [1986] ECR 1651, para 18; Case C-432/05 *Unibet* [2007] ECR I-2271, para 37; Case C-279/09 *DEB*, judgment of 22 December 2010 nyr, para 29. See also, eg Claes, n 1 above at 135–41; Rosas and Armati, n 2 above at 231. It is not possible here to analyse the relationship, as far as the Court's case law is concerned, between the principle of effective judicial protection and what has been termed the 'procedural autonomy' of Member States. On this question see, eg Rosas and Armati, n 2 above, 231–32; S Prechal and R Widdershoven, 'Effectiveness or Effective Judicial Protection: A Poorly Articulated Relationship' in T Baumé et al (eds), *Today's Multi-layered Legal Order: Current Issues and Perspectives. Liber Amicorum in Honour of Arjen WH Meij* (Zutphen, Paris Legal Publishers, 2011) 283.

[17] See notably Case 294/83 *Les Verts v Parliament* [1986] 1339, para 23; Case C-50/00 *Unión de Pequeños Agricultores v Council* [2002] ECR I-6677, para 40; Case C-131/03 P *Reynolds Tobacco v Commission* [2006] ECR I-7795, para 80.

[18] See, eg A Rosas, 'The European Union as a Federative Association', *European Law Lecture 2003* (Durham European Law Institute, University of Durham, 2004) 8–9.

[19] Rosas and Armati, n 2 above at 231–32.

[20] This is often characterised as the 'procedural autonomy' of Member States, see n 16 above.

[21] For an overview of the national judicial systems see, *Les juridictions des États membres de l'Union européenne: Structure et organisation* (Luxembourg, Cour de justice des Communautés européennes, 2008).

One aspect of this question has recently been the subject of an important opinion of the ECJ, given on the basis of Article 218(11) TFEU (opinions on international agreements envisaged). In Opinion 1/09,[22] the Court had to rule on a plan to establish, through an international agreement to be concluded between the EU Member States, the Union itself and third countries, an international court structure with jurisdiction to hear actions related to so-called European as well as Union patents. As the judicial system envisaged was of an international character, involving also non-EU States (third countries), and would, on certain matters, have taken the place of the national courts of the EU Member States, the question arose as to its compatibility with the Union legal order. Could the EU and its Member States in this way 'delegate' or 'outsource' judicial functions to an international organisation which otherwise would have been dealt with by the courts of the Member States, or possibly by a new Union court set up under the provisions of the Treaties?

This question raises fundamental issues relating to the EU constitutional order and its judicial system in particular. The importance the ECJ attached to the Council's request for an opinion is underlined by the decision of the Court to refer the case to the full Court rather than to its Grand Chamber. This is only the second time, since the EU enlargement of 2004, that the Court has used the full Court rather than the Grand Chamber in a case where, according to primary law, such referral would not have been obligatory.[23]

OPINION 1/09: BACKGROUND AND SUMMARY

According to Article 218(11), a Member State, the European Parliament, the Council or the Commission may obtain the opinion of the Court of Justice 'as to whether an agreement envisaged is compatible with the Treaties'.[24] Article 107(2) of the Rules of Procedure of the Court of Justice[25] adds that an opinion may deal not only with the question whether the envisaged agreement is compatible with the provisions of the Treaties but also with the question whether the Union has

[22] Opinion 1/09 of 8 March 2011 (The Draft Agreement on the European and Community Patents Court) nyr.

[23] According to Art 16(4) of the Statute of the Court of Justice of the European Union, the full Court is obligatory when cases are brought pursuant to Art 228(2), Art 245(2), Art 247 or Art 286(6) TFEU. The right of Member States and some Union institutions to request opinions concerning international agreements envisaged is not governed by any of these provisions but by Art 218(11) TFEU. In such a situation, the Court, according to Art 16(5) of the Statute, 'may', after having heard the Advocate General, decide to refer a case to the full Court if it is of 'exceptional importance'. Apart from Opinion 1/09, the only cases referred to the full Court after 2004 were Opinion 1/03 (Lugano Convention on Jurisdiction and the Recognition of Judgments in Civil and Commercial Matters) [2006] ECR I-1145 and Case C-432/04 *Commission v Cresson* [2006] ECR I-6387. The referral of the latter case to the full Court was obligatory under the then Art 213 TEC (now Art 245 TFEU).

[24] On the mechanism of opinions see, in particular, S Adams, *La procédure d'avis devant la Cour de justice de l'Union européenne* (Bruxelles, Éditions Bruylant, 2011).

[25] Rules of Procedure of the Court of Justice, [1991] OJ L176/7 and [1992] OJ L383/117 (corrigenda), with later amendments (most recent amendment [2011] OJ L162/17).

the power to enter into the agreement. The binding character of such opinions is reflected in the requirement, expressed in Article 281(11), that where the opinion of the Court is adverse, the agreement envisaged may not enter into force unless it is amended or the Treaties revised.

The idea of establishing a Union (or before the entry into force of the Treaty of Lisbon, Community) patent has been a subject of long and arduous discussions at the level of the political institutions.[26] Apart from disagreements on the language regime, a fundamental question has concerned the relationship between the Union patent system envisaged and the existing European Patent Convention system. This Convention, signed in 1973 and binding at the time of Opinion 1/09 on 38 States, including all the EU Member States, provides for a unitary procedure for granting so-called European patents by the European Patent Office in Munich. To cite Opinion 1/09, while the procedure for granting a European patent is unitary, this patent 'breaks down into a bundle of national patents, each governed by the domestic law of the States which the holder of the right has designated'.[27] By contrast, the Union patent envisaged, while also being granted by the European Patent Office pursuant to the European Patent Convention, would, again to cite Opinion 1/09, have a 'unitary and autonomous character, producing equal effect throughout the European Union, and could be granted, transferred, declared invalid or lapse only in respect of the whole of that territorial area'.[28]

The ECJ was not called upon to rule on the legality of this construction as such. The request of the Council was limited to the compatibility with the Treaties of the judicial system envisaged, as outlined in a draft agreement creating a unified patent litigation system.[29] This system would have been centred on a European and Community Patent Court (Patent Court) composed of a court of first instance, a court of appeal and a joint registry. For the purposes of this paper, it is important to note that the Court, when hearing a case under the agreement envisaged, would have been obliged to respect Union law and would, for a number of issues enumerated in the draft agreement, have had exclusive jurisdiction, thus replacing the jurisdiction of the national courts of EU Member States as well as that of national courts of other Contracting Parties. According to a draft provision mirroring Article 267 TFEU, the Patent Court would have had, in the case of the court of first instance, a right, and in the case of the court of appeal, a duty to seek preliminary rulings from the ECJ on questions of interpretation of the EU Treaties or the validity and interpretation of acts of the Union institutions.

[26] The historical background is summarised in the Explanatory Memorandum to the Commission Proposal for a Regulation of the European Parliament and of the Council implementing enhanced cooperation in the area of the creation of unitary patent protection, COM(2011) 215 final of 13 April 2011, 1–2.

[27] Opinion 1/09, n 22 above, para 3.

[28] ibid, para 6.

[29] Draft Agreement on the European and Community Patents Court and Draft Statute – Revised Presidency text, Working Document from the General Secretariat of the Council of 23 March 2009, Council doc 7928/09.

As the draft agreement was to be concluded not only by the EU and its Member States but also by third countries such as Balkan countries, Norway, Switzerland and Turkey (and thus including States not parties to the European Economic Area), there was no doubt that the judicial system, in line with the existing Munich regime concerning European patents, would have been of an international character and that the Patent Court would not have constituted a Union court or a national court of one or several Member States. Moreover, the court of first instance would have included regional and local divisions, the latter to be set up in a Contracting State upon its request and the former to be set up for two or more Contracting States upon their request. The judges would have to be nationals of one of the Contracting States; it was not excluded that the majority on a given panel deciding a case would have been nationals of third countries.[30]

As the texts submitted by the Council to the ECJ, notably the draft agreement with a draft statute of the Patent Court and a draft proposal for a Council regulation on the Community patent, did not provide a complete or definitive regulation of the envisaged patent system as a whole (including on the interaction between the European patents regime and the Union patent envisaged), the question arose as to the admissibility of the request. Invoking its earlier case law in this regard, which does not require that the agreement envisaged be definitive in all respects, the Court found the request admissible.[31]

On substance, the Court concluded that the envisaged agreement creating a unified patent litigation system was *not* compatible with the provisions of the TEU and the TFEU. A summary of the principal reasoning is to be found in the last operative paragraph of the Opinion:[32]

> Consequently, the envisaged agreement, by conferring on an international court which is outside the institutional and judicial framework of the European Union an exclusive jurisdiction to hear a significant number of actions brought by individuals in the field of the Community patent and to interpret and apply European Union law in that field, would deprive courts of Member States of their powers in relation to the interpretation and application of European Union law and the Court of its powers to reply, by preliminary ruling, to questions referred by those courts and, consequently, would alter the essential character of the powers which the Treaties confer on the institutions of the European Union and on the Member States and which are indispensable to the preservation of the very nature of European Union law.

Shortly after this negative Opinion, the Commission proposed two regulations, one on the creation of unitary patent protection[33] and the other on the translation

[30] If a local division had been set up in a non-EU State, or a regional division in a group of non-EU States, Art 6 of the draft agreement even required that two out of three judges of a panel of the court of first instance were nationals of the Contracting State(s) concerned.

[31] Opinion 1/09, n 22 above, paras 46–57.

[32] ibid, para 89.

[33] Commission Proposal, n 26 above.

modalities.[34] The proposals build on the existing European patent system (which, as was noted above, provides for a bundle of national patents) but it is added that such a patent could be registered also as a European patent 'with unitary effect', in which case the patent should provide uniform protection and should have equal effect in all participating Member States. Two Member States (Italy and Spain) are opposed to these proposals, as they are based on so-called enhanced cooperation between the participating 25 Member States.[35] At the time of writing, it is not known what solution will be proposed for the judicial system, given that the ECJ ruled out the possibility of outsourcing the judicial functions to an international organisation.

PREVIOUS CASE LAW

The main legal question arising in the context of Opinion 1/09, in other words the outsourcing of the jurisdiction of national courts to apply Union law to an international judicial regime, had not previously been answered by the Court. This also explains why the Court referred the request for an opinion to the full Court. That said, some earlier case law, including two opinions delivered by the Court in the 1990s, are not devoid of relevance for an understanding of the line of reasoning adopted in Opinion 1/09.

Probably the most relevant contribution in this regard is Opinion 1/91 concerning the compatibility with the Treaties of the judicial regime established by the then Draft Agreement relating to the Creation of the European Economic Area (EEA).[36] According to the draft submitted to the Court, the EEA Agreement would have set up an EEA Court and an EEA Court of First Instance, both consisting of judges from the ECJ (for the EEA Court of First Instance, judges of the Court of First Instance of the European Communities) and judges nominated by the EFTA States, that is, the EEA States which were not EU Member States. The EEA Court would have had jurisdiction with respect to the settlement of disputes between the Contracting Parties, actions concerning the surveillance procedure regarding the EFTA States and, in the field of competition, appeals concerning decisions taken by the EFTA Surveillance Authority. In addition, the EFTA States would have been authorised to allow their courts or tribunals to ask the ECJ to give an opinion on the interpretation of the EEA Agreement.

[34] Commission Proposal for a Council Regulation on the implementation of enhanced cooperation in the area of the creation of unitary patent protection with regard to the applicable translation arrangements, COM(2011) 216 final of 13 April 2011.

[35] See Council Decision 2011/167/EU of 10 March 2011 authorising enhanced cooperation in the area of the creation of unitary patent protection, [2011] OJ L76/53. On the notion of enhanced cooperation see, eg Rosas and Armati, n 2 above, 108–10.

[36] Opinion 1/91, Draft agreement between the Community, on the one hand, and the countries of the European Free Trade Association, on the other, relating to the creation of the European Economic Area [1991] ECR I-6079.

The ECJ held that the judicial system envisaged was, on several accounts, incompatible with the EEC Treaty, notably as it undermined the autonomy of the Community legal order. There is no need here to analyse in detail the reasoning in its entirety. For a comparison with the situation with which the Court was confronted in Opinion 1/09, it seems particularly relevant to note the following two elements of the Court's negative findings in Opinion 1/91: the envisaged mechanism for the settlement of disputes between the Contracting Parties and the possibility for EFTA States to allow their national courts to request opinions on the interpretation of the EEA Agreement.

As far as the dispute settlement mechanism was concerned, the Court underlined that the EEA Court would have had to decide whether, in a given context, the expression 'Contracting Party' referred to the Community, the Community and the Member States, or simply the Member States (given that the EEA Agreement was to be concluded as a so-called mixed agreement[37]), in other words on the allocation of competences between the Community and the Member States.[38] While one wonders whether that aspect alone should have led the Court to declare the jurisdiction of the EEA Court incompatible with Community law,[39] the Court in any case went on to analyse the foreseeable effects of the future case law of the EEA Court on the interpretation of Community law.

In this regard, the Court held that, as a matter of principle, the Community *could* submit itself to dispute settlement mechanisms established under international agreements concluded by the Community. Such a power was a necessary consequence of the competence of the Community in the field of international relations and its capacity to conclude international agreements.[40] The problem with the EEA regime, however, was that the EEA Agreement took over 'an essential part' of the rules – including the rules of secondary legislation – which governed economic and trading relations within the Community and which constituted, for the most part, 'fundamental provisions of the Community legal order'.[41] Taking also into account the objective of ensuring homogeneity of the law throughout the EEA, the regime would affect the interpretation not only of the EEA Agreement but also of the corresponding rules of Community law and would thus come into conflict with the then Article 164 of the EEC Treaty (now Article 19(1) TEU), which, as noted above, provides that it is up to the Court of

[37] On mixed agreements see, eg J Heliskoski, *Mixed Agreements as a Technique for Organizing the International Relations of the European Community and its Member States* (The Hague, Kluwer Law International, 2001); C Hillion and P Koutrakos (eds), *Mixed Agreements Revisited: The EU and its Member States in the World* (Oxford, Hart Publishing, 2010).

[38] Opinion 1/91, n 36 above, paras 32–36.

[39] In fact, that conclusion could cast doubts on the legality of dispute settlement mechanisms that the EU has accepted under existing mixed agreements such as the World Trade Organization Agreements and the Energy Charter Treaty; see, on such mechanisms, A Rosas, 'International Dispute Settlement: EU Practices and Procedures' (2003) 46 *German Yearbook of International Law* 284.

[40] Opinion 1/91, n 36 above, paras 39–40.

[41] ibid, para 41.

Justice of the European Union to ensure that in the interpretation and application of Union law, the law is observed.[42]

As to the possibility foreseen in the draft Agreement of authorising EFTA States to allow their national courts to request opinions from the ECJ (rather than the EEA Court), the Court stressed that the regime envisaged did not guarantee that the answers given by the ECJ would be binding on the courts making the reference. Such a system would change the nature of the functions of the ECJ, 'namely that of a court whose judgments are binding',[43] and could also have negative spill-over effects for the national courts in the Community, not only giving rise to uncertainty about the legal value of the advisory opinions for these courts but also entailing the risk of misunderstandings about the legal effects of preliminary rulings under the then Article 177 of the EEC Treaty (now Article 267 TFEU).[44]

These findings, of course, underscore the autonomous and unique character of the Union legal order and the exclusive nature of its judicial system. On the other hand, the Opinion does not exclude the acceptance of any international dispute settlement mechanism set up under international agreements concluded by the Union or the possibility of authorising national courts of third States to request preliminary rulings from the ECJ. After the idea of a mixed EEA Court had been abandoned and the EEA judicial system and dispute settlement mechanisms also modified in other respects, the ECJ rendered a new Opinion (1/92)[45] now holding that the Agreement, including the possibility it provided for EFTA national courts to request a 'ruling'[46] from the ECJ, was compatible with Community law.

The latter possibility was highlighted in Opinion 1/00 concerning a draft multilateral agreement to be concluded between the Community and a group of non-Member States on the establishment of a European Common Aviation Area.[47] In terms of objectives, the draft agreement was comparable to the EEA Agreement in that it, although being limited to the aviation sector, aimed to extend the *acquis communautaire* to new States. Institutionally, the agreement differed from the 'twin pillar' system of the EEA (Community/EFTA) in that it, instead of providing for distinct European Common Aviation Area institutions, would have in many ways extended the powers of the Community institutions to cover the Area as well. In line with what the ECJ had held in Opinion 1/92 on the revised EEA Agreement, the Court found that the common aviation regime envisaged did not

[42] ibid, paras 42–46. The Court added that the mixed composition of the EEA Court, including the EEA Court of First Instance, which also involved judges from the ECJ and the Court of First Instance, would not mitigate but rather accentuate the general problems arising from the EEA court system, ibid, paras 47–53.

[43] ibid, para 61.

[44] ibid, paras 54–65.

[45] Opinion 1/92, Revised draft Agreement on the European Economic Area [1992] ECR I-2821. See also Rosas, n 39 above, 290–91.

[46] The Court stated that the interpretation to be given would be binding on the national court of the EFTA State, ibid, para 34.

[47] Opinion 1/00, Proposed agreement between the European Community and non-Member States on the establishment of a European Common Aviation Area [2002] ECR I-3493. Most of the then non-Member States have subsequently become EU Member States.

adversely affect the autonomy of the Community legal order, notably the essential character of the powers of the Community and its institutions, and that the draft agreement was consequently compatible with the Treaty.

Concerning the role of the Union Courts, in particular, the ECJ observed that the draft agreement did not call into question the Court's exclusive task of reviewing the legality of acts of the Community institutions and that the mechanisms for ensuring uniform interpretation of the rules of the agreement and for resolving disputes would not have the effect of binding the Community, in the exercise of its internal powers, to a particular interpretation of the rules of Community law incorporated in the agreement.[48] As to the possibility foreseen in the draft agreement for the non-Community States to authorise their national courts to request preliminary rulings from the ECJ, the Court, referring to its Opinions on the EEA Agreement, observed that such a system is, in principle, allowed, provided that the answers to be given were binding on the referring court. As this was the case with respect to the draft agreement, the system of preliminary rulings was also compatible with Community law.[49]

With regard to the EU judicial system, two basic conclusions can be drawn from Opinions 1/91, 1/92 and 1/00: 1) an international agreement cannot, in view of Article 19(1) TEU and Article 344 TFEU, call into question the exclusive powers of the Union Courts to review the legality of acts of the Union institutions nor have the effect of binding the Union institutions to a certain interpretation of internal Union law; 2) an international agreement concluded with third countries may *extend* the powers of the Union Courts to settle disputes arising under the agreement or to give binding preliminary rulings on the interpretation and validity of the agreement and the rules established pursuant to it on questions submitted by courts of the third countries concerned.

In this context, a brief reference can also be made to Opinion 2/94 on the competence of the Community to accede to the European Convention on Human Rights.[50] In this case, too, the ECJ was faced with an international agreement which provides for a compulsory dispute settlement mechanism, that is, the European Court of Human Rights (ECtHR). The request for an Opinion focused on the competence of the Community to conclude the agreement. As, according to the Court, there were no Treaty provisions specifically conferring on the Community institutions any general power to enact rules on human rights or to conclude international conventions in this field, the Court turned to the then Article 234 TEC (now Article 352 TFEU), which 'is designed to fill the gap where no specific provisions of the Treaty confer on the Community institutions express or implied powers to act', if such powers are necessary to enable the Union to

[48] ibid, paras 34–45.

[49] ibid, paras 30–33.

[50] Opinion 2/94, Accession of the Community to the Convention for the Protection of Human Rights and Fundamental Freedoms ECR I-1759. See also B Brandtner and A Rosas, 'Human Rights and the External Relations of the European Community: An Analysis of Doctrine and Practice' (1998) 9 *European Journal of International Law* 468 at 471–72.

carry out its functions.[51] The Court concluded that accession to the ECHR would go beyond the scope of Article 235 TEC and could be brought about only by way of Treaty amendment. As Community law stood in the mid-1990s, the Community accordingly had no competence to accede to the Convention.

For the purposes of this paper, it should be noted that the ECJ, while acknowledging that respect for human rights is a condition of the lawfulness of Community acts, held that accession to the ECHR would necessitate a 'substantial change' in the Community system for the protection of human rights in that it would entail 'the entry of the Community into a distinct international institutional system' as well as integration of all the provisions of the Convention into Community law.[52] The 'distinct international institutional system', arguably, refers above all to the ECtHR and its compulsory jurisdiction provided under the Convention. The ECJ does not explain why this mechanism implied a more serious intrusion into the Community legal order than other international dispute settlement mechanisms that the Court had accepted or the EU adhered to in practice (such as the EEA mechanisms – if account is not taken of the planned EEA Court, to which the ECJ said no – or the World Trade Organization system[53]). It can be surmised that the Court was thinking of such elements of the Strasbourg system as the compulsory jurisdiction of the ECtHR and the binding nature of its decisions, right of individual complaint, the likely direct effect of many provisions of the Convention, in combination with the lack of express or implied powers in the Treaties to enact rules on human rights or to conclude international conventions in this field.

The case law considered so far has been preoccupied mainly with the likely effects of international courts and other dispute settlement mechanisms on the Union legal order, in particular on the exclusive powers of the Union Courts to rule on the validity, and to provide the ultimate authoritative interpretation, of Union legal acts, as well as with the powers of the Union to extend Union law mechanisms such as the preliminary ruling procedure to non-EU States.

In addition, it will be recalled that with respect to the role of the *national* Courts of the EU Member States, the ECJ has ruled that every national court must apply Community law in its entirety and protect rights which the latter confers on individuals and that it, in collaboration with the Court of Justice, fulfils a duty entrusted to them both of ensuring that in the interpretation and application of the Treaties, the law is observed.[54] The Court has also held that Article 267 TFEU confers upon each national court an autonomous jurisdiction to make a reference to the ECJ, which remains seized of a reference so long as it has not been revoked or amended by the referring national court.[55]

[51] Opinion 2/94, n 50 above, para 29.

[52] ibid, para 34.

[53] See n 39 above. On the World Trade Organization system and the role of the EU in this regard see also A Rosas, 'Implementation and Enforcement of WTO Dispute Settlement Findings: An EU Perspective' (2001) 4 *Journal of International Economic Law* 129.

[54] See at nn 5–7 above.

[55] See at nn 10–11 above.

While Union law determines which national bodies qualify as courts or tribunals entitled to request preliminary rulings,[56] the institutional structure of the national court system is, in principle, left to be regulated by national law. The ECJ has had the opportunity to specify that a court able to submit questions to the ECJ may be a court common to a number of Member States.[57]

The question arose in the context of a request for a preliminary ruling from a Dutch court of last instance, which asked, inter alia, whether the obligation to refer a case to the ECJ applies to it or to the Benelux Court of Justice, given that the latter has the task of ruling, in a 'Benelux' preliminary ruling procedure, on the interpretation of the Uniform Benelux Law on Trade Marks. As a preliminary question, the ECJ considered whether a court like the Benelux Court may refer questions to the ECJ for a preliminary ruling and, if so, whether it may be obliged to do so. The ECJ motivated its affirmative answer to the first question by recalling that the Benelux Court has the task of ensuring the uniform application of Benelux law and that the procedure before it is a step in the proceedings before the national courts leading to definitive interpretations of common Benelux rules. Moreover, allowing a court such as the Benelux Court to request preliminary rulings from the ECJ would serve the purpose of Article 267 TFEU, which is to ensure the uniform interpretation of Union law.[58] As to an obligation to refer, the ECJ held that both the Dutch national court and the Benelux Court may be obliged to do so, but that if either of them has already received an answer from the ECJ, the authority of the interpretation given by the ECJ may remove from the other court its obligation to submit substantially the same question to the ECJ.

In a recent case, decided after Opinion 1/09, at issue was whether the Complaints Board established under the 1994 Convention defining the Statute of the European Schools is a court or tribunal entitled to request preliminary rulings from the ECJ.[59] While the Court accepted that the Complaints Board is a court or tribunal, the real question was, is it a court or tribunal 'of a Member State', pursuant to Article 267 TFEU. The ECJ's answer was in the negative. The Court observed that the Complaints Board, while required to apply the general principles of EU law, is not a court common to a number of Member States, comparable to the Benelux Court of Justice. This is because it has no direct organic links with the judicial systems of the Member States and, although created by all the Member States and by the Union, 'is a body of an international organisation which, despite the functional links which it has with the Union, remains formally distinct from it and from those Member States'.[60]

[56] See, eg C Naomé, *Le renvoi préjudiciel en droit européen: Guide pratique*, 2nd edn (Bruxelles, Éditions Larcier, 2010) 94–106. For a recent judgment see Case C-196/09 *Miles*, judgment of 14 June 2011 nyr.

[57] Case C-337/95 *Parfums Christian Dior* [1997] ECR I-6013, paras 15–31.

[58] While *Parfums Christian Dior*, n 57 above, came before the ECJ as a request from a Dutch national court, the first request for a preliminary ruling submitted by the Benelux Court itself was Case C-265/00 *Campina Melkunie* [2004] ECR I-1699. See also Naomé, n 56 above, 106.

[59] Case C-196/09 *Miles*, n 56 above.

[60] ibid, paras 41–42.

THE ROLE OF NATIONAL COURTS: CONCLUSION

As noted above, the envisaged agreement creating a unified patent litigation system differed from the institutional solutions considered in previous case law in that it provided for a Patent Court (consisting of a court of first instance and a court of appeal), established by an international agreement concluded between the European Community, the EU Member States and a certain number of third States, which, on certain enumerated matters, would have *replaced* the national courts of the Contracting States, including the national courts of the EU Member States. It will be recalled that in the context of the EEA Agreement and the draft agreement on a Common Aviation Area, the right of the national courts of third States to refer cases to the ECJ would have been an *extension* of the preliminary ruling procedure to third States, without depriving the national courts of the EU Member States to do the same.

In Opinion 1/09, the ECJ first rejected the arguments put forward by some Member States that the unified patent litigation system would be contrary to Articles 262 and 344 TFEU. The Court observed that Article 262 enabled, but did not require, that some of the powers envisaged for the Patent Court (patent litigation between individuals) be entrusted to the Court of Justice of the European Union. As to Article 344, the prohibition for Member States to submit disputes concerning Union law to mechanisms other than those provided for in the Treaties, did not apply to disputes between individuals.[61]

The Court then recalled the fundamental elements of the Union legal order and judicial system. Recalling traditional and well-established case law,[62] the Court observed that the founding Treaties established a new legal order, possessing its own institutions, for the benefit of which the States have limited their sovereign rights, in ever wider fields, and the subjects of which comprise not only Member States but also their nationals. The essential characteristics of this legal order are in particular its primacy over the laws of the Member States and the direct effect of a whole series of provisions.[63]

The Court went on to say that, as Article 19(1) TEU makes clear, the guardians of that legal order and its judicial system 'are the Court of Justice and the courts and tribunals of the Member States'.[64] While it is for the Court of Justice to ensure respect for the autonomy of the legal order, it is up to the Member States, including their national courts and tribunals, to ensure the application of Union law in the Member States and to ensure judicial protection of an individual's rights under that law. Both the Court of Justice *and* the national courts fulfil a duty entrusted to them both of ensuring that in the interpretation and application of

[61] Opinion 1/09, n 22 above, paras 60–63.
[62] Some of this case law is cited at nn 5–7 above.
[63] Opinion 1/09, n 22 above, para 65.
[64] ibid, para 66.

the Treaties, the law is observed. The EU judicial system is a complete system of legal remedies and procedures.[65]

After having summarised the main characteristics of the planned Patent Court, the ECJ recalled that Union law enables the setting up, by international agreement, of international courts called upon to interpret and apply the agreement in question and that the agreement may also confer new judicial powers on the ECJ provided that the essential character of the function of the Court is preserved and that there is no adverse effect on the autonomy of the EU legal order.[66]

The patent litigation system envisaged differed from the regimes considered in earlier case law in two main respects: 1) the Patent Court had the task of interpreting and applying not only the provisions of the agreement setting up the new system but also the future regulation on the Community patent and other instruments of EU law and could be called upon to determine a dispute in the light of the fundamental rights and general principles of Union law, or even to examine the validity of a Union act; 2) the Patent Court, which was outside the institutional and judicial framework of the EU, took the place of national courts and tribunals in the field of its exclusive jurisdiction and thus deprived the national courts of their corresponding powers.[67] The following paragraph deserves to be quoted *in extenso*:

> 80. While it is true that the Court [of Justice] has no jurisdiction to rule on direct actions between individuals in the field of patents, since that jurisdiction is held by the courts of the Member States, nonetheless the Member States cannot confer the jurisdiction to resolve such disputes on a court created by an international agreement which would deprive those courts of their task, as ordinary courts within the European Union legal order, to implement European Union law and, thereby, of the power provided for in Article 267 TFEU or, as the case may be, the obligation, to refer questions for a preliminary ruling in the field concerned.

The patent litigation system differed from the Benelux Court considered in the Dior case, as the latter is a court 'common to a number of Member States and situated, consequently, within the judicial system of the European Union'.[68] As was noted above, in a judgment rendered after Opinion 1/09, the ECJ also held that a body created by the Member States and by the Union (but not by third States), that is, the Complaints Board of the European Schools, could be disqualified as a judicial body of the Member States if the link to their national judicial systems was tenuous.[69]

However, 'outsourcing' the functions of the national courts of the EU Member States to a court outside the institutional and judicial framework of the EU was a different matter. The Court observed that Article 267 TFEU requires 'direct cooperation' between it and national courts as part of which national courts are 'closely

[65] ibid, paras 68–69.
[66] ibid, paras 71–76.
[67] ibid, paras 77–79.
[68] ibid, para 82. See also *Parfums Christian Dior*, n 57 above.
[69] See, concerning *Miles*, n 56 above.

involved in the correct application and uniform interpretation of European Union law and also in the protection of individual rights conferred by that legal order'.[70] And so the tasks attributed to the national courts and to the ECJ respectively are 'indispensable to the preservation of the very nature of the law established by the Treaties'.[71]

To these general observations, building on its previous characterisation of the EU legal order, the Court added two more specific reasons for why one could not equate international mechanisms such as the planned Patent Court with the national courts of the Member States:[72]

1) The principle that Member States may become liable for breaches of Union law, based on the *Francovich* case law,[73] also applies, albeit under specific conditions, to their judicial bodies;[74]
2) If national courts infringed EU law, infringement actions pursuant to Articles 258–260 TFEU could be brought against the Member State concerned.

These possibilities did not exist with respect to the Patent Court.

It is interesting to note that the ECJ referred to the *tasks attributed to the national courts*[75] and to the *powers which the Treaties confer* on the EU institutions *and on the Member States.*[76] The limits of Union competences are, of course, governed by the principle of conferral, under which the Union shall act only within the limits of the competences conferred upon it by the Member States.[77] This, it would appear, does not prevent the Member States from attributing, in the context of the powers they confer upon the Union, tasks to their own organs and bodies such as courts and tribunals. There is, in fact, an increasing tendency in EU law to assign tasks to national political (national Parliaments), administrative and judicial bodies instead of leaving the organisation of the national application and implementation of EU law entirely to the discretion of the Member States.[78]

A commentator has observed that in Opinion 1/09, 'la tonalité de l'argumentaire de la Cour de justice prend des accents constitutionnels, voire fédéralistes, assez remarquables'.[79] It is, in fact, obvious that Opinion 1/09 constitutes one more contribution to the characterisation of the EU legal order as a *constitutional* one.[80] In this respect, it is submitted that the Opinion does not really break new ground, but is an important complement to a long string of case law, exemplified by judg-

[70] Opinion 1/09, n 22 above, para 84.

[71] ibid, para 85.

[72] ibid, paras 86–88.

[73] Joined Cases C-6/90 and C-9/90 *Francovich and ors* [1991] ECR I-5357.

[74] Case C-224/01 *Köbler* [2003] ECR I-10239, paras 31–36; Case C-154/08 *Commission v Spain* [2009] ECR I-187, para 125.

[75] Opinion 1/09, n 22 above, para 84.

[76] ibid, para 89.

[77] See Art 5(1) and (2) TEU.

[78] Rosas, n 18 above, 7–15; Rosas and Armati, n 2 above, 13, 91–96.

[79] D Simon, 'Avis négatif sur le projet de création d'une juridiction des brevets' (CJUE, ass plén, avis no 1/09, 8 mars 2011) *Europe* no 5, Mai 2011, étude 5, 5.

[80] See, eg C Timmermans, 'The Constitutionalization of the European Union' (2001–2002) 21 *Yearbook of European Law* 1; Rosas and Armati, n 2 above, 3.

ments such as *van Gend and Loos*,[81] *Costa v ENEL*,[82] *Stauder*,[83] *Simmenthal*,[84] *Les Verts*,[85] *Francovich*[86] and, last but not least, *Kadi*.[87]

The added value of Opinion 1/09 lies undoubtedly in its emphasis of the essential role played by national courts as integral parts of the Union judicial system. Just as the tasks of the Union Courts cannot be transferred to non-EU bodies, the national courts of the EU Member States have a constitutional mandate which cannot, in principle, be outsourced. Both Union Courts and national courts fulfil a 'duty entrusted to them both' of ensuring that in the interpretation and application of the Treaties the law is observed.[88] That this formulation stems from a judgment of 1981 attests to the fact that Opinion 1/09 is not creating something entirely new but is one of many contributions to a constitutional edifice which has been built up gradually, and in interaction with the evolution of primary law, including Article 19 TEU as modified by the Treaty of Lisbon.

The Opinion is arguably also relevant for an understanding of the EU constitutional order as one corresponding to the notion of 'cooperative federalism'.[89] With regard to the EU judicial system, one can say that the two main levels, the Union Courts in Luxembourg and the national courts, work together, being complementary parts in a shared legal sphere, instead of operating independently in separate spheres.[90] To cite Opinion 1/09 once more, the system set up by Article 267 TFEU establishes between the ECJ and the national courts 'direct cooperation' as part of which the latter are 'closely involved in the correct application and uniform interpretation of European Union law and also in the protection of individual rights conferred by that legal order'.[91] And so the tasks attributed not only to the ECJ but also to the national courts 'are indispensable to the preservation of the very nature of the law established by the Treaties'.[92]

[81] Case 26/62 *van Gend & Loos* [1963] ECR 1.
[82] Case 6/64 *Costa v ENEL* [1964] ECR 1141.
[83] Case 29/69 *Stauder* [1969] ECR 419.
[84] *Simmenthal*, n 5 above.
[85] *Les Verts v Parliament*, n 17 above.
[86] *Francovich and ors*, n 73 above.
[87] Joined Cases C-402/05 P and C-415/05 P *Kadi and Al Barakaat International Foundation v Council and Commission* [2008] ECR I-6351.
[88] *Foglia*, n 7 above, para 16; Opinion 1/09, n 22 above, para 69.
[89] For a discussion of this notion see, in particular, R Schütze, *From Dual to Cooperative Federalism: The Changing Structure of European Law* (Oxford, Oxford University Press, 2009).
[90] *cf* Schütze, n 89 above at 346, who observes that cooperative federalism stands for the idea that the federal government and the State government 'work together: they are complimentary parts in the same legal sphere'.
[91] Opinion 1/09, n 22 above, para 84.
[92] ibid, para 85.

9

Issues of EU Law Raised by National Courts of their Own Motion

AINDRIAS Ó CAOIMH*

INTRODUCTION

THE ROLE OF national courts and tribunals in enforcing European Union (EU) law is a pivotal one. However, the task is not always easy. The interplay between obligations at EU level and national procedural rules gives rise on occasions to difficulty at the national level. One of the more complex issues is the obligation or faculty of national courts to raise issues of EU law of their own motion in proceedings before them.

THE COURT'S INITIAL STEPS IN *VAN SCHIJNDEL* AND *PETERBROECK*

This issue was first raised in the context of two references for preliminary rulings coming before the Court of Justice in which it delivered its judgment on the same day. The proceedings in question were *Peterbroeck*[1] on a reference from the Court of Appeal in Brussels and *van Schijndel*[2] on a reference from the Supreme Court of the Netherlands. These cases illustrate that the treatment of this issue at national level differs considerably from one Member State to another.

In *Peterbroeck* what was at issue was a procedural time limit under the Belgian Income Tax Code which imposed a 60-day time limit on the raising of a new plea of law. In *van Schijndel*, the national court referred questions to the Court of Justice with regard to the power of a national court or tribunal to consider of its own motion the compatibility of a rule of domestic law with certain Treaty provisions. The proceedings before the referring court were proceedings in cassation. The national court indicated that the plaintiffs were relying on various circumstances which were not established by the national court at first instance or relied upon by them in support of their claims before the lower courts. The Supreme

* Judge of the Court of Justice of the European Union.

1 Case C-312/93 *Peterbroeck, van Campenhout & Cie v Belgian State* [1995] ECR I-4599.

2 Joined Cases C-430/93 and C-431/93 *van Schijndel and van Veen v SPF* [1995] ECR I-4705.

Court indicated that, in Dutch law, a plea in cassation by its nature excludes new arguments unless on pure points of law. While Dutch courts might raise points of law, if necessary, of their own motion, a principle of judicial passivity in cases involving civil rights and obligations freely entered into by the parties entails that additional pleas on points of law cannot require courts to go beyond the ambit of the dispute defined by the parties themselves or rely on facts or circumstances other than those on which a claim is based.

Advocate General Jacobs delivered Opinions in both of these cases. As appears from the Opinion in *van Schijndel*, the Court of Justice decided to re-open the oral procedure in that case and to conduct a joint hearing of the references from the two courts. In his earlier Opinion in *Peterbroeck*, which he re-affirmed in his Opinion in *van Schijndel*, Advocate General Jacobs took the view that EC law as it then stood did not require a national court to set aside a rule of national law which, in proceedings pending before it, requires the parties to raise claims based on EC law within a specified time, provided the rule applies to comparable claims based on national law and that it does not make excessively difficult the protection of rights based on EC law.

Advocate General Jacobs referred to the principle of national procedural autonomy under EC law as recognised by the Court of Justice to the effect that,

> in the absence of Community rules, it is for the domestic legal system of each Member State to determine the courts having jurisdiction and the procedural conditions governing actions intended to ensure the protection of directly effective Community rights, provided that those conditions fulfil two requirements: they are not less favourable than the conditions relating to similar actions of a domestic nature; and they do not render virtually impossible or excessively difficult the exercise of rights conferred by Community law.

It can be seen that the Advocate General had regard to both the principles of equivalence and effectiveness as enshrined in the Court's case law.

Advocate General Jacobs addressed certain exceptions, including the issue of *res judicata*, recognised by Belgian law in relation to the application of the time limit in question in light of the first of those requirements, namely the issue of equivalence. While indicating that the principle of equivalence must apply to any such exception, he did not consider on the facts before him that there was any breach of that principle. He then addressed the issue whether national courts can be precluded from raising of their own motion issues of EC law in light of the requirement that procedural rules of national law must not render the protection of Community rights virtually impossible or excessively difficult, namely the principle of effectiveness. He indicated that he was not of the view that a national court must be free to raise an issue of EC law of its own motion irrespective of the time limit imposed by national law.

Advocate General Jacobs noted the position under French law as well as that under Belgian law and then addressed the circumstances in which the Court itself will raise of its own motion issues of law and noted that this depends on the nature of the proceedings. He noted that the case law of the Court establishes a balance between, on the one hand, the need to respect the procedural autonomy of the legal system of the Member States and, on the other hand, the need to ensure the effective protection of Community rights in the national courts. Having examined the *Simmenthal*[3] and *Factortame I*[4] decisions relied upon by the applicant, in the context of the effective protection of Community rights, Advocate General Jacobs concluded that they do not suggest that it must in all circumstances be open to the national court, as a matter of EC law, to raise of its own motion issues which the parties have failed to raise.

With regard to the preliminary ruling procedure, Advocate General Jacobs noted that the Court had previously declined to take up a suggestion of Advocate General Darmon in *Verholen* that a national court has a duty to raise of its own motion the existence of a Community rule.[5] Advocate General Jacobs proposed that the answer to the question referred should be that

> Community law does not preclude a rule of national law which prevents a national court from taking account of an argument based on Community law unless it has been raised by one of the parties to the proceedings within a specified time-limit, provided that that rule applies without discrimination to similar arguments based on national law and that it does not render excessively difficult the protection of rights guaranteed by Community law.

The Court reformulated the question and addressed the first part of the question as reformulated which was limited to the principle of effectiveness. It then referred to its earlier case law with regard to national procedural autonomy and the requirement that the principles of effectiveness and equivalence be respected.

The Court indicated that while the 60-day time limit was not objectionable per se, the special features of the procedure in question had to be emphasised. In this regard it emphasised, firstly, the fact that the Belgian Court of Appeal was the first court which could make a reference to the Court in the context of the tax procedure in question and, secondly, it noted that the 60-day time limit had expired before the Belgian Court of Appeal held its hearing in the case such that it was denied the possibility of considering the question of compatibility of the Belgian tax law with the Treaty provision on the freedom of establishment, and no other Belgian court or tribunal could in subsequent proceedings raise of its own motion the question of compatibility. The Court considered that this restriction was not reasonably justified by principles such as the requirement of legal certainty or the proper conduct of the procedure.

The Court in *Peterbroeck*, accordingly, differed with the Advocate General and answered the question posed as follows

> Community law precludes application of a domestic procedural rule whose effect, in procedural circumstances such as those in question in the main proceedings, is to

[3] Case 106/77 *Simmenthal* [1978] ECR 629.
[4] Case C-213/89 *R v Secretary of State for Transport, ex parte Factortame* [1990] ECR I-2433.
[5] Opinion of AG Darmon, Case C-89/90 *Verholen* [1991] ECR I-3575, para 19.

> prevent the national court, seised of a matter falling within its jurisdiction, from considering of its own motion whether a measure of domestic law is compatible with a provision of Community law when the latter provision has not been invoked by the litigant within a certain period.

In *van Schijndel*, Advocate General Jacobs indicated that the case raised similar issues to those raised in *Peterbroeck*. He again sought to distinguish the case before him from *Simmenthal* and *Factortame*. He took the view that EC law did not require or empower a national court to set aside national procedural rules, applicable without distinction to claims based on national and EC law, preventing it from applying Community provisions not relied upon by the parties where that would require the national court to go outside the ambit of the dispute or to raise issues of fact not pleaded by the parties.

The Court indicated that in proceedings concerning civil rights and obligations freely entered into by the parties, it is for the national court to apply the binding competition rules of the Treaty which are directly applicable in the national legal order even when the party with an interest in application of those provisions has not relied on them, where domestic law allows such application by the national court.

The second question in *van Schijndel* raised the issue whether this obligation also exists where the national court would have to abandon the passive role assigned to it by going beyond the ambit of the dispute defined by the parties themselves and/or by relying on facts and circumstances other than those on which the party to the proceedings with an interest in the application of the provisions of the Treaty bases his claims.

While the Court reiterated some of the considerations that it had advanced in *Peterbroeck*, it emphasised that in the case before it the domestic law limitation on courts raising points of their own motion was justified by the principle that, in a civil law suit, it is for the parties to take the initiative, the court being able to act of its own motion only in exceptional cases where the public interest requires its intervention. That principle reflects conceptions prevailing in most of the Member States as to the relations between the State and the individual; it safeguards the rights of the defence, and it ensures proper conduct of procedure by, in particular, protecting them from the delays inherent in examination of new pleas.

The Court then, in following the Advocate General in *van Schijndel*, ruled that EC law does not require national courts to raise of their own motion an issue concerning the breach of provisions of EC law where examination of that issue would oblige them to abandon the passive role assigned to them by going beyond the ambit of the dispute defined by the parties themselves and relying on facts and circumstances other than those on which the party with an interest in the application of those provisions bases his claim.

In *Eco Swiss*,[6] the Court received a request for a preliminary ruling by the Dutch Supreme Court in which the Court raised a number of questions arising from the Court's decision in *van Schijndel*. At issue was whether, in the case of annulment

[6] Case C-126/97 *Eco Swiss China Time Ltd v Benetton International NV* [1999] ECR I-3055.

proceedings of a final arbitration award, which had the force of *res judicata* as the annulment of that award had not been sought in proper time, a national procedural rule, based upon the principle of *res judicata*, restricting the application for annulment, was compatible with EC law. The Dutch Supreme Court asked to what extent the decision in *van Schijndel* was applicable by analogy in circumstances where, in the arbitration proceedings, the parties made no reference to the provisions of the Treaty on competition law in circumstances where under national procedural law, the arbitrators are not at liberty to apply those provisions of their own motion.

The Court of Justice indicated that where its domestic rules of procedure require a national court to grant an application for annulment of an arbitration award where such an application is founded on failure to observe national rules of public policy, it must also grant such an application where it is founded on failure to comply with the prohibition laid down in the provisions of the Treaty on competition law.[7] The Court recognised the importance of this Treaty article and stated that its provisions may be regarded as a matter of public policy.[8] The Court recognised that the arbitrators, unlike national courts, were unable to make a reference for a preliminary ruling to the Court of Justice.[9]

The Dutch Supreme Court also sought in essence to ascertain whether EC law required a national court to refrain from applying domestic rules of procedure according to which an interim arbitration award – which is in the nature of a final award and in respect of which no application for annulment has been made within the prescribed time limit – acquires the force of *res judicata* and may no longer be called into question in proceedings for annulment of a subsequent arbitration award where this was necessary to examine whether the agreement which the interim award held to be valid in law was nevertheless void under the relevant provision of the Treaty on competition law. The Court held that a three-month period for bringing proceedings to annul the interim arbitration award was not such as to render the exercise of rights conferred by EC law excessively difficult or virtually impossible. The Court indicated that the domestic procedural rules which restrict the possibility of applying for annulment by reference to the application of the principle of *res judicata* in the circumstances of the case to the interim arbitration award are justified by basic principles of legal certainty and acceptance of *res judicata*, which is an expression of that principle.

The differences in outcome between the cases of *van Schijndel* and *Peterbroeck* have since been explained by Advocate General Poiares Maduro in his Opinion in *van der Weerd*.[10] He indicated that the limitation period in *Peterbroek*, considered in its legal and practical context, in effect impaired the possibility of exercising rights conferred by EC law.[11] He added:

[7] ibid, para 37.
[8] ibid, para 39.
[9] ibid, para 40.
[10] Joined Cases C-222/05 to C-225/05 *van der Weerd* [2007] ECR I-4233, 4236.
[11] Opinion of AG Poiares Maduro, *van der Weerd*, n 10 above, para 22.

> The question whether in practice it is excessively difficult to exercise a right can be a matter of a sliding scale – which explains why *Peterbroeck* and *van Schijndel* and *van Veen* resulted in a different outcome on the basis of only a few factors. There are circumstances, however, in which it is apparent that, without the possibility for a national court to raise a plea based on Community law of its own motion, it would be extremely difficult for parties to obtain judicial protection where Community law grants them a right. *Océano Grupo Editorial and Salvat Editores*[12] and *Cofidis*[13] provide an example.[14]

Advocate General Poiares Maduro then indicated that in the cases cited by him above the Court held that the possibility for a court to raise a plea of its own motion may be implied in the terms of a directive, when it is a necessary means to achieve the purpose of that directive. More precisely, the Court held that the power of a national court to determine of its own motion that the jurisdiction clause in a consumer contract amounted to an unfair term was necessary to achieve the purpose of Council Directive 93/13.[15] That purpose, after all, was to protect consumers against unfair terms in consumer contracts. The Court interpreted the Directive in harmony with the principle of effectiveness. Had the Court done otherwise,

> the paradoxical situation would [have arisen] in which the consumer would [have been] obliged to appear before a court in a place other than that where he resides precisely in order to argue that the contractual term obliging him to do so is an unfair term![16]

Advocate General Poiares Maduro then offered the following summary of the case law: the principle of effectiveness does not impose a duty on national courts to raise pleas based on EC/EU law of their own motion, except in circumstances where this would be necessary in order to ensure that judicial protection is available where EC/EU law confers a right. Therefore, national courts have a duty to intervene when it is necessary to guarantee the protection of rights granted by EC/EU law. Yet, the principle of effectiveness does not entail a general duty for national courts to ensure, under all circumstances, the application of rules arising from the Union legal order.

Advocate General Poiares Maduro then referred to the decision in *Eco Swiss*[17] which had been expressly mentioned by the referring Dutch court in *van der Weerd*. He referred to the fact that in the arbitration proceedings, the question whether the agreement might be void under the Treaty provision had not been raised. The decision in that case was an application of the principle of equivalence. Advocate General Poiares Maduro then further explained matters when he

[12] Joined Cases C-240/98 to C-244/98 *Océano Grupo Editorial and Salvat Editores* [2000] ECR I-4941.

[13] Case C-473/00 *Cofidis* [2002] ECR I-10875.

[14] Opinion of AG Poiares Maduro, *van der Weerd*, n 10 above, para 23.

[15] Council Directive 93/13/EEC of 5 April 1993 on unfair terms in consumer contracts, [1993] OJ L95/29.

[16] Opinion of AG Saggio, *Océano Grupo Editorial and Salvat Editores*, n 12 above, para 24.

[17] *Eco Swiss*, n 6 above.

added that it would be mistaken to conclude from *Eco Swiss* that the principle of effectiveness requires that some Community norms, on account of their importance for the Community legal system, must be applied by national courts even where the parties have failed to rely on them:

> Indeed, such a reading of *Eco Swiss* would be irreconcilable with the judgment in *van Schijndel* and *van Veen*. Admittedly, the Court observed in *Eco Swiss* that Article 81 EC constituted 'a fundamental provision which is essential for the accomplishment of the tasks entrusted to the Community'. However, the same provision was also at issue in *van Schijndel* and *van Veen*, and there the Court did not find an obligation to apply Article 81 EC. It follows that the question whether the provision under consideration is one of public policy is not decisive for the purposes of applying the principle of effectiveness.[18]

The Advocate General pointed out that *Eco Swiss* belongs, first and foremost, to the class of cases in which the Court applied the principle of equivalence. The Advocate General then proceeded as follows:

> Still, the Court did make a statement on the principle of effectiveness in *Eco Swiss*. After having decided the case on the basis of the principle of equivalence, the Court further noted that 'questions concerning the interpretation of the prohibition laid down in [Article 81(1) EC] should be open to examination by national courts when asked to determine the validity of an arbitration award'. The Court's main concern appears to have been that a judicial remedy must be available in order to challenge an arbitration award that infringes Article 81 EC. Consequently, a national rule that limits the judicial review of an arbitration award to the grounds on which the applicant had relied during the arbitration proceedings contravenes the principle of effectiveness. The fact that the parties had an opportunity to rely on grounds based on Community law during the arbitration proceedings does not guarantee complete judicial protection, because those proceedings – like the administrative review procedure in *Peterbroeck* – do not constitute *judicial* proceedings in the strict sense.
>
> In sum, the principle of effectiveness does not impose a duty on national courts to raise a plea based on Community law of their own motion, even when the plea would concern a provision of fundamental importance to the Community legal order. However, the principle of effectiveness does require that parties be given a genuine opportunity to raise a plea based on Community law before a national court. Otherwise, the national court must have the power to raise that plea of its own motion.[19]

In *van der Veerd*, the Court addressed the requirement, arising from the principles of equivalence and effectiveness, for a national court to raise of its own motion the validity of an administrative measure on the basis of a plea alleging violation of a directive.

The Court in that case noted that, under Dutch law, a national court could raise of its own motion issues relating to the infringement of the rules of public policy, which were construed under Dutch law as meaning issues concerning the powers of administrative bodies and those of the court itself. The Court indicated that the

[18] *van der Weerd*, n 10 above, para 27.

[19] ibid, paras 28–29.

provisions of the Directive which were in issue in that case did not occupy a similar position within the Community legal order as they did not govern either the conditions under which the administrative procedures could be initiated or the authorities which possessed the power to determine the extent of the rights and obligations of individuals. On this basis, the Court concluded that the provisions in question could not be considered as being equivalent to the national rules of public policy referred to. The Court indicated that the principle of equivalence did not require the national court in the circumstances of this case to conduct of its own motion an examination of the validity of the administrative measures in question by having regard to the criteria based on the Directive.

With regard to the principle of effectiveness, the Court in *van der Weerd* applied the principles established in *van Schijndel* and concluded that the principle of effectiveness does not, in circumstances such as those which arose in the main proceedings, impose a duty on national courts to raise a plea based on a Community provision of their own motion, irrespective of the importance of that provision to the Community legal order, where the parties are given, as was the situation in the case before the national court, a genuine opportunity to raise a plea based on EC law before a national court.

CASES INVOLVING CONSUMER CONTRACTS

A number of cases have come before the Court of Justice relating to the obligation on national courts and arbitrators in the context of consumer contracts involving possible unfair arbitration awards. Directive 93/13 concerns essentially contracts of adhesion.[20] It provides in Article 3(1) that a contract term which has not been individually negotiated shall be regarded as unfair, if, contrary to the requirement of good faith, it causes a significant imbalance in the parties' rights and obligations arising under the contract, to the detriment of the consumer. Article 2 of the Directive provides that a term shall always be regarded as not individually negotiated where it has been drafted in advance and the consumer has therefore not been able to influence the substance of the term, particularly in the context of a pre-formulated standard contract. Article 6 of the Directive provides that Member States shall state that unfair contract terms used in a contract concluded with a consumer by a seller or supplier shall, as provided for under their national law, not be binding on the consumer.

The Court addressed the provisions of Directive 93/13 initially in *Océano Grupo*. In that case, a Spanish court of first instance asked whether, in the context of the Directive, it may determine of its own motion whether the term of a contract is unfair when making its preliminary assessment as to whether a claim should be allowed to proceed before the court seized.

[20] Directive 93/13/EEC, n 15 above.

The Court stated that the system of protection introduced by the Directive is based on the idea that the consumer is in a weak position vis-a-vis the seller or supplier, as regards both his bargaining power and his level of knowledge. This leads to the consumer agreeing to terms drawn up in advance by the seller or supplier without being able to influence the content of the terms.[21] It went on to find that the protection provided for consumers by Directive 93/13 entails the national court being able to determine of its own motion whether a term of a contract before it is unfair when making its preliminary assessment as to whether a claim should be allowed to proceed before the national courts.[22]

Subsequently in *Mostaza Claro*[23] the Court indicated with regard to the same Directive that a national court is required to assess of its own motion whether a contractual term is unfair.[24] In that case, the applicant before the national court had not contested the arbitration agreement, which the national court indicated included an unfair contractual term to the consumer's detriment, but raised the issue in subsequent annulment proceedings before the national court. The Court ruled that the Directive must be interpreted as meaning that a national court seized of an action for annulment of an arbitration award must determine whether the arbitration agreement is void and annul that award where that agreement contains an unfair term, even though the consumer has not pleaded that invalidity in the course of the arbitration proceedings, but only in the action for annulment.[25]

In *Pannon*[26] the Court ruled that Article 6(1) of Directive 93/13 must be interpreted as meaning that an unfair contract term is not binding on the consumer, and it is not necessary, in that regard, for that consumer to have successfully contested the validity of such a term beforehand. Furthermore, the national court is required to examine, of its own motion, the unfairness of a contractual term where it has available to it the legal and factual elements necessary for that task. Where it considers such a term to be unfair it must not apply it, except if the consumer opposes that non-application. That duty is also incumbent on the national court when it is ascertaining its own territorial jurisdiction.

In *Asturcom*[27] the Court of Justice, on a reference from a Spanish court of first instance, called upon to enforce an arbitration award that had become final, had to rule in circumstances where arbitrators were not permitted under Spanish law to examine of their own motion whether unfair arbitration clauses were void. The arbitration award had acquired the force of *res judicata*, albeit it was made in the absence of the consumer.

The Court indicated that the case could be distinguished from *Mostaza Claro* in that the consumer did not in any way become involved in the various proceedings and did not bring an action for annulment of the arbitration award in order to

[21] *Cofidis*, n 13 above, para 25.
[22] ibid, para 29.
[23] Case C-168/05 *Mostaza Claro* [2006] ECR I-10421.
[24] ibid, para 38.
[25] ibid, para 39.
[26] Case C-243/08 *Pannon GSM* [2009] ECR I-4713.
[27] Case C-40/08 *Asturcom Telecomunicaciones* [2009] ECR I-9579.

challenge the arbitration clause on the basis that it was unfair. It was in these circumstances that the arbitration award had attained the force of *res judicata*.[28]

The Court said that it was necessary to determine whether the need to replace the formal balance, which the contract establishes between the rights and obligations of the parties, with an effective balance, which re-establishes equality between them, requires the court or tribunal responsible for enforcement to ensure that the consumer is afforded absolute protection, even where the consumer has not brought any legal proceedings in order to assert his rights and notwithstanding the fact that the domestic rules of procedure apply the principle of *res judicata*.[29] It referred to the importance, both for the Community legal order and for national legal systems, of the principle of *res judicata*.[30] The Court indicated, in referring to its case law, including *Eco Swiss*, that EC law does not require a national court to disapply domestic rules of procedure conferring finality on a decision, even if to do so would make it possible to remedy an infringement of a provision of EC law, regardless of its nature.[31]

The Court, in examining the principle of effectiveness, concluded that a two-month time limit imposed by Spanish law, which started to run from the notification of the arbitration award, was consistent with the principle of effectiveness, since it was not in itself likely to make it virtually impossible or excessively difficult to exercise any rights which the consumer derived from the Directive.[32] It then added that:

> the need to comply with the principle of effectiveness cannot be stretched so far as to mean that, in circumstances such as those in the main proceedings, a national court is required not only to compensate for a procedural omission on the part of a consumer who is unaware of his rights, as in the case which gave rise to the judgment in *Mostaza Claro*, but also to make up fully for the total inertia on the part of the consumer concerned who, like the defendant in the main proceedings, neither participated in the arbitration proceedings nor brought an action for annulment of the arbitration award, which therefore became final.[33]

The Court then examined the principle of equivalence in the light of its decision in *van Schijndel*. It indicated that:

> in view of the nature and importance of the public interest underlying the protection which Directive 93/13 confers on consumers, Article 6 of the directive must be regarded as a provision of equal standing to national rules which rank, within the domestic legal system, as rules of public policy.[34]

[28] ibid, para 33.
[29] ibid, para 34.
[30] ibid, para 35.
[31] ibid, para 37.
[32] ibid, para 46.
[33] ibid, para 47.
[34] ibid, para 52.

The Court then referred to *Pannon* when it added that it followed that:

> inasmuch as the national court or tribunal seized of an action for enforcement of a final arbitration award is required, in accordance with domestic rules of procedure, to assess of its own motion whether an arbitration clause is in conflict with domestic rules of public policy, it is also obliged to assess of its own motion whether that clause is unfair in the light of Article 6 of that directive, where it has available to it the legal and factual elements necessary for that task.[35]

In line with its judgment in *van Schijndel*, the Court indicated that, where such discretion existed, it had to be exercised by the national court or tribunal concerned. The Spanish Government had indicated that a Spanish court enforcing an arbitration award, such as the referring court in that case, had jurisdiction to assess of its own motion whether the arbitration clause was null and void on the ground that such a clause was contrary to national rules on public policy.

This led the Court to rule that Directive 93/13 must be interpreted as meaning that a national court or tribunal hearing an action for enforcement of an arbitration award which has become final and was made in the absence of the consumer is required, where it has available to it the legal and factual elements necessary for that task, to assess of its own motion whether an arbitration clause in a contract concluded between a seller or supplier and a consumer is unfair, in so far as, under national rules of procedure, it can carry out such an assessment in similar actions of a domestic nature. If that is the case, it is for that court or tribunal to establish all the consequences thereby arising under national law, in order to ensure that the consumer is not bound by that clause.

In *VB Pénzügyi Lízing*,[36] a case which had been stayed pending the outcome of *Pannon*, the Court examined whether, with regard to having available to it the legal and factual elements necessary to assess whether the contractual term conferring exclusive territorial jurisdiction is unfair, it is obliged to undertake, of its own motion, an investigation with a view to establishing the necessary factual and legal elements, in circumstances where the national procedural rules permit such an investigation, only if one of the parties so requests.

Referring to its earlier decisions in *Océano Grupo*, *Mostaza Claro* and *Asturcom*, the Court emphasised that there is a two stage process in the examination to be carried out by the national court. In the first place, the national court must establish that any term appearing in the contract conferring exclusive territorial jurisdiction was not individually negotiated. As regards the second stage, the national court must establish that the term conferring exclusive jurisdiction on a court is unfair, in so far as it causes, contrary to the requirement of good faith, a significant imbalance in the parties' rights and obligations arising under the contract, to the detriment of the consumer.

In answer to the question referred, the Court ruled that the national court must investigate of its own motion whether a term conferring exclusive territorial

[35] ibid, para 53.
[36] Case C-137/08 *VB Pénzügyi Lízing*, judgment of 9 November 2010 nyr.

jurisdiction in a contract concluded between a seller or supplier and a consumer, which is the subject of a dispute before it, falls within the scope of the Directive and, if it does, assess of its own motion whether such a term is unfair.

In conclusion, with reference to consumer contracts under Directive 93/13, it is clear that the role of national courts and arbitrators involves a degree of intervention, beyond what is normal for such courts, in the interest of the consumer to ensure that such contracts and, in particular, arbitration clauses are fair and that this requirement results from the object of the Directive itself.

THE OBLIGATION ON NATIONAL COURTS TO RE-OPEN DECISIONS BASED ON A MISINTERPRETATION OF EU LAW

A final issue which arises in the context of this presentation is the issue of when a national court of final instance is required to re-open proceedings where it has misapplied EU law. An examination of this issue reveals the consequences that arise for national courts which fail, of their own motion, to raise issues of EU law and in particular to refer such issues, arising before courts of final instance, to the Court of Justice, where it subsequently transpires that such a court has incorrectly interpreted EU law. Such failure to refer may result in an obligation at the national level to re-open national proceedings that have otherwise become final.

In *Künhe & Heitz*,[37] a Dutch administrative court asked whether the principle of Community solidarity contained in Article 10 EC[38] required an administrative body to reopen a final decision in order to ensure the full operation of EC law, as it is to be interpreted in the light of a subsequent preliminary ruling.

Under Dutch law, an earlier administrative decision of refusal may be re-opened if the applicant shows new facts or a change of circumstances. Furthermore, a court may, on the application by one party, review a final judgment taking account of facts and circumstances which occurred before the judgment but which were not known and which could not reasonably have been known by the applicant before the judgment was delivered and which, if the court had been aware of them, could have led it to deliver a different judgment.

The applicant was required by the Dutch authorities, following reclassification by the authorities, to repay export refunds which it had been paid for the export of poultry meat to third countries. The applicant appealed this decision to the same Dutch court that made the reference and that Court, in 1991, dismissed the appeal on the basis of an interpretation of the common customs tariff, without making a reference to the Court of Justice and without having been requested by the applicant to make a reference. A subsequent ruling of the Court of Justice in

[37] Case C-453/00 *Kühne & Heitz* [2004] ECR I-837.

[38] Repealed by the Lisbon Treaty and replaced in substance by Art 4(3) TEU. Art 10 provided: 'Member States shall take all appropriate measures, whether general or particular, to ensure fulfilment of the obligations arising out of this Treaty or resulting from action taken by the institutions of the Community. They shall facilitate the achievement of the Community's tasks'.

Voogd Vleesimport en -export[39] called into question the earlier ruling of the Dutch court. The applicant in *Künhe & Heitz* made a fresh application to the administrative authorities to pay the refunds. This was refused by the Dutch authorities and the applicant then brought an action to the referring court against this fresh decision.

The Dutch court took the view that an assessment of whether there was an obligation to review a decision must be based upon the principle that judicial decisions given after a final administrative decision, cannot, in themselves, affect the finality of a decision. The national court considered it unacceptable for a final decision to be amended in light of a subsequent ruling of the Court of Justice on the basis that it would give rise to administrative chaos and seriously impair legal certainty. However, the referring court was uncertain whether the Dutch rule on the finality of administrative decisions should be relaxed.

The Court of Justice indicated that legal certainty was one of a number of general principles recognised by EC law. Finality of an administrative decision, which is acquired upon expiry of the reasonable time limits for legal remedies or by exhaustion of those remedies, contributes to such legal certainty and it follows that EC law does not require that administrative bodies be placed under an obligation, in principle, to reopen an administrative decision which has become final in that way.

The Court highlighted, however, the particular circumstances of the main case. First, national law confers on the administrative body competence to reopen a final decision. Second, that decision became final only as a result of a judgment of a national court against whose decisions there is no judicial remedy. Third, that judgment was based on an interpretation of EC law which, in the light of a subsequent judgment of the Court, was incorrect and which was adopted without a question being referred to the Court for a preliminary ruling in accordance with the conditions provided for in the third paragraph of Article 267 TFEU. Fourth, the person concerned complained to the administrative body immediately after becoming aware of that judgment of the Court.[40]

In light of these circumstances the Court indicated that the administrative body concerned was, in accordance with the principle of co-operation arising from Article 10 EC, under an obligation to review that decision in order to take account of the interpretation of the relevant provision of EC/EU law given in the meantime by the Court of Justice. The administrative body had to determine on the basis of the outcome of that review to what extent it was under an obligation to reopen, without adversely affecting the interests of third parties, the decision in question.

The Court accordingly answered the question referred to it to the effect that the principle of co-operation arising from Article 10 EC imposes on an administrative body an obligation to review a final administrative decision, where an application

[39] Case C-151/93 *Voogd Vleesimport en -export* [1994] ECR I-4915.

[40] ibid, para 26.

for such review is made to it, in order to take account of the interpretation of the relevant provision given in the meantime by the Court, subject to the four conditions outlined above.

Following on from the Court's decision in *Künhe & Heitz*, the Finanzgericht Hamburg in *Kempter*,[41] raised the issue whether review and amendment of a final administrative decision, which is intended to take account of the interpretation of Community law made by the Court in the meantime, require the claimant to have relied on Community law in his action before the national court. That Court also asked the Court of Justice whether an application for the review and amendment of a final administrative decision which is contrary to Community law is subject to a time limit.

In *Kempter*, similar to the circumstances in *Künhe & Heitz*, the applicant received export refunds for the export of cattle from the EC to third countries. When it was discovered that some of the cattle had died or been slaughtered out of necessity during transportation or in the course of quarantine in the third countries of destination, the competent customs office demanded the repayment of the export refunds. While Kempter challenged this decision it did not raise a breach of EC law. Its challenge was rejected by the Finanzgericht Hamburg and thereafter by the Bundesfinanzhof on appeal. Neither court made a reference to the Court of Justice for a ruling on the interpretation of the relevant provisions of EC law. In *Emsland-Stärke*, however, the Court subsequently indicated that the earlier decision taken against Kempter was in breach of EC law.[42] In separate proceedings the Bundesfinanzhof delivered judgment in March 2002 applying the interpretation established in *Emsland-Stärke*. Kempter claimed only to have become aware of this judgment in July 2002. In September 2002, Kempter requested the Haupzollamt to review its earlier decision and withdraw the decision requiring the repayment of the export refunds. This application was rejected as was a subsequent administrative appeal. Kempter then brought the matter before the Finanzgericht Hamburg relying on the Court's decision in *Künhe & Heitz.*

The Grand Chamber of the Court indicated that, firstly, in accordance with settled case law, all the authorities of the Member States have the task of ensuring observance of the rules of EC law within the sphere of their competence. Secondly, a preliminary ruling does not create or alter the law, but is purely declaratory, with the consequence that, in principle, it takes effect from the date on which the rule interpreted entered into force. It followed that, in a case such as the main proceedings, a rule of EC law thus interpreted must be applied by an administrative body within the sphere of its competence even to legal relationships which arose and were formed before the Court gave its ruling on the request for interpretation.

However, the Court pointed out that the case law had to be read in the light of the principle of legal certainty. It stressed that the finality of an administrative

[41] Case C-2/06 *Kempter* [2008] ECR I-411.
[42] Case C-110/99 *Emsland-Stärke* [2000] ECR I-11569.

decision, which is acquired upon expiry of reasonable time limits for legal remedies or, as in the main proceedings, by exhaustion of those remedies, contributes to such legal certainty, with the consequence that EC law does not require that administrative bodies be placed under an obligation, in principle, to reopen an administrative decision which has become final in that way.

The Court indicated that it could not be inferred from *Kühne & Heitz* that, for the purposes of the third condition established by that judgment – namely that the judgment under review is, in the light of a decision given by the Court subsequent to it, based on a misinterpretation of EC law which was adopted without a question being referred to the Court for a preliminary ruling – the parties must have raised before the national court the point of EC law in question. In order for that condition to be satisfied, it is sufficient if either the point of EC law, the interpretation of which proved to be incorrect in light of a subsequent judgment of the Court, was considered by the national court ruling at final instance or raised by the latter of its own motion.

The Court then referred to the principle of equivalence as applied in *van Schijndel* in adding that

> while Community law does not require national courts to raise of their own motion a plea alleging infringement of Community provisions where examination of that plea would oblige them to go beyond the ambit of the dispute as defined by the parties, they are obliged to raise of their own motion points of law based on binding Community rules where, under national law, they must or may do so in relation to a binding rule of national law.[43]

The Court thus answered the first question referred by the national court in the negative.

In answer to the second question, the Court noted that the applicant in *Kühne & Heitz* had applied for the review of the administrative decision within three months of becoming aware of the Court's ruling which caused the administrative decision to be unlawful. However, the Court recognised that the fourth condition in *Kühne & Heitz* did not require the application for review to be made within a specified period after the applicant became aware of the decision of the Court on which the application for review was based. In the absence of EC rules the matter is to be governed by domestic rules in accordance with the principle of national procedural autonomy subject to the principles of equivalence and effectiveness.[44]

Finally, it is appropriate to refer to *Heemskerk and Schaap*[45] where the issue arose as to whether EC law requires national courts to examine, of their own motion, pleas in law derived from regulations falling outside the ambit of the dispute. The matter came before the Court on a reference from a Dutch court which indicated that, in accordance with Dutch law, it may not, as a rule, take account of arguments which fall outside the ambit of the dispute as defined by the parties. If

[43] ibid, para 45.
[44] ibid, paras 55–57.
[45] Case C-455/06 *Heemskerk and Schaap* [2008] ECR I-8763.

EC law required it to raise of its own motion pleas based on a certain specified regulation, it might come up against the procedural rule prohibiting *reformatio in pejus* enshrined in Dutch administrative law, according to which an individual who brings an action cannot find himself in a less favourable position than he would have been in had the action not been brought. It did not rule out the possibility that, if those regulations were taken into account, the burden on the applicants in the main proceedings may be increased.

The Court indicated that EC law cannot oblige a national court to apply EC legislation of its own motion where this would have the effect of denying the principle, enshrined in its national procedural law, of the prohibition of *reformatio in pejus*. Such an obligation would be contrary not only to the principles of respect for the rights of the defence, legal certainty and protection of legitimate expectations which underlie the prohibition, but would expose an individual who brought an action against an act adversely affecting him to the risk that such an action would place him in a less favourable position than he would have been in had he not brought that action.

CONCLUSION

An examination of the case law of the Court of Justice indicates the particular difficulties that may arise from the obligation of national courts to raise issues of EU law of their own motion and, in particular, the difficulty of ascertaining to what extent such an obligation exists. An examination of the cases referred to in this article leads one to imagine that the end of this category of cases coming to the Court of Justice has not yet been reached! It may be observed, in view of the third condition laid down in *Kühne & Heitz* relating to the failure of the national court to have made a reference to the Court of Justice and the reference in *Kempter* to the fact that it is sufficient if either the point of EU law the interpretation of which proved to be incorrect in light of a subsequent judgment of the Court was considered by the national court ruling at final instance or raised by the latter of its own motion, that it may present a difficulty for any such court if it has to conceive of a point of EU law which has not been raised by the parties unless it is quite evident that the national court in question should have considered the issue in reaching its decision. This condition may give rise to a greater number of questions being referred by courts of final instance in the future to avoid the difficulties which would otherwise arise.

10

Some Reflections on Mutual Recognition in the Area of Freedom, Security and Justice

LARS BAY LARSEN*

INTRODUCTION

WHEN PERNILLA LINDH joined the European Courts in Luxembourg in January 1995 as the first Swedish judge at the then still fairly new Court of First Instance and thus continued an already remarkable career as a Swedish, Scandinavian and European lawyer, the area of Justice and Home Affairs had only recently been covered by the European Treaties. It was only in November 1993 with the Maastricht Treaty of 1992 (as completed by the Edinburgh Agreement in December 1992), that the area of Justice and Home Affairs had found its way into the European Treaties as the so-called 'third pillar'.

It was a third pillar which was then split in two by the Amsterdam Treaty (1997), following which only the penal half (also including law enforcement co-operation and counter-terrorism) retained – almost fully – its intergovernmental character, while the other half (the 'communitarised' areas of immigration, asylum, border-controls and civil law co-operation) basically just retained a few intergovernmental features for a limited period of time.[1]

This third pillar is now in the process of disappearing completely since the Lisbon Treaty came into force in December 2009. There are, of course, a few not unimportant leftovers in the form of various national opt-outs and opt-ins, complicated further by the crossing lines of what is related to the Schengen *acquis* and its further development and what is not, as well as a transitory regime, which makes the limited jurisdiction governed by Article 35 TEU apply to the ECJ until December 2014 under the conditions set out in Article 10 of Protocol No 36 to the TEU and the TFEU.

The third pillar is thus in the process of becoming legal history, interesting legal history notably for those of us who have devoted a substantial part of our

* Judge of the Court of Justice of the European Union.

[1] See C Elsen, 'From Maastricht to The Hague: The Policies of Judicial and Police Cooperation' (2007) 8 *ERA Forum* 13; L Bay Larsen: 'Judicial Control within the European Penal Area' in S Braum and A Weyembergh (eds), *Le contrôle juridictionnel dans l'espace penal européen* (Brussels, Editions de l'Université de Bruxelles, 2009) 14.

professional existence to live and sometimes suffer – with this sensitive area. And sensitive it still is. This seems to be reflected in the rather high number of governments intervening before the ECJ when a reference for a preliminary ruling involves a question of criminal law. The fact that the third pillar disappears in the constitutional structure of the Union does in no way imply that the legal subjects in this area have become uncontroversial or less sensitive.

At this point in time, as Pernilla Lindh is leaving our Court, almost two decades after Maastricht, and more than one decade after the thematic European Council in Tampere in 1999 and ten years after the terrorist attacks of 11 September 2001, it is perhaps not unjustified to pause briefly and reflect on the way in which the key principle of mutual recognition has been established and applied – both by the EU lawmaker and the European Courts – in this area. I intend to do so, briefly, by using examples mainly from instruments and jurisprudence in the field of EU penal law. Obviously, this contribution cannot provide a complete review of the fast growing case law in this area, but allow me to make a few personal observations and comments on the basis of some of the key judgments on the Framework Decision on the European Arrest Warrant (EAW)[2] – also in the light of recent case law from the ECtHR in Strasbourg.

MUTUAL RECOGNITION AS A KEY PRINCIPLE IN EU PENAL LAW

Following the thematic Tampere meeting of the European Council which favoured a vast application of the principle of mutual recognition over harmonisation and approximation in the third pillar area,[3] a number of new legislative initiatives were launched – and eventually completed.[4] During the negotiations in the Justice and Home Affairs Council it became clear that it is perhaps not legally, but very often politically, difficult for the Member States to accept the principle of mutual recognition fully without at least some form of approximation of national procedural and/or substantive penal law.

The fact of political life that harmonisation or approximation of national laws in this area is rather a means to an end than a goal in itself is now more clearly reflected in the wording of Article 82 TFEU which, in paragraph 1 makes it clear that judicial co-operation in criminal matters in the Union shall be based on the principle of mutual recognition of judgments and judicial decisions, and that it shall include the approximation of the laws and regulations of the Member States in the areas delimitated in paragraph 2 and in Article 83 TFEU. Further to this

[2] Council Framework Decision 2002/584/JHA of 13 June 2002 on the European arrest warrant and the surrender procedures between Member States (OJ 2002 L 190, 1).

[3] The Council held that '[e]nhanced mutual recognition of judicial decisions and judgements and the necessary approximation of legislation would facilitate co-operation between authorities and the judicial protection of individual rights'. See para 33 of the Presidency Conclusions.

[4] See the draft programme of measures to implement the principle of mutual recognition of decisions in criminal matters, [2001] OJ C12/10. See now the Stockholm programme setting out the EU's priorities for the area of justice, freedom and security for the period 2010–2014, [2010] OJ C115/1.

delimitation of the EU legislative power it is emphasised in Article 82(2) TFEU that to the extent necessary to facilitate mutual recognition of judgments and judicial decisions and police and judicial co-operation in criminal matters, the EU legislator may, by means of directives, establish minimum rules harmonising national laws taking into account the differences between the legal traditions of the Member States.[5]

The difficult discussions in the JHA Council on the first drafts of the Framework Decision on the EAW are a clear example of this political link between approximation of national laws and national legislation. The Nordic states had already in the 1950s committed themselves to parallel legislation that went significantly further than the Council of Europe's Convention on Extradition of 1957, as the Nordic States between themselves allowed for extradition of their own nationals, and disregarded to a certain extent the double criminality condition. But that was politically relatively easy to do in a strictly Nordic and rather homogenous context within legal systems of a similar nature. To do the same in a much wider and less homogenous context of 15, 25, 27 or 27-plus Member States is naturally different. Many Member States reflected and hesitated.

11 September 2001, for obvious reasons, had a big impact, including on the EU legislative process. It became an absolute political imperative for the Council to cut quickly through the political and legal problems that blocked certain proposals such as the draft Framework Decision on the EAW. National Parliaments, prosecutors, defence lawyers, national judges and we at the ECJ in Luxembourg have since had to live with the inevitably less than perfect outcome of this intensified process.[6]

It follows from this that a number of interesting new questions were bound to be dealt with before the ECJ in Luxembourg. The lawmaker in Brussels had in reality – by not clearly resolving difficult key questions or sometimes even leaving such questions completely out of the legal text – often delegated legislative power to the ECJ. It is in the very nature of such a delegation of power that, normally, the ECJ cannot avoid explaining how Union law is to be understood when faced with a preliminary question demanding interpretation of a less than complete legal act, as the Court is supposed to provide an answer to the national judge which will enable him to give judgment in the main proceedings. I believe that the Court's case law in the area of Justice and Home Affairs – as well as in other areas – reflects this quite well.[7]

[5] See K Leanerts and P van Nuffel, *European Union Law*, 3rd edn (London, Sweet & Maxwell, 2011) 334.

[6] See, in this context, J Wouters and F Naert, 'Of Arrest Warrants, Terrorist Offences and Extraditions Deals: An Appraisal of the EU's Main Criminal Law Measures Against Terrorism After 11 September' (2004) 41 *CML Rev* 909.

[7] See, in particular, Case C-66/08 *Kozłowski* [2008] ECR I-6041 and Case C-357/09 PPU *Kadzoev* [2009] ECR I-11189 where, in the former it was a problem for the Court that the Framework Decision on the EAW does not make it sufficiently clear whether the Member States are under an obligation to transpose Art 4(6) of this Act which that Court was asked to interpret. In the latter case, the Court was faced with a situation where Directive 2008/115/EC on common standards and procedures in Member States for returning illegally staying third-country nationals, [2008] OJ L348/98, did not contain any

FUNDAMENTAL RIGHTS

In parallel to the efforts by the EU legislator to give substance to the choice made in Tampere in favour of a wide application of the principle of mutual recognition in the area of justice and home affairs, another important development took place. The same European Council also agreed on the composition, method of work and practical arrangements for the body entrusted with drawing up a draft Charter of Fundamental Rights of the European Union following the conclusions from the Cologne European Council in June 1999. The intentions were basically to close the perceived gap in legal protection, as the EU as such had not, due to lack of competence both internally at the EU level and externally in the Council of Europe set-up, acceded to the ECHR. At the time several Member States found that a parallel legal instrument to the ECHR might lead to legal uncertainty or even confusion and, as a compromise, the Charter was drawn up as a political declaration.[8]

The Charter consists, as it follows from its preamble, of rights as they result, in particular, from the constitutional traditions and international obligations common to the Member States, the ECHR and the Social Charters adopted by the Union and by the Council of Europe. Article 52(3) of the Charter provides that the meaning and scope of the Charter rights which correspond to rights guaranteed by the ECHR 'shall be the same as those laid down by the [ECHR]'.

Although not legally bound to do so, the ECJ had, long before the Charter was drawn up and first pronounced at the European Council in Nice (2001), made clear that the Court, when safeguarding fundamental rights, had to look to the constitutional traditions common to the Member States and international treaties concerning the protection of human rights and the common constitutional principles of the Member States. Those Union fundamental rights 'are also binding on the Member States when they implement Community rules'.[9] The fact that the Union already provides a protection of fundamental rights, which can be compared to the protection granted by the ECHR, is also recognised and reflected in the case law of the ECtHR notably as the essential precondition for the *Bosphorus* jurisprudence.[10]

It is one of the curious small paradoxes in the development of EU primary law that with the entry into force of the Treaty of Lisbon in December 2009 two

transitional rules at all which, in reality, left it to the Court to 'invent' such a transitional regime in order to give the Bulgarian referring judge a useful answer to his questions.

[8] See K Lenaerts and P van Nuffel, n 4 above, 830–33.

[9] Case 5/88 *Wachauf* [1989] ECR, para 17 2609 and Case C-260/89 *ERT* [1991] ECR I 2925, para 42.

[10] In *Bosphorus Hava Yollari Turizm ve Ticaret Anonim Sirketi v Ireland* [GC] No 45036/98, § 165 ECHR 2005 VI, 30 June 2005, the ECtHR held that the Union system for the protection of fundamental rights has become equivalent to that of the Convention (see para 165). There is thus a presumption that the EU Member States do not violate the Convention when by way of the Treaties they pool national competences in the EU system, whereby such pooled competences then essentially fall outside the full direct control of the ECtHR in Strasbourg.

important further steps were taken simultaneously: Article 6(2) TEU – and the accompanying Protocol No 8 setting out the key preconditions – makes it clear that the EU is to adhere to the ECHR, and at the same time Article 6(1) TEU gives the Charter 'the same legal value as the Treaties', although these two moves in Tampere were widely perceived as alternative means to the same end.

EUROPEAN ARREST WARRANT – VALIDITY AND INTERPRETATION

So how do fundamental rights and the EAW go together? It is still too early to predict the situation after the accession of the Union to the ECHR, as negotiations towards this end are still pending before the EU and the Council of Europe.[11]

When the Framework Decision on the EAW was agreed as the first concrete measure in the field of criminal law implementing the principle of mutual recognition, the aim was to replace the traditional extradition procedures between Member States with one single and simple mechanism securing 'surrender' of a requested person – including nationals of the requested Member State – in accordance with the basic principle of mutual recognition. The surrender (extradition) of own nationals was, however, not the only key element of the Framework Decision that gave rise to discussions. The abolition, for a list of 32 crimes, of the traditional requirement of dual criminality – found in most extradition arrangements – was equally heavily debated. These 32 crimes, widely defined, are presumed to be punishable in all Member States, but this presumption is not to be verified by the judicial authorities of the requested Member State, who will in fact normally be obliged to surrender the requested person even in a situation where it is clear that the alleged criminal behaviour of this person is not punishable in the requested Member State, provided that the alleged offence corresponds to a crime on the list.

As dual criminality is found as a necessary precondition for extradition in most bilateral and multilateral extradition instruments, it is not surprising that the Court eventually had to decide on the validity of this important part of the instrument. In fact several national constitutional courts had to rule on the compliance of national EAW implementing acts with fundamental rights and constitutional principles and did so without referring preliminary questions to the Court.[12] Only the Belgian Cour d'arbitrage (now Constitutional Court) referred its EAW case to Luxembourg. This case, *Advocaten voor de Wereld*,[13] which did not concern a

[11] See the Joint Communication of 17 January 2011 from Presidents Costa and Skouris.

[12] In 2005, the Polish Constitutional Tribunal ruled that the implementation of the EAW was to be brought into line with the Constitution. In the same year, the German Bundesverfassungsgericht also ruled against the constitutional compatibility of the provisions permitting the surrender of German nationals under the EAW to other Member States. Implementing measures were also challenged before constitutional courts in Greece, Spain, the Czech Republic and before the Supreme Court in Cyprus.

[13] Case C-303/05 *Advocaten voor de Wereld* [2007] ECR I-3633. See for an in-depth analysis of this judgment and further case law on the EAW: S Peers, *EU Justice and Home Affairs Law*, 3rd edn (Oxford, Oxford University Press, 2011) 696.

concrete surrender situation, was particularly important not only because the EAW was the first instrument to implement the principle of mutual recognition as agreed by the European Council in Tampere, but it had also served as a blueprint for other measures that had been adopted in the meantime.[14]

Concerning the first question asked by the Belgian court as to whether a Framework Decision constituted the proper legal instrument I do not feel that, now that the special third pillar toolbox has disappeared, it is relevant to take a closer look at the Court's arguments underlining the Council's procedural freedom of choice. *Advocaten voor de Wereld* had challenged the innovative Article 2(2) of the EAW which removes the possibility of examining 'double criminality' for 32 broadly defined categories of offences, provided, however, that these offences are punishable in the issuing state for a maximum period of at least three years. The claimants argued, inter alia, that legality in criminal matters requires that the offences concerned are precisely defined not only in the penal law of the requesting Member State, but also in the list drawn up in Article 2(2) of the EAW. Further they argued that it would be contrary to principles of equality and non-discrimination that a person surrendered according to Article 2(2) would not be subject to a double criminality check guaranteeing that the acts for which the surrender is requested constitute a criminal offence in both Member States involved, while other persons may find their extradition subject to such a double criminality check.

On both these points the claimant association failed to convince the Court. First, Article 2(2) of the EAW could not infringe the principle of legality as this provision does not seek to harmonise the criminal offences in question. Instead, the definitions of the offences continue to be matters determined by the law of the issuing Member State. It is therefore up to the penal law of each issuing Member State to respect the principle of legality.[15] Surrender of a suspected or convicted

[14] Before the entry into force of the Treaty of Lisbon, the principle of mutual recognition was applied in several Framework Decisions: Framework Decision 2003/577/JHA on the execution in the EU of orders freezing property or evidence, [2003] OJ L196/45, Framework Decision 2005/214/JHA on the application of the principle of mutual recognition to financial penalties, [2005] OJ L76/16, Framework Decision 2006/783/JHA on the application of the principle of mutual recognition to confiscation orders, [2006] OJ L328/59, Framework Decision 2008/909/JHA on the application of the principle of mutual recognition to judgments in criminal matters imposing custodial sentences or measures involving deprivation of liberty for the purpose of their enforcement in the EU, [2008] OJ L327/27, Framework Decision 2008/947/JHA on the application of the principle of mutual recognition to judgments and probation decisions with a view to the supervision of probation measures and alternative sanctions, [2008] OJ L337/102, Framework Decision 2008/978/JHA on the European Evidence Warrant for the purpose of obtaining objects, documents and data for use in proceedings in criminal matters, [2008] OJ L350/72 and Framework Decision 2009/829/JHA on the application, between Member States of the EU, of the principle of mutual recognition to decisions on supervision measures as an alternative to provisional detention, [2009] OJ L294/20.

[15] The Court had used the same argument – that substantial criminal law was not to be harmonised – in its first judgments on the double jeopardy principle ('*ne bis in idem*'). In Joined Cases C-187/01 and C-385/01 *Gözütok and Brügge* [2003] ECR I-1345, the Court ruled that 'there is a necessary implication that each Member State . . . recognises the criminal law in force in the other Member States even when the outcome would be different if its own national law were applied' (para 33). The Court's recognition of the importance of the principle of mutual recognition in Art 54 of the Convention implementing the Schengen Agreement (CISA) has influenced the Court's interpretation of the *ne bis in idem* principle contained in this provision.

person is not in itself a genuine criminal prosecution, but mere procedural assistance – based on mutual trust – to prosecution by another Member State.

Second, the Court did not find it necessary to state whether the situations of persons falling under the double-criminality check and those under the EAW mechanism are comparable. Either way, the distinction would be objectively justified. The justification follows from the seriousness of the offences listed in Article 2(2).

This case is also an example showing that the Court occasionally will have not only to interpret an instrument of international law, but even to judge on the very existence of such an 'instrument' – here an eventual fundamental principle of international law insisting on double criminality. To the English as well as the Scandinavians (who, as mentioned above, have extradited even their own nationals for decades without dual criminality in between them) it will not come as a great surprise that the Court did not succeed in identifying such an international fundamental principle.

In *Kozłowski* and *Wolzenburg*[16] and, more recently, in *IB.*,[17] the Court struggled with the interpretation of Article 4(6) of the EAW and its relation with Article 5(3) of the same Act. These articles concern the possibility of partly turning down an EAW in the sense that a judgment already passed or eventually to be passed in the issuing Member State shall not be served in this Member State, but instead in the executing Member State. I suspect that the EAW in the final phase of its very fast negotiation had so many different layers of mandatory and optional grounds for refusal of an EAW added in such haste – so many Member States realised that they had substantial and sometimes constitutional difficulties in accepting the main principles of mutual recognition, surrender of own nationals and doing away with dual criminality – that the legal quality and coherence of the instrument was affected.

If one takes a survey of the national implementation of the EAW, as the Commission has now done in three reports[18] – and completes the picture with further information on national laws transposing or not transposing Article 4(6) of the EAW, it becomes clear that the actual state of implementation of this important provision is very mixed.[19] Some Member States, like the United Kingdom, opted for a wider application of the main principle of surrender by not implementing Article 4(6) at all. Other Member States have fully implemented this provision – but in very different ways which, of course, makes the situation even more complicated. Some of these Member States have allowed full discretion to the individual national judges responsible for executing EAWs, other Member States have adopted a legal framework for the competent judges' application of

[16] Case 123/08 *Wolzenburg* [2009] ECR I-9621.

[17] Case C-306/09 *IB.*, judgment of 21 October 2010 nyr.

[18] See COM(2005) 63 of 23 February 2005, revised by COM(2006) 8 of 24 January 2006 and COM(2007) 407 of 12 July 2007 and, most recently, COM(2011) 175 of 11 April 2011.

[19] See on implementation in general in a selected number of Member States: G Vernimmem-Van Tiggelen, L Surano and A Weyembergh (eds), *The Future of Mutual Recognition in Criminal Matters in the European Union* (Brussels, Editions de l'Université de Bruxelles, 2009).

this facultative reason for turning down an EAW.[20] Furthermore, in between are various kinds of partial implementation, giving different rights to some or all of the three different groups of persons listed in Article 4(6): own nationals, persons residing in and persons 'staying in' the executing Member State. This was the situation both in Germany (*Kozłowski*) and the Netherlands (*Wolzenburg*).

It is puzzling that the Framework Decision does not provide an answer or at least an indication of how to determine whether Member States are obliged to implement Article 4(6) of the EAW in domestic legislation. Nor does the act contain any formulations indicating why Article 4(6) was drafted differently from Article 5(3) of the EAW which only mentions two of the three groups of persons listed in Article 4(6) – although the interests to be balanced in the respective situations seem identical. Such inexplicable differences in the formulation of important provisions of a legal act do, of course, not facilitate interpretation.

If the EU legislator's intention with Article 4(6) was that Member States, when implementing this provision, should simply allow national judges to apply it freely on a case-by-case basis without further guidance in national law setting out rules for its application – then why was Article 5(3) of the EAW manifestly based on a completely different concept, where a role and a choice for the national legislator is clearly foreseen.

One might further ask if an absence of guidelines in national implementing legislation does necessarily lead to a higher degree of legal protection for the individuals concerned. In my view, the contrary could well be the case. In both *Kozłowski* and *Wolzenburg*, the differential treatment of notably own nationals (German and Dutch respectively) and nationals from other Member States followed directly and with full transparency from day one from the national legislation transposing Article 4(6) of the EAW. Had a similar position instead been developed solely by way of national jurisprudence on a case-by-case basis, it would at least have taken considerably longer before such a practice had been clearly established by a series of individual court decisions.

Obviously, Advocate General Bot in his view in *Kozłowski* (para 175) saw it differently as he proposed that the Court should answer the second question on the compatibility of the German law transposing Article 4(6) of the EAW as follows:

> Article 4(6) of [the EAW] must be interpreted as precluding legislation of a Member State under which the execution of a European arrest warrant issued for the purposes of execution of a custodial sentence is ruled out where that arrest warrant applies to one of its own nationals and he does not consent to his surrender.
>
> In the case before it, the referring court must apply to Mr Kozłowski the provisions of its national law applicable to nationals of the other Member States, in accordance with the objective of [the EAW]. The principle of conforming interpretation precludes the extension to nationals of other Member States, pursuant to the principle of non-

[20] Although Art 4(6) is labelled as an optional ground to 'refuse' a EAW, it should be recalled that it is a firm precondition for the application of this ground in a specific case that the executing Member State undertakes to execute the sentence or detention order in accordance with its domestic law.

discrimination, of the ground for non-execution laid down in national law in favour of German nationals who oppose their surrender. (See point 175(1) of the view)

As it were, the Court found that it did not have to take a position on this difficult question in relation to the German implementing legislation.[21] This was due to the fact that the Court, on the basis of information contained in the reference, held that the links between the Polish national, Mr Kozłowski, and Germany were so weak that – when giving an interpretation of Article 4(6) as a piece of Union law – he had to be considered falling completely outside the field of application of this provision.[22]

In *Wolzenburg*, the situation was different in the sense that the German national, Mr Wolzenburg, was clearly covered by the scope of application of Article 4(6) of the EAW, as he was living (and working) in the Netherlands. However, he had not yet been living there for the five years required by the Dutch implementation legislation in order to be given the same protection as Dutch nationals under Article 4(6) of the EAW. The Court did not find that this different treatment of own nationals and nationals from other Member States was unjustified and came to this conclusion without having to take a clear position on whether there is in fact an obligation for Member States to implement the optional ground in Article 4(6).

However, this question of principle seems to surface once again in Case C-42/11 *Lopes Da Silva Jorge* (pending) concerning an EAW issued by a Portuguese judicial authority in order to enforce a penalty of five years' imprisonment imposed on a Portuguese national residing in France where he, like Kozłowski and Wolzenburg, does not wish to consent to his surrender. Article 695-24 of the French Code of Criminal Procedure provides that the execution of an EAW may be refused if the person sought for the purpose of execution of a sentence is of French nationality and the competent French authorities undertake to carry out that enforcement. The requested person has before the national court with reference to *Wolzenburg* and Article 18 TFEU challenged the French partial implementation of Article 4(6) of the EAW. It is against this background that the French referring court asks, inter alia, whether 'the principle of the implementation in domestic law of the grounds for non-enforcement provided for in Article 4(6) of the EAW [is] a matter for the discretion of the Member States or is . . . compulsory'.

[21] The case was referred because, on the one hand, under Art 80(3) of the German Law on International Mutual Legal Assistance in Criminal Matters (Gesetz über die internationale Rechtshilfe in Strafsachen), as amended by the implementing law on the European Arrest Warrant (Europäisches Haftbefehlsgesetz), a European arrest warrant concerning a German national may not be executed if that person does not consent to his surrender. On the other hand, under Art 83b of that same law, the lack of consent of a national of another Member State can only lead to a refusal if execution of the custodial sentence in Germany is justified by an interest that deserves protection. The referring court pointed out that those provisions, in so far as they favour German nationals and make no distinction with regard to nationals of other Member States and those of third States, where adopted following a judgment of the Bundesverfassungsgericht of 18 July 2005 declaring the earlier law to be unconstitutional on the ground that it infringed, in a disproportionate manner, the fundamental right of every German not to be extradited.

[22] *Kozłowski*, n 6 above, paras 53, 56.

As the Court is again faced with this basic issue, which ought to have been resolved by the EU legislator, it must be recalled that Article 4(6) of the EAW is just one of a fairly long list of optional grounds for refusal of an EAW and that any solution found for Article 4(6) should probably also be applicable to these other grounds.

ON MUTUAL RECOGNITION AND THE PROTECTION OF FUNDAMENTAL RIGHTS

Mutual Trust is Good – But it Has its Limits

When a Member State is handling a traditional request for extradition from a third country, the protection of fundamental rights in the requesting State may become an issue. From time to time it happens that either the administrative or the judicial authorities of the executing State feel compelled to turn down a request for extradition precisely because they consider that the protection of fundamental rights is insufficient in the issuing State – either in general or specifically as concerns the requested person.[23] It is sometimes discussed to what extent the executing Member State is allowed – or even obliged – to carry out a similar control of the protection of fundamental rights in the issuing Member State when confronted with an EAW.

It has been argued that as a general rule, and following the principle of mutual trust as a necessary precondition for mutual recognition, the point of departure is that the executing Member State should normally rely on the checks made in this respect by the judicial authorities in the issuing Member State which has issued the EAW under an obligation to respect the fundamental rights of the requested person.[24] It follows from the Treaties that all Member States of the Union are under an obligation to respect the ECHR and a number of other instruments of international law which form part of the *acquis communautaire*. Against this background it does not seem unjustified to conclude that there is a presumption that an issuing Member State lives up to these basic obligations under primary Union law and respects fundamental rights.

However, this presumption, like any other presumption, can be falsified or it may – due to unfortunate developments in the conditions in a Member State – disappear. Earlier this year the ECtHR passed its judgment in *MSS v Belgium and*

[23] In a judgment of 30 June 2011, the Østre Landsret (Eastern Regional Court, Denmark) decided not to extradite a Danish citizen to India where he was to be prosecuted for having participated in the dumping of weapons from an aircraft in West Bengal. It was due to the existence of a real risk that the requested person would be treated contrary to Art 3 of the ECHR that such request was turned down. See U.2011.2904 Ø.

[24] Art 1(3) of the EAW makes it clear that the Framework Decision 'shall not have the effect of modifying the obligation to respect fundamental rights and fundamental legal principles as enshrined in Art 6 [TEU]'. It follows from recital ten that the mechanism of the EAW may be suspended only in the event of a serious and persistent breach by one of the Member States of the principles set out in Art 6(1) TEU.

Greece (App No 30696/09) involving the Dublin Regulation based on inter-State confidence and directives supplementing this regulation.[25] In this judgment Greece was condemned for lack of respect for the fundamental rights of the asylum seekers present in Greece, including those returned to Greece from other EU Member States in conformity with the Dublin Regulation. Secondly, Belgium was condemned for returning asylum seekers to Greece in spite of the treatment the returned third country nationals were given in Greece. Belgium submitted essentially that it had been justified to assume that another Member State, here Greece, would honour its obligations under the ECHR and comply with EU legislation on asylum. This argument did not convince the judges at the ECtHR. Their judgment must be read to imply that although such a presumption of respect of fundamental rights in another Member State does exist, it had *in concreto* disappeared in the case of the treatment of returned asylum seekers in Greece. The indications of the insufficient treatment of returned asylum seekers in Greece were of such a serious nature that Belgium could no longer ignore them and continue to return asylum seekers under the Dublin Regulation without addressing effectively the issue of fundamental rights.

It must be assumed that the ECtHR will eventually reason in a similar way as concerns the protection of fundamental rights vis-a-vis instruments of EU penal law and penal procedural law, like the Framework Decision on the EAW. The executing Member State can normally rely on a presumption that fundamental rights have been and will be respected by the issuing Member State.[26] But if specific circumstances indicate a serious deterioration of the protection of fundamental rights in the issuing Member State, then a situation might develop where the executing Member State cannot pretend not to see the problem. The requested Member State does not have the right, which the British Admiral Nelson claimed at the occasion of the naval battle at Copenhagen on 2 April 1801, 'to turn a blind eye'.

(Mutual) Trust is Good, but is Control Better?

More recently the ECtHR, in a judgment of 12 July 2011 in *Šneersone and Kampanella v Italy* (App No 14737/09) in another old third pillar area, more specifically in the area of co-operation in civil matters, seems to develop its *Neulinger*

[25] Council Regulation No 343/2003 of 18 February 2003 establishing the criteria and mechanisms for determining the Member State responsible for examining an asylum application lodged on one of the Member States by a third-country national, [2003] OJ L50/1.

[26] This was what the Court held in Case C-261/09 *Mantello*, judgment of 16 November 2010 nyr, on the interpretation of the *ne bis in idem* ground for mandatory non-execution in Art 3(2) of the EAW. An Italian judge had issued an EAW requesting a German judge to surrender a convicted person. The German judge referred a question to the Court wanting to know whether he was allowed to check to which extent it was correct, as the Italian judge held in his request, that the principle of *ne bis in idem* did not apply to the judgment founding the EAW. The Court (see para 51) held that the executing German judicial authority had no reason to apply, in the circumstances of the case, the ground for mandatory non-execution provided for in Art 3(2) of the EAW.

jurisprudence (App No 41615/07) somewhat further in a case concerning parental custody.

In this case, which concerned a young boy, Marko, of an Italian father and a Latvian mother, Italy was condemned by the ECtHR because an Italian court, in breach of the ECHR, had ordered the child, living with his mother in Latvia, to be returned to his Italian father in Italy without taking full account of the family situation of the child in Latvia, although such considerations are not a precondition according to the Hague Convention on the Civil Aspects of International Child Abduction or Regulation No 2201/2003 concerning jurisdiction in matters of parental responsibility.[27]

The facts of the case and the position of the applicants can fairly briefly be summarised as follows. While still living in Italy, the mother was granted custody of Marko in September 2004 by the Rome Youth Court. The father's appeal against this decision was rejected as the Court of Appeal found that the mother was unlikely to take Marko to Latvia without the father's consent. In June 2005 a passport was issued to Marko. In April 2006 the mother returned to Latvia with her son because of lack of financial means. In June 2006 the Rome Youth Court granted the father interim sole custody of Mark and ordered his return to Italy.

In accordance with the Hague Convention, the Italian authorities issued, in January 2007, a request for Marko to be returned to Italy. The Latvian authorities initiated civil proceedings against the mother in accordance with Article 7 of the Hague Convention. In March 2007, the Latvian courts decided that Marko's return to Italy would not be compatible with his best interests. In April 2008 the Rome Youth Court, upon request from the father, ordered Marko's immediate return to Italy on the basis of Regulation No 2201/2003. In August 2008, the Italian authorities invited Latvia to enforce the return order made by the Youth Court in Rome. The mother's appeal of this decision was rejected. In July 2009, the bailiff of the Latvian court charged with the execution of the Rome Youth Court decision from April 2008 invited Marko's father to re-establish contact with his son. Marko's father did not react to this request.

In October 2008, Latvia brought the matter before the European Commission in accordance with Article 227 TEC (now Article 259 TFUE) claiming infringement of EU law. It alleged, in particular, that the proceedings in Italy did not conform to Regulation No 2001/2003. The Commission, in its reasoned opinion, held that Italy had violated neither the Regulation nor the 'general principles of Community law'.

Relying in particular on Article 8 ECHR on the right to family life, the applicants argued before the ECtHR that the Italian court decision ordering Marko's return to Italy did not take into account his best interests and constituted a violation of international and Latvian law.

[27] Regulation (EC) No 2201/2003 of 27 November 2003 concerning jurisdiction and the recognition and enforcement of judgments in matrimonial matters and the matters of parental responsibility, repealing Regulation (EC) No 1347/2000, [2003] OJ L338/1.

On this factual background it is perhaps not difficult to understand that the substance of the case may well give rise to different opinions. This is very often the situation in cases on parental responsibility, where a court decision should normally be, if not the very last resort, then the last but one. It becomes particularly delicate when a court has to balance the need to do justice following a wrongful 'abduction' of the child by one parent against the need to let the interests of the child prevail.

One might say that to establish a coherent European framework on the judicial competences in this highly sensitive area – and thus facilitating this balancing act – is the essential and specific raison d'être behind Regulation No 2201/2003. Articles 8 and 10 of the Regulation, which are not quoted in the judgment of the ECtHR, establishes the general principle that the court(s) in the Member State where the child had its habitual residence before it was wrongfully removed by one parent will retain their jurisdiction in spite of the fact that the child following the wrongful removal is now de facto residing in another Member State. The basic idea behind the Regulation is that the decisions, including interim decisions, are generally best taken in the Member State where the child has so far been legally staying and that a parent should normally not by way of a one-sided, wrongful removal of the child be allowed to go shopping for another forum.

What is normally considered paramount in such cases is the need for a quick and final decision of the venue of law and eventually a quick return of the child. This is because any delay – even a short one – tends to point towards eventually accepting the status quo, as most judges, regardless of their nationality, after the elapse of many months or even several years will be very reluctant to order the surrender of a small child, even if the child was at the outset manifestly unlawfully removed by one of the parents; the welfare of the child must take precedence over the more abstract justice between the parents.

These considerations point towards a rather direct application of the principle of mutual recognition based on mutual trust in respect of a judicial decision that orders the return of the wrongfully removed child.[28] It also has to be admitted that such an application of mutual recognition is hardly compatible with an extensive use of double control proceedings which are essentially based on mutual distrust between the judicial authorities of the Member States. In this respect it seems to me that the judgment in *Šneersone* could be read to imply that a court in the issuing Member State has a far-reaching duty not only to take into account available information on the current situation in another Member State of a wrongfully removed child, but also actively to seek such information before taking, eventually, even an interim decision, on the immediate return of the unlawfully removed child.

Further the *Šneersone* judgment seems to grant the requested Member State a rather wide possibility – perhaps even an obligation – to scrutinise the protection of the child's fundamental rights in the issuing Member State. To the extent that this is a correct reading of the judgment in *Šneersone* there seems to be a real risk

[28] See recitals 2, 12, 17, 21 and 23 of Regulation (EC) No 2201/2003.

that this jurisprudence might severely compromise the *effet utile* of Regulation No 2201/2003 in particular, but not exclusively, in cases of child abductions.

Further Implications of *Šneersone* – Final Remarks

There seems to be no particular reason why such a jurisprudence should be limited to mutual recognition in one specific part of the Area of Freedom, Security and Justice (civil law co-operation on child custody), and should not affect mutual recognition in another part of that area (such as penal law co-operation). It seems to me that the possible implications of the *Šneersone* judgment merit careful reflection not only by the EU legislator when considering future application of the concept of mutual recognition, but also by the European courts in Luxembourg and Strasbourg, when seeking the right balance between mutual recognition and protection of fundamental rights, between mutual trust and controls. This issue is perhaps of such importance for maintaining an '*area of freedom, security and justice with respect for fundamental rights*' (Article 67 TFEU) that it deserves to be given special consideration in the context of the ongoing negotiations on the accession of the EU to the ECHR.

11

Administrative Law as a Key to Market Integration?

JÖRGEN HETTNE*

INTRODUCTION

JUDGE LINDH WAS a Union Judge from 1995 to 2011. In this article I will explore a legal development that has mainly taken place during this period and which is also closely connected with important Swedish cases such as *Franzén* and *Hanner*. We may call it the administrative law influence or the proceduralisation of the Single Market rules, which put a special emphasis on transparency, the obligation to state reasons and the possibility of challenging decisions before an independent board.

THE GROWING IMPORTANCE OF GENERAL PRINCIPLES OF ADMINISTRATIVE LAW

General principles of law, such as legal certainty, good administration, rights of defence, the obligation to state reasons and access to justice have become more and more important in cases regarding free movement, State aid, public procurement and competition law. These principles provided guidance in the early days for the development of Union law especially within the framework of administrative procedures. Such procedures are typically relevant when the Commission is dealing with matters in, for example, the competition and State aid sector and also when power has been attributed to a particular EU authority, such as, for instance, the Office for Harmonisation of the Internal Market (OHIM). A reason why general principles of law have been particularly important in this context is that the EU lacks a general administrative law which normally exists in the Member States. On the basis of general principles of law the ECJ has instead created an *unwritten European administrative law*. The most basic principles are enshrined in the Charter of Fundamental Rights. Article 41, headed 'Right to good administration', is worded as follows:

* Senior Researcher and Deputy Head of Agency at the Swedish Institute for European Policy Studies, SIEPS. Associate Professor of EU Law at the University of Lund.

> 1. Every person has the right to have his or her affairs handled impartially, fairly and within a reasonable time by the institutions, bodies, offices and agencies of the Union.
>
> This right includes:
>
> (a) the right of every person to be heard, before any individual measure which would affect him or her adversely is taken;
> (b) the right of every person to have access to his or her file, while respecting the legitimate interests of confidentiality and of professional and business secrecy;
> (c) the obligation of the administration to give reasons for its decisions.

In addition, Article 47 provides:

> Everyone whose rights and freedoms guaranteed by the Union law are violated has the right to an effective remedy before a tribunal in compliance with the conditions laid down in this Article.
>
> Everyone is entitled to a fair and public hearing within a reasonable time by an independent and impartial tribunal previously established by law. Everyone shall have the possibility of being advised, defended and represented.
>
> Legal aid shall be made available to those who lack sufficient resources in so far as such aid is necessary to ensure effective access to justice.

Of particular interest in the present context is that the general principles of administrative law have importance not only in connection with administrative processes before EU institutions. The ECJ has also referred to general legal principles of an administrative law nature in order to define the meaning of the four freedoms, that is, free movement of goods (including the provisions on State monopolies), services, persons and capital. Moreover, the Charter is applicable when Union law is implemented in the Member States (Article 51). Hence, these general principles limit the scope for Member States to erect barriers to free movement and can therefore be seen as a complement to the basic principles of equal treatment and proportionality. It is therefore permissible to speak of an *administrative law dimension of free movement.*[1]

This dimension has made a particularly important impact in the field of health care services. On the basis of Article 56 TFEU, on the free movement of services, the ECJ has introduced a list of requirements as regards national licensing systems that are comparable with the provisions in national legislation on administrative law in many Member States. Another interesting development concerns the judgments of the ECJ regarding the Swedish alcohol and pharmacy monopolies which will be described next.

[1] *cf* J Hettne, *Rättsprinciper som styrmedel* (Stockholm, Norstedts juridik, 2008) ch 4.

THE SWEDISH RETAIL MONOPOLY ON ALCOHOL

Sweden Accession Negotiations

The discussion whether the Swedish alcohol monopoly was compatible with Union law started during the preparation for the entry into force of the Agreement on the European Economic Area (EEA), which basically contains the same requirements for monopolies of a commercial character as Article 37 TFEU. The Swedish government was initially unresponsive to any adjustment to the alcohol monopoly. In the government Bill regarding the EEA Agreement, the government argued, for example, that:

> The current system of state monopolies for the import, wholesale and retail sale of alcoholic beverages does not contain any elements discriminatory of foreign manufacturers or wholesalers. On the Swedish market domestic and imported goods compete on equal terms. The monopolies are thus not discriminatory in the sense of the Treaty of Rome.

However, prior to the entry into force of the EEA Agreement on 1 January 1994, the accession negotiations with the EU had already begun. The European Commission emphasised during the preparatory talks that Swedish alcohol legislation had to be adjusted in the context of impending membership of the Union. The government Bill on Swedish accession to the EU thus stated:

> During the negotiations regarding membership of the EU, [. . .] an exchange of letters took place between the Commission and the Swedish Government.[2] In this correspondence the Commission claimed that import, export, wholesale trade and manufacturing monopolies are incompatible with the EC treaty. As regards the retail monopoly, the Commission considers that if all elements that are discriminatory between domestic products and those imported from other member countries are removed, there is no reason for the Commission to take measures, on its own initiative, against this monopoly.

After discussion with the Commission the Swedish government revised its views on the need to adjust the national monopoly on alcohol. The government's new approach was to safeguard the retail monopoly, while abolishing the monopolies on import, export, wholesale trade and manufacturing.

In addition, the Swedish retail monopoly had to be changed in order to become consistent with Union law. It had to be tolerable from an internal market perspective. To this end, certain administrative conditions were introduced, the so-called 'elements necessary to ensure non-discrimination'. According to the Commission, non-discrimination entailed objective rules regarding the purchase and sales of alcoholic beverages which were applied equally to every Union citizen and Union product and which were transparent. The Commission underlined that the latter point meant that these rules must be public. The Swedish government accepted

[2] Letter dated 22 December 1993, Meeting with Sweden on Alcohol Monopoly, attached to the Bill on Swedish Accession to the EU (Prop 1994/95:19) annex 12.

this interpretation. In the letter from the Commission, it was finally stated that the measures which should guarantee the objective of non-discrimination discussed during the preparatory talks were not exhaustive but indicative. The minutes of the meeting would thus constitute guidance for Sweden as regards the retail monopoly's obligation to function in a non-discriminatory manner.

In the light of this exchange of letters, an objective product plan for the beverages provided by Systembolaget (the retail monopoly) was introduced. Furthermore, according to the new agreement between the Swedish government and Systembolaget, the beverages should be selected in accordance with predetermined and objective criteria and suppliers who were not allowed to sell their products to Systembolaget should be informed about the reasons for this and be entitled to challenge such decisions before an independent board (Alkoholsortimentsnämnden).

Franzén

The Swedish adaptation to EU requirements, and in particular the maintenance of Systembolaget, was however contested immediately following Sweden's entry into the EU. This occurred in the *Franzén* case.[3] Harry Franzén was prosecuted in Landskrona tingsrätt (Landskrona District Court) for having sold, in his own retail store on 1 January 1995, the day when Sweden joined the EU, wine that the prosecutor claimed he had either bought at Systembolaget or imported from Denmark. The District Court requested a preliminary ruling from the ECJ.

The ECJ reviewed the retail monopoly in accordance with the requirements set during the Swedish negotiations. As regards Article 37 TFEU (at that time Article 31 EC), the ECJ pointed out that the organisation and operation of the monopoly should be arranged:

so as to exclude any discrimination between nationals of Member States as regards conditions of supply and outlets,
so that trade in goods from other Member States is not put at a disadvantage, in law or in fact, in relation to that in domestic goods and
so that competition between the economies of the Member States is not distorted.

Thereafter, the Court noted that it was not contested that, in aiming to protect public health against the harm caused by alcohol, a domestic monopoly on the retail of alcoholic beverages, such as that conferred on Systembolaget, pursued a public interest aim.

Next, the Court assessed the Swedish system and drew attention in particular to the following circumstances:

- There was an objective product plan for beverages provided by Systembolaget.
- The beverages were selected by Systembolaget on the basis of predetermined and objective criteria (commercial criteria and qualitative criteria).

[3] Case C-189/95 *Franzén* [1997] ECR I-5909.

- There were alternative ways for traders to have their products marketed by the monopoly: those whose offers were not selected by Systembolaget could ask for their products to undergo a second qualitative test before a panel of consumers.
- Traders were entitled to be informed about the reasons for decisions taken by the monopoly.
- There was a possibility to challenge decisions before a board offering every guarantee of independence (Alkoholsortimentsnämnden).

In light of this, the ECJ concluded that the criteria and selection methods used by Systembolaget did not appear to be either discriminatory or apt to put imported products at a disadvantage.

Hanner

A couple of years later, the Swedish monopoly on pharmacies was also challenged. Krister Hanner, general manager of Bringwell International AB, had been accused of having sold non-prescription medicines (Nicorette patches and chewing gum) in a health store in violation of Swedish law which reserved retail sales of these kinds of products to *Apoteket* (the State owned monopoly on pharmacies). The case came before Stockholms tingsrätt (Stockholm District Court), which requested a preliminary ruling from the ECJ.

The ECJ tested the Swedish monopoly on pharmacies by the same yardstick as in *Franzén*. The Court pointed out that Article 37 TFEU (at that time Article 31 EC) does not require total abolition of state monopolies of a commercial character; they only have to be adjusted in such a way as to ensure that no discrimination regarding the conditions under which goods are procured and marketed exists between nationals of Member States.[4]

As was also stressed in *Franzén*, the Court underlined that the purpose of Article 37 is to reconcile the possibility for Member States to maintain certain monopolies of a commercial character as instruments for the pursuit of public interest aims with the requirements of the establishment and functioning of the common market. The Court pointed out that Article 37 aims to eliminate obstacles to the free movement of goods, save, however, for restrictions on trade which are inherent in the existence of the monopolies in question. Monopolies are not allowed if they are arranged in such a way as to put at a disadvantage, in law or in fact, trade in goods from other Member States as compared with trade in domestic goods.

Thereafter, the Court assessed whether the contested sales regime was arranged in such a way as to exclude any discrimination against goods from other Member States. In particular, the Court examined whether the way in which the State monopoly in question was organised and operated was liable to place medicinal preparations from other Member States at a disadvantage.

[4] Case C-438/02 *Hanner* [2005] ECR I-4551.

The Court pointed out that it followed from its judgment in *Franzén* that the selection system of a sales monopoly must be based on criteria that are independent from the origin of the products and *must be transparent by providing both for an obligation to state reasons for decisions and for an independent monitoring procedure*. Moreover, the retail network of such a monopoly must be organised in such a way that the number of sales outlets is not limited to the point of compromising consumers' procurement of supplies and, finally, such a monopoly's marketing and advertising measures must be impartial and independent of the origin of the products and must endeavour to make new products known to consumers.

Since the monopoly on pharmacies had not been adjusted at all in accordance with the EU legal requirements listed in *Franzén*, the Court limited itself to stating that the Swedish system for the retail sale of medicinal preparations did not contain any provision for a purchasing plan or for a system of 'calls for tenders' within the framework of which producers whose products are not selected would be entitled to be apprised of the reasons for the selection decision. Nor does it provide for any opportunity to contest such decisions before an independent supervisory authority. The Court considered that, on the contrary, under Swedish law, Apoteket appeared, in principle, to be entirely free to select a product range of its choice.

The Court found that those circumstances constituted a sufficient basis for finding that the way in which Apoteket was organised and operated, and more particularly its system of selecting medicinal preparations, was liable to place trade in medicinal preparations from other Member States at a disadvantage as compared with trade in Swedish medicinal preparations. Thus, that State monopoly was not arranged in such a way as to exclude any discrimination against medicinal preparations from other Member States.

Accordingly, the ECJ compared Apoteket with Systembolaget and required that it should be adjusted correspondingly. The ruling should be interpreted in such a way that if a product plan is established and a system of 'calls for tenders' (or other system that guarantees every independence and an objective selection of products) as well as requirements on motivation and legal review by an independent supervisory body, the Swedish monopoly should be considered to be designed in such a way that it prima facie is consistent with Article 37 TFEU. However, if de facto discrimination is revealed, the monopoly is not consistent with Article 37 TFEU.[5]

DEVELOPMENT OF ADMINISTRATIVE LAW IN OTHER AREAS

In order to explain the importance of the administrative law dimension of free movement, examples from different areas will now be presented. At the same

[5] See J Hettne, 'Transforming Monopolies: EU-Adjustment or Social Changes?' in S Gustavsson, L Oxelheim and L Pehrson (eds), *How Unified Is the European Union? – European Integration Between Visions and Popular Legitimacy* (Berlin, Springer, 2009) 106.

time, this illustrates the *general application* of these principles. In the following, cases regarding public procurement, health care and gaming monopolies will be described.

Public Procurement

The clearest link between the principle of equal treatment and transparency is probably to be found in the area of procurement. In this context, the Member States cannot uphold exemptions from the principles of free movement, but the contracting authorities are attributed a significant margin of discretion in the selection of tenders, which put these authorities in a similar position to a regulatory authority having power to impede access to the market. To limit this discretion and make sure that the procurement process is fair, that is, meets the requirement of equal treatment, contracting authorities must carefully formulate criteria for evaluation of tenders and award of contracts in advance. Against this background, the ECJ has held:

> that the principle of equal treatment, which underlies the directives on procedures for the award of public contracts, implies in particular an obligation of transparency in order to enable verification that it has been complied with.[6]

Furthermore, the Court has emphasised that the obligation of transparency consists of ensuring, for the benefit of any potential tenderer, a degree of advertising sufficient to enable the services market to be opened up to competition and the impartiality of procurement procedures to be reviewed.[7] Therefore, the procedure for comparing tenders has to comply at every stage with both the principle of the equal treatment of tenderers and the principle of transparency so as to afford equality of opportunity to all tenderers when formulating their tenders.[8]

The Court has explained its case law by stating that the grant of a concession, in the absence of any transparency, to an operator located in the Member State of the awarding authority constitutes a difference in treatment to the detriment of operators located in other Member States, who have no real possibility of manifesting their interest in obtaining the concession in question. Such a difference in treatment is contrary to the principle of equal treatment and the prohibition of discrimination on grounds of nationality, and constitutes indirect discrimination on grounds of nationality prohibited by Articles 43 EC and 49 EC (now Articles 49 and 56 TFEU), unless it is justified by objective circumstances.[9] The Court's

[6] See, eg Case C-275/98 *Unitron Scandinavia and 3-S v Ministeriet for Fødevarer, Landbrug og Fiskeri* [1999] ECR I-8291, para 31; Case C-324/98 *Telaustria and Telefonadress v Telekom Austria* [2000] ECR I-10745, para 61.

[7] *Telaustria and Telefonadress v Telekom Austria*, n 6 above, para 62.

[8] *cf* J Hettne and U Öberg, 'Fritt skön och domstolskontroll vid offentlig upphandling' (2005) *Svensk Juristtidning* 192; BJ Drijber and H Stergiou, 'Public Procurement Law and Internal Market Law' (2009) 46 *CML Rev* 805.

[9] See, eg Case C-347/06 *ASM Brescia* [2008] ECR I-5641, paras 59–60.

approach is thus very critical towards non transparent schemes, since they lack all guarantees of equal treatment.

Health Care

As has already been mentioned, the administrative law dimension of free movement has had a particularly important impact in the field of health care services. The development started with the rulings from the ECJ in *Decker* and *Kohl.*[10] It came as a surprise for many Member States that the ECJ in these judgments rejected a requirement of prior authorisation for health care in another Member State. The Court based its conclusions on the right for EU citizens to receive services in other Member States, including health services. The Court ruled that the requirement for prior authorisation impedes the exercise of medical services and will therefore be in conflict with the present Article 56 TFEU on the free movement of services. Therefore, the conditions attached to the grant of such authorisation must be justified in the light of the overriding considerations to society and must satisfy the requirement of proportionality.

The Court found that the requirement for prior authorisation for medical treatment abroad could not be justified at all as regards non-hospital (extramural) care, such as orthodontics. The Court has, however, in subsequent cases, established a difference between such care and hospital (intramural) care. It is only when care is provided by hospitals that a requirement for prior authorisation can be justified. The reason for this is that the care provided by hospitals has certain characteristics that care provided in a doctor's practice or at home visits do not have. In the case of hospital care it is considered that the Member States have an urge to control and plan the number of hospitals, their geographical distribution, the way in which they are organised and the facilities with which they are provided, and even the nature of the medical services which they are able to offer. The Court considers that such planning seeks to ensure that there is sufficient and permanent access to a balanced range of high-quality hospital treatment in the State concerned. For another thing, it assists in meeting a desire to control costs and to prevent, as far as possible, any wastage of financial, technical and human resources.

Nevertheless – and importantly in the present context – if a condition of a system of prior authorisation is applied, it must in any event be based on *objective, non-discriminatory criteria which are known in advance, in such a way as to circumscribe the exercise of the national authorities' discretion, so that it is not used arbitrarily.* Such a system must furthermore be based on a procedural system which is easily accessible and capable of ensuring that a request for authorisation will be dealt with objectively and impartially within a reasonable time *and refusals to grant authorisation must also be capable of being challenged in judicial or quasi-*

[10] Case C-120/95 *Decker* [1998] ECR I-1831; Case C-158/96 *Kohll* [1988] ECR I-1931.

judicial proceedings.[11] To that end, refusals to grant authorisation, or the advice on which such refusals may be based, must refer to the specific provisions on which they are based and be properly reasoned in accordance with them. Likewise, courts or tribunals hearing actions against such refusals must be able, if they consider it necessary for the purpose of carrying out the review which it is incumbent on them to make, to seek the advice of wholly objective and impartial independent experts.[12]

Gaming Monopolies

As regards lotteries and gaming, state monopolies or other types of exclusive rights are common in the Member States of the EU. The ECJ has for a long time taken a prudent approach. Illustrative of this cautious approach is the following statement in the *Schindler* case:

> First of all, it is not possible to disregard the moral, religious or cultural aspects of lotteries, like other types of gambling, in all the Member States. The general tendency of the Member States is to restrict, or even prohibit, the practice of gambling and to prevent it from being a source of private profit. Secondly, lotteries involve a high risk of crime or fraud, given the size of the amounts which can be staked and of the winnings which they can hold out to the players, particularly when they are operated on a large scale. Thirdly, they are an incitement to spend which may have damaging individual and social consequences. A final ground which is not without relevance, although it cannot in itself be regarded as an objective justification, is that lotteries may make a significant contribution to the financing of benevolent or public interest activities such as social works, charitable works, sport or culture.

Those particular factors justify national authorities having a *sufficient degree of latitude* to determine what is required to protect the players and, more generally, in the light of the specific social and cultural features of each Member State, to maintain order in society, as regards the manner in which lotteries are operated, the size of the stakes, and the allocation of the profits they yield. In those circumstances, it is for them to assess not only whether it is necessary to restrict the activities of lotteries but also whether they should be prohibited, provided that those restrictions are not discriminatory.

In subsequent cases regarding similar issues, the Court has asked the national court which requested the preliminary ruling to carry out this seemingly limited proportionality test itself. However, in some cases the Court has given clear indications of the circumstances which the national court should take into account when it carries out that proportionality test.

Also in this area, the Court has tried to circumscribe the exercise of the national authorities' discretion, so that it is not used arbitrarily. The Court has declared

[11] See Case C-157/99 *Smits and Peerbooms* [2001] ECR I-5473, para 90; Case C-385/99 *Müller-Fauré and van Riet* [2003] ECR I-4509, para 85; Case C-372/04 *Watts* [2006] ECR I-4325, para 116.

[12] See Case C-56/01 *Inizan* [2003] ECR I-12403, para 49.

that as regards licences to operate gaming establishments, *the obligation of transparency* amounts to a condition which must be met before a Member State can exercise its right to award licences. According to the Court, when a licensing system pursuing legitimate objectives recognised by the case law is introduced in a Member State, such licensing system cannot render legitimate discretionary conduct on the part of the national authorities which is liable to negate the effectiveness of provisions of Union law, in particular those relating to the fundamental freedoms.[13]

The Court pointed out that it has consistently been held that if a prior administrative authorisation scheme is to be justified even though it derogates from such fundamental freedoms, *it must be based on objective, non-discriminatory criteria known in advance, in such a way as to circumscribe the exercise of the national authorities' discretion so that it is not used arbitrarily*. Furthermore, any person affected by a restrictive measure based on such derogation must have an *effective judicial remedy available to him*.[14]

SERVICE DIRECTIVE

The administrative conditions mentioned above have also found their way into the Service Directive[15] and are therefore now codified and generally applicable in a large part of the service sector. Article 9 in the Directive introduces conditions for 'Authorisation schemes'. According to this Article:

1. Member States shall not make access to a service activity or the exercise thereof subject to an authorisation scheme unless the following conditions are satisfied:
   (a) the authorisation scheme does not discriminate against the provider in question;
   (b) the need for an authorisation scheme is justified by an overriding reason relating to the public interest;
   (c) the objective pursued cannot be attained by means of a less restrictive measure, in particular because an a posteriori inspection would take place too late to be genuinely effective.

Article 10 provides the necessary conditions for the granting of authorisation. This Article is worded in the following way:

1. Authorisation schemes shall be based on criteria which preclude the competent authorities from exercising their power of assessment in an arbitrary manner.
2. The criteria referred to in paragraph 1 shall be:

[13] See, in particular, Case C-203/08 *Sporting Exchange*, judgment of 3 June 2010 nyr, para 49; Case C-46/08 *Carmen Media Group*, judgment of 8 September 2010 nyr, para 86; Case C-64/08 *Engelmann*, judgment of 9 September 2010 nyr, para 54.

[14] See *Sporting Exchange*, n 13 above, para 50; *Carmen Media Group*, n 13 above, para 87; *Engelmann*, n 13 above, para 55.

[15] Directive 2006/123/EC of the European Parliament and of the Council of 12 December 2006 on services in the internal market, [2006] OJ L376/36.

(a) non-discriminatory;
(b) justified by an overriding reason relating to the public interest;
(c) proportionate to that public interest objective;
(d) clear and unambiguous;
(e) objective;
(f) made public in advance;
(g) transparent and accessible.

Under paragraph 6 it is added that except in the case of the granting of an authorisation, any decision from the competent authorities, including refusal or withdrawal of an authorisation, shall be *fully reasoned and shall be open to challenge before the courts or other instances of appeal.*

Article 13 in the Directive concerns authorisation procedures:

1. Authorisation procedures and formalities shall be clear, made public in advance and be such as to provide the applicants with a guarantee that their application will be dealt with objectively and impartially.
2. Authorisation procedures and formalities shall not be dissuasive and shall not unduly complicate or delay the provision of the service. They shall be easily accessible and any charges which the applicants may incur from their application shall be reasonable and proportionate to the cost of the authorisation procedures in question and shall not exceed the cost of the procedures.
3. Authorisation procedures and formalities shall provide applicants with a guarantee that their application will be processed as quickly as possible and, in any event, within a reasonable period which is fixed and made public in advance. The period shall run only from the time when all documentation has been submitted. When justified by the complexity of the issue, the time period may be extended once, by the competent authority, for a limited time. The extension and its duration shall be duly motivated and shall be notified to the applicant before the original period has expired. [. . .]
5. All applications for authorisation shall be acknowledged as quickly as possible. The acknowledgement must specify the following:

   (a) the period referred to in paragraph 3;
   (b) the available means of redress;
   (c) where applicable, a statement that in the absence of a response within the period specified, the authorisation shall be deemed to have been granted.

CONCLUSION

It can be concluded that the requirements imposed on Systembolaget under Article 37 TFEU are comparable with the requirements imposed on an authority responsible for an authorisation scheme according to the Service Directive. Furthermore, similar conditions have been applied in the area of public procurement, gaming monopolies and in the cases regarding cross-border health care. The motive for applying the conditions regarding transparency, motivation and access to justice in these different contexts is that it is important from a legal perspective to limit the discretion conferred on national authorities and monopolies and make sure that they do not act arbitrarily.[16] This development is also highly visible in the Service Directive which makes these conditions generally applicable within its scope. One advantage of this development is that individuals and enterprises affected by a state regulation or another state measure will have an insight into the way in which the measure works and affects its activities. Moreover, if these individuals or enterprises are given the opportunity to appeal against decisions that disadvantage them, such procedure will expose any factual conditions that might perhaps be in conflict with Union law. For the right of appeal to function it is further required that the reasons for decisions should be stated. Supervisory authorities and courts can then check that the state measure is consistent with Union law. Requirements for transparency, statements of reasons and legal remedies are thus important elements in the process of establishing a fully functioning Single Market.

The proper legal context of this development can be discussed. Barnard has called it *proceduralisation of proportionality*.[17] She considers that this line of case law suggests an increasing emphasis on 'good governance' in the states' approach to the question of proportionality. This is perfectly true but I do not think it is entirely correct to see this development *exclusively* as an aspect of proportionality. In cases like *Franzén* and *Hanner*, the principle of proportionality was not even mentioned. In these cases the ECJ seemed rather to draw the administrative requirements from the principle of equality of treatment. They could therefore be termed *structural guarantees for equality of treatment* in the context of these judgments.[18] I believe that a more correct description of this development is that it adds structural or procedural guarantees to the application of different substantive Union law principles, such as equal treatment, proportionality or mutual recognition,[19] depending on the circumstances of each case.

It should also be mentioned that although these structural guarantees are outflows of general principles of law, particularly the principle of good administration or legal certainty, they appear in some cases to be somewhat unforeseeable. As Union law must function in 27 Member States, the standard of clarity and predictability demanded is necessarily high. Legal development through case law does not always create an adequate degree of predictability. If, for example, these requirements apply to the licensing system in respect of prior authorisation in the area of health care (as we know they do), they should logically also apply to all other similar systems that restrict the free movement of services within the single market. It is doubtful if this is generally considered to be the present state of

[16] See A Ericsson, 'Structural Guarantees – the Union's Last Best Hope against National Arbitrariness' (2010) *Europarättslig tidskrift* 237 *ff.*

[17] See C Barnard, *The Substantive Law of the EU – The Four Freedoms*, 2nd edn (Oxford, Oxford University Press, 2007) 85.

[18] See J Hettne, n 1 above; Ericsson, n 16 above.

[19] *cf* Regulation (EC) No 764/2008 of the European Parliament and of the Council of 9 July 2008 laying down procedures relating to the application of certain national technical rules to products lawfully marketed in another Member State and repealing Decision No 3052/95/EC, [2008] OJ L218/21.

Union law. In this regard, the development through the above-mentioned Service Directive is welcomed as it generalises the application of these requirements. Similar development is also visible in the directive on the application of patients' rights in cross-border health care[20] and in the so-called *Altmark* package.[21] However, it seems more appropriate to consolidate and develop the unwritten principles of administrative law in a more general and systematic way. That would then lead to greater predictability and increased legal certainty. A good base for such a development is the Code of Good Administrative Behaviour adopted by the ombudsman. A legal base for the adoption of a regulation with similar content is Article 298 TFEU. This article is, however, directed expressly towards the institutions, bodies, offices and agencies of the Union. A supplementary legal basis seems therefore to be needed in order to include requirements concerning the Member States when they apply Union law.

The administrative dimension is potentially an important key to market integration in the EU. However, the administrative law requirements must not become ends in themselves. They should always promote the purpose, and guarantee the application, of the substantive rules on free movement and fair competition.

[20] Directive 2011/24/EU of the European Parliament and of the Council of 9 March 2011 on the application of patients' rights in cross-border health care, [2010] OJ L88/45.

[21] See, eg the Commission Decision 2012/21/EU of 20 December 2011 on the application of Article 106(2) of the Treaty on the Functioning of the European Union to State aid in the form of public service compensation granted to certain undertakings entrusted with the operation of services of general economic interest [2011] OJ L 7/3.

12

French Administrative Courts and Union Law

JEAN-CLAUDE BONICHOT*

IT IS WIDELY accepted that French administrative law has influenced a number of mechanisms of Community – now Union – law. For example, the recours pour excès de pouvoir (ultra vires action), which is the common form of judicial review in France, is certainly the origin of the action for annulment of Article 263 TFEU. In a similar view the role of the commissaire du gouvernement may be considered as the forerunner to that of the Advocate General at the ECJ. In the mix of the different legal systems of the founding Member States there is no doubt that German and French administrative law were used as the foundation of Union law. However, the relationship between French administrative courts and Union law was not always an easy one. In general, Union law has been applied correctly by these national courts from the outset. Nevertheless, French administrative judges have sometimes been reluctant to agree entirely with some decisions of the ECJ. That was, for example, the case – as, incidentally, in other Member States – with the direct effect of directives. The same can be said about the issue of the relationship between Union law and subsequent national statutes. Although these difficulties have been overcome, it is useful to recall them as they are, one might say, the counterpart of the benefits of French administrative law and of the particular position occupied by administrative courts in France.[1]

From this point of view, two elements must be highlighted. First, throughout the course of history, French administrative courts have developed a set of simple and efficient remedies at the disposal of all citizens. Among these, the well-known recours pour excès de pouvoir has played a major role. Any individual regarded as having an interest – even the slightest – can, without any formality, and notably without legal representation, challenge an administrative act, even a regulatory act, and, if successful, obtain its annulment. One of the foremost experts on French administrative law once noted that: 'the general principles of substantive administrative law are judge-made law, and continue to be developed by the

* Judge of the Court of Justice of the European Union.

[1] For an overview see R Mehdi, 'French Supreme Courts and European Union Law: Between Historical Compromise and Accepted Loyalty' (2011) 48 *CML Rev* 439.

judges'.[2] There is no doubt that it is more difficult in such a situation to depart from time-honoured practices that have proved their worth. Furthermore, under the 'French conception of separation of powers', administrative courts have a great respect for the statutes voted by Parliament. They have built their capacity to review executive acts and their authority over the executive branch and its agencies by relying on Parliament, the embodiment of democracy and the seat of sovereignty. Last but not least, the effectiveness of judicial review itself has led French administrative judges to err on the side of caution. Since the remedies at their disposal are so brutal, their implementation without a minimum of restraint could jeopardise all administrative law.[3]

Today the structure of the administrative court system can be described as follows. At the top is the Conseil d'État, at once court of appeal, legal adviser to the government and even, to a certain extent since the latest modification of the French Constitution,[4] to the Parliament. These functions are obviously carried out in a manner designed to prevent any interference between these advisory and judicial functions, notably by their clear separation based on the fundamental statute governing the administrative judiciary – the law of 24 May 1872. Lower courts are the administrative courts of first instance and, since 1987, the eight administrative courts of appeal. The Conseil d'État now essentially plays the role of a supreme administrative court, hearing appeals against judgments of the administrative courts of appeal on points of law only. However, it also has some exclusive fields of jurisdiction. For example, an action for annulment against a national regulatory act can only be brought before the Conseil d'État. In 2010, more than 175,000 cases in total were brought before the administrative courts of first instance, 27,000 before the courts of appeal, and 9,000 before the Conseil d'État. In the framework of its advisory function in legislative and administrative matters, it has examined 128 statutes and more than 810 regulations.[5]

What can be said about European law? The Conseil d'État, as legal adviser, has always intervened in Union law matters. Administrative judges today ensure full compliance with Union law. Furthermore, it must be pointed out that, in what has become a tradition, some administrative law judges serve in different European institutions.

The three pillars of the Union legal order – primacy, unity and direct effect[6] – are fully taken into account by the administrative courts. After having maintained for some time its refusal to allow Union law to prevail over a more recent statute, the Conseil d'État changed its case law in 1989, in the seminal *Nicolo* judgment.[7] Since then, administrative judges are bound to set aside a national statute which is

[2] J Bell, *Judiciaries within Europe, a Comparative Review* (Cambridge, Cambridge University Press, 2006) 71.

[3] For a description of the current state of the question, see B Genevois, 'L'application du droit communautaire par le Conseil d'État' (2009) *Revue Française de droit administratif* 201.

[4] Constitutional Amendments of 23 July 2008.

[5] For further information see the website of the Conseil d'État: www.conseil-etat.fr.

[6] See A Rosas and L Armati, *EU Constitutional Law* (Oxford, Hart Publishing, 2010) 54 ff.

[7] Conseil d'État, judgment of 20 October 1989, *Nicolo*, Rec CE 190.

incompatible with Union law, even where the national statute was adopted after the relevant provision of Union law. A few months before *Nicolo*, the Conseil d'État had delivered another important judgment stating that the government is obliged to repeal a regulation contrary to Union law or which has become contrary to it, for example when Union law has evolved. In such a case, the refusal to repeal the regulation can be challenged and, when annulled, the court can order the competent authority to repeal it.[8] This case law is general in scope and the Conseil d'État has, for example, examined the compatibility of a statute with a Council decision.[9]

Moreover, French administrative law has long recognised on the simple basis of its own principles, the principle of State liability for loss or damage caused by a breach of Union law.[10] This solution was extended in 2007 when the Conseil d'État held that the State is under the obligation to redress damage caused by any statute breaching any international commitment made by France.[11] In line with the case law of the ECJ deriving from *Köbler*,[12] State liability also exists where the breach of Union law is caused by a court of last resort as stated in *Gestas*.[13] The latter is all the more significant because, although French administrative law does admit State liability for damage caused in the course of judicial functions, it normally excludes it when the damage results from a judgment, under the doctrine of *res judicata*. Thus *Gestas* constitutes an exception in favour of Union law.

The highest French court, the Tribunal des conflits has recently drawn far-reaching consequences from the principle of primacy. It is well known that France, unlike several other European countries, does not have a single body of professional judges. A distinction must be drawn between ordinary civil and criminal courts on the one hand and administrative courts on the other.[14] Each set of courts has its own hierarchy and its own supreme court, the Cour de cassation for civil and criminal courts, and the Conseil d'État for administrative courts. Each branch has is its own field of competences and its own jurisdiction. When a question on the respective competences of both categories arises, it has to be brought before the Tribunal des conflits, where judges from the Conseil d'État sit with an equal number of members of the Cour de cassation. When a case is brought before a court lacking jurisdiction over the matter in dispute, that court must stay the proceedings and the parties are obliged to refer the matter to the competent court of the other branch for a preliminary ruling. For example, that is the case when, in a civil or a criminal case, the legality of an administrative act is called into question, or where, in an administrative case, a question relating to a

[8] Conseil d'État, judgment of 3 February 1989, *Compagnie Alitalia*, Rec CE 44.

[9] Conseil d'État, judgment of 10 January 2001, *Région Guadeloupe*, Rec CE 7.

[10] Conseil d'État, judgment of 28 February 1992, *Société Arizona produits et Philip Morris France*, Rec CE 78.

[11] Conseil d'État, judgment of 8 February 2007, *Gardedieu*, Rec CE 78.

[12] Case C-224/01 *Köbler* [2003] ECR I-10239.

[13] Conseil d'État, judgment of 18 June 2008, *Gestas*, Rec CE 230.

[14] France is not the only State with a system of administrative courts distinct from the judiciary.

civil matter, such as property or nationality, arises. In a recent judgment,[15] the Tribunal des conflits stated that an exception had to be made in cases where the issue relates to the compatibility of a measure with Union law. In that case, a judge from a civil court had been asked to release a farmer from payment of a tax which had been foreseen in a professional agreement between pig producers, and made compulsory by the government, on the ground that the government decision was contrary to Union law. According to the Tribunal des conflits, it flows from the principle of effectiveness of Union law that, as noted in the famous *Simmenthal*[16] judgment, every national court must, in a case falling within its jurisdiction, apply Union law in its entirety and protect the rights which the latter confers on individuals and must accordingly set aside any provision of national law which may conflict with it, whether prior or subsequent to the relevant provision of Union law. Therefore, a civil court, which would normally stay the proceedings and leave the question of the legality of the administrative decisions to be decided by the administrative courts, is entitled to review the legality of the administrative act and to draw all inferences from its finding.[17]

The prevalence of Union law over national law is not, however, boundless. As in other states, French judges have never accepted the absolute authority of Union law over national law. Even if these limits seem rather theoretical, they have led to some interesting legal constructions. In an important case called *Société Arcelor*,[18] the Conseil d'État had to deal with the Union regulatory framework governing greenhouse gas emission quotas. The applicants sought the annulment of a decision refusing to repeal the national regulation implementing Directive 2003/87 relating to the quotas exchange system. They claimed that the directive infringed the constitutional principle of equality since some industrial branches did not fall within the scope of the system and were therefore exempt from its charges. The Conseil d'État stated that, so long as Union law ensures the same level of protection of fundamental rights as in national law – for example constitutional law – it follows from France's membership of the European Union that it is the task of the ECJ, and the ECJ alone, to rule on the validity of the directive. This stand is very close to that of the German constitutional court in its *Solange* judgment. It must be pointed out that the case law of the French constitutional court, the Conseil constitutionnel, takes a similar position. When examining the constitutionality of a statute implementing a directive, it states that since the implementation derives from a constitutional duty, it is not within its remit to call into question the validity of the directive by monitoring the national statute. The only limit is that the implementing measures, and thus the directive itself, cannot infringe a rule or principle 'inherent to the constitutional identity of France'.[19] The scope of this formula, which corresponds to

[15] Tribunal des conflits, judgment of 17 October 2011, *Préfet de la region Bretagne*, nos 3828 and 2829 nyr.

[16] Case 106/77 *Simmenthal* [1978] ECR 629.

[17] See F Donnat, 'Abandon de la jurisprudence *Septfonds*: Le droit de l'Union en demandait-il autant?' *Recueil Dalloz* no 44, 22 December 2011, 3046.

[18] Conseil d'État, judgment of 8 February 2007, *Société Arcelor*, Rec CE 55.

[19] Conseil constitutionnel, judgment of 12 May 2010, no 2010-605 DC.

that of the Treaty itself,[20] is not very clear. It is generally understood, in France, as encompassing at least the principle of secularity.

Concerning the relationship between constitutional law and Union law, the Conseil d'État has also rendered an important judgment drawing the limits between constitutional and administrative review. Since 2008,[21] questions can be referred to the French constitutional court by the Conseil d'État or the Cour de cassation when issues of constitutionality arise, for example where one litigant alleges that a statute is contrary to the Constitution. In its *M'Rida* judgment, the Conseil d'État held that when a statute has been considered compatible with the Constitution, or when the constitutional court offers remedies despite the unconstitutionality of a statute,[22] it is up to the court deciding on the merits to verify, in addition, whether the statute is also compatible with Union law, since it is not part of the competences of the constitutional court to do so.[23]

Finally, it must be pointed out that administrative judges also apply the general principles of Union law such as legal certainty, proportionality or protection of legitimate expectation.[24] These principles are considered as having, in accordance with the case law of the ECJ, the same value as primary law. The government is thus bound by the principle of protection of legitimate expectation when it implements a regulation in the area of the Common Agricultural Policy. However, general principles of Union law apply only where they are in a nexus with Union law. That is not the case when an applicant seeks the annulment of a national regulation on waste which is not aimed at implementing Union law.[25] In addition, a general principle of Union law cannot prevail over a constitutional rule[26] since the Constitution is, in the French national legal order, the supreme rule.[27]

As expressly provided by the Treaties, EU regulations have general application and are directly applicable in all Member States. French administrative law fully reflects this situation. National authorities are bound by regulations and have no margin of discretion in implementing them, even if national measures have been adopted in order to implement them. Therefore, the State cannot be held liable for loss or damage caused to individuals or undertakings by an EU regulation.[28]

The Conseil d'État has always held that national regulations must comply with EU directives. Regulatory measures which are not compliant can be subject to

[20] See Art 4 TEU and Preamble of the Charter of Fundamental Rights.

[21] Constitutional Amendments of 23 July 2008.

[22] For example, when a court enjoins an agency to redress a situation within a set time limit.

[23] Conseil d'État, judgment of 13 May 2011, no 316734 nyr.

[24] See K Lenaerts and P van Nuffel, *European Union Law*, 3rd edn (London, Sweet & Maxwell, 2001) 851.

[25] Conseil d'État, judgment of 1 February 2001, *Entreprise personnelle de transports Freymuth*, Rec CE 865.

[26] Conseil d'État, judgment of 3 December 2001, *Syndicat national de l'industrie pharmaceutique*, Rec CE 624.

[27] Conseil d'État, judgment of 30 October 2998, *Sarran et Levacher*, Rec CE 368.

[28] Conseil d'État, judgment of 5 November 1971, *Comptoir agricole du Pays-Bas-Normand*, Rec CE 1187; Conseil d'État, judgment of 12 May 2004, *Société Gillot*, Rec CE 221.

annulment[29] and may also be set aside in individual cases. As mentioned earlier, any interested party can also request that the administrative authority that adopted such act withdraw it. From this perspective, French case law goes beyond the requirements of Union law. In fact, these rules come into play not only when the directive (or its relevant provision) has direct effect. They apply more generally when the national regulation or even the national statute can be seen as contrary to the objectives of the directive. It is also possible to invoke a directive against an unwritten principle of national law, such as the principle according to which the award of public supply contracts is not subject to any rule of procedure.[30]

However, for many years the Conseil d'État consistently held that a directive could not be invoked against an individual act. This line of cases dated back to the 1978 *Cohn Bendit* ruling[31] in which a student of fame contested a deportation order taken in the course of the events of 1968. The reason the Conseil d'État did not simply apply the case law of the ECJ in *SACE*[32] and *Van Duyn*,[33] was that it had resulted from confusion between Union regulations and Union directives. The Conseil d'État thought that it could continue to stick to the letter of the treaty, which provides that a directive 'shall be binding, as to the result to be achieved, upon each Member State'.

The Conseil d'État finally altered its position in the recent *Perreux* case[34] concerning a decision relating to the career of a magistrate. The applicant claimed that she had been discriminated against and invoked Directive 2000/78, pointing out that, according to the directive, it was incumbent on the administration to prove that there has not been any discrimination. The judgment recognises that, in principle, this could be argued, but nonetheless that the provisions of the directive concerning the burden of proof left a margin of discretion to the Member States and that, in the French administrative system, it is for the judge to lead the investigation. Consequently, as a result of this ruling, administrative case law can now be seen as fully in line with that of the ECJ.

When French administrative courts apply directives, they take due account of the interpretation given by the ECJ. The *Ordre des Barreaux francophones et germanophones* case[35] provides a fine example. In this case the Belgian Constitutional Court, which had serious doubts about the validity of the directive relating to money laundering, referred the case to the ECJ for a preliminary ruling. The

[29] Conseil d'État, judgment of 7 December 1984, *Fédération française des sociétés de protection de la nature*, Rec CE 410.

[30] Conseil d'État, judgment of 6 February 1998, *Tête et Association de sauvegarde de l'Ouest Lyonnais*, Rec CE 30.

[31] Conseil d'État, judgment of 22 December 1978, *Cohn Berdit*, Rec CE 528.

[32] Case C-33/70, *Sace* [1970] ECR 1213.

[33] Case 41/74 *Van Duyn v Home Office* [1974] ECR 1337.

[34] Conseil d'État, judgment of 30 October 2009, *Perreux*, Rec CE 407; (2010) *Revue trimestrielle du Droit Européen* 223, case note from D Ritleng.

[35] Case C-305/05, *Ordre des barreaux francophones et germanophones* [2007] ECR I-5305; see case note from E Broussy, F Donnat and C Lambert, (2007) *Actualité Juridique Droit Administratif* 2248.

ECJ found the directive compatible with fundamental rights. The Conseil d'État, relying on this interpretation, rejected the action for annulment put before it against the national measures implementing the directive.[36]

What can be said about the unity of Union law? Nowadays, administrative judges are no longer reluctant to refer questions to the ECJ for a preliminary ruling. They frequently rely expressly on authorities from the ECJ, often criticising its case law directly in their judgments. If French courts can reject a claim of invalidity of a Union act,[37] they do also refer such claims to the ECJ in the presence of serious doubts. Administrative judges also interpret national law as far as possible in conformity with the directives and, more generally, with Union law, in accordance with the case law of the ECJ. This obligation is also incumbent on the public authorities themselves, as held in the *Costanzo* case.[38]

The French administrative courts were for a long time very reluctant to take into account a preliminary ruling from the ECJ if they considered that the latter had gone beyond the scope of the question raised by the referring judge. This was, for example, the case when the ECJ circumscribed the effects of a declaration of invalidity of a Union act, without having been asked to do so.[39] However, the Conseil d'État has changed its position and now states that, even if the ECJ has given a response which is broader than the question referred to it, the national court is bound by the judgment of the ECJ.[40]

Two other points are worth mentioning. The first is that in the framework of interim relief, and especially when administrative judges are bound to rule within a statutory time limit, a reference to the ECJ could be incompatible with this requirement; it is up to them to interpret Union law directly, at least for the time being.[41] Secondly, the Conseil d'État has adopted an interesting position where the ECJ confirms the validity of a Union act. According to the *Zuckerfabrick Südendithmarschen* case law,[42] a national judge who is asked to set aside a national act adopted to implement a Union regulation can do so on an interim basis, and order its suspension, provided that he has serious doubts about the validity of the Union act and that he refers the matter to the ECJ for a preliminary ruling. If the national judge does so, and the ECJ confirms the validity of the Union act, the national judge must then reject the claim and put an end to the suspension. However, it may happen that the Union regulation itself provides for provisional measures or a certain delay for its full application. If the national judge has suspended the national implementing measure, the time limit provided for under the Union regulation may run out. In this case, the Conseil d'État has, boldly but

[36] Conseil d'État, judgment of 10 April 2008, *Conseil national des Barreaux et autres et Conseil des Barreaux européens*, Rec CE 129.

[37] Conseil d'État, judgment of 16 November 2005, *Société métallurgique du Rhin*, Rec CE 775.

[38] Conseil d'État, judgment of 30 July 2003, *Association 'Avenir de la lange française'*, Rec CE 347.

[39] Conseil d'État, judgment of 26 July 1985, *Office national interprofessionnel des céréales*, Rec CE 233.

[40] Conseil d'État, judgment of 11 December 2006, *de Groot En Slot Allium BV, and Société Bejo Zaden BV*, Rec CE 512.

[41] Conseil d'État, judgment of 18 October 2006, *Djabrailova*, Rec CE 431.

[42] Case C-143/88 & C-92/89, *Zuckerfabrik Süderdithmarschen et Zuckerfabrik Soest* [1991] ECR I-415.

wisely, decided in the name of legal certainty that a new time limit should be given to persons concerned.[43]

The French administrative courts have pursued an active dialogue with the ECJ. They did not hesitate to point out to the ECJ the ruling which they deemed inadequate and have referred cases back to the ECJ with arguments justifying the ECJ to reverse its position. This, for example, led the ECJ, in the *Olazabal* case,[44] to refine its case law in *Rutili*.[45]

The Conseil d'État in its advisory capacity – both vis-a-vis the government and, since the modification of the Constitution in 2008, the Parliament – examines all legislative proposals tabled by the government. The presidents of both houses of Parliament can also submit a proposal to the Conseil d'État for an opinion. The Conseil d'État can also be consulted by ministers on any questions. In this framework, it has rendered important advisory opinions. For example, its opinion on the Schengen Agreement relating to Asylum Seekers led to a modification of the French Constitution. So did its opinion concerning the European Arrest Warrant.[46] However, what is important to note is that dealing with European matters has become routine work for the Conseil d'État. In 2011, it received more than 1,400 documents from the European institutions; of these 77 were draft directives, 247 draft regulations, and 309 draft decisions. All these documents are analysed and referred to the competent authorities where necessary. To this end, a delegation on European affairs and a committee for European affairs have been created. Many draft statutes or regulations give rise to comments. For example, the Conseil d'État frequently draws to the attention of the government the incompatibility of a draft measure with European law, or the necessity of following a specific procedure, such as in the notification of State aid.[47] The Conseil d'État's annual report contains not only a wealth of examples similar to those noted here, but also a general survey on a given topic. In 2003, as in 2006, this survey was devoted to European law. The first related to 'Local public bodies and Community law', the second to 'French public administration and the European Union'.[48] As pointed out by the President of the Conseil d'État, the French supreme administrative court clearly contributes to the respect and the implementation of Union law.[49]

One would not give a complete idea of the role of the French administrative courts without speaking of the personal involvement of their members in European

[43] Conseil d'État, judgment of 27 October 2006, *Société Techna*, Rec CE 451.

[44] Case C-100/01 *Oteiza Olazabal* [2002] ECR I-10981; see Y Robineau 'De l'affaire Rutili à l'affaire Olazabal' in *Le dialogue des juges, Mélanges offerts à Bruno Genevois* (Paris, Dalloz, 2009) 903.

[45] Case 36/75 *Rutili* [1975] ECR 1219.

[46] See B Stirn, *Les sources constitutionnelles du droit administratif* (Paris, LGDJ, 2011) 32.

[47] JL Sauron, 'La contribution des formations consultatives du Conseil d'État à l'élaboration et à l'application du droit communautaire' (2009) *Gazette du Palais* 16.

[48] J Biancarelli, E Lannes, E Maréchal, P Martin, 'La place du droit communautaire dans les études et les rapports du Conseil d'État' (2009) *Gazette du Palais* 24.

[49] JM Sauvé, 'Le juge administratif, la démocratie et l'Union européenne' (2010) 540 *Revue du Marché commun et de l'Union européenne* 413.

affairs.[50] For a long time, judges of the French administrative court, and especially the Conseil d'État, have played key roles. At the ECJ, traditionally, the two French members are a member of the Conseil d'État and a magistrate from the judiciary. Jean-Louis Dewost was for a time the Legal Advisor to the European Council and for ten years Director General of the legal service of the Commission.[51] When he was appointed to the Council, as Deputy Legal Advisor, in 1973, he took over from Jean-Pierre Puissochet who became judge of the ECJ in 1994 after having been Director of the Legal Service of the French Ministry of Foreign Affairs. The current Legal Advisor to the European Council, Hubert Legal, is also a member of the Conseil d'État, and was formerly a judge at the General Court of the EU. Another Conseil d'État member was until recently a judge at the EU Civil Service Tribunal. As a tradition too, members of the administrative court system are part of the French judges' chambers,[52] and a good number are legal assistants in other cabinets of members of the ECJ as well as in cabinets of members of the General Court, or the Civil Service Tribunal.[53] Administrative judges are often seconded as national experts to the European Commission for two years. The presence of members of the administrative courts is also common in national bodies dealing with EU affairs such as the Secretariat General for European Affairs, a body attached to the Prime Minister's office, as well as at the French Permanent Representation to the EU in Brussels or at the presidency of the French Republic. For many years these exchanges have developed a thorough knowledge of EU affairs in the administrative courts.

If, as stated at the beginning of this article, French administrative law has influenced Union law, the converse is also true, obviously.[54] EU law has played a great role in accelerating some changes which where necessary but that French society was reluctant to make. It has improved the administrative law system, already quite a good one, but whose limitations were becoming ever more apparent. For example if the creation, in 2000, of a completely new set of rules in the field of interim relief is not directly due to Union law, it is obvious that the general context has led to this major change. The same can be noted regarding the introduction into French law of new principles such as that of legal certainty,[55] the application of which was not unusual in administrative law, but which was not accepted in itself. In applying Union law the French administrative courts have found the means to renew themselves.

[50] B Stirn, 'Le Conseil d'État et l'Europe' in *L'État de droit, Mélanges en l'honneur de Guy Braibant* (Paris, Dalloz, 1996) 653.

[51] JL Dewost, 'Vingt cinq ans de conseil juridique au service de l'Europe' in *L'État souverain dans le monde d'aujourd'hui, Mélanges en l'honneur de JP Puissochet* (Pedone, 2008) 59.

[52] Usually a member of the Conseil d'État, and a president of an administrative court.

[53] On the role of the legal assistants, see S Gervasoni, 'Des référendaires et de la magistrature communautaire' in *L'État souverain dans le monde d'aujourd'hui*, n 49 above, 105.

[54] As is the case in other Member States, such as Italy: see A Tizzano, 'L'influence du droit communautaire sur le droit administrative italien' (1996) *Actualité juridique Droit Administratif* 129. On France, see O Dubos, 'Droit administratif et droit communautaire', in *Jurisclasseur administratif* (Paris, Jurisclasseur, 2007) vol 24.

[55] Conseil d'État, judgment of 24 March 2006, *Société KPMG et Société Ernst et Young et autres*, Rec CE 154.

13

Preliminary References and Swedish Courts: What Explains the Continuing Restrictive Attitude?

ULF BERNITZ*

INTRODUCTION

SWEDEN IS NOW in its eighteenth year of EU membership (1995–2012). However, there is still a clear reluctance within the Swedish court system to ask the ECJ for preliminary rulings. The practice of the Swedish courts when it comes to preliminary rulings is of core importance for the actual application and impact of EU law within the Swedish legal system. It constitutes the basis for the ongoing co-operation and dialogue between the national courts, being the national arm of the European legal order, and the ECJ. As pointed out by the Court in the *Lyckeskog* case, the obligation to refer cases to the ECJ 'is in particular designed to prevent a body of national case-law that is not in accordance with the rules of Community law from coming into existence in any Member State'.[1]

After more than 17 years of membership there is much information available in relation to the Swedish application of the preliminary ruling system. Swedish courts have been criticised for being too restrictive in requesting preliminary rulings and, when doing so, referring the cases unnecessarily late in the litigation process. In total, the ECJ has decided 70–75 preliminary ruling cases in the years 1995 to 2010 inclusive at the request of Swedish courts, that is, less than five cases per year.[2] The situation has not changed; the ECJ decided four preliminary references from Swedish courts in 2010 and six in 2011. By May 2012 six–seven preliminary references from Swedish courts were pending at the ECJ. There is no lack of cases in which lawyers litigating cases before Swedish courts request the Swedish court to refer the case to the ECJ, but it is a well-known fact that in the overwhelming majority of those cases the courts decide to reject the application for

* Professor of European Law, Stockholm University, Jur Dr, Drjurh c (Copenhagen), MA (Oxon), Senior Associate Fellow, St Hilda's College, University of Oxford.

[1] Case C-99/00 *Public Prosecutor v Lyckeskog* [2002] ECR I-4876, para 14.

[2] There are a few cases which have been referred to the ECJ from Swedish courts but which have not resulted in a judgment or order by the Court.

referral. To get a positive decision by a Swedish court to bring a legal matter before the ECJ is like passing through the eye of a needle.

Sweden belongs to those Member States where courts request preliminary rulings rather infrequently, although the situation is by no means unique. The object of this article is to analyse the issue and the reasons behind it. It is not a new or unknown problem. On the contrary, in 2004 the Commission took the unique step of starting infringement proceedings against Sweden based on the EC Treaty arguing that the Swedish supreme courts were too restrictive in their application of the preliminary ruling procedure.[3] Later in this chapter, I will describe in brief, as a starting point, the action by the Commission and its outcome and discuss whether or not the Commission's action has had any effect. In particular, I will examine the newly enacted legislation making it compulsory for Swedish courts of last resort to state their reasons in cases involving EU law in which they do not grant admission and thus do not refer the case to the ECJ.

I will also look at the Swedish cases that have been referred to the ECJ. This section is based on the findings in a Report in the Swedish language which I prepared in 2010 for The Swedish Institute for European Policy Studies (Sieps) on Preliminary Rulings by the ECJ – the Attitude and Practice of the Swedish Courts.[4] Some statistics will be presented. The data obtained give quite interesting information about the activities of different types of courts and the areas of law that have been covered. Also, it is possible to point at areas of law in which there have been particularly few, or no, references.

Finally, I will try to draw conclusions and explain and criticise the reasons behind the reluctance within the Swedish court system to co-operate more closely with the ECJ and to put forward the arguments for the need for a change of attitude. In my view the explanations are quite complicated and relate, at least partially, to legal traditions of a constitutional character and the courts' perception of their own role.

THE COMMISSION'S ACTION AGAINST THE ALLEGED PRACTICE OF THE SWEDISH SUPREME COURTS NOT TO REFER CASES TO THE ECJ

As mentioned, in 2004, the Commission started a legal action against Sweden based on the observation that the Swedish courts of last resort, primarily Högsta Domstolen (the Supreme Court) and (to a lesser extent) Högsta Förvaltningsdomstolen (the Supreme Administrative Court) were too restrictive in their application of the preliminary ruling procedure. The case reached the stage of a reasoned opinion, which was submitted to the Swedish government.

[3] I have treated the Commission's action and its background more extensively in my article 'The Duty of Supreme Courts to Refer Cases to the ECJ: The Commission's Action Against Sweden' in N Wahl & P Cramér (eds), *Swedish Studies in European Law*, vol 1 (Oxford, Hart Publishing, 2006) 37.

[4] U Bernitz, 'Förhandsavgöranden av EU-domstolen. Svenska domstolars hållning och praxis' (Preliminary Rulings by the EU Court of Justice – The Attitude and Practice of the Swedish Courts), Sieps Rapport 2010:2 (with an English Summary), available at www.sieps.se.

The reasoned opinion has been made public in Sweden under Swedish law on transparency of public documents.[5]

The Commission mentioned specifically in its reasoned opinion that from 1995 until 31 December 2002 the Supreme Court had only referred two cases to the ECJ and the Supreme Administrative Court 10 cases. In 2003 each court referred only one additional case. The Commission observed in particular that the supreme courts decided on the admissibility of a case without stating any reasons; the supreme courts merely stated in one sentence that they did not grant admission (leave). This made it impossible, including for the Commission, to check if the national courts had observed their obligations under what is now Article 267(3) TFEU. The Commission required that Swedish courts of last resort be obliged to state their reasons if they do not grant leave in cases involving the application of EU law.

The Swedish government rejected these allegations of breach of EU law. However, the government opted for a compromise solution. It proposed special legislation requiring the courts of last resort to give reasons when deciding not to grant leave in a case involving issues of EU law raised by a party. The proposal was opposed by the Supreme Court and the Supreme Administrative Court as an unjustified intrusion, but was supported by the majority of the authorities and organisations heard by the government, among those the law faculties of the Lund, Stockholm and Uppsala universities. A Bill by the government based on the proposal was sent to Parliament where it was accepted without any difficulty, taking legal effect on 1 July 2006. After the legislative amendment had been approved by the Swedish Parliament the Commission withdrew the infringement case, which never reached the ECJ. However, the case seems to be unique.

The specific issue whether the provision on the right to a fair trial in Article 6(1) of the European Convention of Human Rights (ECHR) requires supreme courts to give reasons when they do not grant admission was not raised by the Commission in the legal action or by Sweden in relation to the legislative amendment just mentioned. Obviously, the supreme courts, when opposing the legislative proposal, assumed there was no such requirement. Today, we know the European Court of Human Rights (ECtHR) has taken the opposite view in the recent *Ullens de Schooten* case.[6] In this case, the ECtHR found that Article 6(1) ECHR required the Belgian Cour de cassation to give reasons for its decision not to refer a case to the ECJ.[7] However, the ECtHR found itself satisfied with the reason given by the Belgian court in this particular case. The position taken by the

[5] Commission docket no 2003/2161, C(2004) 3899, dated 13 October 2004. See U Bernitz, n 3 above; M Schmauch, 'Lack of Preliminary Rulings as an Infringement of Art 234 EC? Commission Case COM 2003/2161, Procedure against Kingdom of Sweden' (2005) *European Law Reporter* 445.

[6] Case Nos 3989/07 and 38353/07, *Ullens de SchootenetRezabek v Belgium*, judgment of 20 September 2011.

[7] Para 60 of the decision: 'Ainsi, l'article 6 § 1 met dans ce context à la charge des jurisdictions internes une obligation de motiver au regard du droit applicable les décisions par lesquelles elles refusent de poser une question préjudicielle, d'autant plus lorsque le droit applicable n'admet un tel refus qu'a titre d'exception'.

ECtHR adds a new dimension to the Commission's infringement action and the requirement to motivate a decision not to grant admission.

Now, after five years of application, it is possible to evaluate the importance of the legislative change. What is the importance of the new requirement to give reasons? The matter has been evaluated in a recent law review article by Martin Johansson based on a study of the reasons given by the supreme courts in a substantial number of cases involving EU law in which leave was denied.[8] The study demonstrates clearly that in most cases the reasons given by the supreme courts take the shape of standardised phrases which give little information. In my report for Sieps, mentioned above, I have reached the same conclusion.[9] Different phrases are in use by the supreme courts. Sometimes, the courts simply state that the case does not involve any issue of EU law which makes the court obliged to refer a question to the ECJ. In other cases the supreme courts simply state that there is sufficient EU case law available. Phrases of this kind do not relate properly to the CILFIT criteria[10] and leave open, and unanswered, questions whether the court has found the EU law issues raised in the case at hand to be without relevance or whether the court has found the EU law issues raised to be *acte éclairé* or, alternatively, *acte clair*.

Two decisions taken in 2011 by the Swedish Supreme Court not to grant admission and not to refer the case to the ECJ for a preliminary ruling cast serious doubt as to whether the practice applied is in conformity with European law. Both cases concern issues about the interpretation of important provisions of the EU Charter of Fundamental Rights which had not, so far, been addressed by the ECJ.

In *Hammer*, the Supreme Court decided by three votes to two not to refer the case to the ECJ and denied leave.[11] The case concerned the *ne bis in idem* rule in Article 50 of the Charter, that is, the right not to be tried or punished twice in criminal proceedings for the same criminal offence. According to Swedish law, tax fraud is met with a combination of the levying of a tax surcharge (normally a 40 per cent addition to the tax to be paid) and criminal proceedings, normally resulting in imprisonment for more serious offences. The tax surcharge is decided by the tax authorities and can be appealed to the administrative courts while the criminal proceedings are handled by the ordinary courts. It follows from recent case law of the ECtHR, in particular the *Zolotukhin* case, that a tax surcharge is to be regarded as a penal sanction under Article 4 of the 7th Protocol to the ECHR.[12] The case at hand concerned a tax fraud related to the payment of VAT for commercial transactions. The Supreme Court found the decisive issue to be whether the application of penal sanctions in relation to tax fraud in the VAT field concerned the implementation (or application) of Union law under Article 51(1) of

[8] M Johansson and S Ahmed, 'De högsta domstolsinstansernas motiveringsskyldighet vid beslut att inhämta förhandsavgörande från EU-domstolen – en papperstiger' (2009) *Europarättslig Tidskrift* 769.

[9] ibid, 36 ff.

[10] Case 283/81 *Cilfit v Ministro della Sanitá* [1982] ECR 3415.

[11] Case No B 5312-10, decision of 29 June 2011. The case is published (in Swedish) in Nytt Juridiskt Arkiv (NJA) 2011, 444, also available at www.hogstadomstolen.se.

[12] Case No 14939/03, *Zolotukhin v Russia*, judgment of 10 February 2009.

the Charter. On this point, the Supreme Court was divided. Three judges, forming the majority, argued against and two judges argued in favour of the applicability of the Charter. Both sides presented detailed and lengthy legal reasoning. The majority found that the matter was *acte clair*, while the minority took the opposite view. Thus the Supreme Court actually took a vote on the *acte clair* issue.

In the opinion of the author, this decision amounts to a misuse of the *acte clair* doctrine. The very fact that two supreme court judges, presenting good reasons, find an issue of EU law to be unclear, should be proof that the matter is not *acte clair*.[13] It may be recalled that the *acte clair* doctrine requires the national court to be convinced 'that the matter is equally obvious to the courts of the other Member States and to the Court of Justice'.[14]

The second case, *Landin*,[15] dealt with the last sentence of Article 49(1) of the Charter, according to which '[i]f, subsequent to the commission of a criminal offence, the law provides for a lighter penalty, that penalty shall be applicable.' In this case, several persons had been sentenced severely for customs fraud by declaring incorrectly the origin of products subject to an antidumping duty. The issue in the case was whether the provision cited would cover the situation in which the antidumping regulation had expired after the fraud had been committed. The Supreme Court stated in its decision not to grant leave only that

> the case did not bring to the fore any issue of union law which would give cause for requesting a preliminary ruling from the EU Court.

The motivation requirement is normally better fulfilled in cases in which the supreme courts grant leave but decide the case without making a reference to the ECJ for a preliminary ruling. Although the reasons given might be short, it is normally possible to follow the court's reasoning. However, this is not always the case. As an example the following case on EU law issues of general importance relating to VAT law, decided by the Supreme Administrative Court without reference to the ECJ, may be cited. The court gave the following brief reasons in its opinion:

> The issues of EU law that are brought to the fore in the case can be decided under the guidance of the case law of the ECJ. Thus, reasons to bring the matter before the Court are not present.[16]

It is not possible to point to any judgment or decision taken by the Swedish Supreme Court or Supreme Administrative Court in which either court has engaged in a discussion of how it evaluates the CILFIT criteria or other issues of principle related to the Treaty obligation to refer cases to the ECJ. To conclude, the legislation of 2006 on the duty for Swedish courts of last resort to give reasons

[13] However, a Swedish court of first instance, Haparanda District Court, has referred a similar case to the ECJ for a preliminary ruling, Case C-617/10, *Åkerberg Fransson*. Oral hearing in the case took place in January 2012.

[14] *Cilfit v Ministro della Sanitá*, n 10, para 16.

[15] Case No B-1794-09, decision of 25 August 2011.

[16] Regeringsrättens Årsbok (Yearbook of the Supreme Administrative Court) 2009 no 72.

when deciding not to grant admission in cases involving EU law has not changed the realities much. It is rightly characterised by Martin Johansson in the article mentioned as a 'paper tiger'.

SWEDISH CASES REFERRED TO THE ECJ: NUMBERS AND CHARACTERISTIC FEATURES

It is important to clarify the scope and direction of Swedish case law in the field of preliminary references from a broader EU perspective and against the background of the criticism that has occurred. The 67 cases referred from Sweden and decided by the ECJ during the 15 years from 1995 until 2009 should be compared with the nearly 300 preliminary references decided at that time by the Court every year. As is evidently demonstrated by the statistics, there are essential differences in legal culture between the Member States in relation to referring cases to the ECJ. These are the figures:[17]

Preliminary References from Member States' Courts 1995–2009[18]

	Total number of cases	*Inhabitants in millions*
Austria	363	8.2
Belgium	329	10.4
Denmark	83	5.5
Finland	64	5.3
France	427	64.1
Germany	1074	82.3
Greece	119	10.7
Ireland	25	4.2
Italy	692	58.1
Luxembourg	40	0.5
The Netherlands	348	16.7
Portugal	73	10.7
Spain	203	40.5
Sweden	89	9.3
United Kingdom	319	61.1

As this table shows the number of references differs greatly among countries. Naturally, the large Member States generate more references than the smaller ones. But quite visibly, there are also different judicial cultures on this point in the

[17] The figures are derived from the statistics published in the Annual Report of the ECJ, available at the Court's webpage www.curia.europa.eu.

[18] As Sweden joined the EU on 1 January 1995, 1995 has been chosen as the starting point. The new Member States, which joined in 2005 or 2007, have not been included.

Member States. Thus, there are more references from the older Member States, primarily the six founding ones. On the other hand, Member States from the periphery of the Union tend to have fewer references. It is interesting to note that the situation is quite similar in the three Nordic Member States – Denmark, Finland and Sweden – taking the population differences into account. I will return to that point later on. Austria is a special case. Having a population somewhat smaller than Sweden and having entered the Union at the same date, Austria has generated more than four times as many references. This seems to be a particular aspect of Austrian legal culture. But also Belgium, being of comparable size, has made nearly four times as many references as Sweden.[19]

To conclude, Sweden is not faring particularly badly compared to a number of other Member States such as its Nordic neighbours, Portugal and, in particular, Ireland. However, the number of references from Swedish courts has been rather few. Looking at the general picture, there is scope for a substantial increase in the number of Swedish cases referred without cause for criticism for overburdening the ECJ.

The number of cases referred from Swedish courts has stayed fairly constant over the years. It is not possible to point to any lasting change which could be connected to the Commission's action against Sweden, described above, and following the Swedish legislative amendment. As mentioned, the reasons now given by the supreme courts in cases involving EU law, in which leave is either denied or granted without referral, tend to be very short and not particularly informative.

In my Report for Sieps of 2010, mentioned earlier, I looked at the Swedish cases referred to the ECJ in more detail. Of the 67 Swedish cases referred to and decided by the ECJ by the end of 2009, the lower courts (courts of first instance and courts of appeal), have referred 28 cases, that is, only slightly more than 40 per cent. On this point, there is a discrepancy between Sweden and many other EU countries where the large majority of cases referred to the ECJ emanate from lower courts. In particular, there seems to be an attitude among most Swedish courts of first instance that it is not really their task to refer cases to the ECJ.

Sweden has a special, independent system of administrative courts, similar to what is often the case in continental European countries. The number of references emanating from ordinary courts versus administrative courts is evenly balanced, 30 cases versus 28 cases. The remaining nine cases emanate from courts of special jurisdiction, such as the Labour Court and the Market Court (dealing with competition and marketing law), or from court-like organs. However, the Supreme Administrative Court has referred considerably more cases than the Supreme Court (18 cases versus 12). On the other hand, few cases emanate from the lower Swedish administrative courts, although they are particularly involved with EU law related issues of tax law, social insurance law and public procurement law.

[19] For further statistical data related to the preliminary ruling procedure, see T de la Mare and C Donelly, 'Preliminary Rulings and EU Legal Integration: Evolution and Status' in P Craig and G de Búrca, *The Evolution of EU Law*, 2nd edn (Oxford, Oxford University Press, 2011) 363.

However, the vast majority of the cases referred to the ECJ from Swedish courts have dealt with important legal issues of EU law which have normally been unclear or, in any case, not sufficiently clarified. Once a Swedish court has taken the decision to refer a case to the ECJ, there has nearly always been good reason to do so. The ECJ has been able to deliver clarifying answers in its judgments which have been of fundamental importance, very often completely decisive, for the final judgment in the case by the Swedish court. Only a few of the cases referred to the ECJ have dealt with situations of only limited interest. Among those, we find cases dealing with detailed rules in particular fields having a restrictive effect on the free movement of goods or services. In certain cases of this type, the proper state of the law has been rather obvious. In such cases, Swedish courts seem to have preferred to leave it to the ECJ to set aside the Swedish provision as inconsistent with EU law instead of so doing themselves.

Certain cases referred from Sweden to the ECJ are of particular general interest. One of them is the *Laval* case[20] on the relation between free movement of services and the right to take collective action in a labour law dispute, others are the *Lyckeskog* case[21] on the issue whether a court of appeal should be regarded as a court of last resort because a further appeal requires prior leave, the *Unibet* case on the necessary procedural requirements in order to satisfy access to effective remedies[22] and the *Mickelsson & Roos* case on restrictions of the use of jet-skis on waterways equivalent to a quantitative restriction.[23] In addition, some of the early Swedish tax law cases on the relation between free movement of services and capital merit to be observed, in particular the first case of this type, the *Jessica Safir* case[24] on the taxation of Swedish life insurance policies taken out abroad.

The cases referred to the ECJ by the Swedish courts can be systematised under the following headings: EU constitutional law; Swedish legal monopolies; free movement of goods and services including freedom of establishment; tax cases related to free movement of services and capital; free movement of workers and employees and other labour law cases; competition law; intellectual property law; advertising law; environmental law; international private law; tax; social law; immigration law and agricultural regulation. In most of these fields, we find only a few cases and sometimes just one case.

To what extent are there important fields of law related to EU law in which there are no preliminary references from Swedish courts or only a few? There are a great number of such areas. There is no case in which a Swedish court has referred the interpretation of provisions of Swedish law based on Union law but

[20] Case C-341/05 *Laval un Partneri Ltd v Svenska Byggnadsarbetareförbundet et al* [2007] ECR I-11767; Case Comment by U Bernitz and N Reich, 48 *CML Rev* (2011) 603 ff.

[21] See n 2 above.

[22] Case C-432/05 *Unibet v Justitiekansler (Chancellor of Justice)* [2007] ECR I-2271.

[23] Case C-142/05 *Public Procecutor v P Mickelsson and J Roos* [2009] ECR I-4273.

[24] Case C-118/96 *Jessica Safir v The Tax Authority in the Dalarna County* [1998] ECR I-1897.

applied outside its ambit in accordance with the *Leur-Bloem* principle.[25] Further, there are no cases in which Swedish courts have referred issues related to public procurement, State aid, consumer law or criminal procedure. There is no case so far in which a Swedish court has made use of the urgent preliminary ruling procedure. Turning to areas of law where there are remarkably few cases referred from Sweden one might mention environmental law, social law and migration law. Naturally, this list is not exhaustive.

However, Swedish courts have fully accepted the principles of the precedence and direct effect of EU law as well as the principle of interpretation in conformity with the treaties and directives. There are no Swedish cases in which Swedish courts have openly displayed a reluctance to accept the supremacy of EU law. However, sometimes the lack of references might point in this direction, indicating a certain silent resistance.

HOW DO WE EXPLAIN THE RESTRICTIVE ATTITUDE?

To conclude, what is the attitude of the Swedish courts towards requesting preliminary rulings from the ECJ? It seems possible to make the overall assessment that the attitude is more open today than during the first period of Swedish EU membership, but it is still possible, as the statistics clearly demonstrate, to observe a certain caution. New developments influencing legal culture have a tendency not to penetrate so quickly and, as mentioned, the action brought by the Commission and the following legal amendment about the duty for the courts of last instance to give a proper statement of reasons when deciding not to grant leave in cases involving issues of EU law have hardly had the effect intended.

What might be the reasons behind this remaining restrictive attitude? As is well known nowadays, the Swedish courts are no longer only the courts of the Kingdom of Sweden but they are integrated into a European legal and court system comprising the whole of the EU. Within that system, they constitute the national arm of the EU legal order having independent responsibility for its full effect and correct application within Sweden. The Swedish courts have been given a new role which, on the whole, had no equivalent before Sweden's entry into the EEA in 1994 and the EU the year after. However, one might question whether the Swedish courts have fully realised the implications of their new role.

In my view, the underlying explanations are to be found primarily in the differences in legal method and constitutional legal tradition between Swedish law, on the one hand, and European law, on the other.

The Swedish legal method is often characterised as legal positivism.[26] Statutory law is the main source of law, although case law is the predominant source in

[25] Case 28/95, *A Leur-Bloem v Inspecteur der Belastingdienst/Ondernemingen Amsterdam 2* [1997] ECR I-4161. Public procurement law and competition law are areas in which this issue would be of particular practical importance.

[26] For an overview, see, eg M Bogdan (ed), *Swedish Legal System* (Stockholm, 2010) chs 1–3.

certain fields. The *travaux préparatoires* play a very important role. In the government Bills to Parliament the intended interpretation and application of the proposed statutory rules are often explained in detail. These statements are not legally binding but normally the courts read them carefully and follow what they recommend. In particular, this is the case when the legislation is fairly recent. General principles of law do exist but play a much lesser a role than in EU law.[27] Also, there is no counterpart in Swedish law to the division in EU law between primary and secondary law. For Swedish lawyers EU law represents a different type of legal system, applying other and less well-known methods of legal reasoning. In particular, the distinctly different attitudes towards preparatory legislative material are of importance. Most likely, the vast majority of Swedish judges still regard EU law as fairly unfamiliar and difficult; they approach it with caution. Thus, they often remain inclined to apply domestic Swedish law if at all possible.

A particularly important feature of the differences in legal method concerns the different traditions in the field of constitutional law. Sweden has a centralised, non-federal governmental structure and there is no constitutional court or similar. When applying domestic law Swedish courts are only rarely involved in constitutional legal issues, freedom of expression and transparency being the exceptions. In domestic law, the constitutionality of statutes in force is normally taken for granted. Until 1 January 2011 the Swedish Constitution permitted the courts to disregard a statutory provision considered to be unconstitutional only if the unconstitutionality was found to be manifest.[28] However, this requirement was abolished by a revision of the Constitution in 2010. But it is not to be foreseen that this amendment will lead to any radical change in the practice of the courts. In the area of human rights, there is growing Swedish case law based on the application of the European Convention of Human Rights but only a few of these cases are based on domestic Swedish legal sources. In short, Swedish courts are not used to exercising judicial review on issues of constitutional law of an often sensitive nature.

Symptomatically, there is hardly any Swedish case law in relation to European constitutional law issues. Thus, there is no case in which a Swedish court has requested a preliminary ruling in a case about the alleged nullity of an EU legal act. To the best of my knowledge there is no Swedish court case in which the legality of an EU legislative act has even been seriously questioned during the more than 17 years that have elapsed since Sweden joined the EU. This might reflect the general unawareness in the Swedish legal system among practising lawyers, as well as judges, of the possibility of litigating constitutional law issues in the courts.

As mentioned above, the number of references from Danish and Finnish courts to the ECJ is largely of the same moderate size as Sweden's, taking the population difference between the countries into account. On this point, there are strong similarities between the Scandinavian countries in legal method and constitu-

[27] X Groussot, *General Principles of Community Law* (Groningen, Europa Law Publishing, 2006). See ch 9, 'Impact of the General Principles in Swedish Public Law' 384 ff.

[28] Ch 11 Art 14 of the Swedish Constitution. Available as amended in 2010 at www.riksdagen.se (click 'English', then 'Documents and Laws').

tional legal traditions. By contrast, Austria and Belgium, generating so many more references to the ECJ, are both countries with a federal structure.

The connection between the lack of a tradition of constitutional judicial review in the Nordic countries and the restrictive attitude towards referring cases to the ECJ for a preliminary ruling have been observed by several authors in recent Scandinavian legal debate.[29] Behind the decision taken by a national court to refer a case to the ECJ there is very often at least a suspicion that the domestic law at issue is not fully in line with the requirements of EU law. Thus, by referring cases to the ECJ national courts fulfil, to a large extent, a kind of judicial review. This seems to be quite a step to take for a Scandinavian judge.

It would be difficult to regard the present situation as satisfactory. Looking at the overall picture, Swedish courts remain excessively restrictive and sometimes reluctant to refer cases to the ECJ. This tendency is particularly evident among lower courts and might function to the detriment of the legal security of the parties in cases involving EU law. There is scope for a decisive increase in the number of Swedish cases referred to the ECJ without causing any critique for Swedish courts overburdening the latter. The statistics from the different Member States indicate that a doubling of the average number of cases referred by Swedish courts from five to ten per year would fall well within what can be considered as normal European practice in this regard. However, it might take time to bring about a change in attitudes. As I have tried to explain, this restrictive attitude is not just the result of lack of knowledge or some type of general hostility but has explanations of a more profound nature, related to the differences in legal method and the lack of a developed constitutional law practice in the courts of Sweden.

Hopefully, the picture is slowly changing. The decisive role of the *travaux préparatoires* is gradually losing importance in Swedish domestic law and the Swedish courts have been given a wider scope for the application of constitutional law. General principles of law seem to have become more important than before and the courts are gradually becoming more and more involved in human rights issues. In short, there is an ongoing Europeanisation of Swedish law which should have an effect also on the attitudes towards asking the ECJ for preliminary rulings, at least in the longer term.

Finally, it is my hope that Swedish and other Nordic courts will realise that active participation in the preliminary ruling process is a way to influence the ongoing evolution of European law. A substantive referral rate offers the opportunity for national legal values to be presented, tested and possibly incorporated in the preliminary ruling discursive process. Swedish judges should not hesitate to take part in this particularly important development of the law. In particular, one would wish the supreme courts to take a more proactive role in this regard.

[29] M Wind, 'The Nordics, the EU and the Reluctance Towards Supranational Judicial Review' 2010 *JCMS* 1039 ff; J Nergelius, 'Laval, Metock and the Recent Nordic Debate on Judicial Review' in *Europe. The New Legal Realism. Essays in Honour of Hjalte Rasmussen* (Copenhagen, 2010) 527; O Zetterquist, 'Rättens rike och EG-rätten – Envälde eller dubbelmonarki?' [The Realm of Law and EU-Law – Autocracy or Double Monarchy?], *Liber Amicorum Kjell Å Modeer* (Lund, 2007) 735.

14

The Swedish Market Court

CHRISTER H:SON FALLENIUS*

INTRODUCTION

AS A NATIONAL court of last resort, Marknadsdomstolen, the Swedish Market Court, has a particular responsibility to follow the judgments of the ECJ and ask for preliminary rulings, when necessary. Pernilla Lindh was, until 2006, a member of the Court of First Instance (now General Court) and earlier, during her service at the Swedish Ministry for Foreign Affairs, she was an alternate member of the Market Court. With her great knowledge of questions dealt with by the Market Court she has always been a valuable source of inspiration, not least on matters of competition. Being a close friend she has always been open to all sorts of discussions concerning Union law, the ECJ and the General Court. In the first part of my contribution I will give a short overview of the Market Court, and of some competition cases, as well as cases relating to fair marketing that we have had to handle during my Chairmanship, leaving, however, all analysis of the judgments to others. I will also present some thoughts about the raison d'être of specialised courts. In the second part of my contribution I will present a personal portrait of Pernilla Lindh who has been a dear friend since we met in 1974.

THE MARKET COURT

The Market Court was founded in the early seventies at a time when consumer protection became increasingly important and remedies in that area had to be strengthened. The Market Court which has now reached middle age after having been in action for forty years has two principal spheres of competence, namely unfair commercial practices and competition. As a court of last instance, it is responsible for making jurisprudence in those areas which are not dealt with by the Högsta Domstolen, Sweden's Supreme Court. In earlier times, litigation matters relating to unfair commercial practices and competition were not handled by regular courts but rather by dispute settlement bodies composed of representatives from interest groups and organisations.

* Former Chairman, Swedish Market Court.

What are the differences between ordinary courts and specialised courts? In short, the only difference lies, at least as far as Sweden is concerned, in the nature of the cases falling within their respective jurisdictions. The Market Court is one of four specialised courts in Sweden, the others being the Arbetsdomstolen (Labour Court), the Patentbesvärsrätten (Court of Patent Appeals) and the Statens inspektion av Försvarunderrättelsedornstolen (Foreign Intelligence Court). At the outset, the Market Court was formed as a collegial body composed of a chairman and members drawn from various professional and industrial organisations. This set-up remained until the beginning of the 1990s. Since then, however, members of the court are no longer affiliated with special interest groups.

Nowadays, the Market Court comprises seven members: a chairman, a vice chairman and five 'special members'. The chairman, the vice chairman and one of the special members must have a legal background and be experienced judges. The other special members are experts in economics, often with a relevant university background. There are also a number of alternate members. All members are appointed by the government for three-year terms. All seven members normally participate in hearings. The chairman is a full time employee of the court, whereas for the other six members it is an extra assignment. Young lawyers serve as legal secretaries and the court has its own administrative office.

Two particular pieces of legislation are central for the Court, the Marknadsföringslagen[1] (Marketing Act) and the Konkurrenslagen[2] (Competition Act), as in force since 2008. The Marketing Act implements Directive 2005/29/EC concerning unfair business-to-consumer commercial practices in the internal market.[3] The Market Court also deals with matters covered by other legislative instruments, the so-called 'annex-Acts', regulating specific products. The Alkohollagen[4] (Alcohol Act) is a good example, containing rules regulating alcohol advertising. If the advertising of alcohol is claimed to be unfair, the case has to be brought to the Market Court. I will later go into an interesting case concerning advertising of alcohol, the *Gourmet*[5] case. The remedy against unfair marketing is a prohibition subject to a penalty fine, an administrative fine (also called a market disruption charge) or an indemnity. Most frequently, the Market Court issues prohibition orders, acting as both first and last instance court. Claimants are usually either affected competitors, or the *Konsumentombudsmannen* (Consumer Ombudsman), whose task is to safeguard consumer interests and pursue legal remedies in the courts. Administrative fines are usually requested in instances

[1] SFS 2008:579.

[2] SFS 2008:486.

[3] Directive 2005/29/EC of the European Parliament and of the Council of 11 May 2005 concerning unfair business-to-consumer commercial practices in the internal market and amending Council Directive 84/450/EEC, Directives 97/7/EC, 98/27/EC and 2002/65/EC of the European Parliament and of the Council and Regulation (EC) No 2006/2004 of the European Parliament and of the Council ('Unfair Commercial Practices Directive') (Text with EEA relevance) OJ L 149 22–39.

[4] SFS 1994:1738.

[5] Case C-405/98 *Gourmet International Products* [2001] ECR I-1795.

when the Consumer Ombudsman is the claimant. In such cases, the Market Court has final jurisdiction over appeals from the Stockholms tingsrätt (Stockholm District Court). Claims for indemnification can be brought before the district court where the respondent has its legal seat. Under certain circumstances, companies may also request an administrative fine.

Since the beginning of the 1990s, the competition rules in Sweden mirror Union law and prohibit anti-competitive co-operation between undertakings and abuses of dominant position. The remedies available can take the form of injunctions (prohibition or obligation) or the payment of an administrative fine. The competition authorities in Sweden are the Konkurrensverket (Competition Authority), the Stockholm District Court and – as last instance – the Market Court. In order to impose administrative fines, the Competition Authority must file a petition to the Stockholm District Court whose judgment may then be appealed to the Market Court. However, leave of appeal is required. In certain cases, the Competition Authority has the right to order an undertaking to pay an administrative fine under the condition that the material circumstances regarding the infringement are clear and the company in question agrees in essence to a kind of settlement. The Competition Authority may also oblige a company to terminate an infringement with or without penalty of a fine, subject to a right of appeal to the Market Court. Besides this, there are cases of a particular kind: those having their ground in Chapter 3 Article 2 of the Swedish Competition Act (see below).

As a court of last instance, the Market Court is under an obligation to refer questions of interpretation of Union law to the ECJ for a preliminary ruling when necessary. Some cases have been referred to the ECJ, inter alia, the *Gourmet* case and *Ving Sverige*[6], a case about requisites for the legal concept 'invitation to purchase' in connection with the marketing of a special journey in which the price was indicated as 'New York from 7.820:-'. The concept of 'invitation to purchase', which is found in the Marketing Act of 2008, has been interpreted somewhat differently among Member States during the process establishing the Unfair Commercial Practices Directive. The ECJ delivered its preliminary ruling (C-122/10) in May 2011 and the Market Court heard the case in December 2011. The Court found that the marketing had to be seen as an 'invitation to purchase' and that all the information given in the advertisement together with information on the website of the travel company, Ving, was sufficient not to be misleading. Accordingly the suit from the Consumer Ombudsman was dismissed.

Under Chapter 3 Article 2 of the Swedish Competition Act a company that considers itself affected by a measure of alleged unfair competition from a competitor can bring a claim for an obligation directly to the last instance, the Market Court, under the condition that the Competition Authority beforehand has decided not to investigate or to go further into the matter. This particular right for the company is called a 'special action' or a 'subsidiary claim'.

[6] MD 2011:30, *Konsumentombudsmannen mot Ving Sverige AB.*

Article 1(1) and Article 2 of Chapter 3 of the Swedish Competition Act read as follows:

> The Competition Authority may require an undertaking to terminate an infringement of any of the prohibitions laid down in Chapter 2 Article 1 or 7, or Article 101 or 102 in the EC Treaty.
>
> If the Competition Authority decides in a particular case not to impose an obligation in accordance with Article 1, the Market Court may do so at the request of an undertaking that is affected by the infringement.

The Competition Authority's decision is a declaration of intent that it will not investigate the matter further or take any action on the complaint brought to it. Consequently it cannot be formally appealed. If the company disapproves of the position of the Competition Authority, the company is directed to apply to the Market Court.

This particular right has been questioned by different parties. Some are of the opinion that the Competition Authority ought at least to take a formal decision which can be appealed. Others have argued that the company has to wait until the Competition Authority has delivered its opinion. When the Authority has done so, the company can bring the case directly to the Market Court. The right for a company to turn to the Market Court directly must be seen in light of the Competition Authority discretion with respect to the treatment of complaints. The subsidiary claim allows a company that considers itself affected by a competitor to have its claim tested in court and to obtain relatively quickly a judgment prohibiting the other company from continuing the infringement. However, it is the affected undertaking which bears the burden of proof and has to investigate the matter, to present facts and evidence, since the Market Court is a court – as opposed to the Competition Authority which is an administrative authority dotted with investigation powers – and therefore cannot and will not carry out any investigation beyond the task of ensuring that the facts and motions presented by the parties are explained and clear, thus allowing the court to rule on the case. This can often be quite expensive and burdensome, particularly for smaller undertakings. The chances of success of such claims are therefore restricted to those cases where the facts are fairly clear.

The Market Court has handled some 'subsidiary claim' cases, the latest example involving a special rebate system put in place by a company within the Swedish Post group of companies.[7] Posten Meddelande AB is the successor to the former postal monopoly and enjoys a dominant position. It was challenged by another competitor, Bring City Mail Sweden AB. Posten Meddelande AB is obliged to distribute mail to the entire country whereas Bring City Mail only distributes mail in the largest cities (Stockholm, Gothenburg and Malmö) and on the island of Gotland. The rebate was open to large-scale deliveries if the company asking for the rebate did some of the sorting work by itself. The Market Court found that

[7] MD 2011:14, *Bring City Mail AB mot Posten Meddelande AB.*

Posten Meddelande AB could use the fact that it distributed post to the entire country as a means of creating ties of loyalty which prevented customers from using the rebate of Bring City Mail. According to the Market Court the negative side of the rebate went far beyond the advantages of the rebate and therefore constituted an abuse of the dominant position in breach of both Swedish and Union law. If Posten Meddelande AB did not cease the rebate it would have to pay an administrative fine of 100 million Swedish Crowns (approximately €10 million). The conclusion may be that the possibility of initiating an action under Chapter 3 Article 2 of the Competition Act – though called in question – remains a useful means for a company to obtain justice within a relatively brief time span.

The Asphalt Case

In May 2009 the Market Court rendered a judgment on collusion between companies in the construction business.[8] Some of the largest construction companies in the country had been found guilty of having agreed on prices and market shares. So far, this is the largest cartel case in Sweden. Following years of investigation and a 'dawn raid' in the autumn of 2001 against several companies in the asphalt business, the Competition Authority applied to the Stockholm District Court for administrative fines of approximately 1,24 billion Swedish crowns (€124 million).

The Stockholm District Court, in a July 2007 judgment, found that the companies had been colluding from 1997 to March 2001.[9] Some of the companies took a lead role while others just participated episodically. The companies had distributed and allocated among themselves contracts from the private sector as well as from municipalities and the Vägverket (National Road Administration). According to the judgment, the companies agreed which one of them was to be awarded a construction contract in the case of a public procurement. What is more, the companies were also found guilty of having compensated other companies for refraining from bidding.

The 'business', as the companies called it, began with contacts among the leaders discussing the amount of asphalt and construction work which could be estimated to be available the following year by tender at a national level as well as from the private sector and the municipalities. The leaders of the cartel then decided how to divide the work between them and contacted smaller companies. Finally they reached an agreement regarding who should and who should not take part in the bidding and who should quote a high and therefore not competitive price.

According to the Stockholm District Court, 'representatives of the companies deliberately sought to share the market between them and establish price levels for the tenders to be submitted'. The Court also found that a procedure had been established whereby the large companies contacted smaller companies and paid them for not submitting tenders. The individual agreements were so closely linked

[8] MD 2009:11, *NCC Aktiebolag mfl mot Konkurrensverket.*

[9] *Stockholms tingsrätt,* Case T 5467-03.

to each other, the Court declared, that they must be deemed to have been part of an ongoing process in defiance of the law.

Nine companies – including the National Road Administration – were ordered to pay administrative fines of about 460 million Swedish crowns (€46 million). By Swedish standards, the administrative fines imposed were very high indeed. Six of these companies appealed to the Market Court. The ruling of the Market Court made it clear that the companies had been guilty of a very severe infringement and that the cartel had affected trade among Member States.

The total fine set by the Market Court for some of the companies exceeded those of the Stockholm District Court by 40 million Swedish crowns (€4 million). In some cases, the fines were modified – upwards or downwards – due to the presence of aggravating or mitigating circumstances. The claim of the Competition Authority regarding one company was dismissed entirely.

The case raised a couple of interesting problems, one of which was about the participation of the National Road Administration in the cartel. The National Road Administration had four main tasks: traffic security, exercise of public authority, building and maintenance of roads in Sweden. Could the National Road Administration be characterised legally as an undertaking and could it be part of a cartel acting against its own interest? In a separate judgment the Market Court found that the National Road Administration in the particular circumstances at hand was an undertaking and therefore could act in the case and be responsible for participation in an alleged unlawful collusion. After the judgment of the Market Court, several cases were brought to the Stockholm District Court by municipalities seeking damages from the construction companies claiming that they had been affected by excessive prices due to the operation of the cartel. In some of those cases the parties have reached a settlement, others are still pending.

Gourmet, the Case that Changed Sweden's Legislation on Alcohol Advertising

Gourmet is a Swedish magazine, published in two editions, one intended for subscribers and another sold in shops. An issue from 1997 of the first mentioned edition contained three pages of advertisements for alcoholic beverages, one for red wine and two for whisky. Those advertisements did not appear in the edition sold in shops. The Consumer Ombudsman applied to the Stockholm District Court for an injunction restraining the publisher of Gourmet from contributing to the marketing of alcoholic beverages to consumers by means of such advertisements in contravention of Swedish law. The rule in question, Article 2 of the Swedish Alcohol Act, was very strict and in general only allowed marketing with particular moderation so as not to encourage alcohol consumption. Advertising was not permitted for spirits, wines or strong beers with the exception of publications distributed solely at the point of sale of such beverages. The defendant company contended that the application should be dismissed because the proceeding brought against it was based on legislation contrary to Union law. After having asked the ECJ if the Swedish general prohibition on alcohol advertising was proportionate and in line with Union law,[10] the Stockholm District Court in its judgment rejected the claim from the Consumer Ombudsman. The Swedish prohibition was too far-reaching and thereby not in line with Union law. Consequently the claim of the Consumer Ombudsman was rejected.

The Ombudsman appealed to the Market Court. In its judgment the Market Court came to the same conclusion as the Stockholm District Court, that is, that the Swedish legislation was not in conformity with Union law. The stated purpose of limiting alcohol consumption when compared to its effect as an obstacle to trade was deemed too far-reaching and not proportionate according to Union law.

The judgment of the Market Court received much attention from the Swedish press and politicians. In general the Swedish policy on alcohol is, from an international perspective, strict and has always been the subject of intense debate. Even cabinet ministers participated in the debate, declaring – after the judgment of the Market Court – that the organisation of the Market Court had to be looked into and possibly changed on the ground that alcohol policy was too important to be left for judges to decide. One can regard this as an anecdote but it is nonetheless remarkable in the light of the general restrictions in the Regeringsformen (Swedish Constitution) for anyone to interfere with a judgment from a Swedish court. If there is a disagreement with the way a court has interpreted the law, the solution for the lawmakers is to change the law. The political result in the end was a revised Alcohol Act allowing advertisement of alcoholic beverages up to 15 per cent volume/alcohol, with the restriction that marketing may not show the alcohol in a context that may be interpreted as an invitation to buy. In general, this means that only the bottle and the price may be shown.

Some Other Cases

As I mentioned above, the Market Court consists of members with both judicial and economic backgrounds. The need for special competence in economics was particularly evident in a case appealed by the Competition Authority to the Market Court after a judgment of the Stockholm District Court, in which Volvo and Renault car dealers had been cleared of accusations of unlawful price fixing and market sharing.[11] There had in fact been co-operation between the companies but no effect had been demonstrated. Both parties presented in depth economic analyses of the relevant market, vertical steering and the positive and negative effect respectively of a co-operation in sales of new cars and the market for the maintenance and repair of cars. The Market Court found in a judgment of 10 September 2008 – contrary to the Stockholm District Court – that there had been unlawful co-operation affecting trade among EU Member States and fined them 21 million Swedish crowns (€2.1 million).

[10] *Gourmet International Products*, n 5 above.

[11] MD 2008:12, *Konkurrensverket mot AB Bil-Bengtsson mfl.*

The Market Court has also clarified the meaning of some expressions often used in advertisements. The meaning of a 'transaction decision' was defined in the case of *Toyota Sweden AB v Volvo Personbilar Sverige AB.*[12] According to the Marketing Act, which implemented the Unfair Commercial Practices Directive, a 'transaction decision' is a decision made by a consumer or a trader concerning whether, how and under what conditions a product is to be bought, if all or part of the purchase sum is to be paid, if the product is to be retained or transferred, or if a contractual right in connection with the product is to be exercised, regardless of whether the consumer or trader decides to make a transaction or refrain from making a transaction. The Market Court in its judgment of 12 March 2010 stressed that a 'transaction decision' naturally means much more than a decision to buy. As an example, the Market Court mentioned a situation when a consumer decides to take a further step due to an advertisement, for example to visit a shop to get more information.

It is rather common that advertisers want to stress their merchandise's environmental advantages. In *The Consumer Ombudsman v Mercedes-Benz Sverige AB* the claims 'environmentally friendly', 'favourable to the environment' and 'good for the environment' among others were challenged.[13] The Market Court, in a judgment of 31 May 2011, stated that such claims have to be used with caution – not least in connection with cars – as motor vehicles in general affect the environment. With reference, inter alia, to the rules of the International Chamber of Commerce, the Market Court stated – as the claim 'environmentally friendly' has such a variety of meanings – that in order to be justified in advertisements, the expression normally has to be followed by an explanation of what the advertiser means by the expression. In some of the advertisements in question, the claims were found to be too general to be acceptable. However, the Market Court found that the claims included in a leaflet focusing on improvements in a new generation of Mercedes cars in this particular case were acceptable.

Whither Specialised Courts? Some Remarks

The raison d'être of specialised courts in Sweden has from time to time been debated and called into question, along two main lines of criticism. The first – and orthodox one – postulates that the general court system should be able to deal with all sorts of cases and argues that, consequently, there is no need for specialised courts. The other line of criticism focuses on the fact that smaller courts – such as the specialised courts in Sweden – spend comparatively more resources on administration and, because they are thinly staffed, are more vulnerable to employees' sick leave and other bouts of absenteeism. From the bar, lawyers who are specialists in specific matters emphasise the importance of fast and secure procedures before a court with technical skills and competence in the subject matter. This, they argue, is often difficult to achieve within the ordinary court system

[12] MD 2010:8, *Toyota Sweden AB mot Volvo Personbilar Sverige Aktiebolag.*

[13] MD 2011:12, *Konsumentpmbudsmannen mot Mercedes-Benz Sverige AB.*

where their cases have to compete with other important cases due to the courts' limited resources. Specialised courts can concentrate on their problems and are therefore more efficient at settling technical disputes, or so they claim.

The debate will go on. My personal view is that the advantages of specialised courts have been well documented and that these critiques have not provided any real evidence showing that specialised courts are particularly exposed to staffing constraints. To my knowledge, the Market Court has never been in the situation where a session had to be cancelled or postponed due to shortage of resources. Delays may occur due to the parties' way of handling the proceedings, for example, by presenting new evidence at a late stage. It can be argued that there is a need to look closer into the court organisation when it comes to areas of intellectual property and unfair commercial practices as well as some other particular areas where a there are possibilities for greater co-ordination or even optimisation within a specialised court.

PORTRAIT OF A FRIEND

Pernilla Lindh was already at Svea Hovrätt (Svea Court of Appeal) when I arrived to start my training to become a judge in April 1974. She had a very pleasant sense of humour and, according to my Stockholm taste, a funny accent from the south of Sweden. We soon became very good friends, a friendship which has continued over the years.

After being approved as reporting clerks at the Court of Appeal we took different roads but have from time to time worked together. Being one of the best, Pernilla was engaged in the administration of the Court of Appeal and was later entrusted with the task of informing organisations and courts all over Sweden about the new legislation on the right of co-determination in working life. This assignment was followed by a position with the Justitiekanslern (Chancellor of Justice) at the same time as I had a corresponding position with the Justitieombudsmannen (Parliamentary Ombudsman).

During that period you could find us working in one of the basement floors of the Stockholm District Court dealing with cases about debt recovery. At the same time we made serious attempts to quit smoking but were not successful, at least not at that time. Sitting opposite Pernilla and knowing her competence, I naturally turned to her with quite a number of questions. It was, in my experience, an excellent and reliable way to find the solution to legal problems that arose. Even then I admired her great competence and efficiency.

After a second period in the Court of Appeal, at that time obligatory in order to become a judge, Pernilla was asked to join the then Ministry of Trade. She began in July 1981 and was initially working, among other things, with industrial and intellectual property law. Some months later, when I had finished my second period in the Court of Appeal, I joined Pernilla at the Legal Secretariat of the Ministry. After the elections of 1982, matters of foreign trade were transferred to the Ministry for

Foreign Affairs and to a new established Foreign Trade Department. Pernilla and I and our head, the Director General for Legal Affairs Jörgen Holgersson, joined the Foreign Trade Department. A Parliamentary Commission rendered its report on new legislation on manufacturing and export of war material. Pernilla was given the task of writing a Bill for the Parliament. Despite being a very complicated legal area as well as politically delicate, according to my memory, the Bill passed both the Council on Legislation and the Parliament with only minor corrections.

At the same time I was engaged with another piece of politically delicate legislation regarding sanctions against apartheid in South Africa. Pernilla was at my side, always willing to assist me when I got stuck with all sorts of difficulties connected with legislation regarding Swedish companies' engagement in another part of the world.

Pernilla continued to handle the legal issues attached to the war material legislation, which was later complemented also with rules on importation of such material. The area became more and more infected in particular in relation to a special *affaire*, arising from the exportation of guns from the Swedish company Bofors to India and related bribery allegations. Sensitive Swedish, Indian and other interests were in the balance; handling them required extreme tact and careful consideration. In 1988 Pernilla succeeded Jörgen Holgersson as Director General for Legal Affairs of the Foreign Trade Department. She also succeeded him as an alternate member of the Market Court.

During the 1980s both the EFTA countries and the EU wished to expand their co-operation beyond free trade and towards a single market for goods, services, capital and persons. Pernilla took part in this work, on the legal side, discussing inter alia the principle of direct effect and a mechanism of settlement of conflicts between the EU and the EFTA countries. After the Swedish application for membership to the European Union, Pernilla was engaged in the preparation and the implementation of the EU *acquis* where she played a central role in the co-ordination of the legal questions in Sweden. Having been a member of a special working group for legal questions she subsequently became chairperson of the group.

This was no easy task as it required trying to strike a balance between different views, with input from politicians as well as other Ministries. For some politicians, the legal questions had to be handled swiftly, once they had solved the big problems, a view which did not always suit Pernilla's ambition for perfection. She resisted every attempt to rush matters.

On 1 January 1995, Sweden became a member of the EU and Pernilla was appointed to the Court of First Instance. In 2006 when a new Swedish judge for the ECJ was to be appointed the only person the Swedish Government could propose – in my view – was Pernilla Lindh. I was very pleased indeed when it happened.

In spite of the difficulties she has had to fight during her years as a judge of the ECJ with its intensive work, she has kept her marvellous sense of humour and self-irony for the benefit and joy of us all, not least for me. Coming back to Sweden and being such a prominent judge I am convinced she can continue to play an important role when it comes to information about the ECJ and Union law in different fora.

Part II

Citizenship and Fundamental Rights

15

A propos European Citizenship: The Right to Move and Reside Freely

JOSÉ NARCISO DA CUNHA RODRIGUES*

ARTICLE 45 OF the Charter of Fundamental Rights of the EU lays down the historic '*acquis*' on the right to move and reside freely within the Union. Progressing from a 'fundamental freedom' to a 'fundamental right' has consequences. Questions arise on three levels: a) the wording of the right; b) the link of the right with the economic freedom of workers laid down in the Treaties; and c) the meaning and evolution of the right within the context of European citizenship.

THE WORDING OF THE RIGHT

The right to free movement of persons is set out in many international agreements. The Universal Declaration of Human Rights, adopted on 10 December 1948, proclaimed it in Article 13. The International Covenant on Civil and Political Rights of 1966 made reference to it. The Council of Europe accorded it particular importance in the European Convention on Human Rights adopted on 13 December 1955 and in Article 1 of the European Agreement on Regulations governing the movement of persons between Member States of the Council of Europe signed on 13 December 1957. Protocol No 4 of the Convention for the Protection of Human Rights and Fundamental Freedoms (ECHR), adopted on 16 September 1963, established the right in Article 2. The movement of foreigners within the Member States has been the subject of numerous developments at the Council of Europe by way of recommendations and resolutions.

* Judge of the Court of Justice of the European Union. All opinions expressed herein are personal to the author.

THE LINK OF THE RIGHT WITH THE ECONOMIC FREEDOM OF WORKERS LAID DOWN IN THE TREATIES

The Treaties define the free movement of persons in terms of economic activity. Holders of this right are workers (Articles 45 to 48 TFEU), self-employed persons (Articles 49, 54 and 56 TFEU) and members of their families. Secondary legislation has regulated various categories of beneficiaries, while maintaining the economic references underlying this fundamental freedom. Besides conditions of employment and work, right-holders benefit from the same social and fiscal rights conferred on other workers in the same Member States. Their family members are not subject to any conditions regarding their nationality. In certain circumstances, depending on co-operation and association agreements, workers from third countries may benefit from these rights.

There is substantial ECJ case law on the matter, notably concerning the notions of 'worker' and 'family' and of the prohibition of discrimination under the Treaty. The field of application regarding the persons covered by the concept of freedom of movement is progressively widening. In general, it can be affirmed that, currently, the right to free movement and residence for Union nationals is unconditional for those who work in another Member State. Residence for those Union nationals seeking work in another Member State is limited within certain time limits which the Member States must determine in a reasonable manner. Inactive nationals must demonstrate that they have sufficient resources and valid health insurance. Students are subject to similar conditions.

Irrespective of the status of citizenship, freedom of movement underwent its first adaptation to classic fundamental rights with the application of the ECHR and the case law of the ECJ. This led in some cases to a widening of some notions of Union law (such as barriers) and in others to the recognition of third country nationals' rights to move and reside freely within the Union.[1]

Article 21 (ex Art 18 EC) provides that every citizen of the Union shall have the right to move and reside freely within the territory of the Member States, subject to the limitations and conditions laid down in this Treaty and by the measures adopted to give it effect. The creation of European citizenship enshrined in the Treaty of Maastricht and its inherent declaration of the right to move and reside freely in the European Community irrespective of socio-economic criteria was, in

[1] Case C-60/00 *Carpenter* [2002] ECR I-6279 illustrates the extension of the notions of Community law regarding the application of fundamental rights. It concerned the deportation of a spouse of a Member State national, established in the State concerned, who provided services in other Member State, whose spouse was a national of a third country. In Case C-459/99 *MRAX* [2002] ECR I-6591, concerning third country nationals who are spouses of Union nationals and their right to move and reside freely, the Court ruled that a Member State may not send back at a border a third country national married to a Member State national, on the grounds of lack of a valid identity card, passport or, where required, visa, when the spouse was in a position to prove her identity and conjugal ties and there was no evidence of a risk to public policy, public security or public health within the meaning of Art 10 of Directive 68/360 and Art 8 of Directive 73/148. Such action by the Member State was considered disproportionate given the importance the Community legislator attaches to family life.

itself, of symbolic value, albeit relative. In fact, the right was subject to limitations and conditions set down in the Treaty and by the measures adopted to give it effect and, to that extent, it was structured according to the conditions and limits of the earlier *acquis*.

It was therefore reasonable to ask whether Article 18 EC could be considered a specific legal basis likely to alter the impact of secondary law which, in this area, defined the right to move and reside freely. The ECJ answered this question in recognising the direct effect of Article 18 in the *Baumbast*[2] judgment delivered on 17 September 2002. Restating the case law in *Grzelczyk*,[3] the court held that the status of European Union citizen is the fundamental status of Member State nationals and stressed that the right to move and reside freely provided for in Article 18(1) EC is granted to every Union citizen, which is clearly stated in the Treaty, simply by being a national of a Member State and, thus, a Union citizen.

MEANING AND EVOLUTION OF THE RIGHT WITHIN THE CONTEXT OF EUROPEAN CITIZENSHIP

The notion of European citizenship has always been a controversial matter.[4] Reservations have been expressed in many ways. The concept of European citizenship has been considered as 'having no teeth', or 'lacking in substance' or being 'in favour of the Market citizen, inherited by the European Union as an '*acquis*' from the European Economic Communities'.[5] It has also been described as 'confusing',[6] a 'cynical exercise',[7] 'polysemy'[8] and 'an unidentified political object'.[9] Still others have drawn attention to the methodological aspects of the development of the concept of citizenship as regards the process of its development, subordinated in terms of status and incomplete in its content.[10] It has been

[2] Case C-413/99 *Baumbast and R* [2002] ECR I-7091.

[3] Case C-184/99 *Grzelczyk* [2001] ECR I-6193.

[4] See JN Cunha Rodrigues, 'Entre a Europa das liberdades e a Europa dos cidadãos', in *Estudos jurídicos e Económicos em homenagem ao Professor Doutor António de Sousa Franco* (Coimbra, Coimbra editora, 2006) 675.

[5] E Delaney and L Barani, 'The Promotion of 'Symmetrical' European Citizenship: A Federal Perspective' (2003) 25 *Journal of European Integration* 95.

[6] A Mattera, '"Civis europaeus sum": la libertà di circolazione e di soggiorno dei cittadini europei e la diretta applicabilità dell'articolo 18 (ex articolo 8 A) del Trattato CE' (1999) 3 *Il Diritto dell'Unione europea* 451.

[7] J Weiker, quoted by CWA Timmermans, 'Lifting the Veil of Union Citizens' Rights' in N Colneric, D Edward, JP Puisochet, D Ruiz-Jarabo (eds), *Une Communauté de Droit: Festschrift für Gil Carlos Rodriguez Iglesias* (Berlin, Berliner Wissenschafts-Verlag, 2003) 196.

[8] M Fraile Ortiz mentions the loss of the meaning of the concept of European citizenship, condemned to act as a synonym of belonging to a grouping of geometric variables. M Fraile Ortiz, *El Significado de la Ciudadania Europea*' (Madrid, Centro de Estudios Políticos y Constitucionales, 2003) 25.

[9] JD Mouton, *La citoyenneté de l'Union: passé, présent et avenir*' in G Ress, T Stein (eds), *Vorträge, Reden und Berichte aus dem Europa-Institut* (Saarbrücken, Europa-Institut der Universität des Saarlandes, 1996) 3.

[10] R Kovar, 'L'émergence et l'affirmation du concept de citoyenneté européenne dans le processus d'intégration européenne' in C Philip, P Soldatos and C Blumann (eds), *La citoyenneté européenne* (Montréal, Université de Montréal, 2000) 82.

suggested that the legitimisation of Union decisions would continue to be made on the basis of nationality rather than citizenship.[11] Critics have also focused on the wording of the Maastricht Treaty, calling it 'confused and hasty' oriented rather towards citizenship as membership, as opposed to a '*status iuris*' made up of rights and obligations; a sort of 'pathos' insufflated in those reluctant to cut the umbilical cord that ties them to their own country.[12]

It is historically correct that European citizenship is genetically a superposed citizenship and that it endures as an imbalanced asymmetric notion in favour of economic factors. Habermas has identified three ways of understanding citizenship: in terms of the market, in ethno-cultural terms (favouring shared cultural ties) and in terms of civic responsibility (aimed at sharing norms and values). The process of building European citizenship has faced difficulties in each of these areas.

The first observation one can make regarding the origins and evolution of the aspirations which shaped the notion of European citizenship is that, dating back to the 1970s, they have long maintained a high degree of homogeneity, even in the terms of their formal expression.[13] From the beginning, the difficulties were understood as legal questions, on the one hand, and as questions concerning other matters such as belonging and identity on the other. Legally, one can say that what emerged from an initial reading of the notion of European citizenship was the secondary nature of its link and the apparent completeness of conferred rights, going beyond the economic functionalisation.

However, the succinctness of this reading contrasts with the widening of the doctrinal speculation and the results obtained, in particular due to the ECJ case law. The assertion that the 'edifice' had been slow in finding a solid foundation, remaining anchored to the general principle of non-discrimination based on the nationality which each economic freedom expresses[14] was probably correct. Nevertheless, one should not over-exaggerate its merits.

[11] C Close, 'The Concept of Citizenship in the Treaty on European Union' 29 *CML Rev* 1168, 1169.

[12] A Mattera, 'Civis europaeus sum, Citoyenneté européenne, droit de circulation et séjour, applicabilité directe de l'article 8 A du Traité CE' (1998) 3 *Revue du Marché Unique Européen* 16.

[13] The first proposition dating back to the Paris summit was on the initiative of the Italian government. Andreotti contended that this type of citizenship should supplement that of each Member State and allow Community citizens, after a determined period of residence in a Member State, to enjoy certain political rights, such as voting in local elections. G Coletta, 'La residenza nell'individuazione del cittadino europeo' in (2000) *Sovranità rappresentanza democracia* 467. Regarding the origins, see also, V Constantinesco, R Kovar and D Simon, *Traité sur l'Union Européenne* (Paris, Economica, 1995) 129; K Lenaerts and P Van Nuffel, *Constitutional Law of the European Union*, 2nd edn (London, Sweet & Maxwell, 2005) 539; M Condinanzi et al, *Cittadinanza dell'Unione e libera circolazione delle persone* (Milano, Giuffrè Editore, 2003) 1; M Gorjão-Henriques, *Direito comunitário*, 4th edn (Coimbra, Almedina, 2007) 405.

[14] J Shaw, 'The Problem of Membership in European Union Citizenship' in L Kalliomaa-Puha (ed), *Perspectives of Equality: Work, Women and Family in the Nordic Countries and EU* (Copenhagen, Nordic Council of Ministers, 2000) 236. See also P Garrone, 'Les droits du citoyen européen: l'acquis communautaire et l'apport du traité de Maastricht' (1993) *Revue suisse de droit international et de droit européen* 251; R Witterwulghe, 'Du concept économique de travailleur au concept politique de citoyen européen' in C Philip et al (eds), n 10 above, 115, 221; S Hennion-Moreau, 'Le travail ou les limites de la citoyenneté européenne' in *Drôles de droits: Mélanges en l'honneur de Elie Alfandari* (Paris, Dalloz, 2000) 300; L Moccia, 'Du marché à la citoyenneté: à la recherche d'un droit privé européen durable et de sa base juridique' (2004) 2 *Revue internationale de droit comparé* 296.

On the one hand, the achievement of the internal market was founded on economic freedoms based on free movement, and the principle of non-discrimination was the key to the removal of restrictions and barriers. On the other hand, the decline in social fabric cast a distinctive light on the problem of non-discrimination.[15]

In any case, the principle of equal treatment, although limited to economic operators, afforded the possibility of promoting a wider vision of Community law, with the Treaty of Maastricht favouring advancement in the areas of the protection of workers' health, protection of public health (Title X), protection of the workplace and the working environment, protection of the environment (Title XVI), consumer protection (Title XI), and education, vocational training and youth (Title VIII).

The case law has quickly explored other avenues and this has resulted, in the short term, in qualitatively different solutions. The historical legacy has determined the legal context and continues to explain why economic dimensions have had more influence on the status of 'social policy'. However, that legacy also explains why the presence of the condition of economic order caused by a 'quasi superstition' has gradually disappeared given the new realities brought about by changes in the world of work and migration, connected to the transformations which have occurred. This has happened in several areas; the concept of 'worker' is but one example.

In this general area the Court has adopted a broad interpretation resulting in the prohibition of discrimination based on nationality and the barriers to free movement leading to a widening of the rights of those not engaged in economic activity. Encouraged by this case law, the Community legislator has laid down legislation which evolves in the same direction.[16]

Certainly, many of these changes recognised the constitutional features of Article 21 TFEU, characteristics which are faithful to the letter of the Treaty and better adapted to European integration. This constitutional dimension, based on a new legal and political approach towards the recognition of 'special rights', has underlined the transition from the status of a person as merely a recipient of norms to a status central to the process of European construction. The Union legislator has taken this route, following an evolutionary or progressive clause in consonance with the 'plastic' or 'dynamic' character of the status of citizenship, which can be adapted as the process develops.

For some, citizenship could be the legal foundation for systematic harmonisation, according to a (comparative) method, targeting autonomous self-concepts,

[15] See F Cerrone, 'La cittadinanza europea fra costituzione ed immaginario sociale' (2002) *Rivista critica del diritto privato* 495.

[16] Directive 2004/38/EC of the European Parliament and of the Council of 29 April 2004 on the right of citizens of the Union and their family members to move and reside freely within the territory of the Member States, [2004] OJ L158/77, illustrates this approach. The Community legislator referred to the Court's case law in points 9, 16 and 27 of the preamble. The Directive appears as a 'progressive' text which has largely condensed the existing case law in this area.

identified by their substantial capacity to adapt to the Union legal order. Thus it has moved away from the conceptions that dominated the early years.

At that time, European citizenship was associated with a functional logic and tried to compensate for the 'democratic deficit' of which the process of European construction had been accused. The basis and the driving force of the notion of citizenship rested exclusively on the freedom of movement of workers. It is this freedom which served as the testing ground, accompanying the transition of free movement to include the right to reside freely and the passage of the central notion of 'worker' to that of 'person'.

However, at the beginning, European citizenship was already much more than that. It was an instrument of integration. It sought equality between individuals, while preserving cultural diversity. It was closely linked to fundamental rights. In a certain sense, the origin and the common destinies of citizenship and fundamental rights constituted the values on which the Union should be based. The perception of this evolution is essential to the interpretation of current events and to the understanding of the instruments used to date for the broadening of the concept of European citizenship. One of the most important aspects of this methodological continuum is the importance attributed to the right to move freely and the use of the principle of non-discrimination as a factor in widening this right. We will see how these conditions have been reflected in the jurisprudence of the Court.

As is generally recognised, the status of citizenship was largely developed by the ECJ case law. An examination of the most important judgments illustrates the expansion of the notion of citizenship and also a certain argumentative discontinuity. From the point of view of form, the Community legislator used a definition of citizenship based on positive elements. As a result, the notion presents itself as a 'sum of new rights', even if, in certain cases, some Member States had already conferred such rights on nationals of other Member States. The question that arose was whether the legislator had established and defined citizenship as encompassing an exhaustive catalogue of rights, or as an open category with a normative content able to produce autonomous effects and influence the interpretation of other measures.

The first decision in which the Court used citizenship as a criterion in deciding a case was handed down in *Martínez Sala*.[17] The novelty of the *Martínez Sala* judgment and its potential did not pass unnoticed. It was recalled, quite rightly, that, notwithstanding the apparent limitation of community legislation, the Court's reinterpretation relating to the intersection of material and personal objectives of Community law, combined with the principle of non-discrimination, showed

[17] Case C-85/96 *Martínez Sala* [1998] ECR I-2691. The Court, contrary to the conclusions of the AG considered that it was not necessary to widen the interpretation of Art 18 EC and considered that Art 17(2) EC, affords Union citizens the rights and duties set down in the Treaty, notably not to suffer discrimination on grounds of nationality within the scope of application *ratione materiae* of the Treaty (Art 12 EC). Having been lawfully authorised to reside in Germany Mrs Sala benefited from the application of Art 17(2) EC on the ban on discrimination on the ground of nationality (Art 12 EC) as the allowance claimed comes under the application *ratione materiae* of Community law.

that 'something close to a universal right of access' to the benefits of the social state for all European Union citizens legally resident in a Member State 'has now taken root in EC Law'.[18] *Martínez Sala* had brought the real borders of European citizenships closer to the geographical borders, by virtue of non-discrimination based on nationality and the leverage afforded by citizenship.[19]

The problem of citizenship arose once more in the *Bickel and Franz* case.[20] The Court's decision evolved in comparison to the stand taken in *Martínez Sala*. The point at issue in *Bickel and Franz* was not linked to a specific right conferred by the Treaty, but to the association that the Court established between the point at issue (usage of a language) and an economic freedom (the right to move and reside freely). What is particularly important in this construction is that the right to move and reside freely was a two-fold issue. One the hand, it determined the personal field of the Treaty (that of citizenship), whilst on the other hand (in association with usage of language), it triggered the material field, highlighting the principle of non-discrimination.

Another significant stage was reached in *Grzelczyk*.[21] It is in this ruling that, for the first time, the Court asserted that

> Union citizenship is destined to be the fundamental status of the nationals of Member States enabling those who find themselves in the same situation to enjoy the same treatment in law irrespective of their nationality, subject to such exceptions as are expressly provided for.

As has been observed, this ruling represented a 'turning point', the main aspects of which are the following:

- Union citizenship is assumed to be the fundamental status of nationals of Member States, in a formula which sheds light on the dynamic character of the concept;
- the non-requirement of subordination of the activity of the national to an economic objective is repeated, as it had been outlined in *Bickel and Franz*.

[18] Shaw, n 14 above, 257.

[19] ibid, 269.

[20] Case C-274/96 *Bickel and Franz* [1998] ECR I-7637. The Court, citing Case 137/84 *Mutsch* [1985] ECR 2681, began by recalling that, in the context of a Community based on the principles of freedom of movement for persons and freedom of establishment, the protection of the linguistic rights and privileges of individuals is of particular importance. In the opinion of the Court, exercising that right is enhanced if Union citizens can communicate with the judicial authorities in another Member State on the same basis accorded to nationals of the host State. Under those circumstances, Bickel and Franz were able to invoke the protection of Art 12 EC. In this judgment the Court established a link between the linguistic regime used in court proceedings and exercised the rights set down in the Treaty – freedom of movement.

[21] *Grzelczyk*, n 3 above. The Court considered that a social security benefit which guarantees a minimum level of income, such as that laid down in the relevant Belgian law, constitutes a welfare benefit in the sense of Regulation (EEC) No 1612/68 of the Council of 15 October 1968 on freedom of movement for workers within the Community, [1968] OJ L257/2, and the fact that Mr Grzelczyk was not of Belgian nationality was the only obstacle to the granting of this benefit. Discrimination of this kind is forbidden in principle by Art 12 EC. According to the Court, in the case at issue, this article must be read in conjunction with the provisions of the Treaty concerning citizenship of the Union in order to determine its sphere of application.

In short, the Court recognised that Union citizens have the right to invoke the norms of Community law, since the allegedly suffered damage questions the freedoms guaranteed to citizens of the Union by the EC Treaty. In a certain sense, the ECJ extended the field of application *ratione personae* and made the criterion *ratione materiae* more flexible.[22] *D´Hoop*[23] followed, in the main part, the orientations of *Grzelczyk*. In *Baumbast and R*[24] the Court, as has been noted, laid down an important aspect of the notion of citizenship, assuming the direct effect of Article 18 EC. *Garcia Avello*,[25] *Collins*,[26] *Trojani*,[27] *Zhu and Chen*,[28] *Bidar*[29] and *Grunkin and Paul*[30] illustrate significant developments in the case law.

Several elements show this evolution. Firstly, a widening of the status of European citizenship, either resulting from the recognised 'nuclear' function in Article 17(1) EC or in the application of the 'programme' which the Court defined in the *Grzelczyk* ruling and later reiterated several times: citizenship 'expands' to being the fundamental status of Member State nationals. Secondly, the examination of the internal or community character of situations is based on normative criteria which exempt mobility and, concretely, do not require the right-holder to move. Thirdly, the link between the *sub judice* situation and the Union legal order no longer means that the right be expressly established by this order. Indirect protection is sufficient, in the sense that, if the denial of the right hinders a freedom set down in the Treaty, the conditions for citizenship to operate as a complementary status of Member State nationals are fulfilled. This causal link can be indirect or potential. Fourthly, Article 21 TFEU has direct effect; it follows that secondary legislation cannot establish limitations or conditions to the right of residence which undermine the essential content of this right. Fifthly, the effects of Union law can be withdrawn on the ground of the status of citizenship by a method of interpretation which gets closer to the 'interpretation in conformity'. Finally, the status of citizenship exceptionally entails the balancing of the relative value of the standards of secondary legislation, finding the best solution, in the case at issue, from the point of view of the realisation of this status.

The Charter, proclaimed in 2000, acquired legal force on 1 December 2009 when the Treaty of Lisbon entered into effect.[31] The absence of a reference in Article 45(1) regarding the conditions and limitations set down in the treaties or

[22] See F David, 'La citoyenneté de l'Union, statut fondamental des ressortissants des États membres' (2003) *Revue trimestrielle de droit européen* 562, 564, 576.

[23] Case C-224/98 *D´Hoop* [2002] ECR I-6191.

[24] *Baumbast and R*, n 2 above.

[25] Case C-148/02 *Garcia Avello* [2003] ECR I-11613.

[26] Case C-138/02 *Collins* [2004] ECR I-2703.

[27] Case C-456/02 *Trojani* [2004] ECR I-7573.

[28] Case C-200/02 *Zhu and Chen* [2004] ECR I-9925.

[29] Case C-209/03 *Bidar* [2005] ECR I-2119.

[30] Case C-353/06 *Grunkin and Paul* [2008] ECR I-7639.

[31] Art 45 of the Charter of Fundamental Rights of the European Union provides: '1. Every citizen of the Union has the right to move and reside freely within the territory of the Member States. 2. Freedom of movement and residence may be granted, in accordance with the Treaty establishing the European Community, to nationals of third countries legally resident in the territory of a Member State'.

in secondary legislation, confers on the proclamation of the right to move and reside freely something that is akin to classic civil and political fundamental rights. Any limitation of these rights must be statutory and respect the substantive content of the aforementioned rights.[32] However, although not appearing in the statement, the problem of the conditions and the limitations resurfaces in the application of Article 52(2) of the Charter.

The Charter represents a substantial modification only on the axiological plan defined by the norms. It intervenes in the new context of the Treaty of Lisbon, in which dynamics criss-cross: the path towards further integration, produced by the abolition of pillars and the strengthening of the scope of fundamental rights (eg by the adhesion of the Union to the ECHR) and the logic of increased Member State participation, in particular within the framework of the principle of subsidiarity.

Recent case law of the Court would appear to reflect these dynamics as regards the right to move and reside freely. This can be noted in the *Rottmann*, *Ruiz Zambrano*, and *McCarthy* judgments. The *Rottmann*[33] ruling confirmed the principle according to which the definition of the conditions for withdrawing nationality belongs to Member States, which are obliged to respect Union law. Its contribution to the evolution of the notion of citizenship was to specify the range of jurisdictional control when the combined effect of the law of two Member States causes a person with the nationality of these two States to lose both nationalities and, consequently, his European citizenship.

One of the objections expressed regarding this ruling concerned the purely internal character of the situation. Another referred to the competences of Member States regarding nationality. The Court appraised these two objections and, after having considered that the matter fell within the scope of Union law, concluded that, given the fraudulent behaviour of the party concerned, the Union law did not oppose the withdrawal of the naturalisation of one of the Member States involved and did not impose the reinstatement of the nationality of the other Member State. However, the Court stated that the national jurisdiction should take into account the possible consequences which the decision would entail for the interested party and, if relevant, for the members of his family as regards the loss of the rights enjoyed by every citizen of the Union. It was important in this respect to verify, in particular, if this loss was justified with regard to the gravity of the deception committed by Mr Rottmann, given the time that elapsed between the decision to grant naturalisation and the decision to withdraw it, as well as the possibility of his recovering his nationality of origin. As this concerned a case involving the right of nationality which threatened that of European citizenship, it was sufficient to consider that the situation was not purely internal.

In the *Ruiz Zambrano*[34] ruling the Court considered that Article 20 TFEU must be interpreted in the sense that it precludes a Member State from, on the one hand, refusing a national of a third State with dependent children who are citizens

[32] This is confirmed in Art 52(1) of the Charter.
[33] Case C-135/08 *Rottmann* [2010] ECR I-1449.
[34] Case C-34/09 *Ruiz Zambrano*, judgment of 8 March 2011 nyr.

of the Union, the right to reside in the Member State of residence and nationality of those children and, on the other hand, refusing to issue a work permit to a national of a third State, as such decisions would deprive the aforementioned children of the effective enjoyment of the substantive rights attached to the status of Union citizenship.[35] Reiterating once again that the status of Union citizenship is the fundamental status of the nationals of Member States, the Court concludes, quoting the *Rottmann* judgment, that Article 20 TFEU opposes national measures having the effect of depriving the citizens of the Union of the effective enjoyment of the substantive rights conferred by their status as citizens of the Union. The refusal to grant residence for a person, a national of a third State, in the Member State where his very young dependent children live, and are nationals of that Member State, as well as the refusal to issue a work permit, have this effect.

The Court emphasised the fact that Union citizenship confers a fundamental and individual right to move and reside freely on the territory of Member States, the exercise of which does not depend on measures of secondary law. Implicitly, the ruling considers that it is not a purely internal situation and dispels any possible doubts about the necessity of a previous exercise of the right to move, in recognition of the right to reside freely in light of the status of citizenship. The Court did not take a stand on the question of whether the Zambrano children's right of residence ensued from the internal law, or directly from the status of citizenship. Neither did the Court appraise the question whether, with the Treaty of Lisbon which represents a new stage in the status of citizenship (with the integration of the TFEU and the TEU, mentioned in Title II of the TEU, under the epigraph 'Provisions on Democratic Principles'), it would still be necessary to examine the need for previous movement.[36] Another issue that will need to be clarified in the future concerns the relations which can become established between *complementarity* (Articles 9 TEU and 20(1) TFEU) and *subsidiarity* (Article 5(3) TEU and Protocol No 2) and Article 51(1) of the Charter.

The *McCarthy*[37] ruling of 5 May 2011 had, as its object, the interpretation of Articles 3(1) and (16) of Directive 2004/38/EC of 29 April 2004 on the right of citizens of the Union and their family members to move and reside freely within the territory of Member States. The Court ruled that Article 3(1) of this Directive must be interpreted in the sense that it is not applicable to a citizen of the Union who has never made use of her right of freedom of movement traffic, who has always resided in a Member State the nationality of which she possesses and who enjoys, at the same time, the nationality of another Member State.

The Court examined the question relative to Art 21 TFEU. It first observed that the situation of a citizen of the Union who, like Mrs McCarthy, did not invoke the right to free movement, for that reason alone, had to be assimilated to a purely

[35] The questions referred for a preliminary ruling aimed essentially at clarifying the right to move and reside freely within the Union.

[36] For an interesting application on the status of citizenship, concerning the question of national identity, see Case C-208/09 *Sayn-Wittgenstein*, judgment of 22 December 2010 nyr.

[37] Case C-434/09 *McCarthy*, judgment of 5 May 2011 nyr.

internal situation. As a citizen of at least one Member State, a person like Mrs McCarthy enjoys the status of a Union citizen under Art 20(1) TFEU, and may thus rely on the rights pertaining to that status, including against her Member State of origin, and the rights relative to such a status, in particular the right to move and reside freely on the territory of Member States. However, no element of Mrs McCarthy's situation, as described by the national court, revealed that the national measure at issue in the main proceedings had the effect of depriving her of the genuine enjoyment of the substance of the rights associated with her status as a Union citizen, or of impeding the exercise of her right to move and reside freely within the territory of the Member States. The Court explained, moreover, that in the *Zambrano* and *Garcia Avello* cases, the national measure at issue had the effect of depriving citizens of the Union of the effective enjoyment of the substance of the rights conferred by this status or of hindering the exercise of their right to circulate and reside freely within the territory of the Member States. The situation of a person such as Mrs McCarthy presented no factor linking it with any of the situations governed by Union law and the situation is confined in all relevant aspects within a single Member State.

It follows that the question of the subordination of the exercise of citizenship to a precondition of free movement between Member States, if it ever had foundation, is henceforth resolved. Moreover, the right to move and reside freely remains fertile ground for a favourable evolution of the status of citizenship. It is not difficult to anticipate that due to the expansion of the status of European citizenship, the peculiarities of regulations concerning third country nationals may require, in certain cases, a reconfiguration of the notion of a 'purely internal situation'.

16

'Civis Europaeus Sum': *From the Cross-border Link to the Status of Citizen of the Union*

KOEN LENAERTS*

INTRODUCTION

TRADITIONALLY, THE APPLICATION of the provisions on EU citizenship was conditioned on the existence of a cross-border element. Just as with the provisions on the fundamental freedoms, purely internal situations fell outside the scope of application of the provisions on EU citizenship.[1] A 'purely internal' situation was one lacking any links with EU law. Accordingly, in the absence of a cross-border element, nothing in the Treaties prevented a Member State from discriminating against its own citizens (so-called 'reverse discrimination').

The first section of this chapter is devoted to exploring how the ECJ has determined the existence of such a link. In this regard, it is submitted that the ECJ has followed a broad approach when it comes to identifying a 'cross-border' element. However, some scholars posit that such a broad approach is at odds with the principle of legal certainty. They argue that it is very difficult to draw the external contours of the Treaty provisions on free movement and EU citizenship given that, in order to promote the protection of fundamental rights, the ECJ is too eager to find cross-border elements, which are, more often than not, artificially constructed.[2]

* Judge and President of Chamber at the European Court of Justice, and Professor of European Union Law, Leuven University. All opinions expressed herein are personal to the author.

[1] See Joined Cases C-64/96 and C-65/96 *Uecker and Jacquet* [1997] ECR I-3171, para 23.

[2] See, eg C Dautricourt and S Thomas, 'Reverse Discrimination and Free Movement of Persons under Community Law: All for Ulysses, Nothing for Penelope?' (2009) 34 *EL Rev* 433; N Nic Shuibhne, 'Free Movement of Persons and the Wholly Internal Rule: Time to Move On?' (2002) 39 *CML Rev* 731; E Spaventa, 'Seeing the Wood Despite the Trees? On the Scope of Union Citizenship and its Constitutional Effects' (2008) 45 *CML Rev* 13; A Tryfonidou, 'Reverse Discrimination in Purely Internal Situations: An Incongruity in a Citizens' Europe' (2008) 35 *Legal Issues of Economic Integration* 43.

In *Ruiz Zambrano*,[3] Advocate General Sharpston echoed those critical views, putting forward two approaches. She opined that the ECJ should pursue the trend initiated in *Rottmann*[4] where the ECJ opted for a reading of Article 20 TFEU which focused on interpreting EU citizenship as 'the fundamental status of nationals of the Member States'[5] rather than as the freedom to move of economically inactive citizens. Alternatively, she invited the ECJ to interpret Article 20 TFEU so as to prohibit national measures which, though applied in a purely internal context, give rise to reverse discrimination.[6]

Departing from its traditional approach, the ECJ agreed with the first alternative set out in the Opinion of Advocate General Sharpston. In *Ruiz Zambrano*, the ECJ made it clear that it does not follow from the fact that a situation lacks a cross-border dimension that it has no links with EU law. Regardless of the factual context in which Article 20 TFEU is invoked, a link with EU law exists in so far as a national measure has 'the effect of depriving citizens of the Union of the genuine enjoyment of the substance of the rights conferred by virtue of their status as citizens of the Union'.[7] Whilst it is too soon to identify all of the implications flowing from this seminal judgment, this contribution supports the contention that *Ruiz Zambrano* has emancipated EU citizenship from the constraints inherent in its free movement origins.

GENERAL OBSERVATIONS

A feature shared by both the Treaty provisions on free movement and the Treaty provisions on EU citizenship is that there must be 'a link' or nexus with EU law. For the fundamental freedoms, no link exists where the situation at issue is purely internal.[8] As the ECJ pointed out in *Saunders*,

> [t]he provisions of the Treaty on freedom of movement for workers cannot therefore be applied to situations which are wholly internal to a Member State, in other words, where there is no factor connecting them to any of the situations envisaged by [EU] law.[9]

[3] Case C-34/09 *Ruiz Zambrano*, judgment of 8 March 2011 nyr.

[4] Case C-135/08 *Rottmann* [2010] ECR I-1449.

[5] Case C-184/99 *Grzelczyk* [2001] ECR I-6193, para 31.

[6] Opinion of AG Sharpston, *Ruiz Zambrano*, n 3 above.

[7] *Ruiz Zambrano*, n 3 above, para 42.

[8] In relation to *goods*, see, eg Case 98/86 *Mathot* [1987] ECR 809; Case 286/81 *Oosthoek's Uitgeversmaatschappij* [1982] ECR 4575. As to *establishment*, see, eg Case 204/87 *Bekaert* [1988] ECR 2029; Joined Cases C-54/88, C-91/88 and C-14/89 *Nino* [1990] ECR I-3537. As to *workers*, see, eg Case 175/78 *R* v *Saunders* [1979] ECR 1129; Joined Cases 35/82 and 36/82 *Morson and Jhanjan* v *State of the Netherlands* [1982] ECR 3723; Case C-132/93 *Steen II* [1994] ECR I-2715. Regarding *services*, see, eg Case C-108/98 *RI SAN* [1999] ECR I-5219; Case C-97/98 *Jägerskiöld* [1999] ECR I-7319; Case C-245/09 *Omalet*, judgment of 22 December 2010 nyr. As to *capital*, see Joined Cases C-515/99, C-519/99 to C-524/99 and C-526/99 to C-540/99 *Reisch and ors* [2002] ECR I-2157. In relation to *citizenship*, see *Uecker and Jacquet*, n 1 above; Case C-127/08 *Metock and ors* [2008] ECR I-6241.

[9] *R* v *Saunders*, n 8 above, para 11.

For example, in *Jägerskiöld*, the ECJ found that, since the legal proceedings pending before the referring court concerned a dispute between two Finnish nationals, both established in Finland, regarding the right of one of them to fish in waters belonging to the other situated in Finland, such a situation did not present any link to any of the situations envisaged by EU law in relation to the freedom to provide services.[10]

Originally, the incorporation of the provisions on EU citizenship into the Treaty in 1993 changed nothing in this respect. In this regard, in paragraph 23 of *Uecker and Jacquet*, the ECJ held that

> citizenship of the Union . . . is not intended to extend the scope *ratione materiae* of the Treaty also to internal situations which have no link with [EU] law. . . . Any discrimination which nationals of a Member State may suffer under the law of that State falls within the scope of that law and must therefore be dealt with within the framework of the internal legal system of that State.[11]

It has been argued that the 'cross-border' link requirement amounts to a reformulation of the principle of conferral for the judicial enforcement of Treaty limits imposed upon the Member States.[12] As Ritter explains, extending the application of the fundamental freedoms to purely internal situations would result in a new incursion into national competences, which would deprive the Member States of the power to regulate the factors of production by reference to policy objectives other than those recognised as legitimate by EU law.[13]

The truth is that determining the presence or absence of a link with EU law has significant repercussions for the vertical allocation of powers. The more broadly the 'link' with EU law is interpreted, the wider the material scope of the substantive law of the Union becomes, and the fewer situations there are where reverse discrimination may arise. From a federal perspective, a broad interpretation of the concept of a link with EU law would significantly restrict the exercise of competences pertaining to the Member States.[14] On the contrary, a restrictive interpretation would leave more room for the national legislator.

The case law relating to free movement and EU citizenship indicates that the ECJ has opted for a rather broad interpretation of the required EU link. This has been done in different ways. Five types of cases illustrate this point. Firstly, the

[10] *Jägerskiöld*, n 8 above, paras 42–44.

[11] *Uecker and Jacquet*, n 1 above, para 23. See also Case C-148/02 *Garcia Avello* [2003] ECR I-11613, para 26; Case C-403/03 *Schempp* [2005] ECR I-6421, para 20; Case C-192/05 *Tas-Hagen et Tas* [2006] ECR I-10451, para 23; Case C-212/06 *Gouvernement de la Communauté française et gouvernement wallon* [2008] ECR I-1683, para 39; Case C-499/06 *Nerkowska* [2008] ECR I-3993, para 25.

[12] Others have argued that it enshrines the principle of subsidiarity. See P Oliver, 'Some Further Reflections on the Scope of Articles 28–30 (ex 30–36) EC' (1999) 36 *CML Rev* 783.

[13] C Ritter, 'Purely Internal Situations, Reverse Discrimination, *Guimont, Dzodzi* and Article 234' (2006) 31 *EL Rev* 690, 692.

[14] S O'Leary, *The Evolving Concept of Community Citizenship: From the Free Movement of Persons to Union Citizenship, 13 European Monographs* (Amsterdam, Kluwer Law International, 1996) 276. See also K Lenaerts, 'Federalism and the Rule of Law: Perspectives from the European Court of Justice' (2010) 33 *Fordham International Law Journal* 1338.

ECJ has applied EU law to situations where barriers are erected to insulate a territory from other parts of the same Member State.[15] Secondly, the ECJ has also adopted a relaxed approach when examining whether a contested national measure has a deterrent effect on the exercise of EU rights.[16] Thirdly, cases like *D'Hoop* show that EU law applies when free movers return to their own Member State.[17] Fourthly, it is possible for a person to invoke the EU rights of a third party, in so far as there is a 'direct link' between the legal position of that person and the rights of the third party.[18] Last, but not least, the ECJ has applied the Treaty provisions on EU citizenship in cases where there is no physical movement from one Member State to another, but there are other elements that serve as a sufficient connecting factor to EU law. Since the absence of physical movement played an important role in the rationale of the ECJ in its recent judgments in *Rottmann*, *Ruiz Zambrano* and *McCarthy*,[19] it is worth looking at how a link with EU law was established in those situations in previous cases.

For example, in *Garcia Avello*,[20] one of the first cases of this trend, Mr Garcia Avello and Ms Weber – a Spanish-Belgian couple living in Belgium – decided to follow Spanish law when naming their son and daughter; they used the first surname of the father followed by the first surname of the mother ('Garcia Weber'). However, their application to register the children under that name was rejected by the Belgian Registrar for Births, Marriages and Deaths, on the ground that, in Belgium, children bear their father's surname. Before the ECJ, Belgium argued that there was no link with EU law as the situation of the children of Mr Garcia Avello was purely internal: they were two Belgian nationals residing in Belgium. However, the ECJ rejected that argument. First, it observed that the children of Mr Garcia Avello were also Spanish nationals lawfully residing in Belgium.[21] Second, the ECJ held that Belgian law contravened Articles 18 and 20 TFEU, by putting children with dual nationality at a disadvantage, given that they would have to cope with difficulties resulting from having two different names, both on the professional and on the private level, in using, in one Member State of which they were nationals, the documents or diplomas obtained in another Member State of which they were also nationals.[22]

[15] See, eg Case C-163/90 *Legros and ors* [1992] ECR I-4625; Joined Cases C-363/93 and C-407/93 to C-411/93 *Lancry and ors* [1994] ECR I-3957, Joined Cases C-485/93 and C-486/93 *Simitzi* [1995] ECR I-2655; Case C-281/98 *Angonese* [2000] ECR I-4139.

[16] Case C-60/00 *Carpenter* [2002] ECR I-6279; Case C-1/05 *Jia* [2007] ECR I-1.

[17] See, eg Case C-224/98 *D'Hoop* [2002] ECR I-6191. See also Case C-520/04 *Turpeinen* [2006] ECR I-10685; Joined Cases C-11/06 and C-12/06 *Morgan and Bucher* [2007] ECR I-9161; Case C-353/06 *Grunkin and Paul* [2008] ECR I-7639.

[18] *Schempp*, n 11 above.

[19] Case C-434/09 *McCarthy*, judgment of 5 May 2011 nyr.

[20] *Garcia Avello*, n 11 above.

[21] ibid, paras 27–28, where the ECJ pointed out that the fact that the children also have Belgian nationality was irrelevant. In any event, the ECJ indicated that Belgium could not deny recognition of their Spanish nationality '*by imposing additional requirements, with a view to the exercise of fundamental freedoms provided for in the Treaty*' (emphasis added). See Case C-369/90 *Micheletti and ors* [1992] ECR I-4239, para 10.

[22] ibid, para 36.

In the same way, in *Zhu and Chen*,[23] the ECJ ruled that Article 21 TFEU precluded British authorities from deporting Mrs Chen, a Chinese citizen, who was the mother of Catherine Zhu, an Irish infant, and had sufficient resources to support herself and her daughter. The fact that Catherine – who had acquired Irish nationality as a result of being born in Northern Ireland – had never left the UK had no bearing on the ECJ's findings.[24]

REVERSE DISCRIMINATION

The Traditional Approach to Reverse Discrimination

Traditionally, situations that remained purely internal were entirely governed by national law.[25] This meant that a Member State was free to discriminate against persons not benefiting from the protection of EU law, that is, against nationals who had never exercised their right to move. As explained above, the principle of conferral provides an explanation as to why the ECJ decided not to apply the Treaties to situations which are confined, in all relevant respects, to a single Member State. A traditional discourse on reverse discrimination supports the contention that there are sufficient political or judicial means at national level to tackle such unequal treatment. In addition, the Member States can act together 'as members of the EU legislature to address the problem of reverse discrimination'.[26]

Unlike situations where a national measure discriminates against EU citizens of other Member States, nationals who are adversely affected by reverse discrimination have access to the political process of their home Member State. Where reverse discrimination affects a majority of nationals, it will be very unlikely to persist. Politicians will be obliged to adopt new policies in compliance with the views of that majority. But what happens where reverse discrimination only affects a minority of nationals? Although the political process does not seem a viable alternative in systems suffering from a 'majoritarian bias',[27] such a minority may still rely on the judicial remedies provided for by national law. In this regard, the ECJ held in *Steen II* that

[23] Case C-200/02 *Zhu and Chen* [2004] ECR I-9925.

[24] ibid, para 19 (holding that '[t]he situation of a national of a Member State who was born in the host Member State and has not made use of the right to freedom of movement cannot, for that reason alone, be assimilated to a purely internal situation, thereby depriving that national of the benefit in the host Member State of the provisions of [EU] law on freedom of movement and of residence').

[25] See, eg *R* v *Saunders*, n 8 above, paras 9 ff.

[26] AP Van der Mei, 'Editorial: Combating Reverse Discrimination: Who Should Do the Job?' (2009) 16 *Maastricht Journal of European and Comparative Law* 379, 382 (who argues that '[a]s significant as Union citizenship may be, it is not a magic judicial tool that can be used to fix any legal problem of the nationals of the Member States. The Court's current view is that it is first and foremost for the Member States, either acting on their own or in their capacity as members of the EU legislature, to address the problem of reverse discrimination. Should the [ECJ] alter its view? Is this truly a job for the [ECJ]?').

[27] M Poiares Maduro, 'The Scope of European Remedies: The Case of Reverse Discrimination and Purely Internal Situations' in C Kilpatrick, T Novitz and P Skidmore (eds), *The Future of Remedies in Europe* (Oxford, Hart Publishing, 2000) 117.

> [i]t is for the national court, faced with a question of national law, to determine whether there is any discrimination under that law and whether that discrimination must be eliminated and, if so, how.[28]

Notably, the members of such a minority could try to enforce the constitutional principle of equality.[29] For example, that approach has been embraced in Italy,[30] Austria[31] and France.[32] However, in contrast to the situation where national rules conflict with directly effective EU rights, not all national courts are empowered to set aside national law conflicting with the constitution; nor are they able to rely on the EU principles of equivalence and effectiveness to overcome obstacles inherent in the very nature of the legal systems concerned.[33]

Moreover, where a national court relies on national law with a view to prohibiting reverse discrimination, it can still benefit from the guidance of the ECJ. Indeed, in accordance with *Guimont*, the ECJ will not declare inadmissible questions referred by a national court, where

> it is not obvious that the interpretation of [EU] law requested is not necessary for the national court. Such a reply might be useful to it if its national law were to require, in proceedings such as those in this case, that a national producer must be allowed to enjoy the same rights as those which a producer of another Member State would derive from [EU] law in the same situation.[34]

In other words, the ruling of the ECJ will determine whether the national measure at issue in the main proceedings runs counter to EU law. In the affirmative, the contested national measure will give rise to reverse discrimination and thus the national court will have to decide whether such unequal treatment is constitutionally admissible.[35] The rationale underpinning the *Guimont* line of cases is similar to that in *Dzodzi.*[36] They both reflect the fact that it is of paramount

[28] *Steen II*, n 8 above, para 10.

[29] Poiares Maduro, n 27 above, 137 ff (who is in favour of national courts stepping up).

[30] Corte costituzionale, judgment no 443 of 30 December 1997 (relying on the constitutional principle of equality).

[31] Verfassungsgerichtshof Österreich, judgment no G 42/99 y 135/99 of 9 December 1999 (relying on Art 7 of the Austrian Constitution).

[32] Conseil d'État, judgment of 6 October 2008, *Compagnie des architectes en chefs des monuments historiques* et al re no 310146.

[33] Opinion of AG Poiares Maduro in Case C-72/03 *Carbonati Apuani* [2004] ECR I-8027, para 57.

[34] Case C-448/98 *Guimont* [2000] ECR I-10663, para 23. See also *Reisch and ors*, n 8 above, para 26; Case C-6/01 *Anomar and ors* [2003] ECR I-8621, para 41; Case C-451/03 *Servizi Ausiliari Dottori Commercialisti* [2006] ECR I-2941, para 29; Joined Cases C-94/04 and C-202/04 *Cipolla and ors* [2006] ECR I-11421, para 30; Case C-380/05 *Centro Europa 7* [2008] ECR I-349, para 69; Joined Cases C-570/07 and C-571/07 *Blanco Pérez and Charo Gómez*, judgment of 1 June 2010 nyr, para 39.

[35] Opinion of AG Sharpston in *Ruiz Zambrano*, n 6 above, para 43.

[36] Case 297/88 *Dzodzi* [1990] ECR I-3763. But see Ritter, n 13 above, 698, who argues that 'the Dzodzi principle and the Guimont principle have been co-existing for several years even though they are essentially similar – except for one difference: under the Guimont principle, the [ECJ] does not actually check whether national law prohibits reverse discrimination; nor does it require the national court to show that its national law prohibits reverse discrimination. Whereas under the Dzodzi principle the Court requires an express, absolute and unconditional reference to [EU] law in the national provision. Therefore, one may view Guimont as a relaxed version of Dzodzi'. In his view, the Guimont principle should be abandoned in favour of the Dzodzi principle, since the latter could address the same

importance for the ECJ to forestall future differences of interpretation of EU law, even in situations where the Treaties are applied as a logical prerequisite to the application of, or by virtue of a reference made by, national law.[37]

In addition, where the EU enjoys relevant competences, the EU legislator may adopt harmonising measures that put an end to reverse discrimination. However, that possibility provides only a partial solution to the problem. Indeed, the fundamental freedoms and EU citizenship also apply to situations where the EU legislator lacks the powers to intervene. It is settled case law that, in relation to 'matters coming within the competence of the Member States, the latter must none the less, when exercising that competence, comply with EU law'.[38] For example, whilst the Member States retain the power to adopt national rules in the sphere of criminal legislation, national rules of criminal procedure, national rules governing a person's name, national rules relating to direct taxation, or national rules determining the persons entitled to vote and to stand as candidates in elections to the European Parliament, those national rules may constitute obstacles to free movement,[39] and, as the case may be, give rise to reverse discrimination, without the EU legislator having the power to adopt measures at EU level.

Arguments against Reverse Discrimination

Several authors and Advocates General have urged the ECJ to depart from its traditional approach to reverse discrimination.[40] In their view, reverse discrimination *as such* should be prohibited by the Treaties. Stated differently, an individual should be able to rely on the Treaty provisions on EU citizenship in order to combat reverse discrimination, regardless of whether his or her situation is confined in all relevant respects to a single Member State.

Those scholars argue that, ever since the provisions on EU citizenship were incorporated into the Treaties in 1993, the ECJ has sought to broaden the concept of a 'cross-border' link so as to avoid situations which may give rise to reverse discrimination. Whilst recognising the ECJ's efforts to prevent reverse discrimination, they believe that 'the expansionist momentum that has characterised the ECJ's stance on the free movement of persons'[41] has led to the establishment of tenuous, even artificial, connections with free movement that not only blur the

problems as the former, while preventing the ECJ from exercising its jurisdiction in cases where national law does not actually prohibit reverse discrimination. See also Opinion of AG Poiares Maduro in *Carbonati Apuani*, n 33 above, para 57.

[37] *Dzodzi*, n 36 above, para 37. See Case C-130/95 *Giloy* [1997] ECR I-4291, para 28; Case C-300/01 *Salzmann* [2003] ECR I-4899, para 34; Case C-222/01 *British American Tobacco* [2004] ECR I-4683, para 40.

[38] See, eg Case C-274/96 *Bickel and Franz* [1998] ECR I-7637, para 17; *Garcia Avello*, n 11 above, para 17; *Schempp*, n 11 above, para 19; Case C-145/04 *Spain v United Kingdom* [2006] ECR I-7917, para 78.

[39] *Rottmann*, n 4 above, para 41.

[40] See, eg Dautricourt and Thomas, n 2 above; Nic Shuibhne, n 2 above; Spaventa, n 2 above; Tryfonidou, n 2 above.

[41] Nic Shuibhne, n 2 above, 770.

scope of application of EU law, but also give rise to abusive practices.[42] In their view, the ECJ should adopt a more straightforward and clear stand against reverse discrimination.

Originally, reverse discrimination served to draw the distinction between persons contributing directly to the establishment and functioning of the internal market and those who were not. Accordingly, since 'static' persons did not engage in the development of intra-Community trade, there was no reason why EU law should protect them.[43] However, the incorporation of the provisions on EU citizenship into the Treaty is said to have opened the door to a new paradigm, according to which the right to move and reside in the EU is no longer reserved to economically active persons exercising a cross-border activity, but is to be enjoyed by all EU citizens.[44] According to this view, the objectives of the EU have evolved beyond market integration, so that they now include the prohibition of any 'discrimination arising as a result of the process of European integration.'[45] Accordingly, if the ECJ were to abandon its traditional approach to reverse discrimination, it would be redefining the constitutional role played by EU citizenship. The potential of Article 20 TFEU would then transcend market-integration rhetoric, transforming into a living truth the idea that Union citizenship is destined to become the fundamental status of Member States' nationals.[46]

The Opinions of Advocate General Sharpston

In her Opinion in *Government of the French Community and Walloon Government*, Advocate General Sharpston also urged the ECJ to abandon its traditional approach to reverse discrimination. After advocating the application, by analogy, of the prohibition on internal tariff barriers[47] to the realm of the free movement of persons,[48] the Advocate General sought to base her arguments on the status of citizen of the Union.

First, Advocate General Sharpston argued that it does not follow from the fact that a situation is 'internal' that there is 'no link' with EU law. For example, Article 157 TFEU on equal pay for men and women applies to situations which are normally wholly internal.[49] Second, she called into question the reference to ex Article

[42] Tryfonidou, n 2 above, 52.

[43] ibid, 54.

[44] Nic Shuibhne, n 2 above, 757 ff.

[45] Tryfonidou, n 2 above, 61.

[46] Spaventa, n 2 above, 31.

[47] See, eg *Legros and ors*, n 15 above; *Lancry and ors*, n 15 above; *Simitzi* n 15 above; *Carbonati Apuani*, n 33 above.

[48] Opinion of AG Sharpston in *Gouvernement de la Communauté française et gouvernement wallon*, n 11 above, para 122 ff. In her view, just as with Arts 28 and 30 TFEU, Art 45 TFEU should be read together with Art 26(2) TFEU so that all obstacles, internal and external, to the free movement of workers fall within the scope of EU law.

[49] ibid, para 136.

47 EU contained in paragraph 23 of *Uecker and Jacquet*.[50] In her view, that provision only operated to protect the *acquis communautaire* from being affected by Common Foreign and Security Policy ('CFSP') and Police and Judicial Cooperation in Criminal Matters ('PJCC') measures. It would clearly have been wrong to conceive that ex Article 47 EU was intended to protect certain parts of the existing EC Treaty from other parts, such as the Articles on EU citizenship that were inserted by amendment into that same Treaty by the Maastricht Treaty.[51] Third, the Advocate General observed that nothing in the wording of Article 20 TFEU prevented the ECJ from reading that provision as conferring on every citizen the 'right to *both* move and *to* reside' within the territory of the Member States (as opposed to the more limited right to 'move and *then* reside'). Echoing the Opinion of Advocate General Poiares Maduro in *Carbonati Apuani*, for whom 'it is now clearly one of the fundamental objectives of the [Union] to ensure that no discrimination of any kind should arise as a result of the application of its own rules',[52] Advocate General Sharpston posited that, in light of Article 21 of the Charter and Article 19 TFEU, '[d]iscrimination is thus generally perceived to be repugnant and something that should be prohibited'.[53]

In *Ruiz Zambrano*,[54] Advocate General Sharpston took the opportunity to develop her thesis further. In that case, the referring court asked, in essence, whether Mr Ruiz Zambrano, a Colombian national residing illegally in Belgium, could rely on the Treaty provisions on EU citizenship with a view to obtaining a derivative right of residence as the father of two Belgian children. By obtaining such a derivative right, Mr Ruiz Zambrano also sought to obtain a work permit to which, as an illegal immigrant, he was not entitled under Belgian law. The referring court also asked whether EU law opposes reverse discrimination, implicitly on the assumption that the situation of Mr Ruiz Zambrano was to be qualified as purely internal. The facts in *Ruiz Zambrano* may be distinguished from those in *Zhu and Chen*. Whilst both cases dealt with EU citizens who were infants, had never exercised their right to free movement, and were dependent on a relative in the ascending line who was a national of a third country, only *Ruiz Zambrano* involved EU citizens residing in the Member State of which they were nationals.

The Advocate General urged the ECJ to reply in the affirmative. As will be explained below, she opined that the situation of Mr Ruiz Zambrano was not purely internal. In addition, she argued that even if the ECJ were to hold that the situation of Mr Ruiz Zambrano was purely internal, Article 18 TFEU, read in con-

[50] *Uecker and Jacquet*, n 1 above, para 23: '[i]n that regard, it must be noted that citizenship of the Union, established by Article [17] of the EC Treaty, is not intended to extend the scope ratione materiae of the Treaty also to internal situations which have no link with Community law. Furthermore, Article [47] of the Treaty on European Union provides that nothing in that Treaty is to affect the Treaties establishing the European Communities, subject to the provisions expressly amending those treaties'.

[51] Opinion of AG Sharpston in *Gouvernement de la Communauté française et gouvernement wallon*, n 11 above, para 138.

[52] See also Opinion of AG Poiares Maduro in *Carbonati Apuani*, n 33 above, para 63.

[53] Opinion of AG Sharpston in *Gouvernement de la Communauté française et gouvernement wallon*, n 11 above, para 147 ff (referring to Case C-300/04 *Eman and Sevinger* [2006] ECR I-8055).

[54] Opinion of AG Sharpston in *Ruiz Zambrano*, n 6 above.

junction with Article 21 TFEU, would prohibit reverse discrimination. In her view, cases like *Carpenter*, *Zhu and Chen*, and *Metock*[55] suggest that, by embracing the traditional approach to reverse discrimination, the ECJ is caught on the horns of a constitutional dilemma. Those cases create legal uncertainty in a delicate area of both EU law and domestic law, as they are based on a broad and unpredictable interpretation of Article 21 TFEU intended to promote the protection of fundamental rights, notably the right to a family life.[56] For the Advocate General, a more proactive and straightforward approach to reverse discrimination could have the best of both worlds, since it would put an end to the uncertainty surrounding that line of case law without undermining the protection of fundamental rights. Advocate General Sharpston opined that

> Article 18 TFEU should be interpreted as prohibiting reverse discrimination caused by the interaction between Article 21 TFEU and national law that entails a violation of a fundamental right protected under EU law, where at least equivalent protection is not available under national law.[57]

In accordance with her approach, three cumulative conditions must be met. First, reverse discrimination would only arise where the EU citizen concerned resided in his or her home Member State and had not yet exercised his or her right to move.[58] Second, there would need to be a violation of his or her fundamental rights, as protected by the ECHR.[59] This means that minor instances of reverse discrimination would not fall within the scope of application of Article 18 TFEU. Finally, the Treaty provisions on EU citizenship would only apply if national law failed to provide effective remedies capable of eliminating the wrongs caused by reverse discrimination. Stated differently, Article 18 TFEU would operate as a subsidiary remedy.[60]

THE ADVENT OF A NEW APPROACH: *ROTTMANN*

Rottmann is a landmark judgment which opens a new stage in the law on EU citizenship. In this case, the ECJ focuses on the 'status of citizen of the Union' rather than on the existence of elements demonstrating a cross-border situation. The facts of the case are as follows. Whilst being the subject of judicial investigations in Austria, Dr Rottmann, an Austrian national, moved to Germany in 1995. Two years later, Austria issued an arrest warrant against him. In February 1999, he acquired German nationality by naturalisation, which meant losing his Austrian nationality at the same time. However, in August 1999, Austria informed Germany of the arrest warrant issued against Dr Rottmann. Taking the view that by with-

[55] *Carpenter*, n 16 above; *Zhu and Chen*, n 23 above; *Metock*, n 8 above.
[56] Opinion of AG Sharpston in *Ruiz Zambrano*, n 6 above, para 141.
[57] ibid, para 144.
[58] ibid, para 146.
[59] ibid, para 147.
[60] ibid, para 148.

holding that information Dr Rottmann had obtained German nationality by deception, Germany revoked that nationality and, since the original nationality did not revive, Dr Rottmann became stateless. Dr Rottmann challenged that decision before the German courts. In essence, the referring court asked the ECJ whether, in a situation such as that of Dr Rottmann, it was contrary to Article 20 TFEU for a Member State to withdraw from a citizen of the Union the nationality of that State acquired by naturalisation and obtained by deception inasmuch as that withdrawal deprived the person concerned of the status of citizen of the Union and of the benefit of the rights attaching thereto by rendering him stateless, acquisition of that nationality having caused that person to lose the nationality of his Member State of origin.

At the outset, several Member States posited that the rules on the acquisition and loss of nationality do not fall within the scope of application of EU law, as those rules remain within the realm of national sovereignty.[61] However, the ECJ dismissed that argument, recalling that the powers retained by the Member States may be circumscribed by the substantive law of the EU. For the case at hand, this meant that the Member States must, when exercising their powers in the sphere of nationality, have due regard to EU law.[62] Moreover, Germany and Austria urged the ECJ to declare the preliminary reference inadmissible as all the elements of the case at hand were confined to a single Member State, namely Germany: at the time the contested decision was adopted Dr Rottmann was a German national, living in Germany, to whom an administrative act was addressed by a German authority. However, Advocate General Poiares Maduro opined that the ECJ should reject that objection of admissibility, focusing on 'the origins of [Dr] Rottmann's situation'.[63] For the Advocate General,

> the exercise by [Dr] Rottmann of his right, as a citizen of the Union, to move and reside in another Member State had an impact on the change in his civil status: it was because he transferred his residence to Germany that he had been able to satisfy the conditions for acquiring German nationality, namely, lawful habitual residence within that country's territory.[64]

Like the Advocate General, the ECJ dismissed the argument put forward by Germany and Austria. In so doing, however, it adopted a different approach. In contrast to Advocate General Poiares Maduro, the ECJ 'disregard[ed Dr Rottmann's] earlier move and look[ed] exclusively to the future effects that withdrawal of German citizenship would have by rendering [Dr] Rottmann stateless.'[65] In the key passage of the judgment, the ECJ held that

> [i]t is clear that the situation of a citizen of the Union who, like the applicant in the main proceedings, is faced with a decision withdrawing his naturalisation, adopted by

[61] *Rottmann*, n 4 above, para 37.
[62] ibid, para 41.
[63] Opinion of AG Poiares Maduro in *Rottmann*, n 4 above, para 11.
[64] ibid, para 13.
[65] Opinion of AG Sharpston in *Ruiz Zambrano*, n 6 above, para 78.

> the authorities of one Member State, and placing him, after he has lost the nationality of another Member State that he originally possessed, in a position capable of causing him to lose the status conferred by Article [20 TFEU] and the rights attaching thereto falls, by reason of its nature and its consequences, within the ambit of [EU] law.[66]

In reaching that conclusion, the ECJ stressed once again that 'citizenship of the Union is intended to be the fundamental status of nationals of the Member States'.[67] With a view to transforming this postulate into a living truth, the ECJ places weight on the status of citizen of the Union *as such* rather than on free movement. In light of *Rottmann*, even if there is no actual physical movement across a frontier, national measures which deprive an individual of his or her status of citizen of the Union and thereby of the rights attaching to that status, fall within the scope of application of the Treaty provisions on EU citizenship.

'CIVIS EUROPAEUS SUM': *RUIZ ZAMBRANO*

Rottmann left open the question whether the absence of a cross-border element prevents the application of Article 20 TFEU where a national measure does not deprive an individual of his or her status as an EU citizen but, in practical terms, produces the same effect. Stated simply, was the rationale underpinning *Rottmann* to be limited to national measures whose application results in a legal deprivation of the status of citizen of the Union or did it also extend to measures that deprived an EU citizen of the genuine enjoyment of the substance of the rights attaching to that status? In *Ruiz Zambrano*, the ECJ was confronted with that very question. Since the facts of the case have been explained above, for the sake of brevity there is no need to repeat them here.

All intervening Member States and the Commission argued that the situation of Mr Ruiz Zambrano was one that was purely internal to Belgium: the son and daughter of Mr Ruiz Zambrano were two Belgian citizens who had never exercised their right to move. However, Advocate General Sharpston did not share that view. For her, cases like *Garcia Avello*, *Zhu and Chen*, and *Rottmann* show that the Treaty provisions on EU citizenship have been applied in spite of the fact that 'the element of true movement was either barely discernable or frankly non-existent'.[68] She also criticised the traditional approach of the ECJ by saying that '[l]ottery rather than logic would seem to govern the exercise of EU citizenship rights'.[69] As to the question whether the situation of Mr Ruiz Zambrano was to be treated as a purely internal one, she urged the ECJ to read *Rottmann* in conjunction with its findings in *Zhu and Chen*. The Advocate General conceded that, unlike the contested decision in *Rottmann*, the Belgian legislation at issue did not deprive the son and daughter of

[66] *Rottmann*, n 4 above, para 42.
[67] ibid, para 43.
[68] Opinion of AG Sharpston in *Ruiz Zambrano*, n 6 above, para 77.
[69] ibid, para 88.

Mr Ruiz Zambrano of their status as EU citizens. However, bearing in mind that the deportation of Mr Ruiz Zambrano to Colombia (or to any other third country) would require his son and daughter to leave the territory of the EU with him, Advocate General Sharpston argued that

> [t]hat would, in practical terms, place [such children] in a position capable of causing them to lose the status conferred [by their citizenship of the Union] and the rights attaching thereto. [Hence,] the children's situation 'falls, by reason of its nature and its consequences, within the ambit of EU law'.[70]

In the same way as in the situation of Catherine Zhu in *Zhu and Chen*, it would be impossible for the son and daughter of Mr Ruiz Zambrano to exercise their rights to move and reside in any Member State without the support of their father.[71] Therefore, Advocate General Sharpston concluded that Article 20 TFEU was applicable to a situation such as that of Mr Ruiz Zambrano. Moreover, she found that the Belgian legislation at issue was an interference with the rights of his son and daughter to move and reside in the EU, which could not be justified as it failed to comply with the principle of proportionality.[72] The ECJ agreed with the Advocate General, ruling that Article 20 TFEU was applicable to the situation of Mr Ruiz Zambrano. The ECJ began by noting that Article 3 of Directive 2004/38,[73] which defines the persons benefiting from the rights contained therein, was not applicable to the case at hand, since that provision applies to EU citizens 'who move to or reside in a Member State other than that of which they are a national, and to their family members'.[74] Next, the ECJ held that, since the son and daughter of Mr Ruiz Zambrano were Belgian nationals, Article 20 TFEU conferred the status of citizen of the Union on them.[75] After stressing that 'citizenship of the Union is intended to be the fundamental status of nationals of the Member States',[76] the ECJ ruled, in the key passage of the judgment, that

> Article 20 TFEU precludes national measures which have the effect of depriving citizens of the Union of the genuine enjoyment of the substance of the rights conferred by virtue of their status as citizens of the Union.[77]

For the case at hand this meant that a refusal to grant a right of residence to a third country national with dependent minor children in the Member State where those children are nationals and reside, and also a refusal to grant such a person a

[70] ibid, para 95.
[71] ibid, para 96.
[72] ibid, para 98 ff.
[73] Directive 2004/38/EC of the European Parliament and of the Council of 29 April 2004 on the right of citizens of the Union and their family members to move and reside freely within the territory of the Member States amending Regulation (EEC) No 1612/68 and repealing Directives 64/221/EEC, 68/360/EEC, 72/194/EEC, 73/148/EEC, 75/34/EEC, 75/35/EEC, 90/364/EEC, 90/365/EEC and 93/96/EEC, OJ [2004] L 158/77.
[74] *Ruiz Zambrano*, n 3 above, para 39.
[75] ibid, para 40.
[76] ibid, para 41.
[77] ibid, para 42 (referring to *Rottmann*, n 4 above, para 42).

work permit, has such an effect.[78] Thus, Mr Ruiz Zambrano had a derivative right of residence in Belgium.

Whilst it is too early to forecast the full impact of *Ruiz Zambrano* on EU citizenship, I would like, however, to make six observations. First, it follows from *Ruiz Zambrano* that Article 20 TFEU applies to EU citizens who reside in their home Member State but have not exercised their right to move, provided that the national measure at issue deprives that citizen of 'the genuine enjoyment of the substance of the rights conferred by virtue of their status as citizens of the Union' (in French: privation 'de la jouissance effective de l'essentiel des droits conférés par leur statut de citoyen de l'Union'). Contrary to the traditional approach, *Ruiz Zambrano* stresses that a link with EU citizenship may exist in spite of the absence of physical movement across the border of the home Member State.

Second, although the ECJ referred to 'the genuine enjoyment of the substance of the rights conferred by virtue of' EU citizenship, I believe that the rationale underpinning *Ruiz Zambrano* also applies to national measures the effect of which are to deprive an EU citizen of the genuine enjoyment of the substance of some, but not all, of the rights attaching to that status. Indeed, for example, the national measure at issue in *Ruiz Zambrano* did not deprive Mr Ruiz Zambrano's son and daughter of their right to seek diplomatic and consular protection in the territory of a third country as provided for by Article 23 TFEU.

Third, *Ruiz Zambrano* illustrates that EU citizenship not only operates under a pro-integrationist rhetoric, but also emulates the rationale under which human rights apply. In light of *Ruiz Zambrano*, any EU citizen is

> entitled to say 'civis europeus sum' [to all the Member States, including his or her own,] and to invoke [the Treaty provisions on EU citizenship] in order to oppose any [deprivation of the genuine enjoyment of the substance of the rights conferred by virtue of EU citizenship].[79]

Like human rights in democratic societies, the rights attaching to EU citizenship operate as a protective umbrella that stays with EU citizens, regardless of whether they move or stand still. Hence, the fact that the deprivation of those rights takes place in a context lacking a cross-border dimension is not decisive.

Fourth, in contrast to its previous ruling in *Rottmann* and the Opinion of Advocate General Sharpston, the ECJ held that Article 20 TFEU opposed a national measure such as that at issue in the main proceedings, without first determining whether it complied with the principle of proportionality. However, this does not mean that the new approach developed in *Ruiz Zambrano* makes no room for that principle. In my view, the reason why the national measure in question was not examined under the principle of proportionality lies in that Belgium did not provide any justification as to the compatibility of that measure with Article 20 TFEU. Instead, it limited itself to arguing that Article 20 TFEU did not

[78] ibid, para 43.

[79] Opinion of AG Jacobs in Case C-168/91 *Konstantinidis* [1993] ECR I-1191, para 46.

apply to the case at hand. Be that as it may, it seems very difficult for a national measure, which causes the de facto loss of the status of citizen of the Union, to pass muster under the proportionality principle, given that 'citizenship of the Union is intended to be the fundamental status of nationals of the Member States'.

Fifth, an *a contrario* interpretation of *Ruiz Zambrano* suggests that there is no link with EU law where there is no deprivation of 'the genuine enjoyment of the substance of the rights conferred by virtue of their status as citizens of the Union.' Such an interpretation leaves open two different, albeit interconnected, questions. The first question is whether the expression 'national measures which have the effect of depriving . . .' is to be interpreted as a synonym of the expression 'national measures which are liable to hinder or make less attractive the exercise of [rights attaching to the status of citizen of the Union] guaranteed by the Treaty' (broad interpretation),[80] or whether the expression 'national measures which have the effect of depriving . . .' refers to situations in which EU citizens have de facto lost a right attaching to the status of citizen of the Union (restrictive interpretation). As to the second question, it seems that the deprivation of a right attaching to the status of EU citizenship must relate to the 'substance' of those rights. Obviously, a restrictive interpretation of the expression 'national measures which have the effect of depriving . . .' would render the term 'substance' redundant, as a de facto loss of a right attaching to the status of citizen of the Union would, by definition, affect its substance. Conversely, the term 'substance' would be of paramount importance, if the expression 'national measures which have the effect of depriving . . .' were to be interpreted broadly. In accordance with such a broad interpretation, the ECJ will be called upon to draw the distinction between violations affecting the substance of a right attaching to EU citizenship and violations which do not.

Last, but not least, it is worth noting that, unlike the Opinion of Advocate General Sharpston, the ECJ did not address the issue of reverse discrimination. Perhaps, once it held that the situation of Mr Ruiz Zambrano was not purely internal, the ECJ reasoned that it was no longer necessary to determine the role played by reverse discrimination in the context of EU citizenship. However, one might also argue that the ECJ evaluated the alternatives put forward by Advocate General Sharpston, choosing an approach based on the status of citizen of the Union over one that relied on the prohibition of reverse discrimination. It is true that in the case at hand both approaches led to the same solution. That will not always be the case, however: reverse discrimination may arise even in situations where there is no deprivation for EU citizens of 'the genuine enjoyment of the substance of the rights conferred by virtue of their status as citizens of the Union'.

[80] That expression is commonly used by the ECJ in the context of the Treaty provisions on free movement. See, eg Case C-19/92 *Kraus* [1993] ECR I-1663, para 32.

THE EPILOGUE: *MCCARTHY*

In *McCarthy*,[81] the ECJ had for the first time the opportunity to apply its new approach to EU citizenship. In so doing, the ECJ clarified some of the issues that *Ruiz Zambrano* left open, notably the interaction between Articles 20 and 21 TFEU, and the interpretation of the expression 'national measures which have the effect of depriving . . .'. The facts of the case may be summarised as follows. Mrs McCarthy, a dual Irish and UK national, was born and had always lived in the UK, that is, she had never exercised her right of free movement. Mrs McCarthy married a Jamaican national who lacked leave to remain in the UK in accordance with that Member State's immigration laws. In order to prevent his deportation, Mrs and Mr McCarthy applied to the Secretary of State for a residence permit and residence document under EU law as, respectively, a Union citizen and the spouse of a Union citizen. However, their application was rejected on the ground that Mrs McCarthy was neither economically active nor self-sufficient, as she was a recipient of State benefits. The referring court asked, in essence,

> whether Article 3(1) of Directive 2004/38 or Article 21 TFEU [was] applicable to the situation of a Union citizen who [had] never exercised [her] right of free movement, who [had] always resided in a Member State of which [she was] a national and who [was] also a national of another Member State.

If so, the referring court also asked whether that Union citizen could be considered to be a legal resident for the purposes of Article 16 of Directive 2004/38, in spite of the fact that she did not satisfy the requirements of Article 7 thereof.

The ECJ began by recalling that a Union citizen in a situation such as that of Mrs McCarthy is not covered by the concept of 'beneficiary' as provided for by Article 3(1) of Directive 2004/38. In addition to relying on the wording of that provision, the ECJ found that a teleological and contextual interpretation of Article 3(1) also led to a negative reply to the first question referred by the national court. In this regard, the ECJ noted that the residence of a person residing in the Member State of which he is a national cannot be made subject to conditions, since this would run counter to the principle of international law,[82] recognised by EU law, which precludes a Member State from refusing its own nationals the right to enter its territory and remain there for any reason, or expelling its own nationals from its territory, or refusing their right to reside in that territory, or making such right conditional.[83] Accordingly, since Directive 2004/38 sets out the conditions governing the exercise of the right to move and reside freely within the territory of the Member States, it cannot apply to a Union citizen who enjoys an unconditional right of residence due to the fact that he resides in the Member State of which he is a national.[84]

[81] *McCarthy*, n 19 above.
[82] That principle is reaffirmed in Art 3 of Protocol No 4 to the ECHR.
[83] *McCarthy*, n 19 above, para 29.
[84] ibid, para 34.

As to the applicability of Article 21 TFEU, the ECJ held that EU law does not apply to situations 'which have no factor linking them with situations governed by [EU] law and which are confined in all relevant respects within a single Member State'.[85] However, the ECJ pointed out that even if a Union citizen, like Mrs McCarthy, has not made use of her right of free movement, it does not follow that her situation is, for that reason alone, to be considered as purely internal.[86] Quoting the key passage of *Ruiz Zambrano*, the ECJ held that

> Article 20 TFEU precludes national measures which have the effect of depriving Union citizens of the genuine enjoyment of the substance of the rights conferred by virtue of that status.[87]

Needless to say, among the rights attaching to the status of citizen of the Union, there is the right to move and reside freely within the territory of the Member States, which is enshrined in Article 21 TFEU. However, the ECJ held that

> no element of the situation of Mrs McCarthy, as described by the national court, indicates that the national measure at issue in the main proceedings has the effect of *depriving* her of the genuine enjoyment of the substance of the rights associated with her status as a Union citizen, or of *impeding* the exercise of her right to move and reside freely within the territory of the Member States, in accordance with Article 21 TFEU.[88] (emphasis added)

Indeed, the failure by the UK authorities to take into account Mrs McCarthy's Irish nationality had in no way affected her right to move and reside freely within the EU.

Next, the ECJ went on to distinguish the facts of the case at hand from those in *Ruiz Zambrano* and *Garcia Avello*. In contrast to *Ruiz Zambrano*, the ECJ observed that the national measure at issue in the main proceedings did not have the effect of obliging Mrs McCarthy to leave the EU.[89] As to *Garcia Avello*, the ECJ explained that what mattered in that case was not whether the discrepancy in surnames was the result of the dual nationality of the persons concerned, but the fact that that discrepancy was liable to cause serious inconvenience for the Union citizens concerned that constituted an obstacle to freedom of movement that could be justified only if it was based on objective considerations and was proportionate to the legitimate aim pursued.[90] Stated differently, the ECJ ruled that dual nationality is not in itself a sufficient connecting factor with EU law.[91] Accordingly, the ECJ ruled that the situation of a person such as Mrs McCarthy had no factor linking it with any of the situations governed by EU law and was thus confined in all relevant respects within a single Member State.

[85] ibid, para 45.
[86] ibid, para 46.
[87] ibid, para 47.
[88] ibid, para 49.
[89] ibid, para 50.
[90] ibid, para 52 (*Grunkin and Paul*, n 17 above, paras 23, 24 and 29).
[91] ibid, para 54.

In accordance with the ruling of the ECJ in *McCarthy*, one may argue that a combined reading of Articles 20 and 21 TFEU suggests that in order for a national measure to fall within the scope of EU law, the latter must produce either a 'deprivation effect' or an 'impeding effect'. In my view, the 'impeding effect' refers to the traditional line of case law according to which the application of the Treaty provisions on EU citizenship requires the existence of a cross-border link. Thus, the 'impeding effect' requires a cross-border link but it does not require the national measure in question to cause the loss, in practice, of the status of citizen of the Union. As *Garcia Avello* shows, it suffices that the national measure at issue is liable to cause 'serious inconvenience' to a right attaching to the status of citizen of the Union. By contrast, as *Ruiz Zambrano* made clear, the 'deprivation effect' does not depend on the existence of such a link, but focuses on the rights attaching to the status of EU citizen. Or, in other words, the 'deprivation effect' does not require a cross-border link but requires the national measure to cause more than 'serious inconvenience'. That effect requires a de facto loss of one of the rights attaching to the status of citizen of the Union. It follows from the foregoing that the 'impeding' and 'deprivation' effect are subject to different requirements which are not, however, mutually exclusive: it is still possible for a national measure which applies in a cross-border context to cause the loss of the status of EU citizen, thus producing both types of effect.

Furthermore, it is worth noting that the ECJ did not expressly refer to *Zhu and Chen*. However, that silence should not be interpreted as a sign of inconsistency. On the contrary, in my view, a close reading of *Zhu and Chen* suggests that the latter is actually consistent with *McCarthy*. In that case, one should recall that the application of the national measure in question would have caused a 'deprivation effect': just like the children of Mr Ruiz Zambrano, the deportation of Mrs Chen would have forced Catherine Zhu to leave the territory of the Union. The deportation of her mother would indeed have had 'the effect of depriving her of the genuine enjoyment of the substance of the rights associated with her status as a Union citizen'. Hence, her Irish nationality provided a sufficient connecting factor with EU law, but not because she was an Irish national living in the UK, but owing to the fact that her Irish nationality allowed her to benefit from the rights attaching to her status as an EU citizen. Accordingly, since the national measure at issue caused the de facto loss of a right attaching to her status as an EU citizen, namely her right to move, that measure fell within the scope of Article 21 TFEU.[92]

Moreover, it is true that in *Ruiz Zambrano*, instead of having recourse to Article 21 TFEU, the ECJ grounded the 'deprivation effect' in Article 20 TFEU. However, given that Article 21 TFEU limits itself to giving expression to a right already laid down in Article 20(2)(a) TFEU, one may argue that Article 21 TFEU also opposes

[92] Today, an EU citizen in the same situation as that of Catherine Zhu would fall within the scope of Art 3(1) of Directive 2004/38, as that person, unlike Ms McCarthy, would only have the Irish nationality. Hence, he or she would be an Irish national challenging an administrative decision adopted by the UK authorities.

a national measure which has 'the effect of depriving a Union citizen of the genuine enjoyment of the substance of [the right to move]'.[93]

CONCLUSION

In light of *Rottmann*, *Ruiz Zambrano*, and *McCarthy*, the Treaty provisions on EU citizenship are something more than a 'fifth freedom' which protects economically inactive free movers. In contrast to the Treaty provisions on free movement, a link with EU citizenship may exist in the absence of a cross-border element. 'Article 20 TFEU precludes national measures which have the effect of depriving citizens of the Union of the genuine enjoyment of the substance of the rights conferred by virtue of their status as citizens of the Union',[94] even if such measures apply in respect of an EU citizen who resides in his or her home Member State and has never exercised his or her right to free movement. Moreover, *McCarthy* made clear that in order for a national measure to fall within the scope of Article 21 TFEU, the latter must produce either a 'deprivation effect' or an 'impeding effect'. Whilst the latter effect is still governed by the rhetoric of free movement, the former focuses on the status of citizen of the Union. *McCarthy* also suggests that the approach put forward by the ECJ in *Ruiz Zambrano* is limited to cases where a national measure produces a de facto deprivation of one of the rights listed in Article 20(2) TFEU. Therefore, the ECJ has opted for a restrictive interpretation of the expression 'national measures which have the effect of depriving . . .'. In my view, this is a positive development, since otherwise the ECJ would run the risk of excessively loosening the requirement of a connecting factor for the application of the Treaty provisions on EU citizenship, thus disturbing the vertical allocation of powers sought by the Treaties.

As a postscript, a brief reference should be made to the recently decided *Dereci* case in which the Grand Chamber of the ECJ made an integrated reading of *Ruiz Zambrano* and *McCarthy* and expressly confirmed the restrictive interpretation of the 'deprivation effect'.[95] Such effect will only occur in a situation in which an EU citizen has, in fact, to leave not only the territory of the Member State of which he or she is a national but also the territory of the Union as a whole. And only when – exceptionally[96] – such 'deprivation effect' takes place will the situation of the EU citizen concerned fall within the scope of EU law for the purposes of Article 51(1) of the Charter of Fundamental Rights of the European Union and will such citizen be entitled to raise a plea against his or her Member State founded on Article 7 of the Charter concerning respect for private and family life. This means, in essence, that this fundamental right plays no role when determining whether a 'deprivation effect' exists. The latter depends rather on the factual circumstances of the case.

[93] *Ruiz Zambrano*, n 3 above, para 42.
[94] *Ruiz Zambrano*, n 3 above, para 42 (referring to *Rottmann*, n 4 above, para 42).
[95] Case C-256/11 *Dereci*, judgment of 15 November 2011 nyr.
[96] ibid, para 67.

When the facts of the case trigger a 'deprivation effect', a material link with the rights attaching to the status of EU citizen is established as a result of which the provisions of the Charter can be applied to the legal relationship between such citizen and the Member State of which he or she is a national. If the ECJ had opted for an inverse order, the material link with EU law would have been derived from the Charter itself and such approach would have conflicted with Article 51(1) thereof.[97] Indeed, the risk would then have become real that provisions of the Charter could be invoked even outside the material scope of the application of EU law, in every internal legal relationship between an EU citizen and the Member State of which he or she is a national. The drafters of the Charter expressly sought to avoid such risk.

The ECJ neutralised that risk. In doing so, however, it stressed the complementary role of the legal orders adjacent to the Union legal order, providing a real-life illustration of the legal doctrine of 'constitutional pluralism'. According to this doctrine each legal order, within its sphere of competence, bears responsibility for the protection of fundamental rights. In *Dereci* the ECJ therefore indicated that its ruling was without prejudice to the question whether, on the basis of other criteria, inter alia, by virtue of the right to the protection of family life as provided for in the national constitution or in the ECHR, a right of residence had to be granted to the citizen of a third country.[98]

[97] ibid, paras 70–72.
[98] ibid, paras 69, 72–73.

17

Zambrano, *An Unexpected Ruling*

PAOLO MENGOZZI*

THE IMPORTANT ECJ judgment in *Zambrano*[1] has already been the object of many scholarly commentaries. In one of the most substantial of those, R Palladino does not pretend to give an exhaustive interpretation[2] but raises a fundamental question: whether and on what basis the Court recognises to the benefit of a third country national, father of two very young children who are citizens of a Member State, the right to obtain, in that same Member State, both a residence and a work permit? This question is worthy of a reply. First of all, the answer concerns the allocation of powers between the Member States and the EU as far as citizenship and, particularly, immigration policy are concerned. Secondly, it is appropriate to verify Palladino's suggestion that the judgment *appears* to shape the right of residence of the father as stemming from the same right attributed to his children because of their status as Union citizens, autonomously from their right of free movement from one Member State to another. In order to proceed to such verification it is useful to start with a brief summary of the facts of the

* Advocate General of the Court of Justice of the European Union, Professor of International Law and Union Law, University of Bologna.

[1] Case C-34/09 *Zambrano*, judgment of 8 March 2011, nyr.

[2] See R Palladino, 'Il diritto di soggiorno nel "proprio" Stato membro quale (nuovo) corollario della cittadinanza europea?' in (2011) *Studi sull'integrazione europea* 331. On the same judgment see also R Grand, 'Consécration d'un droit de séjour européen independent de la libre circulation' (2011) *L'Actualité Juridique Droit Administratif* 38; F Picod, 'Reconnaissance d'un droit de séjour à un ressortissant colombien père de deux enfants devenus citoyens de l'Union' (2011) *La Semaine Juridique – édition générale* 543; J Cavallini, 'Portée de la citoyenneté européenne' (2011) *La Semaine Juridique – Social* 25; S Corneloup, 'Citoyenneté européenne: la Cour de justice apporte une nouvelle pierre à son édifice' (2011) *Recueil Dalloz* 1325; M Aubert, E Broussy, F Donnat, 'Chronique de jurisprudence de la CJUE. Citoyenneté de l'Union' (2011) *L'Actualité Juridique Droit Administratif* 1007; R de Meo, 'Status di cittadino europeo del figlio e diritto derivato di soggiorno del genitore' (2011) *Giurisprudenza italiana Gr Sez Col* 763; A Rigaux, 'Article 20 TFUE' (2011) *Europe* (May 2011) Commentaires 12; M Houser, 'De la lutte contre les discriminations à rebours à la protection des droits fondamentaux par l'Union européenne. Le pas est presque franchi, mais . . .' (2011) *L'Actualité Juridique Droit Administratif* 1084; D Martin, 'L'actualité de la jurisprudence européenne et internationale. La Cour de Justice et les situations internes à un Etat membre: vive la révolution?' (2011) *Revue de jurisprudence sociale* 450; A Hinajeros, 'Extending Citizenship and the Scope of EU Law' (2011) 70 *Cambridge Law Journal* 309; C Boutayeb, A Raccah, 'Le bénéfice du regroupement familial élargi aux parents étrangers d'enfants citoyens de l'Union' (2011) *Revue de droit sanitaire et social* 449; K Hailbronner and D Thym, 'Case C-34/09, Gerardo Ruiz Zambrano v Office National de l'Emploi (ONEm), Judgment of the Court of Justice (Grand Chamber) of 8 March 2011' (2011) 48 *CML Rev* 1253.

Zambrano case and of the stands taken, prior to this judgment, by the Court on the subject of Union citizenship. These positions constitute the background of this ruling. Once this has been done, it will be possible to better understand its content as well as its consequences and its limits.

BACKGROUND

In the *Zambrano* case two minors, born in Belgium of Colombian parents without the right of residence in Belgium, had acquired Belgian citizenship as their parents had voluntarily omitted to declare them at the Colombian Embassy. The Belgian State, at that time, in order to minimise cases of statelessness, attributed its citizenship to stateless persons born within its territory. The issue which had arisen before the Belgian courts concerned Mr Zambrano's request to obtain both a residence permit and a work permit as he was supporting his two children, who are both Belgian citizens, and, therefore, Union citizens. On the basis of their Union citizenship, he invoked the right to reside in Belgium, notwithstanding the fact that none of the children had exercised the right to move freely within the Union. Mr Zambrano's request having been rejected, he appealed to the Tribunal du Travail (Labour Court) of Brussels, which referred the matter to the ECJ for a preliminary ruling under Article 267 TFEU. Before the ECJ, all the Member States intervening in the proceedings, as well as the Commission, clearly supported Belgium. They agreed that the situation in question was merely internal as the children lived in – and had never left – the Member State of their nationality. Accordingly, Belgium argued that the reference was inadmissible.

Similar points had been raised by some Member States and by the Commission in the *Rottman*[3] case. Mr Rottman, an Austrian national, left Austria and took up residence in Bavaria, Germany, where he successfully applied for naturalisation as a German citizen. He was later deprived of his German nationality on account of the fact that it had been obtained fraudulently. Under Austrian law, the acquisition of foreign citizenship causes the loss of Austrian nationality. Germany's Bundesverwaltungsgericht referred the matter to the ECJ for a preliminary ruling asking whether Union law prohibits a Member State from withdrawing its nationality when doing so would cause the person concerned to lose his Union citizenship and the rights and fundamental freedoms attached thereto, resulting in statelessness because this person cannot recover the nationality of the Member State which he originally possessed.

As far as the admissibility of the German reference was concerned, the Court concurred with the Advocate General.[4] However, it did so after having identified a different link with Union law. The Court did not attribute any relevance to what had happened before the naturalisation. It did not take into consideration that

[3] Case C-135/08 *Rottman* [2010] ECR I-1449.

[4] See *Rottman*, n 3 above, para 46.

Mr Rottman had exercised his right to move from Austria to Germany. Instead, the Court deemed that the nexus with Union law was constituted by the fact that stripping Mr Rottman of his German citizenship would have had a negative impact on his legal status as a Union citizen: he would have lost his Union citizenship because the loss of his German citizenship would have been added to the loss of his Austrian one and to the impossibility of recovering it.

The fact that both the Advocate General and the ECJ had deemed the referral for a preliminary ruling by the Bundesverwaltungsgericht as admissible does not diminish the significance of the difference in reasoning in order to arrive at the same result. It warrants careful examination as regards a fundamental problem concerning not only the exercise of the functions of EU judges but the delineation of the scopes of Union and national law. Furthermore, it is linked to the many lively discussions on the application of the principle of conferral.[5]

Advocate General Poiares Maduro stressed the fact that the decision to grant and subsequently withdraw German nationality to Mr Rottmann had been determined in the continuity of his exercise of the freedom of movement – Mr Rottmann's moving from Austria to Germany. The Advocate General stated, without offering any specific reasoning, that the link with Union law was sufficient to trigger its application, because Mr Rottmann's situation undoubtedly presented a cross-border dimension. The Court, on the other hand, ignored what had happened before the German naturalisation. It held that the situation of a person, even though determined by a Member State acting within its exclusive sphere of competence, can justify that the apparent lack of a cross-border character be disregarded. The Court found it decisive that a person was affected by a national measure which was going to have a negative impact on his Union status and on the rights attaching thereto.[6]

This was not the first time that the Court had expressed such an idea, having already done so in the *Garcia Avello*[7] and *Zhu and Chen*[8] rulings. Advocate General Sharpston pointed this out in her opinion in the *Zambrano*[9] case, stressing that in these two prior cases it was claimed that EU law was not applicable because purely internal situations were involved. In *Garcia Avello*, the problem was that of ascertaining the conformity with Union law of a Belgian measure denying to two minors of Spanish-Belgian dual nationality the right to use the family name which Spain had attributed to them. Because they were born in Belgium and they had never left that Member State, the Belgian authorities deemed that their situation was purely internal. In *Zhu and Chen*, a similar problem had appeared with reference to the refusal of a right of residence in the United Kingdom to a minor born in Northern Ireland and who, after moving within the United Kingdom, had

[5] See, in this respect, Pieralberto Mengozzi, *Il principio personalista nel diritto dell'Unione europea* (Padova, Cedam, 2010).

[6] See *Rottman*, n 3 above, paras 41–42.

[7] Case C-148/02 *Garcia Avello* [2003] ECR I-11613.

[8] Case C-200/02 *Zhu and Chen* [2004] ECR I-9925.

[9] Opinion of AG Sharpston in *Zambrano*, n 1 above.

demanded such a right for herself and for her mother, a third country national. The minor was invoking her Union citizenship, relying on the fact that her birth in Northern Ireland had made her an Irish citizen.

In *Zambrano*, the Advocate General stressed that, in the two above-mentioned rulings, the element of movement from one Member State to another was barely perceivable or almost non-existent. In spite of this, the Court decided that Union law was applicable and the reference for a preliminary ruling was admissible. In the same opinion, the Advocate General added that, in *Rottmann*, the Court had already followed the position taken in *Garcia Avello* and *Zhu and Chen* and deemed Union law applicable because of the negative consequences the decisions at issue had on Union citizenship rights. The Advocate General suggested in *Zambrano* that the Court reject the plea of inadmissibility raised by the Belgian Government on account of the fact that *Garcia Avello* and *Zhu and Chen* had already established a judicial policy according to which Union law can be applied in situations governed by national law irrespective of the movement of a person from one Member State to another.

Beyond these appearances, other decisive elements led the Court to apply Union law in the *Garcia Avello* and *Zhu and Chen* cases. In *Garcia Avello* and *Zhu and Chen*, the Court found that the circumstances fell under the scope of Union law because it could then apply the principle of non-discrimination on ground of nationality in order to hold the Belgian measure as incompatible with Union law. This measure treated identically (only one surname) two distinct categories of citizens (Belgian nationals and dual nationals). The situation was such that, even if the freedom of movement of the minors in question had not yet been affected, the threat was very real: it was clear that the two minors and their family would periodically move from Belgium to Spain. The discrepancy in surnames caused by the Belgian measure was

> liable to cause [in the future] serious inconvenience for those concerned at both professional and private levels resulting from, inter alia, difficulties in benefiting, in one Member State of which they are nationals, from the legal effects of diplomas or documents drawn up in the surname recognised in another Member State of which they are also nationals.[10]

In *Zhu and Chen*, the minor with Irish citizenship had never left the United Kingdom. Her situation fell within the scope of Union law because, as a citizen of the Union, she could assert the right of establishment in the United Kingdom – as a Member State different from the one of her nationality – and the refusal of a residence permit in this country for her and her mother negatively affected her right of establishment.

In *Rottmann*, the Court held that the withdrawal of the applicant's German naturalisation fell within the scope of EU law, because it had negative effects on

[10] *Garcia Avello*, n 7 above, para 36.

his Union citizenship and on the rights inherent therein.[11] Therefore, the situation was similar to that of the *Garcia Avello* and *Zhu and Chen* cases. The consequence is that the *Rottman* ruling adds to the two earlier cases in order to confirm – without going beyond – the traditional case law which defines the conditions under which the Court has jurisdiction over references for preliminary rulings and which applies Union law when national measures affect the rights it confers on individuals.

In *Rottmann*, the national judge asked the Court to clarify the effects of the *Micheletti*[12] ruling according to which the Member States must exercise their competence, as far as citizenship is concerned, in respect of EU law. Advocate General Poiares Maduro started from the premise that Union citizenship, although linked to a Member State's citizenship, is independent of it. He drew the conclusion that Union citizenship determines Union rights and obligations constituting a body which cannot be limited in an unjustified manner by the exercise of a Member State's competence to regulate the citizenship attributed to individuals.[13] In his view, it cannot reasonably be inferred that it is absolutely impossible for a Member State to deprive a person of nationality where such deprivation would entail the loss of Union citizenship. This impossibility may result from general principles of law, from the necessity to protect fundamental rights, from any rule of the EU legal order and from international law rules binding on the EU. In particular, he recalled the Convention on the Reduction of Statelessness of 30 August 1961 and the European Convention on Nationality, adopted by the Council of Europe on 6 November 1997, which seek to establish the principle that statelessness must be avoided. However, he remarked that these conventions authorise States, by way of exception, to deprive an individual of his nationality even if that deprivation would render him stateless, when the nationality was acquired as a result of deception or of providing false information.

The Court, taking into account the elements underlined by Advocate General Poiares Maduro decided that, in principle, a decision withdrawing naturalisation based on deception 'could be compatible with European Union law'[14] even though that withdrawal could cause the person in question to lose, in addition to the nationality of the Member State of naturalisation, his or her Union citizenship.[15] However, it affirmed that

[11] For a preview of the doctrinal plan of submitting to the judicial control of the Court the withdrawal of a Member State's citizenship because of its repercussions on rights descending from Union citizenship, see G de Groot, 'Towards a European Nationality Law' (2004) 8 *Electronic Journal of Comparative Law* 14.

[12] See Case C-369/90 *Micheletti* [1992] I-4239, para 10. On this ruling, see, among others, E Bergamini, 'Il difficile equilibrio tra riconoscimento del diritto alla libera circolazione rispetto alla vita familiare e abuso del diritto' (2006) *Il diritto dell'Unione europea*, 347 ff; Pieralberto Mengozzi, 'Il diritto alla continuità di cognome dei minori provvisti della cittadinanza di uno Stato non membro della Comunità e della cittadinanza italiana', (2009) *Rivista di diritto internazionale privato e processuale*, 69 ff and, above all, C Morviducci, *I diritti dei cittadini europei* (Torino, G Giappichelli Editore, 2010) 15 ff.

[13] See Opinion of AG Poiares Maduro in *Rottman*, n 3 above, para 23.

[14] *Rottman*, n 3 above, para 50.

[15] For comments on the basis on which the German authorities, given the circumstances of the case at issue, adopted the measure in question 'en conformité de principe' with Union law see M Aubert,

> it is [. . .]for the national court to ascertain whether [such] withdrawal decision [. . .] observes the principle of proportionality so far as concerns the consequences it entails for the situation of the person concerned.[16]

In so doing, the Court specified – in an innovative way – that this principle, which is a general principle of Union law, tends to constitute a limit on the adoption of national measures not only when they pursue a treaty objective, an act or a principle of the Union, but also when, within the framework of an exclusive Member State competence, they negatively affect the status and rights conferred by Union law on individuals.

In addition, the Court remarkably enriched this important clarification. Despite its apparent deference towards the national court, the Court affirmed that it was for the latter to ascertain whether the decision of Land of Bavaria complied with the principle of proportionality. First of all, it indicated in detail the elements that the national court had to take into account while making such an assessment. Specifically, the Court identified a) the consequences that a decision withdrawing naturalisation would entail for the person concerned and for the members of his family, b) the gravity of the offence committed, c) the lapse of time between the naturalisation decision and the withdrawal decision and d) the possibility of the person concerned recovering his original nationality. Secondly, the Court specified that it is also for the national court to determine whether, having regard to these elements, 'observance of the principle of proportionality requires the person concerned to be afforded a reasonable period of time in order to try to recover the nationality of his Member State of origin'.[17]

These recommendations go beyond the general criterion which, according to the traditional case law of the Court, must be used for the application of the principle of proportionality, with reference to the legitimacy of acts of the EU institutions but which can also be widened to that of Member States' acts of EU relevance. According to such traditional criterion the principle in question

> requires that measures adopted by Community institutions should not exceed the limits of what is appropriate and necessary in order to attain the objectives pursued by the

E Broussy and F Donnat, 'La perte de la nationalité d'un Etat member peut entraîner la perte de la citoyenneté de l'Union' (2010) *L'Actualité Juridique Droit Administratif* 938. According to F Fabbrini, 'La Corte di giustizia europea e la cittadinanza dell'Unione' (2010) *Giornale di diritto amministrativo* 708 ff, the Court, in considering the German measure as, in principle, lawful, went a little bit too far in favour of the principle of sovereignty and leaving to the national judge the decision on the proportionality of such measure, seems to put him in a position 'like Pontius Pilate'. M Castellaneta, 'Lo Stato deve valutare gli effetti sul cittadino del provvedimento di revoca della naturalizzazione', *Guida al diritto, Il Sole 24 Ore*, 10 April 2010, 99, stresses the fact that the Court linked the qualification of the withdrawal at issue as legitimate, in principle, with the affirmation that a Member State may legitimately wish to protect the special relationship of solidarity and loyalty between its citizens and itself as well as the reciprocity of rights and duties which are at the heart of the bond of citizenship.

[16] *Rottman*, n 3 above, para 55. For an analysis of the stand taken by the Court to this purpose see Morviducci, n 13 above, 36 ff. See also R Cafari Panico, 'La cittadinanza dell'Unione europea e il federalismo fiscale' in MC Baruffi (ed), *Cittadinanza e diversità culturale nello spazio giuridico europeo* (Padova, Cedam, 2010) 50 at n 65.

[17] *Rottman*, n 3 above, para 58.

legislation in question, and where there is a choice between several appropriate measures, recourse must be had to the least onerous, and the disadvantages caused must not be disproportionate to the aims pursued.[18]

Such criterion only imposes a limit on the exercise of a competence existing *a priori*. On the contrary, the application of the principle of proportionality utilised by the Court in *Rottman* gave place *ex novo* to an obligation alien to a tradition which considered the issuance and withdrawal of citizenship as falling under national sovereignty and, therefore, within Member States' exclusive competence.

The Court's application of the principle of proportionality is the result of a hybridisation of that principle with two other principles. The first one is the principle according to which even the Member States' exercise of conferred powers must respect Union law and the rights that the latter confers on individuals. The second one, more innovative, is inspired by the idea of co-operation and the spirit of mutual trust. This binds a Member State which intends to withdraw the naturalisation of another Member State's citizen who, because of such naturalisation, has lost his State of origin's citizenship, to allow him a reasonable period of time in order to recover the citizenship of his Member State of origin.

The Court indeed admits that the Member States are, in principle, competent to grant (and withdraw) naturalisation. However, considering the consequences of such competence in terms of loss of Union citizenship, the Court imposes its own criteria about the way in which, through their national courts, Member States must assure the correct exercise of their competence. By affirming that the withdrawal of a person's nationality from a given Member State can have a negative effect on that person's Union citizenship only proportionately to the legitimate interest of the States to apply sanctions against instances of fraud in matters concerning the acquisition of a nationality, the Court clearly indicates the criteria on the basis of which national courts are obliged to ensure that these criteria are respected.[19]

One cannot help but notice that, with this new ruling, which goes even further than all prior predictions, the Court gave a new, tangible, consistency to the principle

[18] Joined Cases C-27/00 and C-122/00 *Omega Air and ors* [2002] ECR I-2569, para 62.

[19] Noticeably, the Court referred to the criteria usually reserved to justify a national measure in principle unlawful or concretise a restriction to the exercise of freedoms granted by Union law, specifically a) the legitimacy of the objective pursued by the State, b) the necessity of the examined measure and c) its proportionality in respect of the pursued objective. Yet, the Court indicated to the national court not to follow those criteria in that capacity. This nuance must be underlined as it clearly shows how the Court appreciated the delicate nature of the problem and the need to balance through the soft tone that it adopted, the advanced – if not invasive – character of the directions it obliged the national courts to follow. For a similar remark see ME Bartoloni, 'Competenza degli Stati in material di cittadinanza e limiti posti dal diritto dell'Unione europea: il caso Rottman' (2010) *Diritti umani e il diritto internazionale* 428, according to whom, in the *Rottman* case, the ECJ would not have indicated to the national court to apply the principle of proportionality to ascertain the conformity of the withdrawal of the naturalisation decision with the treaties; the Court would have committed the national court to verifying, on the basis of such principle, if this measure, although a legitimate exercise of State sovereignty even in the light of Union law, has unacceptable consequences in the sphere of the subjective positions deriving from the status of European citizen.

oft-affirmed – since *Grzelczyk*[20] – according to which Union citizenship constitutes the fundamental status of Member States' citizens. However, the Court could only get so far because it fused the application of the principle of proportionality with the way in which it traditionally co-ordinates the respect of the principle of conferred powers with that of respect of Union law as well as those of co-operation and of mutual trust. It did so considering that Germany, in withdrawing naturalisation could exceptionally affect an individual situation resulting from Union law as it was authorised to do so by the latter, and that it could do so solely by respecting the principle of proportionality.

CONTENT

In *Zambrano*, Advocate General Sharpston proposed that the Court decide that the reference was admissible and – as in *Rottmann* – did not concern a purely internal situation. The Advocate General further suggested that the Belgian measures were incompatible with Union law. She considered, mainly, that the Court should assimilate the case at issue into *Rottmann*. In her view, the denial of a residence permit to a third country citizen, father of two very young children who are Union citizens, would have opened up the perspective of the necessity for the whole family to be forced to leave the Union, with the consequence of placing, '*in practical terms*' those children in a 'position capable of causing them to lose the status conferred [by their citizenship of the Union] and the rights attaching thereto'.[21]

This position is characterised by the indication that those minors were only '*in practical terms*' in such situation, that is, in a situation which is similar to that which was determined by the withdrawal of Mr Rottmann's naturalisation by the German authorities. There is, actually, an important difference between these two situations. In *Rottmann*, the German measure was unequivocally going to deprive a person of his status as a citizen of the Union whereas in *Zambrano*, the status of Mr Zambrano's children as Union citizens was never in question even if they had all been required to leave the Union. That is why Advocate General Sharpston integrates the reference to *Rottmann* with the assumption that Mr Zambrano's right derives from the right of residence which must be attributed to his children as linked to their right to invoke throughout the Union the fundamental rights attributed to them by Union law[22] *even in the Member State of which they are nationals.* Such right of residence is seen as a fundamental right protected by

[20] Case C-184/99 *Grzelczyk* [2001] ECR I-6193.

[21] Opinion of AG Sharpston in *Zambrano*, n 1 above, para 95.

[22] On the autonomous and wider character that the category of fundamental rights safeguarded by Union order and by its judicial bodies presents compared to that of fundamental rights granted by the international conventions to which Union law pays attention in order to use them see P Mengozzi, 'Les caractéristiques spécifiques de l'Union européenne dans la perspective de son adhesion à la CEDH' (2010) *Il diritto dell'Unione europea* 236 ff. I make reference to that article as far as problems of balance between fundamental rights are concerned.

Union law independently from the right to move freely from one Member State to another.

This reasoning is fascinating indeed. It specifically highlights the fact that it would be absurd that Mr Zambrano's children could claim residence in Belgium and invoke fundamental rights according to Union law had they paid a short visit to France or to Great Britain but could not do so in the absence of such insubstantial circumstances. The Court paid attention to this. However, it is necessary to specify in which sense and to what extent it did so.

In her essay, Palladino argues that the Court paid attention to these remarks in affirming that the ruling at issue *appears* to recognise Mr Zambrano's right to obtain, in Belgium, a residence permit and a work permit as deriving from the residency enjoyed by his children because of their status as Union citizens independently from their movement from one Member State to another.[23] According to Palladino, the consistency of such *appearance* is remarkable. Firstly, it illustrates the general evolution of the Court towards a 'personalistic' approach and the need to protect the useful effect of the right of residence of minors as Union citizens. Secondly, because of the analogy with what was done for the minor concerned in the *Zhu and Chen* ruling. If one can agree, as far as the personalistic approach in *Zambrano* and *Zhu and Chen* is concerned, one must nonetheless disagree with the analogies drawn between these two rulings. As I mentioned above, in *Zhu and Chen*, unlike in *Zambrano*, the right of residence was invoked in a Member State in favour of a minor who was a national of another Member State, who could legitimately and undoubtedly claim such right. In *Zambrano*, the right of residence of the claimant's children could not rest on any such assumption. The Court could not radically ignore what it had affirmed in *Garcia Avello* where it had stressed that Union citizenship cannot 'extend the scope *ratione materiae* of the Treaty also to internal situations which have no link with Community law'.[24]

In order to avoid drastically neglecting what it had affirmed in *Garcia Avello*, the Court merely considered the particular situation of the two children in *Zambrano*, referring to the practical consequences of this ruling with respect to their own situation. After having once again reaffirmed what it had specified in *Grzelczyk* – Union citizenship constitutes 'the fundamental status of nationals of the Member States'[25] – in order to show very clearly that it had no intention to 'extend the scope *ratione materiae* of the Treaty', the Court founded its stand on a combined interpretation of Articles 20(2) and 25(2) TFEU. Considering that, according to the latter, only the Council, acting unanimously after obtaining the consent of the European Parliament, may adopt provisions to complete the rights listed in Article 20(2), the Court gave a careful interpretation of the rights of citizens of the Union. The Court interpreted such provision in the sense that the status of Union citizens can be

[23] Palladino, n 2 above, 351.

[24] *Garcia Avello*, n 7 above, para 26. See MC Baruffi, 'La cittadinanza dell'Unione e i diritti di minori nello spazio giuridico europeo', in Baruffi, n 16 above, 78.

[25] *Grzelczyk*, n 20 above, para 31.

enriched only by a particularly rigid legislative procedure. Yet, Union citizenship cannot be deprived of its useful contents and, therefore, cannot be infringed by national measures. For this reason, the Court affirmed that the status of Union citizens must be safeguarded so that its 'genuine enjoyment' is not hindered in any aspects which, albeit not covered by rights specifically listed in Article 20(2) TFEU, must be considered as pertaining to 'the substance of the rights' attaching to the same status. The Court did so, evidently considering that national measures which have such effect do not lead to merely internal situations and the 'substance of the rights' includes the right of two minors of a young age, as citizens of the Union, not to lose the support of their father, the only support they could rely on. It did not consider the father's right of residence or his right to a work permit as deriving from his children's status as Union citizens, but as functional to ensure that their status was not concretely deprived of content and to avoid forcing them to leave the territory of the Union in circumstances that would not be the result of free choice as they 'cannot decide their own fate'.[26]

Moreover, it is also important to note that, by deducing these rights directly from Union citizenship or, at least, from the substantial core of it (*'l'essentiel des droits'*), the Court indicated that Belgium must grant a right of residence and a work permit to the father of these Union citizens independent of any limitation and condition under which the Union legal order subordinates the grant of the right of residence of its citizens in the framework of the freedom of movement, and of their family members who are third country nationals legitimately residing in the territory of the Union.

CONSEQUENCES AND LIMITS

The consequence of *Zambrano* is that the criterion of the protection of the substantive core of rights (*'l'essentiel des droits'*) concerning Union citizenship may, in the future, extend the scope of Union law beyond situations presenting a cross-border character. A further problem thus arises: what are the limits?

A first answer to this may be found in the recent *McCarthy*[27] ruling. This case concerned a citizen of the United Kingdom who was a recipient of State benefits since she was unable to provide for her needs. She was also an Irish citizen although she had never resided in any State other than the United Kingdom. Mrs McCarthy and her husband of Jamaican nationality applied to the United Kingdom authorities for a residence permit and a residence document under Union law as, respectively, a Union citizen and the spouse of a Union citizen. Following Mrs McCarthy's appeal against the rejection of such application, the

[26] Hailbronner and Thym, n 2 above, 1256.

[27] Case C-434/09 *McCarthy*, judgment of 5 May 2011 nyr. On this ruling see J Cavallini, 'Inapplicapilité du droit de l'Union aux situations purement internes' (2011) *La Semaine Juridique Sociale*, 1363; D Simon, 'La Cour ne se prononce pas sur le mécanisme belge de question incidente de constitutionnalité pour des raisons de compétence' (2011) *Europe* (Mai 2011) 16 ff.

question of the legitimacy of her request reached the Supreme Court of the United Kingdom which referred the matter to the Court for a preliminary ruling. First of all the Court observed, in accordance with *Zambrano*, that the mere fact that a Union citizen has not exercised his right of free movement does not mean that the situation which concerns him must be considered as a purely internal situation. Secondly, the Court examined whether the measure adopted by the United Kingdom could deprive Mrs McCarthy of the genuine enjoyment of the substance of the rights ('*l'essentiel des droits*') conferred by virtue of her status as Union citizen. The Court denied any such negative impact since the national measures did not necessarily force her to leave Union territory.

The Court's answer is important in two respects. First, it stresses the distinct character of the situation: a third country national cannot obtain a residence permit because a member of his family is a Union citizen unless this family member is in a state of absolute dependency. Secondly, it implies that respect for family life in relation to family reunification is not included among the essential rights attached to Union citizenship in situations that a) do not fall within the scope of Union law which expressly provide for it or b) are not similar to that considered in the *Zambrano* case.[28] Beyond the limits stated in *McCarthy*, the criterion of the 'substance of the rights' will operate in cases in which national measures produce effects analogous to those in *Zambrano*, that is, when they severely and adversely impact on the substance of the Union citizenship.

After the *McCarthy* ruling, legal commentators, looking at the case law which preceded *Zambrano* with the benefit of hindsight, have argued that, firstly, *Garcia Avello* and *Grunkin Paul*[29] could have been motivated on the basis of the 'substance of the right' criterion. Indeed, the national measures taken in these two instances were sufficient to deter (potentially in *Garcia Avello* and actually in *Grunkin Paul*) the exercise of the rights and freedoms granted to the minors by Union law. Secondly, the *Rottmann* ruling could also have been decided on the basis of the same criterion since the withdrawal of the German nationality at issue would also have led to the loss of Union citizenship.[30]

[28] As to whether respect for family life, as provided for by Art 8(1) of the ECHR, constitutes an obligation of the Member States established by such Convention with the consequence that the ascertainment of a violation of this obligation must be made by national judges under the control of the ECtHR, see *McCarthy*, n 27 above, para 60, and my view of 29 September 2011 in Case C-256/11, *Dereci and ors*, judgment of 15 November 2011 nyr.

[29] Case C-353/06 *Grunkin and Paul* [2008] ECR I-7639. In this case the minor Leonhard Mathias was often moving from Denmark (the country where he was born, lived and attended school) to Germany (the country of which he was a national). His parents had asked that the child could bear the same surname (Grunkin-Paul) entered in his Danish birth certificate in the family register in Germany. This was refused by the German authorities on the ground that German law does not allow a child to bear a double-barrelled surname composed of the surnames of both the father and the mother. The case was brought before the German judges who referred the matter to the Court of Justice for a preliminary ruling. The latter deemed that such request had to be satisfied as '[h]aving to use a surname, in the Member State of which the person concerned is a national, that is different from that conferred and registered in the Member State of birth and residence is liable to hamper the exercise of the right, established in Article 18 EC, to move and reside freely within the territory of the Member State' (para 22).

[30] See *McCarthy*, n 27 above, paras 51–53; Hailbronner and Thym, n 2 above, 1257; Cavallini, n 27 above, 3.

Speculating on futures cases, one can reasonably deem that the criterion of the 'substance of the rights' could find further applications in situations of absolute dependence from a third country national, not only for a Union citizen of young age, but also for adults or disabled persons who cannot provide autonomously for their own support. This same criterion could further be applied in situations where national measures have an impact, at least potentially, on the exercise of rights which the Union legal order attributes to its citizens, with a gravity comparable to that in *Zambrano*. In this sense, it could be provided that in the situations concerned it does not imply an enrichment of a person's status as Union citizen, but limits itself to avoiding that such status loses its useful effect or is even deprived of content.

The fact that Union citizens, who have neither exercised nor concretely allowed for a real possibility of exercising the freedom of movement, can see a member of their family, a third country national, benefit from the *Zambrano* treatment only under the negative and positive conditions indicated above, may seem paradoxical. It can appear contrary to what was established by Council Directive 2003/109/EC of 25 November 2003 concerning the status of third country nationals who are long-term residents[31] and by Council Directive 1990/364/EC of 28 November 2003 on the right of residence.[32] But such impression would be misplaced. Firstly, these directives do not automatically recognise a right of residence for the members of the Union citizens' families. Second, because the Union legal order rests on the principle of conferral, the Court leaves the resolution of issues which do not fall within its jurisdiction to national legal orders and to the international rules to which Member States they are bound. Consequently, the legitimacy of national measures which might appear in conflict with the principles of the respect of family life and of the protection of children under the European Convention on Human Rights must be ascertained by the national courts. The caution with which the Court has proceeded has led to various criticisms from those who would like to see it take a more active role in the protection of fundamental rights.[33] However, this prudence is understandable if one considers that after *Zhu and Chen*, Ireland modified its law on citizenship in a restrictive way and that Belgium acted similarly before the request for a preliminary ruling in *Zambrano* had reached the court. In both countries these modifications led to a deterioration in the legal status of a large number of persons.[34]

[31] Council Directive 2003/109/EC of 25 November 2003 concerning the status of third country nationals who are long-term residents, [2004] OJ L16/44.

[32] Council Directive 1990/364/EC of 28 November 2003 on the right of residence, [1990] OJ L180/26.

[33] For a criticism of the stand taken by the Court in this respect, on the same wavelength as the Opinion of AG Sharpston in *Zambrano*, n 1 above, see Houser, n 2 above, 1085.

[34] Corneloup, n 2 above, 1337; Rigaux, n 2 above, 12.

18

Citizenship and Fundamental Rights – Pandora's Box or a Natural Step Towards Maturity?

ELEANOR SHARPSTON*

WHEN THE MEMBER States decided to include, amongst the changes brought about by the Treaty of Maastricht, the concept of 'citizenship of the Union', what did they really have in mind? Intergovernmental conferences are, generically, the place for hard-nosed negotiation, based on balancing national interests within the context of developing EU law. They are not usually the place for 'blue-sky thinking'. What emerges at the end of the process is often unpredicted at the start. Sometimes – as with the reinforcement of the drive towards the single market through the adoption of the Single European Act – the changes are very significant indeed. At other times, what happens may unkindly be described more as 'tinkering with the system' than as anything really new.

Into which category does citizenship of the Union fall? Was it – as certain delegations may have hoped – intended to be a mere sound bite, a nice political phrase that would add nothing of substance to what was already there? Or did it (perhaps, unwittingly) represent the foundation stone for something infinitely more important – a wholly different concept of the relationship between the individual and the European Union?

CITIZENSHIP – AN EVOCATIVE WORD

A moment's reflection shows that 'citizen' and the associated descriptive abstract noun 'citizenship' are not terms to be used lightly (at least, not in Western democracies). Being a citizen matters. It is fundamental. It is important. A few examples will suffice to illustrate the point.

* The author serves as an Advocate General at the Court of Justice of the European Union. The views expressed are personal. I should like to express my gratitude to two dear friends, James O'Reilly SC and Fionnuala O'Reilly, who tolerated the unscheduled overlap between finishing this contribution to Judge Lindh's Festschrift and my visit to Dublin with unruffled courtesy and good humour (and who sustained the writing process with unflagging hospitality).

The transfer of power from the oligarchs to the demos marked the real beginnings of the city-state that was ancient Athens. The (rather limited) group of citizens[1] had a status, power, influence and responsibility beyond the reach of less happy mortals, such as resident foreigners ('metics'), slaves and women. Pericles' Funeral Oration[2] is permeated with references to the values Athens had built on the democratic foundations of citizenship – values for which those being commemorated had, indeed, just laid down their lives at the beginning of Athens' disastrous conflict with Sparta in the Peloponnesian War.

The Roman Empire distinguished sharply between those with, and without, Roman citizenship. If one was not lucky enough to possess it from the outset, citizenship was a prize that could be obtained (for example, after 20 years' service as an auxiliary in the Roman army) and that was proudly passed on to one's descendants. St Paul, finding himself in a decidedly sticky situation in Jerusalem, played his trump card by claiming (accurately) 'civis Romanus sum' and was immediately set free.[3] When evangelising and explaining to new converts to Christianity the real meaning of the step that they had taken in converting, St Paul reached naturally for the citizenship analogy: 'ye are citizens of heaven'.[4] St Augustine's 'City of God' is part of the same intellectual current.

Moving forward in time, with the revolutionary movements towards the end of the eighteenth century, the emotional weight of the term 'citizen' became, if anything, even stronger. In the turmoil of the French revolution, the fact that both ordinary people and '*aristos*' (the former bearers of elaborate courtesy titles) were now addressed using the same term, '*citoyen*', was of enormous importance.

Not so long ago, Michael D Higgins (now President of Ireland) put the evocative values of citizenship eloquently in the modern context when, in an address delivered to Trinity College Politics Society on 3 November 1988, he said:

> A case must be urgently made therefore for a new and vibrant citizenship that can vindicate such values as solidarity, community, democracy, justice, freedom and equality, and give them practical expression. At the heart of this conception is *the respect for the life of the person as having a shared public value beyond the narrow consumer power of the individual.* Such an approach to citizenship stands for *the right of every citizen to partici-*

[1] Estimates as to the actual number of citizens in Athens at the height of her powers varies. The most widely used figures that I have found suggest that in the mid-5th century BC there may have been as many as 60,000 but that the number fell sharply during the Peloponnesian War. During the 4th century BC the total population of Attica may well have been some 250,000–300,000 people, of whom 'citizen families' may have accounted for around 100,000. Within that number, there may therefore have been around 30,000 actual male citizens, of whom perhaps 5000–6000 would normally turn up to vote at the ἐκκλησία (assembly). These figures are also consistent with the physical dimensions of the *Pynx* (the assembly meeting place).

[2] A very readable translation is to be found in Fordham University's Ancient History Sourcebook, available at www.fordham.edu/halsall/ancient/pericles-funeralspeech.asp.

[3] See Acts 22:25–30. The exchange between St Paul and the chief captain only underscores the value of Roman citizenship.

[4] Philippians 3:20. In the same vein see, eg Philippians 1:27 (referring to πολιτευεσθαι – to discharge one's duty as citizen); Philippians 3:20 (πολιτευμα); and Ephesians 2:19 (citizenship in God's πολις).

> *pate in society and to have the opportunity to develop their personal and social selves in conditions of freedom and communal solidarity.*[5] (emphasis added)

Citizenship is the core in the creation of cohesive community. Citizens should not be mere subjects who do what they have to do, have circumscribed rights, get on with their lives, get what they can out of the system and feel that they play no part in (and therefore bear no responsibility for) that system being what it is. Citizens 'belong' to the community that they are part of. They are responsible for it. They have rights and duties.

Against that background, we should perhaps approach the concept of 'citizenship of the Union' with more awareness – and possibly also more respect. When citizenship meets fundamental rights, something is probably going to happen.

FUNDAMENTAL RIGHTS WITHIN EU LAW

The evolution of fundamental rights protection within the EU legal order is too well known to require much exposition. Initially, these rights were incorporated into EEC law by the Court through its case law, from *Internationale Handelsgesellschaft*[6] and *Nold*[7] onwards, drawing on the constitutional traditions of the Member States and also particularly on the ECHR. This case law was given expression at treaty level in the TEU.[8] Gradually, over the years from the Treaty of Maastricht to the Treaty of Lisbon, these rights have been refined and elaborated further and are now enshrined, in the Charter, at the level of primary law of the Union.[9]

THE RUN-UP TO THE INTRODUCTION OF CITIZENSHIP OF THE UNION IN THE TEU

Citizenship of the Union was not a sudden, last-minute addition to an otherwise rational economic programme (or, to put the same point another way, it did not spring like Athena fully armed from the head of Zeus). On the contrary: the gestation period was a lengthy one.[10]

Thus, as early as 1968 the Commission described the free movement provisions of the EEC Treaty (especially those relating to the free movement of workers) as the first step in creating 'an incipient form of European citizenship'.[11] The Paris

[5] MD Higgins, 'Citizenship: The Space of Politics Recovered' in *Causes for Concern* (Dublin, Liberties Press, 2006) 53–55.

[6] Case 11/70 *Internationale Handelsgesellschaft* [1970] ECR 1125.

[7] Case 4/73 *Nold v Commission* [1974] ECR 491.

[8] Art F(2) TEU (in the original 1992 numbering). See Art 6(3) TEU.

[9] See the post-Lisbon version of Art 6(1) TEU.

[10] The content of the narrative in the next few paragraphs is drawn primarily from D O'Keeffe, 'Union Citizenship' in D O'Keeffe and P Twomey (eds), *Legal Issues of the Maastricht Treaty* (London, Chancery, 1993) ch 6.

[11] Bull EC 11-1968, 5–9. See also R Plender, 'An Incipient Form of Citizenship' in F Jacobs (ed), *European Law and the Individual* (Oxford, North Holland, 1976).

summit in 1974 set up a working group to study the conditions 'under which the citizens of the Member States could be given *special rights* as members of the Community'.[12] (emphasis added) The Tindemans Report on European Union[13] advocated granting special rights to nationals of the Member States, consisting of certain civic and political rights including the right to vote and eligibility for public office. This was followed, in the same vein, by the European Parliament's Scelba Report.[14] The Second Addonino Report on 'A People's Europe'[15] dealt with the special rights of Community citizens from the stance of education, culture, communication exchanges and the image and identity of the Community. The Commission Guidelines for a Community Policy on Migration stated that the free movement of persons should go beyond a Community employment market and should embrace the concept of European citizenship.[16]

In the process preceding the Intergovernmental Conference on the Treaty of European Union at Maastricht, the citizenship debate gathered momentum. The Belgian memorandum on institutional re-launch[17] contained elements such as the inclusion of human rights in the Treaties, accession to the ECHR and provisions to allow Community nationals to vote in local and European Parliament elections in their country of residence. The Dublin Summit (June 1990) endorsed the concept of citizenship in principle and asked the Council to examine the question:

> How will the Union include and extend the notion of *Community citizenship* carrying with it *specific rights* (*human, political, social, the right of complete free movement and residence etc*) for the citizens of the Member States by virtue of these States belonging to the Union?[18] (emphasis added)

The Spanish Government produced a detailed 'Memorandum on European Citizenship',[19] urging the creation and grant of European citizenship to the citizens of Member States, who would thereby acquire additional rights and duties. In December 1990 the Rome Summit decided that the concept of citizenship should be examined as part of the process of creating the Union. Human rights were not, however, to form part of the 'citizenship package' as such. That approach was opposed both by the Commission[20] and by the European Parliament.[21] In particular, the European Parliament's rapporteur, Rosy Bindi, considered that citizenship should be based on the expansion of fundamental rights.

[12] Bull EC 12-1974, para 111.

[13] 1975.

[14] EP Working Documents 1977–78, Doc 346/77, 10.

[15] Reports of the Ad Hoc Committee on a People's Europe to the European Council, Supp 7/85-Bull EC, 18.

[16] COM (88) 351 final.

[17] *Europe Documents* No 1608, 29 March 1990.

[18] *Europe* No 5252, 11 May 1990.

[19] 'Towards a European Citizenship', *Europe Documents* No 1653, 2 October 1990.

[20] '*Union Citizenship*': Contribution by the Commission to the Intergovernmental Conference, Supp 2/91 – Bull EC. The Commission maintained that citizens should be able to invoke the rights guaranteed under the ECHR, to which there should be explicit reference, and recalled the proposal for the Community to accede to the ECHR.

[21] See the Bindi Report on Union Citizenship, PE Doc A 3-0139/91 (23 May 1991).

Over this extended gestation period, a number of different strands emerged in the debate. Four are perhaps particularly worthy of mention here.

First, are nationals of 'other' Member States to be treated merely as *privileged foreigners* (the situation under 'classic' rights of free movement'), or should there be a move towards something more (European *citizenship*) that would define the rights of individuals affected by the transfer of competences from Member States to the Union?

Second, what rights should be identified and included as part of citizenship? Specifically, three distinct types of rights were identified fairly readily as intrinsic elements of citizenship: (a) *civic rights*, such as participation in local and European Parliament elections; (b) *social and economic rights*, such as freedom of movement and residence and equal treatment; and (c) *joint diplomatic protection* of Community nationals in third countries by their own and by other Member States' consular services.

Third, there was the question of how to deal with fundamental rights. Were they (or were they not) to be 'attached' to the citizenship provisions? The conclusion appears to have been that fundamental rights are distinct and separate from citizenship as such; and that they should be extended to all persons present on the territory of the Union. At all events, fundamental rights were not included in the citizenship 'package' but were dealt with in a separate provision (Article F(2)). Nevertheless, that fact should not obscure the real significance of the introduction of fundamental rights provisions into the Treaty on European Union at Maastricht at exactly the same moment as the citizenship provisions.

Finally, there was some abstract discussion of the possibility that citizens of the Union might have duties as well as rights (after all, the two go together as part of normal citizenship of a Member State). Partial reflection of this strand of the discussion is perhaps to be found in the provisions conferring voting rights (remembering that in some Member States, voting is not only a right but expressly a duty). By performing their duty to vote in the election of the European Parliament, citizens are contributing directly to reducing the 'democratic deficit' within the European Union.

After all the reports, the working groups, the guidelines, the proposals, the memoranda and the summit declarations, 'citizenship of the Union' finally found its way into the Treaty on European Union at Maastricht in 1992.[22]

THE TREATY PROVISIONS

The wording of the treaty provisions themselves was – in some respects – both ambiguous and circumspect.

[22] The timing – coinciding as it did with the move from the 'EC' to the creation of the 'European Union' – is itself significant. One cannot be a citizen of a mere economic community, whereas one can plausibly be a citizen of the European Union.

Thus, Article 8(1) EC (subsequently Article 17(1) EC and now part of Article 20 TFEU) states that, '[c]itizenship of the Union is hereby established. Every person holding the nationality of a Member State shall be a citizen of the Union. Citizenship of the Union shall complement and not replace national citizenship'.[23] Article 8(2)[24] expanded – or did not expand – on that statement by proclaiming that, '[c]itizens of the Union shall enjoy the rights conferred by this Treaty and shall be subject to the duties imposed thereby'. That immediately begs the question, was citizenship of the Union going to add anything new (and, if so, what)? Nevertheless, Article 8 taken as a whole did clearly establish the *status* of 'citizen of the Union'.

In a non-exhaustive list, the draftsman proceeded to set out a summary of the specific rights that citizens of the Union were to enjoy: (a) the right to move and reside freely within the territory of the Member States; (b) the right to vote and to stand as candidates in elections to the European Parliament and in municipal elections in their Member State of residence, under the same conditions as nationals of that State; (c) the right to enjoy, in the territory of a third country in which the Member State of which they are nationals is not represented, the protection of the diplomatic and consular authorities of any Member State on the same conditions as the nationals of that State; and (d) the right to petition the European Parliament, to apply to the European Ombudsman, and to address the institutions and advisory bodies of the Union in any of the Treaty languages and to obtain a reply in the same language. Separate provisions – of which the most litigated by far has been that pertaining to the right to move and reside freely within the territory of the Member States[25] – then spelt out these rights.

THE EARLY CASE LAW

In three early cases, the Court looked at the consequences of combining citizenship of the Union with the provision prescribing equal treatment (a Treaty expression of a well-recognised fundamental right).[26]

In *Martinez Sala*,[27] a Spanish national living in Germany, where she had previously worked, made an application for child-raising allowance. Her application was rejected on the grounds that she did not have German nationality, a residence entitlement or a residence permit. The national court making the reference thought that

[23] The apparently simple question of who is a 'national of a Member State' when asked in the context of the United Kingdom's (very complicated) rules on nationality gave rise to some excitement in Case C-192/99 *Manjit Kaur* [2001] ECR I-1237. On the 'complementary' nature of citizenship of the Union, see also Art F(1) TEU: 'The Union shall respect the identities of the Member States . . .'.

[24] Subsequently Art 17(2) and now part of Art 20 TFEU.

[25] Art 8a EC, subsequently Art 18 EC and now Art 21 TFEU.

[26] I have tried elsewhere (in my Opinion in Case C-427/06 *Bartsch* [2008] ECR I-7245, paras 42–46), to offer some thoughts as to the way in which equal treatment has evolved over time as a fundamental right.

[27] Case C-85/96 *Martínez Sala* [1998] ECR I-2691.

she might perhaps be able to rely on Regulation 1408/71 or Regulation 1612/68. In its questions, it did not ask specifically about the citizenship provisions.

The Court first determined that the benefit claimed fell within the scope *ratione materiae* of Community law. However, it was not clear from the facts whether Ms Martinez Sala would qualify for it, either as a worker (Article 48 and Regulation 1612/68) or as an employed person (Regulation 1408/71). The Commission raised the question of whether she might be able to rely on Article 8a (right to move and reside freely) and claim a right of residence under that provision since she was, under Article 8(1), a citizen of the Union.

The Court picked up the citizenship issue, but dealt with it even more directly, stating that it was

> not necessary to examine whether the person concerned can rely on Article 8a of the Treaty in order to obtain recognition of a new right to reside in the territory of the Member State concerned, since it is common ground that she has already been authorised to reside there, although she has been refused issue of a residence permit. [61] As a national of a Member State lawfully residing in the territory of another Member State, the appellant in the main proceedings comes within the scope *ratione personae* of the provisions of the Treaty on European citizenship.'[28] It went on to hold that: 'Article 8(2) of the Treaty attaches to the status of citizen of the Union the rights and duties laid down by the Treaty, including the right, laid down in Article 6 of the Treaty, not to suffer discrimination on grounds of nationality within the scope of application ratione materiae of the Treaty. [63] It follows that a citizen of the European Union, such as the appellant in the main proceedings, lawfully resident in the territory of the host Member State, can rely on Article 6 of the Treaty in all situations which fall within the scope *ratione materiae* of Community law . . .[29]

The discrimination in issue (refusal of a benefit that had already been found to fall within the scope *ratione materiae* of Community law) thus came within the scope of the Treaty. It could not be considered to be justified. It was direct discrimination on grounds of nationality and in any event nothing to justify such unequal treatment had been put before the Court.[30] The Court therefore held that Community law precluded a Member State from requiring nationals of other Member States authorised to reside in its territory to produce a formal residence permit issued by the national authorities in order to receive a child-raising allowance, whereas that Member State's own nationals were only required to be permanently or ordinarily resident in that Member State.

In *Martinez Sala*, the Court thus built directly on the applicant's *status* as a citizen of the Union (Article 8) and combined that with the Treaty enunciation (in Article 6) of a fundamental right (equal treatment) in order to find that the claimant was entitled to the same child-raising benefit as nationals of the host Member State.

[28] ibid, paras 60–61.

[29] ibid, paras 62–63.

[30] This was possibly a slip of the pen: other case law states consistently that whereas *indirect* discrimination can sometimes be justified, *direct* discrimination cannot be.

Bickel and Franz[31] concerned, respectively, an Austrian and a German national who were charged in criminal proceedings in the Alto-Adige region of Italy, where (for historical reasons)[32] local residents have the right to use German rather than Italian in court proceedings. The defendants requested that the proceedings against them be conducted in German. Their requests were turned down. In considering whether Articles 6, 8a and 59 EC precluded such treatment, the Court pointed out that the exercise of the right to move and reside freely in another Member State is enhanced if citizens of the Union are able to use a given language to communicate with the administrative and judicial authorities of a State on the same footing as its nationals. Persons such as the defendants who had exercised that free movement right were in principle entitled, pursuant to Article 6 of the Treaty, to treatment no less favourable than that accorded to nationals of the host State so far as concerns the use of languages which are spoken there. Whilst criminal legislation and the rules of criminal procedure (such as the national rules governing the language of proceedings) fell within Member State competence, such legislative provisions nevertheless could not violate the principle of equal treatment or restrict the fundamental freedoms guaranteed by Community law.[33] Consequently, in so far as they might compromise the right of nationals of other Member States to equal treatment in the exercise of their right to move and reside freely in another Member State, national rules concerning the language to be used in criminal proceedings in the host State fell within the scope of the Treaty and had to comply with Article 6 thereof.[34]

The Court went on to hold that the rules in question were discriminatory because they favoured nationals over non-nationals (through the residence requirement); and the residence requirement was not justified, because it was not based on objective considerations independent of the nationality of the persons concerned and was not proportionate to the legitimate aim of the national provisions.

This time, equal treatment (Article 6) was combined with free movement (Article 8a) in order to ensure that rules of criminal procedure that fell, unquestionably, within the competence of the Member State were applied in a way that protected another fundamental right (the right to a fair criminal trial, as provided for by Article 6 ECHR). It is perhaps worth pointing out that the Court did *not* take a minimalist approach, hold that the situation fell outwith EC law and suggest that Messrs Bickel and Franz would nevertheless find adequate protection under national constitutional law and/or under the ECHR.[35] The Court clearly opted instead for an approach that combined the new citizenship provisions with the protection of fundamental rights.

[31] Case C-274/96 *Bickel and Franz* [1998] ECR I-7637.

[32] The area was formerly the Süd-Tirol and belonged to the Austro-Hungarian Empire.

[33] *Bickel and Franz*, n 31 above, paras 16–17.

[34] ibid, paras 18–19.

[35] Art 6(3)(a) of the ECHR guarantees everyone charged with a criminal offence the right 'to be informed promptly, in a language which he understands and in detail, of the nature and cause of the accusation against him'; and Art 6(3)(e) the right 'to have the free assistance of an interpreter if he cannot understand or speak the language used in court'.

In his Opinion in that case, Advocate General Jacobs made it clear that he, for one, viewed citizenship and protection of fundamental rights as inextricably linked. Whilst carefully leaving open the question of whether *all* criminal proceedings against a citizen of the Union fell within the scope of application of the Treaty for the purposes of Article 6 (non-discrimination), even where that citizen has not exercised his right to free movement, he declared:

> It may be . . . that the time has come for even that question to be answered affirmatively. The notion of citizenship of the Union implies a commonality of rights and obligations uniting Union citizens by a common bond transcending Member State nationality. The introduction of that notion was largely inspired by the concern to bring the Union closer to its citizens and to give expression to its character as more than a purely economic union. That concern is reflected in the removal of the word 'economic' from the Community's name (also effected by the Treaty on European Union) and by the progressive introduction into the EC Treaty of a wide range of activities and policies transcending the field of the economy.
>
> Against that background it would be difficult to explain to a citizen of the Union how, despite the language of Articles 6, 8 and 8a [now 18, 20 and 21 TFEU], a Member State other than his own could be permitted to discriminate against him on grounds of his nationality in any criminal proceedings brought against him within its territory. Freedom from discrimination on grounds of nationality is the most fundamental right conferred by the Treaty and must be seen as a basic ingredient of Union citizenship.[36]

In *Grzelczyk*,[37] the Court took a significant further step. Mr Grzelzcyk was a French fourth year student residing and studying in Belgium. After three years combining work and studying, he applied to be given the '*minimex*' (the minimum subsistence allowance) to help finance the final year of his course. He was refused on the basis that, as a non-Belgian, he was only entitled to claim the *minimex* if he could show entitlement through Regulation 1612/68 (which he apparently could not do).[38] Had he been a Belgian student, he would have been entitled to claim the *minimex*.

In a phrase which has since become almost a mantra in the citizenship case law,[39] the Court declared that,

> Union citizenship is destined to be the fundamental status of nationals of the Member States, enabling those who find themselves in the same situation to enjoy the same

[36] Opinion of AG Jacobs in *Bickel and Franz*, n 31 above, paras 23–24.

[37] Case C-184/99 *Grzelczyk* [2001] ECR I-6193.

[38] The parties to the main proceedings, the Member States that intervened and the Commission all devoted substantial effort to examining whether the fact that during the first three years of his studies Mr Grzelczyk took various paid jobs was sufficient to enable him to be classified as a 'worker' for the purposes of Community law, which would have enabled the problem to have been solved without tackling the thorny question of citizenship of the Union. However, the Court stuck to the analysis and questions provided by the referring court (see paras 15–17 of the judgment).

[39] See, eg Case C-413/99 *Baumbast and R* [2002] ECR I-7091, para 82; Case C-148/02 *Garcia Avello* [2003] ECR I-11613, para 22; Case C-200/02 *Zhu and Chen* [2004] ECR I-9925, para 25; Case C-135/08 *Rottmann* [2010] ECR I-1449, para 43; Case C-34/09 *Ruiz Zambrano*, judgment of 8 March 2011 nyr, para 41.

> treatment in law irrespective of their nationality, subject to such exceptions as are expressly provided for . . .[40]

Drawing on *Martinez Sala* and *Bickel and Franz*, the Court went on to hold that Articles 6 and 8 of the Treaty precluded entitlement to a non-contributory social benefit, such as the *minimex*, from being made conditional, in the case of nationals of Member States other than the host State where they are legally resident, on their falling within the scope of Regulation No 1612/68 when no such condition applies to nationals of the host Member State.

Thus, the *status* of citizenship, taken in conjunction with the prohibition on discrimination on grounds of nationality, enabled Mr Grzelczyk to claim equal treatment with a Belgian national in the same situation and hence to benefit from the *minimex*.[41] The national court had asked, in the alternative, about the interpretation of Article 6 read in conjunction with Article 8a (freedom to move and reside freely) but, in the light of the answer given on Articles 6 and 8, it became unnecessary to answer that question.

Let us pause there to take stock. First, these three early cases – *Grzelczyk* most clearly – supply the foundations on which the subsequent citizenship case law has been built. Second, none of the three judgments makes express mention of fundamental rights. Third, all three nevertheless combine fundamental rights thinking (equal treatment, protection of the rights of the defence) with the new citizenship principles – either the status of citizenship (*Martinez Sala*, *Grzelczyk*) or the exercise of one specific citizenship right, namely the right to move and reside freely (*Bickel and Franz*) so as to produce a result that would *not* have been arrived at under the classic economic free movement rights.

Has the Court, then – like M Jourdain in Molière's *Le Bourgeois Gentilhomme*,[42] who discovered that he has been speaking prose for more than forty years without knowing it – already been applying fundamental rights to citizenship implicitly?

It seems to me that in two areas – cases on names and cases involving 'non-moving' citizens (that is, cases in which no trans-border movement, in the classic sense, can be discerned) – what the Court has already done supports this thesis.

THE CASE LAW ON NAMES

A person's name is a key part of their identity. The problem of the name someone is known by first came to the fore in a case involving the exercise of a 'classic' free movement right: *Konstantinidis*,[43] which concerned a Greek masseur working in

[40] *Grzelczyk*, n 37 above, para 31.

[41] The rights under Art 6 read with Art 8 therefore enabled the requirements of Directive 93/96 on student residence to be read in a way that reflected solidarity rather than tight budgetary constraints.

[42] Act II, scene 4, during the lesson with his philosophy teacher: 'Par ma foi! Il y a plus de quarante ans que je dis de la prose sans que j'en susse rien, et je vous suis le plus obligé du monde de m'avoir appris çela'.

[43] Case C-168/91 *Konstantinidis* [1993] ECR I-1191.

Germany who claimed that the official transliteration of his name breached his rights under EU law. Thanks to Advocate General Jacobs, *Konstantinidis* ceased to be merely a case about discrimination on grounds of nationality and became a case about the fundamental right to personal identity. In an elegant and much-quoted passage, he declared,

> A Community national who goes to another Member State is entitled not just to pursue his trade or profession and to enjoy the same living and working conditions as nationals of the host state: he is in addition entitled to assume that . . . he will be treated in accordance with a common code of fundamental values, in particular those laid down in the European Convention on Human Rights. In other words, he is entitled to say "*civis Europeus sum*" and to invoke that status in order to oppose any violation of his fundamental rights.[44]

The Court, more prosaically, told the national court that Article 52 of the Treaty must be interpreted as meaning that it is contrary to that provision for a Greek national to be obliged, under the applicable national legislation, to use, in the pursuit of his occupation, a spelling of his name whereby its pronunciation is modified and the resulting distortion exposes him to the risk that potential clients may confuse him with other persons.

In *Garcia Avello*, the Court was asked to consider a bizarre situation arising from different national traditions as to how children are named. The Garcia Avello children, born in Belgium, possessed through their parents the nationality of two Member States (Spain and Belgium). On registration of their births in Belgium, they were (in accordance with the Belgian rules) given the double surname borne by their father, Garcia Avello (a double name composed of the first element of the father's own father's surname and the first element of his mother's surname). The parents subsequently applied to the Belgian authorities to have the children's surname changed to Garcia Weber, so that it reflected the Spanish pattern and comprised the first element of their father's surname (Garcia) followed by their mother's maiden surname (Weber).[45] The Belgian authorities refused, indicating that they would be prepared to accept plain Garcia as a compromise. The parents rejected that peace overture; and in due course the Conseil d'État made a reference.

The Court started with the observation that, as dual nationals, the Garcia Avello children were also citizens of the Union.[46] Although the rules governing a person's surname were matters coming within the competence of the Member States, the latter must none the less, when exercising that competence, comply with Community law.[47] It was true that citizenship of the Union was not intended to

[44] ibid, Opinion of AG Jacobs, para 46.

[45] As AG Jacobs pointed out at para 55 of his Opinion, the 'Belgian name' Garcia Avello meant that within the Spanish community the children's surname would lead to them being identified not as Mr Garcia Avello's children but as his siblings.

[46] *Garcia Avello*, n 39 above, para 25.

[47] The Court applied a not dissimilar analysis later in Case C-192/05 *Tas-Hagen* [2006] ECR I-10451. There, Dutch nationals (hence, citizens of the Union) who had made use of their right to move and reside to establish themselves in Spain had been refused benefits for civilian war victims that were *not*

extend the scope *ratione materiae* of the Treaty to internal situations which had no link with Community law. However, the necessary link with Community law did exist because of the children's dual nationality: despite having never moved, they were therefore nationals of one Member State lawfully resident in the territory of another Member State.[48]

The Court went on to hold that, because those with two nationalities (like the Garcia Avello children) had the right to seek to be treated differently from those with only one (the ordinary Belgian national), there had been discrimination that was not justified and/or was disproportionate. The Court therefore ruled that Articles 12 EC and 17 EC precluded, in circumstances such as those of the main proceedings, the administrative authority of a Member State from refusing to grant an application for a change of surname made on behalf of minor children resident in that State and having dual nationality of that State and of another Member State, where the purpose of that application was to enable those children to bear the surname to which they were entitled according to the law and tradition of the second Member State.

Advocate General Jacobs had devoted significant space, in his Opinion, to exploring naming systems and their personal and cultural significance.[49] Against that background, it would have been difficult for the Court to have been unaware of the fundamental rights issues behind the questions that it was answering.

Grunkin and Paul required the Court to take a further, cautious, step forward. Leonhard Matthias was the child, born in Denmark, of two German nationals. Under Danish rules on names, it was perfectly possible for him to be registered with the surnames of both parents, as 'Leonhard Matthias Grunkin-Paul'. Like his parents, he had German nationality.[50] Unfortunately, his parents subsequently separated, one remaining in Denmark whilst the other returned to live in Germany. They applied for Leonard Matthias to be issued with a German passport, so that he would have the necessary travel document to be able to cross the border between Denmark and Germany and spend time with each parent. Applying German legislation on names to a German national, the German authorities informed them that they were not prepared to recognise the surname 'Grunkin-Paul'. Either Grunkin or Paul would be fine; but not both together.

Applying *Garcia Avello*, the Court stated that Leonhard Matthias could rely in principle, as against the Member State of which he was a national, on the right

covered by EU benefits legislation, on precisely the grounds that they did not satisfy the residence criterion of residence in the Netherlands. The Court nevertheless held that they could rely on Art 18(1) EC. Member States must exercise their admitted competence in relation to such benefits in a way that was compatible with EU law. The residence criterion placed the claimants at a disadvantage precisely because they had exercised their rights of free movement as EU citizens. The residence criterion was not appropriate to attain its objective; therefore, it was disproportionate and not capable of justification.

[48] *Garcia Avello*, n 39 above, paras 26–27.

[49] ibid, paras 5–22.

[50] Unlike, for example, Ireland and Belgium (and the rules which gave rise, respectively, to *Zhu and Chen*, n 39 above, and to *Ruiz Zambrano*, n 39 above), Denmark does not operate a *jus soli* rule on nationality.

conferred by Article 12 EC not to be discriminated against on grounds of nationality and on the right, established in Article 18 EC, to move and reside freely within the territory of the Member States.[51] That said, there was here no discrimination on grounds of nationality (so Article 12 EC was not engaged). Nevertheless, national legislation which placed certain nationals of the Member State concerned at a disadvantage simply because they had exercised their freedom to move and to reside in another Member State was a restriction on the freedoms conferred by Article 18(1) EC on every citizen of the Union.[52]

If Leonhard Matthias was obliged to have a German passport showing a name other than that on his Danish birth certificate (and other than the name that would in due course probably appear on his school certificates and perhaps on his university diploma), ordinary life for him as a citizen would be unnecessarily complicated.[53] The various justifications advanced by the German Government did not suffice to justify the obstacle to freedom of movement.[54] The Court concluded that Article 18 EC precluded the authorities of a Member State, in applying national law, from refusing to recognise a child's surname, as determined and registered in a second Member State in which the child – who, like his parents, had only the nationality of the first Member State – was born and had been resident since birth.

The judgment is framed solely in terms of the existence of an obstacle to the exercise of free movement rights (as in *Garcia Avello*). But it seems plausible that the Court had in mind fundamental rights when reaching its decision.[55]

Sayn-Wittgenstein[56] followed swiftly on the heels of *Grunkin and Paul*. Here, an enterprising Austrian lady had, following her adoption as an adult by a German aristocrat, set herself up in the prestige end of the real estate market, with a business card identifying her as 'Fürstin von Sayn-Wittgenstein', selling castles and stately homes. She had however retained her Austrian nationality. The dispute arose from the Austrian authorities' belated decision[57] in 2007, following a decision of the Austrian Verfassungsgerichtshof in a similar case, to correct the entry in the register of civil status so as to remove the title of nobility ('*Fürst*') and the nobiliary particle ('*von*') from her name.

[51] Case C-353/06 *Grunkin and Paul* [2008] ECR I-7639, para 18.

[52] ibid, para 21.

[53] ibid, paras 23–28.

[54] ibid, paras 29–38.

[55] ibid, paras 64–71 of my Opinion, in which I set out my reasons for thinking that there might be a violation of the general principle of equal treatment. I also referred (at para 87) to the need for the German authorities and courts to have regard to the child's best interests as a primary consideration, in accordance with Art 3(1) of the United Nations Convention on the Rights of the Child and Art 24(2) of the Charter.

[56] Case C-208/09 *Sayn-Wittgenstein*, judgment of 22 December 2010 nyr.

[57] ibid, paras 23–24. Following her adoption, the Austrian authorities had initially registered her in the Austrian register of civil status as 'Ilonka Fürstin von Sayn-Wittgenstein'. She had been issued with a German driving licence and formed a company in Germany under that name. In addition, her Austrian passport had been renewed at least once, in the course of 2001, in the name of Ilonka Fürstin von Sayn-Wittgenstein and two certificates of nationality had been issued by the Austrian consular authorities in Germany in that name.

Both Austrian and German national law contain provisions (introduced in the immediate aftermath of the First World War, when both became republics) for the abolition of the nobility and all the privileges and titles pertaining thereto. However, the exact rules differ in the two Member States. For Austrian nationals, it has been unlawful since then, as a matter of constitutional law, to bear any title of nobility, a prohibition which extends to the use of such particles as '*von*' or '*zu*' as part of a surname. In Germany, however, a different approach was taken. Existing titles, although they could no longer be borne as such, became part of the family surname, transmitted to all children, subject only to variations according to the sex of the child where an element has both a masculine and a feminine form – for example *Fürst* (Prince) and *Fürstin* (Princess). The Kreisgericht Worbis (Germany) had accordingly stated in 1992 that, following the adoption, the applicant had acquired the surname of her adoptive father as her name at birth, in the form 'Fürstin von Sayn-Wittgenstein', which would be the name she would use; and she had used that name from 1992 onwards.

Although, given the lady's professional activities, it would have been possible to approach the matter from the perspective of Article 56 TFEU, the Court decided the case on the basis of Article 21 TFEU alone. It commenced its answer with fundamental rights:

> It must be noted as a preliminary point that a person's name is a constituent element of his identity and of his private life, the protection of which is enshrined in Article 7 of the Charter of Fundamental Rights of the European Union and in Article 8 of the European Convention for the Protection of Human Rights and Fundamental Freedoms. Even though Article 8 of that convention does not refer to it explicitly, a person's name, as a means of personal identification and a link to a family, none the less concerns his or her private and family life (see, inter alia, European Court of Human Rights judgments *Burghartz v. Switzerland* of 22 February 1994, Series A No 280-B, p. 28, § 24, and *Stjerna v. Finland* of 25 November 1994, Series A No 299-B, p. 60, § 37).[58]

The Court went on to trace a delicate line between competing values. The national legislation was a restriction on free movement,[59] and it was clear – particularly given the passage of time – that being forced to change names would cause the claimant serious inconvenience.[60] At the same time, the public policy justification was a weighty one. After a careful and lengthy analysis, the Court concluded that

> the refusal, by the authorities of a Member State, to recognise all the elements of the surname of a national of that State,[61] as determined in another Member State – in which that national resides – at the time of his or her adoption as an adult by a national of that other Member State, where that surname includes a title of nobility which is not permitted in the first Member State under its constitutional law cannot be regarded as a

[58] ibid, para 52.
[59] ibid, paras 53–54.
[60] ibid, paras 55–71. See also my Opinion at paras 40–50.
[61] ibid, paras 36–48.

> measure unjustifiably undermining the freedom to move and reside enjoyed by citizens of the Union.[62]

Such a measure was *not*, therefore, precluded by Article 21 TFEU, provided that the measures adopted by the authorities in that context were justified on public policy grounds, that is to say, necessary for the protection of the interests which they were intended to secure and proportionate to the legitimate aim pursued.[63]

Certain Member States were nevertheless getting decidedly worried about how far this right-to-a-name trend might be going – notably Lithuania, which had intervened in both *Grunkin and Paul* and *Sayn-Wittgenstein* and whose national system for names seemed a likely next target. Sure enough, in *Runevič-Vardyn and Wardyn*[64] the Lithuanian naming rules came before the Court. That case arose out of proceedings between, on the one hand, a Lithuanian national of Polish ethnic origin (Malgožata Runevič-Vardyn), and her husband, a Polish national (Łukasz Paweł Wardyn), and, on the other, the responsible civic authorities in Vilnius, who had refused to amend the forenames and surnames of the interested parties as entered on the birth and marriage certificates issued to them. The bone of contention was how, under Lithuanian and Polish rules, their names were written.

Having decided that the situation was not covered by Directive 2000/43 on eliminating discrimination based on racial or ethnic origin, the Court initially addressed the questions referred (which related to Articles 18 and 21 TFEU) from the perspective of the case law on the status of citizenship (Article 20 TFEU).[65] Since both applicants had exercised their free movement rights, however, the Court then returned to the analysis under Article 21 TFEU. It recalled the principles laid down in its decisions in *Garcia Avello*, *Grunkin and Paul* and *Sayn-Wittgenstein*, and then passed back to the national court the decision as to whether the Lithuanian rules that precluded amendment of the joint surname of the applicants created a real risk of serious inconvenience for them: if so, those rules would constitute a restriction under Article 21 TFEU.[66] The Court went on to give the national court strong guidance that, even if there were such a restriction, the national rules were still justified and probably proportionate.[67]

In his Opinion, Advocate General Jääskinen had again emphasised the importance of surnames and forenames, for both individuals and states.[68] When taken in

[62] ibid, para 94.

[63] ibid, para 95 and operative part of the judgment. In my Opinion, I had suggested (at paras 67–68) that the final decision on proportionality must be for the national court, because there were a number of legal and factual issues to decide which would determine whether, in this particular case, rectification of a name after 15 years of use was disproportionate. I do not know the end of the story.

[64] Case C-391/09 *Runevič-Vardyn and Wardyn*, judgment of 12 May 2011 nyr.

[65] ibid, paras 59–61.

[66] ibid, paras 77–78. This was one of three complaints. The others involved a request for the lady's forename and maiden name to be changed on her birth and marriage certificates; and a request for the gentleman's forenames to be entered on his marriage certificate with the diacritical marks (thus, 'Łukasz Paweł' instead of 'Lukasz Pawel'). Both those complaints were dismissed.

[67] ibid, paras 83–94.

[68] ibid, see Opinion of AG Jääskinen, paras 5–6 and 77–79, examining the case law of the Strasbourg court on names and Art 8 ECHR.

conjunction with the Court's deliberate digression (in an Article 21 TFEU case) in order to invoke the Article 20 TFEU case law on the status of citizen, that provides compelling evidence of the underlying basis for the Court's decision (citizenship with fundamental rights; derogation from rights on legitimate public policy grounds; proportionality test).

'NON-MOVING' CITIZENS OF THE UNION

The future baby Catherine Xhu[69] was blessed with Chinese parents who took excellent legal advice. In consequence, they arranged for their daughter to be born in Belfast – part of the United Kingdom of Great Britain and Northern Ireland. Under Irish constitutional law as it then stood, because the child was born on the territory of the island of Ireland (viewed as an indivisible whole), she became upon birth an Irish citizen. She did not qualify for, and thus did not acquire, British nationality. Although she and her mother never crossed a border, Catherine was thus a citizen of one Member State (Ireland) residing in another Member State (the United Kingdom). On that basis, her mother sought to obtain a permanent residence permit to live in the United Kingdom (in Cardiff) in order to be able to care for her baby daughter there.

The Court's decision is well known. It held that Catherine (irrespective of age) could take advantage of the Treaty's provisions on movement and residence.[70] She was a citizen of the Union, with a right to reside freely in the territory of the Member States and, thanks to her mother, she had both sickness insurance and sufficient resources for her not to become a burden on the social assistance system of the host Member State.[71] There had been no abuse of rights.[72] Refusing Mrs Chen a right of residence to look after Catherine would deprive the child's right of residence as a Union citizen of any useful effect; therefore, for that reason alone, where (as here), Article 18 EC and Directive 90/364 granted a right to reside for an indefinite period in the host Member State to a young minor who was a national of another Member State, those same provisions allowed a parent who was that minor's primary carer to reside with the child in the host Member State.[73]

In his Opinion, Advocate General Tizzano had argued that Mrs Chen must be able to invoke a right of residence derived from her daughter, because 'the opposite conclusion would be manifestly contrary to the interests of the minor and to

[69] *Zhu and Chen*, n 39 above. Having delved into the national file for that case whilst writing my Opinion in *Ruiz Zambrano*, I can confirm that, as the daughter of Mr Guoqing Zu (known as Hopkins Zhu) and Lavette Man Chen, the baby was Catherine Zhu and *not* Catherine Chen (she was, indeed, correctly so identified by AG Tizzano at the start of his Opinion). However, she has probably been known to practitioners of EU law as 'baby Chen' for too long for this footnote to serve any purpose beyond the strictly academic!

[70] ibid, paras 18–20.

[71] ibid, paras 25–33.

[72] ibid, paras 34–40.

[73] ibid, paras 45–47.

the requirement of respecting the unity of family life' and 'would deprive of any useful effect the right of residence conferred by the Treaty upon Catherine because clearly, since she cannot remain alone in the United Kingdom, she would otherwise ultimately be unable to enjoy that right'.[74] The Court must therefore have reached its decision against the background of being aware of the fundamental rights issues, even though it did not refer to them expressly.

In contrast, *Government of the French Community and Walloon Government*[75] concerned a system of care insurance benefits established by the Flemish Community. The rules governing those benefits made their grant conditional on residence in the territory of Flanders or in the territory of another Member State, thereby excluding persons working in Flanders who were resident in another part of the national territory of Belgium. The reference arose out of actions brought by the Government of the French Community and the Walloon Government before the Court of Arbitration (which later became the Constitutional Court) for the annulment of the relevant Flemish legislation. No fundamental rights issues directly affecting individuals were involved.

In my Opinion, I concluded that the care insurance scheme fell within the scope *ratione materiae* of Regulation No 1408/71 and that, so far as nationals of other Member States working in Belgium and Belgian nationals who had exercised rights of freedom of movement were concerned, Articles 39 and 43 EC and Article 3 of Regulation No 1408/71 precluded an autonomous Community (Flanders) of a federal Member State (Belgium) from adopting provisions which, in the exercise of its powers, allow only persons residing in the territory for which that autonomous Community is competent or in another Member State to be insured under and covered by a social security scheme within the meaning of that regulation, to the exclusion of persons, whatever their nationality, who reside in a part of the territory of the same federal State for which another autonomous Community is competent.

I then went on to examine the situation of Belgian citizens who had *not* made use of their free movement rights. I suggested that, in a post single-market world in which frontiers between Member States have been abolished, it was a little odd to go on drawing such a sharp distinction between citizens who cross frontiers and those who do not; and I invited the Court to consider whether, in the light of the citizenship provisions, 'static' citizens of the Union could really be regarded as being in a 'purely internal situation'.[76]

The Court refused to be drawn down that path. It excluded from consideration Belgian nationals working in Flanders but living elsewhere in Belgium who had never exercised their freedom to move within the European Community. Community law 'clearly' could not apply to those purely internal situations, although its interpretation might possibly help such persons to obtain protection

[74] ibid, Opinion of AG Tizzano, paras 90 and 91–94, which link the analysis to Art 8 ECHR.

[75] Case C-212/06 *Gouvernement de la Communauté française et gouvernement wallon* [2008] ECR I-1683.

[76] ibid, my Opinion at paras 112–57.

against reverse discrimination from national laws on equal treatment.[77] The Court then turned to examine the position of nationals of other Member States working in Belgium and Belgian nationals who *had* exercised free movement rights. The Court held that such legislation was likely to have a restrictive effect on the exercise of free movement rights,[78] and that it could not be justified as pursuing a legitimate objective in the public interest in a proportionate way.[79]

Apart from the equal treatment issue that is inherent in any case which includes the possibility of reverse discrimination (here, against 'static' Belgians), the case raised no issues of fundamental rights; and it was not, strictly speaking, necessary to explore the issue of how 'static' citizens of the Union fared in order to resolve the questions referred. It is therefore unsurprising that the Court stuck to a classic free movement analysis and steered clear of Articles 17 and 18 EC (even though these were expressly raised and relied upon by the Government of the French Community).[80] Outside Belgium, the Court's decision attracted relatively little attention.

In contrast, *Ruiz Zambrano*[81] is a case that has aroused passionate debate. At first sight, it involved a 'purely internal situation': an application in Belgium by a third country national to be paid the unemployment benefit to which he had contributed for five years through his taxes and social security payments, but which had been refused on the basis that during that period, he had held neither a work permit nor a residence permit. Behind that simple storyline, however, was the fact that since their arrival in Belgium the Ruiz Zambranos had had two further children (Diego and Jessica), who both – under Belgian nationality law – were entitled to and held Belgian nationality. As Belgians, Diego and Jessica were therefore also citizens of the Union.

The wider picture – as the national judge making the reference correctly realised – was therefore less simple and was *not* (despite the protestations of the intervening Member States and, indeed, the Commission) a purely internal situation. If Mr Ruiz Zambrano found himself unable to stay and work in Belgium, the family as a unit would have to leave that country, thus uprooting Diego and Jessica. It seemed, on the facts, implausible to suppose that they could readily move to another Member State that would welcome them all (the Union citizen children and their third country national parents) with open arms and allow them to settle. Rather, it seemed all too likely that they would be unable to move to, or reside in, *any* EU Member State. What, then, of the children's rights as 'citizens of the Union'?

The Court dealt with the problem much more shortly than its Advocate General.[82] It started from the (clearly correct) observation that, since Diego and Jessica had acquired Belgian nationality perfectly legitimately under national law,

[77] ibid, my Opinion at paras 37–40.
[78] ibid, paras 41–54.
[79] ibid, paras 55–60.
[80] ibid, para 39.
[81] *Ruiz Zambrano*, n 39 above.
[82] ibid, my Opinion, which runs to 178 paras.

they undeniably enjoyed the status of citizens of the Union.[83] Since citizenship of the Union is intended to be the fundamental status of nationals of the Member States, it follows that 'Article 20 TFEU precludes national measures which have the effect of depriving citizens of the Union of the genuine enjoyment of the substance of the rights conferred by virtue of their status as citizens of the Union'.[84] A refusal to grant a right of residence to a third country national with dependent minor children in the Member State where those children are nationals and reside, and also a refusal to grant such a person a work permit, has such an effect.[85] The Court pointed out that both those decisions would, it must be assumed, lead to the children having to leave the territory of the Union and that 'those citizens of the Union would, as a result, be unable to exercise the substance of the rights conferred on them by virtue of their status as citizens of the Union'.[86] Article 20 TFEU therefore precluded a Member State from refusing a third country national upon whom his minor children, who are European Union citizens, are dependent, a right of residence and a work permit, 'in so far as such decisions deprive those children of the genuine enjoyment of the substance of the rights attaching to the status of European Union citizen'.[87]

In arriving at that conclusion, the Court built on its recent decision in *Rottmann*.[88] In that case, the crucial citizenship (German citizenship by naturalisation, rather than his earlier Austrian citizenship by birth) was acquired by Dr Rottmann after he had moved to Germany from Austria. The judgment disregards that earlier move and looks exclusively to the *future* effects that withdrawal of German citizenship would have on Dr Rottmann's *status* as a citizen of the Union by rendering him stateless.

Like *Rottmann*, the judgment in *Ruiz Zambrano* looks to the future and focuses exclusively on the *status* of citizenship and its consequences. There is no mention in the reasoning in *Ruiz Zambrano* of fundamental rights. It is nevertheless difficult to suppose (in the light of the observations lodged, the hearing and the Opinion) that the Grand Chamber's decision was not influenced by such considerations.

Shortly afterwards, the Third Chamber gave judgment in *McCarthy*.[89] The claimant in that case was an adult British national on social benefits who had never moved from the UK. Following her marriage to a Jamaican national who lacked leave to remain in the United Kingdom under the immigration rules, she applied for an Irish passport for the first time and obtained it. She and her husband then applied for a residence permit and residence document under EU law as, respectively, a Union citizen and the spouse of a Union citizen. In other words, Mrs McCarthy claimed that she was resident *in the UK* on the basis of her Irish

[83] ibid, para 40.
[84] ibid, paras 41–42.
[85] ibid, para 43.
[86] ibid, para 44.
[87] ibid, para 45 and operative part of the judgment.
[88] *Rottmann*, n 39 above.
[89] Case C-434/09 *McCarthy*, judgment of 5 May 2011 nyr.

(rather than her British) nationality and that her third country national husband should, on that basis, also be granted residence rights.

One suspects that Mrs and Mr McCarthy may have appeared to be less obvious candidates for sympathetic treatment than the Ruiz Zambrano children. Still, one might reasonably ask the question, 'did she not have spousal rights?' (such as had assisted Mrs Carpenter to remain with her services-providing husband).[90]

Although the national court had limited itself[91] to enquiring as to the proper construction of Directive 2004/38, the Court decided that an analysis of Article 21 TFEU would also be of assistance. In a much more extended judgment than *Ruiz Zambrano*, the Court first established that Directive 2004/38 did not apply. It then turned its attention to 'whether Article 21 TFEU is applicable to a Union citizen who has never exercised his right of free movement, who has always resided in a Member State of which he is a national and who is also a national of another Member State'.[92] The analysis is thus ostensibly based on movement, not on status; but it would be fair to say that to some extent it weaves the two together.

The Court started by invoking Article 20 TFEU, *Schempp*[93] and the Court's ruling in *Ruiz Zambrano* in order to establish that this might not be a purely internal situation.[94] It then combined Article 21 TFEU with *Ruiz Zambrano* dicta. Since Mrs McCarthy was able to reside in the United Kingdom by virtue of her British nationality, the authorities' refusal of her request for EU residence documents did *not* have

> the effect of depriving her of the genuine enjoyment of the substance of the rights associated with her status as a Union citizen, or of impeding the exercise of her right to move and reside freely within the territory of the Member States, in accordance with Article 21 TFEU.[95]

Nor (unlike the national measures in *Ruiz Zambrano*) did it oblige her to leave the territory of the EU.

Next, the Court drew on *Garcia Avello* and *Grunkin and Paul* for its analysis of whether there was any serious risk of impediments to the exercise of rights of movement,[96] before combining *Garcia Avello* and *Ruiz Zambrano* to explain its conclusion:

> Thus, in Ruiz Zambrano and García Avello, the national measure at issue had the effect of depriving Union citizens of the genuine enjoyment of the substance of the rights

[90] Case C-60/00 *Carpenter* [2002] ECR I-6279. Whilst it is clear that Mr Carpenter was economically active whereas Mrs McCarthy was not (and indeed that Mrs Carpenter's presence helped Mr Carpenter to engage in the provision of services), it is less clear that the presence or absence of economic activity should be determinative of whether an applicant can invoke spousal rights.

[91] As, essentially, had AG Kokott in her Opinion in *McCarthy*, n 89 above; indeed, she suggested that if the Court really wished to explore the citizenship arguments further, it should reopen the oral procedure (para 46).

[92] *McCarthy*, n 89 above, para 44.

[93] Case C-403/03 *Schempp* [2005] ECR I-6421, para 22.

[94] *McCarthy*, n 89 above, paras 46–50.

[95] ibid, para 49.

[96] ibid, paras 51–52.

> conferred by virtue of that status or of impeding the exercise of their right of free movement and residence within the territory of the Member States.
>
> As stated [above] . . ., the fact that Mrs McCarthy, in addition to being a national of the United Kingdom, is also a national of Ireland does not mean that a Member State has applied measures that have the effect of depriving her of the genuine enjoyment of the substance of the rights conferred by virtue of her status as a Union citizen or of impeding the exercise of her right of free movement and residence within the territory of the Member States. Accordingly, in such a context, such a factor is not sufficient, in itself, for a finding that the situation of the person concerned is covered by Article 21 TFEU.
>
> In those circumstances, the situation of a person such as Mrs McCarthy has no factor linking it with any of the situations governed by European Union law and the situation is confined in all relevant respects within a single Member State.[97] (emphasis added)

Accordingly, the Court concluded that

> Article 21 TFEU is not applicable to a Union citizen who has never exercised his right of free movement, who has always resided in a Member State of which he is a national and who is also a national of another Member State, provided that the situation of that citizen does not include the application of measures by a Member State that would have the effect of depriving him of the genuine enjoyment of the substance of the rights conferred by virtue of his status as a Union citizen or of impeding the exercise of his right of free movement and residence within the territory of the Member States.

An interesting analogy may perhaps be drawn here with the evolution of the case law on free movement of goods. That case law initially interpreted the free movement principle[98] very widely,[99] so that many commercial and marketing rules were caught, including ones that had only a marginal or incidental effect on free trade,[100] and then, after examination, exonerated a number of those measures under Article 36 EEC[101] or the 'mandatory requirements'[102] derogations. In *Keck and Mithouard*, the Court reversed its earlier thinking, stating that 'contrary to what has previously been decided, the application to products from other Member States of national provisions restricting or prohibiting certain selling arrangements' that apply in the

[97] ibid, paras 53–55. In Case C-369/90 *Micheletti and ors* [1992] ECR I-4239, the Court insisted that a person who holds dual nationality in the form of the nationality of a Member State and the nationality of a third country *can* rely on their Member State nationality to invoke rights under EU law (*cf Zhu and Chen*, n 39 above). See now, in the context of dual Member State nationality and Turkish nationality, Joined Cases C-7/10 and C-9/10 *Kahveci and Inan* (pending).

[98] Originally Art 30 EEC, then Art 30 EC, then Art 28 EC, now Art 34 TFEU.

[99] The inevitable result of applying the '*Dassonville* formula' which catches any measure that 'directly or indirectly, actually or potentially' hinders trade between Member States: Case 8/74 *Procureur du Roi v Dassonville* [1974] ECR 837, para 5.

[100] On the stream of 'Sunday trading cases', see, eg Case 145/88 *Torfaen Borough Council v B&Q* [1989] ECR 3851.

[101] Originally Art 36 EEC/EC; then (confusingly) Art 30 EC; now reassuringly, for those of us who are bad at remembering numbers, Art 36 TFEU.

[102] Created by the Court in Case 120/78 *Rewe-ZentraleAG v Bundesmonopolverwaltung für Branntwein* ('*Cassis de Dijon*') [1979] ECR 649 as a non-exhaustive list of additional good reasons for not having unlimited free trade.

same manner, both in law and in fact, to all traders within the national territory was not caught by the free movement principle.[103]

The decision in *McCarthy* suggests that with citizenship rights, the Court may be trying to avoid a flood of cases that are really 'purely internal situations with a possible EU twist' by doing its fundamental rights analysis, à la *Keck and Mithouard*, at the beginning of the story; and only allowing citizenship rights for 'static' EU citizens to be invoked where the violation of fundamental rights if they *cannot* be invoked would be flagrant. If that is not the case, the situation – it seems – will continue to be classified as internal; and the rights that indubitably attach to the status of citizen of the Union will not be triggered.

In *Dereci*[104], decided whilst this book was in press, the Grand Chamber was invited (in essence) to explain how to reconcile *Ruiz Zambrano* and *McCarthy*. Unfortunately the decision came too late for me to be able to do it justice in this essay. Suffice it to say that the Grand Chamber (a) confirmed that the situation of a 'static citizen' cannot necessarily be assimilated to a 'purely internal situation'; (b) reiterated (endorsing *Ruiz Zambrano*) that Article 20 TFEU indeed precludes national measures which have the effect of depriving Union citizens of the genuine enjoyment of the substance of the rights conferred by virtue of that status, but went on to say that (c) 'the criterion relating to the denial of the genuine enjoyment of the substance of the rights conferred by virtue of European Union citizen status refers to situations in which the Union citizen has, in fact, to leave not only the territory of the Member State of which he is a national but also the territory of the Union as a whole'.[105] The Court passed back to the national court the task of deciding whether the situation of the applicants in the main proceedings was covered by EU law, thus triggering the application of Article 7 of the Charter (on respect for private and family life) or whether it was not (in which case the national court was invited to apply Article 8 ECHR).

Important though it undoubtedly is, *Dereci* leaves a number of questions unanswered. A series of pending cases (such as *O, S and L*[106], *Alopka and Others*[107] and *Ymeraga*[108]) will afford the Court further opportunities to clarify its case law. Perhaps it will define more clearly whether the *only* circumstance in which the 'substance' of the citizenship rights of a 'static' citizen is threatened is where an infant EU citizen would have to leave the territory of the EU as a whole. Perhaps it will explore further the distinction (if distinction there be) between the *status* of citizen and what should attach to it (Article 20 TFEU) and the specific issue of rights of *movement and residence* (Article 21 TFEU). Since there are a number of possible permutations of factual circumstances which might give rise to litigation in this area, it is probable that *Ruiz Zambrano*, *McCarthy* and *Dereci* represent the

[103] Joined Cases C-267 and C-268/91 *Keck and Mithouard* [1993] ECR I-6097, paras 16–17.

[104] Case C-256/11 *Dereci and others* (judgment 15 November 2011).

[105] Para 66 of the judgment.

[106] Joined Cases C-356/11 and C-357/111 *O and S* (pending). C-356/11 O&S, & C-357/11 L (pending).

[107] Case C-86/12 *Alopka and Others* (pending).

[108] Case C-87/12 *Ymeraga* (pending).

start, rather than the conclusion, of this chapter in the continuing story of citizenship of the Union.

Behind (perhaps, beyond) the articulation of individual 'rights' attaching to citizenship lies the bigger question of what the *status* of citizenship entails. That question looks both backwards and forwards. It looks back to concepts of citizenship: to what is 'special' about being a citizen and what distinguishes the citizen from the mere economic factor of production. It looks forward, to what is likely to be the impact – in terms of the citizen being able to enjoy the benefits of his status – of particular national measures. Do they not matter too much (so, can the Member State be left unhindered to apply them)? Or are they likely to undermine the very essence of what that status should confer? To recall the test laid down by the Court in *Ruiz Zambrano*: in any particular case, will the contested national measure 'have the effect of depriving citizens of the genuine enjoyment of the substance of the rights conferred on them by virtue of their status as citizens of the Union'? It seems to me that, when trying to answer that question, the Court will inevitably have regard to fundamental rights, whether it states this expressly in its reasoning or not.

APPLYING FUNDAMENTAL RIGHTS TO THE CITIZENSHIP PROVISIONS – SOME BROADER REFLECTIONS

In retrospect, it may perhaps seem obvious that the Court would necessarily bear in mind fundamental rights when interpreting the Treaty's provisions on citizenship of the Union. Whilst a civilised society extends the protection afforded by fundamental rights guarantees to all those who are present on their territory, this does not alter the fact that the people who (par excellence) have rights – including, of course, fundamental rights – are citizens. Article 19(1) TEU (originally Article 164 EEC) states that '[t]he Court of Justice . . . shall ensure that in the interpretation and application of the Treaties the law is observed'. Viewed in that light, it becomes clear that it would be unthinkable for the Court to interpret the scope and content of the citizenship provisions of the Treaty without recourse to fundamental rights.

However, fundamental rights within EU law as enshrined in the Charter are only part of the story. National constitutional law (whether written or unwritten) tends generically to afford fundamental rights protection. The 27 Member States of the EU are all members of the Council of Europe and also signatories to the ECHR. One is therefore looking at a system with overlapping layers of protection from different sources: national constitutional law, the ECHR and EU law.

How should the Court of Justice handle a case that is viewed as being 'on the margins' – that might be considered to fall within the scope of EU law but that does not do so automatically and obviously in the classic sense – and that raises questions of fundamental rights?

Should it adopt a minimalist, 'hands off' approach (along the lines of 'provided protection may plausibly be available under either national constitutional law or the ECHR, there's no need for EU law to get involved')? The Court is not, after all, a 'human rights court'. That function is fulfilled by the European Court of Human Rights, some 200 kilometres down the road in Strasbourg. (I would argue that, as the supreme interpreter of EU law, the Court nevertheless has a permanent responsibility to ensure respect for such rights within the sphere of EU competence.)[109]

Following such an approach would mean, as I see it, that the Court would indeed step in (but would only step in) if there were no other protection available (usually, an unlikely scenario) and if the facts of the case could, with a little ingenuity, be construed as falling *ratione personae* and *ratione materiae* within the scope of application of EU law. Where possible, however, it would leave the fundamental rights problem to be dealt with elsewhere by construing the idea of the 'purely internal situation' broadly and, correspondingly, construing 'the scope of EU law' restrictively.

I think that the minimalist approach comes with a number of disadvantages attached.

First, such an approach seems strange when viewed historically, in the light of the evolution of EEC/EC/EU law thus far. During that evolution, fundamental rights protection and EU law itself have grown together. The Court has naturally and instinctively drawn on the constitutional traditions of the Member States and the ECHR in order to endow first EEC, and then EC and EU, law with the fundamental rights that are an integral part of a civilised legal system, at the same time as it has delineated the boundaries of EU law. Second, such an approach might produce case law based on a rather artificial analysis of how the facts of the case fell within the scope of EU law.[110] Third, it is quite difficult to reconcile such an approach with the Charter (even as 'soft law', and still less now that the Charter has been elevated to the same status as the Treaty itself). Fourthly, it might perhaps re-ignite the old debate about whether national legal systems and national supreme constitutional courts whose duty is, inter alia, to safeguard fundamental rights within their respective Member States can and should afford primacy to EU law, if the Court were seen no longer to care so much about fundamental rights protection.[111]

There is a further argument that I find compelling. Such an approach would sit ill with the concept that the nationals of the Member States have also been, for nearly 20 years, citizens of the Union. Citizens with no fundamental rights? That looks like a contradiction in terms.

Should the Court, then, regard the three types of fundamental rights protection (national, EU, ECHR) as complementary pieces of the jigsaw? On that basis, cases

[109] See my Opinion in *Ruiz Zambrano*, n 39 above, para 155.

[110] The Court's decision in *Carpenter*, n 90 above, is often cited and criticised as an illustration of such an artificial approach. *Zhu and Chen*, n 39 above, has also not been without its detractors.

[111] The well-known historical example is the Bundesverfassungsgericht (in the *Solange I*, *Solange II* and the *Maastricht* and *Lisbon* judgments), but other constitutional courts – for example, in Italy, Spain, Poland and the Czech Republic – have also legitimately addressed questions that are not so dissimilar.

that were purely internal to the Member State would attract national and ECHR protection; whilst cases that fell within the scope of EU law would be protected under EU fundamental rights (and, as/when the EU accedes to the ECHR, under the ECHR as well).

Such an approach seems neat and simple, which obviously commends it. It does leave certain issues untouched, of which the most obvious is reverse discrimination caused by the interaction of national law with EU law, with the result that 'static' citizens are left in a worse position than their 'mobile' counterparts, even though in all other respects their circumstances may be similar or identical. I have suggested elsewhere[112] that Article 18 TFEU (the prohibition on discrimination) should be interpreted as prohibiting reverse discrimination caused by the interaction between Article 21 TFEU (the EU citizen's right to move and reside freely) and national law that entails a violation of a fundamental right protected under EU law, where at least equivalent protection is not available under national law.

Specifically, fundamental rights protection under Article 18 TFEU would be triggered when (but only when) three cumulative conditions were met. First, the claimant would have to be a 'static' Union citizen resident in his Member State of nationality whose situation was comparable, in other material respects, to that of other 'mobile' citizens of the Union in the same Member State (who would already be able to invoke rights under Article 21 TFEU) – thus, the reverse discrimination at issue would, effectively, be *caused by* EU law. Second, the reverse discrimination would have to entail a violation of a fundamental right protected under EU law. Third, Article 18 TFEU would be available only as a subsidiary remedy, confined to situations in which national law did not afford adequate fundamental rights protection.

Whether that solution or some other is adopted, some solution *is* required to the problem of reverse discrimination if a 'complementary rights' approach is to be followed.

A further possibility is to regard the different sources of fundamental rights protection as cumulative. Under such an approach, just as ECHR protection comes 'on top' of the protection afforded by national constitutional law, fundamental rights protection under EU law would add a further layer. The Member State citizen/EU citizen would therefore be able to invoke the protection afforded by all three systems automatically. Whether or not, in a particular case, he obtained a finding that his right(s) had been violated would depend on where the court drew the boundary between the protected right and the permitted derogation.[113] As I see it, this scenario implies taking as one's premiss that EU law

[112] See the section of my Opinion in *Ruiz Zambrano* dealing with reverse discrimination (paras 123–50), in particular paras 144–48.

[113] Within all three systems of protection – national, EU and ECHR – *most* rights are not absolute, but can be derogated from in the general interest. In the context of EU law, it may perhaps be less easy than in the national or the ECHR context (applying the 'margin of appreciation') to tell precisely where the boundary should be drawn between the citizen's right to rely on his individual protected right and the Member State's right to derogate from that individual right in the general interest.

provides (or should provide) a completely autonomous, free-standing set of fundamental rights. Such rights would presumably be accessed by EU citizens through the portal *ratione personae* of their EU citizenship; but what about the *ratione materiae* component of the equation? And how and when would those rights benefit non-EU citizens present within the territory of the Union?

Here we come back round to the issues of competence and conferral. According to settled case law, EU fundamental rights may be invoked when (but only when) the contested measure comes within the scope of EU law.[114] The EU operates on the basis of conferred, not intrinsic, powers. Under this system, competence remains with the Member States unless and until it is agreed either to transfer the competence fully to the EU (resulting in exclusive EU competence) or to give the EU competence in parallel with the Member States (shared competence). The 'purely internal situation' rule is a convenient expression of the idea that the Court is looking at a situation which involves no element of EU law *because* Member States retain full competence.[115] Exclusive EU competence, too, is relatively easy to deal with (at least conceptually). If only the EU is competent to act in a particular field, protection of fundamental rights in that field should presumably also come from EU law (and now, specifically, from the Charter). But how should the Court approach situations where the EU enjoys shared competence with the Member States, particularly where it has not yet exercised that competence?

I have suggested elsewhere[116] that, in the long run, the clearest rule would be one that made the availability of EU fundamental rights protection dependent neither on whether a Treaty provision was directly applicable nor on whether EU secondary legislation had been enacted, but rather on *the existence and scope of a material EU competence*. To put the point another way: the rule would be that, provided that the EU had competence (whether exclusive or shared) in a particular area of law, EU fundamental rights should protect the citizen of the EU *even if such competence has not yet been exercised*.[117]

As I see it, such a rule would have a number of advantages. It avoids the need to create or promote fictitious or hypothetical 'links with Union law' and deals, once and for all, with the problem of reverse discrimination. It keeps the EU within the four corners of its powers. It might encourage Member States to move forward to legislate in areas of particular sensitivity that already fall within shared competence, rather than leaving fundamental rights problems to be solved by the Court

[114] See Case 36/75 *Rutili* [1975] ECR 1219, para 26; Case 222/84 *Johnston* [1986] ECR 1651, paras 17–19; Case 222/86 *Heylens and ors* [1987] ECR 4097, paras 14–15.

[115] For an elegant, clear and compelling analysis, see the excellent paper by S O'Leary entitled 'The Past, Present and Future of the Purely Internal Rule in EU Law' presented at the ICEL seminar 'Union Citizenship in Practice', Dublin, 3 November 2011. An updated version is to be published in M Dougan, N Nic Shuibhne and E Spaventa (eds), *Empowerment and Disempowerment of EU Citizens* (Oxford, Hart Publishing, forthcoming, 2012).

[116] See the final section of my Opinion in *Ruiz Zambrano*, dealing with fundamental rights (paras 151 ff), in particular paras 163–70.

[117] It is a pleasure to be able to acknowledge here the contribution which Daniel Sarmiento, the référendaire serving with AG Ruiz-Jarabo Colomer who worked with me on the Opinion in *Ruiz Zambrano* after the latter's untimely death, made to the development and refinement of this analysis.

on an *ad hoc* basis, as and when they are litigated. And it would also be coherent with the full implications of citizenship of the Union as the fundamental status of the nationals of Member States.

It is, I freely admit, a bold approach and one that involves introducing an overtly federal element into the structure of the EU's legal and political system. For some, that is an unacceptable crossing of the Rubicon.[118] It was an approach that was not appropriate to adopt in *Ruiz Zambrano* because of the timeline. The relevant date there was the birth of the first child to acquire Belgian nationality (Diego) on 1 September 2003. At that stage, several important developments in fundamental rights protection in EU law had not yet occurred.[119] It is however – as I have already ventured to suggest – a question that will probably require to be answered in the not too distant future.[120]

CONCLUSION

It is both understandable and sensible of the Court to tread warily. Citizenship with fundamental rights is a potent combination – perhaps more potent even than the tried and tested 'pincer' effect of combining rights of movement with the right not to be discriminated against. I do not venture to predict exactly how this case law will develop over the next few years. Pretending to possession of a crystal ball (even in a Festschrift) is always dangerous! However, it seems likely that, if the Court approaches the Charter so as to give real substance to the rights that it lists, the Charter will inevitably have a significant impact on the outcome of such cases.

To return to the title of this contribution: will this be 'opening Pandora's Box'? Personally, I do not think so (not least because, so far as I can see, the lid on the box is already well ajar!). Is it, rather, 'a natural step towards maturity'? Provided that the Court works out a sensible and consistent intellectual structure within which to afford the appropriate fundamental rights protection to citizens of the Union, I would answer that question with a fervent 'yes'.

[118] By leaving his province (Cisalpine Gaul) with his army and crossing the Rubicon on 11 January 49 BC without the Senate's authorisation, Caesar broke a fundamental law and thereby challenged the Senate for the governance of Rome. It was indeed the point of no return and the die was cast: 'alea jacta est'. See, eg Lucan, *Civil War (Pharsalia)*, 1.215 ff, (text in Latin and antique English translation available at www.archive.org/stream/lucancivilwarboo00lucauoft/lucancivilwarboo00lucauoft_djvu.txt).

[119] See my Opinion in *Ruiz Zambrano* n 39 above, para 175, for a more detailed analysis.

[120] ibid, my Opinion, para 177.

19

The European Arrest Warrant: The Impact of the Charter

FIDELMA MACKEN*

FOR MANY YEARS the extradition of persons from one Member State to any other Member State has been governed by three possible legal instruments: the European Convention on Extradition of 13 September 1957, the Convention Implementing the Schengen Agreement of 14 June 1985: and the Convention on the Simplified Extradition Procedure between the Member States of the Union of the 10 March 1995. However, the effects of the events of 11 September 2001 in New York and other parts of the United States, appear to have been the impetus for the Council decision to include a specific proposal for a Community wide arrest warrant in its 'European Action Plan to Combat Terrorism'. This eventually led to the Framework Decision creating the European Arrest Warrant (EAW), the subject of this Chapter. This new and quite radical system has, so far as Member States are concerned, replaced the earlier arrangements, mainly bilateral treaties or analogous arrangements negotiated between sovereign governments, such as the above conventions. This Chapter examines the origins of the new system, its main provisions and issues of fundamental rights, which are of especial interest to competent authorities in Member States.

ORIGINS OF THE EUROPEAN ARREST WARRANT

The origins of the Framework Decision had already been the subject of the Tampere Conclusions of the European Council held in October 1999 which evidenced the Council's policy on the issue of extradition. The Tampere Conclusions were followed by the Laeken Council meetings of December 2001, where a final agreement was reached. The Council announced that:

> European Union Member States' Judiciary will no longer have to go through the formal extradition procedure in order to forcibly transfer a person from one Member State to another before conducting a criminal prosecution . . . A high level of mutual trust and

* Judge of the Supreme Court of Ireland. Judge of the Court of Justice (1999–2004).

> co-operation between Member States who share the same highly demanding conception of the rule of law has made it possible to simplify and improve the surrendering procedure. In doing so, they are developing the European Union into a single European judicial area.

The EAW Framework Decision was finally adopted by the Council on 13 June 2002. It was the first specific measure implementing, on a Union wide basis, the principle of mutual recognition in the field of criminal law. Of significance is that the Framework Decision has introduced a common system of extradition, although this is now called 'surrender' between a very large number of States by means of the EAW. It is now the basis for the law of extradition in all the Member States.

Although inspired to some extent by the threat of terrorism, the EAW is not limited to such offences at all, but covers the entire gamut of offences existing in each Member State. As will be seen later, the EAW itself divides the offences into two groups; those which list all those offences accepted by Member States as representing the most serious criminal offences, in respect of which the EAW in its pro forma example sets them out in list form, and all other offences. The system provides for surrender either to face prosecution or to serve a sentence already imposed, or about to be.

This entirely new and common binding system of surrender of suspects now spans all 27 Member States. A Framework Decision, as opposed to a Directive, was the mechanism adopted in respect of this topic, perhaps stemming from the very disparate nature of extradition arrangements then existing between the many different legal systems, and from the fact that it includes extradition for criminal matters not in any way 'harmonised' until then. The Council adopted 'mutual recognition of judicial decisions' as the 'cornerstone of judicial co-operation', and the decision of a judicial body of one Member State, and its recognition by another Member State, the fundamental basis consists of the EAW.

In respect of criminal matters, which I am concerned with in this chapter, the Framework Decision proposed the possibility of 'fast track extradition procedures', while recognising 'the principle of fair trial'. This reference to a 'fair trial' must be to one occurring in the issuing Member State. For reasons which are mentioned later, it is silent, however, on procedural aspects of the system from the perspective of the executing Member State, and its impact on well recognised, substantive rights.

The need to establish a proper balance between the pursuit of criminals moving between Member States, and the obligation to respect established principles of fairness and justice is always at the centre of any discussion on the EAW, and has been the subject of numerous writings and reports. The enlargement of the Union and the inevitable but significant increase in the free movement of persons between Member States – even on a fairly temporary basis – has inevitably increased the number of those involved in crime also moving. This phenomenon could only be met by an appropriate political and legislative programme, such as that found in the Framework Decision, which is based on both political and legal solutions, although many of those adopted are more obviously political, because references in the Framework Decision to such essentially legal issues such as respect for fundamental rights or even for the principle of a fair trial are rather scant.

The EAW is firmly positioned within the third pillar. A cynical person considering the EAW might be driven to the view that when adopting such a legal mechanism Member States were anxious to restrict the influence of Community institutions, including even the ECJ. There are several unusual features worth drawing attention to: the reduced role of the European Parliament in the legislative process; the absence of any right for individuals to seek annulment of Union acts before the Union courts; and the absence of any power in the Commission to bring infringement actions against Member States. Unlike the position concerning the implementation of Directives, it has no remedy at its disposal, equivalent to Article 226 of the EC Treaty, to bring Member States before the ECJ for infringement of the Framework Decision. Finally, there is the absence of a binding provision conferring the power of interpretation on the ECJ. The Court has, nonetheless, followed a jurisprudential line which tends to the integration, so far as possible, of Title VI with the Community Treaty, correctly in my view. The Court has also, at least in more recent Opinions and Judgments, gone to some lengths to consider respect for fundamental rights in the implementation of the EAW.

The EAW has existed now for more than nine years. In the context of the growing influence of co-operation between Member States, its existence, its increasing use and the extent to which it is affected by the Charter merits particular consideration. Before examining this, it is useful to look at the figures. There has been a significant growth in the number of EAWs, both those issued, and those executed. According to the most recent report of the Commission,[1] the growth in the numbers of both issued and executed EAWs is remarkable. Not all Member States provided statistics in the first years after the implementation of the Framework Decision, but according to that report, the total numbers issued and executed in the Member States had each increased by 50 per cent from 2007. This is in line with the increases seen at Member State level in almost all cases, including in Ireland, the jurisdiction with which I am most familiar. Only Malta appears to linger at the very low end of the growth figures. These numbers are likely to increase further.

The EAW system operates on the doctrine of 'mutual recognition'. According to Scott Siegel at New York University:

> Mutual recognition in the area of criminal and justice affairs has led to a 'horizontal transfer of sovereignty' in that judicial decisions are enforceable in another country's territory (Lavenex 2007). This implies that the methods, procedures and decisions of other prosecutors, and courts are not only immediately enforceable in another member state, but it also requires one EU Member State to assume that all other members States protect and respect a citizen's right and legal privileges to the same degree as the surrendering State, albeit with different methods.[2]

[1] Report from the Commission to the European Parliament and the Council on the Implementation since 2007 of the Council Framework Decision of 13 June 2002 on the European arrest warrant and the surrender procedures between Member States, Com (2011) 175 final.

[2] S Siegel 'Courts and Compliance in the European Union: The European Arrest Warrant in National Constitutional Courts', New York University School of Law Jean Monnet working paper 5/08, www.jeanmonnetprogram.org/paper/08.080501.html, 16 August 2011.

Extradition, now called surrender, between Member States is now effected exclusively pursuant to the EAW process. This process is subjected to dual scrutiny, according to applicable procedures in both the issuing and the executing Member States. It is interesting to note that not all Member States require that an EAW, whether issued or executed, must be scrutinised by a Court, even though an EAW is defined in the Framework Decision as a 'judicial decision'. The Framework Decision, by Article 6, designates the issuing judicial authority, and the executing judicial authority, as being the respective authorities 'competent' to issue or execute an EAW. In some Member States, a competent issuing authority may include a police authority. In Ireland, it is always a court.

Already prior to the entry into force of the Lisbon Treaty, the ECJ had acknowledged that acts of institutions adopted in the field of justice and home affairs, falling within the Union's third pillar, were required to be compatible with the Treaties and with general principles of Union law. In *Advocaten voor de Wereld*,[3] the Court held it had jurisdiction to review the validity of the Framework Decision. It did so in light of the principles of the legality of criminal offences and penalties, and the principle of equality and non-discrimination. The Court made its first express reference to the then non-binding Charter, observing that these principles were reaffirmed in Articles 49, 20 and 21 of the Treaty, although even prior to that time, both the General Court (as the then Court of First Instance) in its judgments, as well as several Advocates General of the ECJ had already invoked the Charter's then provisions in their opinions. While it is natural that the EAW should be assessed according to its legality and effectiveness, I propose to concentrate on the sometimes difficult interface between its effectiveness and the principle of respect for fundamental rights, in particular for an executing judicial authority, having regard to the Charter. Following the entry into force of the Lisbon Treaty on 1 December 2009, the Charter[4] has the same value as the Treaties. Since that date the ECJ has, at the time of writing, delivered two judgments on the Framework Decision, and two further cases are pending. I deal with these later in this chapter.

At this stage, however, I want to return to the Dutch case, decided before the entry into force of the Lisbon Treaty, and prior to when the Charter became binding, and consider how issues of fundamental rights were then dealt with in the ECJ. Advocate General Ruiz-Jarabo, in his Opinion in the case of *Advocaten voor de Wereld,* looked at the issue of extradition, and he distinguished what he called 'traditional' extradition, the nature of which he considered to be the 'exercise of an uncontrolled sovereign power' from the surrender provisions found in the Framework Decision. While his opinion contains a very interesting exposé of a particular and perhaps peculiar view of extradition, it has to be said that it did not examine the nature of extradition as gleaned from any of the several treaties mentioned at the commencement of this chapter, which he did not appear to consider of any particular relevance. But his exposé is also interesting because it does not

[3] Case C-303/05 *Advocaten voor de Wereld* [2007] ECR I-3633.

[4] Charter of Fundamental Rights of the European Union, [2010] OJ C 83/389.

necessarily concur with the nature of extradition in many Member States. In the system with which I am most familiar, namely Ireland, where extradition (especially between Ireland and the United Kingdom) has been the subject of a very significant number of cases – in particular those invoking constitutional rights – the nature of extradition has been considered on several occasions by the Supreme Court including, almost 30 years ago, in the following terms:

> Extradition is the formal surrender, based upon reciprocating arrangements, by one nation to another of an individual accused or convicted of an offence who is within the jurisdiction of the requested country when the requesting country being competent to try and punish him, demands his surrender. The formal arrangements by which this may be secured and the principle of reciprocity enshrined, are either by way of treaties or by reciprocal legislation. But, whichever system exists, in every case in which the matter comes into the courts of the requested State, they must inquire whether the stipulations of the treaty or the requirements of the legislation, as the case may be, have been fulfilled.[5]

Following the adoption of the Framework Decision, the surrender of a person can no longer be equated with his rendition pursuant to the exercise of an uncontrolled sovereign power. Instead, there is the application of objective, ascertainable and predictable legal norms or rules, within a judicial process. The 8th recital in the preamble to the Framework Decision recognises this:

> Decisions on the execution of the European arrest warrant must be subject to sufficient controls, which means that a judicial authority of the Member State where the requested person has been arrested will have to take the decision on his or her surrender.

RESPECT FOR FUNDAMENTAL RIGHTS

How does a national court or judicial authority, charged with implementing the Framework Decision, approach the obligation to surrender a requested person, having regard at the same time to the provisions of the Charter? The Charter states, at Article 19(2):

> No one may be . . . extradited to a State where there is a serious risk that he or she would be subjected to . . . torture or other inhuman or degrading treatment or punishment.

Article 47 reads as follows:

> Everyone whose rights and freedoms guaranteed by the law of the Union are violated has the right to an effective remedy before a tribunal in compliance with the conditions laid down in this Article.
>
> Everyone is entitled to a fair and public hearing within a reasonable time by an independent and impartial tribunal previously established by law. Everyone shall have the possibility of being advised, defended and represented.

[5] *Wyatt v McLaughlin* [1974] IR 378.

> Legal aid shall be made available to those who lack sufficient resources in so far as such aid is necessary to ensure effective access to justice.

Article 48 provides:

1. Everyone who has been charged shall be presumed innocent until proved guilty according to law.
2. Respect for the rights of the defence of anyone who has been charged shall be guaranteed.

The term 'respect for fundamental rights' is intended by me to cover all aspects of fairness, procedural and substantive, including those requirements flowing from the ECHR[6] ('the Convention') to which all Member States are signatories, as well as the Charter. Having regard to the content of these, the substantive terms of the Framework Decision are open to some valid criticism.

Article 1.3 of the Framework Decision declares that:

> This Framework Decision shall not have the effect of modifying the obligation to respect fundamental rights and fundamental legal principles as enshrined in Article 6 of the Treaty on European Union.

This article is expressed in the negative, notwithstanding the provisions of the Preamble, perhaps because of the then status of the inchoate earlier Charter document. On the other hand, recitals 12 to 14 of the preamble of the Framework Decision are couched in positive terms:

> (12) This Framework Decision respects fundamental rights and observes the principles recognised by Article 6 of the Treaty on European Union and reflected in the Charter of Fundamental Rights of the European Union, in particular Chapter VI thereof. Nothing in this Framework Decision may be interpreted as prohibiting refusal to surrender a person for whom a European arrest warrant has been issued when there are reasons to believe, on the basis of objective elements, that the said arrest warrant has been issued for the purpose of prosecuting or punishing a person on the grounds of his or her sex, race, religion, ethnic origin, nationality, language, political opinions or sexual orientation, or that that person's position may be prejudiced for any of these reasons.
>
> This Framework Decision does not prevent a Member State from applying its constitutional rules relating to due process, freedom of association, freedom of the press and freedom of expression in other media.
>
> (13) No person should be removed, expelled or extradited to a State where there is a serious risk that he or she would be subjected to the death penalty, torture or other inhuman or degrading treatment or punishment.
>
> (14) Since all Member States have ratified the Council of Europe Convention of 28 January 1981 for the protection of individuals with regard to automatic processing of personal data, the personal data processed in the context of the implementation of this Framework Decision should be protected in accordance with the principles of the said Convention.

[6] Signed 4 November 1950.

How are these recitals and the provision of the Charter to be applied to the EAW arrest and surrender procedures within the Member States? These provide for the following: (a) issue of an arrest warrant (Article 1.1(b)); (b) contents are to be as in Article 8 (and as close as possible to the pro forma Warrant annexed to the Framework Decision itself); (c) transmission of the arrest warrant (Articles 9 and 10); (d) arrest of requested person (Article 11); (e) hearing by the executing judicial authority, in accordance with the law of the executing Member State (Article 14); (f) decision on surrender (Article 15). The requested person is entitled to be provided with legal assistance and an interpreter. He/she may be detained, or released provisionally. He/she may raise at a 'judicial proceeding' any grounds against the validity of the procedure or any non-compliance with the requirements of the EAW. By Articles 3 and 4, both mandatory and optional grounds for non-execution of a warrant, such as an amnesty, statute of limitations or decisions not to prosecute, are provided for. None of the articles, however, expressly permits an executing judicial authority to refuse surrender on the basis that to do so may lead to a failure to respect fundamental human rights in the issuing Member State. How then is Article 1.3 of the Framework Decision to be interpreted and applied?

Recitals 12, 13 and 14 of the Framework Decision appear to permit an executing authority to refuse surrender in a number of situations. First, they permit general reference to, and application of, the provisions of the Convention (indirectly through the application of Article 6 TEU) and the Charter, in spite of its then, perhaps uncertain, legal status. Secondly, recital 12 envisages refusal on the ground of a wide range of possible types of discrimination by the issuing Member State. Thirdly, and perhaps most unusually, recital 12 permits a Member State to apply its constitutional rules relating [inter alia] to 'due process'. Recital 13 expressly mandates refusal where there is a 'serious risk' of 'inhuman or degrading treatment or punishment', but it is unclear what these phrases are intended to include. Does this mean that although nowhere specified in any Article of the Framework Decision, a person can be protected against surrender in cases where it is established, objectively, that the prison conditions he will face are degrading? If so, is it sufficient for an executing judicial authority to accept findings of the European Court of Human Rights which condemn a Member State in respect of those conditions?

These recitals, and in particular their effects, if any, are obscure. First, does the preamble have any effect at all in the absence of substantive provisions to the same effect, of which there are none? Secondly, do they permit a court to refuse to surrender a person by reason of conditions or deficiencies existing in the issuing State? If so, does this relate to all features concerning a fair trial, or even conditions of incarceration, which do not comply with the views of the executing judicial authority's requirements of fairness, as mandated by the law of the executing Member State, or by reference to the Convention? Is recital 12 limited to the procedures to be followed by the judicial authority in the execution process towards surrender? How should an executing court treat the other factors mentioned such as 'freedom of association, freedom of the press and freedom of expression'? Does this permit a court to refuse surrender, if the offence invoked by the issuing Member State would infringe any of these specified freedoms? If it does so permit, then according to which law is the freedom to be assessed and determined?

The problem of resolving the tensions which arise in the interface between the Framework Decision and the provisions of the Charter and/or the Convention, are also compounded by the variety of methods of implementation of the Framework Decision in Member States. I take, for example, the legislation with which I am most familiar. This is not necessarily so in all Member States, and it is not necessarily undesirable that there should be a considerable degree of variation. The Framework Decision must be able to accommodate the diverse legal traditions of all Member States. Irish legislation expressly prohibits surrender on a wide range of human-rights related grounds. To cite one example, it prohibits surrender of the person if 'his or her surrender would constitute a contravention of any provision of the Constitution . . .'. The right to a fair trial under the Irish Constitution includes the right, by oneself or one's counsel, to cross-examine accusers. It is easy to imagine an argument being advanced, and such arguments have been advanced, that a trial in the issuing Member State would not meet these requirements. Of course, such a trial might not meet the requirements of Article 6 of the Convention either, since this too enshrines, as part of fair trial procedures, the right to challenge an accuser. But does the fact that the recital to the Framework Decision recognises that all Member States are signatories to the Convention have as its consequence that an executing judicial authority of a Member State must assume compliance by the issuing State with the guarantee in Article 6 to a fair trial, including within a reasonable period of time? If not, the problem of interpretation and application arises.

According to the decision of the ECJ in *Pupino*,[7] national courts are bound to interpret rules of national law 'so far as possible, in the light of the wording and purpose of the Framework Decision'. This case is followed, and its principles applied as standard practice, by all relevant courts in my jurisdiction. However, this broad statement does not necessarily resolve all the difficulties. The ECJ had occasion to consider the Framework Decision in the recent past. To date the ECJ has delivered seven judgments on the EAW.[8] From a search of the Court's website there are (as of mid August 2011) three cases on the EAW pending before the Court.[9] Not all Member States have made the declaration (necessary under Article 35.2 TEU) to confer preliminary-ruling jurisdiction on the ECJ. A person, even one 'personally and individually' affected by an EAW issued pursuant to the Framework Decision, would have no legal right to mount a similar challenge to the validity of the latter. Nonetheless, in *Advocaten voor de Wereld* a reference for a preliminary ruling was made and admitted.

[7] Case C-105/03 *Pupino* [2005] ECR I-5285.

[8] *Advocaten voor de Wereld*, n 4 above; Case C-66/08 *Kozłowski* [2008] ECR I-6041; Case C-296/08 PPU *Santesteban Goicoechea* [2008] ECR I-6307; Case C-338/08 PPU *Leymann and Pustovarov* [2008] ECR I-8993; Case C-123/08 *Wolzenburg* [2009] ECR I-9621; Case C-306/09 *IB*, judgment of 21 October 2010 nyr; Case C-261/09 *Mantello*, judgment of 16 November 2010 nyr.

[9] Case C-42/11 *Lopes da Silva Jorge*; Case C-396/11 *Radu*; Case C-399/11 *Melloni*.

The decision of the ECJ in that case is of importance. It was decided at the time of the 'old' Charter. The Court was considering the Framework Decision in its context as a measure adopted pursuant to Title VI of the TEU which confers legitimacy and recognition on the EAW. While it acknowledged that the questions referred 'revealed no factor capable of affecting the validity of' the Framework Decision, nevertheless the Court expressed significant views as to its legality.

Advocaten voor de Wereld, a non-profit making association, brought an action seeking the annulment of the Belgian implementing law. The Arbitragehof of Belgium referred two questions. The first concerned the competence to adopt the Framework Decision, the second related to its contents. The questions were:

> (1) Is Framework Decision 2002/584 . . . compatible with Article 34(2)(b) EU, under which framework decisions may be adopted only for the purpose of approximation of the laws and regulations of the Member States?
>
> (2) Is Article 2(2) of Framework Decision 2002/584 . . . in so far as it sets aside verification of the requirement of double criminality for the offences listed therein, compatible with Article 6(2) EU and, more specifically, with the principle of legality in criminal proceedings guaranteed by that provisions and with the principle of equality and non-discrimination?

I consider the case from the point of view of comments made by the Court about the effect of the Framework Decision, and the question of fundamental rights. The ECJ stated that the use of the principle of mutual recognition

> requires the approximation of the laws and regulations of the Member States with regard to judicial cooperation in criminal matters and more specifically, of *the rules relating to the conditions, procedures and effects of surrender as between national authorities.*[10] (emphasis added)

This statement seems to me to be broader than the Advocate General's opinion, which was to the effect that only the 'arrest procedures' were to be harmonised by the Framework Decision.

As to the principles of legality in criminal matters and of equality and non-discrimination, the ECJ stated that both principles are among those protected by the general principles of law of the European Union:

> It must be noted at the outset that, by virtue of Article 6 EU, the Union is founded on the principle of the rule of law and it respects fundamental rights, as guaranteed by the European Convention for the Protection of Human Rights and Fundamental Freedoms, signed in Rome on 4 November 1950, and as they result from the constitutional provisions common to the Member States, as general principles of Community law.[11]

The Court went on to accept that these principles were 'reaffirmed respectively in Articles 49, 20 and 21 of the Charter of Fundamental Rights of the European

[10] *Advocaten voor de Wereld*, n 4 above, para 29.

[11] ibid, para 45.

Union, proclaimed in Nice on 7 December 2000'. This was the first clear statement by the ECJ on the status of the then Charter. In his opinion, the Advocate General had called on the Court to 'break its silence and recognise the authority of the Charter as an interpretative tool at the forefront of the protection of fundamental rights which are part of the heritage of the Member States'. The Court also restated that the issuing Member State 'as is . . . stated in Article 1(3) of the Framework Decision, must respect fundamental rights and fundamental legal principles as enshrined in Article 6 EU, and, consequently, the principle of the legality of criminal offences and penalties'.

From the point of view of a national judge, the meaning of this last statement is not entirely clear. Since it refers specifically to the Framework Decision, it appears to envisage that the obligation to respect fundamental rights arises at the time of the issuing of the warrant, rather than at the time of surrender. This may be because the Court was considering the principle of legality in the context of the issuing Member State and the offences listed at Article 2(2), or was referring to the position of the issuing Member State, post surrender. What is clear, however, is that the Court did not refer to the role of the judicial authority of the executing Member State. This is rather regrettable, since it is here that most of the issues of fundamental rights arise. Once a person has been surrendered, he becomes available for prosecution and trial in the issuing Member State, and the Framework Decision has no further relevance, save in very limited circumstances. The Court did not have to, and did not, in fact, consider, in *Advocaten voor de Wereld*, the effect, if any, of recitals 12 to 14.

The Court did, however, restate that 'comparable situations must not be treated differently and that different situations must not be treated in the same way unless such treatment is objectively justified', pursuant to the principle of equality and non-discrimination. The argument advanced was that this principle was infringed to the extent that 'double criminality' was dispensed with for the offences listed in Article 2(2) but not for all other offences. In respect of the latter, surrender may be made subject to verification that the offence in question is also an offence in the executing Member State. The Court observed, correctly, in my view:

> [. . .] the Council was able to form the view, on the basis of the principle of mutual recognition and in the light of the high degree of trust and solidarity between the Member States, that, whether by reason of their inherent nature or by reason of the punishment incurred of a maximum of at least three years, the categories of offences in question feature among those the seriousness of which in terms of adversely affecting public order and public safety justifies dispensing with the verification of double criminality.

Even on the assumption, therefore, that the situation of a person sought for an offence listed in Article 2(2) was comparable with that of a person sought for an offence not on that list, the distinction was objectively justified.

Express references to the Charter as an interpretative tool have been extremely limited in the case law of the ECJ, whether on the EAW or on other issues. Of the seven judgments on the EAW listed above, at the time of writing, only two have been delivered since that date: *IB*[12] and *Mantello*.[13]

In *IB*,[14] the referring court made a reference precisely on the interpretation of the EAW in light of the fundamental rights obligations in the Union legal order. The Court was asked to consider whether the execution of an EAW issued for the purposes of serving a sentence rendered *in absentia* could be made subject to the condition that the individual, a national or resident of the executing Member State, be returned to serve the sentence in that latter State. The Advocate General made express reference to the new legal context governing the interpretation of the Framework Decision, in the light of fundamental rights having become more imperative since the entry into force of the Charter. In its judgment, the Court followed the recommendation of the Advocate General. The question posed was, however, resolved without any express consideration of the Charter.

IB was a Romanian national sentenced in 2001 to four years' imprisonment for 'trafficking nuclear and radioactive materials'. The sentence was curiously (and not explained in the judgment) to be served 'at his workplace'. This may be a reference to a suspended sentence subject to a condition. It would have been helpful to know if there was a condition, because he left Romania – in unclear circumstances – and moved to Belgium. If the suspension was subject to a condition which had been breached, this might be a factor to be taken into account by an executing Member State. The Supreme Court of Romania, on appeal, ordered a custodial sentence. That decision was rendered *in absentia*, (presumably because of *IB*'s absence in Belgium), and he was not notified of the date or place of the hearing. *IB* argued that the judicial decisions were rendered in serious breach of procedural guarantees.

The referring court asked, essentially, whether, in circumstances where a warrant is issued for the purposes of execution of a sentence imposed *in absentia*, and guarantees under Article 5(1) of the Framework Decision were required, it was precluded from attaching a further condition whereby execution of the EAW would be subject to the sentence being served in the executing Member State. If national courts are so precluded, the referring court also asked whether Articles 4(6) and 5(3) of the Framework Decision were compatible with Article 6(2) TEU and the principles of equality and non-discrimination.

In his Opinion, Advocate General Cruz Villalón stated that:

> the protection of fundamental rights and freedoms is a precondition which gives legitimacy to the existence and development of [the area of security, freedom and justice]. The Framework Decision repeatedly states as much in Recitals 10, 12, 13 and 14, and in Article 1(3). Consequently, although Article 5(1) contains a guarantee which is recognised by the European Court of Human Rights regarding decisions rendered in absentia, it must to be emphasised too that Articles 4(6) and 5(3) also reflect a requirement

[12] *IB*, n 8 above.
[13] *Mantello*, n 8 above.
[14] *IB*, n 8 above.

> contemplated by the European Convention on Human Rights and by the case-law of the associated Court. (para 43)

The Advocate General further considered that:

> the need to interpret the Framework Decision in the light of fundamental rights has become more imperative since the entry into force of the Charter of Fundamental Rights, Article 7 of which covers the right to private and family life. Until now the case-law of the ECJ on this issue has related very specifically to the free movement of persons but has not involved itself directly in the relationship between this right and judicial cooperation in criminal matters. The fact that the *Kozlowski* and *Wolzenburg* judgments preceded the entry into force of the Charter is linked logically to that result. *Nevertheless, from 1 December 2009, it is imperative that Articles 4(6) and 5(3) of the Framework Decision should be interpreted in the light of Article 7 of the Charter.* This being the case, the narrow interpretation put forward in points 38 to 40 of this Opinion cannot prevail. (para 44, emphasis added)

Paragraphs 38 to 40 considered the issue of mutual recognition, and the apparent guidance of the ECJ that optional grounds of surrender under the Framework Decision must be interpreted narrowly.

The Court (Grand Chamber), in its judgment, observed that while the system established by the Framework Decision is based on the principle of mutual recognition, that recognition does not, as is clear from Articles 3 to 5, mean that there is an absolute obligation to execute the warrant. The Court also held that Articles 4(6) and 5(3) make it possible for the Member States to allow the competent judicial authorities, in specific situations, to decide that a sentence must be served on the territory of the executing Member State, and there was nothing to indicate that the Union legislator had sought to exclude persons from this possibility on the basis that they been sentenced *in absentia*.

In the second case, *Mantello*, the Court was required to interpret the principle of *ne bis in idem* (the rule against double jeopardy) as set out in Article 3(2) of the Framework Decision. In his Opinion, Advocate General Bot recalled that this principle constitutes a fundamental right enshrined in several international instruments, and in particular, Article 50 of the Charter. Although the EAW system relies on a high degree of mutual trust, the fact remains that the surrender of an individual stems from a decision by a judicial authority, and must be taken in a manner consistent with fundamental rights. The Court concluded that the German executing judicial authority had no reason to apply the ground for mandatory non-execution provided for in Article 3(2) of the Framework Decision in respect of the 'same acts'.

Mr Mantello was an Italian national residing in Germany, accused of various criminal offences relating to dealing and trafficking in drugs between 2004 and 2005. The charges related to undertaking such activities as part of a criminal organisation with at least 10 other persons, an offence punishable by imprisonment for a minimum of 20 years. In November 2008, the Italian Court issued an EAW on the basis of a domestic warrant issued there in September 2008. He opposed his surrender.

Article 3(2) of the Framework Decision provides that the judicial authority of the executing Member State shall refuse to execute the EAW if it is informed that the requested person has been finally judged by a Member State in respect of 'the same acts' provided that, where there has been a sentence, that sentence has been served or is currently being served, or may no longer be executed under the law of the sentencing Member State.

In the course of the national procedure, a question arose as to whether the principle of *ne bis in idem* precluded execution of the EAW. Mr Mantello had previously been arrested and tried in Italy in 2005 for possession of drugs for onward sale (a more minor offence to that forming the offence on the EAW which concerned drug trafficking in the context of a criminal organisation). He had been sentenced and had served a short term of imprisonment. At the time of his arrest in 2005, the investigators had sufficient evidence to charge and prosecute him in connection with the more serious charges set out in the EAW, but did not disclose this to the investigating judge, in order to preserve ongoing investigations which sought to dismantle trafficking networks, and arrest others involved.

As a matter of German law, an offence relating to participation in a criminal organisation may be the subject of a separate and subsequent prosecution. The referring German court considered, however, that a separate prosecution could only be permitted if at the time of the judicial decision in 2005, the investigators were unaware of the facts constituting the more serious offences relating to participation in a criminal organisation. This was manifestly not the case. It made a reference seeking to ascertain whether the term 'same acts' in Article 3(2) is to be determined on the basis of the law of the issuing Member State, the executing Member State, or on an autonomous interpretation. The referring court also asked whether the unlawful importation of narcotics constituted the 'same acts', in the circumstances set out above.

In his Opinion delivered on 7 September 2010, Advocate General Bot considered the extent to which EU fundamental rights norms apply to judicial authorities considering an EAW, recalling that the *ne bis in idem* principle constitutes a fundamental right recognised by the legal systems of all the Member States, and enshrined in the Charter. He also observed that the principle is enshrined in Article 50 of the Charter as a bar to being sentenced twice, either by the courts of the same Member State or of different Member States, provided that the situation is covered by European Union law. Article 50 of the Charter states:

> No one shall be liable to be tried or punished again in criminal proceedings for an offence for which he or she has already been finally acquitted or convicted within the Union in accordance with the law.

Advocate General Bot further stated that:

> It is settled case-law that the Member States, when implementing EU law, must do so in a manner consistent with fundamental rights. That case-law is not limited to measures adopted in the context of the EC Treaty. It applies to all the measures taken in the context of the European Union, since, by virtue of Article 6 EU, the Union is founded on

> the principle of the rule of law and it respects fundamental rights, as guaranteed by the European Convention for the Protection of Human Rights and Fundamental Freedoms, signed in Rome on 4 November 1950, and as they result from the constitutional traditions common to the Member States.
>
> Consequently, in the same way as the lawfulness of a measure adopted under the Third Pillar, such as the Framework Decision, may be reviewed in the light of fundamental rights, the action of the Member States, when they implement such a measure, must be consistent with those same rights. The executing judicial authority is therefore bound by that obligation where it is responsible for executing a European arrest warrant, as is expressly stated in Article 1(3) of the Framework Decision.

The Advocate General considered that:

> although the system of the European Arrest Warrant does indeed rely on a high degree of mutual trust, the fact remains that the surrender of the person referred to in such a warrant stems from a decision by the judicial authority of the executing Member State, which must be taken in a manner consistent with fundamental rights.

The Court's case law on the Convention Implementing the Schengen *acquis*, and in particular on the rule against double jeopardy, based on the *ne bis in idem* principle, are considered by the Court as relevant, and have been applied to cases concerning the Framework Decision, since it also incorporates the same rule. For the sake of completeness, there have been eight such decisions by the ECJ on the Convention Implementing Schengen,[15] all concerning this principle.

In its judgment, the Court held that the concept of 'same acts' in Article 3(2) of the Framework Decision is an autonomous concept of Union law, which could not be left to the discretion of the judicial authorities of each Member State on the basis of their national law. The Court further held that the concept of 'same acts' is the same as that concept forming part of the Convention Implementing the Schengen Agreement ('CISA'), relying, by analogy, on its judgment in *Kozlowski*[16]. I am not convinced that this bald statement by the Court in its judgment is sufficiently sophisticated to merit a finding that the concept of 'same acts' is an autonomous concept of Union law, in light of the basis upon which the Framework Decision is founded. There, a two tier system operates under which a clear distinction is drawn between those offences which all contracting parties accept will, on the basis of mutual respect and regardless of what facts constitute those offences, oblige the executing State to surrender a person sought, provided of course, all other conditions are met. They are specifically found listed in the Annex to the Framework Decision itself. How then can an autonomous definition of 'same acts' operate in such circumstances? Or is the Court merely stating that, when deciding what constitute such same acts, certain criteria must be adopted. If

[15] Joined Cases C-187/01 and C-385/01 *Gözütok and Brügge* [2003] ECR I-1345; Case C-469/03 *Miraglia* [2005] ECR I-2009; Case C 436/04 *Van Esbroeck* [2006] ECR I 2333; Case C 467/04 *Gasparini* [2006] ECR I-9199; Case C-150/05 *Van Straaten* [2006] ECR I-9327; Case C-288/05 *Kretzinger* [2007] ECR I-06441; Case C-367/05 *Kraaijenbrink* [2007] ECR I-6619; Case C-491/07 *Turanský* [2008] ECR I-11039.

[16] *Kozlowski*, n 8 above.

the latter, this does not appear to be clear from the Court's judgment. Nor is there any analysis as to why the matter should be determined by reference to the terms of the Schengen Agreement, although clearly this agreement might properly inform the Court's approach, provided that the unusual terms of the Framework Decision are taken into account. The Court appears to have considered, implicitly, that the acts here were different, since the earlier 'acts' related to the possession and onward supply of cocaine, while the acts forming part of the EAW concerned participation in a criminal organisation, and that those acts had not been 'finally judged'. Whether or not the acts had been finally judged does not, however, assist a national court in determing whether the acts are the 'same acts' and by reference to which law. It will be important to see how the Court interprets the Framework Decision on this issue in future cases. Of course, it is also the case that the matter may be determined or clarified, ultimately, in any new Regulation governing the surrender of suspects or convicted persons in the future.

In *Wolzenburg*,[17] in a somewhat similar case to *IB*, but raising issues of non-discrimination, the ECJ was asked to interpret the scope of Article 4(6) of the Framework Decision. Article 4(6) provides that:

> The executing judicial authority may refuse to execute the European arrest warrant [. . .] if the European arrest warrant has been issued for the purposes of execution of a custodial sentence or detention order, where the requested person is staying in, or is a national or a resident of the executing Member State and that State undertakes to execute the sentence or detention order in accordance with its domestic law.

Mr Wolzenburg was wanted by the German authorities to serve a sentence imposed on him for importation of marijuana into Germany. The sentences had been suspended, but were reactivated following a breach of the terms attaching to their suspension. He was by then residing in the Netherlands and opposed his surrender. According to Dutch law, the competent judicial authorities are required to exercise Article 4(6), and must refuse to execute an EAW in respect of a Dutch national. The same prohibition only applies to residents if, among other requirements, they are in possession of a residence permit of indefinite duration (obtained by being lawfully resident for a continuous period of five years immediately prior to application).

The national court made a reference asking whether this differentiation in treatment between nationals and residents, and in particular the requirement for the possession of a residence permit of indefinite duration, is compatible with the principle of non-discrimination enshrined in Article 12 EC (now Article 18 TFEU).

In his Opinion, Advocate General Bot considered that a Member State cannot, in the context of implementing a framework decision, undermine the principle of non-discrimination as a fundamental principle enshrined, inter alia, in Article 14 of the Convention. The Court agreed. The Member State could not therefore impose such a condition on residents where it is not imposed on nationals. Although the Court adopted the recommendation of the Advocate General, it

[17] *Wolzenburg*, n 8 above.

nevertheless emphasised the limitations inherent in the executing Member States' powers to expand the limits imposed in respect of non-surrender under Article 4, pointing out in paragraphs 57–62 the importance attaching to the mandatory non-return provisions (Article 3), the limits permitted to be placed on the optional non-return choices, and on the extent to which other objectives may impact on those limitations.

It will be seen therefore that the Court emphasised the essential basis for the existence of Article 4 of the Framework Decision, and only in limited circumstances permits this to be overridden by other objectives, such as those set out above. It is essential to recognise, therefore, the Court's approach to the structure of the system and the importance it attaches to retaining the effectiveness of the EAW system.

FUTURE DEVELOPMENTS

It seems clear that the EAW is going to continue to provide ammunition for references to the ECJ. In its report,[18] the Commission emphasises the numbers of submissions it received from lawyers, NGOs, defendants, human rights organisations, and others, concerning the need to protect and strengthen the procedural rights of suspects and of accused persons in criminal proceedings. In particular the Commission has considered that, although the law and criminal procedures of all Member States are subject to the standards of the Convention, there are often doubts about standards being similar across the EU. The right to complain to the ECtHR has not, it concluded, resulted in an effective means of ensuring that signatories comply with the Convention's standards.

Some courts, including the Supreme Court of Ireland, have recently had to consider the test to be applied where a party invokes the provisions of Article 3(2) of the Charter,[19] on the basis that the issuing Member State had already been the subject of condemnation by the ECtHR, in particular in relation to the conditions of the sometimes lengthy incarceration prior to the trial, and relying also on international human rights evidence in the form of published material. I imagine this is the type of question which may be referred to the ECJ in the future. So too, the precise effect and ambit of the contents of the recitals, especially when there are no corresponding substantive rights declared by any of the articles of the Framework Decision. I also see questions arising in relation to the issue of 'same acts' where these relate to offences the subject of Article 2.2 of the Framework Decision, as opposed to other offences. Many of the likely issues are the subject of the Commission's Roadmap, mentioned in the Commission's Report on the Framework Decision and the European Arrest Warrant. It is certain that the ECJ

[18] Report from the Commission to the European Parliament and the Council on the Implementation since 2007 of the Council Framework Decision of 13 June 2002 on the European arrest warrant and the surrender procedures between Member States, n 2 above.

[19] *MJELR v Rettinger* [2010] IESC 45.

will be busy with such matters, in a burgeoning area of criminal law, for which it has not, in the past, been called upon to consider to any great extent, and in respect of which it has not, in the past, sought expertise in its judges. Future appointments to the Court may well have to be considered in the light of the growing ambit of its criminal law jurisdiction, especially after the transitional period expires in 2014.

20

The Scope of Application of the Charter of Fundamental Rights of the European Union in the Member States

HEIDI KAILA*

INTRODUCTION

PROTECTION OF FUNDAMENTAL rights is a founding principle of the European Union (EU). The obligation to respect fundamental rights, as guaranteed by the European Convention for the Protection of Human Rights and Fundamental Freedoms (ECHR) and as they result from the constitutional traditions common to the Member States, has been confirmed by the Court of Justice of the European Union (ECJ) in its case law as well as by the successive Treaties,[1] most recently by Article 6 TEU.[2] The Charter of Fundamental Rights of the European Union (Charter) enshrines this common heritage by reaffirming and codifying in a single text the civil, political, economic and social rights of European citizens and persons residing legally within the EU.[3] It makes the overriding importance and relevance of those rights more visible to everyone.[4]

Proclaimed in Nice on 7 December 2000[5] by the European Parliament, the Council and the Commission, the Charter, though not binding per se, had a high political value. It sought to strengthen the democratic legitimacy of the EU before the deepening of EU integration and the new wave of accessions.[6] In political terms it was also imperative for the EU, highlighting the importance of human

* Legal Secretary (référendaire), Court of Justice of the European Union. The views expressed in this contribution are personal to the author. I am indebted to S O' Leary and D Sarmiento Ramirez-Escudero for their valuable suggestions and comments on a previous draft.

[1] The principles established by that case law were for the first time reaffirmed in the preamble to the Single European Act 1986, [1987] OJ L169.

[2] Art F(2) TEU. See now Art 6(3) TEU.

[3] K Lenaerts and E De Smijter, 'A Bill of Rights for the European Union' (2001) 38 *CML Rev* 273, 290.

[4] See Presidency Conclusions, Cologne European Council, 3 and 4 June 1999, Annex IV, doc SN 150/99 and the preamble of the Charter.

[5] [2000] OJ C 364.

[6] O Le Bot, 'Charte de l'Union européenne et Convention de sauvegarde des droits de l'homme: la coexistence de deux catalogues de droits fondamentaux' (2003) 14 *Revue trimestrielle des droits de l'homme* 785, 781.

rights in its external relations, to consolidate its own commitments in this respect.[7] The effects the Charter could produce as a political declaration were however incomplete.[8] On 1 December 2009, with the entry into force of the Treaty of Lisbon, the Charter[9] became legally binding. Its new status was welcomed as it enhanced judicial protection and increased legal certainty.[10] Thanks to the reform, individuals could invoke fundamental rights more easily and authorities could apply those rights in a more coherent and efficient manner. The adoption of a legally binding Bill of rights was also an important step in EU constitution-building[11] and in the creation of an ever closer Union among the peoples of Europe. Such a catalogue affirmed the autonomous nature of the EU legal order[12] and established a direct legal relation between the citizens and those exercising power on their behalf and upon them.[13] There was also a link between the conferral of a mandatory character to the Charter and the proposal of reaffirming the principle of primacy of EU law in the Treaties.[14]

The Charter applies primarily to the EU institutions. Despite the broad range of competences they had been entrusted with, including within the area of freedom, security and justice, until December 2000 they were not bound by any written catalogue of fundamental rights. However, in line with the ECJ's case law they had to observe fundamental rights as general principles of EU law. Without going into details, it should be recalled that the ECJ recognised in 1969, in *Stauder*,[15] notably in order to defend the primacy of European Economic Community (EEC) law over national law, that fundamental rights are enshrined in the general principles of law guaranteed under EEC law and protected by the Court.[16]

[7] See A Cassese, C Lalumière, P Leuprecht and M Robinson, 'Montrer l'exemple: Un programme d'action sur les droits de l'homme pour l'Union européenne de l'an 2000' in P Alston, M Bustelo and J Heenan (eds), *L'Union européenne et les droits de l'homme* (Bruylant, Brussels, 2001) 957.

[8] See C Ladenburger, 'L'application pratique de la Charte par la Commission européenne (2002) 14 *Revue européenne de droit public* 817, 818.

[9] [2007] OJ C 303; [2010] OJ C 83.

[10] LS Rossi, 'Les rapports entre la Charte des droits fondamentaux et le traité de Lisbonne' in *Chemins d'Europe: mélanges en l'honneur de Jean-Paul Jacqué* (Paris, Dalloz, 2010) 609, 620.

[11] See, eg point V of the Resolution of the European Parliament on the Drafting of a European Union Charter of Fundamental Rights (C5-0058/1999–1999/2064(COS)) of 16 March 2000 which reads as follows: 'Whereas the Charter of Fundamental Rights should be regarded as a basic component of the necessary process of equipping the European Union with a constitution'. See also Lenaerts and De Smijter, n 3 above, 274.

[12] G Di Federico, 'Preface' in G Di Federico (ed), *The EU Charter of Fundamental Rights: From Declaration to Binding Instrument* (Wien New York, Springer, 2011) v, vi.

[13] I Pernice, 'The Treaty of Lisbon and Fundamental Rights' in S Griller and J Ziller (eds), *The Lisbon Treaty. EU Constitution Without a Constitutional Treaty* (Wien New York, Springer, 2008) 235, 252.

[14] This idea was abandoned but Declaration No 17 concerning primacy was annexed to the Final Act of the Intergovernmental Conference which adopted the Treaty of Lisbon. See Pernice, n 13 above, 239; T Von Danwitz, 'Grundrechtsschutz im Anwendungsbereich des Gemeinschaftsrechts nach der Charta der Grundrechte' in H Herdegen, H Klein, HJ Papier and R Scholz (eds), *Staatsrecht und Politik: Festschrift für Roman Herzog zum 75 Geburtstag* (München, Verlag C H Beck, 2009) 19.

[15] Case 29/69 *Stauder* [1969] ECR 419, para 7.

[16] See also Case 11/70 *Internationale Handelsgesellschaft* [1970] ECR 1125.

According to *Nold*,[17] in safeguarding these rights, the ECJ is bound to draw inspiration from constitutional traditions common to the Member States and from the international Treaties for the protection of human rights on which the latter have collaborated or of which they are signatories.

The Charter has to be observed, within certain limits, also by the Member States. Such an obligation is crucial as implementation and application of EU law relies essentially upon national legal orders. The ECJ's case law reflects this reality. According to *Wachauf*, delivered in 1989, the requirements for the protection of fundamental rights are binding on the Member States when they implement Community rules (the 'Agency situation').[18] The ECJ widened the scope of this obligation in *ERT*,[19] ruling that fundamental rights have to be respected when a Member State derogates from a fundamental economic freedom guaranteed by the Treaties (the 'Derogation situation'). In its subsequent jurisprudence, the ECJ has required Member States to respect fundamental rights as general principles of EU law also in some other situations having a sufficient connection to EU law. However, the exact scope of this obligation is subject to controversy. This case law takes EU fundamental law protection into the sphere of each Member State where it coexists with the standards of fundamental rights protection enshrined in national law or in the ECHR.[20]

Defining to what extent the Member States should be bound by the Charter was a politically difficult and awkward exercise. A number of sensitive issues arose during the drafting process of the instrument and still do. As the EU is a supranational legal order based on the principle of conferred competences and as the Member States have their own autonomous tasks and competences, the possible impact of the Charter on the division of powers within the EU was necessarily on the agenda.[21] The relation between the Charter and other sources of fundamental rights (including the ECHR and the Member States' Constitutions), the level of protection to be ensured, as well as the possibility of providing for limitations to the rights to be codified by the instrument, were also extensively debated.

The provisions of the Charter governing its scope of application are the result of a delicate compromise. According to Article 51(1) the provisions of the Charter are addressed to the Member States 'only when they are implementing Union

[17] Case 4/73 *Nold v Commission* [1974] ECR 491, para 13. The ECJ was most likely influenced by the Italian and German constitutional courts, see the Frontini judgment of the Italian Corte Costituzionale of 27 December 1973, No 183/73 and the judgment of the German Bundesverfassungsgericht of 29 May 1974, known as *Solange I* (2 BvL 52/71). See also T Von Danwitz, n 14 above, 1; K Lenaerts and Smijter, n 3 above, 276.

[18] It has been argued that the foundations for this development were laid in Case 36/75 *Rutili* [1975] ECR 1219, where the ECJ alluded to fundamental rights considerations in the context of Member State action, see J Coppel and A O'Neill, 'The European Court of Justice: Taking Rights Seriously?' (1992) 12 *Legal Studies*, 227, 230; Opinion of AG Trabucchi in Case 118/75 *Watson and Bellman* [1976] ECR 1185.

[19] Case C-260/89 *ERT* [1991] ECR I-2925.

[20] Opinions of AG Sharpston in Case C-427/06 *Bartsch* [2008] ECR I-7245, para 69 and Case C-34/09 *Ruiz Zambrano*, judgment of 8 March 2011 nyr, para 156.

[21] See further A Knook, 'The Court, the Charter, and the Vertical Division of Powers in the European Union' (2005) 42 *CML Rev* 367.

law'. This formulation lends itself to different interpretations and academic opinion is divided on the proper reading thereof.

This article explores the scope of application of the Charter as regards the Member States. After having recalled the drafting process of Article 51(1), this contribution explores to what extent the latter are or should be bound by that instrument in the light of the provision at issue, the explanations relating to it as well as recent ECJ case law. To complete the overall picture, consideration is given to possible implications of the Charter in situations falling outside its field of application. Finally, some concluding remarks are presented.

THE GENESIS OF THE GENERAL PROVISIONS OF THE CHARTER AND ARTICLE 51(1) THEREOF

Towards a Political Declaration

The Charter was negotiated outside the traditional intergovernmental framework in order to increase transparency and popular legitimacy of the drafting process and its outcome. The Convention, entrusted with this task by the Cologne European Council,[22] held its constituent meeting in December 1999 and adopted the draft Charter in less than one year, in October 2000.[23] This was a major achievement as neither agreeing on the scope *ratione materiae* of the instrument, nor reaching a compromise on the most central horizontal questions, was easy.

Title VII of the Charter, titled 'General provisions' (Articles 51 to 54) constitutes its cornerstone. It comprises provisions governing the field of application of the instrument, the scope and interpretation of the rights and principles reaffirmed by it as well as the level of protection to be ensured. It also lays down a prohibition of abuse of rights. The drafting process of that Title was complicated by the fact that its provisions accommodate simultaneously regressive and progressive interests.[24]

On the one hand, the general provisions of the Charter were aimed at hindering and restricting an uncontrolled development of the EU legal system. Even if it was stressed right from the beginning that the purpose of the exercise was not to alter the responsibilities of the EU,[25] several Member States were suspicious. In fact, past experiences with Bills of rights in federal States show that such instruments have a strong centralising effect.[26] It could be argued that the drafting process of

[22] See Presidency Conclusions, Cologne European Council, n 4 above. See also Presidency Conclusions, Tampere European Council, 15 and 16 October 1999, SN 200/99.

[23] The draft was approved by the Biarritz European Council held on 13 and 14 October 2000.

[24] P Helander, 'Perusoikeuskirjan yleiset määräykset ja perusoikeuksien konstitutionaalinen konteksti' in L Nieminen (ed), *Perusoikeudet EU:ssa* (Helsinki, Lakimiesliiton kustannus, 2001) 89, 94.

[25] Charte 4105/00, Body 1, 13 January 2000. See Knook, n 21 above, 372. This principle was also in conformity with the Presidency Conclusions of the Cologne European Council which underlined that the Charter should consolidate fundamental rights applicable at EU level, n 4 above.

[26] P Eeckhout, 'The EU Charter of Fundamental Rights and the Federal Question' (2002) 39 *CML Rev* 945, 945. See also Opinion of AG Sharpston in *Ruiz Zambrano*, n 20 above, paras 172–73; K Lenaerts, 'Exploring the Limits of the EU Charter of Fundamental Rights', forthcoming in the *Irish Journal of European Law*.

those provisions gave the Member States an opportunity to gain a certain form of control on the development of the ECJ's case law in the future.[27] It has been argued that had the Charter been drawn up with the sole purpose of remaining a political statement the general provisions thereof would have been superfluous.[28] It is difficult to agree with this view given the political sensibility of the issues at stake.

On the other hand, the general provisions paved the way for the adoption of a legally binding Bill of rights. As is well known, the Charter was formulated 'as if' it was subsequently to be incorporated into the EU Treaties with legally binding status.[29] Such a drafting technique was in conformity with the mandate issued by the Cologne European Council and reaffirmed in Nice,[30] that is, the commitment to consider whether and, if so, how the Charter should be integrated into the Treaties. Thus, the substantive rights and principles had to be formulated carefully and several horizontal questions had to be addressed by the instrument itself.[31] It was also necessary to ensure that the outcome would be consistent with the Treaties.[32]

Drafting Article 51(1) of the Charter proved to be difficult. While there was no doubt that, according to Article 6 TEU and to the ECJ's case law, the Member States have to respect fundamental rights as general principles of EU law, the fact remains that the relation between those principles and the fundamental rights and principles reaffirmed by the Charter is not unambiguous. On the one hand, it could be argued that fundamental rights are a subset of general principles of EU law.[33] On the other, the Charter comprises rights which might not necessarily qualify as such principles. Besides, the general principles of law are often unwritten, rather indeterminate and have to be fleshed out in a concrete case, whereas the Charter establishes a written, sharply defined framework for the protection of fundamental rights.[34] Thus, simply drawing a parallel between the fields of application of these two regimes of protection of fundamental rights did not seem to be a realistic option.

[27] J Van der Velde, 'The Protection of Fundamental Rights within the European Union: A Historical Approach' in J Wouters, L Verhey and PH Kiiver (eds), *European Constitutionalism beyond Lisbon* (Antwerpen, Intersentia, 2009) 61, 79.

[28] See Communication from the Commission on the Legal Nature of the Charter of Fundamental Rights of the European Union, COM(2000) 644 final.

[29] Record of the first meeting of the Body to draw up a draft Charter of Fundamental Rights of the European Union, held in Brussels, 17 December 1999, Charte 4105/00, Body 1, 13 January 2000.

[30] This commitment was reaffirmed by the Nice European Council. See Presidency Conclusions, Nice European Council, 7, 8 and 9 December 2000, SN 400/00, point I.

[31] J Dutheil de la Rochère, 'Droits fondamentaux: quelle place dans l'architecture de l'Union,' in *Chemins d'Europe: mélanges en l'honneur de Jean-Paul Jacqué* (Paris, Dalloz, 2010) 263, 268; Le Bot, n 6 above, 781.

[32] Charte 4111/00, Body 3 of 20 January 2000, 2.

[33] See A Prechal, 'Competence Creep and General Principles of Law' (2010) 3 *Review of European Administrative Law* 5, 7–8. On a discussion on the constitutional status of the general principles of EU law see Case C-101/08 *Audiolux and ors* [2009] ECR I-9823; A Prechal above, 21, and S O'Leary in this volume.

[34] A Prechal, n 33 above, 21.

Yet, the ECJ's case law on fundamental rights provided valuable guidance to the Convention. It offered various drafting options due to its gradual evolution and to the fact that each clause reflects the circumstances of the litigation at issue and the wording of the question referred to the ECJ.[35] Interestingly, underpinning different clauses are central issues concerning the development of both European fundamental rights protection and EU constitutional law.[36]

Discussions were launched in January 2000 with an information note on certain horizontal questions prepared by the Secretariat of the Convention.[37] In this note, it was made clear that the Charter was not intended to apply to 'activities of Member States falling outside the scope of EC or EU legislation'. It was also recalled that the latter were bound to respect fundamental rights whenever they acted within the scope of the Treaties for the purposes either of implementing EC (or EU) legislation or derogating from it.

According to a proposal presented to the Convention for discussion in February 2000, the provisions of the Charter would have been binding on the Member States only when the latter transpose or apply EU law.[38] The clause was meant to be inserted either into the preamble of the Charter or into its first article. The statement of reasons attached to that proposal indicated that the aim was to avoid any application of the Charter to the Member States when they were acting within their own jurisdiction. It also referred to the case law as set out in *Cinéthèque*[39] and *Kremzow.*[40] In *Cinéthèque* reference is made to an area which falls within the jurisdiction of the national legislator and in *Kremzov* to a situation not falling within the field of application of EU law. Three months later the clause had changed to read as follows: 'The provisions of this Charter are addressed to the Member States exclusively within the framework of implementing Community law'.[41] After having recalled that according to the ECJ's case law the requirement to respect fundamental rights is binding on the Member States when they act within the context of Community law, the statement of reasons quoted the restrictive phrase used in *Wachauf* 'when they implement Community rules' (ie, the Agency situation).

Intermediate proposals were broader in order to reflect more directly the relevant EU law.[42] In a document presented for discussion in May 2000,[43] the clause at

[35] See especially Coppel and O'Neill, n 18 above, 227–45.

[36] Eeckhout, n 26 above, 953.

[37] Charte 4111/00, Body 3 of 20 January 2000, 2. See also Eeckhout, n 26 above, 954; De Burca, 'The Drafting of the European Union Charter of Fundamental Rights' (2001) 26 *EL Rev*, 126, 136.

[38] Charte 4123/1/00, Convent 5 of 15 February 2000.

[39] Joined Cases 60 and 61/84 *Cinéthèque v Fédération Nationale des Cinémas Français* [1985] ECR 2605, para 26. See Coppel and O'Neill, n 18 above, 235; Opinion of AG van Gerven in Case C-159/90 *Society for the Protection of Unborn Children Ireland v Grogan* [1991] ECR I-4685, para 31.

[40] Case C-299/95 *Kremzow* [1997] ECR I-2629. In points 16 to 18 of this judgment, the ECJ pointed out that Mr Kremzow's situation was not connected in any way with any of the situations contemplated by the Treaty provisions on freedom of movement for persons.

[41] Charte 4235/00, Convent 27 of 18 April 2000.

[42] See De Burca, n 37 above, 137; Eeckhout, n 26 above, 955.

[43] Charte 4316/00, Convent 34 of 16 May 2000.

issue was drafted as follows: 'The provisions of the Charter are addressed to the Member States exclusively within the scope of Union law'. This formulation clearly covers situations where Member States are implementing and applying EU law, and where they are derogating from it, as well as other situations falling within its realm. The clause was however criticised for being too malleable.[44] The statement of reasons was identical to the former version except for the addition of a reference to *Karlsson*[45] where the formulation 'when they implement Community rules' is used in line with *Wachauf*. The provision was designated to be placed in the final part of the Charter.

The subsequent formulations were more restrictive due to an emergent reluctance among the Member States to commit themselves to observing the provisions of the Charter in cases other than those most closely linked to the EU.[46] Interestingly, the June draft distinguished, in the relevant article, between, on the one hand, the Charter generally and, on the other, the social rights and principles set out in it.[47] It stated that the Charter was addressed to the Member States exclusively when they implement Union law. The Member States would have had to respect social rights and implement social principles. This approach was explained by the sensitive character of such rights and principles, including the question of the possible positive obligations to which they could give rise.[48] The proposal was however not retained.

The clause which ultimately made its way into Article 51(1) of the Charter was debated in July, August and September 2000.[49] It reflected the restrictive wording of *Wachauf* and read as follows: 'The provisions of the Charter are addressed to the Member States only when they are implementing Union law'. Adding the word 'only' illustrated the minimalist approach of some Member States.[50] Referring to 'Union law' instead of 'Community law' was an improvement as it made clear that all EU pillars were covered.[51] A reference to 'Community' would in any case have become untenable with the entry into force of the Treaty of Lisbon in 2009 as the name 'Community' was replaced by the name 'Union'.

The explanations relating to Article 51(1) of the Charter prepared at the instigation of the Presidium of the Convention recalled that the obligation to respect fundamental rights defined in the framework of the EU is only binding on Member States 'when acting in the scope of Union law'. Instead of limiting itself to *Wachauf*, the document also refers to *ERT* corresponding to the 'Derogation situation' and to

[44] C Ladenburger, 'Artikel 51 GRCh (Art II–111 VVE) Anwendungsbereich' in PJ Tettinger and K Stern (eds), *Kölner Gemeinschaftskommentar zur Europäischen Grundrechte-Charta* (München, Verlag C H Beck, 2006) 759, 764.

[45] Case C-292/97 *Karlsson and ors* [2000] ECR I-2737.

[46] See De Burca, n 37 above, 137; see also C De Burca, 'The Evolution of EU Human Rights Law' in P Craig and C De Burca (eds), *The Evolution of EU Law* (Oxford, Oxford University Press, 2011) 465, 484; Knook, n 21 above, 373.

[47] Charte 4373/00, Convent 40 of 23 June 2000.

[48] Van der Velde, n 27 above, 74.

[49] Charte 4422/00, Convent 45 of 28 July 2000; Charte 4470/00, Convent 47 of 14 September 2000.

[50] On the meaning of the word 'only' see Von Danwitz, n 14 above, 26.

[51] De Burca, n 37 above, 137.

Annibaldi[52] where the formulation 'within the scope of Community law' is used. The relation between the Charter and the explanations thereof will be discussed below.

Article 51 of the Charter also established other guarantees in order to prevent an undesired shift in the division of powers between the EU and the Member States. In terms of its first paragraph, the addressees of the Charter shall respect the rights, observe the principles and promote the application thereof in accordance with their respective powers. In other words, the provisions of the Charter are not only formulated as guarantees against interference by its addressees but they also serve in the process of enacting legislation and developing policies.[53] As regards the EU institutions and bodies, a reference to the principle of subsidiarity was made. The second paragraph of that article underlined the principle of conferral by stating that the Charter does not establish any new powers or tasks at EU level and nor does it modify existing powers.[54] Although respect for fundamental rights is a condition for the legality of EU acts, those rights cannot in themselves have the effect of extending the scope of the Treaty provisions beyond the competences of the EU.[55]

These different limitations and guarantees constituted a counterweight to the material content of the Charter.[56] Tailor-made for the EU in light of changes in society, social progress and scientific and technological developments,[57] it contains a wide range of rights, freedoms and principles. Its scope *ratione materiae* is broader than the scope of the ECJ's fundamental rights case law[58] as it reaffirms rights not having been previously considered, expressly or impliedly, as fundamental by the ECJ.[59] Further, the rights and freedoms are very varied in nature. Some articles deal with issues where the EU has no or only limited competence to act.[60] Moreover, not all provisions of the Charter are formulated identically to the corresponding provisions in the sources thereof, which leaves room for differing interpretations.[61] While it could be argued that drafting a modern catalogue of fundamental rights but limiting its effects can create false expectations among the citizens, there is no doubt that addressing horizontal questions in the Charter itself increased legal certainty.

[52] Case C-309/96 *Annibaldi* [1997] ECR I-7493.

[53] Van der Velde, n 27 above, 68; Pernice, n 13 above, 253.

[54] Knook, n 21 above, 374.

[55] Opinion 2/94, Accession by the Community to the European Convention for the Protection of Human Rights and Fundamental Freedoms [1996] ECR I-1759, paras 34–35; Case C-249/96 *Grant* [1998] ECR I-621, para 45.

[56] Knook, n 21 above, 371.

[57] See the preamble of the Charter.

[58] It contains fewer rights than the ECJ could have guaranteed on the basis of Art 6(2) TEU juncto Art 46(d) TEU; see K Lenaerts and De Smijter, n 3 above, 273; Knook, n 21 above, 371.

[59] Eeckhout, n 26 above, 951.

[60] See further House of Lords, Sixth Report, *The Future Status of the EU Charter of Fundamental Rights*, 3 February 2003, 54.

[61] The explanations to Art 52 of the Charter contain a list of rights which may at the present stage, without precluding developments in the law, legislation and the Treaties, be regarded as corresponding to rights in the ECHR.

Towards a Legally Binding Bill of Rights

As agreed by the Cologne[62] and Nice[63] European Councils, the status of the Charter was on the agenda of the debate on the future of the EU.[64] This reflection was launched in December 2001 by the Laeken European Council, which declared that thought would have to be given to whether the Charter should be included in the basic Treaty. The process culminated in the adoption of the Treaty Establishing a Constitution for Europe in June 2004,[65] and the signature thereof in October of that year.

The Charter, slightly amended, was integrated into the Draft Constitutional Treaty as its Title II. In order that the 'Charter-sceptic Member States'[66] could also accept it becoming legally binding, the preamble and the general provisions thereof had to be adjusted.[67] The equivalent of Article 51 of today's Charter, namely Article II-111, was strengthened so as to ensure that such incorporation would not entail an extension of the EU's competences. Its first paragraph was complemented by a reference to the necessity to respect the limits of the powers of the EU as conferred on it by the Treaties. The logic underlying this addition was that when incorporated into the Treaties, the substantive articles of the Charter would have legal force equivalent to that of the articles of the Treaties. Thus, there was a need to clarify that the provisions of the Treaties 'prevail' over those of the Charter.[68] The list of the addressees of the Charter was complemented by a mention of EU offices and agencies.[69] The equivalent of Article 52(5) of today's Charter, namely Article II-112(5) governing the implementation of the Charter provisions which contain principles, was introduced. Like Article 51(1) it comprised a reference to Member States when they are implementing EU law.[70] The explanations of the Charter were updated in the light of the drafting adjustments

[62] See Presidency Conclusions, Cologne European Council, n 4 above, Annex IV.

[63] See Presidency Conclusions, Nice European Council, n 30 above.

[64] See Declaration No 23 on the future of the Union annexed to the Final Act of the Intergovernmental Conference which adopted the Treaty of Nice. See Presidency Conclusions, Laeken European Council, 14 and 15 December 2001, SN 300/1/01 Rev 1. In October 2000, when the Convention delivered its draft Charter, representatives of the Member States had already been considering Treaty changes in order to ensure that the EU would have properly functioning, efficient and legitimate institutions after the upcoming enlargement. There was however no consensus to add the question on the status of the Charter to the agenda of the ongoing Intergovernmental Conference which led to the adoption of the Treaty of Nice. See further Lenaerts and de Smijter, n 3 above, 298.

[65] [2004] OJ C 310.

[66] See C Ladenburger, 'Fundamental Rights and Citizenship of the Union' in G Amato, H Briosia and B de Witte (eds), *Genèse et destinée de la Constitution européenne* (Brussels, Bruylant, 2007) 311, 313; J Ziller, 'Le fabuleux destin des explications relatives à la Charte des droits fondamentaux de l'Union européenne' in *Chemins d'Europe: mélanges en l'honneur de Jean-Paul Jacqué* (Paris, Dalloz, 2010) 765, 769.

[67] See further M Dougan, 'The Treaty of Lisbon 2007: Winning Minds, not Hearts' (2008) 45 *CML Rev* 617, 661.

[68] WG II–WD 13, 5 September 2002, Working Group II 'Incorporation of the Charter/Accession to the ECHR', Auditions of MM Schoo, Piris and Petite, 23 July 2002, 23, 27.

[69] The expression 'bodies, offices and agencies' is commonly used in the Treaties to refer to all the authorities set up by the Treaties or by secondary legislation, see explanations to Art 51(1) of the Charter.

[70] Van der Velde, n 27 above, 76.

made to the instrument and of further developments of EU law. In particular, the texts relating to the general provisions were clarified and complemented.[71]

The possible constitutional implications of the integration of the Charter into the Treaties were thoroughly scrutinised by some constitutional courts.[72] The general provisions thereof played a crucial role when carrying out such impact assessments. As the ratification process of the EU Constitution failed due to the negative referenda in France in May 2005 and in the Netherlands in June of that year,[73] the status of the Charter remained unchanged until the Treaty of Lisbon,[74] signed on 13 December 2007, entered into force on 1 December 2009.

The Treaty of Lisbon was negotiated from the premise that the Treaties will not have a constitutional character.[75] The idea of incorporating the Charter as such into the Treaties was abandoned. Instead, it was declared in Article 6(1) TEU that the EU recognises the rights, freedoms and principles set out in the Charter, as adapted, which shall have the same legal value as the Treaties.[76] An adapted version of the instrument was proclaimed at Strasbourg, on 12 December 2007.[77] The compatibility of the Lisbon Treaty with national Constitutions was evaluated by several constitutional courts.[78]

In order to meet the concerns of the Member States which feared that the conferral of a legally binding character to the Charter would have an impact on their sovereignty, a number of guarantees were inserted into Article 6(1) TEU. Firstly, it was confirmed that the provisions of the instrument shall not extend in any way the competences of the EU as defined in the Treaties. This clause corresponds to the formulation inserted into Article 51(2) of the Charter and to the principle of conferral in Article 5 TEU. Secondly, it was made clear that the rights, freedoms and principles enshrined in the Charter have to be interpreted in accordance with the general provisions thereof. Thirdly, a reference to the explanations prepared under the authority of the Presidium of the Convention was made. The provisions of the Charter would have to be interpreted with due regard to that document which sets out the sources thereof. The explanations were updated in 2007.[79] A reference to them is also to be found in the preamble of the Charter and in its Article 52(7). The importance of the explanations should not be underestimated. Not only do they

[71] Ziller, n 66 above, 774.

[72] Décision du Conseil constitutionnel (France), 19 November 2004; Declaración del Pleno del Tribunal Constitucional 1/2004, 13 December 2004, DCT 1/2004. See V Bazzocchi, 'The European Charter of Fundamental Rights and the Courts' in G Di Federico (ed), *The EU Charter of Fundamental Rights: From Declaration to Binding Instrument* (Wien New York, Springer, 2011) 55, 73; Ziller, n 66 above, 775.

[73] See further Dougan, n 67 above, 619.

[74] [2007] OJ C306, [2010] OJ C83.

[75] Presidency Conclusions, Brussels European Council, 21 and 22 June 2007, 11177/1/07 Rev 1, Annex I.

[76] A similar proposal had already been presented by the European Parliament at the Intergovernmental Conference 2000, see CONFER 4804/00, 16 November 2000.

[77] [2007] JO C303. See also [2010] JO C83.

[78] Conseil constitutionnel (France), décision no 2007-560 DC, 20 December 2007; Constitutional Court of the Czech Republic, decision P1.US 19/08; Bundesverfassungsgericht, 2 BvE 2/08 vom 30.6.2009. See Bazzocchi, n 72 above, 74; Ziller, n 66 above, 779.

[79] [2007] JO C303/17.

provide a limitative framework for the interpretation of the Charter, they also facilitate a uniform application thereof at national and EU level. These guarantees were reaffirmed in different instruments annexed to the Treaties or to the Final Act of the Intergovernmental Conference which adopted the Treaty of Lisbon.[80]

Some Member States were granted additional guarantees for political reasons. As regards Poland and the United Kingdom, Protocol No 30 of the Treaty and several declarations annexed to the Final Act of the Intergovernmental Conference ostensibly aimed at restricting the interpretation of the Charter by the ECJ and the national courts of these two Member States, in particular as regards the economic and social rights contained in Title IV on Solidarity.[81] The Czech Republic declared its intention to join the protocol fearing that the Charter would allow those displaced after the Second World War from the territory of the modern day Czech Republic to raise property claims before the EU jurisdictions.[82] A declaration by that Member State was annexed to the Final Act of the Intergovernmental Conference. It underlines, among other things, that the provisions of the Charter are not addressed to the Member States when they are adopting and implementing national law independently from EU law.[83] The concerns expressed by the Irish people in the negative referendum on the Treaty of Lisbon in 2008, such as the necessity to ensure the protection of the right to life, were addressed at the European Council in Brussels in June 2009.[84] The Czech and Irish governments have recently submitted to the Council proposals for a forthcoming amendment of the Treaties.[85]

[80] See especially Protocol No 30 on the Application of the Charter of Fundamental Rights of the European Union to Poland and to the United Kingdom, Declaration No 1 concerning the Charter of Fundamental Rights of the European Union and Declaration No 18 in relation to the delimitation of competences.

[81] See Declaration No 61 by the Republic of Poland on the Charter of Fundamental Rights of the European Union and Declaration No 62 by the Republic of Poland concerning the Protocol on the application of the Charter of Fundamental Rights of the European Union in relation to Poland and the United Kingdom. See further Dougan, n 67 above, 665.

[82] See the statement of President Václav Klaus on the ratification of the Treaty of Lisbon, 10 September 2009, Prague Castle. See also Presidency Conclusions, Brussels European Council, 29 and 30 October 2009, 15265/09 Rev 1 Concl 3. The Heads of State or Government agreed that they will, at the time of the conclusion of the next Accession Treaty and in accordance with their respective constitutional requirements, attach to the TEU and the TFEU, the Protocol in Annex I of the conclusions. According to it, Protocol No 30 on the application of the Charter to Poland and the United Kingdom shall apply to the Czech Republic. See further A Rosas and L Armati, *EU Constitutional Law: An Introduction* (Oxford, Hart Publishing, 2010) 156.

[83] Declaration No 53 by the Czech Republic on the Charter of Fundamental Rights of the European Union.

[84] See Presidency Conclusions, Brussels European Council, 18 and 19 June 2009, 11225/2/09 Rev 2 Concl 2 and their Annex 1 (Decision of the Heads of State or Government of the 27 Member States of the EU, meeting within the European Council, on the concerns of the Irish People on the Treaty of Lisbon), Annex 2 (Solemn Declaration on the Workers' Rights, Social Policy and other Issues) and Annex 3 (National Declaration by Ireland). See also Protocol No 35 on Article 40.3.3 of the Constitution of Ireland, annexed to the Treaties.

[85] See Amendment of the Treaties – Protocol on the Application of the Charter of Fundamental Rights of the European Union to the Czech Republic, CO Eur-Prep 33 Polgen 133 Inst 400, 6 September 2011 and Amendment of the Treaties – Protocol on the Concerns of the Irish people on the Treaty of Lisbon, 13181/11 CO Eur-Prep 32 Polgen 127 Inst 378, 2 September 2011. The Irish protocol was signed on 16 May 2012.

Finally, it should be recalled that Article 6(1) TEU is closely linked to other provisions of the Treaties, as amended by the Treaty of Lisbon. To name a few, Article 2 TEU recalls the values on which the EU is founded, including the respect for human rights. Article 6(2) TEU provides for the accession of the EU to the ECHR. The third paragraph thereof reaffirms that fundamental rights, as guaranteed by the ECHR and as they result from the constitutional traditions common to the Member States, constitute general principles of EU law. This provision establishes a safety net[86] as it ensures that the ECJ can still draw on those two sources to recognise fundamental rights not codified by the Charter. Such an approach is in line with the conception that catalogues of fundamental rights in Constitutions are not exhaustive and permit the development, through case law, of additional rights as society changes.[87] Articles 3(5) and 21 TEU highlight the role of human rights in EU external relations. Article 7 TEU provides for a mechanism enabling EU institutions to act when there is a serious and persistent breach by a Member State of the values referred to in Article 2 TEU. Article 49 TEU states that those values have to be respected by the European States applying for membership of the EU. Article 263 TFEU on the right of action of natural and legal persons and Article 19(1) TEU on the obligation of the Member States to provide remedies sufficient to ensure effective legal protection in the fields covered by EU law are also crucial.[88]

THE SCOPE OF APPLICATION OF THE CHARTER

The Situations Covered by *Wachauf*, *ERT* and *Annibaldi*

The Charter can only apply where the measure at issue falls within the scope of EU law. This is a logical consequence of the principle of conferred competences.[89] As long as the powers of the EU remain based on the principle of conferral, EU fundamental rights must respect the limits of that conferral.[90] Yet, a broader scope of application for the Charter was urged by some NGOs in order to give added value to the instrument.[91] Such an evolution would have been a revolution. The EU is not to be converted into a human rights organisation.[92]

[86] Prechal, n 33 above, 20.

[87] Conv 354/02, WG II 16, 22 October 2002, Final Report of Working Group II, pp 9, 10.

[88] See also Art 47 of the Charter.

[89] Opinion 2/94, n 55 above, para 23.

[90] See Opinion of AG Sharpston in *Ruiz Zambrano*, n 26 above, para 162. See Case C-376/98 *Germany v Parliament and Council* [2000] ECR I-8419, para 83; Joined Cases C-402/05 P and C-415/05 P *Kadi and Al Barakaat International Foundation v Council and Commission* [2008] ECR I-6351, para 203; Joined Cases C-393/07 and C-9/08 *Italy v Parliament* [2009] ECR I-3679, para 67; Case C-370/07 *Commission v Council* [2009] ECR I-8917, para 46.

[91] See Charte 4290/00, Contrib 162, 10 May 2000, by Amnesty International; Eeckhout, n 26 above, 957.

[92] See K Lenaerts and J A Gutiérrez-Fons, 'The Constitutional Allocation of Powers and General Principles of EU Law' (2010) 47 *CML Rev* 1629, 1656.

The actions of EU institutions, bodies, offices and agencies fall within the scope of EU law when the latter are exercising powers conferred by or pursuant to the Treaties.[93] The obligation to observe the Charter concerns in particular the legislative work of the Commission, the European Parliament and the Council.[94] Interestingly, some of the provisions of the Charter only seem to apply to this group of addressees.[95]

As regards the measures adopted by the Member States, in other words, the national central authorities, the regional and local bodies, as well as public organisations,[96] the situation is more complicated. The EU and the Member States each have their autonomous tasks and competences. Nevertheless, those compartments are not watertight. EU law and national law are mutually integrated.[97] The ECJ is repeatedly confronted with difficult questions relating to the delimitation between situations falling within the scope of EU law and those remaining within purely national competence.[98] The Treaty of Lisbon constituted an attempt to clarify that demarcation line.[99] Nonetheless, several interesting questions remain unanswered. In this respect, the playing field of 'traditional' international organisations, such as the European Council, is admittedly less complex.

EU fundamental rights protection comes into play when the contested national measure has a sufficient connection to EU law. The clause 'only when they are implementing Union law' as referred to in Article 51(1) of the Charter limits the obligation of the Member States to respect the provisions thereof to implementation of EU law.[100] However, the situation is far from clear, as the notion of implementation is vague. In addition, there are slight discrepancies between different

[93] See Case C-377/98 *Netherlands v Parliament and Council* [2001] ECR I-7079; Case C-404/92 P, *X v Commission* [1994] ECR I-4737; Case C-185/95 P *Baustahlgewebe v Commission* [1998] ECR I-8417; Editorial, 'The Scope of Application of the General Principles of Union Law: An Ever Expanding Union' (2010) 47 *CML Rev* 1589, 1590.

[94] Communication from the Commission: Strategy for the Effective Implementation of the Charter of Fundamental Rights by the European Union, Brussels, COM(2010) 573 final, 3.

[95] Art 41(4) (Right to write to the institutions of the Union in one of the languages of the Treaties and to have an answer in the same language), Art 42 (Right of access to documents), Art 43 (Ombudsman) and Art 44 (Right to petition). See Ladenburger, n 44 above, 761. According to him the situation is less clear as far as Art 41(1) and (2) are concerned (Right to have his or her affairs handled impartially, fairly and within a reasonable time by the institutions and bodies of the Union).

[96] See explanations to Art 51(1) of the Charter.

[97] Eeckhout, n 26 above, 953.

[98] Opinion of AG Jääskinen in Case C-393/08 *Sbarigia*, judgment of 1 July 2010 nyr, paras 29–33; Opinion of AG Mengozzi in Case C-439/08 *VEBIC*, judgment of 7 December 2010, para 36. See also Cases C-144/04 *Mangold* [2005] ECR I-9981; C-427/06 *Bartsch* [2008] ECR I-7245; *Ruiz Zambrano*, n 20 above; C-256/11, *Dereci and ors*, judgment of 15 November 2011 nyr.

[99] See especially Art 5(1) and (2) TEU.

[100] See also Council Regulation (EC) No 168/2007 of 15 February 2007 establishing a European Union Agency for Fundamental Rights, [2007] OJ L 53. As far as the Member States are concerned, the competence of the Agency is limited to the situations where they are implementing Community law. See A Williams, 'Respecting Fundamental Rights in the New Union: A Review' in C Barnard (ed), *The Fundamental Rights of EU Law Revisited: Assessing the Impact of the Constitutional Debate* (Oxford, Oxford University Press, 2007) 71, 80; De Burca, n 46 above, 485.

language versions of the clause at issue. According to some versions[101] the provisions of the Charter are addressed to the Member States 'only when they are applying Union law'. Besides, there seems to be a tension between the provision at issue and the explanations relating to it. The latter recall that the obligation to respect fundamental rights defined in the framework of the EU is only binding on Member States 'when acting in the scope of Union law' and refers to *Wachauf*, *ERT* and *Annibaldi*.[102] It is hardly surprising that different readings of the provision at issue have been put forward.

According to a restrictive understanding of Article 51(1) of the Charter it only applies to the Agency situation. The *Wachauf* line of cases reflects the fact that EU law is to a great extent based on the conception of 'shared administration'. When Member States implement EU law – which is the standard mode of delivering such law[103] – they act as agents of the EU and should be subject to same constraints as the EU legislator as far as protection of fundamental rights is concerned.[104] Not to review such acts would be legally inconsistent and arbitrary.[105]

If *Wachauf* concerned the execution of regulations in the field of common agricultural policy,[106] the ECJ confirmed in *Booker Aquaculture and Hydro Seafood*[107] that the same principle applies to the transposition and implementation of directives.[108] This is logical as the choice of form and methods left to the Member States in such acts should not include the choice whether or not to violate fundamental rights. Vice versa, respect for fundamental rights is an implicit part of the 'result to be achieved' under the directive.[109] In the light of *Lindqvist*[110] it is for the national authorities not only to implement directives but also to make sure they do not rely upon an interpretation of directives which would be in conflict with fundamental rights as general principles of EU law.[111]

[101] See the Spanish (aplicar), Finnish (soveltavat) and Swedish (tillämpar) language versions. See also J Kokott and C Sobotta, 'Die Charta der Grundrechte der Europäischen Union nach Inkrafttreten des Vertrags von Lissabon' 2010 *Europäische Grundrechte-Zeitschrift* 265, 268; A Rosas and H Kaila, 'L'application de la Charte des droits fondamentaux de l'Union européenne par la Cour de justice: un premier bilan' (2011) *Il diritto dell'Unione europea* 1, 19.

[102] Case C-309/96 *Annibaldi* [1997] ECR I-7493.

[103] Eeckhout, n 26 above, 952.

[104] Opinion of AG Jacobs in Case 5/88 *Wachauf*, para 22.

[105] JHH Weiler and S Fries, 'A Human Rights Policy for the European Community and Union: The Question of Competences' in Alston, M Bustelo, J Heenan (eds), *The EU and Human Rights* (Oxford, Oxford University Press, 1999) 147, 162.

[106] Case 5/88 Wachauf [1989] ECR 2609. See also Joined Cases 201/85 and 202/85 *Klensch* [1986] ECR 3477, paras 10–11; Case C-2/92 *Bostock* [1994] ECR I-955, para 16; Joined Cases C-31/91 to C-44/91 *Lageder and ors* [1993] ECR I-1761; Case C-186/96 *Demand* [1998] ECR I-8529, para 35.

[107] Joined Cases C-20/00 and C-64/00 *Booker Aquaculture and Hydro Seafood* [2003] ECR I-7411, paras 88–93.

[108] Case C-442/00 *Caballero* [2002] ECR I-11915, para 31; Case C-144/04 *Mangold* [2005] ECR I-9981, paras 75–77; Case C-427/06 *Bartsch* [2008] ECR I-7245; Case C-555/07 *Kücükdeveci* [2010] ECR I-365.

[109] Opinion of AG Mischo in Joined Cases C-20/00 and C-64/00 *Booker Aquaculture and Hydro Seafood*, n 107 above.

[110] Case C-101/01 *Lindqvist* [2003] ECR I-12971.

[111] See also Joined Cases C-465/00, C-138/01 and C-139/01 *Österreichischer Rundfunk and ors* [2003] ECR I-4989.

The ECJ has subsequently extended the *Wachauf* type of reasoning to the adoption of measures aimed at giving effects to regulations[112] and other EU law provisions.[113] It has also confirmed that this case law applies irrespective of the degree of discretion the Member States enjoy and whether the national measure goes beyond what is strictly necessary for implementation.[114]

A broader reading of Article 51(1) of the Charter would mean that the *ERT* type Derogation situation is also covered.[115] The principle that fundamental rights have to be respected when a Member State derogates from a EU fundamental freedom applies where justifications set out in the Treaties are being put forward, but also, as confirmed in *Familiapress*,[116] where the so-called imperative or overriding requirements, recognised by the case law initiated in 'Cassis de Dijon', are relied upon.[117] Similarly, when a Member State invokes respect for and protection of a fundamental right as a direct justification for a derogation as in *Schmidberger*[118] such a justification must be interpreted in the light of the general principles of EU law.

The philosophy underlying the *ERT* case law[119] is that defining what constitutes a violation of the fundamental freedoms is a matter of EU law. The scope of the derogation and the conditions for applying it are 'creatures' of that law.[120] The Member State is in a sense implementing a power of defence or derogation provided by EU law.[121] Consequently, when it avails itself of a derogation under EU law it also has to respect fundamental rights as general principles of that law.[122] This finding is not undermined by the fact that some grounds of derogation, such as the reasons of public policy and public security, are closely linked with national sovereignty. It would be difficult to apprehend the notion of public policy without considering fundamental rights.[123]

According to the broadest understanding of Article 51(1), the field of application of the rights and principles reaffirmed by the Charter coincides with the

[112] See Case C-345/06 *Heinrich* [2009] ECR I-1659, para 45; Case C-384/05 *Piek* [2007] ECR I-289, paras 32–34; Case C-16/89 *Spronk* [1990] ECR I-3185, para 13. See Prechal, n 33 above, 8.

[113] Case C-309/96 *Annibaldi* [1997] ECR I-2925, paras 14–21; Case C-300/04 *Eman and Sevinger* [2006] ECR I-8055, paras 44–45, 52–53, 61.

[114] Joined Cases C-378/07 to C-380/07 *Angelidaki and ors* [2009] ECR I-3071; Case C-81/05 *Alonso* [2006] ECR I-7569. See also Opinion of AG Trstenjak in Case C-411/10 *NS*, paras 69–83, pending at time of writing.

[115] On the hierarchical position of fundamental rights in this case law compared with their position in *Wachauf*, see Coppel and O'Neill, n 18 above, 238.

[116] Case C-368/95 *Familiapress* [1997] ECR I-3689, para 24.

[117] Case 120/78 *Rewe-Zentral* [1979] ECR 649.

[118] Case C-112/00 *Schmidberger* [2003] ECR I-5659. See Knook, n 21 above, 370.

[119] Case C-60/00 *Carpenter* [2002] ECR I-6279, para 40; Joined Cases C-482/01 and C-493/01 *Orfanopoulos and Oliveri* [2004] ECR I-5257, para 97.

[120] Weiler and Fries, n 105 above, 163.

[121] P Craig, 'The ECJ and Ultra Vires Action: A Conceptual Analysis' (2011) 48 *CML Rev*, 2, 395, 430–31.

[122] *ERT* was foreshadowed by the opinion of AG Van Gerven of 11 June 1991 in Case C-159/90 *Society for the Protection of Unborn Children Ireland v Grogan*. See also Lenaerts and Gutiérrez-Fons, n 92 above, 1659.

[123] Lenaerts and Gutiérrez-Fons, n 92 above, 1659; Eeckhout, n 26 above, 977.

scope of application of EU law. Member States would thus be bound by the Charter whenever they act within the realm of that law.[124] What would be important is the existence of a sufficient connecting link with it. [125] Such a link does exist notably where a specific substantive rule of EU law is applicable to the situation.[126]

In Search of a Correct Interpretation

The narrow interpretation finds some support in the drafting process of the Charter.[127] As explained above, the broader clauses presented for discussion in spring 2000 were rejected by some Member States wishing to limit the obligation to observe the provisions thereof to cases where they have little or no autonomy.[128] The same tendency could be observed in the negotiation processes of the EU Constitution and the Treaty of Lisbon. It could also be argued that the use of the word 'only' advocates a narrow approach.

At the same time, the explanations of the Charter point in favour of a broader reading of Article 51(1). In the light of the reference to *ERT* it could be argued that the Member States are bound by the Charter both when they implement EU rules and in the context of national derogations to the fundamental freedoms.[129] The phrase 'when acting in the scope of Union law' used in *Annibaldi* could be interpreted as meaning that the provision at issue does not intend to exclude from the application of the Charter any situation where general principles of EU law are applicable. As stated above, after the entry into force of the Treaty of Lisbon the provisions of the Charter have to be interpreted with due regard to that document. It is no longer tenable to argue that those explanations 'do not have any legal value [and] are simply designed to clarify the provisions of the Charter in the light of the discussions which took place within the convention'.[130]

The different readings of Article 51(1) are a logical consequence of the vagueness of the concept of implementation. According to Advocate General Bot the concept of implementation should be understood as referring to

[124] Craig, n 121 above, 430.

[125] See, eg Case C-60/00 *Carpenter* [2002] ECR I-6279; Case C-117/01 KB [2004] ECR I-541; Case C-71/02 *Karner* [2004] ECR I-3025; Case C-144/04 *Mangold* [2005] ECR I-9981. See further A Rosas and Armati, n 82 above, 147.

[126] See Opinion of AG Sharpston in Case C-427/06 *Bartsch*, para 69. See also Case C-71/02 *Karner* [2004] ECR I-3025, paras 48–53 (potential impediment to intra-Community trade); Case 804/79 *Commission v United Kingdom* [1981] ECR 1045, paras 23–30 (Member States acting as trustees of the Community in an area of exclusive Community competence); Joined Cases C-286/94, C-340/95, C-401/95 and C-47/96 *Molenheide and ors* [1997] ECR I-7281, paras 45–48 (measures adopted by a Member State in the exercise of its competences relating to VAT).

[127] See Lenaerts and Gutiérrez-Fons, n 92 above, 1657.

[128] De Búrca, n 37 above, 137.

[129] See Opinion of AG Trstenjak in *NS*, n 114 above, para 76.

[130] Opinion of AG Mischo in Joined Cases C-122/99 P and C-125/99 P *D and Kingdom of Sweden v Council of the European Union*, para 97. The explanations were drawn up by the Secretariat on the basis of instructions from the Praesidium, which requested that they be as factual as possible, setting out the texts or case law used as sources for the wording of each article and refraining from any attempt to interpret the Charter. See Charte 4423/00, Convent 46, 31 July 2000; Ziller, n 66 above, 768.

> subsequent and specific applications of rules laid down by a directive, as well as, more generally, to all situations in which national legislation concerns or affects a matter governed by a directive the period for the transposition of which has expired.[131]

Several reasons seem to plead for an understanding of Article 51(1) implying that the field of application of the rights and principles reaffirmed by the Charter coincides with the scope of application of EU law. Such an interpretation would ensure that the EU provisions cannot be interpreted in a way which tolerates violations of fundamental rights.[132]

Firstly, it should be recalled that fundamental rights are part of EU primary law. They should, like any norm of EU law, be respected whenever this body of law, or national measures adopted to implement this law, are applied by legislative, executive and judicial authorities of the Member States.[133] If an EU norm, other than a provision of the Charter, is to be directly applied or interpreted, it would be inconceivable that that norm would have to be applied or interpreted by the EU institutions in the light of the Charter, whereas such application or interpretation by national authorities could take place without regard to that instrument.

Secondly, a restrictive interpretation of the provision at issue would mean that the scope of application of the Charter would be narrower than that of the general principles of EU law.[134] Those principles would take over where the scope of application of the Charter ends.[135] This would lead to the creation of two separate systems of protection of fundamental rights within the EU, according to whether they stem from the Charter or from such general principles[136] – a demarcation line which itself is not clear-cut. It would also constitute a step backwards as regards the ECJ's case law on fundamental rights, although nothing in the Treaty of Lisbon has overruled the latter.[137] Such a weakening of the level of protection of those rights could be regarded as being contrary to the wording of Article 53 of the Charter. It establishes a 'standstill clause' by providing that nothing in that instrument shall be interpreted as restricting or adversely affecting human rights and fundamental freedoms as recognised, in their respective fields of application, by EU law.

Thirdly, a restrictive reading would imply that the scope of application of the Charter would be narrower than that of the provisions governing EU citizenship[138] and of the principle of non-discrimination.[139] The relevant ECJ case law applies within the scope of application of EU law or in situations envisaged by or governed by EU law.[140]

[131] See Opinion of AG Bot in Case C-108/10 *Scattolon*, para 119.

[132] See further Lenaerts and Gutiérrez-Fons, n 92 above, 1659; Eeckhout, n 26 above, 977.

[133] Rosas and Armati, n 82 above, 148.

[134] Lenaerts and Gutiérrez-Fons, n 92 above, 1657.

[135] ibid, 1659.

[136] See Opinion of AG Bot in *Scattolon*, n 131 above, para 120; Lenaerts and Gutiérrez-Fons, n 92 above, 1658.

[137] Craig, n 121 above, 431.

[138] See further Eeckhout, n 26 above, 969–75; Craig, n 121 above, 412.

[139] See further Eeckhout, n 26 above, 986.

[140] See further K Lenaerts and E Sharpston in this volume.

Fourthly, the right to effective legal protection, as recognised by Article 19 TEU and Article 47 of the Charter, should not be undermined. These provisions guarantee the right to an effective remedy before a court in the fields covered by EU law. If the concept of implementation is understood narrowly, the level of protection would differ on the basis of whether a Member State adopts a positive measure in order to give effect to EU law provisions or whether it abstains from doing so. Such a situation would not be consistent with the need to ensure a uniform and efficient protection of individuals and economic operators within the EU.[141]

Moreover, the ECJ has already used the phrase 'implementing Community rules' as synonymous with Member State rules that fall within the scope of EU law.[142] The broad interpretation also finds some support in the most recent case law which will be briefly discussed below.

Yet, it should be borne in mind that the field of application of the Charter is interrelated with the scope of the British and Polish reservations on the application thereof. A broad reading of Article 51(1) would also entail that those reservations have a wide field of application. However, the implications of such a finding are not quite as dramatic as it might seem. Protocol No 30 is not an opt-out from the Charter.[143] If the interpretation of the Charter may be affected by the terms of that Protocol, the fact remains that the Member States concerned are, in any event, bound by Articles 2 TEU, 6(3) TEU and 7 TEU[144] and by the principle of loyal co-operation enshrined in Article 4(3) TEU,[145] as well as by EU secondary legislation touching on fundamental rights and the ECJ's case law on general principles of EU law.

APPLICATION OF THE CHARTER BY THE MEMBER STATES

Application of the Charter as a Political Declaration

The Charter played an important role as a political declaration. It was beyond doubt that the three main political EU institutions had committed themselves to respect the instrument by proclaiming it. The Charter was also taken into consideration by the other EU institutions and organs as well as by the Member States. This is hardly surprising as it constituted 'the expression, at the highest level, of a democratically established political consensus on what must be considered as the

[141] See JP Jacqué, 'La Charte des droits fondamentaux de l'Union européenne: présentation générale' in LS Rossi (ed), *Carta dei diritti fondamentali e Costituzione dell'Unione europea* (Milano, Giuffrè, 2002) 55, 76.

[142] See Craig, n 122 above, 431 and Case C-442/00 *Caballero* [2002] ECR I-11915.

[143] See JP Jacqué, 'Les droits fondamentaux dans le traité de Lisbonne' (2010) *L'observateur de Bruxelles* 17, 19; House of Lords, 'The Treaty of Lisbon: An Impact Assessment', European Union Committee, 10th Report of Session 2007–08, Vol I: Rep, 102.

[144] Rossi, n 10 above, 618.

[145] R Barents, 'The Court of Justice after the Treaty of Lisbon' (2010) 47 *CML Rev* 709, 721.

catalogue of fundamental rights guaranteed by the EU legal order'.[146] It should also be recalled that a number of its provisions already had a mandatory character due to their sources.

The European Parliament[147] and the Commission[148] declared without delay their intention to take the Charter as a point of reference for their acts. The Commission decided that legislative proposals and draft instruments having a specific link to fundamental rights would incorporate a recital as a formal statement of compatibility. Such references are not without legal consequences for the application and interpretation of the instrument.[149] In the first case where the ECJ referred to the Charter, namely in *Parliament v Council*,[150] the preamble of the contested regulation[151] contained an explicit reference to the Charter.[152]

Subsequently, the Charter became a source of inspiration for national jurisdictions including several constitutional courts. The Tribunal Constitucional de España[153] referred to the Charter in 2000 and was followed by the Corte Costitutionale (Italy),[154] the Tribunal Constitucional (Portugal)[155] and, after some hesitation,[156] the Cour constitutionnelle (Belgium)[157].

As to the ECJ, the vast majority of its judgments from the pre-Lisbon era citing the Charter concern the application of EU law at a national level and more

[146] See Opinion of AG Mischo in Case C-20/00 *Booker Aquacultur Ltd* [2003] ECR I-7411, para 126; Eeckhout, n 26 above, 950.

[147] See statement by Mrs Nicole Fontaine, President of the European Parliament, on 7 December 2000. See also Resolution of the European Parliament of 15 March 2007 on the Compliance with the Charter of Fundamental Rights in *Commission Legislative Proposals: Methodology for Systematic and Rigorous Monitoring* (2005/2169(INI)), [2007] JO C 301 E/229.

[148] See statement by R Prodi, President of the Commission, on 7 December 2000. See document SEC(2001) 380/3, Commission Communication on the Charter of Fundamental Rights of the European Union, COM(2000) 559 final, of 13 September 2000; Commission Communication on the Legal Nature of the Charter of Fundamental Rights of the European Union, COM(2000) 644 final of 11 October 2000. See also Communication from the Commission – Compliance with the Charter of Fundamental Rights in Commission Legislative Proposals – Methodology for Systematic and Rigorous Monitoring, COM(2005) 172 final of 27 April 2005. See also Report on the Practical Operation of the Methodology for a Systematic and Rigorous Monitoring of Compliance with the Charter of Fundamental Rights COM(2009) 205 final du 29 avril 2009.

[149] See S O'Leary in this volume.

[150] Case C-540/03 *Parliament v Council* [2006] ECR I-5769, para 38.

[151] Council Directive 2003/86/EC of 22 September 2003 on the right to family reunification, [2003] OJ L251/12.

[152] As far as the EU Courts are concerned, the first substantive reference made in a judgment dates back to 2002. Having previously had to draw inspiration from disparate sources of fundamental rights, the Court of First Instance (General Court) relied upon the Charter in Case T-54/99 *max.mobil v Commission* [2002] ECR II-313, para 48. The Charter was mentioned by the Court of First Instance for the very first time in Case T-112/98 *Mannesmannröhren-Werke v Commission* [2001] ECR II-729. See further Rosas and Kaila, n 101 above, 4–7.

[153] Sentencia no 292/2000 de Tribunal Constitucional, Pleno, 30 November 2000. See also Bazzocchi, n 72 above, 70–71.

[154] Sentenza no 135/2002 della Corte costituzionale, 24 April 2002. See also Bazzocchi, n 72 above, 71.

[155] Acórdão no 275/02 do Tribunal Constitucional, 19 June 2002.

[156] See Case C-305/05 *Ordre des barreaux francophones et germanophone and ors* [2007] ECR I-5305; Arrêt no 10/2008 de la Cour Constitutionnelle, 23 January 2008.

[157] Arrêt no 58/2009 de la Cour Constitutionnelle, 19 March 2009.

precisely, the compatibility with EU law of national provisions adopted in the Agency situation.[158] *Viking*[159] and *Laval*[160] seem to make an exception as they deal with the possibility of derogating from fundamental freedoms. During that era, when interpreting the provisions of the Charter, the ECJ relied upon them largely in combination with other sources of fundamental rights, such as the general principles of EU law, the EU Treaties, the ECHR and the European Social Charter.

The application of the Charter by the Member States raises questions on the overlapping levels of protection under EU law, national constitutional law and the ECHR, and the level of EU fundamental rights protection. This complex issue has been widely debated in legal doctrine and will not be discussed here.[161] It will suffice to recall the European Court of Human Rights' (ECtHR) judgment in *Bosphorus*[162] where it held that, although not fully binding, the provisions of the Charter are substantially inspired by those of the ECHR, and that the Charter recognises the ECHR as establishing the minimum human rights standards. Considering the protection of fundamental rights by EU law to be 'equivalent' to that of the ECHR system, it established a 'presumption of equivalent protection'.

Application of the Charter as a Legally Binding Instrument

In order to take due account of the legally binding status of the Charter, the European Parliament[163] and the Commission[164] agreed to develop, promote and reinforce a genuine culture of fundamental rights in their field action. The Commission underlined that legislative and non-legislative measures should be subject to checks on their compatibility with the Charter. It also declared its deter-

[158] See, eg Case C-432/05 *Unibet* [2007] ECR I-2271, para 37; Case C-303/05 *Advocaten voor de Wereld* [2007] ECR I-3633, para 46; Case C-275/06 *Promusicae* [2008] ECR I-271, paras 33, 41, 42, 46, 61, 64; Case C-450/06 *Varec* [2008] ECR I-581, para 48; Case C-244/06 *Dynamic Medien* [2008] ECR I-505, para 41; Case C-12/08 *Mono Car Styling* [2009] ECR I-6653, para 47.

[159] Case C-438/05 *International Transport Workers' Federation and Finnish Seamen's Union, ('Viking Line')* [2007] ECR I-10779, paras 43–44.

[160] Case C-341/05 *Laval un Partneri* [2007] ECR I-11767, paras 90–91.

[161] See Opinion of AG Sharpston in Case C-34/09 *Ruiz Zambrano*, n 20 above, para 156; Von Danwitz, n 14 above, 31–33. See also the judgments of the German Bundesverfassungsgericht of 29 May 1974, known as *Solange I* (2 BvL 52/71) and of 22 October 1986, known as *Solange II* (2 BvR 197/83); the judgment of the Italian Corte Costituzionale of 21 April 1989 (No 232, Fragd, in *Foro it*, 1990, I, 1855); the declaration of the Spanish *Tribunal Constitucional* of 13 December 2004 (DTC 1/2004).

[162] *Bosphorus Hava Yollari Turizm ve Ticaret Anonim Sirketi v Ireland* [GC] No 45036/98, § 165 ECHR 2005 VI (30 June 2005).

[163] See the Report on the Situation of Fundamental Rights in the European Union (2009-2010) – Institutional Aspects after the entry into force of the Treaty of Lisbon (2009/2161(INI)), Committee on Civil Liberties, Justice and Home Affairs; Resolution of 15 December on the Situation of Fundamental Rights in the European Union (2009-2010) – Effective Implementation after the entry into force of the Treaty of Lisbon.

[164] Commission Communication on the Strategy for the Effective Implementation of the Charter of Fundamental Rights by the European Union, COM(2010) 573 final of 19 October 2010.

mination to use all the means at its disposal to ensure that the Charter is adhered to by the Member States when they implement EU law.[165]

Applying and interpreting the Charter soon became a matter of daily business for national and EU jurisdictions. As a legally binding instrument the Act fulfils, in principle, three functions: it serves as an aid to interpretation of EU law, it may be relied upon as grounds for judicial review and it can operate as a source for the discovery of general principles of EU law.[166] In its case law the ECJ has had to interpret several material rights recognised by the Charter[167] as well as the general provisions thereof. The ECJ has also ruled on the validity of certain EU law provisions with regard to the provisions of the Charter.[168]

As to the general provisions of the Charter, the ECJ seems to have adopted a rather broad understanding of Article 51(1) thereof. For example, *Kücükdeveci*[169] is based on the conception that, for the Charter to be applicable, it is sufficient that the national legislation falls within the scope of Directive 2000/78/EC.[170] Similarly, *Sayn-Wittgenstein*,[171] *DEB Deutsche Energiehandels- und Beratungsgesellschaft mb*,[172] *McB*[173] and *Dereci*[174] could be read as implying that the Charter has to be observed also in other circumstances than those falling within the scope of the Agency situation, *stricto sensu*. According to *Dereci*

> if the referring court considers, in the light of the circumstances of the disputes in the main proceedings, that the situation of the applicants in the main proceedings is covered by European Union law, it must examine whether the refusal of their right of residence undermines the right to respect for private and family life provided for in Article 7 of the Charter.

DEB Deutsche Energiehandels- und Beratungsgesellschaft mb, *McB* and *Dereci* contain an explicit reference to Article 51(1) of the Charter.

This impression is reinforced by the wording of the orders in *Asparuhov Estov and Others*[175] and *Chartry*.[176] In the former, after having recalled Articles 6(1) TEU and 51(1) of the Charter, the ECJ held that its jurisdiction to interpret the Charter

[165] Whenever necessary it will start infringement procedures against Member States for non-compliance with the Charter. Those infringement proceedings which raise issues of principle or which have a particularly far-reaching negative impact for citizens will be given priority. See COM(2010) 573 final of 19 October 2010.

[166] Lenaerts and Gutiérrez-Fons, n 92 above, 1656.

[167] See further Rosas and Kaila, n 101 above, 13–17.

[168] Joined Cases C-92/09 and C-93/09 *Volker and Markus Schecke*, judgment of 9 November 2010 nyr; Case C-236/09 *Association belge des Consommateurs Test-Achats and ors*, judgment of 1 March 2011 nyr.

[169] The facts in this case date from the period before the entry into force of the Treaty of Lisbon.

[170] Council Directive 2000/78/EC of 27 November 2000 establishing a general framework for equal treatment in employment and occupation, [2000] OJ L 303/16.

[171] Case C-208/09 *Sayn-Wittgenstein*, judgment of 22 December 2010 nyr.

[172] Case C-279/09 *DEB*, judgment of 22 December 2010 nyr.

[173] Case C-400/10 PPU *McB*, judgment of 5 October 2010 nyr.

[174] Case C-256/11 *Dereci and ors*, n 98 above.

[175] Case C-339/10 *Asparuhov Estov and ors*, order of 12 November 2010 nyr, para 14.

[176] Case C-457/09 *Chartry*, order of 1 March 2011 nyr, para 25. See also Joined Cases C-267/10 and C-268/10 *Rossius and ors*, order of 23 May 2011, para 19.

was not established, in so far as the order for reference contained nothing showing that the national decision at issue 'constitutes a measure implementing EU law or contains other connections with the latter'. The reference to 'other connections' with EU law rather supports a broader understanding by the ECJ of its jurisdiction to interpret the Charter.[177] The ECJ has been explicitly called upon to rule on the scope of the Member States' obligations in some pending cases, namely in *NS*[178] and in *Åkerberg Fransson*.[179] This implies that is too early to draw any firm conclusions on its position on the issue at state.

The ECJ has referred to other general provisions of the Charter as well, such as Article 51(2) providing that the Charter does not extend the field of application of EU law,[180] Article 52(1) on the possibility of imposing restrictions on the exercise of fundamental rights,[181] Article 52(3) on the need to ensure consistency between the Charter and the ECHR[182] and Article 52(6) on the necessity of taking full account of national laws and practices as specified in the Charter.[183] Recently, the ECJ relied upon the explanations of the Charter.[184] Besides, in several pending cases, interesting horizontal questions are being raised, including the distinction between rights and principles resulting from Articles 51(1) and 52(5), the direct effect of the provisions of the Charter,[185] the possibility of affording a greater level of protection than that deriving from EU law in order to avoid an interpretation which would restrict or adversely affect a fundamental right recognised by a national Constitution[186] and the application of the Charter to the United Kingdom.[187]

Influence of the Charter in Situations Falling Outside its Scope of Application

Where a national measure falls outside the field of application of EU law, it is up to the Member States to ensure compliance with fundamental rights in accordance with their national constitutional systems and international obligations. However, this does not mean that the Charter would be irrelevant.[188]

There is no reason why, in such cases, the Charter could not serve as a source of inspiration for national legislative, executive and judicial authorities. The fact that it was not integrated into the EU Treaties as such but has an independent existence is likely to encourage different actors to use it as a reference for the pro-

[177] Opinion of AG Bot in *Scattolon*, n 131 above.
[178] See Opinion of AG Trstenjak in Joined Cases C-411/10 and C-493/10 *NS*.
[179] Case C-617/10 *Åkerberg Fransson* [2011] OJ C 72/14.
[180] *McB*, n 173 above, para 51.
[181] Case C-407/08 P *Knauf Gips v Commission*, judgment of 1 July 2010 nyr ECR, para 91.
[182] Case C-279/09 *DEB*, n 172 above, para 35; Case C-400/10 *PPU McB*, n 173 above, 53.
[183] Case C-271/08 *Commission v Germany*, judgment of 15 July 2010 nyr, para 38.
[184] Case C-279/09 *DEB*, n 172 above, para 32.
[185] Opinion of AG Trstenjak of 8 September 2011 in Case C-282/10 *Dominguez*.
[186] Case C-399/11 *Melloni* (OJ C290/5).
[187] *NS*, n 178 above.
[188] In the interests of simplicity, this presentation is based on the premise that the field of application of the Charter coincides with the scope of application of EU law.

tection of fundamental rights.[189] Relying upon the Charter as a soft law instrument could give rise to some degree of de facto harmonisation of human rights law in the Member States.[190]

It could also be discussed what effect the incorporation of the Charter, as such, into the national legal order would have. Interestingly, the Spanish law authorising the ratification of the Treaty of Lisbon[191] contains an article declaring that the rules relating to the fundamental rights and freedoms recognised by the Constitution shall be interpreted in conformity with the provisions of the Charter. The complete text of the latter is reproduced in that article. The question arises whether the Charter could or should be applied also in situations falling outside the scope of EU law.[192]

As regards international obligations, all Member States having acceded to the ECHR and the rights reaffirmed by the Charter overlapping to a significant extent with those recognised by that convention, its role should not be underestimated.[193] If it was in the interest of the authors of the Charter to ensure the necessary consistency between the latter and the ECHR, the same is true as far as the interpretation or application of the ECHR is concerned. The content of the fundamental rights applicable in the Member States should not differ, in a given situation, on the basis of whether they stem from the Charter or from the ECHR. Such a state of affairs would be even more unacceptable after the forthcoming accession of the EU to the ECHR. The ECtHR has drawn inspiration from the Charter in a number of judgments.[194] It mentioned the Charter for the first time in 2002 in *Goodwin*[195] when enumerating instruments in the field of human rights protection. Two other judgments should not go unmentioned. *Bosphorus*[196] was already referred to above. In *Eskelinen*[197] the EctHR recognised that the explanations of the Charter are a 'valuable tool of interpretation intended to clarify the provisions

[189] Pernice, n 13 above, 241.

[190] Williams, n 100 above, 89.

[191] Ley orgánica 1/2008, de 30 de julio, por la que se autoriza la ratificación por España del Tratado de Lisboa, por el que se modifican el Tratado de la Unión Europea y el Tratado Constitutivo de la Comunidad Europea, firmado en la capital portuguesa el 13 de diciembre de 2007, BOE núm 184, Jueves 31 julio 2008.

[192] See further S Ripol Carulla, 'La Carta de derechos fundamentales de la Unión Europea en el Boe (Consideraciones sobre el artículo 2 de la lo 1/2008, por la que se autoriza la ratificación del Tratado de Lisboa)' (2010) *Revista de Derecho Comunitario Europeo* 845. See also Joined Cases C-297/88 and C-197/89 *Dzodzi* [1990] ECR I-3763. In its judgment of 14 March 2012 the Austrian Constitutional Court declared that it will consider the fundamental rights of the charter to be an integral part of the constitutional order.

[193] See further L Wildhaber and J Callewaert, 'Espace constitutionnel européen et droits fondamentaux: une vision globale pour une pluralité de droits et de juges' in N Colneric, D Edward, JP Puissochet, D Ruiz-Jarabo Colomer (eds), *Une communauté de droit: Festschrift für Gil Carlos Rodríguez Iglesias* (Berlin, Berliner Wissenschafts-Verlag, 2003) 61, 65, 71, 75–76.

[194] See further Rosas and Kaila, n 101 above, 7–8.

[195] *Goodwin v United Kingdom* No 28957/95, ECHR 2002 (3 July 2002).

[196] *Bosphorus Hava Yollari Turizm ve Ticaret Anonim Sirketi v Ireland*, n 162 above.

[197] *Vilho Eskelinen and ors v Finland* [GC] No 63235/00, § 30 ECHR 2007. See also Ziller, n 66 above, 776–77.

of the Charter'. The Charter has recently also been mentioned by the EFTA Court.[198]

Given the overlap between the provisions of the Charter and those of the ECHR as well as the spillover and cross-fertilisation effects of those instruments,[199] one could ask whether the division of competences between the ECJ and the ECtHR is a question of purely academic interest. The answer is clearly no. This demarcation line is significant notably as regards the remedies available to the individuals and to the courts in which they can be secured[200] and the questions of liability.

In the absence of a sufficient connection to EU law, the ECJ declares itself incompetent, usually by a reasoned order.[201] It is hardly surprising that, after the entry into force of the Treaty of Lisbon, there has been a rise in ECJ references invoking the Charter. As to the Commission, in such situations, it does not have the power to intervene as guardian of the Treaties.[202] In 2010, the Commission received more than 4,000 letters from the public regarding fundamental rights. Approximately three quarters of these concerned cases outside the remit of EU law.[203] The European Parliament is confronted with a similar phenomenon.[204]

Finally, it should be recalled that the non-applicability of the Charter does not preclude the enforcement mechanism provided for in Article 7 TEU from being used when there is a clear risk of a serious and persistent breach of the values referred to in Article 2 TEU, including the respect for human rights.[205]

The fields where EU law can be said to have no influence are becoming fewer. By exercising their renewed competences after the entry into force of the Treaty of Lisbon the EU institutions will increasingly bring national legislation and practice

[198] EFTA Court judgment of 26 July 2011 in Case E-4/11, *Clauder*, para 49.

[199] Rossi, n 10 above, 621; Bazzocchi, n 72 above, 75.

[200] See further House of Lords, Sixth Report, *The Future Status of the EU Charter of Fundamental Rights*, 3 February 2003, 26–27.

[201] See, eg Case C-328/04 *Vajnai* [2005] ECR I-8577; Case C-302/06 *Koval'ský* [2007] ECR I-11; Case C-287/08 *Savia and ors* [2008] ECR I-136; Case C-361/07 *Polier* [2008] ECR I-6; Case C-217/08 *Mariano* [2009] ECR I-35; Case C-333/09 *Noël* [2009] ECR I-205; Case C-339/10 *Asparuhov Estov and ors*, n 175 above; Case C-457/09 *Chartry*, n 176 above; Joined Cases C-267/10 and C-268/10 *Rossius and ors*, n 176 above.

[202] See COM(2010) 573 final of 19 October 2010, 11. See Rosas and Armati, n 82 above, 151.

[203] Report from the Commission to the European Parliament, the Council, the European Economic and Social Committee and the Committee of the Regions, 2010 Report on the Application of the EU Charter of Fundamental Rights, COM(2011) 160 final of 30 March 2011, 3. See also Ladenburger, n 8 above.

[204] See further F Camporesi, 'The European Parliament and the EU Charter of Fundamental Rights' in G Di Federico (ed), *The EU Charter of Fundamental Rights: From Declaration to Binding Instrument* (Wien New York, Springer, 2011) 77, 90.

[205] See Communication from the Commission to the Council and the European Parliament on Art 7 of the Treaty on European Union Respect for and promotion of the values on which the Union is based and the Resolution on it C5-0594/2003 (2003/2249(INI)). See also Rossi, n 10 above, 615; Ladenburger, n 8 above, 827. For an interesting discussion on the scope of the application of EU law where there is a clear risk of a serious or a serious and persistent breach of the values referred to in Article 2 TEU see Opinion of AG Poiares Maduro in Case C-380/05 *Centro Europa* 7, para 66; X Groussot, L Pech and GT Petursson, 'The Scope of Application of Fundamental Rights on Member States' Action: In Search of Certainty in EU Adjudication', Working Paper, July 2011. It is interesting to note that the Three Wise Men's Report on Austria from September 2000 referred to the Charter. See also WG II WD 13, 5 September 2002, Working Group II 'Incorporation of the Charter/Accession to the ECHR, Auditions of MM Schoo, Piris and Petite on 23 July 2002, 29.

within the scope of application of EU law and thus indirectly extend the scope of the Charter.[206]

CONCLUSION

The conferral of a legally binding status to the Charter enhanced judicial protection and sought to increase legal certainty. Much will depend however on how the instrument will be put into practice.[207] The Member States play a central role in this respect. Any doubt among national legislative, executive and judicial authorities on the interpretation of Article 51(1) of the Charter may hamper an effective, coherent and predictable enforcement of the rights reaffirmed by the act. A clear and uniform interpretation of that provision would also be in the interest of EU institutions and organs which are frequently confronted with questions on the demarcation line between situations falling within the scope of application of the Charter and those remaining outside.

The recent case law of the ECJ on the Charter constitutes a first step towards a common understanding of Article 51(1). However, the interpretation of the clause 'only when they are implementing Union law' will need to be developed further in order to ensure legal certainty. Should the outcome of that reflection be that the field of application of the rights and principles reaffirmed by the Charter coincides with the scope of application of EU law, other crucial questions still await an unambiguous answer, such as how the exact scope of EU law should be defined and what constitutes a sufficient connection to that law. This implies – as Judge P Lindh would put it – that the show must go on. And it certainly will.

[206] Di Federico, n 12 above, vii.

[207] See further Report from the Commission to the European Parliament, the Council, the European Economic and Social Committee and the Committee of the Regions: 2010 Report on the Application of the EU Charter of Fundamental Rights, COM(2011) 160 final of 30 March 2011.

21

The Charter and the Future Contours of EU Social and Employment Law

SÍOFRA O'LEARY*

INTRODUCTION

THE STORY OF the genesis of the Charter of Fundamental Rights of the European Union (Charter) is widely known and does not need to be rehearsed.[1] As the Convention which drafted the Charter indicated and the provisions of the Charter themselves underline, the Member States' limited ambitions extended to consolidating, reaffirming and rendering more visible fundamental rights already protected in the European Union (EU). Those rights resulted from constitutional traditions and international obligations common to the Member States, in particular the European Convention for the Protection of Human Rights and Fundamental Freedoms (ECHR), but also the Social Charters previously adopted by the Community and the Council of Europe.[2] It has been argued that the Charter, like Article 6(2) of the TEU, introduced by the Treaty of Maastricht, did little more than codify the principles established by the case law of the Court of Justice since the latter first recognised, in the 1960s, that fundamental human rights are enshrined in the general principles of EU law, the observance of which the Court of Justice is entrusted to ensure.[3] The Charter did not appear to seek to alter the system of rights conferred by the Treaties or extend EU competences. It does not therefore extend the field of application of EU law beyond the powers of the EU, establish any new EU power or task, or modify the powers and tasks as defined in the Treaties. Article 6(1) TEU and 51(2) of the Charter are, in fact, a clear reminder, as regards fundamental rights, of the principle of conferral which the Member States were at such pains to introduce in the opening

* Legal Secretary of the Court of Justice of the European Union; Visiting Professor, College of Europe (Bruges). The views expressed in this paper are purely personal to the author.

[1] First signed in Nice on 7 December 2000, [2000] OJ C364/1 and amended in Strasbourg on 12 December 2007, [2010] OJ C83/389.

[2] See the Charter of the Fundamental Social Rights of Workers (1989) and the European Social Charter signed at Turin on 18 October 1961, both of which are referred to in the opening provision of Title X TFEU on social policy. See also Case C-540/03 *Parliament* v *Council* [2006] ECR I-5769, para 38.

[3] Case 29/69 *Stauder* [1969] ECR 419, para 7.

provisions of the TEU.[4] In the relatively short time since the entry into force of the Treaty of Lisbon, the Court has demonstrated the effects of Article 51(2) of the Charter for the Court's jurisdiction in disputes where fundamental rights and compliance with the Charter's provisions are raised. In *McB* it emphasised, with reference to this provision, that the Court is merely called upon to interpret EU law, in the light of the Charter, within the limits of the powers conferred on it.[5]

Other limitations on the scope and effects of the Charter and thus on its potentially centripetal, integrative force[6] can be found elsewhere in its general provisions. The Charter is addressed to the EU and its institutions, writ large, and applies to the Member States only when 'they are implementing Union law'.[7] In so far as the Charter contains rights which correspond to those guaranteed by the ECHR, the meaning and scope of those rights shall be the same as those laid down by that Convention.[8] In the social sphere, the limited ambitions of the Charter and, consequently, its limited intended impact, can be seen most patently in the distinction drawn between rights, freedoms and principles. Article 52(5) of the Charter, which was introduced prior to the integration of the Charter into the since defunct draft constitutional Treaty, provides that

> the provisions of this Charter which contain principles may be implemented by legislative and executive acts taken by institutions, bodies, offices and agencies of the Union, and by acts of Member States when they are implementing Union law, in the exercise of their respective powers. They shall be judicially cognisable only in the interpretation of such acts and in the ruling on their legality.[9]

The insertion of this general provision was specifically intended to ensure that the socio-economic principles included, in the main, in the Solidarity Title of the Charter, could not be interpreted as establishing subjective rights with direct effect.[10] Article 52(5) of the Charter, as clearly expressed in the explanations

[4] Art 5(1) and (2) TEU provide that the limits of EU competence are governed by the principle of conferral pursuant to which the EU shall act only within the limits of the competence conferred upon it by the Member States in the Treaties to attain the objectives set out therein. Competences not conferred upon the EU in the Treaties remain with the Member States.

[5] Case C-400/10 PPU *McB*, judgment of 5 October 2010 nyr, para 51. See also Case C-161/11 *Vino*, order of 22 June 2011, paras 24–25, 37–38.

[6] See further K Lenaerts, 'Exploring the Limits of the EU Charter of Fundamental Rights', forthcoming in the *Irish Journal of European Law*.

[7] Art 51(1) Charter. For an overview of the narrow and broader constructions of this phrase see P Craig, 'The ECJ and *Ultra Vires* Action: A Conceptual Analysis' (2011) 48 *CML Rev* 395–437, 430 ff and H Kaila's chapter in this volume.

[8] Art 52(3) Charter, reflecting some of the terms of Art 6(3) TEU. See also Case C-256/11 *Dereci*, judgment of 15 November 2011 nyr, para 70.

[9] The distinction between rights and principles in Art 52(5) Charter is further emphasised in the reference in Art 51(1) Charter to rights, which must be respected, and principles, which must be observed.

[10] See, for example, Goldsmith, 'A Charter of Rights, Freedoms and Principles' (2001) 38 *CML Rev* 1201–16. For a discussion of the traditional distinction between different 'generations' of rights, according to which socio-economic rights are generally regarded as being positive (in that they require state expenditure for their realisation), programmatic (in that they merely express goals or objectives to be achieved) and non-justiciable, see TK Hervey and J Kenner (eds), *Economic and Social Rights under the EU Charter of Fundamental Rights – A Legal Perspective* (Oxford, Hart Publishing, 2003).

drawn up as interpretative guidance, sought to ensure that principles only give rise to rights to the extent that they are implemented by national law or, in the areas in which the EU enjoys competence, by EU law.

Given the terms of the Charter, particularly the general provisions in Articles 51 and 52, is it possible to contend that it will have much added value in the social and employment field?[11] This chapter seeks to tease out some of the issues which may prove of particular interest in coming years as the effects of the Charter on the scope and development of EU social and employment law come to be tested. If one examines the Court's case law on fundamental and social and employment rights to date – with reference to the Court's methods of interpretation, style, reasoning and the thrust of its decisions – it would appear unwise to discount the effects for EU social policy of the recognition in the Treaty of Lisbon that the Charter has the same legal status as the Treaties.

REFERENCES TO THE CHARTER WHEN ADOPTING SOCIAL AND EMPLOYMENT LEGISLATION

One of the first and most obvious consequences of the entry into force of the Treaty of Lisbon is the likelihood of more frequent references to the Charter both by the EU legislature when proposing and adopting legislation and by the Court of Justice when interpreting EU law.[12]

As regards the legislature, evidence of this can already be seen in numerous directives, including some in the social and employment field, adopted in recent years. In the general considerations of the revised Parental Leave Directive, adopted in 2010, reference is made to Articles 23 and 33 of the Charter which relate to equality between men and women and the need for reconciliation of professional, private and family life.[13] A similar reference is made by the Commission in its proposed amendment of the Pregnancy and Maternity Directive.[14] These provisions of the Charter do not of course provide a legal basis for the adoption of these directives and nor do they expand the scope of the EU to

[11] See also, in this respect, the Protocol on the Application of the Charter in the United Kingdom and Poland, discussed in the House of Lords, European Union Committee, *The Treaty of Lisbon: An Impact Assessment*, 10th Report of Session 2007–2008, vol 1, 101 ff which provides, inter alia, that nothing in Title IV of the Charter (Solidarity) creates justiciable rights applicable to these two Member States except in so far as those rights are provided for in their national laws. For the legal effects of the Protocol see Case C-411/10 *NS*, judgment of 21 December 2011 nyr, paras 118–22.

[12] The Commission indicated after the Charter was first proclaimed in 2000 that it would proceed as if the Charter had binding legal effect or would acquire such effect as part of the general principles jurisprudence of the Court, COM (2000) 644 final. Many directives predating the entry into force of the Treaty of Lisbon incorporated references to the Charter. See further C Ladenburger, 'L'application pratique de la Charte des droits fondamentaux par la Commission européenne' (2002) *Revue européenne de droit public* 817–39.

[13] Council Directive 2010/18/EU of 8 March 2010 implementing the revised Framework Agreement on parental leave concluded by BUSINESSEUROPE, UEAPME, CEEP and ETUC and repealing Directive 96/34/EC [2010] OJ L68/13.

[14] COM (2008) 600/4.

act beyond the powers already conferred and circumscribed by the Social Policy Title of the TFEU. It is Articles 153 and 154 TFEU which provide the necessary legal bases. Nevertheless, provisions of the Charter do furnish the Commission, when proposing legislation or the social partners when negotiating framework agreements and the Council and European Parliament when adopting those agreements and proposals in the form of directives, with a powerful basis with reference to which they can, indeed must, model and frame their different positions. Even if, as De Witte points out, the Charter admits no new EU *competences* in the social sphere, that may not, indeed in his view, cannot, mean that the EU's *policies* remain unaffected by it. When mainstreaming social policy or protection objectives, as the EU is required to do by Article 9 TFEU, the Charter may reorientate existing values and policies and infuse other new ones.[15]

The Commission's Communication on the Strategy for the Effective Implementation of the Charter of Fundamental Rights by the European Union is illustrative of this point.[16] The Commission makes clear that legislative proposals that have a particular link with fundamental rights must include specific recitals that explain how the proposals comply with the Charter. It indicates that the role of these recitals is to explain the reasoning behind the adoption of the act in question and so enable and facilitate judicial review of the conformity of the act with the Charter. A reference to the Charter in an EU directive is not without legal consequences. Having avoided citing the Charter for many years after it was proclaimed but before it was recognised as constituting, or being equivalent to, primary EU law,[17] the Court of Justice cited it for the first time in the case of *European Parliament* v *Council* on the right to family reunification of minor children of third country nationals.[18] It was presumably no coincidence that the Directive on Family Reunification made a clear reference to the Charter in its preamble.[19] As the Court's case law reveals, recitals of directives play a key role when it is forced, as it often is, to go beyond the literal wording of a provision and examine the overall system to which it belongs, the genesis of the norm and the teleology which supports it. The 1989 Social Charter, which lacked binding legal effect, proved to have legal consequences for the drafting and adoption of legislation as well as for its interpretation.[20]

[15] See B de Witte, 'The Trajectory of Fundamental Social Rights in the European Union' in G de Búrca and B de Witte (eds), *Social Rights in Europe* (Oxford, Oxford University Press, 2005) 153, 163, 165–66.

[16] COM (2010) 573 final.

[17] See Lenaerts, n 6 above.

[18] Case C-540/03 [2006] ECR I-5769, paras 38, 58. The Court of First Instance had preceded the Court by several years. See Case T-112/98 *Mannesmannröhren-Werke v Commission* [2001] ECR II-729.

[19] See the second recital of Council Directive 2003/86/EC of 22 September 2003 on the right to family reunification, [2003] OJ L251/12.

[20] See the discussion in J Kenner, 'Economic and Social Rights in the EU Legal Order: The Mirage of Indivisibility' in Hervey and Kenner, n 10 above, 1–25.

THE CHARTER, EU SOCIAL AND EMPLOYMENT LAW AND TELEOLOGICAL INTERPRETATION

To understand how the Charter may influence the Court's interpretation of EU social and employment law in the future, one need look no further than the trilogy of gender equality cases introduced in the 1970s by a Belgian air hostess, Gabrielle Defrenne. The decisions of the Court in those cases are widely regarded as having formed the cornerstones of EU social law. They established, on the one hand, that the principle prohibiting discrimination on grounds of gender in the field of pay is both horizontally and vertically directly effective and, on the other, that the elimination of this form of discrimination forms part of the fundamental rights and thus the general principles of EU law.[21] At the heart of the Court's reasoning in these cases was the teleological perspective which it adopted – the principle of equal pay was examined in the light of its nature, the aim it pursues and its place in the scheme of the EEC Treaty – and the social, and not merely economic, aims which the Court identified as underpinning the principle. These social aims were, according to the Court, evident in the Member States' commitment, to be found in the preamble of the EEC, to ensure social progress and seek the constant improvement of the living and working conditions of their peoples.[22]

Teleological interpretation and the dual social and economic underpinnings of the Treaties' commitment and obligations in the field of EU social policy have dominated the Court's case law in that field ever since. In *BECTU*, the Court held, with regard to the objective of the Working Time Directive and to its scheme, that paid annual leave of a minimum duration of four weeks constitutes a social right directly conferred by that directive on every worker as the minimum requirement necessary to ensure protection of his health and safety. Although the relevant provision of the Working Time Directive indicated that this right was granted 'in accordance with the conditions for entitlement to, and granting of, such leave laid down by national legislation and/or practice', the Court held that that expression must be construed as referring only to the arrangements for paid annual leave adopted in the various Member States. In other words, Member States could condition the exercise of the right to paid annual leave but not its existence.[23] In *Meerts*, on the Parental Leave Directive, the Court held that Clause 2.6 of the framework agreement annexed to that directive, which provides that rights acquired or in the process of being acquired by the worker on the date on which

[21] See Case 43/75 *Defrenne II* [1976] ECR 455, paras 24–40; Case C-149/77 *Defrenne III* [1978] ECR 1365, para 27.

[22] *Defrenne II*, n 21 above, para 10.

[23] Case C-173/99 *BECTU* [2001] ECR I-4881, paras 36, 47, 50, 53, interpreting Art 7(1) of the Working Time Directive (now Directive 2003/88 of 4 November 2003 concerning certain aspects of the organisation of working time, [2003] OJ L299/9). This decision may be of considerable significance when the Court comes to interpret the socio-economic rights and principles which feature in the Charter, many of which are hedged by a similar proviso relating to the conditions established by EU law and national laws and practice.

parental leave starts are to be maintained as they stand until the end of parental leave, articulates a particularly important principle of EU social law which cannot be interpreted restrictively.[24] In all of these cases, the Court attaches considerable importance to the recitals of the directives under examination, to any commitment to fundamental rights referred to therein, whether the source of that commitment is the Charter, the 1989 Social Charter, or the European Social Charter to which Article 151 TFEU makes direct reference. While the Court has stopped short of qualifying many of these social rights conferred by directives as fundamental rights, preferring instead the rather more ambiguous designation as 'particularly important principles of [EU] social law', the fact remains that their appearance in fundamental rights texts has influenced the manner in which the provision of EU secondary law which articulates or gives expression to the right is interpreted.

To suggest that the Charter will confirm, consolidate and even further reinforce this particular style or method of interpretation and legal reasoning in the social field is hardly surprising in the light of Article 6(1) TEU. The inclusion of a subject matter, whether in the form of a right or a principle, in the Charter, will of necessity influence the manner in which the Court will consider the precise content of the right or principle in question, its range of application and the weighing of conflicting interests. Consider, once again, the right to paid annual leave at issue in the *BECTU* case. At the time of that decision, the right in question was provided by a directive, decided by qualified majority, whose legal basis authorised the adoption of minimum requirement directives to encourage improvements, especially in the working environment, as regards the health and safety of workers.[25] While the EU's competence to regulate working time continues to be located in Article 153 TFEU and not in Article 31(2) of the Charter, the reference to a right to an annual period of paid leave in the Treaties themselves may clearly influence any future interpretation of that right; a right previously only found in secondary legislation, albeit legislation referring to social charters lacking binding legal effect.[26]

[24] Case C-116/08 *Meerts* [2009] ECR I-10063, paras 38–42.

[25] See the text of Article 118(a) and (b) EEC, inserted by the Single European Act. The legal basis for the adoption of legislation in this field can now be found in Art 153(2) TFEU or Art 153(4) TFEU, should the social partners decide to negotiate a framework agreement.

[26] See further A Rosas and H Kaila, 'L'application de la Charte des droits fondamentaux de l'Union européenne par la Cour de justice: un premier bilan' (2011) *Il Diritto dell'Unione Europea* 1, who detail the Court's increasing reference to the Charter as the point of departure for the analysis of respect for fundamental rights in the EU. In the field of social and employment law see, for example, Case C-323/08 *Rodrígeuz Mayor* [2009] ECR I-11621 (collective redundancy); Case C-555/07 *Kücükdeveci* [2010] ECR I-365; Joined Cases C-159/10 and C-160/10 *Fuchs and Köhler*, judgment of 21 July 2011 nyr; Case C-149/10 *Chatzi*, judgment of 16 September 2010 nyr (parental leave); Case C-232/09 *Danosa*, judgment of 11 November 2010 nyr (dismissal on grounds of pregnancy); Joined Cases C-444/09 and C-456/09 *Gavieiro Gavieiro and Iglesias Torres*, judgment of 22 December 2010 nyr (right to effective judicial protection for fixed term workers); Case C-243/09 *Fuß*, judgment of 14 October 2010 nyr (right to effective judicial protection in the context of the Working Time Directive); Cases C-20/10 and C-161/11 *Vino*, orders of 11 November 2010 and 22 June 2011, respectively, nyr (fixed term contracts); Case C-236/09 *Assocation Belge des Consommateurs Test-Achats*, judgment of 1 March 2011 nyr and Case C-104/10 *Kelly*, judgment of 21 July 2011 nyr (gender equality).

The balancing of social and economic objectives is inherent in almost all, if not all, EU social policy legislation. The Directive on the Transfer of Undertakings seeks to protect employees in the event of a change of employer but recognises that changes to the structures of undertakings through transfers of undertakings or businesses are mandated by economic trends at national and EU level. It authorises the dismissal of employees following the change of an employer where the dismissal is for economic, technical or organisational reasons.[27] The Working Time Directive speaks of the need to provide for flexibility in the application of certain provisions of the directive, whilst ensuring compliance with the principles of protecting the safety and health of workers.[28] In the Posted Workers Directive, the balance to be struck is even starker and the difficulties faced by the Court when striking that balance have become the stuff of EU legal legend. Recital 5 of Directive 1996/71 makes clear that the promotion of the transnational provision of services requires a climate of fair competition and measures guaranteeing respect for the rights of workers.[29] Given the terms of Articles 151 and 153 TFEU, this balancing act could be regarded as part of the DNA of EU social policy legislation. For, on the one hand, the relevant provisions of the TFEU indicate the need to both promote employment and improved living and working conditions, while, on the other, they identify the need to maintain the competitiveness of the EU's economy and avoid legislation which would impose administrative, financial and legal constraints in a way which would hold back the creation and development of small and medium-sized undertakings.[30]

The elevation of the Charter by the Treaty of Lisbon may serve not only to reinforce the teleological perspective of the Court in social and employment cases; it may also influence the identification of the objectives underpinning the legislation which the Court may subsequently be asked to interpret and the balancing of the objectives which, as outlined above, is part of the Court's daily bread in the interpretation of secondary legislation in the social and employment sphere.[31] When it comes to this balancing exercise it could be argued that the designation of a provision of the Charter as incorporating a right or a principle or the limiting effects of Article 52(5) of the Charter will be of little relevance. What will be important is whether the inclusion, albeit in broad and principled terms, of a social right in the Charter, will influence the balance struck between the social and

[27] See recitals 2 and 3 and Art 4(1) of Council Directive 2001/23/EC of 12 March 2001 on the approximation of the laws of the Member States relating to the safeguarding of employees' rights in the event of transfers of undertakings, businesses or parts of undertakings or businesses, [2001]OJ L82/16.

[28] Directive 2003/88, recital 15.

[29] Directive 96/71/EC of the European Parliament and of the Council of 16 December 1996 concerning the posting of workers in the framework of the provision of services, [1996] OJ L18/1. For the striking of the balance by the Court see Case C-341/05 *Laval* [2007] ECR I-11767; Case C-438/05 *International Transport Workers' Federation and Finnish Seamen's Union ('Viking Line')* [2007] ECR I-10779.

[30] See Arts 151, line 2, and 153(2)(b) TFEU.

[31] See the balancing of social and economic objectives, with the social at times trumping the economic, in case law on equal pay (Joined Cases C-270/97 and C-271/97 *Deutsche Post* [2000] ECR I-2267); the protection of the health and safety of workers (*BECTU*, n 23 above); the transfer of undertakings (Case C-51/00 *Temco Service Industries* [2002] ECR I-969); the insulation of collective bargaining from the provisions on competition (Case C-67/96 *Albany International* [1999] ECR I-5751).

the economic, between, for example, the need for worker protection and the need for greater flexibility.[32] Derogations and opt-outs, which are often numerous in social and employment legislation and whose inclusion reflects the compromises inherent in the quest for a qualified majority, might be viewed in a different and perhaps stricter light if the right from which they derogate has been included in the Charter as a fundamental right to which the EU adheres. The type of balance struck in the *Laval* and *Viking* cases might be a good illustration of the point. In those decisions, the Court was famously required to balance the economic fundamental freedoms guaranteed by the Treaty in the context of the internal market with the right, characterised by the Court for the first time as a fundamental right to be respected by EU law, to engage in collective strike action for the protection of workers' rights.[33] Academic literature widely regards the Court as having struck a balance which favoured the former freedoms over the latter fundamental right.[34] In *Laval*, the Posted Workers Directive which the Court was interpreting was a piece of internal market legislation, adopted on the basis of Articles 57(2) and 66 EEC.[35] One can only surmise whether the adoption of that legislation on a dual internal market and social policy legal basis, relying also, for example, on Article 153(2) TFEU and referring to Articles 12 and 28 of the Charter, would or could have influenced the Court's reasoning.[36] Similarly, one can only wonder whether the Charter, following the Treaty of Lisbon, would require the Court to reassess its application of the principle of proportionality in those cases, allowing the trade unions to rely on their fundamental right to collective action as a sword and not

[32] See, in this regard, J Hunt, 'Fair and Just Working Conditions' in Hervey and Kenner, n 10 above, 45; AJ Menéndez, 'Chartering Europe: Legal Status and Policy Implications of the Charter of Fundamental Rights of the European Union' (2002) *Journal of Common Market Studies* 471, to the effect that the Charter could herald and concretise a shift in the normative underpinnings of the EU as a polity.

[33] See the identification of the economic and social objectives at stake in *Laval*, n 29 above, paras 58, 74–77. It could be argued that the *Laval* decision, like other decisions on the free provision of services and the posting of workers, contains an unresolved contradiction between whether the objective pursued is that of protecting the interests of posted workers (see paras 57, 76–77) or of workers generally (paras 102, 103, 106–07). See also Joined Cases C-49/98, C-50/98, C-52 to 54/98 and C-68 to 71/98 *Finalarte Sociedade de Construção Civil Lda* [2001] ECR I-7831, paras 33, 58, 69, 72 (protection of workers) and paras 41–42, 49–50 (protection of posted workers). The interests of the two groups do not necessarily coincide as P Davies explains in his article on the Posted Workers Directive and the Court's case law on the free provision of services – 'Posted Workers: Single Market or Protection of National Labour Law Systems' (1997) 34 *CML Rev* 571–602.

[34] See the various contributions to the special edition of (2007–2008) 10 *Cambridge Yearbook of European Legal Studies*; C Kilpatrick, 'The ECJ and Labour Law: A 2008 Retrospective' (2009) 38 *Industrial Law Journal* 180–208, 194–202; J Malmberg and T Sigeman, 'Industrial Actions and EU Economic Freedoms: The Autonomous Collective Bargaining Model Curtailed by the European Court of Justice' (2008) 45 *CML Rev* 1115–46. *cf* the more nuanced approach of A Rosas, 'Finis Europae socialis?' in *Chemins d'Europe: mélanges en l'honneur de Jean-Paul Jacqué* (Paris, Dalloz, 2010) 591, and the prescient article of Davies, n 33 above.

[35] Now, albeit amended and reordered, Arts 50(1) and 62 TFEU.

[36] In March 2012, the Commission adopted a proposal for a council regulation on the exercise of the right to collective action within the context of the freedom of establishment and the freedom to provide services, com (2012) 130 final. The proposed legal basis is Article 352 TFEU. See the resolution of the ETUC calling for revision of the Posted Workers Directive and, in particular, a broader social policy legal basis and restoration of the directive as providing for a minimum floor of rights rather than a maximum ceiling (www.etuc.org).

just a shield.[37] In *Santos Palhota*, a case on posted workers postdating *Laval*, Advocate General Cruz Villalón maintained that, given the status of the Charter following the entry into force of the Treaty of Lisbon, insofar as the protection of workers is a matter which warrants protection under the Treaties themselves, it is not a simple derogation from a freedom, still less an unwritten exception inferred from the Court's case law and it cannot, as such, be interpreted strictly.[38]

The *Test-Achats* case on the Directive on Equal Access to Goods and Services is also a recent example of how the Charter can show it has teeth. That directive expressly referred in its recitals to the principle of equality enumerated in the Charter in Articles 21 and 23. The Court thus assessed the validity of the impugned provision of the directive in the light of those articles. Since the provision in question permitted Member States to derogate from the principle of equality indefinitely, the Court concluded that it worked against the achievement of the objective which it was the purpose of the directive to achieve and was thus incompatible with Articles 21 and 23 of the Charter.[39] The difficulty for the Court in the future may be that, as Hunt points out, while the Charter provides space for a more robust protection and promotion of social rights, now that both economic and social rights are regarded as fundamental, there is little if anything in the Charter to guide the Court in balancing these rights.[40]

THE CHARTER, THE EU LEGISLATURE AND THE EFFECTS OF ARTICLE 53

Article 53 of the Charter provides that

> Nothing in this Charter shall be interpreted as restricting or adversely affecting human rights and fundamental freedoms as recognised, in their respective fields of application, by EU law and international law and by international agreements to which the Union or all the Member States are party, including the [ECHR], and by Member States' constitutions.

The nature and effect of this provision is, as yet, unclear.[41] One question which could be asked is the possible effect of this provision on the social and employment legislation adopted by the EU legislature.

[37] For criticism of this aspect of the Court's decisions in *Laval* and *Viking*, see, for example, ACL Davies, 'One Step Forward, Two Steps Back? The *Viking* and *Laval* cases in the ECJ' (2008) 37 *Industrial Law Journal* 126–49.

[38] Opinion of AG Cruz Villalón in Case C-515/08 *Santos Palhota*, paras 51–52.

[39] *Test-Achats*, n 26 above, paras 17, 31–32. This decision could be regarded not just as an example of the coming of age of the Charter but as the coming of age of EU equality law generally. In *Deutsche Post*, n 31 above, paras 56–57, the Court held that, in view of the designation of the right not to be discriminated against on grounds of gender as a fundamental human right, the social aim pursued by Art 157 TFEU (ex 119 EEC) had to be given preference. Despite this relegation of the provision's economic aim, many commentators had lamented the Court's failure to match its actions to its words in subsequent cases. See, for example, E Ellis, 'The Recent Jurisprudence of the Court of Justice in the Field of Sex Equality' (2000) 37 *CML Rev* 1403–26.

[40] See Hunt in Hervey and Kenner, n 10 above, 65.

[41] The nature and effect of Art 53 is the subject of a reference from the Spanish Constitutional Court in Case C-399/11 *Melloni* [2011] OJ C290/5.

The Working Time Directive provides, once again, a good example of what may be at stake. Adopted in 1993, the Directive defined working time as 'any period during which the worker is working, at the employer's disposal and carrying out his activity or duties, in accordance with national laws and/or practice'.[42] The Court of Justice has held that the concept of working time must be given an autonomous EU interpretation in order to secure the full efficacy of the Directive and secure uniform application of that concept in all the Member States. On-call duty performed by a worker where he is required to be physically present on the employer's premises must be regarded in its entirety as working time within the meaning of the Working Time Directive, regardless of the work actually done by the person concerned during that on-call duty and regardless of whether the employer makes available a rest room where the employee may rest when not actively providing his services.[43] This interpretation has had significant consequences for the organisation of, in particular, the emergency services. If all on-call time spent at the employer's disposal qualifies as working time, the maximum weekly working time of 48 hours established by the directive as the generally applicable rule is fast exceeded. As a consequence, the Court's judgments on the definition of working time were met with consternation in several Member States which had previously distinguished between active and inactive on-call time.[44] Several sought, at least for certain sectors, to opt out of the 48 hour weekly working time rule. In 2004, the Commission proposed the amendment of the Working Time Directive, introducing separate definitions of on-call time (that period during which a worker must be available to work, if required to do so by his/her employer) and inactive on-call time (when a worker who is on call is not actually carrying out his duties). It was proposed that only the former would now be regarded as working time.[45] The European Parliament and Council failed to reach agreement on this and other proposed amendments and, despite recourse to the conciliation procedure, the proposal had to be abandoned with the result that the 2003 version of the directive, and the Court's interpretation thereof, remain in force. The amendment procedure demonstrated the existence of real disagreement between certain Member States as regards the definition of working time and the importance to be attributed to the protection of the health and safety of workers.

Prior to the recognition of the equal legal status of the Charter one could argue that the EU legislature could, without legal difficulties, amend a provision of secondary law adopted on the basis of Article 153 TFEU, even if the effect of that amendment was to overrule a decision of the Court of Justice interpreting that secondary legislation (in this instance the judgments on the definition of working

[42] Art 2(1) of Directive 93/104 (now Art 2(1) of Directive 2003/88).

[43] See Case C-303/98 *SIMAP* [2000] ECR I-7963; Case C-151/02 *Jaeger* [2003] ECR I-8389.

[44] For an idea of the alleged costs entailed by this definition of working time see para 44 of the Opinion of AG Ruiz Jarabo Colomer in *Jaeger*, n 43 above. See also the discussion in the British Medical Journal of how working time restrictions may affect the training of surgeons and doctors reported in *The Daily Telegraph*, 6 November 2009.

[45] COM (2004) 607 final.

time in *SIMAP* and *Jaeger*). The competence to adopt legislation in this field lies, by virtue of this provision of the Treaty, with the EU legislature and, in certain circumstances, the social partners at EU level. Consequently, the competence to amend the same legislation also appertains to those bodies. However, one might now wonder what the effect could be of Article 6(1) TEU (recognition of equal legal value for the Charter) combined with Articles 31 (fair and just working conditions including the right to a limitation of maximum working hours) and 53 (a possible standstill clause). Do these provisions render more difficult the amendment of a directive which constitutes the specific recognition or implementation of a right affirmed in the Charter? Does it make any difference in this respect that the Court in *Jaeger* regarded its definition of working time as 'the *only* interpretation which accords with the objective of [the D]irective which is to secure effective protection of the safety and health of employees by allowing them to enjoy minimum periods of rest'?[46] Of course it is the sovereign right of the EU legislature also to amend the objectives pursued by the Working Time Directive or indeed any other piece of social policy legislation. The exercise of this competence is subject, however, to respect for the requirements of EU primary law, including, since the Treaty of Lisbon, the Charter.[47] In the first phase of the new consultation procedure initiated by the Commission following the failure to amend the Working Time Directive, the Commission appears to be proposing such a reassessment. It focuses heavily in its communication on the need to reassess the directive in the light of fundamental changes that have taken place in working patterns since it was originally conceived and of the prospective needs of workers, businesses and consumers in the twenty-first century.[48] It recognises that while the regulation of working time has traditionally pursued health and safety objectives, the time has come to examine whether regulation in the EU has kept pace with developments in the workplace according to which working time is also regarded as a crucial element of, inter alia, improving productivity and enhancing competitiveness. However, again, one might ask to what extent the leeway of the EU legislature may be affected, even circumscribed, by the reference in the Charter to a right to limitation of maximum working hours, daily and weekly rest periods and paid annual leave. In the Charter, these 'rights' are located squarely within a provision on the establishment of fair and just working conditions which respect workers' health, safety and dignity. They make no reference to competitiveness, productivity or flexibility. Given that the Working Time Directive which was the subject of cases like *SIMAP* and *Jaeger* established the minimum floor of rights in this field, is it possible, where those rights are now reflected, albeit in broad terms, in the Charter, to lower the floor? The decision in *Test-Achats* could suggest different possible answers to this question. On the one hand, the Court indicated, unequivocally, that it is the EU legislature which, in the light of the tasks conferred on the EU by the TFEU, determines when it will take action in any given

[46] *Jaeger*, n 43 above, para 70.
[47] See, in this regard, *Test-Achats*, n 26 above, para 17.
[48] COM (2010) 106 final.

field. In taking that decision, the legislature must have due regard 'to the development of economic and social conditions within the EU', suggesting that a reorientation of the objectives pursued by the legislation in question may be warranted depending on those conditions. On the other hand, the Court emphasised that 'when [legislative] action is decided upon, it must contribute, in a coherent manner, to the achievement of the intended objective . . .'.[49]

THE CHARTER AND EU COMPETENCE IN THE SOCIAL AND EMPLOYMENT SPHERE

As pointed out previously, the Charter very clearly states that it does not extend the field of application of EU law beyond the powers of the EU or establish any new power or task for the Union. The limits of EU competence are governed by the principle of conferral. Article 4 TFEU sets out the areas of competence shared between the EU and the Member States, of which social policy is one. Unlike any other area of shared competence, Article 4(2)(b) TFEU explicitly states that social policy is an area of shared competence 'for the aspects defined in this Treaty'. Both this provision of the TFEU and the general provisions of the Charter which seek to circumscribe its effects as regards socio-economic principles reflect a concern by Member States that the scope of EU social policy remains within clear and defined limits.[50] Despite this concern, it cannot be excluded, if one examines samples of the Court's existing case law, that the definition and delimitation of the field of EU social and employment law might be influenced by the existence of the Charter generally and/or by specific provisions thereof.

In the case of *P v S*, the applicant, a teacher working for Cornwall County Council, claimed that her dismissal, due to the fact that she was undergoing gender reassignment, was contrary to EU gender equality legislation.[51] There was, at that time, no express reference to transsexuals in the EU directives regulating the principles of equal pay and equal treatment for male and female workers. The case turned, therefore, on whether the applicant's discrimination claim could be accommodated within the scope of application of existing EU gender equality law. The sequence of the Court's reasoning in the case is instructive. It recalled that the Equal Treatment Directive was but the expression, in a particular field, of the principle of equality, which is one of the fundamental principles of EU law and that the right not to be discriminated against on grounds of gender is one of

[49] *Test-Achats*, n 26 above, paras 20–21.

[50] See, for similar express limits to EU competence in this field, the prohibitions of discrimination in Arts 18 and 19 TFEU or the clear statement in Art 3(1) of Directive 2000/78, adopted on the basis of the latter provision, that the Directive applies '[w]ithin the limits of the areas of competence conferred on the [EU], this Directive shall apply to all persons, as regards both the public and private sectors, including public bodies . . .'.

[51] Art 5 of Directive 76/207 prohibited direct and indirect discrimination as regards conditions governing dismissal.

the fundamental human rights whose observance the Court has a duty to ensure.[52] In answer to the pivotal question raised by the case – whether discrimination on grounds of gender within the meaning of EU law extended to discrimination on grounds of gender reassignment – the Court's answer was brief:

> the scope of the [Equal Treatment Directive] cannot be confined simply to discrimination based on the fact that a person is of one or other gender. In view of its purpose and the nature of the rights which it seeks to safeguard, the scope of the directive is also such as to apply to discrimination arising, as in this case, from the gender reassignment of the person concerned.[53]

In the words of the Court, to tolerate discrimination based on gender assignment would be tantamount to a failure to respect the dignity and freedom to which he or she is entitled, and which the Court has a duty to safeguard. This language, reminiscent of that found in the case law of the Strasbourg court, was less familiar in the context of the EU, where the extent of the Court's duty to observe fundamental rights had been clearly and somewhat strictly circumscribed in its case law.[54] In *P v S*, the Court appeared to rely on the need to respect fundamental rights when determining the scope of application of EU gender equality law, rather than determining as a preliminary issue the scope of application of EU gender equality law, confirming whether or not the situation of the applicant came within that scope and thereafter verifying whether fundamental rights had, in that context, been respected.[55]

It should be stressed that in a subsequent sexual orientation discrimination case, where the applicant was also seeking to fit her own discrimination claim within the boundaries of the same EU gender equality legislation, the Court quickly reverted to its more orthodox position on the protection of fundamental rights within the scope of application of EU law.[56] However, *P v S*, albeit one of the most forcible examples of the possible influence of fundamental rights and general principles on the Court's definition of the scope of application of EU law, is not necessarily an isolated case. Strains of its melody can still be heard, even if indistinctly, in more recent cases in the social field.[57] Furthermore, like *P v S*, decisions in other areas of EU law serve to underline the inchoate nature of 'the scope

[52] Case C-13/94 *P v S* [1996] ECR I-2143, paras 18–19.

[53] ibid, para 20.

[54] See, for example, Case C-299/95 *Kremzow* [1997] ECR I-2629, para 15: '... where national legislation falls within the field of application of [EU] law, the Court ... must give the national court all the guidance as to interpretation necessary to enable it to assess the compatibility of that legislation with fundamental rights – as laid down in particular in the [ECHR] – whose observance the Court ensures. However, the Court has no such jurisdiction with regard to national legislation lying outside the scope of [EU] law'.

[55] See further C Barnard, 'P v S: Kite-flying or New Constitutional Approach?' in A Dashwood and S O'Leary (eds), *The Principle of Equal Treatment in EC Law* (London, Sweet & Maxwell, 1997) 59.

[56] See Case C-249/96 *Grant* [1998] ECR I-621, para 45: '... although respect for the fundamental rights which form an integral part of those general principles of law is a condition of the legality of [Union] acts, those rights cannot in themselves have the effect of extending the scope of the Treaty provisions beyond the competences of the [EU]'.

[57] See Case C-144/04 *Mangold* [2005] ECR I-9981; Case C-555/07 *Kücükdeveci*, n 26 above.

of application of EU law'. In the context of the Court's case law on Union citizenship – a status introduced by the Maastricht Treaty whose meaning and effects have been the subject of extensive litigation since the mid-1990s – the definition of the scope of application of EU law has been of fundamental importance as regards application of the prohibition of discrimination on grounds of nationality in Article 18 TFEU. The Court has repeatedly stated that Union citizenship 'is not intended to extend the scope *ratione materiae* of the Treaty also to internal situations which have no link with Community law'.[58] Nevertheless, two strands of jurisprudence could be cited to call into question the completeness of this statement. On the one hand, the Court seems to have breached or slightly altered the purely internal rule – according to which EU citizenship and free movement law do not apply where there is no factor linking a case with any of the situations governed by EU law and/or all of the elements of the case are purely internal to a single Member State – in certain circumstances. In *Rottmann* and *Ruiz Zambrano* it has indicated that Article 20 TFEU will preclude national measures which, even in situations which appear to be *prima facie* purely internal to one Member State, have the effect of depriving Union citizens of the genuine enjoyment of the substance of the rights conferred by their status as Union citizens.[59] On the other hand, in a line of cases concerning the entitlement of Union citizens to social benefits on an equal basis with the nationals of the Member State which hosts them, the Court has relied on the introduction of the status of Union citizenship to overturn previous decisions which had limited the extent to which economically inactive Member State nationals were entitled to equal treatment as regards unemployment benefit or student maintenance grants in Member States in which they reside but do not work and of which they are not nationals.[60] In those cases, the Court framed its revision of its prior case law in terms of 'the establishment of citizenship of the Union and the interpretation in the case law of the right to equal treatment enjoyed by citizens of the Union'.[61]

These cases demonstrate that what corresponds to the field or scope of application of EU law is more fluid than might at first sight appear to be the case. The Court will examine whether a case comes within the scope of application of EU

[58] Joined Cases 64/96 and C-65/96 *Uecker and Jacquet* [1997] ECR I-3171. Recently reiterated by the Grand Chamber in Case C-212/06 *Flemish Welfare Aid* [2008] ECR I-1683, paras 38–39; Case C-127/08 *Metock* [2008] ECR I-6241, paras 77–78.

[59] See Cases C-135/08 *Rottmann* [2010] ECR I-1449; C-34/09 *Ruiz Zambrano*, judgment of 8 March 2011 nyr. Discussed further in S O'Leary, 'The Past, Present and Future of the Purely Internal Rule in EU Law' (2010) *Irish Jurist* 13–46. See also the recent decision of the Court in Case C-434/09, *McCarthy*, judgment of 5 May 2011 nyr, in which the Court appears to revert to the standard formulation and consequences of the purely internal rule in the case of a British/Irish dual national who had always resided in the UK. While *Rottmann* and *Ruiz Zambrano* were decided with reference to Art 20 TFEU and concentrated on the *status* of EU citizenship, *McCarthy* turned on the interpretation of Art 21 TFEU, a provision which may mandate prior *movement*. See further the chapters by K Lenaerts and P Mengozzi in this volume.

[60] See, eg Cases C-138/02 *Collins* [2004] ECR I-2703 (equal treatment and entitlement of job-seeking Union citizens to employment benefit); C-209/03 *Bidar* [2005] ECR I-2119 (equal treatment and the entitlement of Union citizen/students to maintenance grants and study loans).

[61] *Collins*, n 60 above, para 63.

law and, in this regard, will look for the existence of some sort of link or point of attachment with that law. In the social and employment sphere, where the EU has enjoyed only limited competence when it comes to the adoption of legislation providing for substantive, as distinct from procedural, rights, the establishment of that link or attachment may have far-reaching consequences. With a proliferation of equality legislation now adopted at EU level,[62] the nature of the relevant attachment with EU law in the employment sphere can be varied and indeed tenuous. In *Mangold*, for example, a case principally about age discrimination, the national court sought an interpretation of Directive 2000/78 in relation to facts which took place at a time when that Directive had not yet been transposed into national law. This did not deter the Court from regarding the case as coming within the scope of application of EU law and therefore subject to the general principle of equality (Directive 2000/78 being but a specific expression of that principle), albeit its decision to do so proved controversial. The necessary link with the scope of application of EU law in *Mangold* was furnished by the fact that the national judge had also raised a question concerning the lawfulness of the fixed term contract concluded with the applicant employee in that case in the light of the provisions of the Directive on Fixed Term Work.[63]

The *Kükükdeveci* case further demonstrates the expanding scope of EU law, specifically EU social and employment law, and thus the expanding potential for application of the Charter. At issue in *Kükükdeveci* was national legislation which distinguished, on the basis of age, between different workers as regards calculation of the notice period for dismissal. Unfair dismissal legislation remains, in the main, a matter for national law. The EU legislature may adopt legislation relating to the protection of workers where their employment contracts are terminated but such legislation is subject to unanimity in Council and the European

[62] See Directive 2000/43/EC implementing the principle of equal treatment between persons irrespective of racial or ethnic origin, [2000] OJ L180/22; Directive 2000/78/EC implementing a general framework for equal treatment in employment and occupation, [2000] OJ L303/16; Directive 2004/113 of 13 December 2004 implementing the principle of equal treatment between men and women in the access to and supply of goods and services, [2004] OJ L373/37, which were adopted on the basis of Art 19 TFEU. See also Directive 2006/54 of 5 July 2006 on the implementation of the principle of equal opportunities and equal treatment of men and women in matters of employment and occupation (recast), [2006] OJ L204/23; Directive 2010/41 of 7 July 2010 on the application of the principle of equal treatment between men and women engaged in an activity in a self-employed capacity and repealing Council Directive 86/613/EEC, [2010] OJ L180/1, which were adopted on the basis of Art 157(3) TFEU (ex Art 141(3) EC). Only the Race Directive and the Directive on Equal Access to Goods and Services extend beyond the employment field.

[63] Contrast the decision in *Mangold*, n 57 above, with that in Case C-427/06 *Bartsch* [2008] ECR I-7245. In the latter case, the applicant relied only on Directive 2000/78 and the Court thus concluded that, prior to the transposition of that directive into national law, her case could not succeed. Had she claimed indirect gender discrimination and not just age discrimination, her case would arguably have fallen within the scope of EU law and thus been subject to the general principle applied in *Mangold*. A closer examination of the latter decision suggests that the establishment of the necessary link in that case could also be open to question. The assertion in para 75 of *Mangold* that the impugned German law was a measure implementing the Fixed Term Workers Directive seems to conflict with the preliminary conclusion at paras 52–53 that that legislation was not mandated by the implementation of the framework agreement annexed to the directive.

Parliament is excluded from the procedure as co-legislator.[64] Directives on insolvency and redundancy have touched on the edges of this area of national law, providing, in the main, procedural guarantees rather than far-reaching substantive protection.[65] However, the material scope of application of Directive 2000/78 is very broadly defined in Article 3. Like most of the other equality directives listed above, it covers conditions for access to employment, to self-employment or to occupation, including selection criteria and recruitment conditions and promotion; access to all types and to all levels of vocational guidance, vocational training, advanced vocational training and retraining, including practical work experience; employment and working conditions, including dismissals and pay, and membership of, and involvement in, an organisation of workers or employers, or any organisation whose members carry on a particular profession, including the benefits provided for by such organisations. The national provision at issue in *Kücükdeveci* affected the conditions of dismissal of employees and, as such, came within the scope of application of the Directive and thus the general EU principle of equality. Thus, despite the limits to EU competence in the employment law field, the constitutional and horizontal principle of equality, identified in *Kükükdeveci* as having its origins, inter alia, in the Charter, can reach into the farthest corners of national employment legislation.

The application of Directive 2000/78 (as distinct from the issue of the enforceability of the applicant's rights in a horizontal situation) was relatively clear-cut in *Kükükdeveci.* In other cases, the necessary attachment with EU law which might bring a case within its scope of application may be less clear or non-existent.[66] In such cases, the Court may declare itself manifestly incompetent by way of order and, as such, decline to answer the questions referred. However, the dividing line between a case with no connecting factor which is disposed of summarily in this manner and a case raising fundamentally important questions of EU law destined for the Grand Chamber is often less straightforward than Court watchers might suspect.

This is not to suggest that the type of reasoning one sees in *P v S* or *Ruiz Zambrano* will become more prevalent with the entry into force and recognition of the Charter. However, neither is it likely to disappear. The extent and nature of the competences of the EU in the social and employment sphere are at the heart of many, if not most, of the litigation which has made its way to the Court over the years. While in some cases the debate is covert, hidden in arguments about the extent of Member States' margin of manoeuvre when implementing directives,[67] in others it is overt and unembellished. The annulment action brought by the United Kingdom against the Working Time Directive was all about who was competent, to what extent and on what basis to regulate the organisation of

[64] Arts 153(1) and (2) TFEU.

[65] See, for example, Directive 98/59 ([1998] OJ L225/16) on collective redundancies and Directive 2002/74 ([2002] OJ L270/10) on workers' rights in the event of insolvency.

[66] In the employment sphere see, for example, Case C-217/08 *Mariano* [2009] ECR I-35; C-333/09 *Noël* [2009] ECR I-205.

[67] See, for example, *BECTU*, n 23 above, on the conditions attached by UK legislation to the right to paid annual leave.

working time.[68] Given the provisions of the Charter and the values and objectives of the EU as expressed in the opening provisions of the TEU, a question now worth reflecting on is the potential effect of the Charter on the Court's view of EU competence in the social and employment sphere and its identification in individual cases of the necessary links or attachment with EU law? This question is but a subset of the larger debate, to which the provisions of the TEU and TFEU on the principle of conferral relate, about the limits to EU competence and Member State's continued autonomy in certain fields.[69] As Craig emphasises, the 'fit' between the injunctions in the TEU and TFEU regarding the limits of EU competences and the substantive provisions of the Charter is sometimes far from perfect. The Court will be drawn inexorably to resolving the difficulties to which this imperfect fit gives rise.[70]

WHAT'S IN A NAME? RIGHTS, FREEDOMS AND PRINCIPLES

As indicated previously, the Member States provided, in Article 52(5) of the Charter, that provisions which contain principles are only justiciable when they have been implemented by EU legislative and executive acts and by acts of the Member States when they are implementing EU law. The purpose of this general provision, added in 2007 when the Charter was to be integrated into the draft Constitutional Treaty, was to ensure that certain rights or principles listed in the Charter, particularly socio-economic ones, perhaps requiring positive action and expenditure on the part of Member States, were not transformed into directly effective fundamental rights.

The problem of course is that the Charter does not distinguish clearly between rights, freedoms and principles.[71] As the explanations relating to the Charter indicate, some provisions may contain elements of both a right and a principle. Furthermore, in the social and employment field, where the distinction between rights and principles may be of particular importance given the provisions of the Solidarity Title, the interpretative challenge which this distinction may pose for the Court of Justice in years to come is not helped by the Court's use of similar or related terminology in its case law in the past. In *Defrenne II*, the Member States had argued that use of the term 'principle' in Article 119 EEC highlighted the programmatic nature of this provision and precluded the Court from deducing any subjective, directly effective, right. The Court came to the opposite conclusion, concluding: 'in the language of the Treaty, [the term principle] is specifically used

[68] Case C-84/94 *United Kingdom* v *Council* [1996] ECR I-5755.

[69] See further Editorial Comments, 'The Scope of Application of the General Principles of Union Law: an Ever Expanding Union?' (2010) 47 *CML Rev* 1589–96; S Prechal, 'Competence Creep and the General Principles of Law' (2010) 3 *Review of European Administrative Law* 5–22.

[70] See Craig, n 7 above, 429.

[71] See further G De Búrca, 'Fundamental Rights and Citizenship' in B de Witte (eds), *Ten Reflections on the Constitutional Treaty for Europe* (Florence, European University Institute, 2003) 11 at 22–25.

in order to indicate the fundamental nature of certain provisions'.[72] This stance is borne out in more recent social and employment decisions, where the Court has designated certain rights conferred by directives in this field as 'particularly important principles of EU social law'.[73] To confuse matters further, the principles in question appeared, in the main, to enjoy direct effect.

Apart from the distinction drawn in the general provisions of the Charter between rights and principles, the Court will have to clarify how the Charter fits within its existing jurisprudence on fundamental rights and general principles. Article 6 TEU not only recognises the Charter as being of equal legal value, it also reiterates the EU's *acquis* on the protection of fundamental rights as guaranteed by the ECHR and as they result from the constitutional traditions common to the Member States. The latter shall constitute general principles of EU law.[74] Since the Charter enumerates rights which are now, within the EU, to be considered fundamental, can that mean that all the Charter provisions encapsulate general principles? The answer to this simple, indeed simplistic, question must be no. Adapting the words of the Court in its *Audiolux* decision, in which it rejected the existence of a general principle for the protection of minority shareholders, many of the Charter's provisions do not possess the general, comprehensive character which is naturally inherent in general principles of law which, moreover, in the words of the Court, have a constitutional status.[75] This question is an important one since, as the Court held in *Kükükdeveci*, when a directive gives specific expression to, but does not lay down, a general principle of EU law, a national court, even in a dispute between two individuals, must disapply a national provision falling within the scope of EU law which it considers to be incompatible with that principle and which cannot be interpreted in conformity with that principle.[76]

In a recent case before the Court – *Dominguez* – it was asked precisely what are, following the entry into force of the Treaty of Lisbon, the consequences of the Charter (and its *Kücükdeveci* judgment) for social and employment rights.[77] Given the provisions of the Solidarity Title and the existence of directives which give specific expression to some of those provisions, when, where and how will the reasoning behind *Kücükdeveci* apply? At issue in *Dominguez* was the right to paid

[72] *Defrenne II*, n 21 above, para 28.

[73] See *BECTU*, n 23 above, para 43; Joined Cases C-350/06 and C-520/06 *Schultz-Hoff* [2009] ECR I-179, para 22 (right to paid annual leave in Art 7(1) of the Working Time Directive); Case C-307/05 *Del Cerro Alonso* [2007] ECR I-7109, para 38; Case C-268/06 *Impact* [2008] ECR I-2483, para 114; *Gavieiro Gavieiro and Iglesias Torres*, n 26 above, para 49 (right of fixed term workers not to be discriminated against in clause 4 of the Fixed Term Workers Directive); *Meerts* n 24 above, para 26 (the right to maintain rights acquired or in the process of being acquired pursuant to Clause 2.6 of the Parental Leave Directive).

[74] Article 6(3) TEU.

[75] Case C-101/08 *Audiolux ea* [2009] ECR I-9823, paras 42, 50, 63. See also *Vino*, n 5 above, para 39, on the distinction between a principle and a general principle.

[76] *Kücükdeveci*, n 26 above, paras 50–54 and the discussion of general principles of EU law in K Lenaerts and JA Gutierrez-Fons, 'The Constitutional Allocation of Powers and the General Principles of EU Law' (2010) 47 *CML Rev* 1629.

[77] Case C-282/10 *Dominguez*, judgment of 24 January 2012 nyr.

annual leave in Article 7(1) of the Working Time Directive, the provision first interpreted in *BECTU*. A general but undetailed reference to the right to paid annual leave is contained in Article 31(2) of the Charter. The applicant wished to enforce her right – described by the Court to date as a particularly important principle of EU social law – against her private sector employer. Does a particularly important principle of EU social law constitute a general principle within the meaning of the *Kücükdeveci* judgment? Is the Working Time Directive the specific expression of a general principle whose foundation can be found in Article 31 of the Charter? In the event, the Court effectively limited itself to the absence of horizontal direct effect of directives and shied away from discussing the Charter. Regardless of the outcome of the case, however what *Dominguez* does demonstrate is that although the type of dispute in the field of EU social and employment law may remain the same following the entry into force of the Treaty of Lisbon, the terms of those disputes have irrevocably altered due, in the main, to the Charter.

CONCLUSION

It will take time, patience and, no doubt, trial and error, to establish the overall effects of the entry into force of the Treaty of Lisbon and the recognition of the equal legal status of the Charter for EU social and employment law. Claims such as those made in national debates on the ratification of the draft constitutional treaty to the effect that that document, which incorporated the Charter, would have little or no effect on this sphere of EU law, should nevertheless be questioned. EU social and employment law is a curious and quite unique area of shared competence which requires the EU legislature and, consequently, the Court, to engage in a constant balancing of economic and social objectives. This is a delicate exercise and one which does not always produce easily reconciled or harmonious results. Nevertheless, a review of the Court's case law in this field reveals that, for all the cacophony, there is a certain recurring harmony, even a melody, in its social and employment jurisprudence. This can be witnessed, in particular, in the fact and the manner of the Court's recurring examination of the teleology of EU law in this field. For all the questions raised by this chapter – and there are many more questions raised than answers provided – it seems inevitable that the entry into force of the Treaty of Lisbon and the new status accorded the Charter will shape EU social and employment law in years to come. The extent of their influence is likely to be determined not by distinctions between rights and principles or between commonplace principles and general principles of a higher pedigree. Instead, we should look to whether the Charter will modify or affect the overall framework within which the EU legislature, and its component parts, define policies and objectives and exercise competence in the social and employment field and whether the Court will, in turn, when adjudicating the disputes which come before it – disputes inevitably constructed in terms of the Charter as primary law – recognise the altered framework.

22

How is the EU Concept of Discrimination Implemented and Applied in Sweden?

ANNA FALK*

INTRODUCTION

THE AIM OF this contribution is to illustrate how the EU principle of equality as expressed and fleshed out by the prohibition of discrimination in secondary EU law, in particular Directive 2000/43/EC,[1] Directive 2000/78/EC,[2] Directive 2004/113/EC[3] and Directive 2006/54/EC,[4] has been implemented and applied in Sweden, paying particular attention to the more recent prohibition of age discrimination.

The area of anti-discrimination law has known important developments through the judgments of the ECJ during the mandate of Judge Pernilla Lindh. She has been judge rapporteur in several important cases decided by the Grand Chamber, in particular in the area of age discrimination such as *Kücükdeveci*,[5] *Wolf*,[6] *Petersen*,[7] *Andersen*,[8] *Rosenbladt*[9] and *Prigge*.[10] What lessons will be learnt in her home country from this emerging case law remain to be seen. While discrimination on grounds of sex, ethnic origin, religious belief, disability and sexual orientation has been forbidden by law in Sweden for the last decade or more, it

* Director at the Swedish Ministry for Foreign Affairs, Legal Secretariat, Acting Agent before the Court of Justice of the European Union. All opinions expressed herein are personal to the author.

[1] Council Directive 2000/43/EC of 29 June 2000 implementing the principle of equal treatment between persons irrespective of racial or ethnic origin, [2000] OJ L180/22.

[2] Council Directive 2000/78/EC of 27 November 2000 establishing a general framework for equal treatment in employment and occupation, [2000] OJ L303/16.

[3] Council Directive 2004/113/EC of 13 December 2004 implementing the principle of equal treatment between men and women in the access to and supply of goods and services, [2004] OJ L373/37.

[4] Directive 2006/54/EC of the European Parliament and of the Council of 5 July 2006 on the implementation of the principle of equal opportunities and equal treatment of men and women in matters of employment and occupation (recast), [2006] OJ L204/23.

[5] Case C-555/07 *Kücükdeveci* [2010] ECR I-365.

[6] Case C-229/08 *Wolf*, [2010] ECR I-1.

[7] Case C-341/08 *Petersen*, [2010] ECR I-47.

[8] Case C-499/08 *Andersen*, judgment of 12 October 2010 nyr.

[9] Case C-45/09 *Rosenbladt*, judgment of 12 October 2010 nyr.

[10] Case C-447/09 *Prigge*, judgment of 13 September 2011 nyr.

was only on 1 January 2009 that age discrimination was prohibited.[11] Hence judgments from Swedish courts on age discrimination are still scarce and the jurisprudence remains to be developed.

Nevertheless the Arbetsdomstolen (Swedish Labour Court) on 4 May 2011[12] ruled on whether an age-related ground for dismissals was compatible with the prohibition of age discrimination, having close regard to the case law of the ECJ. Furthermore, a Swedish district court asked the ECJ on 21 March 2011 whether the general principle of law on the prohibition of age discrimination and Article 6 of Directive 2000/78 prevent a national rule such as the age limit of 67 years in the Swedish Employment Protection Act, beyond which the ordinary rules against unfair dismissal cease to apply, with the practical consequences that employers do not have to give objective reasons to terminate the employment of an employee who has reached that age.

After a brief background describing the legal framework implementing the above mentioned Directives, the interpretation and application of the concept of discrimination will be addressed – following the three step approach chosen by the Swedish legislator; disadvantage, comparison and causation – and the issue of burden of proof. The aim is not to give a complete or even half a picture of the legal situation in Sweden regarding these complex and broad matters, but rather to produce a snapshot based on some judgments of Swedish courts which in recent years have attracted some attention. While the concept of discrimination in Sweden covers not only direct and indirect discrimination but also harassment and instruction to discriminate, this contribution is limited to the former two.

Background

The anti-discrimination regulation in civil law has undergone important developments during its 30 years of existence in Sweden. Since the early 1980s, when the Act on equal treatment of men and women in employment[13] was adopted, the Swedish legislator has moved from a piecemeal approach towards uniformity in regulating anti-discrimination. On 1 January 2009 the new Discrimination Act[14] entered into force and replaced seven legislative instruments regulating anti-discrimination.[15] To

[11] On the same date, a prohibition of discrimination on grounds of transgender identity and expression also entered into force.

[12] Arbetsdomstolen, Case A 110/10, *Diskrimineringsombudsmannen v Flygarbetsgivarna och SAS*, judgment 37/11 of 4 May 2011.

[13] SFS 1979:1118.

[14] SFS 2008:567.

[15] The Equal Opportunities Act (SFS 1991:433); the Act on Measures against Discrimination in Working Life on Grounds of Ethnic Origin, Religion or Other Religious Faith (SFS 1999:130); the Prohibition of Discrimination in Working Life on Grounds of Disability Act (SFS 1999:132); the Prohibition of Discrimination in Working Life on Grounds of Sexual Orientation Act (SFS 1999:133); the Equal Treatment of Students at Universities Act (SFS 2001:1286); the Prohibition of Discrimination Act (SFS 2003:307); the Act Prohibiting Discriminatory and Other Degrading Treatment of Children and School Students (SFS 2006:67).

the existing grounds of discrimination on the basis of sex, ethnic origin, religion or other belief, disability and sexual orientation, the new Act added age[16] and transgender identity or expression. While the new Discrimination Act generally prohibits discrimination in a vast number of situations of everyday life,[17] the scope of the prohibition as regards age is more limited.[18]

The adoption of the Discrimination Act completed the implementation in Sweden of Directive 2000/78 establishing a general framework for equal treatment in employment and occupation, Directive 2000/43 implementing the principle of equal treatment between persons irrespective of racial or ethnic origin and Directive 2002/73 amending Council Directive 76/207 on the implementation of the principle of equal treatment for men and women as regards access to employment, vocational training and promotion, and working conditions. The entry into force of the Discrimination Act also put an end to two of the three infringement proceedings the European Commission had initiated against Sweden regarding the implementation of these directives.[19]

Moreover, on 1 January 2009 a new agency, the Diskrimineringsombudsmannen, the Equality Ombudsman, was established to supervise compliance with the Discrimination Act, superseding and amalgamating the supervisory tasks of four different Ombudsmen (the Equal Opportunities Ombudsman, the Ombudsman against Ethnic Discrimination, the Disability Ombudsman and the Ombudsman against Discrimination because of Sexual Orientation). Among other functions, the Equality Ombudsman will bring actions before the courts on the basis of complaints of discrimination from private parties in order to have the discriminatory measure annulled and/or to seek pecuniary compensation for the damage the discriminatory behaviour has caused.

The express and obvious object of the Discrimination Act was to strengthen the protection against discrimination. According to the legislator it was important to ensure as far as possible equal treatment between the different grounds of discrimination – no ranking among them should in principle exist. A common concept of discrimination should apply, although not without certain differences in scope of application and extent, in particular with regard to exceptions notably in the field of age discrimination.

[16] According to Art 18 of Directive 2000/78 Member States could prolong the deadline for implementing the provisions of the Directive on age and disability discrimination until 2 December 2009.

[17] Working life, educational activities, labour market policy activities and employment, services not under public contracts, starting or running a business, professional recognition, membership of certain organisations, goods, services and housing, meetings and public events, health and medical care, social services, social insurance, unemployment insurance, financial support for studies, national military service and civilian service and public employment.

[18] The Act prohibits age discrimination in working life, educational activities, labour market policy activities and employment services not under public contracts, starting or running a business, professional recognition and membership of certain organisations.

[19] While the European Commission in 2010 decided to close these proceedings regarding Directive 2000/43 and Directive 2000/78, its complaint (2006/2537) regarding the implementation of Directive 2002/73 remains open. Sweden considers however that Directive 2002/73 has been fully implemented by the entry into force of the Discrimination Act.

This development mirrors the evolution at EU level, where a uniform definition of discrimination has been adopted through the EU directives based on Article 13 EC[20] (now Article 19 TFEU) and on Article 141 EC (now Article 157 TFEU). The use of equality as a general principle of law requires in essence that similar situations are treated alike unless there are objectively justified reasons for a difference in treatment. These directives address the more specific issue of unequal treatment between groups of individuals and specify the general principle further. According to the directives the principle of equal treatment means that there shall be no direct or indirect discrimination whatsoever on any of the prescribed grounds within the respective areas covered by each directive.[21] As regards direct discrimination there are no possibilities for justification other than those expressly stated in the directives, while indirect discrimination may be objectively justified by a legitimate aim where the means of that aim are appropriate and necessary. In relation to age, Directive 2000/78 permits further justifications for differences in treatment directly based on age if they are objectively and reasonably justified by a legitimate aim including legitimate employment policy, labour market and vocational training objectives, and if the means of achieving that aim are appropriate and necessary.[22]

From these justifications, a certain hierarchy may be inferred as to which differential treatment the legislator regards the most condemnable. Direct discrimination shall not occur unless expressly permitted while indirect discrimination may be tolerated when justified according to an open-ended formula and discrimination on the ground of age may to a significant degree still be accepted. This structure is corroborated by the greater difficulties in providing sufficient evidence of indirect discrimination in relation to direct discrimination, which all the more indicates the importance for a complainant that a particular difference in treatment is subsumed under the correct concept as well as the correct ground of discrimination.

DIRECT AND INDIRECT DISCRIMINATION

According to the EU directives direct discrimination occurs where a person is treated less favourably than another is, has been or would have been in a comparable situation on any of the indicated grounds.[23] This definition has been implemented in slightly different terms by Chapter 1, Section 4.1 of the Swedish Discrimination Act. According to that provision, direct discrimination means that someone is disadvantaged by being treated less favourably than somebody else is

[20] Directive 2000/43, Directive 2000/78; Directive 2004/113.

[21] Art 2(1) of Directive 2000/43; Art 2(1) of Directive 2000/78; Art 4(1) of Directive 2004/113; Art 1 together with Arts 4, 5 and 14 of Directive 2006/54.

[22] Art 6 of Directive 2000/78.

[23] Art 2(2)(a) of Directive 2000/43; Art 2(2)(a) of Directive 2000/78; Art 2(a) of Directive 2004/113; Art 2(1)(a) of Directive 2006/54.

treated, has been treated or would have been treated in a comparable situation if this disadvantage is associated with the enumerated grounds. This definition is based on the same threefold assessment involving the existence of a disadvantage, a comparator/comparable situation and a causal link between the disadvantage and a prohibited ground of discrimination, as were the seven different anti-discrimination laws that preceded the Discrimination Act. Since the legislator considered that this approach amounted to the same content and result as the definitions in the relevant EU directives, the Discrimination Act meant no amendment in this regard.[24] In consequence there is no need to distinguish between cases assessed by Swedish courts according to the Discrimination Act and according to the former anti-discrimination legislation when for the purposes here we consider how the concept of discrimination has been interpreted and applied.

As far as indirect discrimination is concerned Chapter 1, Section 4.2 of the Discrimination Act stipulates that indirect discrimination means that someone is disadvantaged by the application of a provision, a criterion or a procedure that appears neutral but that may put people of a certain sex, a certain transgender identity or expression, a certain ethnicity, a certain religion or other belief, a certain disability, a certain sexual orientation or a certain age at a particular disadvantage, unless the provision, criterion or procedure has a legitimate purpose and the means that are used are appropriate and necessary to achieve that purpose.

The definition corresponds in all essential aspects to the definition in the relevant directives. While indirect discrimination aims to catch the wider problem of discrimination where a particular group of people is disadvantaged by the way society works – measures that are discriminatory in effect – it conceptually consists of the same basic elements as direct discrimination, namely disadvantage, comparison and causation. It will therefore not be treated separately in the discussion of these elements below.

The boundaries of the concept of discrimination will be discussed in terms of the three-step test established by the Swedish legislator, (1) the existence of a disadvantage, (2) the existence of a comparator in a comparable situation and (3) the existence of a causal link between the disadvantage and the alleged ground of discrimination.

DISADVANTAGE

Indisputably, the concept of discrimination requires that a person has been disadvantaged. Since this requirement is closely related to the comparative analysis – whether somebody has been treated less favourably than another person – the ECJ does not in general consider the disadvantage separately in the same way as Swedish courts do. However, the assessment whether somebody has been disadvantaged is straightforward and does not raise any major issues. According to

[24] Government Bill prop 2007/08:95 *Ett starkare skydd mot diskriminering* 99.

the Swedish legislator the decisive element is that a negative effect has occurred for the person concerned. The particular reasons behind the occurrence of this effect are of no relevance and the disadvantageous treatment could be the result of both active measures and failure to act.

One question that has arisen is whether the disadvantage must reach a certain threshold in order to trigger the prohibition of discrimination. There is nothing in the statement of legislative intent accompanying the government Bill that indicates that this was indeed the intention of the legislator – the requirement of disadvantage being described as a treatment that typically is considered as a disadvantage or harm to an individual.

In practice there are, however, examples pointing towards a different approach. In one case, it was argued in a dissenting opinion that the negative effect had been too trivial to amount to a disadvantage in the sense of the definition of direct discrimination in the Discrimination Act. The case concerned a woman of Romany origin who was attending a conference at a hotel and who had been asked by the hotel management whether she belonged to the hotel guests three times in a day, when serving herself coffee from the coffee machines in the hotel lobby, but had not actually been denied free coffee at the hotel.[25]

A less straightforward situation occurred in a case where a homosexual had applied for and been granted the right to adopt her partner's child. For the district court to grant adoption, the municipal social committee had to be heard beforehand. In this instance one member of the social committee had voted against the adoption since the applicants were of the same sex. The same member also made a reservation against the final favourable opinion of the social committee. Considering that this behaviour of the member of the committee had increased the risk for a negative outcome of the court's decision and had caused the couple discomfort, the Ombudsman against Discrimination based on Sexual Orientation brought an action against the municipality for damages. The question then arose whether the couple had suffered a disadvantage within the meaning of the concept of discrimination. The Court of Appeal explained that the notion of disadvantage should be understood as requiring the existence both of treatment that objectively could lead to harm or disadvantage to an individual and of an effect of such a treatment.[26] A subjective sense of discomfort is not sufficient. Since the Court of Appeal disagreed with the Ombudsman that there was an objective risk for a negative outcome due to the behaviour of the committee member, it did not find that the Ombudsman had proven that the couple had been subject to direct discrimination.

COMPARABLE SITUATIONS

According to the definition of discrimination in both the Directives and the Discrimination Act the disadvantaged person must find him- or herself in a situ-

[25] *Göta Hovrätt*, judgment of 19 May 2010 in case T-3065-09.

[26] *Hovrätten för Övre Norrland*, judgment of 1 September 2009 in case T-441-07, RH 2008:62.

ation comparable to another actual or fictive person. In other words a complainant needs to refer to a comparator (actual or potential) in a comparable situation. During the elaboration of the Discrimination Act the question was raised whether a comparison was at all necessary when defining direct discrimination. According to this view the existence of a disadvantage and a causal link between that disadvantage and one of the grounds of discrimination would be sufficient to establish direct discrimination. It was argued that the comparison only served the purpose of showing the connection to a particular ground of discrimination and therefore it did not have any independent function for the definition of discrimination.

In view of the express wording of the EU directives the Swedish legislator however maintained the reference to a comparator in a comparable situation pointing to the fact that by keeping close to the wording of the definitions in the directives the full implementation of EU law would become clear.[27] It has also been opined that the element of comparability is important for reasons of objectivity, since without that element the discretion placed in the hands of the courts would be too vast.[28] It would also conceptually seem hard to disregard completely an element of comparison when defining discrimination in general terms, as it inherently means a difference in treatment and presupposes a point of reference to which a particular treatment may be compared.

Even with the component of comparability as an element of the definition of discrimination, the courts are left with broad discretion as the situations need not be identical but only comparable. According to the ECJ the comparability must be examined having regard, inter alia, to the subject matter and object of the rules establishing the difference in treatment.[29] As a consequence the importance of the requirement of a comparator and a comparable situation will depend on the situation at hand. If the measure is such as to hit the large majority or the entirety of the population, such as an age limit for when employment may end without further requirements, the need for an actual comparison hardly seems necessary. Rather the existence of a disadvantage and a causal link between the disadvantage and a particular ground of discrimination would be decisive and sufficient. To insist on the existence of a comparable situation also points at the possibility of construing them so narrowly that no discrimination is taken to occur. The prime example is pregnant women: since a man cannot be pregnant there could be no comparable situation and no sex discrimination, hence the need for express rules on pregnancy and maternity.[30] The ECJ has long discarded the solution of comparing pregnant women to men similarly incapable for medical reasons.[31] Rather difference in treatment by reasons of pregnancy is to be considered as directly discriminatory on grounds of sex since pregnancy is inextricably linked to the female gender.

[27] Government Bill 2007/08:95, 101.

[28] E Ellis, 'The Definition of Discrimination in European Community Sex Equality Law' *EL Rev* 563.

[29] Case C-356/09 *Kleist*, judgment of 18 November 2010 nyr, para 34; Case C-127/07 *Société Arcelor Atlantique et Lorraine et al* [2008] ECR I-9895, para 26.

[30] See, eg Art 4(1)(a) of Directive 2004/113; Art 2(2)(c) and 15 of Directive 2006/54.

[31] See, eg Case C-177/88 *Dekker* [1990] ECR I-3941; Case C-32/93 *Webb* [1994] ECR I-3567, para 24.

In practice Swedish courts have confirmed the necessity of an element of comparability in order for discrimination to be established, having regard both to the wording of the definition of discrimination according to the law applicable at the time[32] and the ordinary meaning of the concept.[33] This, in combination with the particular situation of pregnant women, has caused a Swedish court to have recourse to such a highly hypothetical comparator as an 'unpregnant man'. Four women had been subject to a more restrictive assessment when applying for sickness allowances for health problems related to their pregnancies, than persons with health problems unrelated to pregnancy. This, according to the court, constituted direct discrimination on grounds of sex since the women had been disadvantaged in comparison to an 'unpregnant man', and in consequence the four women were awarded damages.[34]

A less clearcut situation arose when the Ombudsman against Discrimination based on Sexual Orientation brought an action on behalf of a lesbian couple against a county council (Landsting) for preventing one of the women from receiving the remaining three out of six insemination treatments that couples were allowed when her partner could not receive them due to her age. The district court found that the situation of the woman who had been refused treatment should be compared to that of another woman living together with another person irrespective of sexual orientation. Since the County Council's rules meant that all women living together with a man could be inseminated but only one of the women living together with another woman, it concluded that these rules resulted in disadvantaging half of the population of lesbian women both as regards the population of heterosexual women and as regards the other half of the population of lesbian women. After having dismissed the plea on direct discrimination on formal grounds, the Court of Appeal, assessing whether indirect discrimination had occurred, held that the situation of the lesbian couple should be compared to the situation of a heterosexual couple, who would not have been able to transfer treatments after the woman had passed the prescribed age limit to the other part of the couple since he was a man. No discrimination therefore existed and the action was dismissed.[35]

Another perhaps more illustrative example of two courts reaching diverging conclusions when presented with the same facts was the dismissal of pilots and cabin crew employed by Scandinavian Airline Systems (SAS). SAS had to cut down personnel and therefore decided, in agreement with the relevant labour organisations, to draw up lists of personnel that would have to be let go, and the order in which they would be dismissed. The decisive factor was the entitlement to a right to a pension, which meant in fact that only persons above a certain age were to be dismissed.

[32] Act on Prohibition of Discrimination, SFS 2003:307.

[33] See, eg *Svea Hovrätt*, judgments of 30 September 2010 in case T-9430-09 and of 5 November 2011 in case T-9187-08.

[34] *Svea Hovrätt*, judgment of 30 September 2010 in case T-9430-09.

[35] *Svea Hovrätt*, judgment of 5 November 2011 in case T-9187-08.

A group of pilots challenged this system before a district court on grounds of age discrimination. The District Court dismissed the action since it was of the opinion that no age discrimination had occurred. The criterion chosen to select the pilots to be let go did not amount to age discrimination. Neither did it constitute indirect discrimination since the aim of the measure – to protect younger pilots from unemployment and low income at the expense of those who were eligible to a pension – was legitimate.

Subsequently, in a second case, a group of cabin crew represented by the Ombudsman against Discrimination brought a similar action against SAS, but before the Labour Court. According to that court, the cabin crew who had been dismissed should be compared to those who had been able to remain employed. The Labour Court did not agree with the defendant that a distinction could be made with reference to the entitlement to a right to a pension and that in consequence persons with such a right were not in a comparable situation to those who did not. In contrast to the District Court, the Labour Court held that the criterion of a right to a pension was inseparably linked to age and hence that there was direct discrimination. After having considered that no exception to the prohibition of direct discrimination applied it granted the action and annulled the dismissals.

In the latter case the Labour Court drew a parallel with the judgment of the ECJ in the case of *Andersen*,[36] when it considered that the use of the contested measure was inextricably linked to an age limit and concluded that there was direct discrimination. By this more generous interpretation of direct discrimination the delimitation between direct and indirect discrimination is pushed to the advantage of the former over the latter. This kind of approach also works to the advantage of complainants, who are generally in a more difficult situation when it comes to establishing the occurrence of indirect discrimination than of direct discrimination. Furthermore the judgment of the Labour Court, in contrast to the District Court's judgment, avoids the use of entitlement to a pension right which is directly linked to age, in order to establish that a dismissed group of employees was not comparable to employees who were not dismissed. As follows from the case law of the ECJ, the criterion by which situations may be distinguished so as to be not comparable to one another, must be independent of the discrimination ground at stake.[37]

CAUSAL LINK

The third and clearly fundamental element of the definition of discrimination is the existence of a causal link between the disadvantage and the alleged ground of discrimination. There is no indication in the definition of discrimination in the directives that an element of intent to discriminate is required. It is the discriminatory

[36] *Andersen*, n 8 above.

[37] See, eg Case C-227/04 *P Lindorfer v Council* [2007] ECR I-6767, para 54; Opinion of AG Kokott in *Kleist*, n 29 above, para 43.

effect of a certain behaviour (in the large sense of the word) that is decisive. This is consistent with a long line of cases from the ECJ.[38] The Swedish legislator also pointed out that no intent to discriminate is necessary in order for discrimination to be established.[39] Such an intent may, however, serve to show the existence of the necessary causal link between a certain behaviour and a ground of discrimination. A causal link may also exist when somebody wrongly assumes that a person belongs to one of the protected groups, for example when a person is disadvantaged because somebody wrongly assumes the person to be homosexual.

The opposite situation, when the alleged discriminator was not conscious of the existence of the ground of discrimination, was tried in a case before the Svea Court of Appeal.[40] In that instance the personnel of a restaurant did not realise that a woman was suffering from a spastic disease, but assumed that she was drunk and consequently denied her entry to the restaurant. According to the Court of Appeal the requirement of a causal link between the disadvantage of being denied entrance to the restaurant and the disability as a ground of discrimination, means that the discriminator must actually have been aware of the discrimination ground. It would not suffice that the discriminator objectively should have been aware of the ground. The action was hence dismissed due to the lack of the required causal link between the disadvantage and the ground of discrimination.

It is not to be unexpected that age discrimination in particular may raise questions of causation, since age is often an underlying factor of different criteria for selection to employment, education, promotion and the like. Experience, years of employment and maturity tend to be of advantage to older people while criteria like physical fitness, strength, IT knowledge, extensive travelling would tend to advantage the young. Unless the criteria would be considered as inseparably linked to age, the relation to age in these instances would be of an indirect nature and should be assessed according to the rules on indirect discrimination.

BURDEN OF PROOF

Chapter 6, Section 3 of the Discrimination Act states

> If a person who considers that he or she has been discriminated against or subjected to reprisals demonstrates circumstances that give reason to presume that he or she has been discriminated against or subjected to reprisals, the defendant is required to show that discrimination or reprisals have not occurred.

This rule implements and corresponds to the rules on burden of proof in the EU directives.[41]

[38] See, eg *Dekker*, n 31 above.

[39] Government Bill 2007/08:95, 488; Government Bill 2002/03:65, 85.

[40] *Svea Hovrätt*, judgment of 2 June 2009 in case T-7752-08.

[41] See Art 4 of the now repealed Council Directive 97/80 on the burden of proof in cases of discrimination based on sex (OJ L14/6); Art 8.1 of Directive 2000/4; Art 10(1) of Directive 2000/78; Art 9 of Directive 2004/113; Art 19(1) of Directive 2006/54.

With the aim of alleviating the burden of proof resting on plaintiffs,[42] the rule stipulates a two-step method for the assessment of evidence. Instead of having to prove both the facts which would constitute a disadvantage in comparable situations and a causal link between the questioned measure and the ground of discrimination, the plaintiff must only establish the facts required for the first limb and, if so established, the causal link will be presumed.

According to the Swedish legislator,[43] the burden of proof for the plaintiff and the defendant should correspond to the burden of proof expressed in the EU directives.[44] This would be so in spite of the different wording in the directives, according to which it shall suffice that the plaintiff *establishes facts* from which it may be presumed that there has been direct or indirect discrimination, and if so, it shall be for the respondent *to prove* that there has been no breach of the principle of equal treatment. In contrast to the wording of the Swedish Discrimination Act, this language may suggest a different level of the burden of proof for the different parties – a lighter requirement for the plaintiff when it comes to the facts from which the discrimination may be presumed, and a heavier requirement for the defendant in relation to facts refuting that discrimination has occurred. The practical impact of these differences in the texts should not however be exaggerated in view of the legislator's express intent and the courts obligation to interpret to Discrimination Act in light of the directives.

The significance of the interpretation of the rule on burden of proof is illustrated by the different approaches that have been present in the Swedish preparatory works to the legislation and in cases before the Swedish courts. While the Swedish legislator[45] has repeatedly explained this rule in terms of a shared burden of proof, the Swedish Supreme Court in a judgment in 2006 regards it as a presumption.[46] In its judgment the Supreme Court first referred to the relevant directives and the purpose of the rule to alleviate the burden of proof of the plaintiff. It then agreed with the criticism put forward in the literature that the burden of proof could hardly be shared between the two parties with regard to one and the same fact. Rather the rule should apply as a presumption: once certain facts are established by the plaintiff, discrimination could be presumed and these facts are distinct from the facts to be refuted.

This case attracted some public attention, not so much because of the ruling on the burden of proof, as because of the facts of the case. The owner of a restaurant had asked one of his guests, a lesbian woman, to stop kissing her female partner and

[42] See Art 1 of Directive 97/80 and recitals 17 and 18; see also recital 21 of Directive 2000/43; recital 31 of Directive 2000/78; recital 22 of Directive 2004/113; recital 30 of Directive 2006/54.

[43] Government Bill 2007/08:95, 446.

[44] See Art 8(1) of Directive 2000/43; Art 10(1) of Directive 2000/78; Art 9 of Directive 2004/113; Art 19(1) of Directive 2006/54.

[45] Government Bill 2002/03:65, 104; Government Bill 2004/05:147, 138; Government Bill 2005/06:38, 121; and Government Bill 2007/08:95, 443–44 and 561 where a more nuanced view is presented.

[46] *Högsta Domstolen*, judgment of 28 March 2006 in case T 2100-05, NJA 2006 170. The case concerned the former Act on Prohibition of Discrimination which contained a similar rule on burden of proof.

then made her leave the establishment. The Ombudsman against Discrimination based on Sexual Orientation brought an action against the owner of the restaurant for discrimination which ended up before the Supreme Court. Applying the rule on burden of proof the Supreme Court found that the plaintiff had established that the woman had been treated in a way in which the guests of the restaurant normally would not be. It was then for the defendant to prove that the request to stop kissing and the dismissal were the result of other factors than her sexual orientation. Since the defendant could not provide any objectively acceptable reasons for the measures, the woman was awarded damages for having been subject to direct discrimination.

Moreover, in general, allegations of indirect discrimination will mean an increased burden of proof for the complainant since he or she will have to produce evidence of the fact that an apparently neutral rule in fact adversely affects a particular group of people in comparison to others. According to the Swedish legislator the difference between those who are able to fulfil a certain requirement and those who cannot must be 'significant' in order to establish that a person from that latter group has been disadvantaged. It is also stressed that there must be a factual and not a hypothetical comparison between the relevant groups. The exact meaning of a significant difference is left to the assessments of the courts.[47]

This may be contrasted with the wording in Chapter 1, Section 4.2 in the Discrimination Act as well as in the EU directives,[48] where the use of a measure 'that may put' and 'would put' people at a particular disadvantage, indicates that proof of a potential disadvantage would suffice and that a 'significant difference' may be shown to exist also without necessarily having recourse to statistics.[49]

Court cases in which the question of indirect discrimination has been assessed in Sweden are also significantly fewer than those where direct discrimination has been assessed.[50] One possible explanation may be the difficulty of producing sufficient evidence in combination with the wider possibilities for justification for the defendants.[51]

Finally, systematic differences in the application of the rule on burden of proof have been found to occur in cases tried by the Arbetsdomstolen, the Labour Court, on the one hand and the general courts on the other.[52] A study from 2010

[47] Government Bill 2007/08, 490.

[48] Art 2(2)(b) of Directive 2000/43; Art 2(2)(b) of Directive 2000/78; Art 2(1)(b) Directive 2006/54; Art 2(b) of Directive 2004/113.

[49] See in this respect C Barnard, *EC Employment Law* (London, Oxford University Press, 2006) 325 ff.

[50] Integrations- och jämställdhetsdepartementet, *Domar i diskrimineringsmål 1999–2009 En förstudie*, Dnr IJ2009/1961/DISK, 7. Out of 41 cases before the Labour Court, 35 concerned direct discrimination and 15 indirect discrimination. Out of 24 cases before the ordinary courts all concerned direct discrimination and three indirect discrimination.

[51] See, eg *Svea hovrätt*, judgment of 28 February 2011 in case T-3073-10 in which the plaintiff was not able to prove that the rule in question disadvantaged men to a greater extent than women.

[52] In this context it could be useful to recall that according to Swedish rules of procedure, actions on labour law issues are brought before the Labour Court either directly at first and last instance, or on appeal against a judgment from a district court which has heard the case at first instance. There would be no further possibilities of appeal. Actions concerning discrimination in fields other than labour law

on the case law from 1999 until 2009 in the field of discrimination,[53] reports clear differences in the application of the rule of burden of proof between the two types of jurisdiction. While the general courts follow the approach in the ruling of the Supreme Court from 2006, the Labour Court tends to apply a shared burden of proof method at the expense of the foreseen two-step assessment. The study also indicates that plaintiffs have been more successful when having their cases tried by the general courts than by the Labour Court. Whether this difference will persist remains to be seen since, for example, the Labour Court in the SAS case did apply the rule on burden of proof in conformity with the application in the general courts.

CONCLUSION

Certainly the legislator has made significant efforts to specify further the general principle of equality through the anti-discrimination directives at the EU level and the Swedish Discrimination Act at the national level in order to ensure that discrimination does not occur between different groups of persons. Still the full effect of the prohibition of discrimination seems hard to achieve.

In spite of Swedish long-standing ambitions to ensure the effective implementation and enforcement of the principle of non-discrimination, the European Commission started infringement proceedings against Sweden for not fully implementing these directives. One of these files still remains open and Sweden got a complementary letter of formal notice as late as in May 2011.

Moreover discrimination is defined in broad and general terms – the necessary consequence of a formula that should cover the manifold circumstances in which the prohibited behaviour may occur. While a uniform and symmetrical approach to discrimination has been established in order to enhance the protection from discriminatory behaviour, the flexibility that such a concept leaves when applied entails at the same time risks of disparity in its factual application and practical effect. A coherent jurisprudence is therefore a necessary complement to the road chosen by the legislator.

In Sweden this risk of lack of coherence in the application is, however, somehow mitigated by the tradition of Swedish judges to look closely at the legislator's intent as expressed in the preparatory works when interpreting the law. It is also clear from the reasoning in the judgments from Swedish courts that the Swedish judge will indeed follow the three-step test set out in the legislative preparatory works when assessing cases on discrimination.

are brought before the general courts, ie district court, court of appeal and the Supreme Court. This means that cases concerning discrimination will be assessed by two different types of jurisdiction with two distinct last instances, the Labour Court and the Supreme Court.

[53] Integrations- och jämställdhetsdepartementet, n 50 above.

Furthermore it is interesting to note that no Swedish reference for a preliminary ruling on anti-discrimination law has been referred to the ECJ for a decade.[54] It was not until March 2011 that the Södertörns tingsrätt, the District Court of Södertörn, lodged a reference for a preliminary ruling to the Court of Justice on the justification and proportionality of the Swedish rule according to which the normal protection of employment ends when an employee has reached the age of 67.[55] This reference does not, however, raise the issues that have been discussed above since the rule in question clearly entails a difference in treatment on grounds of age, but whether it may be justified in accordance with Article 6 of Directive 2000/78. On this question in particular the cases *Palacios de la Villa*[56], *Age Concern England*,[57] *Petersen*,[58] *Andersen*,[59] *Rosenbladt* and *Georgiev*[60] already shed some considerable light.

As is evidenced by this reference the introduction of age as a ground of discrimination may provide increased reasons for Swedish courts to turn to the Court of Justice for advice to end the lack of judicial dialogue. The use of age limits in working life together with the more extensive exceptions of age discrimination under Directive 2000/78 would support such a development.

[54] Case C-407/98 *Abrahamsson and Anderson* [2000] ECR I-5539 on the compatibility of positive action as regards the employment of women with Directive 76/207/EEC was the latest case concerning anti-discrimination law in which a Swedish court sent a reference for a preliminary ruling to the Court of Justice.

[55] Section 32a of the Employment Protection Act, Swedish Code of Statues 1982:80; Case C-141/11 *Hörnfeldt v Posten Meddelande AB*, pending at the time of writing.

[56] Case C-411/05 *Palacios de la Villa* [2007] ECR I-8531.

[57] Case C-388/07 *Age Concern England* [2009] ECR I-1569.

[58] *Petersen*, n 7 above.

[59] *Andersen*, n 8 above.

[60] Joined Cases C-250/09 and C-268/09 *Georgiev*, judgment of 18 November 2010 nyr.

23

Age Discrimination – Four Nordic Cases

MARTIN JOHANSSON*

INTRODUCTION

AGE AS A discrimination ground is a relatively recent phenomenon in international discrimination law. In Article 2 of the UN Universal Declaration on Human Rights, age is not mentioned as an example along the traditional discrimination grounds of race, colour, sex, language and religion. Similarly, in the ECHR, Article 14 on the prohibition of discrimination does not list age among the examples mentioned. The ECtHR has, however, explicitly recognised that age discrimination is covered by Article 14.[1]

In the EU, age as a discrimination ground was first mentioned in Article 13 EC (now Article 19(1) TFEU), introduced by the Treaty of Amsterdam on 1 May 1999. Article 13 EC enabled the Council to take appropriate action to combat discrimination based on sex, racial or ethnic origin, religion or belief, disability, age or sexual orientation. On the basis of this provision, the Council adopted two anti-discrimination directives in 2000: the Race Equality Directive[2] and the Employment Framework Directive.[3] In addition, age is included in the non-exhaustive list of prohibited grounds of discrimination in Article 21 of the Charter of Fundamental Rights of the European Union, which through Article 6(1) TEU, since the entry into force of the Lisbon Treaty, on 1 December 2009, enjoys the same legal value as the treaties.

The principle of non-discrimination on grounds of age was recognised as a general principle of EU law by the ECJ in *Mangold*.[4] However, for the principle to be

* Advokat, Partner, Advokatfirman Vinge, Brussels. Formerly, inter alia, Legal Secretary at the ECJ, the General Court and the EFTA Court. The author was one of the lawyers representing SAS in Attunda Tingsrätt, Case T-6787/08 *Andersson and ors v SAS*, judgment of 18 November 2009; and in Arbetsdomstolen, Case A 110/10, *Diskrimineringsombudsmannen v Flygarbetsgivarna och SAS*, judgment 37/11 of 4 May 2011. The author wishes to thank jur kand Andreas Johansson, at the time trainee at the Brussels office of Vinge, for his help with this article.

[1] See *Schwizgebel v Switzerland*, App no 25762/07, judgment of 10 June 2010 nyr.

[2] Council Directive 2000/43/EC of 29 June 2000 implementing the principle of equal treatment between persons irrespective of racial or ethnic origin, [2000] OJ L180/22.

[3] Council Directive 2000/78/EC of 27 November 2000 establishing a general framework for equal treatment in employment and occupation, [2000] OJ L303/16.

[4] Case C-144/04 *Mangold and Helm* [2005] ECR I-9981, para 74.

applicable the national rules at issue need to fall within the scope of application of the Treaties[5] and the principle is applied as given expression by Directive 2000/78.[6] The ECJ has given a number of judgments interpreting the provisions on age discrimination in the Employment Framework Directive, especially during the last two to three years. In the Nordic countries, those provisions have come up lately in four cases involving the airline sector, none of which gave rise to a reference to the ECJ for a preliminary ruling or to the EFTA Court for an advisory opinion.

The present article first briefly sets out the relevant provisions of the Employment Framework Directive. Thereafter follows a short presentation of the different cases. The last part of the article contains an analysis of the judgments, mainly in the light of the case law of the ECJ, as it stood at the time of writing, in July 2011.

THE EMPLOYMENT FRAMEWORK DIRECTIVE

Article 1 of the Employment Framework Directive states that:

> The purpose of this Directive is to lay down a general framework for combating discrimination on the grounds of religion or belief, disability, age or sexual orientation as regards employment and occupation, with a view to putting into effect in the Member States the principle of equal treatment.

Article 2(1) defines the 'principle of equal treatment' to mean that 'there shall be no direct or indirect discrimination whatsoever on any of the grounds referred to in Article 1'.

According to Article 2(2)(a), 'direct discrimination' occurs where one person is treated less favourably than another is, has been or would be treated in a comparable situation.

According to Article 2(2)(b), 'indirect discrimination' occurs:

> where an apparently neutral provision, criterion or practice would put persons having a particular religion or belief, a particular disability, a particular age, or a particular sexual orientation at a particular disadvantage compared with other persons unless:
>
> (i) that provision, criterion or practice is objectively justified by a legitimate aim and the means of achieving that aim are appropriate and necessary, . . .

It is clear from the Directive that age is considered to be different from the other discrimination grounds.[7] Recital 25 points out that 'differences in treatment in connection with age may be justified under certain circumstances' and differences in treatment 'require specific provisions which may vary in accordance with the situation in Member States'. For this reason, it is necessary to

[5] Case C-427/06 *Bartsch* [2008] ECR I-7245, paras 23–25.

[6] See, eg Case C-555/07 *Kücükdevici* [2010] ECR I-365, paras 50–51.

[7] This has been underlined by the ECJ. In Case C-388/07 *Age Concern England* [2009] ECR I-1569, para 60, the Court notes that Art 6 of the Directive 'establishes a scheme of derogation specific to differences of treatment on grounds of age, on account of the recognized specificity of age among the grounds of discrimination prohibited by the directive'.

> distinguish between differences in treatment which are justified, in particular by legitimate employment policy, labour market and vocational training objectives, and discrimination which must be prohibited.

Article 6, on the justification of differences of treatment on grounds of age, therefore provides:

> Notwithstanding Article 2(2), Member States may provide that differences of treatment on grounds of age shall not constitute discrimination, if, within the context of national law, they are objectively and reasonably justified by a legitimate aim, including legitimate employment policy, labour market and vocational training objectives, and if the means of achieving that aim are appropriate and necessary.

It follows from Article 3(1)(c) that the Directive applies to all persons, whether in the public or the private sector, in relation to 'employment and working conditions, including dismissals and pay'. The ECJ has held that the principle of non-discrimination on grounds of age, as given expression in Directive 2000/78, has horizontal direct effect and can thus be invoked in disputes between individuals.[8]

FOUR NORDIC CASES

All four cases concerned situations in which there was shortage of work[9] and the question was thus who was to be dismissed, the last employed or those who were entitled to a pension from a pension scheme to which the employer had contributed under a collective agreement.

Attunda Tingsrätt

At the time of the disputed dismissals in the judgment of the Attunda Tingsrätt (the first instance court of Attunda, Stockholm) in *Andersson and others v SAS*,[10] Sweden had not yet implemented the Employment Framework Directive.[11] The Tingsrätt, however, interpreted applicable Swedish law in the light of the Directive.

In this case, the Attunda Tingsrätt found that it had been proven that there was a shortage of work. For the carrying out of the necessary dismissals, the pilot union concerned and the defendant had agreed a new order of priority for dismissal, deviating from the normal rule in the Swedish Employment Protection Act – last in, first out.[12] The agreement provided that the employees having attained the age of 60 would be dismissed before those not having attained that

[8] *Kücükdevici*, n 6 above, para 56.

[9] This fact was either not contested or the court concerned concluded that this was the case.

[10] Attunda Tingsrätt, Case T-6787/08 *Andersson and ors v SAS*, judgment of 18 November 2009.

[11] The Swedish Discrimination Act (*diskrimineringslag 2008:567*) entered into force on 1 January 2009.

[12] *Lag (1982:80) om anställningsskydd*, s 22 (for a non-official translation, see www.sweden.gov.se/content/1/c6/07/65/36/9b9ee182.pdf).

age. The Tingsrätt held that it was not age, in itself, that had governed the selection of the employees to be dismissed, but the question of which employees had their means of support secured through retirement benefit under a pension scheme to which the defendant had contributed under a collective agreement. There was thus no difference of treatment based on age in itself and thereby no direct discrimination. However, the Tingsrätt found that the criteria relating to secure means of support constituted indirect discrimination, being indirectly disadvantageous to those belonging to a certain age group, that is, those having attained the age of 60 years.

The Tingsrätt noted that the justifications invoked by the defendant were of a social character and that the assessment made was based on what was the best solution for the group of employees concerned as a whole. It stated that the main aim of the agreement was to protect the younger pilots from unemployment and, as a consequence, a low salary. That this was done at the expense of the older employees was motivated by the fact that the latter were provided for by the abovementioned pension. The Tingsrätt considered that such an aim must be considered legitimate since the disadvantaged group was provided for in a way that the younger employees could not be. The fact that the older employees were already entitled to the pension under the collective agreement, and did not get anything on top of this by reason of their dismissal, did not change this assessment.

The Tingsrätt considered the means of achieving the aim to be appropriate and necessary, in particular since, on the one hand, the dismissals were part of a necessary reduction of the number of employees and, on the other, the disadvantaged group was entitled to advantageous pensions. The Tingsrätt concluded that the dismissals constituted neither direct nor indirect discrimination since they were justified by a legitimate aim and that aim could be achieved in an appropriate and necessary manner. Consequently, they were not contrary to the Employment Framework Directive. With regard to the principle of non-discrimination on grounds of age invoked by the applicants, the Tingsrätt, referring to the judgment of the ECJ in *Palacios de la Villa*,[13] held that the principle could not be interpreted on its own as its content and scope had been specified in the Employment Framework Directive.

Københavns Byret

In *Ligebehandlingsnævnets sekretariat and others v SAS*, the Københavns Byret[14] (the first instance court of Copenhagen) found that it appeared from the collective agreement between the defendant and Dansk pilotforening (the Danish pilots' union) that an old-age pension was paid to the pilots after they had attained the age of 60 and that pilots employed by the defendant were consequently enti-

[13] Case C-411/05 *Palacios de la Villa* [2007] ECR I-8531, para 76.

[14] Københavns Byret, Case BS 32C-1356/2010, *Ligebehandlingsnævnets sekretariat and ors v SAS*, judgment of 11 February 2011.

tled to a pension when they attained that age. The Byret noted from the conclusion in the three protocols concerned in the proceedings that the pilots who should be dismissed were those who were entitled to a pension, one of the protocols specifying 'ie until the pilot turns 60'. The list containing the order of priority also showed that all the dismissed pilots were over the age of 60.

The Københavns Byret came to the conclusion that the criterion 'entitled to a pension', used when the pilots concerned were dismissed, clearly is directly and inextricably linked to the age of the employees. The criterion was therefore not neutral, or apparently neutral, within the meaning of the Danish Act on Equal Treatment. The Byret therefore found that the employees concerned, because of their being over 60, had been treated less favourably than others in a comparable situation and that, consequently, there had been a direct difference in treatment based on age.

The Byret further found that it had not be shown that there was support in Danish law or in the Employment Framework Directive for the assumption that the parties or their organisations generally, in advance, may agree on a deviation from the rules on discrimination in the Danish Act on Equal Treatment,[15] which constitute a general principle of Union law. The pilots were therefore not bound by the agreement between Dansk pilotforening and the defendant.

Arbetsdomstolen

Diskrimineringsombudsmannen v SAS[16] concerned an agreement concluded between the defendant and the local organisation of the SAS cabin crew union for reasons of shortage of work. The agreement deviated from the normal priority rules in the Swedish Act on Employment Security, providing for the dismissal of cabin crew entitled to an occupational pension.

The Arbetsdomstolen (the Swedish Labour Court), referring to the judgment of the ECJ in *Andersen*,[17] first found that the employees concerned were selected for dismissal on the ground that, unlike the other employees, they were entitled to a pension. Since the only employees entitled to the pension were those who had attained the age of 60 years, the criterion based on the entitlement to a pension must be considered to be inextricably linked to the age of the employees. The dismissed employees were thus the subject of direct discrimination.

Secondly, the Arbetsdomstolen noted that the defendant and the cabin crew union had agreed that the existing redundancy of cabin crew should be dealt with through the dismissal of employees entitled to a pension, since they had a right to a full occupational pension. Contrary to younger employees, they had access to a

[15] *Lov om forbud mod forskelsbehandling på arbejdsmarkedet mv* (LBK 31 of 12 January 2005, with the amendments that follow from Act 240 of 27 March 2006, Act 1542 of 20 December 2006 and Section 17 in Act 387 of 27 May 2008).

[16] Arbetsdomstolen, Case A 110/10, *Diskrimineringsombudsmannen v Flygarbetsgivarna och SAS*, judgment 37/11 of 4 May 2011.

[17] Case C-499/08 *Andersen*, judgment of 12 October 2010 nyr.

guaranteed income in the form of an old-age pension stipulated by collective agreement and the younger employees avoided becoming unemployed. The aim invoked by the defendant, that is, to secure the means of support for all cabin crew, should be considered legitimate as part of the national employment policy to promote access to employment by better distributing this access between the generations, something which according to the ECJ may constitute an objective justification for a Member State to prescribe differences of treatment on grounds of age.

The Arbetsdomstolen nevertheless declared that the agreement was not appropriate to achieve the aim pursued, since it was contrary to the objective and the content of a binding provision of national law, namely Section 32a of the Employment Protection Act,[18] which provides that an employee is entitled to remain in employment up to the end of the month when he or she attains the age of 67 years.

Further, the Arbetsdomstolen, referring to the part of the judgment in *Andersen* where the ECJ examines whether the proportionality criterion is met, declared that the dismissal of all the cabin crew entitled to a pension would be too far-reaching. The dismissal could be said to constitute a form of forced retirement. Notwithstanding their entitlement to an occupational pension, the dismissed employees must be considered as unemployed at the end of the period of notice. The Arbetsdomstolen stressed that, furthermore, it was not disputed that the employees were not even asked whether they wished to take out their old-age pension and terminate their employment or if they would be prepared to terminate their employment in exchange for some form of economic compensation in addition to the occupational pension. The fact that some of the employees having been dismissed might already have started to draw on their occupational pension did not change the assessment, since this was the effect of the pension agreement between the defendant and the unions, giving the right to those entitled to receive the occupational pension to draw on that pension while still being employed with the defendant.

Norges Høyesterett

The Employment Framework Directive is not part of the EEA Agreement, but Norway has implemented it in the Act on the Working Environment,[19] independently of its obligations under the EEA Agreement. The Norges Høyesterett (the Norwegian Supreme Court) has held that national courts should relate to the Directive when deciding the requirements that have to be fulfilled for a provision on age limits to be upheld and that they have to assess on an independent basis whether there is age discrimination, using the same sources of law that would be applicable had the question been put before the ECJ.[20]

[18] See n 12 above.

[19] *LOV 2005-06-17 nr 62: Lov om arbeidsmiljø, arbeidstid og stillingsvern mv* (arbeidsmiljøloven).

[20] Norges Høyesterett, Case 2009/1594 *A v X AS*, HR-2010-00303-A, judgment of 18 February 2010, paras 55–56, confirmed in the judgment of the Høyesterett commented on in this article.

In *Bottolvs and others v SAS*,[21] the Norges Høyesterett found that the three Norwegian pilot unions concerned and the defendant had agreed not to use seniority as the principle of selection for deciding who should be dismissed, but that the pilots who were entitled to a pension should be dismissed before those at the bottom of the seniority list. Pilots who had turned 60 were thus dismissed. The Høyesterett considered this selection criterion to be so closely linked to age that there could be no doubt that the agreement implied age discrimination. Against the background of the judgment of the ECJ in *Andersen*,[22] the selection criterion was probably to be considered as inextricably linked to age and thus as direct discrimination. However, the classification of the difference of treatment as direct or indirect was not considered to be decisive for the outcome of the case.

The Høyesterett then analysed whether the conditions for the exception from the prohibition of differences of treatment on grounds of age were fulfilled and referred in this context to Article 6(1) of the Employment Framework Directive. It found that the aim of the agreement between the unions concerned and the defendant was to establish which employees would suffer the least from a dismissal. The Høyesterett declared that it is a legitimate aim within the context of Norwegian law to attach importance to considerations of social policy such as the possibilities for the individual to support himself after a possible dismissal.

Thereafter it examined whether the proportionality criteria had been met. It pointed out that the problem in the case before it was somewhat different from that in cases concerning termination of employment at the attainment of a certain age. The case before it concerned the selection of the employees to be given notice of dismissal because of shortage of work and the weighing up of the interests of different groups of employees. The assessment must necessarily be influenced by what the alternative was to the dismissal of the pilots having attained the age for being entitled to the pension.

Again referring to the judgment of the ECJ in *Andersen*,[23] the *Høyesteret* also noted in its assessment that it was not to examine which selection criterion the defendant should have found to be the optimal choice on the basis of an ideal standard, but whether the chosen solution was inappropriate. The Høyesterett attached a certain importance to the fact that the solution chosen had been negotiated through a collective agreement with organisations representing 95 per cent of the SAS pilots, referring to the judgment of the ECJ in *Rosenbladt*.[24] It also emphasised that the selection criterion was objective. The Høyesterett found that the situation of the older pilots had been weighed against that of the younger and great importance had been attached to the fact that the older pilots were entitled to considerable pension benefits. It pointed out that this argument can be of importance in the proportionality assessment, referring to the judgments of the

[21] Norges Høyesterett, Case 2010/1676, HR-2011-0091-A, judgment of 5 May 2011.
[22] *Andersen*, n 17 above, para 23.
[23] ibid, para 35.
[24] Case C-45/09 *Rosenbladt*, judgment of 12 October 2010 nyr, para 49.

ECJ in *Rosenbladt* and in *Palacios de la Villa*.[25] In addition, the dismissed pilots could start a new job without losing their right to the pension payments.[26] The Høyesterett concluded that the agreement negotiated between the pilot unions concerned and the defendant was not contrary to the Norwegian legislation on age discrimination read in the light of the Employment Framework Directive.

CONFORMITY WITH THE CASE LAW OF THE ECJ

The four judgments described above contain somewhat different interpretations of the Employment Framework Directive and the principle of non-discrimination on grounds of age. As to the latter principle, it is not clear whether the Københavns Byret is of the view that there are no exceptions to that principle. It is submitted that this would not be correct. It is clear from the case law of the ECJ that the principle is not applicable on a standalone basis, but 'as given expression by' the Employment Framework Directive.[27] The national legislation implementing the principle thus has to be interpreted in the light of the Directive (and the relevant case law of the ECJ). It is, in this regard, interesting to note that the Norwegian Supreme Court has concluded that in the application and interpretation of the Norwegian legislation implementing (on a voluntary basis) the Employment Framework Directive, Norwegian courts should use the same sources of law as the ECJ. They should consequently interpret that legislation in the light of the Directive and the case law of the ECJ.

As to the interpretation of the definition of direct and indirect discrimination, the Attunda Tingsrätt came to the conclusion that since, in the case before it, there was no difference of treatment based on age in itself, there was no direct discrimination. However, in the three other judgments, which were all given after the judgment of the ECJ in *Andersen*,[28] it was held that the criterion used to decide which employees should be dismissed was inextricably linked to age and that the difference of treatment thus constituted direct discrimination.

In *Andersen*, the provision concerned deprived the workers of their right to a severance allowance on the sole ground that they were entitled to draw, on termination of the employment relationship, an old-age pension from their employer.[29] The entitlement to that pension was subject to a minimum age requirement, which in the case at hand was set under a collective agreement at 60 years. Thus, the requirement for the entitlement to the pension, which *automatically* excluded the right to the severance allowance, was the attainment of the age of 60 years. That provision was therefore considered to be based on a criterion which was inextricably linked to the age of the employees.

[25] ibid, para 48; *Palacios de la Villa*, n 13 above, para 73.

[26] The Norges Høyesterett again referred to *Rosenbladt*, n 24 above, paras 75–76.

[27] See, eg *Kücükdevici*, n 6 above, paras 51–56.

[28] *Andersen*, n 17 above.

[29] ibid, para 23.

It may nevertheless be questioned whether, in a situation of shortage of work, a system that bases the selection of the employees that must be dismissed on the criterion that the result shall secure the means of support for the group of employees concerned as a whole (dismissed as well as not dismissed), although resulting in a difference of treatment linked to age, that difference of treatment could really be said to be inextricably linked to the age of the employees and thus be *directly* based on age.[30]

However, as indicated in the judgment of the Norges Høyesterett, the classification of a difference of treatment as direct or indirect discrimination might not always be that important for the outcome of the case. What is more important is whether the difference of treatment can be objectively justified by a legitimate aim and whether the means of achieving that aim are appropriate and necessary within the meaning of the Employment Framework Directive.[31]

With regard to the question of whether the aim pursued by the measures concerned was legitimate, all three of the judgments, that in their analysis went beyond the establishment of whether the difference in treatment was direct or indirect, agree that securing the means of support for the group of employees concerned as a whole (dismissed as well as non-dismissed) constitutes a legitimate aim. It is submitted that such an aim clearly constitutes a social policy objective as required under Article 6(1) of the Employment Framework Directive.[32]

However, those judgments come to different conclusions with regard to what is required in order for the means to achieve that aim to be appropriate and necessary. The Attunda Tingsrätt is rather short in its analysis, simply pointing to the fact that the dismissals were part of a necessary reduction of the number of pilots and that the members of the disadvantaged group of employees were entitled to an advantageous pension financed by their employers under a collective agreement.

The Norges Høyesterett carries out a more detailed analysis, stressing, as a point of departure, that the chosen solution must not be inappropriate. It emphasises that the assessment must be influenced by what the alternative solution would have been. It underlines that the solution chosen had been negotiated

[30] In this context it can be noted that while the Employment Framework Directive provides that direct discrimination occurs where one person is treated less favorably than another on any of the discrimination grounds covered by the Directive, the Swedish Discrimination Act provides that direct discrimination occurs if that treatment *is related to* any of those grounds (see ch 1, s 4, para 1).

[31] In this regard, the Københavns Byret appears to hold that the Danish Act on Equal Treatment (n 15 above) does not contain a provision allowing the parties to deviate from the prohibition of difference of treatment based on age. However, s 5a, para 3 of the Act seems to contain such a provision, setting out that, notwithstanding para 1 (providing that provisions in individual or collective agreements that are contrary to the prohibition of discrimination are invalid), the Act does not preclude the application of age limits established in, or agreed in connection to, collective agreements, on condition that such age limits are objectively and reasonably justified by a legitimate aim within the context of Danish law and the means of achieving that aim are appropriate and necessary ('Uanset bestemmelsen i stk. 1 er loven ikke til hinder for opretholdelsen af gældende aldersgrænser fastsat i eller aftalt i henhold til kollektive aftaler og overenskomster, forudsat at disse aldersgrænser er objektivt og rimeligt begrundet i et legitimt formål inden for rammerne af dansk ret, og midlerne til at opfylde det pågældende formål er hensigtsmæssige og nødvendige').

[32] See, eg *Age Concern England*, n 7 above, para 46.

through a collective agreement with organisations representing 95 per cent of the employees concerned. Furthermore the selection criterion used was objective. Moreover the situation of the older employees had been weighed against that of the younger and great importance had been attached to the fact that the older employees were entitled to considerable pension benefits. In addition, the dismissed pilots could start a new job without losing their right to the (parallel) payments under the pension scheme.

All these facts seem to be elements that, according to the case law of the ECJ, should be taken into consideration when examining whether the aim concerned is appropriate and necessary. However, the Arbetsdomstolen, when carrying out that analysis, points out that the agreement concerned was contrary to a binding provision of national law and that the agreement can therefore not be considered appropriate to achieve its aim. It is argued that the fact that the agreement, according to the Arbetsdomstolen, was contrary to art 32a of the Employment Protection Act[33] cannot influence the examination of whether the agreement was 'appropriate and necessary'. First, the conclusion of the Arbetsdomstolen on this point in fact has the effect of declaring Chapter 2, Section 2, paragraph 4, of the Discrimination Act, which implements Article 6(1) of the Employment Framework Directive in Swedish law, null and void.[34] However, Section 32a of the Employment Protection Act provides 'unless otherwise prescribed by this Act' and Section 2, first paragraph, of the Act reads:

> Separate provisions contained in other statutes or regulations enacted by statutory authority that deviate from this Act shall have precedence over conflicting provisions contained in this Act.

According to the Arbetsdomstolen, any difference in treatment based on age and implying that employees would have to leave their employment (on a non-voluntary basis) before the age of 67 is contrary to Article 32a of the Employment Protection Act and therefore also to Section 2, Article 2, paragraph 4, of the Discrimination Act. Such a difference in treatment is not 'appropriate' and thus cannot be justified by way of derogation from the prohibition of discrimination on grounds of age. This reasoning changes the order of precedence set out in the provision quoted above and thereby also leads to a circular reasoning. With this reasoning, the Arbetsdomstolen actually did not need to examine at all whether the agreement pursued a legitimate aim. It would have been enough to state that the agreement was contrary to Section 32a of the Employment Protection Act and that Chapter 2, Section 2, paragraph 4, of the Discrimination Act therefore was not applicable.

[33] See n 12 above.

[34] Ch 2, s 2, para 4 of the Discrimination Act provides that, notwithstanding the prohibition of discrimination, differences of treatment on grounds of age are allowed if they have a legitimate aim and the means used to achieve the aim are appropriate and necessary ('förbudet mot diskriminering hindrar inte 'särbehandling på grund av ålder, om den har ett berättigat syfte och de medel som används är lämpliga och nödvändiga för att uppnå syftet').

Not only does the reasoning of the Arbetsdomstolen on this point seem to be contrary to the principle of legal certainty, requiring, on the one hand, that rules of law must be clear and precise and, on the other, that their application must be foreseeable by those subject to them,[35] but the question is also whether it is in line with Swedish constitutional law. It should be noted that the case law of the ECJ would seem to indicate that what should have been ascertained was whether the agreement was *manifestly* inappropriate for attaining the established legitimate aim.[36] Moreover, it follows from the judgment of the ECJ in *Andersen*,[37] that what the Arbetsdomstolen should have been examined is whether the agreement enabled the attainment of a legitimate aim pursued by the agreement without unduly prejudicing the legitimate interests of the employees concerned who, as a result of the agreement, found themselves deprived of their employment on the ground that they were entitled to an old-age pension to which the employer had contributed.

The Arbetsdomstolen should thus have examined whether dismissing those workers who were entitled to the occupational pension appeared unreasonable in the light of the objective of promoting access to employment by better distributing this access between the generations within the scope of the national employment policy. It is submitted that if the Arbetsdomstolen had carried out such an analysis, it is not unlikely that it would have come to the same conclusion as the ECJ in *Andersen*, that is, that the measure concerned did not appear to be manifestly inappropriate for attaining the legitimate aim pursued.

When it comes to the question of whether or not the agreement was proportionate, the Arbetsdomstolen recalled that the ECJ in *Andersen*[38] held that by not permitting payment of the severance allowance to workers who, although eligible for an old-age pension from their employer, nonetheless wish to waive their right to such a pension temporarily in order to continue with their career, the measure in question unduly prejudiced the legitimate interests of workers in such a situation and thus went beyond what was necessary to attain the social policy aims pursued by it. Basing itself on this conclusion of the ECJ, the Arbetsdomstolen held that giving notice to all the employees being entitled to a pension went beyond what was necessary and compared this measure to a forced retirement. The Arbetsdomstolen emphasised that the employees concerned were not even asked whether they wished to take out their old-age pension and leave their employment, or if they would consider leaving their employment in exchange for some kind of economic compensation in addition to the occupational pension. It especially underlined that the fact that some of the employees who had been given notice had already started to draw on their occupational pension did not change

[35] That requirement must be observed all the more strictly in the case of rules liable to entail financial consequences, in order for those concerned to know precisely the extent of the obligations which those rules impose on them. See, eg Case C-201/08 *Plantanol* [2009] ECR I-8343, para 46.

[36] See *Andersen*, n 17 above, para 35. The Norges Høyesterett referred to this paragraph when stating that it should only examine whether the chosen solution was inappropriate and not whether it was the optimal solution.

[37] *Andersen*, n 17 above, para 32.

[38] ibid, para 47.

the conclusion, because this was simply an effect of the pension agreement between the unions and the defendant, which gave the employees a right to draw on the pension while still employed by the defendant.

It is submitted that this interpretation of *Andersen* is questionable. What the ECJ pointed out was the fact that the workers who wished to waive their right to the old-age pension temporarily, and thus would not receive such benefits, would be deprived of the severance payment anyway.[39] In the case before the Arbetsdomstolen, this would, at the most, have meant that the agreement should only have covered those workers who actually were, or would be, drawing on the pension from the defendant.

Nevertheless, the situations were not the same. The logic of the agreement concerned in the case before the Arbetsdomstolen was that those employees who were entitled to receive the occupational pension were guaranteed a reasonable income and that, therefore, by giving notice to those workers, and thereby allowing the younger workers to keep their employment, the agreement ensured the best solution for the group of employees concerned as a whole. The logic behind the measure concerned in *Anderson* was, in principle, to prevent the severance pay from being claimed by persons who were not seeking new employment but would receive a replacement income in the form of the old-age pension from their employer. In the latter case, the reasoning of the ECJ makes sense, but in the former it does not.

It would also seem to follow from the reasoning of the ECJ that in *Andersen* the question of whether or not workers decide to draw on the occupational old-age pension actually was relevant to the examination of the proportionality of the measure in question.

In addition, the measures suggested by the Arbetsdomstolen as being less restrictive are not very clear. Would it have been enough if the defendant had first asked the employees concerned if any of them wished to draw on the occupational pension and leave their employment? Or would they have had to offer them 'some form of economic compensation' in addition to the pension? How much should that have been? Five per cent of their salary? What about those who would not accept? Could they then have been given notice anyway (which would be the same thing as forcing them to accept the offer)? Or would it then not be possible to give notice to those employees, implying that before the employees attain the age of 67 years only voluntary retirements are allowed, that is, once again coming to the conclusion that Chapter 2, Section 2, paragraph 4, of the Discrimination Act simply is inapplicable to differences in treatment based on age.

CONCLUSION

It appears from the four judgments analysed above, that the Nordic courts tend to follow rather well the case law of the ECJ interpreting the Employment Framework

[39] ibid, paras 44–47.

Directive. The only major question marks concern the interpretation of the definition of direct discrimination, the proportionality analysis and, possibly, the application of the principle of non-discrimination on grounds of age.

With regard to the definition of direct discrimination, it is submitted that after the judgment of the ECJ in *Andersen*, it is not quite clear how wide the scope of this definition is. The conclusion of the Court appears to indicate that the definition covers any situation in which the result of a measure is that employees who are below a certain age and those who are above are treated differently. It is nevertheless submitted that such a wide definition would seem to go beyond what is set out in the Employment Framework Directive.

As to the proportionality analysis, it always implies a difficult weighing of different interests. Nevertheless, it is argued that the analysis by the Arbetsdomstolen of whether or not the agreement concerned was 'appropriate and necessary' to achieve its legitimate aim is contrary to the case law of the ECJ, in particular the judgment in *Andersen*.

Finally, contrary to what seems to have been the view of the Københavns Byret, the principle of non-discrimination on grounds of age cannot be applied on a standalone basis. It follows from the case law of the ECJ that it has to be applied as given expression by the Employment Framework Directive.

PART III

PROCEDURE AND DUE PROCESS

24

Thoughts on Proportionality and Coherence in the Jurisprudence of the Court of Justice

THOMAS VON DANWITZ*

LONG BEFORE ITS explicit incorporation into the primary law of the European Union by the Treaty of Maastricht, the principle of proportionality had been acknowledged by the ECJ as a fundamental principle of the Community legal order.[1] Consequently the principle of proportionality has found expression in numerous judgments and permeates various fields of the Union's legislation.[2] It can justifiably be said that out of the general legal principles it is the most frequently invoked before and examined by the Court.[3] While the principle of proportionality unequivocally found its origin in German legal thinking,[4] it has nowadays become a genuine principle of European law, shaped according to the

* Prof Dr Dr HC, Judge of the Court of Justice of the European Union. All opinions expressed herein are personal to the author.

[1] Case 11/70 *Internationale Handelsgesellschaft* [1970] ECR 1125, paras 4, 15; Case 122/78 *Buitoni v Forma* [1979] ECR 677, paras 16 ff; Case 147/81 *Merkur Fleisch-Import* [1982] ECR 1389, para 12; Case 261/81 *Rau* [1982] ECR 3961, paras 17 ff; Case 66/82 *Fromançais v Forma* [1983] ECR 395, para 8; Case 15/83 *Denkavit Nederland v Hoofproduktschap voor Akkerbouwprodukten* [1984] ECR 2171, paras 24–32; Case 56/86 *Société pour l'exportation des sucres v OBEA* [1987] ECR 1423, paras 27 ff; Case 265/87 *Schräder v Hauptzollamt Gronau* [1989] ECR 2237, paras 21–24; Case C-174/89 *Hoche* [1990] ECR I-2681, para 14; Case C-155/89 *Philipp Brothers* [1990] ECR I-3265, paras 33 ff; Case C-24/90 *Faust* [1991] ECR I-4905, para 12.

[2] See, eg concerning the internal market, especially the four freedoms: Case 302/86 *Commission v Denmark* [1988] ECR 4607, para 21; Case C-331/88 *Fedesa and ors* [1990] ECR I-4023, paras 12 ff; Case C-51/93 *Meyhui* [1994] ECR I-3879, para 10; Case C-27/95 *Bakers of Nailsea* [1997] ECR I-1847, para 17; Case C-158/96 *Kohll* [1998] ECR I-1931, paras 52 ff; concerning fundamental rights: Case 136/79 *National Panasonic v Commission* [1980] ECR 2033, paras 28 ff; Case C-44/94 *Fishermen's Organisations and ors* [1995] ECR I-3115, para 57; Case C-22/94 *Irish Farmers Association and ors* [1997] ECR I-1809, paras 30 ff; Case C-114/96 *Kieffer and Thill* [1997] ECR I-3629, paras 31 ff; Case C-293/97 *Standley and ors* [1999] ECR I-2603, paras 46 ff; Case C-285/98 *Kreil* [2000] ECR I-69, para 29; concerning sanctions: *Buitoni v Forma*, n 1 above, paras 19 ff; Case 288/85 *Hauptzollamt Hamburg-Jonas v Plange Kraftfutterwerke* [1987] ECR 611, para 15; *Philipp Brothers*, n 1 above, paras 33 ff.

[3] See O Koch, *Der Grundsatz der Verhältnismäßigkeit in der Rechtsprechung des Gerichtshofes der Europäischen Gemeinschaften* (Berlin, Duncker & Humblot, 2003).

[4] T Koopmans, 'The Birth of European Law at the Crossroads of Legal Traditions' (1991) 39 *AJIL* 493 (501); H Kutscher, *Der Grundsatz der Verhältnismäßigkeit in den europäischen Rechtsordnungen* (Heidelberg, Müller, 1985).

specific conditions under which the Court exercises its mission, rather than the dogmatism of its native legal order. Exploring and understanding jurisprudence presents an enticing challenge, which might be of some value for the 'jubilee' of our esteemed colleague and dear friend Pernilla Lindh, who has proven her profound expertise in the matter in a vast number of her judgments.

I. WHY REFLECT ON THE COURT'S APPROACH ON PROPORTIONALITY AND COHERENCE?

This contribution will not outline the jurisprudence of the ECJ on the principle of proportionality in all its profound details, but will focus on the 'reasons behind the reasons', and in particular deal with the considerations a judge inevitably needs to take into account when applying a legal standard such as the principle of proportionality whose flexibility and diversity allows it to appear continuously in new forms, oscillating between consistency and subcutaneous change in nature.

Nevertheless, the following considerations are not meant to be interpreted as favouring judicial randomness in the application of the principle of proportionality, for this would inevitably lead to a justification of judicial arbitrariness, superficially clad as the rule of law, since this would certainly run contrary to the pronounced goal of the European integration to which it has been historically, politically, and legally committed from its origins. The following observations will instead be devoted to those considerations that guide the application of the proportionality principle in the judicial practice of the Union. At the same time, this approach will enable us to conduct a proper verification of the coherence of the Court's case law in order to prevent a 'selective rule of law'[5] and to guarantee a European jurisprudence, by which justice is conveyed 'discursively', willing to listen to criticism and receptive to rational examination. Only in this way can a uniform application of judicial findings be preserved and the trust in the ECJ be maintained against the hostility with which it has been met as a 'foreign jurisdiction'.

II. THE PROPORTIONALITY TEST

The principle of proportionality found its early recognition in the European legal order as a general principle of law.[6] However, the significance of this characterisation which appears rather unspectacular today, says little about its nature and

[5] E Schmidt-Aßmann, *Das allgemeine Verwaltungsrecht als Ordnungsidee und System* (Heidelberg, Müller, 1982) 16; from an administrative-scientific perspective: F Wagener, 'Der öffentliche Dienst im Staat der Gegenwart' (1979) 37 *VVDStRL* 215.

[6] *Internationale Handelsgesellschaft*, n 1 above, paras 4, 15; *Buitoni v Forma*, n 1 above, paras 16–23; Case 240/78 *Atalanta v Produktschap voor Vee en Vlees* [1979] ECR 2137, paras 15 ff; *Fromançais v Forma*, n 1 above, para 8; *Denkavit Nederland v Hoofproduktschap voor Akkerbouwprodukten*, n 1 above, paras 24–32; Case 21/85 *Maas v Bundesanstalt für landwirtschaftliche Marktordnung* [1986] ECR 3537, paras 15 ff; *Schräder v Hauptzollamt Gronau*, n 1 above, paras 21–24.

content. It reflects the process of creating precedents by means of comparative law[7] due to the lack of a statutory basis and denotes certain openness when it comes to the determination of its normative substance.

1. Foundations

The principle of proportionality was, at first, aligned with the requirements of the *Rechtsstaat.* It originated[8] in legal difficulties connected with the forfeiture of a security in the context of the Common Agricultural Policy. The Court applied the principle of proportionality with considerable assertiveness in these early cases.[9] Meanwhile the jurisprudence spread from this initial ground of a merely administrative nature and the principle of proportionality soon advanced to become a key requirement of constitutional nature as a standard for the judicial review of legislative acts.[10] The consequences which the Court drew from this major change will be discussed hereafter in contextual and dogmatic terms.

A second, particularly distinctive change can be seen in the acknowledgement of proportionality as 'the' legal standard for the justification of an interference with fundamental rights.[11] Based upon this jurisprudence,[12] the specific task of proportionality as a limitation for justified restrictions of fundamental rights has been given a highly symbolic significance in Article 52(1) of the Charter of Fundamental Rights. The inclusion of this general rule on limitations to fundamental rights explicitly signifies the Charter's commitment to insurmountable

[7] Concerning legitimation and function, see Joined Cases 7/56 and 3/57 to 7/57 *Algera* [1957] ECR 83; see also T von Danwitz, 'Der Einfluss des nationalen Rechts und der Rechtsprechung der Gerichte der Mitgliedstaaten auf die Auslegung des Gemeinschaftsrechts' (2008) *ZESAR* 57.

[8] *Internationale Handelsgesellschaft*, n 1 above, paras 4, 15; *Buitoni v Forma*, n 1 above, paras 16–23; *Atalanta v Produktschap voor Vee en* Vlees, n 6 above, paras 15 ff; *Fromançais v Forma*, n 1 above, para 8; *Denkavit Nederland v Hoofproduktschap voor Akkerbouwprodukten*, n 1 above, paras 24–32; *Maas v Bundesanstalt für landwirtschaftliche Marktordnung*, n 6 above, paras 15, 28; *Schräder v Hauptzollamt Gronau*, n 1 above, paras 21–24.

[9] *Buitoni v Forma*, n 1 above, paras 16–23; *Atalanta v Produktschap voor Vee en Vlees*, n 6 above, paras 15 ff; *Maas v Bundesanstalt für landwirtschaftliche Marktordnung*, n 6 above, paras 15, 28; Case C-118/89 *Lingenfelser* [1990] ECR I-2637, paras 12–15; Case C-319/90 *Pressler* [1992] ECR I-203, paras 12–17.

[10] Case C-280/93 *Germany v Council* [1994] ECR I-4973, paras 88 ff; Case C-84/94 *United Kingdom v Council* [1996] ECR I-5755, paras 50 ff; Case C-233/94 *Germany v Parliament and Council* [1997] ECR I-2405, paras 50 ff; Case C-434/02 *Arnold André* [2004] ECR I-11825, paras 45 ff; Case C-210/03 *Swedish Match* [2004] ECR I-11893, paras 47 ff; Case C-58/08, *Vodafone*, judgment of 8 June 2010 nyr, paras 51 ff; Case C-176/09 *Luxembourg*, judgment of 12 May 2011 nyr, paras 61 ff. As a nuance it may be added that the authorities cited in n 8 above are also linked to these matters.

[11] E Stieglitz, *Allgemeine Lehren im Grundrechtsverständnis nach der EMRK und der Grundrechtsjudikatur des EuGH* (Baden-Baden, Nomos, 2002) 138; A Emmerich-Fritsche, *Der Grundsatz der Verhältnismäßigkeit als Direktive und Schranke der EG-Rechtsetzung* (Berlin, Duncker & Humblot, 2000) 337; T von Danwitz, 'Der Grundsatz der Verhältnismäßigkeit im Gemeinschaftsrecht' (2003) *EWS* 393.

[12] *Buitoni v Forma*, n 1 above, paras 16–23; *Schräder v Hauptzollamt Gronau*, n 1 above, para 15; Joined Cases 46/87 and 227/88 *Hoechst v Commission* [1989] ECR 2859, para 19; *Fishermen's Organisations and ors*, n 2 above, para 55; *Standley and ors*, n 2 above, para 54; Case C-292/97 *Karlsson* [2000] ECR I-2737, para 45; Case C-491/01 *British American Tobacco (Investments) and Imperial Tobacco* [2002] ECR I-11453, paras 122 ff; Case C-112/00 *Schmidberger* [2003] ECR I-5659, para 79.

limitations for the Union's legislative power; namely the principle of proportionality, the necessity for a statutory basis of law and the respect for the essence of fundamental rights and freedoms. The mandate to ensure the observance of the law in the interpretation of the Treaties, which was already included in the Founding Treaties, hereby experiences an accented view reflecting the specific mandate of a constitutional justice in the best tradition of *Marbury v Madison*.[13] Without the guarantee of an effective constitutional review, the practical effectiveness of fundamental rights would be neglected, thus missing the historically anchored[14] purpose of the Charter. Despite the fact that this reorientation has not yet been reflected in the jurisprudence, the case law concerning proportionality as counter limits[15] elaborated in the pre-Charter era indicates what kind of challenges the Court will have to face in that regard.

In the Treaty of Lisbon the principle of proportionality – distinctly more pronounced than was the case under Article 5(3) of the EC Treaty – is embedded in the context of legal powers attributed to the EU and, as well as the principle of subsidiarity, it is regarded as a limitation for the Community's exercise of competences.[16] Under the principle of proportionality, the content and form of Union action shall not exceed what is necessary to achieve the objectives of the Treaties.[17] In the field of fundamental rights, the principle of proportionality requires that the Court determines what is necessary to achieve the objectives of the Treaties in order to comply with the obligation cited above. But how will it cope with this challenge? How will the Court navigate between the Scylla of a *déni de justice* and a Charybdis of a *gouvernement des juges*? Given the diversity of challenges attributed to the principle of proportionality by European primary law it may be stated at the very outset that it seems quite unreasonable to praise a uniformity of sequence and intensity for the judicial application of this standard by the ECJ. This would reveal nothing but the attempt to force the wisdom of proportionality into a Procrustean bed – from the very beginning doomed to failure. This finding, however, contains no surprises for daily judicial business.

[13] *Marbury v Madison*, 5 US 137 (1803).

[14] According to the decision of the European Council adopted on 3 and 4 June 1999 in Cologne (clauses 44, 45 and Annex IV) the Charter shall make fundamental rights' 'overriding importance and relevance more visible to the Union's citizens'; see JP Jacqué, 'La démarche initiée par le Conseil européen de Cologne' (2000) *RUDH* 3.

[15] M Zuleeg, 'Die Rechtsprechung des Europäischen Gerichtshofs zum Europarecht im Lichte des Grundgesetzes und seiner Dogmatik' in U Battis and ors (eds), *Das Grundgesetz im internationalen Wirkungszusammenhang der Verfassungen 40 Jahre Grundgesetz* (Berlin, Duncker & Humblot, 1990) 227–38; R Streinz, *Bundesverfassungsgerichtlicher Grundrechtsschutz und Europäisches Gemeinschaftsrecht – die Überprüfung grundrechtsbeschränkender deutscher Begründungs- und Vollzugsakte von Europäischem Gemeinschaftsrecht durch das Bundesverfassungsgericht* (Baden-Baden, Nomos, 1989) 411.

[16] Art 5(5) TEU.

[17] Art 5(4) TEU.

2. The Different Stages of Proportionality

In search of an appropriate response to the questions arising from the variety of tasks assigned to the principle of proportionality by primary law, a concise recollection of its fundamental function seems essential. Underlying the application of the principle of proportionality is the plain but crucial understanding that the general right to freedom of a Union's citizen may be restricted only in so far as it is indispensable to interests of general welfare.[18] The requirement of proportionality is designed to protect one's individual rights from needless – that is inappropriate, unnecessary and disproportionate – interference by governmental authorities.[19] This idea has found expression in terms of a classical formula in the established jurisprudence of the court, whereupon actions by a governmental authority can only be found lawful if the objectives which the measure in question is pursuing are appropriate and necessary as such. Where a choice of numerous appropriate measures is presented, the least onerous one needs to be chosen. In addition to that, the burden inflicted on the individual needs to be arranged in reasonable proportion to the intended objectives.[20]

These conditions require a case specific examination of the following aspects: the clarification of the preliminary question of proportionality concerning whether the measure under examination is pursuing a legitimate aim of general welfare, which is, as such, approved by the European legal order. Beyond this, the Court applies a conventional three-step analysis.[21] A sovereign measure is appropriate if the objectives pursued can be reached by the measure in question. Given the choice between a variety of appropriate measures, it has to be considered to be necessary. The threshold of necessity is met if no less restrictive measure can be

[18] *cf* for the early recognition in German constitutional law in BVerfGE 19, 342 (348 f).

[19] See, eg P Badura, *Staatsrecht*, 4th edn (München, Beck, 2010) D para 52; see generally P Lerche, *Übermaß und Verfassungsrecht* (Köln, Heymann, 1961).

[20] See, eg *Schräder v Hauptzollamt Gronau*, n 1 above, para 21; *Lingenfelser*, n 9 above, para 12; *Fedesa and ors*, n 2 above, para 13; *Faust*, n 1 above, para 12; Case C-25/90 *Wünsche* [1991] ECR I-4939, para 13; *Pressler*, n 9 above, para 12; Joined Cases C-133/93, C-300/93 and C-362/93 *Crispoltoni and ors* [1994] ECR I- 4863, para 41; Joined Cases C-296/93 and C-307/93 *France and Ireland v Commission* [1996] ECR I-795, para 30; Joined Cases C-254/94, C-255/94 and C-269/94 *Fattoria Autonoma Tabacco* [1996] ECR I-4235, para 55; Case C-157/96 *National Farmers' Union and ors* [1998] ECR-I 2211, para 60; Case C-180/96 *United Kingdom v Commission* [1998] ECR I-2265, para 96; Case C-101/98 *UDL* [1999] ECR I-8841, para 30; Case C-189/01 *Jippes and ors* [2001] ECR I-5689, para 81; Joined Cases C-27/00, C-122/00 *Omega Air and ors* [2002] ECR I-2569, para 63; Case C-220/01 *Lennox* [2003] ECR I-7091, para 76; Joined Cases C-96/03 and C-97/03 *Tempelman and van Schajik* [2005] ECR I-1897, para 47; Case C-504/04 *Agrarproduktion Staebelow* [2006] ECR I-679, para 35; Case C-310/04 *Spain v Counsel* [2006] ECR I-7285, para 97; Case C-45/05 *Maatschap Schonewille-Prins* [2007] ECR I-3997, para 48; Case C-375/05 *Geuting* [2007] ECR I-7983, para 45; Case C-37/06 *Viamex Agrar Handel and ZVK* [2008] ECR I-69, para 35; Case C-534/06 *Industria Lavorazione Carni Ovine* [2008] ECR I-4129, para 25; Case C-33/08 *Agrana Zucker* [2009] ECR I-5035, para 31; Case C-562/08 *Müller Fleisch*, judgment of 25 February 2010 nyr, para 43; Case C-379/08 *TAR Sicilia v Italy*, judgment of 9 March 2010 nyr, para 86; *EGC* jurisprudence concerning this matter includes Joined Cases T-481/93 and T-484/93 *Exporteurs in Levende Varkens and ors* [1995] ECR II-2941, para 119; Case T-390/94 *Schröder and ors v Commission* [1997] ECR II-501, para 138; Joined Cases T-125/96 and T-152/96 *Boehringer v Council and Commission* [1999] ECR II-3427, para 73.

[21] See, eg *Vodafone*, n 10 above, paras 51 ff; *Luxembourg*, n 10 above, paras 66–72.

identified which would ensure that this objective is attained with equal effectiveness.[22] Ultimately, the principle of proportionality requires a judicial finding that the disadvantages caused are not disproportionate to the aims pursued.[23]

Appropriateness is based on a rather simple means-ends-relationship, in which the effect of the chosen measure is analysed with regard to whether the objectives of general welfare can be achieved effectively. In contrast, the evaluation of necessity requires a comparative view of the measure held against other appropriate measures of equivalent effectiveness. Compared to those, the chosen measure may not be more restrictive in order to pass the test of necessity. The test of adequacy exceeds a rigid perspective by requiring that the disadvantages caused by the measure under scrutiny are proportionate to the aims pursued.[24] In order to qualify a given measure as proportionate, one needs to weigh up the importance of the exercised jurisdiction and its burdening effects in comparison to the weight and urgency of the reasons advanced as overriding public interests for its justification.[25] Correspondingly it is acknowledged in the settled case law of the Court that the importance of the objectives pursued by a governmental measure can justify negative consequences even of a substantial nature.[26] Ultimately, this examination requires a lawful cost/benefit ratio[27] based upon a judicial finding on the constitutional value of the private interest which is restricted by the governmental measure under scrutiny. This seems rather apparent when it comes to the justification of a measure interfering with fundamental rights which, under given circumstances, has to be balanced against the public interests which the governmental measure claims to be overriding. It is likewise obvious that such an assessment appears to be of a genuinely constitutional judicial nature and therefore can only be carried out under the authority of the Court, rather than being left to the discretion of the Union's legislator.

3. The Court's Approach

The case law of the Court is quite irritating, since it only addresses the elements of appropriateness and necessity in a significant number of judgments in which

[22] See, eg *Luxembourg*, n 10 above, para 67.

[23] See n 20 above.

[24] *Groppera Radio AG and ors v Switzerland*, judgment, Series A no 173, 28 March 1990, § 72; *Buitoni v Forma*, n 1 above, paras 19 ff; *Crispoltoni and ors*, n 20 above, para 41; *Jippes and ors*, n 20 above, para 81; *Lennox*, n 20 above, para 76; *Viamex Agrar Handel and ZVK*, n 20 above, para 35.

[25] *cf* Case 5/73 *Balkan-Import-Export v Hauptzollamt Berlin-Packhof* [1973] ECR 1091, para 22; *Jippes and ors*, n 20 above, para 99; Case C-127/07 *Arcelor Atlantique et Lorraine and ors* [2008] ECR I-9895, para 59; Case C-208/09, *Ilonka Sayn-Wittgenstein*, judgment of 22 December 2010 nyr, para 93. Examples of national case law are to be found in BVerfGE 30, 292 (316) as well as in Conseil d'Etat, judgment of 28 May 1971 of Conseil d'Etat *Ville nouvelle Est* in Long et al (eds), *Les grands arrêts de la jurisprudence administrative* (Paris, Sirey, 1990) no 107.

[26] *Fedesa and ors*, n 2 above, para 17; Case C-84/95 *Bosphorus* [1996] ECR I-3953, para 23; Case C-86/03 *Greece v Commission* [2005] ECR I-10979, para 96; *Arcelor Atlantique et Lorraine and ors*, n 25 above, para 59.

[27] Concerning the so-called 'théorie du bilan avantages-couts', see the judgment in *Ville nouvelle Est*, n 25 above.

measures of secondary legislation are subject to review under the principle of proportionality.[28] However, these decisions do not shed light on why judicial review is limited to these aspects. Also, neither the structure of the rulings nor the documented approach of the Court indicates whether this two-step review of proportionality seeks to establish a restrictive approach based upon a conceptual understanding which would eliminate the element of proportionateness from being an integral part of the judicial application of proportionality. The assumption that these judgments would indeed want to exempt the element of proportionateness from the judicial review of proportionality however seems not only excessive but rather far-fetched to me. This incoherence of the Court's jurisprudence might certainly be deplorable since the principal mission of the Court is to ensure a uniform interpretation of the law of the Union and to guarantee legal security.[29] But, such a misleading interpretation can be overcome. The practical reasons for the different formulas used by the Court seem to be rather easy to explain. On one hand, it needs to be taken into account that the Court structures its examination of the principle of proportionality in a two-fold manner. The general description of its normative content is followed by a separate statement concerning its judicial review, before the Court then proceeds with the actual test of proportionality. Therefore one should not understand the general description of the normative content of proportionality as a 'major premise' meant to determine fully the subsequent examination. This understanding is supported by the fact that the Court appreciates the element of proportionateness even when it has not made a corresponding announcement before.[30] This is also backed up by the fact that the legal description of the principle of proportionality in Article 5(4) TEU and Article 52(1) of the Charter of Fundamental Rights does not explicitly contain a reference to the element of proportionateness. On the other hand, it is crucial that a review of proportionateness only becomes mandatory, according to general procedural practice of the Court, in so far as it is confronted with a corresponding submission from the parties. A closer look at the Court's jurisprudence shows that the limitation of the judicial review of proportionality to appropriateness and necessity[31] can fully explain this.

The principle of proportionality has been applied in a rather peculiar way in *Schecke and Eifert*. In this judgment the Court did not examine the proportionateness of the fundamental right of the respect of privacy and the protection of personal data as such, which had been invoked by recipients of subsidies of the

[28] Case 170/84 *Bilka* [1986] ECR 1607, para 37; Case 116/82 *Wein* [1986] ECR 2519, paras 21 ff; Case 281/84 *Zuckerfabrik Bedburg* [1987] ECR 49, para 36; *Philipp Brothers*, n 1 above, para 34; Case C-288/89 *Collective Antennevooziening Gouda* [1991] ECR I-4007, para 15; Case C-126/91 *Yves Rocher* [1993] ECR I-2361, para 15; Case C-271/92 *LPO* [1993] I-2899, para 12; Case C-259/91 *Allué* [1993] ECR I-4309, para 15.

[29] This applies all the more from a dogmatic perspective.

[30] *Vodafone*, n 10 above, paras 51, 69; *Luxembourg*, n 10 above, paras 61, 68 ff.

[31] *Wein*, n 28 above, paras 2525 ff; no 25; *Zuckerfabrik Bedburg*, n 28 above, para 59; *Collective Antennevoorziening Gouda*, n 28 above; *Yves Rocher*, n 28 above, paras 2364 ff; *Allué*, n 28 above, paras 4317 ff.

Common Agricultural Policy. Instead, the Court investigated whether the Council and the Commission had carried out considerations of the necessity to protect privacy and personal data when adopting the regulation in question.[32] The Court invalidated the regulation based on the finding of a deficiency of motivation which enjoys priority over a substantive balancing of the involved interests, thus making a statement on grounds of material proportionateness dispensable. The Court's approach appears preferable in so far as it does not rule out the possibility that the interests involved could eventually be balanced in conformity with fundamental rights requirements. In the present context it remains, however, decisive that this particular approach of review may not be (mis-) interpreted as an implicit rejection of the need for a substantive assessment of the proportionateness of secondary legislation by the Court.

III. JUDICIAL REVIEW OF PROPORTIONALITY

The academic discussion is dominated by the question whether the judicial review of proportionality offers a sufficient intensity or, to the contrary, whether it might not ensure effective judicial protection.[33] As a preliminary remark it should be noted that the determination of an adequate intensity of legal scrutiny is often regarded as a matter of judicial discretion and even as an arcanum of judicial decision-making, which is deeply rooted in the self-conception of the judicial branch of government resulting from different national traditions. The great differences existing in that respect amongst the Member States of the European Union might be considered a mere platitude, but these are definitely calling for a genuine determination of the parameters governing judicial review under Union law. In light of these circumstances, the extensive canonisation of factors relating to the intensity of scrutiny as it is exposed in the jurisprudence of the Federal

[32] Joined Cases C-92/09 and C-93/09, *Schecke and Eifert*, judgment of 9 November 2010 nyr, paras 77, 80–81.

[33] For a critical assessment of Case C-280/93 (Bananas I) from German authors, see M Nettesheim, Grundrechtliche Prüfdichte durch den EuGH, (1995) *EuZW* 106 ff; G Berrisch, 'Zum "Bananen" – Urteil des EuGH vom 5 10 1994 – Rs C-280/93, Deutschland/Rat der Europäischen Union' (1994) *EuR* 29, 461, 465 ff; U Everling, 'Will Europe Slip on Bananas? The Bananas Judgment of the Court of Justice and National Courts' (1996) 33 *CMLR* 410, 417, 419; P Huber, 'Das Kooperationsverhältnis zwischen BVerfG und EuGH in Grundrechtsfragen' (1997) *EuZW* 517, 521; S Storr, 'Zur Bonität des Grundrechtsschutzes in der Europäischen Union' (1997) 36 *Der Staat* 547, 552 ff; W Pauly, 'Strukturfragen des unionsrechtlichen Grundrechtsschutzes' (1998) 33 *EuR* 242, 256 ff; P Selmer, *Die Gewährleistung der unabdingbaren Grundrechtsstandards durch den EuGH* (Baden-Baden, Nomos, 1998) 96 ff, 118 ff; T Stein, 'Bananen-Split' (1998) *EuZW* 261, 262; W Leisner, 'Der europäische Eigentumsbegriff: schwächerer Eigentumsschutz als in Deutschland?' in *Verfassungrecht im Wandel, Wiedervereinigung Deutschlands, Deutschland in der Europäischen Union. Verfassungstaat und Föderalismus. Zum 180 jährigen Bestehen der Carl Heymans Verlag KG* (Carl Heymans Verlag, 1995) 395; C Tomuschat, 'Aller guten Dinge sind III?' (1990) 25 *EuR* 340 ff; for further critical voices from France, Spain and Belgium, respectively: M Donny, 'L'affaire des bananes' (1995) *Cahiers de droit européen* 461, 491 ff; F Castillo de la Torre, 'The Status of GATT in EC Law, Revisited – The Consequences of the Judgment on the Banana Import Regime for the Enforcement of the Uruguay Round Agreements' (1995) *Journal of World Trade* 53.

German Constitutional Court[34] cannot be regarded as a *communis opinio* amongst judicial traditions in Europe. This is *a fortiori* true for the distinct self-conception of this constitutional court claiming to have its proper share in the conduct of government.[35] The antithesis is represented by legal systems where no constitutional court exists at all or where only restricted powers to review legislative acts have been constitutionally granted to the judiciary.[36] Even if there can be no doubt that the European legal order has assigned the Court with far-reaching powers to review the validity of Union law and with a corresponding responsibility for the respect of constitutional guarantees which are equivalent to those accredited to the constitutional courts of the Member States, traditional patterns of judicial self-conception remain of significant relevance for the determination of the role assigned to the Court by the treaties and the specific conditions under which it reviews secondary EU law.

1. Safeguarding the Discretion of the Community Legislature

Despite these uncertainties, the jurisprudence of the Court is based on the firm conviction that the way in which the judicial review of the principle of proportionality has to be conducted requires a specific determination in each individual case. However, on the whole, the Court is exercising a review of secondary legislation which is restricted in nature. In that regard, the Court has accepted that

> in the exercise of the powers . . . the Community legislature must be allowed a broad discretion in areas in which its action involves political, economic and social choices and in which it is called upon to undertake complex assessments and evaluations.

Thus, the test of proportionality is not designed to determine whether the measure under scrutiny was the only or the best measure possible, since its legality can only be affected if the measure is manifestly inappropriate with regard to the objective

[34] BVerfGE 50, 290 (332 f): 'In detail, the legislator's competence to decide is dependent on different factors, especially: the peculiarity of the concerned functional area, the possibilities of forming an adequate opinion, and the meaning of the object of legal protection that is at stake. Accordingly, the judicature of the Federal Constitutional Court took sophisticated standards as a basis of the judgment of the legislator's predictions. These standards vary from evidence control (for example: decision of the *Federal Constitutional Court* 36, 1 (17) – primary contract; 37, 1 (20) – the stock of stabilisation; 40, 196 (223) – the bill of road haulage), a control of tenability (for example: decision of the *Federal Constitutional Court* 25, 1 (12 f, 17) – bill of mills; 30, 250 (263) – bill of safeguarding; 39, 210 (225 f) – bill of the structure of mills) to an intensive control with regard to content (for example: decision of the *Federal Constitutional Court* 7, 377 (415) – pharmacies; 11, 30 (45) – CHI physicians; 17, 269 (267 ff) – pharmaceutical law; 39, 1 (46, 51 ff) – § 218 criminal code; 45, 187 (238) – life sentence)'; *cf* also *BVerfGE* 57, 139 (159 ff); 62, 1 (50 f); 90, 145 (173); 99, 367 (389 f).

[35] *cf* the so-called status report of the German Federal Constitutional Court, JöR NF vol 6 (1957) 109 ff.

[36] See for the United Kingdom: W Spoerr, 'Verwaltungsrechtsschutz in Großbritannien' (1991) 82 *Verwaltungsarchiv* 25, 30; *cf* for Denmark: Koch, n 3 above, Verhältnismäßigkeit, 127 ff; Streinz, n 15 above; Grundrechtsschutz, 138; Art 120 of the Dutch Constitution provides, that '[t]he constitutionality of Acts of Parliament and treaties shall not be reviewed by the courts'.

pursued.[37] Even though it has a broad discretion, the Community legislature must base its choice on objective criteria. Furthermore, in assessing the burdens associated with various possible measures, it must examine whether objectives pursued by the measure chosen are such as to justify even substantial negative economic consequences for certain operators.[38] Moreover, the established jurisprudence is based upon the understanding that the Court might not, when applying the principle of proportionality, replace the appreciation of the competent authority, which has to weigh the different interests in its own responsibility.[39]

Summarising these lessons, a 'control grid' becomes apparent, which can certainly not be found to be expressed in the same terms and with equal determination in every decision of the Court. Thus, it should be emphasised from the outset that the Court does not derive the restriction of its judicial review on proportionality requirements by a standard reference to its limited institutional legitimacy in comparison to the legislator. In fact it explicitly refers to the need for complex evaluations in order to justify its limited control.[40] Only when reviewing legislative acts based upon a competence which confers comprehensive legislative powers to the legislator, as is namely the case in the common transport policy, maritime and air transport, the mere dimension of such powers reflecting the specific responsibilities of the Union[41] is sufficient to justify the limitation of the Court's review. In contrast to this particular case, a limitation of the judicial review relating to proportionality requirements is in general conditioned by a specific statement of the Court that the Union legislator enjoys a wide margin of discretion reflecting the need for complex assessments and evaluations.

This jurisprudence of the Court corresponds with a classical attitude, well known from the jurisprudence of the constitutional courts of Member States, in which a prerogative of the two 'political' branches of government to determine the factual basis of legislation and to balance the interests affected by a governmental measure, is expressly recognised. At the same time the Court emphasises in its jurisprudence that the recognition of a prerogative of the Union's legislator in these respects does not absolve it from the obligation to base its decisions upon objective criteria and to examine whether the objectives pursued by a particular measure can justify even significant disadvantages for the stakeholders. In particular, the measures enacted on the basis of a prerogative conceded to the Union's legislator may not produce results which are clearly less proportionate than those produced by other measures which prove to be equally appropriate to reach the

[37] *Vodafone*, n 10 above, para 52; see also *Jippes and ors*, n 20 above, paras 82 ff; *British American Tobacco (Investments) and Imperial Tobacco*, n 12 above, para 123; Joined Cases C-154/04 and C-155/04 *Alliance for Natural Health and ors* [2005] ECR I-6451, para 52; Case C-558/07 *SPCM and ors* [2009] ECR I-5783, para 42.

[38] *Vodafone*, n 10 above, para 53; see also *Tempelman and van Schajik*, n 20 above, para 48; *Greece v Commission*, n 26 above, para 96; *Agrarproduktion Staebelow*, n 20 above, para 37; see also *Arcelor atlantique et lorraine and ors*, n 25 above, para 59; *Luxembourg*, n 10 above, para 63.

[39] Case C-150/94 *United Kingdom v Council* [1998] ECR I-7235, paras 87, 91.

[40] *Vodafone*, n 10 above, para 52.

[41] Art 100 (2) TFEU provides: 'The European Parliament and the Council, acting in accordance with the ordinary legislative procedure, may lay down appropriate provisions for sea and air transport'.

objectives pursued.[42] When it comes to the specific application of these standards to particular cases, a certain degree of variation in the jurisprudence of the Court has to be acknowledged.[43] But this is a phenomenon which belongs to the essence of the case-related function of any jurisdiction and therefore appears to be somewhat inevitable. Thus, the jurisprudence concerning the Court's review of proportionality requirements is found to be thoroughly in harmony with traditional patterns of reasoning derived from the jurisprudence of national courts. In particular, it does not seem justified to assume a fundamental deficit of judicial review.

Less evident, however, is the finding of how the Court actually proceeds in examining the proportionateness of a given measure. As clear as recent jurisdiction indicates a return to the need for this control element,[44] it still remains somewhat unclear what position the Court takes on the question of how it has to implement a precise application of the requirement of adequacy. Of key importance in this regard is an aspect which has often been neglected in earlier discussions and which is directly related to the understanding of the Court as a constitutional court of the Union, a role which has experienced an increased importance after the legally binding enactment of the Charter of Fundamental Rights. Essentially, striking the balance between the objectives of the general welfare pursued by Union legislation on the one hand and interests which are legally protected as fundamental rights on the other hand constitutes an assignment of genuinely judicial nature which can only be attributed to a constitutional court.

Although the Union legislator is fully legitimised to stress the relevance and importance of a particular objective of general welfare, including its protection as a fundamental right, the determination of whether such an objective *indeed* has to be qualified accordingly is a sole matter of interpretation of the Constitution and may therefore only be determined under the authority of the Court. This conclusion applies *a fortiori* to the question what significance has to be attributed to legal interests which are limited or even 'sacrificed' by a legislative act and, finally, whether the balance between conflicting public and private interests has been affected in a way which neglects the importance of fundamental rights. If one wanted to grant the Union's legislator a far-reaching prerogative relating to the assessment of interests and their adequate balancing, this would ultimately lead to a situation in which the importance of the rights granted to EU citizens by the Treaty and by the Charter of Fundamental Rights were ultimately left to the discretion of the Union legislator; a consequence which could hardly be brought into accordance with the fundamental conception of the Treaty to subordinate the Union's legislator to a proper system of constitutional justice.

[42] *Fedesa and ors*, n 2 above, paras 15–17; *Greece v Commission*, n 26 above, para 96.

[43] See, eg *Germany v Council*, n 10 above, paras 90 ff; *Arcelor atlantique et lorraine and ors*, n 25 above, paras 57 ff.

[44] *Viamex Agrar Handel and ZVK*, n 20 above, para 35; *Industria Lavorazione Carni Ovine*, n 20 above, para 25; *Agrana Zucker*, n 20 above, para 31; *Müller Fleisch*, n 20 above, para 43.

2. Proportionality of National Measures

While the preceding considerations on the judicial review of the proportionality requirements were related to legislative acts of the Union's legislature, the application of the principle of proportionality to measures of Member States has so far been deliberately left out of consideration, though there is an abundance of rulings of the Court dealing with fundamental freedoms to which the principle of proportionality has been applied.[45] A comprehensive survey of this jurisprudence would undoubtedly go beyond the limited conception of this contribution. It should however be noted that ever since the judgment in *Cassis de Dijon* was given, the principle of proportionality is considered as a key element in the justification of restrictions of fundamental freedoms by the Member States.[46] The decisive aspect in the course of reviewing a restriction of fundamental freedoms is the scrutiny of the necessity of a national limitation,[47] which the Court only considers if the desired purpose 'can not be achieved by measures that restrict the intra-Community trade less'.[48] In principle, the Court places strict requirements on the need for a national measure restricting fundamental freedoms.[49] In particular, the Member States are not awarded with a prerogative to assess the necessity of a measure, contrary to what is conceded to the Union legislator. However, the proportionality of a regulation of a Member State restricting a fundamental freedom on the grounds of public policy or public security may not be banned for the simple reason that a Member State has established a particularly high level of

[45] See for free movement of goods: Case C-320/03 *Commission v Austria* [2005] ECR I-9871, paras 70 ff; Case C-244/06 *Dynamic Medien* [2008] ECR I-505, para 42; Case C-161/09 *Kakavetsos-Fragkopoulos*, judgment of 3 March 2011 nyr, paras 39 ff; for freedom of establishment: Case C-161/07 *Commission v Austria* [2008] ECR I-10671, para 36; Case C-438/08 *Commission v Portugal* [2009] ECR I-10219, para 47; Case C-400/08 *Commission v Spain*, judgment of 24 March 2011 nyr, para 83; for free movement of services: Case C-319/06 *Commission v Luxembourg* [2008] ECR I-4323, para 51; Case C-137/09, *Marc Michel Josemans*, judgment of 16 December 2010 nyr, para 69; for free movement of capital: Joined Cases C-515/99, C-519/99 to C-524/99 and C-526/99 to C-540/99 *Reisch and ors* [2002] ECR I-2141, para 33; Case C-463/00 *Commission v Spain* [2003] ECR-I 4581, para 68; Case C-98/01 *Commission v United Kingdom* [2003] ECR I-4641, para 49.

[46] See, eg Case 120/78 *Rewe-Zentral* [1979] ECR 649; Case 27/80 *Fietje* [1980] ECR 3839; Case 130/80 *Keldermann* [1981] ECR 527; see also *Koch*, n 3 above, 415; Case 29/72 *Marimex* [1972] ECR 1309; Case 33/74 *Binsbergen* [1974] ECR 1299; Case C-463/01 *Commission v Germany* [2004] ECR I-11705, para 75; Case C-309/02 *Radlberger Getränkegesellschaft and S Spitz* [2004] ECR I-11763, para 75; *Commission v Austria*, n 45 above, para 70; Case C-531/06 *Commission v Italy* [2009] ECR I-4103, para 49; *Commission v Portugal*, n 45 above, para 47.

[47] See W Schroeder in *Streinz* (ed), (2003) EUV/EGV Art 30 EGV, para 53; Koch, n 3 above, 416 ff, listing typical constellations where necessity is to be proved; T Kingreen in *Calliess/Ruffert* (ed), (2011) EUV/AEUV, 4th edn, Arts 34–36 AEUV, para 93; W Frenz, 'Grundfreiheiten und Grundrechte' (2002) *EuR* 603, 610.

[48] See, eg Case 25/88 *Wurmser* [1989] ECR 1105, paras 13 ff; Case C-470/93 *Mars* [1995] ECR I-1923, para 15; Case C-67/97 *Bluhme* [1998] ECR I-8033, para 35; Case C-473/98 *Toolex* [2000] ECR I-5681, para 40; Case C-510/99 *Tridon* [2001] ECR I-7777, para 53; Case C-322/01 *Deutscher Apothekerverband* [2003] ECR I-14887, para 104; Case C-192/01 *Commission v Denmark* [2003] ECR I-9693, para 45; Case C-170/04 *Rosengren and ors* [2007] ECR I-4071, para 43; Case C-219/07 *Nationale Raad van Dierenkwekers en Liefhebbers und Andibel* [2008] ECR I-4475, para 42.

[49] Case C-65/05 *Commission v Greece* [2006] ECR I-10341, paras 38 ff; *Rosengren and ors*, n 48 above, para 57; Schroeder, n 47 above.

protection.[50] Concerning the protection of human health, the Court has now expressly granted the Member States a certain scope of evaluation[51] after having already limited its review in that respect for some time.[52] The same applies to the field of road safety.[53] Recently, the question has been raised whether such a prerogative should be conceded to the Member States in the field of environmental protection responsibilities resulting from Directives 92/62 and 1990/30.[54] Doubtless, it is one of the principal tasks for the Court in the future to monitor closely the coherence of its case law in order to ensure a uniform application of EU law.

3. Division of Labour between the ECJ and National Courts

Finally, an aspect of great relevance for the judicial practice has to be highlighted despite it having received little attention in the judicial literature so far. It concerns the division of judicial responsibilities between the ECJ and the national courts in reviewing whether the requirements of the principle of proportionality are observed *in concreto*. In that respect, it should be recalled that the courts of the Member States are exclusively competent for the determination of the facts and, in principle, for the application of the Court's interpretation of Union law in cases pending before national courts.[55] In order to form an opinion of whether requirements of proportionality are met under given circumstances, an evaluation of the facts as they are present in an individual case is, as a rule, mandatory. National courts therefore play an indispensable role in the application of proportionality requirements. Following these guidelines on the division of labour between the two levels of jurisdiction, the Court has on several occasions refrained from determining in greater detail specific indications on how to handle the proportionality test derived from European Union law and, instead, left room to the courts of the Member States for such findings.[56] In particular, in respect of difficult situations

[50] Case C-443/02 *Schreiber* [2004] ECR I-7275, para 48; Case C-36/02 *Omega* [2004] ECR I-9609, para 38; Case C-141/07 *Commission v Germany* [2008] ECR I-6935, para 51; Case C-110/05 *Commission v Italy* [2009] ECR I-519, para 65.

[51] *Commission v Germany*, n 50 above, paras 46, 51; Case C-169/07 *Hartlauer* [2009] ECR I-1721, para 30; Joined Cases C-171/07 and C-172/07 *Apothekerkammer des Saarlandes and ors* [2009] ECR I-4171, para 19; Case C-333/08, *Commission v France*, judgment of 28 January 2010 nyr, paras 90, 91.

[52] *Schreiber*, n 50 above, paras 47–49; Case C-41/02 *Commission v Netherlands* [2004] ECR I-11375, paras 42, 49, 51; Case 188/84 *Commission v France* [1986] ECR 419, paras 16 ff.

[53] *Commission v Italy*, n 50 above, paras 61, 65.

[54] See Case C-28/09 *Commission v Austria*, pending.

[55] GC Rodríguez Iglesias, 'Der EuGH und die Gerichte der Mitgliedstaaten – Komponenten der richterlichen Gewalt in der Europäischen Union' (2000) *NJW*, 1889; *cf* G Hirsch, 'Die Rolle des Europäischen Gerichtshofs bei der europäischen Integration' (2001) 49 *JöR NF*, 79.

[56] Joined Cases C-286/94, C-340/95, C-401/95 and C-47/96 *Molenheide and ors* [1997] ECR I-7281, paras 48 ff; Case C-405/98 *Gourmet International Products* [2001] ECR I-1795, para 41; Case C-243/01 *Gambelli and ors* [2003] ECR I-13031, para 75; Joined Cases C-338/04, C-359/04 and C-360/04 *Placanica and ors* [2007] ECR I-1891, para 58; Case C-438/05 *International Transport Workers' Federation and Finnish Seamen's Union ('Viking Line')* [2007] ECR I-10779, para 85; Case C-135/08, *Rottmann*, judgment of 2 March 2010 nyr, para 58; Case C-258/08 *Ladbrokes*, judgment of 3 June 2010 nyr, para 22.

of collision which may arise between basic freedoms and fundamental rights, the Court has stated that the conflicting interests have to be balanced according to the principle of proportionality, but has left it to the national courts to determine the specific *modus operandi* without making detailed findings on this so far.[57] Hereby, the Court has introduced an important element into the dialogue of judges by which the co-operation between judges in Europe has been developed under the auspices of judicial subsidiarity.

IV. COHERENCE

More recently, a requirement has been introduced into the proportionality test which is often referred to as the concept of coherence. In the jurisprudence of the Court, the requirement of coherence, which was initially developed to get along with the rather specific problems of EU law in gambling cases, has now found a generalised recognition as an explicit condition for national legislation which can only be considered as appropriate 'if it genuinely reflects a concern to attain that objective in a consistent and systematic manner'.[58]

1. State of Jurisprudence

This classic formula of the Court's case law makes it quite clear that the 'consistency requirement' of the recent jurisprudence is in no way a free-handed 'invention' of a new and hitherto unknown legal standard in the jurisprudence of the Court which has to be understood and applied as an autonomous requirement, independent from the principle of proportionality. Already the precise wording of the jurisprudence on coherence shows that it is neither a supplement nor an alternative to the test of proportionality. The consistency requirement is rather an element firmly embedded in the proportionality test and located on the level of appropriateness. Its objective is to give further guidance for the application of the proportionality test in so far as the objectives of a measure taken by Member States must be pursued in a coherent and systematic manner. Initial comments in the academic literature have posed the quite understandable question whether the Court has, by introducing the requirement of coherence, launched a significant intensification of its scrutiny over restrictions on fundamental freedoms by the Member States.[59]

[57] *International Transport Workers' Federation and Finnish Seamen's Union*, n 56 above, para 85; von Danwitz, 'Grundfreiheiten und Kollektivautonomie' (2010) *EuZA* 6.

[58] *Apothekerkammer des Saarlandes and ors*, n 51 above, para 42; See also *Placanica and ors*, n 56 above, paras 53, 58; Case C-500/06 *Corporación Dermoestética* [2008] ECR I-5785, paras 39 ff; *Hartlauer*, n 51 above, para 55.

[59] U Forsthoff in E Grabitz, M Hilf et al, *Das Recht der Europäischen Union*, 42nd supp (München, Beck, 2010) para 402.

In response to such questions it appears useful, as a general rule, to suggest a cautious approach for an application of the requirement of coherence. Without neglecting the fact that it may seem entirely justified and reasonable to subordinate the restriction of fundamental freedoms by a Member State to the requirement of a coherent pursuit of overriding reasons of general welfare, problems related to the practical implementation of this requirement should not be left out of sight. Even if it might seem exaggerated, it may nonetheless be stated that for any legislation, be it of the Member States or of the European Union, that a 'perfect' law pursuing objectives of general welfare in a thoroughly consistent and systematic manner is a mere fiction which would in practice be impossible to enact. In this respect the famous dictum of *Bismarck* needs to be recalled; that it would be better if fewer people knew how sausages and laws are made. It is therefore crucial to apply the requirement of coherence in a realistic manner.

2. Analysis

Looking at the jurisprudence of the Court on coherence under these auspices, initially it is worth noting that the development of a consistency requirement has taken place in areas where the Court granted the Member States a margin of appreciation in the first place, namely in the field of health protection and in the field of gambling with respect to combating criminality and addiction.[60] Taking this setting into consideration, the requirement of coherence does not really seem to reflect an intensification of the proportionality test as it is operated by the Court, but rather an attempt to apply the criterion of appropriateness adequately under conditions which are characterised by a margin of appreciation granted to Member States. The real explanation behind the application of the requirement of coherence therefore is less likely to be found in intensification, but rather in search for an adequate compensation of judicial review resulting from a margin of appreciation having been conceded to Member States. In essence, it may be concluded that the coherence is designed to object to rules which are found to be self-contradictory or, at least, manifestly inappropriate without questioning the legitimate scope left to Member States by the Union law. The interdependence both of the recognition of a margin of appreciation and the requirement of coherence may become apparent in future case law.[61] However, there are also judgments which show a tendency to over-compensation.[62]

[60] Concerning health protection: *Hartlauer*, n 51 above, para 61; Case C-341/08, *Petersen*, judgment of 12 January 2010 nyr, para 53; concerning gambling: *Gambelli and ors*, n 56 above, para 67; *Placanica and ors*, n 56 above, para 53; Case C-42/07 *Liga Portuguesa de Futebol Professional and Bwin International* [2009] ECR I-7633, para 61; Case C-46/08, *Carmen Media*, judgment of 8 October 2010 nyr, para 64.

[61] See Case C-28/09 *Commission v Austria*, pending.

[62] Case C-384/08 *Attanasio Group*, judgment of 11 March 2010 nyr, para 53; Joined Cases C-570/07 and C-571/07, *Blanco Pérez*, judgment of 1 June 2010 nyr, paras 95–103.

3. Challenges

Finally it should be noted that the actual implementation of the requirements for a coherent pursuit of objectives of general welfare by national law may amount to challenges which might not be visible at first sight. Thus, the question whether national laws pursue a certain objective of general welfare coherently may not only in exceptional cases require a quite sophisticated analysis on what reasons a differentiation in national law is based and in how far distinctions may seem plausible with regard to the objectives pursued. The same difficulty may occur in qualifying whether a coherent pursuit of such objectives is contradicted to an extent which will challenge the effectiveness of a national measure as such. This consideration is particularly relevant in tax law. In particular, national measures which go beyond the requirements of Union law cannot be taken into account in order to challenge the coherence of a national rule designed to ensure the requirements of Union law.[63] In conclusion, it has to be noted that it might often appear legitimate and even plausible from the perspective of Union law to challenge the coherence of national measures. But it is not at all self-evident to answer all questions arising from the requirement of coherence in a satisfactory or even convincing manner. *Quidquid agis, prudenter agas et respice finem.*

V. CONCLUSION

It follows from the considerations above that one conclusion appears to be particularly important: the need for a stringent, consistent and thus more coherent application of the principle of proportionality taking all relevant elements into account. It is without doubt one of the most distinguished duties of the Court to accentuate legitimate interests of legal certainty, legal clarity and consistency with respect to its proper jurisprudence on the principle of proportionality and its further evolution in order to achieve a greater coherence of its jurisprudence. It is as unfortunate as it is unchangeable that the Court has to accomplish this important task without the sage voice of Pernilla Lindh. But her wise advice can be heard by the Court at any time.

[63] Joined Cases C-436/08 and C-437/08, *Haribo*, judgment of 10 February 2011 nyr, para 71.

25

Unlimited Jurisdiction: What Does it Mean Today?

ALEXANDER ARABADJIEV*

INTRODUCTION

ECHOING ANOTHER ARTICLE on the same subject[1], the reference to *today* in the title of the present contribution seeks to shed a new light on certain aspects of a problem which has been widely discussed.[2] It is clear that 'today' refers to the entry into force of the Lisbon Treaty. By virtue of Article 6(1) of the Treaty on European Union (TEU), the Charter of Fundamental Rights of the European Union (Charter) has become a legally binding instrument of primary EU law ('shall have the same legal value as the Treaties') and Article 6(2) TEU provides for the accession of the Union to the European Convention for the Protection of Human Rights and Fundamental Freedoms (ECHR or Convention).

According to some commentators this amounts to a new constitutional situation further to which the way Union courts exercise judicial review on Commission

* Judge of the Court of Justice of the European Union.

[1] See B Vesterdorf, 'The Court of Justice and Unlimited Jurisdiction: What does it Mean in Practice' (2009) 2 *Competition Policy International*, available at www.competitionpolicyinternational.com/june-092.

[2] See, eg M Jaeger, 'Standard of Review in Competition Cases: Can the General Court Increase Coherence in the European Union Judicial System?' in T Baumé (ed), *Today's Multilayered Legal Order: Liber Amicorum in Honour of Arjen WH Meij* (Paris, Legal Publishers, 2011) 115; P Mengozzi, 'La compétence de pleine juridiction du juge communautaire' in *Liber amicorum en l'honneur de Bo Vesterdorf* (Brussels, Bruylant, 2007) 219; D Slater, S Thomas and D Waelbroeck, 'Competition Law Proceedings Before the European Commission and the Right to a Fair Trial: No Need for Reform?' (2009) 1 *European Competition Law Journal* 97 (previously published as GCLC Working Paper 04/08); D Gerard, 'EU Cartel Law and the Shaking Foundations of Judicial Review' (July 10, 2010), available at ssrn.com/abstract=1675451; IS Forrester, 'A Challenge for Europe's Judges: The Review of Fines in Competition Cases' (2011) 2 *EL Rev* 185; IS Forrester, 'A Bush in Need of Pruning: The Luxuriant Growth of Light Judicial Review' in CD Ehlermann and M Marquis (eds), *European Competition Law Annual 2009: Evaluation of Evidence and its Judicial Review in Competition Cases* 407 (Oxford, Hart Publishing, 2010); JF Bellis, 'Review of the Commission's Decision on Fines by the Community Courts' (2006) 1 *ERA-Forum* 27; D Henry, 'Les amendes de la Commission en droit de la concurrence face à la censure du juge européen' (2006) 1 *Cahiers de droit européen* 35; HJ Freund, 'Application of General Principles of Community Law in the Review of Commission Decisions on Fines by the Community Courts' (2006) 1 *ERA-Forum* 40.

decisions imposing penalties is no longer acceptable. The arguments, which concentrate on the power of the Commission under Article 23(2) of Regulation 1/2003 to impose fines for infringements of Article 101 or Article 102 of the TFEU, may be summarised as follows.

First, the finding of an infringement by the Commission and the imposition of a fine amount to the determination of a criminal charge within the meaning of Article 6(1) of the Convention. In this regard, the current context of the EU competition law enforcement regime is characterised by increasingly large fines leading to de facto 'criminalisation' of competition law.

Secondly, in the absence of significant institutional reforms, which would be needed in order to render the Commission's proceedings fully compliant with Article 6(1) of the Convention, the EU courts must subject the Commission's decisions to a more stringent degree of scrutiny in order to discharge the EU's obligations under Article 47 of the Charter and Article 6 ECHR. This raises the question whether the review provided for in the EU judicial system is broad and intense enough to ensure the degree of protection required by Article 6(1) of the Convention. These two arguments will be addressed successively.

CRIMINALISATION OF EU ANTITRUST PROCEEDINGS

The issue of the criminal nature of antitrust fines within the autonomous meaning of the Convention was raised before the Union courts in the 1980s.[3] Thus, in *Commission v Anic Partecipazioni*[4] the Court recognised the applicability of the principle of personal liability to the competition rules, 'given the nature of the infringements and the nature and degree of severity of the ensuing penalties'. Then in *Hüls v Commission* the Court referred to the principle of presumption of innocence enshrined in Article 6(2) ECHR.[5] In these cases the Court held that, given the nature of the infringements in question and the nature and severity of the ensuing penalties, the principle of presumption of innocence applies to the procedures relating to infringements of the competition rules applicable to undertakings that may result in the imposition of fines or periodic penalty payments.[6] With regard to the principle of non-retroactivity of criminal laws, to give but one more example, the ECJ has held that that principle, enshrined in Article 7 of the ECHR,

> constitutes a general principle of Community law, which must be observed when fines are imposed for infringement of the competition rules and that that principle requires

[3] Opinion of AG Vesterdorf in Joined Cases T-1/89 to T-4/89 and T-6/89 to T-15/89 *Rhône–Poulenc and ors v Commission* [1991] ECR II-867, para 885. AG Léger made the same point in his Opinion in Case C-185/95 P *Baustahlgewebe v Commission* [1998] ECR I-8422, para 31.

[4] Case C-49/92 P *Commission v Anic Partecipazioni* [1999] ECR I-4125, para 78, confirmed on appeal in Case C-97/08 P *Akzo Nobel and ors v Commission* [2009] ECR I-8237, para 77.

[5] Case C-199/92 P *Hüls v Commission* [1999] ECR I-4287, para 150.

[6] The ECJ referred to the *Öztürk* and *Lutz* judgments of the ECtHR.

> that the penalties imposed correspond with those fixed at the time when the infringement was committed.[7]

A longer list of examples may be drawn up regarding the application of the specific guarantees of the right to a fair trial provided in Articles 6, paragraphs 2 and 3, and 7 of the Convention.[8] More recently, relying on the general principle of Union law that everyone is entitled to a fair hearing, as inspired by Article 6(1) of the ECHR, the ECJ has confirmed, in the context of the right to legal process within a reasonable period, that this principle applies to proceedings brought against a Commission decision imposing fines on an undertaking for infringement of competition law.[9]

None of these judgments, which recognise the relevance of general concepts of criminal law consecrated by the ECHR, touches, admittedly, directly upon the sensitive issue of the Commission's role in the area under examination, given its investigatory and decision-making functions. Regardless of some considerations on the part of Advocates General to the effect that

> the procedure [. . .] is covered by 'criminal' within the meaning of Article 6(1) of the European Convention for the protection of human rights and fundamental freedoms and must therefore be subject to the guarantees provided for by the criminal justice component of that provision,[10]

the ECJ has not yet been directly called upon to give a judgment on the question whether the Commission constitutes an 'independent and impartial tribunal established by law' within the meaning of Article 6(1) of the Convention.

It is, however, to be observed, that on a number of occasions the issue of the Commission combining investigative, prosecutorial and adjudicative powers has been raised before the General Court. In *Lafarge SA*, for instance, the undertaking concerned was complaining about a violation of the right to a fair trial as guaranteed by Article 6 of the Convention. By contesting the validity of the then Regulation

[7] Joined Cases C-189/02 P, C-205/02 P to 208/02 P and C-213/02 P *Dansk Rørindustri and ors v Commission* [2005] ECR I-5425, para 202.

[8] These include the right to be heard, and more generally, the right of defence, the privilege against self-incrimination, the presumption of innocence and the *ne bis in idem* principle.

[9] Joined Cases Case C-403/04 P and C-405/04 P *Sumitomoto Metal Industries Ltd and ors v Commission* [2007] ECR I-729, para 115, with a reference to Joined Cases C-238/99 P, C-244/99 P, C-245/99 P, C-247/99 P, C-250/99 P to C-252/99 P and C-254/99 P *Limburgse Vinyl Maaatschappij and ors v Commission* [2002] ECR I-8375, para 179; Case C-194/99 P *Thyssen Stahl v Commission* [2003] ECR I-10821, para 154.

[10] Opinion of AG Bot in Case C-352/09 P *ThyssenKrupp Nirosta GmbH v Commission*, judgment of 29 March 2011 nyr, para 49; Opinion of AG Bot in Joined Cases C-201/09 P and C-216/09 P *ArcelorMittal Luxembourg SA v Commission*, judgment of 29 March 2011 nyr, para 41. While the ECJ has refrained in these two cases from explicitly addressing the topic, this approach was endorsed by AG Sharpston in her Opinion in Case C-272/09 P *KME Germany AG and ors v Commission*, still pending at the time of writing. By contrast, AG Mazak has maintained that 'in the light of the clear, express will of the Community legislator – Article 15(4) of regulation No 17 – any strict analogy between criminal sanctions and sanctions imposed by the Commission for infringement of the rules of competition law should be avoided'. See Opinion of AG Mazak in Case C-413/08 P *Lafarge SA v Commission*, judgment of 17 June 2010 nyr, para 107.

No 17, the applicant put forward arguments as to the serious consequences attached to the Commission's decision with a view of which even subsequent judicial control could not justify and remedy the defects of the procedure. The General Court dismissed the plea[11] by finding that the EU antitrust enforcement regime satisfied the requirements of the right to a fair trial. It pointed out, on the one hand, that the right to a fair trial had been recognized by the Court of Justice as a general principle of Union law.[12]

On the other hand, the General Court held that Article 6 ECHR was not determinative in that case in so far as the Commission was not a 'tribunal' in the sense of that provision and, in addition, alluded to Article 15(4) of Regulation No 17,[13] which provides that the European Commission's antitrust fining decisions 'shall not be of a criminal law nature'. Rejecting thus the argument that the Commission's decision was illegal on the sole ground of being taken in the framework of a system which combines accusatorial with decision-making functions, the Court further examined its own status as an independent and impartial jurisdiction as well as its unlimited jurisdiction to review decisions of the Commission conferred on it by Article 17 of Regulation No 17. In the light of these latter considerations the General Court concluded that the regulation which confers on the Commission the power to impose fines was not illegal on that ground.

A similar plea alleging that the antitrust fining procedure before the Commission did not satisfy the requirements of Article 6(1) of the Convention was examined and also rejected in a more recent judgment of the General Court.[14] In that judgment, in a similar manner, the General Court alluded, first, to the right to a fair legal process as recognised by the ECJ as a general principle of EU law, reaffirmed by Article 47 of the Charter. Secondly, basing itself on the distinction between offences that belong to the hard core of criminal law and those falling outside this hard core, as established by the ECtHR in its *Jusilla* judgment, the General Court pointed to *the less stringent* application of the criminal-head guarantees of Article 6(1) ECHR. Then, though having mentioned the *Engel* criteria, without a reference to this particular judgment, the General Court relied on Article 23(5) of Regulation 1/2003 as to the non-criminal nature of the decisions of the Commission imposing fines for infringements of competition law within the meaning of EU law. Lastly, referring also to an extensive case law of its own to the effect that even though the Commission was not a tribunal within the meaning of Article 6(1) ECHR and the fines were not of a criminal nature, the Commission must nevertheless observe the general principles of Union law during the administrative procedure, the Court held that the

[11] Case T-54/03 *Lafarge v Commission* [2008] ECR II-120, paras 36–47.

[12] The ECJ has consistently held that this principle is inspired by fundamental rights in their capacity as an integral part of general principles of Union law enforced by the ECJ, drawing inspiration from the constitutional principles common to the Member States and from the guidelines supplied, in particular, by the ECHR: see Case C-411/04 P *Salzgitter Mannesmann v Commission* [2007] ECR I-959, paras 40–41; Case C-305/05 *Ordre des barreaux francophones et germanophones* [2007] ECR I-5305, para 29.

[13] Replaced by Art 23(5) of Council Regulation (EC) No 1/2003 of 16 December 2002 on the implementation of the rules on competition laid down in Articles 81 and 82 of the Treaty, [2003] OJ L/1/1.

[14] Case T-138/07 *Schindler Holding Ltd*, judgment of 13 July 2011 nyr.

review of the Commission's decisions exercised by Union courts satisfied the requirements of a fair legal process as consecrated by the said provision. In this latter respect, it also referred to the possibility of bringing such a decision before a judicial body that has full jurisdiction, including the power to quash in all respects, on question of fact and law, the challenged decision[15] (§ 81 of the *Janosevic* judgment of the ECtHR). The control of the legality of a decision finding infringement of Article 101 TFEU involved an examination of factual findings as well as their legal assessment while, with respect to fines, the Court disposed of full jurisdiction pursuant to Articles 261 TFEU and 31 of Regulation 1/2003. These two examples call for some observations.

The ECJ has held that the Commission is not a 'tribunal' within the meaning of Article 6 of the Convention since the 1980s.[16] It is true that this consideration has been put forward to reject as irrelevant an argument against the lawfulness of the Commission's decision being adopted under a system in which the Commission combines the functions of prosecutor and judge which is contrary to Article 6(1) of the Convention. However, it is not meant to purport that the mere fact that the Commission is not a 'tribunal' within the meaning of Article 6(1) means as such that this provision is not applicable to the proceedings at issue. Already in *Musique Diffusion Française* the Court underlined that 'during the administrative procedure before the Commission, the Commission is bound to observe the procedural safeguards provided for by Community law'.[17] The qualification employed by the Court – 'procedural safeguards provided for by Community law' – disregards, seemingly, Convention law but in the final analysis, with a view of the latter's integration into Union law, operated by the ECJ through the concept of general principles of Union law, this criticism is no longer relevant. It cannot simply be said that the Union courts reject summarily arguments alleging violation of Article 6(1) ECHR by considering that the Commission is not a 'tribunal' within the meaning of Article 6(1).

This is clearly confirmed by the analysis carried out in the *Schindler* judgment where, notwithstanding the erroneous reliance on the classification contained in Article 23(5) of Regulation 1/2003,[18] the Court followed the widely defended line of reasoning according to which even if the fining procedure falls within the criminal sphere for the purposes of the ECHR, that is, within the autonomous meaning of criminal under the Convention, it differs from the hard core of criminal law. As is also well known, apart from the disciplinary proceedings the autonomous concept of a 'criminal' offence in Article 6 has, since the *Engel* case, been used to apply the fair trial guarantee in Article 6(1) to regulatory and certain other offences that, although not classified as criminal in their respective legal systems,

[15] See *Janosevic v Sweden*, App no 34619/97, EctHR, 23 July 2002, para 81.

[16] Joined Cases 100 to 103/80 *SA Musique Diffusion Française and ors v Commission* [1983] ECR 1825, para 7, with a reference to Cases 209 to 215 and 218/78 *van Landewyckand ors v Commission* [1980] ECR 3125.

[17] ibid, para 8.

[18] Council Regulation (EC) No 1/2003 of 16 December 2002 on the implementation of the rules on competition laid down in Articles 81 and 82 of the Treaty, [2003] OJ L1/1.

have criminal law characteristics, the leading case on regulatory offences being *Öztürk v Germany*.[19] In later judgments the ECtHR considered that some authorities which are administrative bodies and cannot be considered to satisfy the requirements of Article 6(1) of the Convention may be empowered to impose sanctions, even if they come to large amounts, such a system being not incompatible Article 6(1) so long as the person concerned can bring any such decision before a judicial body that has full jurisdiction, including the power to quash the challenged decision in all respects, on questions of fact and law.[20] In a further, more recent, judgment of 23 November 2006 (*Jusilla v Finland*) the ECtHR seemed to provide a (re)statement of the jurisprudence. It summarises the tendency of '. . . gradually broadening the criminal head to cases not strictly belonging to the traditional categories of the criminal law, for example administrative penalties'. Specifying that this is the result of the autonomous interpretation of the notion of 'criminal charge' by applying the Engel criteria, the Strasbourg Court seems to establish a distinction between hard core criminal law and cases falling outside this hard core, that is, 'cases not strictly belonging to the traditional categories of criminal law' and in which criminal-head guarantees will not necessarily apply with their full stringency. Therefore, it may be found compatible with Article 6(1) of the Convention for criminal penalties to be imposed, in the first instance, by an administrative or non-judicial body, given that a full judicial review of Commission decisions is performed on appeal.

This contribution is not meant to address the issue of the dual role of the Commission as judge and prosecutor. While it cannot be excluded that after the accession of the Union to the Convention the ECtHR may rule otherwise, for the purposes of this contribution, it is submitted that it is not even necessary to speculate on future developments. The more so, since, as it has to be reminded, at least formally speaking, the ECHR has – at the time of writing – different forms of existence in the framework of EU law. It is thus not appropriate to assess the validity of claims that the Convention has been already materially integrated into EU law through the operation of Article 52(3) of the Charter which provides that

> [i]n so far as this Charter contains rights which correspond to rights guaranteed by the Convention for the Protection of Human Rights and Fundamental Freedoms, the meaning and scope of those rights shall be the same as those laid down by the said Convention.[21]

It should, however, be noted that there is a tendency in the ECJ's practice to refer directly and only to Article 47 of the Charter which has introduced into EU law the

[19] See *Öztürk v Germany*, Series A no 73, 1984, referred to by AG Vesterdorf in his Opinion in *Rhône-Poulenc and ors v Commission*, n 3 above, where he raised the issue of the criminal law character of fines and pointed out the necessity '. . . that the Court should seek to bring about a state of affairs not susceptible of any judicial criticism with the European Convention for the Protection of Human Rights'.

[20] See *Bendenoun v France*, Series A no 284, 1994, para 46; *Janosevic v Sweden*, n 15 above, para 81.

[21] See W Weiss, 'Human Rights in the EU: Rethinking the Role of the European Convention on Human Rights After Lisbon' (2011) 1 *European Constitutional Law Review* 64.

guarantees provided for by Article 6(1) of the Convention.[22] As already emphasised, the principle of effective judicial protection constitutes a general principle of EU law which is now embodied in Article 47 of the Charter.[23]

This is also increasingly a guiding principle for Union courts when discharging their duties under the Treaties in the area of antitrust proceedings. Its implementation is examined here in the framework of current treaty arrangements and with a view of *a priori* doubts as to the availability, in this framework, of a working mechanism capable of rendering the whole system compliant with the said principle.

'AT THE VERY LEAST'

At the very least, it has been argued that, even if it were to be concluded that the Commission's procedures are not themselves in breach of Article 6(1), the sanctions imposed by the Commission in antitrust proceedings should be subject to full jurisdictional review by an independent and impartial tribunal in order to comply with Article 6 ECHR and to cure the defects of the proceedings carried out by the Commission. That would require the Union courts to exercise full jurisdiction in conducting any review and to have the power to quash any aspect of the challenged decision on a ground of fact or law.[24]

As already pointed out, the necessity to reform the current institutional system exceeds the objective of this contribution. The question which really deserves closer scrutiny relates to the nature of the judicial review effectively exercised by EU courts on the basis of the competences conferred upon them by the Treaty. It must inevitably be addressed in the light of the due process requirements contained in the Charter and of the prospective accession of the EU to the Convention. Admittedly, the decisions of the Commission in competition matters, and their review by the General Court and the ECJ, may become the first EU practices to be scrutinised by the ECtHR. The requirements a system of judicial review must meet in order to comply with Article 6(1) ECHR have yet to be clarified.[25]

[22] According to the Explanation relating to Art 47 (Right to an effective remedy and to a fair trial) which, in accordance with the third sub-para of Art 6(1) TEU and Art 52(7) of the Charter, has to be taken into account for the interpretation of the Charter, the first paragraph of its Art 47 is based on Art 13 of the ECHR and the second paragraph corresponds to Art 6(1) of the ECHR. Those explanations also state that '[i]n Union law, the right to a fair hearing is not confined to disputes relating to civil law rights and obligations . . . Nevertheless, in all respects other than their scope, the guarantees afforded by the ECHR apply in a similar way to the Union'.

[23] Case C-279/09 *Deutsche Energiehandels- und Beratungsgesellschaft*, judgment of 22 December 2010 nyr, para 53.

[24] See, eg Slater, n 2 above.

[25] As the situation stands now, it is clear that the ECtHR has never had the occasion to apply its own case law as to what is 'criminal' within the autonomous meaning of Art 6(1) ECHR in a case concerning the imposition of a fine by the European Commission for infringement of the EU antitrust prohibitions. By way of example, *Jussila v Finland*, judgment of 23 November 2006, [GC] No 73053/01 also cites competition law as not strictly belonging to the traditional categories of criminal law with a reference to the *Société Stenuit v France* case. As correctly observed by some commentators, it is the former European Commission of Human Rights that held that a fine imposed by a French administrative authority on a company for an infringement of French competition law constituted a criminal penalty

Nevertheless, the EU accession to the Convention is qualified in the second sentence of Article 6(2) TEU and in Article 2 of Protocol No 8 relating to the accession of the Union to the ECHR and to its effect on the competences of the Union and the powers of its institutions *which are to be preserved.* The terms of accession, as provided for by the Treaty, are therefore to be understood as founded on the preservation of the autonomy of the EU legal order, the division of powers between the institutions and of the monopoly of interpretation of Union law by the ECJ. This is an aspect generally overlooked by commentators doubting 'whether the current standard of review exercised by the Community courts in antitrust cases does amount to a full judicial review as required under Article 6 ECHR'[26] and even whether such a full scale judicial review as it is understood by the ECHR is available at all at Union level in antitrust cases. The question therefore is what is meant by 'full judicial review' and whether the 'unlimited jurisdiction' exercised by Union courts under Article 261 TFEU corresponds to (is compatible with) this concept. It is common ground that these two concepts are not identical.[27] It is therefore essential to carry out an in-depth analysis so that on the basis of a comparison of the content of the two notions/concepts, a clear answer is given to the question whether the review exercised by Union courts corresponds to the requirements of 'full jurisdiction' required under the standards of Article 6(1) of the Convention and Article 47 of the Charter. The question is therefore whether EU courts have 'full jurisdiction, including the power to quash in all aspects, on question of fact and of law, the challenged decision', as understood by the ECtHR.

Several commentators have already undertaken a comparison of the two notions, analysing critically the existing EU system of judicial review of decisions imposing fines.[28] According to Wouter Wils,[29] who explores both notions by way of identifying their respective substance, 'there can be no doubt that [the] "unlimited jurisdiction" satisfies the "full jurisdiction test" . . .' Conversely, according to Ian S Forrester, a 'deferential or limited review of compliance of fines with administrative guidelines does not satisfy the [ECHR and Charter] standard'.[30] It is, therefore, appropriate to lay down the essential elements of both notions.

within the meaning of Art 6(1) of the Convention; before the ECtHR the applicant withdrew its application. Wils contends that with *Jussila* the ECtHR endorsed the distinction between hard core criminal law and cases not belonging to it, see W Wils, 'Increased Level of EU Antitrust Fines, Judicial Review and the ECHR' (2010) 1 *World Competition* 5. Quite recently – on 27 September 2011 – the ECtHR delivered a judgment in the Case *Menarrini Diagnostics SRL v Italy* (App no 43509/08) where the complaints concerned access to a tribunal in the sense of Art 6(1) of the Convention in proceedings concerning a fine imposed by the Italian competition authorities.

[26] See Slater, n 2 above, 137.

[27] According to AG Sharpston's Opinion in Case C-272/09 P *KME and ors v Commission*, para 70, although the two concepts are 'different' and 'not to be confused', 'there can be little doubt that the "unlimited jurisdiction" conferred upon the General Court by Art 229 EC and Art 17 of Regulation No 17 meets those requirements as regards the amount of the fines imposed . . .'.

[28] See also AG Mengozzi's Opinion in Case C-511/06 P *Archer Daniels Midland Co v Commission* [2009] ECR I-5843, para 175.

[29] See Wils, n 25 above.

[30] See, IS Forrester, 'A Challenge for Europe's Judges: The Review of Fines in Competition Cases' (2011) 2 *EL Rev* 185.

'UNLIMITED JURISDICTION'[31]

Pursuant to Article 261 TFEU

> regulations adopted jointly by the European Parliament and by the Council, and by the Council, pursuant to the provisions of the Treaties, may give the Court of Justice of the European Union *unlimited jurisdiction* with regard to the penalties provided for in such regulations.[32] (emphasis added)

While there are currently a number of relevant regulations, providing for penalties and coming thus under Article 261 TFEU,[33] the present analysis is limited, as indicated above, to the power of the Commission to impose fines pursuant to Article 23(2)(a) of Regulation 1/2003 of 16 December 2002 on the implementation of the rules of competition laid down in Articles 81 and 82 of the Treaty.[34] The scope of review and the conditions under which full jurisdiction is being exercised are two issues which are in themselves a matter of contention. Regardless of the relatively clear wording of Article 261 TFEU, an argument as to the exact scope of the 'full jurisdiction' and an ambiguity seems to stem from the wording of Article 31 of Regulation 1/2003 which, under the heading 'Review by the Court of Justice', states as follows:

> The Court of Justice shall have unlimited jurisdiction to review *decisions* whereby the Commission has fixed a fine or a periodic penalty payment. It may cancel, reduce or increase the fine or the periodic penalty payment imposed. (emphasis added)

[31] The position defended by the author in the following developments is limited to the effect of the existing EU 'constitutional order'.

[32] This provision corresponds to former Art 229 EC (ex-Art 172).

[33] See Regulation (EU) No 513/2011 of the European Parliament and of the Council of 11 May 2011 amending Regulation (EC) No 1060/2009 on credit rating agencies, [2011] OJ L/145/30, Art 36e; Regulation (EC) No 391/2009 of the European Parliament and of the Council of 23 April 2009 on common rules and standards for ship inspection and survey organisations, [2009] OJ L/131/11, Art 6(4); Regulation (EC) No 80/2009 of the European Parliament and of the Council of 14 January 2009 on a Code of Conduct for computerised reservation systems and repealing Council Regulation (EEC) No 2299/89, [2009] OJ L/35/47, Art 15(5); Regulation(EC) No 216/2008 of the European Parliament and of the Council of 20 February 2008 on common rules in the field of civil aviation and establishing a European Aviation Safety Agency, and repealing Council Directive 91/670 EEC, Regulation (EC) No 1592/2002 and Directive 2004/36/EC, [2008] OJ L/79/1, Art 25(4); Regulation (EC) No 139/2004 of 20 January 2004 on the control of concentrations between undertakings (the EC Merger Regulation), [2004] OJ L/24/1, Art 16; Council Regulation (EC) No 2532/98 of 23 November 1998 concerning the powers of the European Central Bank to impose sanctions, [1998] OJ L/318/4, Art 5; Council Regulation (ECSC, EEC, Euratom) No 1859/76 of 29 June 1976 laying down the Conditions for employment of Staff of the European Centre for the Development of Vocational Training, [1976] OJ L/214/22, Art 18; Council Regulation (ECSC, EEC, Euratom) No 1860/76 of 29 June 1976 laying down the Conditions of Employment for the Improvement of Living and Working Conditions, [1976] OJ L/214/1, Art 18; Regulation No 31 (EEC), 11 (EAEC), laying down the staff Regulations of officials and the conditions of employment of other servants of the European Economic Community and the European Atomic Energy Community, [1962] OJ 45/1387, Arts 22, 91.

[34] This Regulation has been adopted on the basis of Art 83(2)(d) TEC (now Art 103(2)(d) TFEU) according to which regulations 'shall be designed to . . . define the respective functions of the Commission and of the Court of Justice in applying the provisions laid down in this paragraph'.

In this regard, a distinction is made between the decision which finds an infringement of Article 101 TFEU or of Article 102 TFEU, on the one hand, and the decision which imposes a fine or a periodic penalty payment, on the other hand.[35] It is submitted in this regard that Article 31 of Regulation 1/2003 could be understood as covering not only the amount of the fine itself but also the substantial finding of an infringement of Article 101 TFEU or of Article 102 TFEU which is contained in the same decision and which logically constitutes a distinct decision.[36] A judicial confirmation in favour of the wider solution can be found in a judgment of the General Court where it is stated that

> under Article 261 TFEU and Article 31 of Regulation 1/2003, the General Court and the Court of Justice have unlimited jurisdiction in advance brought against decisions whereby the Commission has fixed fines and may thus not only annul the decisions taken by the Commission but also cancel, reduce or increase the fines imposed.[37]

The assertion that follows, namely that 'thus, the Commission's administrative practice is subject to unlimited review by the Union judicature', is seen as a sign that the General Court favours the broader interpretation of that jurisdiction.[38]

The position on this issue, which should also take into consideration the fact that other regulations conferring unlimited jurisdiction on Union courts are variously worded,[39] is to be reserved. More pressing is the question of the interplay between Article 261 and Article 263 TFEU. Both give the Union courts the legal basis to review decisions of the Union institutions. Article 263 TFEU provides four grounds of review of legality: lack of competence, infringement of an essential procedural requirement, infringement of the Treaty or of any rule relating to its application, or misuse of powers. But what is really at issue is whether the finding of illegality is a precondition for the exercise of the unlimited jurisdiction under Article 261 TFEU. It has been maintained – by applicants in some cases, for instance[40] – that a distinction has to be made between an action of annulment

[35] One further element which has been disregarded concerns fines which the Commission may impose under Art 23(1) of Regulation No 1/2003. Decisions imposing those fines are also subject to judicial review and may affect interruption and/or suspension of limitation periods.

[36] There is, indeed, a finding of an infringement which forms the basis of a *decision* of the Commission under Art 7 of Regulation 1/2003, whereby it requires of the undertakings concerned to bring such infringement to an end. There is, on the other hand, a *decision* under Art 23 or Art 24 of Regulation 1/2003 whereby a fine or periodic penalty payment is imposed. The finding of an infringement is also integrated in a decision based on Art 23 of Regulation 1/2003 and forms as such the basis for the imposition of fines, the latter being the corollary of the former. Once the Commission finds that the conditions of Art 101(1) TFEU are fulfilled (see in this respect also Art 10 of Regulation 1/2003), it proceeds to determination and imposition of the fine.

[37] Case T-69/04 *Schunk and Schunk Kohlenstoff – Technik v Commission* [2008] ECR II-2567, para 41.

[38] For a critical assessment of the broader reading of Art 31 of Regulation 1/2003, based on a reference to the preparatory works of the regulation, see Wils, n 25 above.

[39] Art 16 of the Merger Regulation, although contemporaneous and closely related to Regulation 1/2003, uses different punctuation. It is worded as follows: 'The Court of Justice shall have unlimited jurisdiction within the meaning of Article 229 of the Treaty to review decisions whereby the Commission has fixed a fine or periodic penalty payments; it may cancel, reduce or increase the fine or the periodic penalty payment imposed.'

[40] See Case T-253/03 R *Akzo Nobel Chemicals et Akcros Chemicals v Commission* [2003] ECR II-4771.

referred to in Article 263 TFEU and an action under the unlimited jurisdiction of the Court referred to in Article 261. According to this position, which regards Article 261 TFEU as an autonomous legal remedy and not as an 'extension' of Article 263 TFEU, varying the amount of the fine is not conditioned upon a prior finding of illegality (under Article 263).

A judgment of the ECJ of 16 November 2000[41] seems to contain the judicial confirmation of this proposition in so far as the Court explicitly alludes to 'jurisdiction in two respects' over actions contesting Commission decisions imposing fines on undertakings for infringement of the competition rules, the first consisting of the task of reviewing the legality of those decisions under Article 263 TFEU and the second – of the power to assess, in the context of the unlimited jurisdiction accorded to it by Article 261 TFEU, the appropriateness of the amount of the fine. This distinction is further exemplified by the ECJ in a more recent judgment where it states that

> more than a simple review of legality, which merely permits dismissal of the action for annulment or annulment of the contested measure, the unlimited jurisdiction conferred on the General Court by Article 31 of Regulation 1/2003 in accordance with Article 261 TFEU authorises the Court to vary the *contested measure* even without annulling it, by taking into account all the factual circumstances, so as to amend, *for example*, the amount of the fine.[42]

What can be safely deduced from this case law is that when setting a new amount for the fine, the courts act not within the framework of Article 263 TFEU but in the exercise of their unlimited jurisdiction under Article 261 TFEU.[43] In the context of the conventional line of reasoning that would mean that after having exercised its review of the contested decision resulting in the finding of an illegality, the court proceeds to assess the appropriateness of the fine.

The case law under discussion, however, seems to suggest otherwise and to point in another direction, that is, to the possibility of varying the amount of the fine without first annulling the contested decision. This is what seems to follow from a literal reading of the aforementioned case law. In fact, neither in *Prym* nor in *Limburgse Vinyl*, did the ECJ confirm a revision of the fine operated by the General Court without prior annulment of the decision of the Commission, nor did the General Court actually revise such fine. This, of course, does not brush aside the questionability of the said assertions, the more so since these remain unsubstantiated as to the ground on which the Union courts would vary the amount of the fine without annulling it.

These seemingly abstract or even scholastic considerations should be further elaborated. With the coming into legal force of the Charter and of its Article

[41] Case C-297/98 P *SCA Holding v Commission* [2000] ECR I-1010, paras 53–55.

[42] Case C-534/07 P *Prym and Prym Consumer v Commission* [2009] ECR I-7415, para 86, with a reference to *Limburgse Vinyl Maaatschappij and ors v Commission*, n 9 above, para 692.

[43] See Case C-3/06 P *Danone v Commission* [2007] ECR I-1331, para 53.

49(3),[44] the door is indeed open for carrying out a proportionality review of fines. Given the fact that the Charter is now binding, a proportionality review of the amount of the fine may thus either be regarded as being part of the review of legality or considered as absorbing it. This may help to overcome the artificial situation as to which finding comes first.

A further question may arise from the wording of Article 31 of Regulation 1/2003 which, purportedly, goes beyond its legal basis when conferring on the Court of Justice 'unlimited jurisdiction to review decisions whereby the Commission has fixed a fine or a periodic penalty payment'. Though this provision could be understood as covering not only the amount of the fine itself but also the substantial finding of an infringement of Article 101 or 102 TFEU which is contained in the same decision and which logically constitutes a distinct decision, it is not clear what conclusion could or should be drawn if unlimited jurisdiction were understood to cover that 'distinct' decision. Given the relationship between Articles 263 and 261 TFEU, the finding of an infringement could be examined only in the framework of the review of legality of the contested decision.

A good deal of criticism has been levelled at the Union courts, and in particular against the General Court's deferential approach vis-a-vis the Commission. The manner in which Union courts exercise their unlimited jurisdiction is often described as being only a formal exercise of this jurisdiction and an expression of a disproportionate deference to the Commission's so-called margin of appreciation. Some even speak of the existence of a 'judicial deference doctrine', a notion strongly contested by others. It is worth determining, therefore, whether the alleged margin of appreciation is just a mantra or a real obstacle to effective judicial review. Two judgments of the General Court, currently under appeal, illustrate on the one hand the point concerning the alleged deference to the Commission's margin of appreciation, and, on the other hand, the manner in which judicial review has actually been exercised.[45] What merits attention, first, are the preliminary observations, contained in both judgments, which precede the analyses and are not linked to and do not constitute an answer to any specific plea in law.[46] Couched in identical abstract and declaratory terms these observations proceed from the finding that the Commission determined the amount of the fines by applying the method defined in its own guidelines on the method of setting fines.

With regard to the guidelines themselves, a standard – not to say conventional or even clichéd – formula reproduces what the ECJ has held in *Archer Daniels Midland Ingredients v Commission*, namely that

[44] Art 49(3) of the Charter provides that '[t]he severity of penalties must not be disproportionate to the criminal offence'.

[45] Case T-127/04 *KME Germany and ors v Commission* [2009] ECR II-1167 – currently under appeal (Case C-272/09 P *KME Germany AG and ors*). See also Case T-21/05 *Chalkor v Commission*, judgment of 19 May 2010 nyr, appeal pending (Case C-386/10 P *Chalkor)*; Case T-25/05 *KME Germany and ors v Commission*, judgment of 19 May 2010 nyr – currently under appeal (Case C-389/10 P *KME Germany AG and ors v Commission*).

[46] ibid, paras 33–36 of the *KME Germany and Others v Commission* judgment; 59–64 of the *Chalkor v Commission* judgment.

> whilst rules of conduct designed to produce external effects, as is the case of the Guidelines, which are aimed at traders, may not be regarded as rules of law which the administration is always bound to observe, they nevertheless form rules of practice from which the administration may not depart in an individual case without giving reasons which are compatible with the principle of equal treatment.[47]

Then follows a statement as to the subject matter of review of legality of fines which also reflects established case law and which, in fact, focuses criticism over the scope and intensity of judicial review. According to this approach, it is for the General Court to verify whether the Commission exercised its discretion in accordance with the method set out in the guidelines and should it be found to have departed from that method, to verify whether the departure is justified and supported by sufficient legal reasoning. It has been noted in that regard that the validity of the guidelines and the method set out in them have been confirmed by the ECJ. Further it is noted that although having self-limited its discretion with the adoption of the Guidelines, the Commission has maintained a substantial margin of discretion. The flexibility of the Guidelines enables it to exercise its discretion in accordance with the provisions of Regulations No 17 and No 1/2003.[48] The conclusion drawn by the General Court directly concerns the scope and intensity of review:

> Therefore in areas where the Commission has maintained a discretion, [. . .] review of legality is limited to determining the absence of manifest error of assessment.

Notwithstanding this statement, the General Court has underlined that 'the discretion enjoyed by the Commission and the limits which it has imposed in that regard *do not* prejudge the exercise by the Court of its unlimited jurisdiction'. This compendium of a settled approach in the form of a peculiar judicial declaration calls for the following observations.

The Guidelines adopted by the Commission have been recognised by the ECJ as rules of conduct designed to produce external effects from which the Commission cannot depart in an individual case without giving reasons that are compatible with the principle of equal treatment.[49] What is more, the current Guidelines themselves rely on case law when stating that 'in exercising its power to impose fines the Commission enjoys a wide margin of discretion within the limits set by Regulation No1/2003'.[50] The question arises as to the subject matter of the alleged margin of appreciation enjoyed by the Commission 'in exercising its power to impose fines'. This could relate to at least two quite different aspects of the Commission's role in the area of competition. On the one hand, discretion may concern the decision to impose or not to impose a fine. In more general

[47] Case C-397/03 P *Archer Daniels Midland and Archer Daniels Midland Ingredients v Commission*, para 91.

[48] *Dansk Rørindustri and ors v Commission*, n 7 above, para 267.

[49] ibid, paras 209, 210.

[50] See para 2 of the 2006 Commission Fining Guidelines and *Dansk Rørindustri and ors*, n 7 above, para 172.

terms, this is a situation in which the Commission has to decide between different courses of action. The Commission itself considers the power to impose fines as 'one of the means conferred on it in order to carry out the task of supervision entrusted to it by the Treaty'. That task is described as including not only 'the duty to investigate and sanction individual infringements' but also as encompassing 'the duty to pursue a general policy designed to apply, in competition matters, the principles laid down by the Treaty and to steer the conduct of undertakings in the light of those principles'.[51] Here again the Commission relies on the case law of the ECJ in order to underline its supervisory task and the need to ensure that its action has the necessary deterrent effect.[52]

The nature of the elements which must be taken into consideration in the determination of the amount of the fine is a quite different matter. This is the second aspect related to the margin of appreciation allegedly afforded to the Commission. In this regard it has to be admitted that the Union courts have repeatedly held that the Commission has a margin of discretion when fixing fines, including 'a particularly wide discretion as regards the choice of factors to be taken into account for the purposes of determining the amount of fines'.[53] It has been added to this assertion that there was no need for the Commission 'to refer to a binding and exhaustive list of the criteria which must be taken into account'.[54] On other occasions the ECJ has indicated – as has 'consistently been held' – that the gravity of infringements of (Union) competition law must be assessed in the light of numerous factors, such as, inter alia, the particular circumstances of the case, its context and the dissuasive effect of fines, although '*no binding or exhaustive list has been drawn up*'.[55] (emphasis added)

The ECJ itself has had the occasion to indicate a number of factors to be taken into account when assessing 'the gravity and the duration of the infringement', that are the only factors explicitly mentioned by Regulation 1/2003. The Court has thus considered that the determination of the amount of the fine should depend on the established duration of the infringement and of all the factors capable of affecting the assessment of the gravity of the infringement, such as the conduct of each of the undertakings, the role played by each of them in the establishment of the concerted practices, the profit which they were able to derive from those practices, their size, the value of the goods concerned and the threat that infringements of that type pose to the objectives of the Union.[56] The Court has also indicated that objective factors, such as the content and duration of the anticompetitive conduct, the number of incidents and their intensity, the extent of

[51] 2006 Commission Fining Guidelines.

[52] See *Dansk Rørindustri and ors*, n 7 above, para 170; *SA Musique Diffusion Française and ors v Commission*, n 16 above, para 106.

[53] Case C-289/04 P *Showa Denko v Commission* [2006] ECR-I-5859, para 36; Case C-3/06 P *Danone v Commission* [2007] ECR I-1331, para 37.

[54] ibid.

[55] *Prym and Prym Consumer v Commission*, n 43 above, para 54.

[56] See *SA Musique Diffusion Francaises and ors v Commission*, n 16 above, para 129; *Dansk Rørindustri and ors*, n 7 above, para 242; *Prym and Prym Consumer v Commission*, n 43 above, para 96.

the market affected and the damage to the economic public order must also be taken into account. The analysis must also take into consideration the relative importance and market share of the undertakings responsible[57] as well as any repeated infringements.[58] Apart from objective factors, the intentional nature of the behaviour[59] as well as the dissuasive and deterrent effect that is pursued may be also significant.[60] Elsewhere, discretion has been related, apart from the 'numerous factors', more generally to the 'method of calculating fines', or, more specifically, to 'assessing the quality and usefulness of the cooperation provided by the undertaking'.[61]

The fact that the ECJ has repeatedly set itself to establish – though not in the form of a binding and exhaustive list – the factors to be taken into account when fixing the amount of the fine might be regarded as in itself indicative of the existence of a problem that cannot be resolved solely by reference to the particularly wide – or 'certain' – margin of appreciation purportedly enjoyed by the Commission. The problem arises with regard to legal certainty and foreseeability. It is in the light of these principles that the Guidelines of the Commission should be viewed; these are intended to determine in a general and abstract manner the method that the Commission has bound itself to use.[62] The same holds true in respect of the Commission's practice and, finally, the case law of EU courts and the manner in which these courts exercise judicial review over decisions imposing fines. The principle that penalties must have a proper legal basis, which is enshrined now in Article 49 of the Charter,[63] implies that offences and the penalties they attract must be clearly defined by law.[64] Legal certainty could be compromised by incoherent application by the Commission of its own Fining Guidelines, including the choice of factors and the importance attached to them in different cases, but also by Union courts when they decide to depart from the Commission's methodology to set fines. In this latter aspect, a departure from the Commission's methodology combined with a new appraisal should also be based on clearly defined criteria.

[57] See Joined Cases C-204/00 P, C-205/00 P, C-211/00 P, C-213/00 P, C-217/00P and C-219/00 P *Aaalborg, Portland and ors v Commission* [2004] ECR I-123, para 91.

[58] On the notion of a repeated infringement, see *Lafarge SA v Commission*, n 10 above, paras 61–76.

[59] See *Prym and Prym Consumer v Commission*, n 43 above, para 96: 'In particular, factors relating to the intentional aspect may be more significant than those relating to the effects . . .'.

[60] Rather, the Commission Fining Guidelines, para 4, distinguish between *specific* and *general* deterrence.

[61] Case C-328/05 P *SGL Carbon AG* [2007] ECR I-3921, paras 81, 88.

[62] See *Dansk Rørindustri and ors*, n 7 above, para 213; Case C-167/04 P *JCB Service* [2006] ECR I-8935, para 209.

[63] Art 49 of the Charter is entitled 'Principles of legality and proportionality of criminal offences and penalties' and its first paragraph reads as follows: 'No one shall be held guilty of any criminal offence on account of any act or omission which did not constitute a criminal offence under national law or international law at the time when it was committed. Nor shall a heavier penalty be imposed than the one that was applicable at the time the criminal offence was committed. If, subsequent to the commission of a criminal offence, the law provides for a higher penalty, that penalty shall be applicable'. According to the Explanations relating to the Charter of Fundamental Rights. Article 49(1) with the exception of the last sentence and (2) correspond to Article 7 of the ECHR.

[64] See Case C-303/05 *Advocaten voor de Werden VZV* [2007] ECR I-3633, para 50.

The conclusion to be drawn from this current situation is that regardless of the great number of factors that the Commission has to take into account it does not follow from that that it enjoys a discretionary power as to the choice of factors and the importance which is attached to them. As a matter of fact, the ECJ has already had the opportunity to examine the legal nature of the Guidelines precisely in the context of offences and punishments that are to be strictly defined by law (*nullum crimen, nulla poena sine lege*) and has held that these Guidelines 'ensure legal certainty on the part of the undertakings.'[65] It would nevertheless be advisable that a more extensive list of relevant factors is provided by the Union legislator instead of leaving their determination to the administrative body entrusted with application of legislation.

On a more specific level, the issue of assessment of complex economic or technical matters also has to be addressed. With regard to economic matters the ECJ has, on the one hand, on a number of occasions recognised that the Commission has a margin of appreciation which necessarily limits reviews undertaken by the Union judicature to verifying whether the rules on procedure and on statements of reasons have been complied with, whether the facts have been accurately stated and whether there has been any manifest error of appraisal or misuse of powers.[66] On the other hand, though not exactly in the framework of cartel proceedings, these boundaries of judicial review seem to be extended so that Union courts are required to establish not only whether the evidence relied on is factually accurate, reliable and consistent but also whether that evidence contains all the information which must be taken into account in order to assess a complex situation and whether it is capable of substantiating the conclusions drawn from it.[67] In this context, however, a reservation has been made to the effect of preventing the Union judicature from substituting its own economic assessment for that of the Commission.[68] While this observation has been made precisely with regard to complex economic appraisals it is a matter of scope and intensity of judicial control whether the Union judicature has the power to substitute completely its own appraisal for that of the Commission in the wider context of judicial review in antitrust proceedings. The answer to that question may be considered as a key

[65] See *Dansk Rørindustri and ors*, n 7 above, paras 209–17. It is worth noting however, in the light of this judgment, that in a later judgment – *Prym and Prym Consumer v Commission*, n 43 above – the Court held that the 'Commission's practice in previous decisions . . . does not serve as a legal framework for setting fines in competition matters, since the Commission enjoys a wide discretion in that area and, when exercising that discretion, is not bound by its past assessments', see para 98, with a reference to *Dansk Rørindustri and ors*, n 7 above.

[66] See Case C-195/99 P *Krupp Hoesh Stahl v Commission* [2003] ECR I-10937, para 55; Joined Cases C-204/00 P, C-205/00 P, C-211/00 P, C-213/00 P, C-217/00 P and C-219/00 P *Aalborg Portland A/S and ors v Commission* [2004] ECR I-123, para 279.

[67] See Case C-12/03 P *Commission v Tetra Laval* [2005] ECR I-987, para 39; Case C-525/04 P *Spain v Lenzing* [2007] ECR I-9947, paras 56, 57. These two judgments delivered in merger cases are applicable to all decisions involving interpretation of information of an economic nature, the more so since Art 16 of the Merger Regulation also grants unlimited jurisdiction to Union courts.

[68] See *Spain v Lenzing*, n 68 above, para 57; Case C-323/00 P *DSG Dradenauer Stahlgesellschaft v Commission* [2002] ECR I-3919, para 43.

element in the attempt to conceptualise the nature of judicial control in this area for the purpose of delineating its true content.

In this regard, it should be made clear, first, that the assessment of complex economic or technical issues forms part of the review of the legality of the Commission's decisions. In the framework of the review of legality, there are no limits to the examination carried out by Union courts so far as matters of law and fact are concerned. As pointed out above in the context of possible areas of the Commission's discretion, as regards matters of law and fact, Union courts exercise full judicial control and there is no room for any margin of appreciation on the part of the Commission in this respect. So far as complex economic and technical cases assessments are concerned, it is apparently a matter of settled case law that Union courts recognise a margin of discretion for the Commission – with the reservation that this does not mean refraining from review, which consequently, takes account of the discretion. Discretion being 'implicit in the provisions of an economic nature',[69] it limits, accordingly, the 'margin' left to the judicature. Union courts' review of the Commission's interpretation of information of an economic nature is confined to scrutiny to determine whether the appraisal of the Commission of the effect and meaning of a certain set of facts is sufficiently substantiated.

This leaves no room for the Union courts to substitute their own assessment in an area that gives rise to complex economic assessments. Such a substitution of appraisal could effectively be carried out when reviewing the amount of the fine under Article 261 TFEU. This is actually how one should understand the case law which states that

> the unlimited jurisdiction conferred on the General Court . . . authorises that court to vary the contested measure, even without annulling it, by taking into account *all the factual circumstances*, so as to amend, for example, the amount of the fine.[70] (emphasis added)

Furthermore, this is also how the interplay of 'complementarity' between the two types of review works. It is noticeable that this formula was actually used by the ECJ in the *Danone* judgment where the Court held that the Union judicature is empowered, 'in addition to carrying out a mere review of the lawfulness of the penalty, *to substitute its own appraisal for the Commission's* and, consequently, to cancel, reduce or increase the fine or penalty payment imposed.'[71] On that analysis, the control of legality, combined with unlimited jurisdiction as conferred by Article 31 of Regulation No 1/2003 according to Article 261 TFEU, seems to go even further than what is required by the 'full jurisdiction' standard. The judgment of the Strasbourg court in *A Menarini Diagnostics SRL v Italy* on the scope and content of judicial control in a particular national system which does not

[69] *Tetra Laval*, n 68 above, para 38.

[70] See *Prym and Prym Consumer v Commission*, n 43 above, para 86; *Limburgse Vinyl Maaatschappij and ors v Commission*, n 9 above, para 692.

[71] ibid, para 61.

allow the administrative judge to substitute his opinion for that of an independent administrative authority, supports such an assessment. From the perspective of the Strasbourg Court, the fact that the national court had looked into the factual allegations of the complainant and the evidence presented before the authority as well as ascertained that there was no misuse of power on the part of the latter, sufficed to conclude that the Court's competence was not limited to a simple review of legality. The control as to the amount of the sanction was 'unlimited', since the national courts could verify its appropriateness with regard to the infringement and, if the case arose, determine a new sanction on the basis of relevant factors and with a view to the principle of proportionality.

Here one can, first, observe a close similarity as to the structuring and wording of the reasoning. Secondly, there seem to be no fundamental differences with regard to the contents and standard of review compared with judicial review. This observation is not to speculate on allegations according to which the Union courts and, in particular, the General Court can go even further than what is required by Convention standards.

A further particular aspect of the issue of assessment of the amount of the fine and its possible modification on grounds of proportionality and of equity is the power, or the lack thereof, of the ECJ to rule on the allegedly disproportionate nature of the fine when ruling on questions of law in the context of an appeal. The answer to that question given by existing case law reads as follows:

> It is not for the Court of Justice, when ruling on questions of law in the context of an appeal, to substitute, on grounds of fairness, its own assessment for that of the General Court exercising its unlimited jurisdiction to rule on the amount of fines.[72]

According to this case law, the ECJ may carry out an examination as to what extent the General Court took into consideration, in a legally correct manner, all the essential factors to assess the gravity of particular conduct but it is not for this Court to substitute, on grounds of fairness, its own assessment for that of the General Court and it is prevented from carrying out a general re-examination of the fine. An appeal seeking this is considered inadmissible and if that follows from a strict interpretation of the ECJ's competence to rule, in the context of an appeal, on 'points of law', one wonders whether the notions of 'fairness', 'reasonable amount' or 'disproportionate or unjust nature' of the fine are not to be considered as making part of the concept of 'law' in the context under consideration.

CONCLUSION

The ECJ has established a clear distinction and relationship between control of legality under Article 263 TFEU and judicial review of fines under Article 261

[72] Case C-291/98 P *Sarrio SA v Commission*, [2000] ECR I-9991, para 96. See also Case C-219/95 P *Ferriere Nord SpA v Commission*, para 31; Case C-185/95 P *Baustahlgewebe GmbH v Commission*, para 129; *Dansk Rorindustri A/S and ors v Commission*, n 7 above, paras 245–46.

TFEU. It should be pointed out, first, that – at this stage at least – the Court tends to dismiss arguments based on a general critique of the whole EU competition law enforcement system and the role of the General Court, as opposed to precise indication as to the possible failure of the General Court to perform an adequate review. Nevertheless, this general critique has directed the Court's attention to the specific arguments, and there is a clear tendency for those to be assessed in the light of the principles enshrined in the Charter. Following this approach, submissions as to the growing 'criminalisation' of EU antitrust enforcement law as a result of the allegedly enormous number of fines and critiques of the application of the 'margin of appreciation doctrine' and of practising 'judicial restraint' have recently, as already noted, nevertheless given rise to a judicial reply to arguments, set out in the form of grounds of appeal, contesting the principles of judicial control in the area under examination.

In this regard it has rightly been pointed out that the founding Treaties have organised judicial control, including unlimited jurisdiction under Article 261 TFEU. Unlimited jurisdiction supplements, so far as pecuniary sanctions are concerned, the control of legality provided for in Article 263 TFEU. This competence empowers the Union judicature to go beyond a simple control of legality, to substitute its own assessment for that of the Commission and, consequently, to cancel, reduce or increase the fine or the periodic penalty payment. One element of this position which, in principle, is to be fully upheld, needs to be further specified. It concerns the subject matter and the ground(s) for substitution of the assessment on the part of the judicature for that of the Commission.[73] Nevertheless, both review of legality and 'unlimited' review remain subject to a request of one of the parties which is a prerequisite for their exercise. This also concerns challenges of the Commission's decisions on grounds concerning the legal nature of this body or challenges to the legality of the Commission's Fining Guidelines.

The examination of the numerous factors taken into account in the determination of the fine is part of the control of legality. Judicial review is not limited by the Commission's margin of appreciation. In this latter aspect, these factors should be subject, on the part of the Commission, to an in-depth examination and, on the part of the Union judicature, to an in-depth review, both on questions of law and of fact and both with regard to the choice of factors and the estimation of their weight. In this latter aspect, an intervention on the part of the Union legislator could help to clarify the constitutive elements of infringements and sanctions and, as a consequence, enhance legal certainty.

[73] The reference to *Limburgse Vinyl Maaatschappij and ors v Commission*, n 9 above, para 692 is of little avail since this para does not contain any indication in this respect. *Prym and Prym Consumer v Commission*, n 43 above, which cites the same paragraph, seems to be more instructive by stating that 'the unlimited jurisdiction conferred on the General Court by Article 31 of Regulation No 1/2003 in accordance with Article 261 TFEU authorises that court to vary the contested measure even without annulling it, by taking into account all of the factual circumstances, so as to amend, for example, the amount of the fine'. The matter at hand concerns 'all the factual circumstances' and it is difficult to imagine a set of circumstances different from those which are normally taken into account in the determination of the amount of the fine. Consequently, this confirms the position that the two forms of control should not be artificially disconnected.

The Court of Justice seems to abandon reliance on the Commission's margin of appreciation and it should be underlined once again in this regard that the narrower the margin left to the Commission, the wider the scope of judicial control and vice versa. Recently, the Court has even gone as far as to censure the very reference to the notion of 'margin of appreciation'.

In the Court of Justice's own estimate, control of legality complemented by unlimited jurisdiction provided for in Article 31 of Regulation No 1/2003, satisfies the requirements of the principle of an effective remedy as envisaged in Article 47 of the Charter. On a thorough analysis of these latest developments, both in the Convention system and in the system of Union courts, doubts as to whether such a full jurisdictional review, as it is to be understood by the ECtHR, is available at Union level in antitrust cases, have to be considered as unsubstantiated. If one now tries to confront the 'unlimited jurisdiction' as interpreted and exercised by Union courts to the 'full jurisdiction' required under the Convention system with a view to bringing it into line with these requirements, the conclusion that the set of legal instruments that is currently at the disposal of the Union judicature is adequate for those requirements would not be a misjudgement.[74]

The mounting impact of 'today's' developments, such as treaty changes, imminent accession of the EU to the Convention and, admittedly, growing criticism is already producing effect. While there are still questions that remain open, the Union judicature is increasingly prepared to give answers that take into account today's imperatives.

[74] Case C-272/09 P, *KME Germany AG and ors v Commissions* (nyr), para 106.

26

Due Process in European Competition Procedure: A Fundamental Concept or a Mere Formality?

HANS HENRIK LIDGARD*

INTRODUCTION

EUROPEANS HAVE LONG taken a relaxed approach to due process requirements. Mere formalities should not prevent an efficient implementation of competition law, but rather be practical and foreseeable. With the Lisbon Treaty things are changing. A fair process and equality of arms based on fundamental human rights stipulations require that procedural safeguards are ensured. Recent case law development confirms that these matters are given higher priority. Changes in the institutional organisation are also called for.

It is almost 50 years since Regulation 17/62 implementing the European competition law entered into force giving substance to two Treaty provisions with, at the time, fairly unknown meaning. The Regulation provided the Commission with an instrument to control industry practices and prosecute and sanction infringements of Articles 101 and 102 TFEU. It also provided means for the courts to rule upon the legality of these actions.

These 50 years of regulatory activities, tightened control and increased sanctions initially utilised a formalistic approach, gradually turning to a focus on economic effects paralleling US antitrust law's evolution from a reliance on 'per se prohibitions' to a 'rule of reason approach'. This 'modernisation' was given statutory recognition when Regulation 1 replaced Regulation 17 in 2003. With the new regulation the Commission's powers were strengthened at the same time as enforcement powers granted to national authorities were cautiously decentralised. Increased powers require checks and balances and Regulation 1/2003's preamble stipulates:

> (37) This Regulation respects the fundamental rights and observes the principles recognised in particular by the Charter of Fundamental Rights of the European Union.

* Professor, University of Lund. This chapter was completed in June 2011.

> Accordingly, this Regulation should be interpreted and applied with respect to those rights and principles.

The entry into force of the Lisbon Treaty introduced an additional element into the handling of European competition law. The fact that the legislators moved the principles in former Article 3 TEC to an obscure protocol does not appear to change the force of its implementation. Of greater importance is that the Charter of Fundamental Rights of the European Union (Charter) became binding.

These references to human rights impose new requirements on all parties. This contribution's purpose is to investigate if a balance has been achieved between the need for the efficient enforcement of competition rules and procedural safeguards in the process. The focus is on activities over the last two years.

DUE PROCESS REQUIREMENTS

Treaty of Lisbon – A New Deal for Human Rights

In the Treaty of the European Union the signatory States confirm 'their attachment to the principles of liberty, democracy and respect for human rights and fundamental freedoms and of the rule of law'. Further provisions reconfirm this statement. Accordingly, Article 2 TEU establishes that '[t]he Union is founded on the values of respect for human dignity, freedom, democracy, equality, the rule of law and respect for human rights . . .'. Article 6 'recognises the rights, freedoms and principles set out in the Charter of Fundamental Rights of the European Union . . ., which shall have the same legal value as the Treaties'. Article 6 also provides that the Union shall accede to the European Convention for the Protection of Human Rights and Fundamental Freedoms (ECHR). Importantly, before such accession occurs, Article 6 adds that '[f]undamental rights, as guaranteed by the European Convention for the Protection of Human Rights and Fundamental Freedoms and as they result from the constitutional traditions common to the Member States, shall constitute general principles of the Union's law'.[1]

The Charter presently has legally binding force and also contains several fundamental rights guaranteed by the ECHR or resulting from common constitutional traditions. Of interest for competition proceedings are that the Charter ensures non-discrimination, good administration, access to documents, an effective remedy, a fair trial, presumption of innocence, rights of defence, principles of legality and proportionality in addressing offences and penalties as well as the right not to be tried or punished twice for the same criminal offence. Any limitation on the

[1] Human rights provisions are also referred to with respect to international relations and Art 218 TFEU establishes a procedure for negotiation of new agreements including accession to the ECHR. The Council shall adopt a unanimous decision, after obtaining the consent of the European Parliament, which shall then enter into force after it has been approved by the Member States. Protocol No 8 relating to Art 6(2) TEU provides certain conditions and limitations on accession relating to Union competences and powers and Member States' previous derogations from the Convention.

exercise of the rights and freedoms recognised by the Charter must be provided for by law and respect the essence of these rights and freedoms. Limitations must also be necessary and genuinely meet objectives of general interest.[2]

Article 52 of the Charter makes an important connection to the ECHR by stipulating that

> (3) In so far as this Charter contains rights which correspond to rights guaranteed by the Convention for the Protection of Human Rights and Fundamental Freedoms, the meaning and scope of those rights shall be the same as those laid down by the said Convention. This provision shall not prevent Union law providing more extensive protection.
>
> (4) In so far as this Charter recognises fundamental rights as they result from the constitutional traditions common to the Member States, those rights shall be interpreted in harmony with those traditions.

Competition Proceeding Safeguards

The Competition provisions in Article 101 and 102 TFEU do not contain procedural safeguards. Regulation 1/2003, which implements Articles 101 and 102 TFEU, is primarily aimed at creating expedient procedures for the Commission to investigate, prosecute and make decisions regarding competition infringements. Far-reaching investigation powers, collaboration with national competition authorities and stiff remedies underscore the Commission's powers.

However, the Regulation also refers to procedural safeguards. The preamble establishes respect for fundamental rights and observes the principles recognised in particular by the Charter. Undertakings cannot be forced to incriminate themselves; they have a right to be heard; are granted the rights of defence; and rights of access to the file. All decisions by the Commission are subject to judicial review by the Court which has unlimited jurisdiction in respect of decisions where the Commission imposes fines or periodic penalty payments.[3]

The operative parts of Regulation 1/2003 add further fuel by requiring that decisions specify the legal basis for inspections and if inspections are made in, for example, the homes of company officials, a national court must provide the green light. Fines should be fixed with regard to the gravity and the duration of the infringement. The Regulation clarifies that such decisions shall not be of a criminal law nature.

Commission decisions must be based on objections upon which the infringer has been able to comment. Article 27(2) adds a requirement that the rights of defence shall be fully respected in the proceedings. Parties shall have access to the Commission's file, subject to the protection of business secrets, the Commission's confidential information and internal documents.[4]

[2] Charter of Fundamental Rights, [2010] OJ C83/02, Arts 41–50.

[3] Regulation 1/2003, recitals 23, 32, 33, 37.

[4] Transparency requirements limit this restriction. See Case C-506/08 P *Kingdom of Sweden and MyTravel Group v Commission*, judgment of 21 July 2011 nyr.

A Limited Review by the Courts

In line with the Charter's call for effective remedies, Article 31 of Regulation 1/2003 clarifies that the ECJ has unlimited jurisdiction to review decisions whereby the Commission has fixed a fine or periodic penalty payment. It may cancel, reduce or increase the fine or periodic penalty payment imposed. Whether this is to be understood as an unlimited or restrained review[5] is debated.[6] Regulation 1/2003 could be interpreted either way. It is rather the general Treaty provisions which provide limitations. Article 263 TFEU stipulates that EU Courts shall review the legality of binding legislative acts intended to produce legal effects. For that purpose they have jurisdiction on grounds of lack of competence, infringement of an essential procedural requirement, infringement of the Treaties or of any rule of law relating to their application, or misuse of powers. The reference to 'review the legality' only seems to support a limited review. In addition, Article 261 TFEU provides that regulations adopted jointly by the European Parliament and the Council, and by the Council pursuant to the provisions of the Treaties, may give the ECJ unlimited jurisdiction with regard to the penalties provided for in such regulations. The latter provision suggests that a full review is with respect to penalties only.[7]

The explanation for this restricted review has been that of an 'institutional balance'.[8] Whether such a balance was intended by the original drafters or if it is in line with fundamental requirements, such as effective remedies, is doubtful. EU Courts appear to have found a middle ground by reviewing matters as to substance, but leaving the Commission 'a margin of discretion' in complex matters. This margin of discretion is applied irrespective of whether the law mandates a full or a restrained review. In spite of the fact that the Treaty supports a full review by the EU Courts of fining decisions, the reality is that discretion is required.[9] Fines should never result from an automatic and predictable calculation. On the

[5] B Vesterdorf, 'Judicial Review in EC Competition Law: Reflections on the Role of the Community Courts in the EC System of Competition Law Enforcement' (2005) 1 *Global Competition Policy* 1, 10: 'The system envisaged a sort of institutional balance. The Commission and the Courts should focus on their respective primary functions: competition policy and enforcement on the one hand, judicial review on the other. It is a simple, but fundamentally important, premise which is enshrined in the EC Treaty itself'.

[6] D Geradin and N Petit, 'Judicial Review in European Union Competition Law: A Quantitative and Qualitative Assessment', ssrn.com/abstract=1698342,.

[7] Interestingly, under Art 262 TFEU the Council may confer what appears to be unlimited jurisdiction to the ECJ in disputes relating to the application of Acts adopted on the basis of the Treaties which create European intellectual property rights.

[8] B Vesterdorf, n 5 above.

[9] In the US the review of remedies appears more limited – at least in unfair trade cases. See *Jacob Siegel Co v FTC*, 327 US 608, 612–13 (1946): the FTC 'is the expert body to determine what remedy is necessary to eliminate the unfair or deceptive trade practices which have been disclosed. It has wide latitude for judgment and the courts will not interfere except where the remedy selected has no reasonable relation to the unlawful practices found to exist'.

other hand, there is no strong reason to limit the review of substantive issues. But the Treaty has it worded the other way around.

MERE PROCEDURE OR FUNDAMENTAL MATTERS OF A CONSTITUTIONAL CHARACTER?

Efficiency considerations appear as an important driving force in Regulation 1/2003 and procedural safeguards are only accepted to the extent that they do not create serious obstacles to Commission enforcement activities. Europeans have always had an ambivalent approach to procedural safeguards. Where the Americans consider due process to be of constitutional significance,[10] civil law lawyers have a tendency to regard these matters as mere formalities which are required in order to arrive at an expedient procedure.[11] Rules must, under the European perspective, be efficient, clear and foreseeable. Service of process is one example. In *Continental Can*, the Commission sent its statement of objection by registered mail to the US party, which returned it unopened. Little did formalities matter according to the Court. The recipient was aware of the content of the letter and that was all that was required. [12] A US court would have taken a different position.[13]

This dichotomy between a formalistic approach to procedural issues, which are themselves ends for other goals, or a constitutional safeguard to secure individual freedoms as promoted by the Americans, lies behind the discussion in Europe. The different views partly explain the opposed positions in the current debate. The binding force of the Charter and future adherence to the ECHR are providing reasons for reconsideration.

[10] US Constitution 14th and 15th amendments.

[11] The 1968 Brussels Convention identified jurisdictional issues and recognition and enforcement of judgments as mere formalities in need of harmonisation to facilitate efficient operations. This attitude has been preserved throughout the years. Regulation 44/2001 on the same subject regards harmonisation of the rules as necessary and required to secure the free flow of judgments. It is a means for other important ends that can be addressed in secondary legislation. Foreseeability and expediency are driving forces. The Anglo-Saxon approach provides a constitutional dimension to these matters. Due process is fundamental in the US and an explanation as to why the UK and Ireland have remained outside the European collaboration.

[12] Case 6/72 *Europemballage Corp & Continental Can Co Inc v Commission* [1973] ECR 215. Continental Can appealed the decision to the Court based on irregularities in procedure and on misuse of powers. Continental Can suggested that simple communication between the Commission and a foreign company was not a sufficient way of serving the company. Ordinary diplomatic channels should have been used. The Court did not agree. A decision is properly notified under Union law 'if it reaches the addressee and puts the latter in a position to take cognisance of it'. The company could not make use of its own refusal.

[13] See, eg *Jones v Flowers*, 547 US 220, 221 (2006): when process served by certified mail was returned unclaimed, due process considerations required the State to take further available steps to provide the defendant with notice. See also *Robinson v Hanrahan*, 409 US 38 (1972) *per curiam*: service by mail violated due process requirements where the State knew that the defendant was in jail and no longer at the address to which the notice was sent.

A Vivid Academic Debate between Competition Officials and Legal Practitioners

Over the last two years Wouter Wils,[14] Hearing Officer at the Commission, and Ian Forrester[15] and frequent legal counsel in competition matters, have been active participants in the discussion providing interesting and thoughtful, but opposing, views on competition law and due process. Their views are, from my perspective, representative of others' comments in this vivid debate. The former president of the General Court ('GC'), Bo Vesterdorf, adds a perspective advocating some form of middle ground.[16]

Wils, even if expressing a personal view, appears as a solid representative of the Commission. He meticulously penetrates the procedure before the Commission and the courts and compares it with the requirements of the ECHR and the Charter, showing that the procedure as envisioned by the Treaty and its implementing secondary legislation satisfy fundamental requirements. In spite of the wording in Regulation 1/2003, that the competition procedure is administrative and not criminal in nature, he supports the reality under the ECHR that the remedies have a criminal nature. But, with reference to the ECtHR judgment in *Jussila v Finland*,[17] Wils draws the conclusion that a distinction can be made between hard core criminal law and other lesser infringements like tax fraud and competition law. The latter permit a more lenient attitude to due process requirements.

Forrester, on the other hand, takes the view that these proceedings in front of the Commission, which are clearly criminal in nature, are not up to standard. The fact that the Commission acts as investigator, prosecutor and decision-maker inevitably leads to biases and flawed results. The checks and balances introduced into the system are not sufficient to provide a fair hearing for the accused. The Hearing Officer is powerless and the Advisory Committee has never objected to a proposed decision and does not provide a balance to the far-reaching Commission powers.

The two of them also disagree as to the appeals procedure. Wils believes that EU Courts are acting within their mandate under the Treaty and it is only proper that they leave certain complex issues to the Commission's discretion. Forrester, for his part, is utterly unhappy with the situation. He is of the view that there should be no matter too complex for a court to review it. In case of need, the courts should bring in neutral experts.

[14] W Wils, 'The Increased Level of EU Antitrust Fines, Judicial Review, and the European Convention on Human Rights' (2010) 33 *World Competition* 5; W Wils, 'Antitrust Enforcement Powers and Procedural Rights and Guarantees: The Interplay between EU Law, National Law, the Charter of Fundamental Rights of the EU and the European Convention on Human Rights' (2011) 34 *World Competition* 189.

[15] I Forrester, 'Due Process in EC Competition Cases: A Distinguished Institution with Flawed Procedures' (2009) 34 *EL Rev* 817; I Forrester, 'A Bush in Need of Pruning: The Luxuriant Growth of Light Judicial Review' in CD Ehlermann & M Maquis (eds), *European Competition Law Annual (2009), Evaluation of Evidence and its Evaluation in Competition Cases* (Oxford, Hart Publishing, 2010).

[16] B Vesterdorf, n 5 above, 3–27; see also B Vesterdorf, 'The Court of Justice and Unlimited Jurisdiction: What Does it Mean in Practice?' in (2009) *Global Competition Policy*, www.competitionpolicyinternational.com/apr-10.

[17] *Jussila v Finland*, App no 73053/01, judgment of 23 November 2006 (GC).

While Wils believes that the sanctions imposed are well grounded in the limitations set by Regulation 1/2003, the Commission guidance on setting fines[18] and the leniency notice,[19] Forrester believes that they are arbitrary, out of proportion and counterproductive. He underscores the need for specific review of these remedies.

Bo Vesterdorf emphasises that the courts are bound by Treaty provisions, which only mandate a limited review of legality as to questions of substance and a full review of sanctions imposed. Antitrust, as expressed in Articles 101 and 102 TFEU, is backwards looking and repressive. Competition law, as contained in the merger control regulations, is forward looking and preventive. The problem with the former is that violations are severely sanctioned and therefore require a fair process and equality of arms. Forward looking merger control is problematic as it requires a rapidity of decision making, which is difficult to satisfy under the present system. The complexities of antitrust cases are such that he promotes establishing a separate court to deal with competition matters to secure the requisite expertise and speed.

Administrative or Criminal Law?

Much turns on the categorisation of competition law. Should Articles 101 and 102 be regarded as expressions of administrative or criminal law, or is correct to find a middle ground in the 'criminal light' proposal made by Wils based on the distinction in *Jussila v Finland*?[20]

The Union courts have never expressly confirmed that competition fines are criminal. With reference to the ECHR and the Charter, the GC in *Fuji* came close by referring to 'the nature of the infringements in question and the nature and degree of severity of the ensuing penalties', when establishing that the principle of the presumption of innocence applies to the competition process, which may result in the imposition of fines or periodic penalty payments.[21] In other instances the GC seems to hold fast to the idea of administrative law. One such issue concerns the point in time when a suspected party is entitled to know of the agency's suspicion and can organise its defence. The GC held in *Amann & Söhne* that

> In the context of an administrative procedure in a competition matter, it is the notification of the statement of objections, on the one hand, and the access to the file enabling the addressee of the statement of objections to peruse the evidence in the Commission's file, on the other, that ensure the rights of the defence and the right of the undertaking

[18] Commission Guidelines on the method of setting fines imposed pursuant to Article 23(2)(a) of Regulation No 1/2003, [2006] OJ C210/02.

[19] Commission Notice on immunity from fines and reduction of fines in cartel cases, [2002] OJ C45/3.

[20] *Jussila v Finland*, n 17 above.

[21] Case T-132/07 *Fuji Electric v Commission*, judgment of 12 July 2011 nyr, para 89 with reference to Case C-199/92 P *Hüls v Commission* [1999] ECR I-4287, paras 149, 150; Case C-235/92 P *Montecatini v Commission* [1999] ECR I-4539, paras 175, 176; Case T-38/02 *Groupe Danone v Commission* [2005] ECR II-4407, para 216.

> concerned to a fair legal process . . . If the abovementioned rights were extended to the period preceding the notification of the statement of objections, the effectiveness of the Commission's investigation would be undermined . . .[22]

The Commission can, under Article 11 of Regulation 17/1962 compel undertakings to provide all necessary information even if it is used to establish the existence of anti-competitive conduct without running afoul of either Article 6(1) and (2) of the ECHR, or the case law of the ECtHR. Undertakings cannot claim that their right not to incriminate themselves has been infringed where they voluntarily reply to such a request.[23]

The fact that the EU Courts have abstained from expressly stating that competition remedies are criminal in nature appears somewhat outdated. When dealing with insider trading, the ECJ, with Pernilla Lindh as Judge Rapporteur, had no problem in referring to the Engels criteria[24] to state that

> in the light of the nature of the infringements at issue and the degree of severity of the sanctions which may be imposed, such sanctions may, for the purposes of the application of the ECHR, be qualified as criminal sanctions.[25]

The sanctions concerned in total one hundred thousand euro. The question is then why it is difficult for the courts to make the same statements with respect to the competition remedies, where the companies get 'slammed' with sanctions now in the hundred millions? The fact that the Lisbon Treaty has come into force must be of considerable importance also in the competition process.[26] Over the last two years, the Advocates General have paid much attention to procedural requirements in competition matters.[27] AG Sharpston[28] has 'little difficulty in concluding that the procedure whereby a fine is imposed for breach of the prohi-

[22] Case T-446/05 *Amann & Söhne, Cousin Filterie v Commission*, judgment of 28 April 2010 nyr, para 336.

[23] ibid, paras 327–29.

[24] See *Engel ea v The Netherlands*, Series A no 22 (1976).

[25] Case C-45/08 *Spector Photo Group & Van Raemdonck* [2009] ECR I-12073, para 42 with references to the case law of the ECtHR.

[26] Opinion of AG Kokott in Case C-110/10 P *Solvay SA v Commission*, para 73: 'Although the EU Courts have repeatedly been faced with the issue of what constitutes a reasonable time in competition proceedings, the points of law raised by Solvay seem to me to be of special importance. First, they concern a case in which the absolute length of the proceedings, taking into account all stages of the administrative and judicial procedures, was without any doubt particularly long. Secondly, the complaints in this case arise against the background of the entry into force of the Treaty of Lisbon on 1 December 2009, at which time the Charter of Fundamental Rights of the European Union became binding in law (Article 6(1) TEU)'.

[27] During the period from 1 January 2010 to 30 June 2011, some 15 opinions have been delivered, which implicate due process and human rights in competition matters. See, eg Opinion of AG Kokott in Case C-110/10 P *Solvay v Commission*, n 26 above; Opinion of AG Sharpston in Case C-272/09 P *KME v Commission*, nyr; Opinion of AG Mengozzi in Case C-439/08 *VEBIC*, judgment of 7 December 2010 nyr; Opinion of AG Bot in Joined Cases C-201/09 P and C-216/09 P *ArcelorMittal v Commission*, judgment of 29 March 2011 nyr; Opinion of AG Mazàk in Case C-360/09 *Pfleiderer AG v Bundeskartellamt*, judgment of 14 June 2011 nyr; Opinion of AG Mazàk in Case C-407/08 P *Knauf Gips KG v Commission*, judgment of 1 July 2010 nyr; Opinion of AG Mazàk in Case C-413/08 P *Lafarge SA v Commission*, judgment of 17 June 2010 nyr.

[28] Opinion of AG Sharpston in Case C-272/09 P *KME v Commission*, n 27 above, para 64.

bition on price-fixing and market-sharing agreements in Article 81(1) EC falls under the "criminal head" of Article 6 ECHR'. The time is also ripe for the courts and it is not satisfactory to apply different standards during different parts of the procedure.

Criminal or Criminal Light?

Could it be argued that different safeguards apply in competition law compared to other criminal procedures? The concept of 'criminal light' as argued by Wils is finding its way into the discussion. AG Kokott, also referring to *Jussila v Finland*, suggests that the ECtHR does not appear to regard competition law as a traditional category of criminal law. Outside of the 'hard core' of criminal law, the ECtHR assumes that the criminal-law guarantees provided for in Article 6(1) ECHR do not necessarily apply with their full stringency.

Whether *Jussila v Finland* actually permits such a far-reaching interpretation can be doubted. The case concerns tax surcharges and the ECtHR referred to three criteria being required to find that an issue may be classified as criminal, namely where: (i) the classification of the 'offence' is 'criminal' according to the domestic legal system; (ii) the very nature of the offence; and (iii) the degree of severity of the penalty that the person concerned risks incurring.[29]

Tax surcharges were held to qualify under the criteria. The amount at stake in *Jussila v Finland* was only some 300 euro, but that did not prevent the ECtHR from classifying the fine as criminal. In other cases involving larger amounts there was no doubt about the classification.[30]

Further, the Finnish Administrative Court had allowed the parties and their experts to provide written statements regarding all aspects of the case. The Court 'would not exclude that in the criminal sphere the nature of the issues to be dealt with before the tribunal or court may not require an oral hearing'.[31] According to the Court it was self-evident that some criminal cases do not carry any significant degree of stigma. There are clearly 'criminal charges' of differing weight. Tax surcharges differ from the hard core of criminal law; consequently, the criminal-head guarantees will not necessarily apply with their full stringency.[32] The Court also noted the minor sum of money at stake.[33] For this reason and referring to the written submissions, the Court found that the requirements of fairness were complied with and did not, in the particular circumstances of this case, necessitate an oral hearing. It should be emphasised that the ECtHR was divided and the dissenters were not willing to make special provisions for cases even with a lower economic value.

[29] *Jussila v Finland*, n 17 above, citing *Engel and ors v the Netherlands*, n 24 above.
[30] ibid, citing *Bendenoun v France*, Series A no 284, (1994) ECHR 54, § 47.
[31] ibid, para 43.
[32] ibid.
[33] ibid, para 48.

Does *Jussila v Finland* really provide support for categorising European competition law as being in a 'criminal light'? The fact that competition law infringements satisfy fraud requirements under national criminal law; that abuses have been criminalised in certain Member States; and that the stiff penalties provide a substantial degree of stigma, suggest that competition law procedure provides every indicia for hard core criminal law intervention. Therefore procedural requirements under the ECHR and the Charter ought to apply in full.

HUMAN RIGHTS IN EU COURTS

Over the last 18 months the GC and the ECJ have rendered some 80 competition judgments out of which at least 10 appear relevant to this discussion on human rights. They deal with procedure before the Commission, the right to be heard, access to files, the burden of proof, examination of witnesses, the presumption of innocence, the privilege against self-incrimination, and legal certainty. Generally the cases are confirmations of prior case law and only to a limited extent do they indicate another direction.

Little light is cast on the characterisation of competition procedure as an administrative or criminal procedure.[34] All actors seem to agree that high penalties require additional procedural safeguards, even if the courts are reluctant to admit that the procedure is criminal and even expressly make statements to the contrary.[35]

Procedure before the Commission[36]

Under Article 6(1) ECHR '. . . everyone is entitled to a fair and public hearing within a reasonable time by an independent and impartial tribunal established by law'.

[34] Case C-413/08 P *Lafarge v Commission*, judgment of 17 June 2010 nyr, para 75, where the appellant briefly referred to the ECHR judgments in *Öztürk* and *Lutz*, to the effect that a penalty imposed by the Commission under competition law comes within the concept of a 'criminal offence' for the purposes of Art 6 ECHR. However, that argument was unsuccessful. 'Even if a penalty imposed by the Commission under competition law were to be regarded as coming within the ambit of a "criminal offence" for the purposes of Article 6 of that convention, Lafarge has not shown how the General Court infringed its right to a fair hearing as required by that article'.

[35] Case T-446/05 *Amann & Söhne*, n 23 above, paras 328, 336. In Case T-191/06 *FMC Foret SA v Commission*, judgment of 16 June 2011 nyr, para 139, the GC stated: 'As the procedure before the Commission is purely an administrative procedure, the Commission is not required to afford the undertaking concerned the opportunity to cross-examine a particular witness and to analyse his statements at the investigation stage. . . . It is sufficient that the statements used by the Commission were provided in the file sent to the applicant, who is able to challenge them before the judicature of the European Union'. See also *Lafarge*, n 34 above, paras 116, 147–49.

[36] The Charter provides in Art 50 (Right not to be tried or punished twice in criminal proceedings for the same criminal offence): 'No one shall be liable to be tried or punished again in criminal proceedings for an offence for which he or she has already been finally acquitted or convicted within the Union in accordance with the law'.

It has been questioned whether the procedure before the Commission is reliable and if the Commission with its many tasks can be regarded as an independent and impartial tribunal. This challenge was not up for discussion during this period, but auxiliary institutions, such as the Hearing Officer,[37] the Advisory Committee[38] and the College of Commissioners,[39] were under scrutiny to determine if they could provide sufficient balance to a potentially biased DG Competition.

A Fair Trial[40]

The Commission must prove infringements of Article 101(1) TFEU and adduce evidence capable of demonstrating, to the requisite legal standard, the existence of the circumstances constituting an infringement.[41] Doubts must operate to the advantage of the undertaking.[42] General questions regarding legal professional privilege,[43]

[37] Case T-66/01 *Imperial Chemical Industries Ltd v Commission*, judgment of 25 June 2010 nyr, the GC held that a Hearing Officer has a limited task of securing respect for the rights of the defence. His intervention was not required the second time the matter came before the Commission. In *FMC Foret*, n 35 above, para 143, with reference to Case T-161/05 *Hoechst* v *Commission* [2009] ECR II-3555, para 176, the GC observed that the Hearing Officer's report is a purely internal Commission document, which does not constitute a decisive factor which the courts must take into account. Interestingly enough, in *Kingdom of Sweden and MyTravel Group plc v Commission*, n 4 above, the Commission resisted disclosure to the defence of a Hearing Officer's report as its own 'internal document', para 69, and the ECJ agreed that the opinion was created for the Commission's and not the public's use, para 95. Such a close alignment of the Hearing Officer with the interests of the Commission appears to conflict with a Hearing Officer's duty to be objective and uphold the rights of the defence. See, Commission Guidance on Procedure of the Hearing Officers in Proceedings Relating to Art 101 and 102 TFEU (ex-Art 81 and 82 EC), paras 3, 5, ec.europa.eu/competition/antitrust/legislation/legislation.html.

[38] In spite of the wording of Regulation 17 and 2842/98, the Commission is not required to hear the defendant or to consult the Advisory Committee again prior to the adoption of the renewed decision. The fact that members of the Committee have changed did not matter. A change in the composition of an institution does not affect the continuity of the institution itself, and its final or preparatory acts in principle retain their full effect. See *ICI v Commission*, n 37 above, para 170.

[39] Nor did the Court accept that the College of Commissioners should have had the opportunity to consider all the relevant facts, circumstances and legal matters when adopting the contested decision the second time around. ibid; *ICI v Commission*, n 37 above, paras 172–74.

[40] Charter Art 47 (Right to an effective remedy and to a fair trial provides): 'Everyone whose rights and freedoms guaranteed by the law of the Union are violated has the right to an effective remedy before a tribunal in compliance with the conditions laid down in this Article. Everyone is entitled to a fair and public hearing within a reasonable time by an independent and impartial tribunal previously established by law. Everyone shall have the possibility of being advised, defended and represented'.

[41] Case T-110/07 *Siemens v Commission*, judgment of 3 March 2011 nyr, para 43.

[42] *Fuji Electric v Commission*, n 21 above, para 89.

[43] In Case C-550/07 P *Akzo Nobel Chemicals Ltd v Commission*, judgment of 14 September 2010 nyr, the Company, on appeal to the ECJ, claimed protection for employed in-house legal counsel in conflict with prior case law. It argued that recourse to legal advice from an in-house lawyer would not be as valuable and its usefulness would be limited if the exchanges within an undertaking with such a lawyer were not protected by legal professional privilege. The Court emphasised that in all proceedings in which sanctions may be imposed, observance of the rights of the defence is a fundamental principle of EU law. However, the Court was not prepared to extend the privilege because in-house lawyers were not always able to represent the client before a court and an extension of the privilege would require restrictions and rules relating to the exercise of the profession. Any individual seeking advice from a lawyer must accept the restrictions and conditions applicable to the exercise of that profession. The rules on

res judicata,[44] the right to be heard[45] and denial of effective defence due to extreme time delays[46] were reviewed during the two year period basically reaffirming prior case law. The ECJ also took a firm stance against repeat infringements.[47]

Access to the File[48]

Access to the file has two dimensions. On the one hand, access to files during an ongoing proceeding may be restricted in accordance with Regulation 1049/2001 regarding public access to institutional documents.[49] The regulation requires openness to strengthen the principles of democracy and respect for fundamental rights as laid down in Article 6 TEU and the Charter. Public access to documents should be secured, subject to the protection of internal deliberations necessary to safeguard the ability of institutions to carry out their tasks. That is, institutions shall refuse access to a document where disclosure would undermine the protection of court proceedings and legal advice and the purpose of inspections, investigations and audits unless disclosure is required by an overriding public interest.

On the other hand, in matters where the file has been closed, access to files should be more permissive. If a document is partially protected, the remaining parts shall be released.

In competition matters, a request for access to the file is normally made in ongoing matters and restrictions may apply. In *FMC Foret*[50] the GC, in line with Article 27(2) of Regulation 1/2003, reaffirmed that parties are entitled to access the Commission's file, subject to the protection of business secrets. The Commission

legal professional privilege form part of those restrictions and conditions in the procedure before the Commission.

[44] In *ICI v Commission*, n 37 above, para 197, the Court also established that a judgment's status as *res judicata* is such as to bar admissibility of an action if the proceedings disposed of by the judgment in question were between the same parties, had the same purpose and the same legal basis, but the principle extends only to matters of fact and law actually or necessarily settled by the judicial decision in question.

[45] In *Siemens v Commission*, n 41 above, the GC confirmed that under Art 6(2) EU the Union is to respect fundamental rights, as guaranteed by the ECHR and as they result from the constitutional traditions common to the Member States, as general principles of Community law. However, these rules do not require that undertakings be given the opportunity to question, during administrative procedures, witnesses heard by the Commission.

[46] The fact that a period of 10 years elapsed between a prior decision and the contested decision meant, according to the applicant, a denial of protection of the effective rights of the defence and time delays, particularly regarding decisions imposing fines, must be reasonable. The Court did not agree; the delays were caused by the court proceedings rather than attributable to the Commission's decision-making. *ICI v Commission*, n 37 above, paras 132–33.

[47] *Lafarge v Commission*, n 34 above.

[48] The Charter provides in Art 42 (Right of access to documents): 'Any citizen of the Union, and any natural or legal person residing or having its registered office in a Member State, has a right of access to documents of the institutions, bodies, offices and agencies of the Union, whatever their medium'.

[49] Regulation (EC) No 1049/2001 of the European Parliament and of the Council of 30 May 2001 regarding public access to European Parliament, Council and Commission documents, [2001] OJ L145/43.

[50] *FMC Foret v Commission*, n 35 above.

must provide an opportunity to examine all of the documents, both incriminating and exculpatory, in the investigation file that may be relevant for the defence. The right of defence is infringed only if the Commission relied on the document to support its objection. The undertaking that has been denied access must show that the result would have been different if the document was disallowed as evidence. However, if an exculpatory document has not been communicated, the undertaking must only establish that its non-disclosure was able to influence the proceedings to its disadvantage.[51]

In *Airtours* the matter was closed in 2002 with the judgment of the GC.[52] MyTravel intended to claim damages from the Commission for its refusal to approve the merger and requested access to several documents in the possession of the Commission, including a report discussing the potential to appeal, the report of the Hearing Officer and documentation supplied to the Advisory Committee. The GC denied access referring to lack of public interest and the fact that access would hamper the Commission's institutional efficiency.[53] The ECJ annulled the Commission decisions denying access and referred the matter back for the GC to consider the requests for disclosure.[54] Openness was the norm and limitations should be interpreted restrictively and be well motivated.

In order to respect the rights of the defence, the file compiled by the Commission must include all the relevant documents obtained during the investigation. If an exculpatory document is not communicated, the appellant must only establish that its non-disclosure was able to influence, to its disadvantage, the course of the proceedings and the content of the Commission's decision.[55] It is not for the Commission alone to determine the documents that might be of use to the defence.[56] The legality of the decision is, however, only called into question if it might have influenced the proceedings and the contested decision to the disadvantage of the applicant.

[51] ibid, paras 265–66. Case T-58/01 *Solvay v Commission* [2009] ECR II-4781 paras 257–64, where the GC examined whether the absence of five binders misplaced by the Commission gave rise to an infringement of Solvay's rights of defence, answering in the negative. In her opinion of 14 April 2011 in *Solvay v Commission*, AG Kokott disagreed: '[T]he General Court seems to assume that anyone already playing with a bad hand would not have found any trump cards in the remaining parts of the file (point 41). The GC applied the wrong criteria when examining whether the missing documents might be useful to Solvay's defence in conflict with the rights of the defence'.

[52] Case T-342/99 *Airtours v Commission* [2002] ECR II-2585, annulling Commission Decision 2000/276/EC, *Airtours/First Choice*, 22 September 1999, [2000] OJ L93/1, declaring a concentration to be incompatible with the common market.

[53] Case T-403/05 *MyTravel v Commission* [2008] ECR II-2027.

[54] *Sweden and MyTravel Group*, n 4 above.

[55] ibid, para 265.

[56] ibid, para 306.

Presumption of Innocence[57]

The presumption of innocence, as prescribed in Article 6(2) ECHR, constitutes a general principle which applies in competition proceedings[58] and requires precise and consistent evidence to prove an infringement.

Under ordinary rules the burden of proof of the existence of circumstances constituting an infringement of Article 102 TFEU is borne by the Commission, which must adduce evidence capable of demonstrating the existence of the circumstances constituting an infringement.[59] Doubts must benefit the accused undertaking.

In *E.ON Energie*[60] the GC, referring to the type of infringement and the penalty imposed, confirmed that the presumption of innocence as contained in Article 6(2) ECHR forms an integral part of European law as recognised by the TEU and the Charter. The question was whether *E.ON* had broken a Commission seal during an investigation, or if it was rather the seal that was defective. The GC found that the Commission had proven that the seal had been broken and the burden was then on the company to prove the alternative to such an extent that the Commission's evidence was called into question.[61]

Did the Commission really prove its case beyond a reasonable doubt and how high was the requirement on *E.ON* to rebut this? A serious problem in competition cases appears to be that EU law does not characterise the standard of proof applicable and the courts are shying away from giving clear guidance and entangle themselves in very complex formulas.[62]

Examination of Witnesses

Under Article 6(3)(d) ECHR everyone charged with a criminal offence has the right 'to examine or have examined witnesses against him and to obtain the attendance and examination of witnesses on his behalf under the same conditions as witnesses against him'.

[57] Charter Art 48 (Presumption of innocence and right of defence provides): '(1). Everyone who has been charged shall be presumed innocent until proved guilty according to law. (2). Respect for the rights of the defence of anyone who has been charged shall be guaranteed'.

[58] *Siemens v Commission*, n 41 above, para 45.

[59] In *AstraZeneca v Commission*, judgment of 1 July 2010 nyr, paras 474–77, the GC held that given the nature of the infringements and the nature and degree of gravity of the ensuing penalties, the principle of the presumption of innocence applies in particular to the competition procedure. The evidence must be precise and consistent to establish the infringement. This does not mean that the Commission must adduce such evidence in relation to every aspect of the infringement. It is sufficient if the body of evidence relied on by the institution, viewed as a whole, and whose various elements are able to reinforce each other, meets that requirement.

[60] Case T-141/08 *E.ON Energie v Commission*, judgment of 15 December 2010 nyr, appeal pending: Case C-89/11 P [2011] OJ C152/11.

[61] ibid, para 242.

[62] See, eg the reasoning of the GC in *Fuji Electric v Commission*, n 21 above, paras 83 ff.

In *FMC Foret* the GC held that:

> even though the Commission is not a tribunal within the meaning of that article, and even though the fines imposed by the Commission are not of a criminal law nature, the Commission must nevertheless observe the general principles of European Union law during the administrative procedure.[63]

However, the right to hear witnesses does not extend to competition procedure as the Commission 'has a reasonable margin of discretion to decide how expedient it may be to hear persons whose evidence may be relevant to the investigation'.[64] The Commission is not required to hear witnesses put forward by the parties where it considers that the investigation has been sufficient.

The Privilege Against Self-incrimination

Article 6(3) ECHR provides that '[e]veryone charged with a criminal offence shall be presumed innocent until proved guilty according to law'. In *Amann & Söhne* the Court held that even if the Commission has the power to request information it cannot compel an undertaking to provide a self-incriminating answer.[65] The Commission is entitled to request any information, even if the information may be used to establish the existence of anti-competitive conduct. This power, does not, according to the GC, fall foul of Articles 6(1) and (2) of the ECHR or the case law of the ECtHR.

An obligation to answer purely factual questions put by the Commission and to comply with its request for the production of documents cannot constitute a breach of the principle of respect for the rights of the defence or impair the right to fair legal process equivalent to that guaranteed by Article 6 ECHR. Nothing prevents the addressee from showing later during the administrative procedure or in an appeal proceeding that the facts set out in its replies have a different meaning from that ascribed to them by the Commission. Undertakings cannot claim that their right not to incriminate themselves has been infringed where they voluntarily replied to such a request.[66]

[63] *FMC Foret v Commission*, n 35 above, para 138.

[64] ibid, para 137.

[65] *Amann & Söhne v Commission*, n 22 above, para 325. On the other hand, at para 326, the GC held: '[A]n undertaking in receipt of a request for information pursuant to Article 11(5) of Regulation No 17 cannot be recognised as having an absolute right of silence. To acknowledge the existence of such a right would go beyond what is necessary in order to preserve the rights of defence of undertakings and would constitute an unjustified hindrance to the Commission's performance of its duty to ensure that the rules on competition within the common market are observed. A right of silence can be acknowledged only to the extent that the undertaking concerned would be compelled to provide answers which might involve an admission on its part of the existence of an infringement which it is incumbent upon the Commission to prove'.

[66] ibid, paras 327–29.

The Imposition of Penalties[67]

Article 7(1) ECHR establishes that:

> No one shall be held guilty of any criminal offence on account of any act or omission which did not constitute a criminal offence under national or international law at the time when it was committed. Nor shall a heavier penalty be imposed than the one that was applicable at the time the criminal offence was committed.

According to the GC, penalties must also have a proper legal basis under the principle of legal certainty which forms part of the constitutional traditions common to the Member States.[68] Accordingly, Article 7 ECHR must be observed with regard both to penal provisions and to specific instruments imposing administrative penalties or permitting their imposition.

The requirement is satisfied where the individual can tell from the wording of the relevant provision, perhaps as interpreted by a court, what acts and omissions will make him criminally liable.[69] It is not necessary according to the ECtHR that the wording of the provisions be so precise that consequences which may flow from an infringement of those provisions are foreseeable with absolute certainty. The existence of vague terms does not necessarily entail an infringement of the provision. The fact that a law confers discretion is not in itself inconsistent with the requirements of foreseeability. To protect the individual against arbitrary interference, the scope of discretion and the manner of its exercise must be indicated with sufficient clarity.[70] In that connection, apart from the text of the law itself, the ECtHR will take account of whether the indeterminate concepts used have been defined by consistent and published case law.[71]

In *Amann & Söhne*[72] the GC emphasised that under Article 23(2) of Regulation 1/2003 the Commission does not have unlimited discretion in finding that the rules on competition have been infringed or in setting fines. Decisions are amenable to full review by the European judiciary. Where such a finding involves complex economic or technical appraisals, the case law recognises that the Commission has a certain degree of discretion; however such discretion is never unlimited and does not mean that the court must refrain from reviewing the

[67] In Art 49 (Principles of legality and proportionality of criminal offences and penalties), the Charter provides that: '(1). No one shall be held guilty of any criminal offence on account of any act or omission which did not constitute a criminal offence under national law or international law at the time when it was committed. Nor shall a heavier penalty be imposed than the one that was applicable at the time the criminal offence was committed. If, subsequent to the commission of a criminal offence, the law provides for a lighter penalty, that penalty shall be applicable. (2). This Article shall not prejudice the trial and punishment of any person for any act or omission which, at the time when it was committed, was criminal according to the general principles recognised by the community of nations. (3). The severity of penalties must not be disproportionate to the criminal offence'.

[68] *Amann & Söhne v Commission*, n 35 above, paras 124–30.

[69] ibid, citing *Coëme and ors v Belgium*, ECtHR 2000-VII, 1, § 145.

[70] ibid, citing *Margareta and Roger Andersson v Sweden*, Series A no 226 (1992), § 75.

[71] ibid, citing *G v France*, Series A no 325-B (1995), § 25.

[72] *Amann & Söhne v Commission*, n 22 above, paras 30–31 citing Case T-201/04 *Microsoft* v *Commission* [2007] ECR II-3601, para 88. *Lafarge v Commission*, n 34 above, paras 94–95.

Commission's interpretation of economic or technical data. The EU judiciary must establish that the evidence is factually accurate, reliable and consistent, determine that it contains all the relevant data, and that it substantiates the conclusions.

RECENT APPEALS AND ACTIONS

During the period from January until July 2011, 30 actions and appeals relating to competition matters were filed with EU Courts. Out of these, more than 30 per cent argued that the procedure was flawed either in Commission decision-making or in the appellate process before the GC. Parties argue that they are prejudiced due to the fact that decisions have been taken by an administrative body and not an independent and impartial tribunal.[73] Parties also complain that they are unfairly prejudiced by the fact that the Commission holds both investigative and decision-making powers,[74] and that the body of Commissionaires has not reviewed the process or even been present during the procedure before rendering the decision.[75]

According to several complaints, administrative procedures before the Commission fail to meet standards of administrative fairness as provided for under Article 6(1) ECHR. Nor are the requirements of due process satisfied within the meaning of Articles 41, 47, 48, 49 and 50 of the Charter. In addition, Article 296 TFEU and other general principles of EU law are not respected in the process. They argue that the process is not fair and ignores fundamental principles of equal treatment,[76] procedural requirements[77], good administration and the rights of the

[73] See action brought on 25 January 2011 in Case T-62/11 *Air France – KLM v Commission,* [2011] OJ C95/8, alleging infringement of the right to an independent and impartial tribunal resulting from the adoption of the contested decision by an authority which holds simultaneously powers of investigation and sanction, in breach of Art 47(2) of the Charter and Art 6(1) of the ECHR. *cf* Action brought on 25 January 2011 in Case T-43/11 *Singapore Airlines and Singapore Airlines Cargo PTE v Commission,* [2011] OJ C89/21, alleging that the decision breached essential procedural requirements, including the right to an independent and impartial tribunal.

[74] See action brought on 25 January 2011, Case T-56/11 *SAS Cargo Group and ors v Commission,* [2011] OJ C89/23 where I Forrester, on behalf of his clients, alleged a selective and arbitrary prosecution of the applicants raising serious issues under the ECHR and the Charter including the applicants' rights to an independent and impartial tribunal rather than an administrative authority which holds simultaneously powers of investigation and sanction.

[75] See action brought on 24 January 2011 in Case T-40/11 *Lan Airlines and Lan Cargo v Commission,* [2011] OJ C80/27. According to the sixth plea the Commission breached the applicants' right to a fair trial and, as a result, breached Art 47 of the Charter and Art 6 of the ECHR, by denying the applicants the opportunity to cross-examine witnesses; the fine was imposed following an oral hearing that was not public and which the decision-maker did not attend; and the contested decision was adopted by an administrative body, and no judicial body has full jurisdiction to review all aspects of it. *cf* Action in Case T-94/11 *AU Optronics v Commission,* [2011] OJ C120/4.

[76] Interestingly, Case C-14/11 *P,* [2011] OJ C80/22, removed from the register on 14 June 2011, was an appeal brought on 11 January 2011 by the Commission against the judgment of the General Court (Fourth Chamber) delivered on 27 October 2010 in Case T-24/05 *Alliance One International v Commission.* The Commission argued that the contested judgment should be set aside because the GC breached the Commission's rights to an adversarial procedure and misinterpreted the duty to state reasons.

[77] See action brought on 24 January 2011 in Case T-67/11 *Martinair Holland v Commission,* [2011] OJ C95/9. The applicant submits that the Commission decision breaches the right to good administration;

defence.[78] They also complain that Commission procedures do not satisfy principles of non-discrimination, proportionality, equal treatment[79] and equality of arms.[80]

The fact that parties invoke procedural irregularities is certainly not a new phenomenon, but has rather been asserted in competition cases throughout the years. However, the direct and indirect references to fundamental principles and especially the Charter and the ECHR confirm a trend that has been found in recent legal writing. The arguments made in the several Air Cargo appeal cases appear well coordinated and their strength remains to be tested in the pending appeals. It is, however, quite evident that the European courts will have to wrestle with these matters for the foreseeable future and the number of complaints signals that more consideration of them is required.

CONCLUSION

The overview indicates that human rights issues have been prevalent in competition law proceedings over the last decade and that the trend was reinforced by the entry into force of the Treaty of Lisbon. Considering the frequent references in the text, the fact that the Charter has become binding and that the relationship with the ECHR is strengthening, this should come as no surprise. A multitude of books and law review articles deal with not only the detailed due diligence requirements, but also suggest that there may be a more fundamental deficit in the EU system.

The trend is also reaching the EU Courts. Recent case law confirms that the process must be fair in the sense that procedural guarantees operate to give the parties assurance that the process is not arbitrary. What is clear is that courts are now paying more attention to the provisions contained in the Charter and the ECHR as interpreted by the ECtHR. Still, the examinations are done with reservations.

The overriding interest of the Commission is support of an efficient competition process and the courts seem to respect this position – perhaps as a division of responsibilities where surveillance obligations are with the Commission with the courts only reviewing the legality of the Commission's actions. That position finds certain support in the wording of the Treaty, yet on the other hand, the courts also often review substantive issues where they allow a margin of discretion

the right to an effective remedy and to a fair trial and the presumption of innocence and rights of defence pursuant to Arts 41, 47 and 48 of the Charter. *cf* Simultaneous action in Case T-39/11 *Cargolux Airlines v Commission*, [2011] OJ C80/26.

[78] See action brought on 23 January 2011 in Case T-28/11 *Koninklijke Luchtvaart Maatschappij v Commission*, [2011] OJ C72/30, implying that the Commission failed to respect the right to be heard, the right to a fair trial and the presumption of innocence under Arts 41(2)(a), 47 and 48 of the Charter by omitting to hear the addressees on the various changes to the scope of the case and the number of addressees.

[79] See action brought on 24 January 2011 in *Lan Airlines and Lan Cargo v Commission*, n 75 above.

[80] See action brought on 25 January 2011 in *Air France – KLM v Commission*, n 73 above.

to the Commission in what they sometimes refer to as complex issues. When the court will or will not apply this discretion appears somewhat arbitrary.

An equally disquieting point is that the courts appear unclear on how to categorise the competition process. Is it purely administrative or is it criminal? There is no doubt that fundamental provisions can be relied on to provide reasonable safeguards for accused parties, but it is, at the same time, clear that these safeguards must not impair efficiency. To protect competition is to protect a fundamental EU concept and the fact that, after the Lisbon Treaty it may be less fundamental, has not affected the evaluation. The 'criminal light' solution advanced by Wils appears to be a handy solution, where the human rights requirements will be respected – but not in full. Whether there actually is support for such an intermediary position in the interpretation made by the ECtHR can be disputed. Whether it is in line with the requirements of the Lisbon Treaty is also doubtful. It might be useful to recognise the criminal force of antitrust provisions by considering instituting personal sanctions of a criminal nature. Fines do not seem to prevent the re-occurrence of antitrust infringement however high. The consumer interest in seeing companies sentenced to fines of 100 millions of euro is unclear. First the customer suffers from the infringement and then suffers from the company trying to allocate the cost of the fine a second time.

It is clear from all the actions and appeals presently pending that the issue will not go away, but will be on the courts' agendas for the foreseeable future. The future entails more than just securing absolute procedural safeguards. The question is whether or not the entire process is fair. It is quite obvious that many lawyers involved in the process, and not only Ian Forrester, are far from happy with things as they are. Equal arms are missing and the checks and balances are insufficient.

A radical solution would be to deprive the Commission of any decision-making power and require that infringements are dealt with by an impartial tribunal. Even if it works in the US and several Member States that would be perhaps too radical a change to propose for the EU. At a minimum, the procedure in the Commission should be improved. The Hearing Officer and the Advisory Committee are not providing the impartial checks and balances required for a fair process. An alternative might be to seek inspiration from the way the procedure is construed at OHIM. Simply, transform the Advisory Committee from a forum for discussion between representatives from the national competition offices (they meet anyway in the network) to an internal appeals instance that will review contested decisions. Such a measure, combined with a GC which is turning every stone and not shying away from more complex issues would create the type of procedure that would satisfy the requirements of the Lisbon Treaty.

27

Rights of Defence in Cartel Proceedings: Some Ideas for Manageable Improvements

JAVIER RUIZ CALZADO & GIANNI DE STEFANO*

THERE IS NO doubt that cartels are among the most serious violations of antitrust laws and that companies whose participation in a cartel has been proven need to be subject to the appropriate fines. Fighting cartels is a priority for the European Commission (Commission) and antitrust agencies of major jurisdictions around the world, as evidenced by their deployment of tools such as leniency programmes, not to mention the severe fines and sanctions which, in certain jurisdictions (eg the US, the UK and Brazil), include imprisonment, and close co-ordination of investigations among agencies around the world. The purpose of this article in honour of Judge Pernilla Lindh is to signal a number of issues that companies involved in a European cartel investigation may face and to suggest improvements in terms of due process, a cardinal notion that should guide the action of the Commission as well as the European Union courts. This reflection starts from the undisputed principle that any company under investigation benefits from the presumption of innocence. This applies when proving the existence of a cartel and the involvement (extent and duration) of each of its members. The burden of proof is on the Commission. Both during the administrative procedure and before the courts in Luxembourg, the accused must be given the benefit of the doubt. Neither the existence of a cartel nor the participation of individual entities can be established up to the requisite legal standard if there are still any doubts lingering in the decision-maker's mind.[1] Accordingly, the EU Courts have in the past annulled, entirely or partially, cartel decisions for lack of sufficient evidence.[2]

* Javier Ruiz Calzado is a partner and Gianni De Stefano is an associate in Latham & Watkins' Brussels office.

[1] Case T-45/07 *Unipetrol v Commission*, judgment of 13 July 2011 nyr, para 48.

[2] The whole decision was annulled for lack of sufficient proof in Joined Cases C-89/85, C-104/85, C-114/85, C-116/85, C-117/85 and C-125/85 to C-129/85 *Ahlström Osakeyhtiö and ors v Commission*, [1993] ECR I-1307; Case T-337/94 *Enso-Gutzeit v Commission*, [1998] II-1571, paras 144, 148–54; Joined Cases T-44/02 OP, T-54/02 OP, T-56/02 OP, T-60/02 OP and T-61/02 OP *Dresdner Bank and ors v Commission*, [2006] ECR II-3567; Case T-44/07 *Kaucuk v Commission*, judgment of 13 July 2011 nyr, paras 59–68; Case T-45/07 *Unipetrol v Commission*, judgment of 13 July 2011 nyr, paras 59–68; Case T-53/07 *Trade-Stomil v Commission*, judgment of 13 July 2011 nyr, paras 73–78. In other instances

A second obvious starting point to highlight is the importance of the rights of defence for the entity under investigation.[3] The *Cement* judgment, rendered by a Chamber of the Court of First Instance presided over by Judge Pernilla Lindh underlined 'the fundamental principle of Community law that the rights of defence must be respected in all proceedings in which sanctions may be imposed',[4] a reminder of particular importance in the context of ever-increasing fines and other grave consequences attached to cartel decisions.[5]

Cartel investigations by the Commission are shaped by the dynamics and special features of the leniency programme.[6] In a high-stake game, leniency applicants have strong incentives to declare that a cartel existed, to denounce other companies as participants and to provide as much information as possible in order to obtain conditional immunity or leniency and preserve it until the final decision. The success of this programme requires more attention than ever on due process.

We believe improvements are possible, manageable and necessary to protect the credibility of the system and competition law generally. We think that these proposals are feasible notwithstanding the outcome of the controversial discussion on whether the whole European sanctioning model should be changed.[7] In

cartel decisions were partially annulled because the Commission had not taken into account all the evidence brought by the applicant: Case T-185/06 *L'Air liquide v Commission*, judgment of 16 June 2011 nyr, paras 74–83; Case T-196/06 *Edison v Commission*, judgment of 16 June 2011 nyr, paras 87–94.

[3] The importance of due process was pointed out by AG Warner and confirmed by the Court for the first time in 1974 in Case 17/74 *Transocean Marine Paint Association v Commission* [1974] ECR 1063, para 15. Secondary legislation reflects the case law. See, eg Council Regulation (EC) No 1/2003 of 16 December 2002 on the implementation of the rules on competition laid down in Arts 81 and 82 of the Treaty (current Arts 101 and 102 TFEU), [2003] OJ L/1/1, Art 27(2): 'The rights of defence of the parties concerned shall be fully respected in the proceedings'.

[4] Joined Cases T-25/95, T-26/95, T-30/95 to T-32/95, T-34/95 to T-39/95, T-42/95 to T-46/95, T-48/95, T-50/95 to T-65/95, T-68/95 to T-71/95, T-87/95, T-88/95, T-103/95 and T-104/95 *Cimenteries CBR and ors v Commission*, [2000] ECR II-491, para 106.

[5] See statistics on the website of the Commission's Directorate General for Competition, available at ec.europa.eu/competition/cartels/statistics/statistics.pdf, paras 1.2 and 1.4 showing how cartel fines increased by almost 17 times from 1990–94 to 2005–09.

[6] See Commission notice on immunity from fines and reduction of fines in cartel cases, [2006] OJ C/298/17.

[7] While the current system incorporates a number of checks and balances that seek to ensure the impartiality of the Commission's decisions, many argue that the Commission's multiple role in administrative proceedings as judge, jury, legislator and prosecutor infringe the right of the investigated company to an independent and impartial tribunal under Art 47(2) of the Charter of Fundamental Rights of the European Union and Art 6 of the ECHR, as interpreted by the case law of the ECtHR. See I Forrester, 'Due Process in EC Competition Cases: A Distinguished Institution with Flawed Procedures' (2009) 34 *EL Rev* 817; D Slater, S Thomas & D Waelbroeck, 'Competition Law Proceedings before the European Commission and the Right to a Fair Trial: No Need for Reform?' (2008) 04 *Global Competition Law Centre Working Paper*. The Commission argues that the impartial tribunal for competition cases does not need to be at the level of the administrative procedure before the Commission and that the control exerted by the General Court suffices; several authors argue that such standard is not sufficient since EU Courts respect the Commission's margin of appreciation in competition cases with a sort of judicial deference. See D Geradin and N Petit, 'Judicial Review in European Union Competition Law: A Quantitative and Qualitative Assessment' (2011) *TILEC Discussion Paper*, M Siragusa, 'Access to the Courts in a Community Based on the Rule of Law', contribution for the workshop 'Access to Justice' organised on the occasion of the symposium 'Celebration of 20 years of the Court of First Instance of

this regard, in appeals by KME and Chalkor against a copper-tube cartel fine, the Court of Justice has held that the EU's administrative system of imposing antitrust sanctions and having them reviewed in court is in line with fundamental rights.[8]

This reflection is all the more appropriate in the context of the changes introduced by the Lisbon Treaty. Indeed, following the entry into force of the Lisbon Treaty on 1 December 2009, the Charter of Fundamental Rights of the European Union[9] became legally binding on the Commission, the EU Courts and all other EU institutions. The Charter reflects the European Convention for the Protection of Human Rights and Fundamental Freedoms ('ECHR'),[10] as interpreted by the European Court of Human Rights ('ECtHR'),[11] now an influential source of interpretation and protection of the fundamental rights guaranteed by EU law. Furthermore, the EU has begun negotiations to accede to the ECHR.[12] As a result, human rights issues (like the rights of defence) will become even more relevant in proceedings before the Commission and the EU Courts in cartel cases.

RIGHTS OF DEFENCE DURING THE ADMINISTRATIVE PROCEDURE BEFORE THE COMMISSION

The Commission's Directorate General for Competition ('DG Competition') has made significant efforts over recent years to render its processes more transparent and subject to greater internal scrutiny, including the recent publication of best

the European Communities' on 25 September 2009, 129. In a recent article the President of the General Court recognised that 'the General Court exercises a standard of review respectful of the institutional balance as set out in the treaties in applying a marginal review to elements of the Commission's decision that come within the margin of appreciation of this institution'. See M Jaeger, 'The Standard of Review in Competition Cases Involving Complex Economic Assessments: Towards the Marginalisation of the Marginal Review?' (2011) 2 *JECLAP* 295 at 313. The ECtHR has ruled that in any event competition decisions should have to be subject to a full judicial review (*Bistrović v Croatia*, 31 May 2007, § 51; *Kyprianou v Cyprus*, (2007) 44 EHRR 27, 27 January 2004, § 44) examining the different allegations in fact and in law (*Menarini Diagnostics v Italy*, 27 September 2011, § 63).

[8] Cases C-272/09 P *KME Germany and ors v Commission*, C-386/10 P *Chalkor v Commission* and C-389/10 P *KME Germany and ors v Commission*, judgments of 8 December 2011 nyr, para 106. The Court of Justice seems to introduce a stronger standard of review to be applied to antitrust decisions ('in-depth review' at para 102 or 'full and unrestricted review, in law and in fact' at para 109).

[9] Charter of Fundamental Rights of the European Union, [2010] OJ C/83/389.

[10] The Declaration on the Charter provides that '[t]he Charter of Fundamental Rights of the European Union ... confirms the fundamental rights guaranteed by the European Convention for the Protection of Human Rights and Fundamental Freedoms'. See also Arts 52(3) ('[i]n so far as this Charter contains rights which correspond to rights guaranteed by the [ECHR], the meaning and scope of those rights shall be the same as those laid down by the said Convention. This provision shall not prevent Union law providing more extensive protection') and 53 ('nothing in this EU Charter shall be interpreted as restricting or adversely affecting human rights and fundamental freedoms as recognized [by the ECHR]') of the Charter.

[11] The Preamble of the Charter provides that the Charter 'reaffirms' the rights as they result, inter alia, from the case law of the ECtHR.

[12] See www.coe.int/t/dc/files/themes/eu_and_coe/default_EN.asp.

practice guidelines for competition proceedings,[13] and an explanatory note regarding its inspection authorisations,[14] as well as most recently an antitrust manual of procedures.[15] Indeed, these steps are part of a long and gradual evolution towards better and fairer administration of competition proceedings. However, issues of procedural unfairness and rights of defence remain, in particular in relation to dawn raids, access to the file, the role of the Hearing Officer, and the overall duration of the administrative proceedings.

Dawn Raids

In the midst of an unannounced inspection at the very beginning of a Commission investigation, certain procedural steps may have a long lasting adverse impact on a company's right of defence. The case law mandates that the rights of defence must be respected even at this preliminary stage,[16] as dawn raids may infringe certain procedural rights of the inspected companies as interpreted by the ECtHR.[17]

Is the Privacy of Companies Sufficiently Protected?

In 1989, the Court of Justice held that the general right to privacy, as recognised in Article 8(1) ECHR, did not apply to business premises, but only to private dwellings of natural persons as there was no ECHR case law on the matter at the time.[18] Later on, the ECtHR ruled that entering into the applicants' premises by the French competition authorities without prior judicial warrant and without a police officer with judicial investigation powers being present infringed Article 8 ECHR.[19] Subsequently, the Court of Justice acknowledged that businesses may also have a right to privacy, albeit within certain limits. The Court suggested that the exception contained in Article 8(2) ECHR (ie, the right of interference of the investigating authorities) may be more generous where business premises are concerned.[20]

[13] Commission notice on Best Practices for the Conduct of Proceedings Concerning Arts 101 and 102 TFEU, [2011] C/306/6 (the 'Best Practices for Proceedings Concerning Arts 101 and 102 TFEU').

[14] Explanatory Note to an Authorisation to Conduct an Inspection in Execution of a Commission Decision, available at ec.europa.eu/competition/antitrust/legislation/explanatory_note.pdf.

[15] DG Competition's Antitrust Manual of Procedures, March 2012, available at http://ec.europa.eu/competition/antitrust/antitrust_manproc_3_2012_en.pdf.

[16] Case 374/87 *Orkem v Commission*, [1989] ECR 3283, para 33.

[17] See W Wils, 'EU Antitrust Enforcement Powers and Procedural Rights and Guarantees: The Interplay between EU Law, National Law, the Charter of Fundamental Rights of the EU and the European Convention on Human Rights' (2011) 34 *World Competition*; I Aslam and M Ramsden, 'EC Dawn Raids: A Human Rights Violation?' (2008) 5 *Competition Law Review*.

[18] See Joined Cases 46/87 and 227/88 *Hoechst v Commission* [1989] ECR 2859, para 17.

[19] *Niemietz v Germany*, Series A no 251-B, (1993) 16 EHRR 97, § 27–33; *Colas Est and ors v France*, ECHR 2002-III, § 49; (2004) 39 EHRR 17.

[20] Case C-94/00 *Roquette Frères and ors v Commission*, [2002] ECR I-9011, para 29 ('the right of interference' established by Art 8(2) of the ECHR 'might well be more far-reaching where professional or business activities or premises were involved than would otherwise be the case').

Following the entry into force of the Lisbon Treaty, is the general right to privacy, as recognised in Article 8(1) ECHR and now also in Article 7 of the Charter, sufficiently protected by the Commission in the context of dawn raids? The Commission (and the EU Courts) could adopt a more protective approach considering that the ECtHR has held that the right to privacy encompasses the privacy of business premises or offices of legal persons and does not qualify or limit such right in comparison to physical persons.

Self-incrimination and Dawn Raids

Under EU case law, the privilege against self-incrimination, which emanates from the right to a fair trial and the presumption of innocence enshrined in Article 6 ECHR and Articles 47 and 48 of the Charter, prevents the Commission from compelling an undertaking to provide answers which might involve an admission as to its participation in an infringement.[21] The EU Courts have so far extended the protection against self-incrimination only to answers to information requests made in the course of the investigation when answering such questions would result in a direct admission of the existence of an infringement. Under the recently revised mandate of the Hearing Officer, parties who take the view that they should not be compelled to reply to questions that might force them to admit to an infringement may refer the matter to the Hearing Officer, who may adopt a reasoned recommendation as to whether the privilege against self-incrimination applies and inform the director responsible of the conclusions drawn.[22]
However, the courts do not consider that such protection applies to documents discovered during dawn raids or supplied in response to an information request.[23] The ECtHR, however, takes a broader view and applies the privilege to pre-existing documents in certain instances, such as, for example, a situation where an individual would be compelled to provide evidence.[24]

[21] Case 374/87 *Orkem v Commission*, [1989] ECR 3283, paras 34–35. The *Orkem* principle is now essentially reflected in Recital 23 of Regulation 1/2003, which states that: 'when complying with a decision of the Commission, undertakings cannot be forced to admit that they have committed an infringement, but they are in any event obliged to answer factual questions and to provide documents, even if this information may be used to establish against them or against another undertaking the existence of an infringement'. However, applying this apparently straightforward principle, in practice, will inevitably give rise to difficulties in grey areas.

[22] Art 4(2)(b) of the Decision of the President of the European Commission of 13 October 2011 on the Function and Terms of Reference of the Hearing Officer in Certain Competition Proceedings, [2011] OJ L/275/29 (the 'Terms of Reference of the Hearing Officer').

[23] *Orkem v Commission*, n 21 above, in Case C-301/04 *Commission v SGL Carbon* [2006] ECR I-5915. For the application of the privilege against self-incrimination as concerns information requests, see Case T-446/05 *Amann & Söhne v Commission*, [2010] ECR II-1255, para 329.

[24] In *Funke* (*Funke v France*, Series A no 256-A, (1993) 16 EHRR 297), the ECtHR held that Mr Funke's rights under Art 6 ECHR were violated when he was required to produce bank statements by customs authorities investigating charges against him and then convicted for refusing to supply those documents. The scope of the *Funke* ruling was cast into doubt by the subsequent ECtHR judgment in *Saunders* (*Saunders v the United Kingdom*, Reports 1996-VI, (1997) 23 EHRR 313), where the ECtHR held that the use in criminal proceedings against Mr Saunders of answers obtained under compulsion from him during an investigation by inspectors was a violation of his rights under Art 6 ECHR; the

Are the Safeguards Against Fishing Expeditions Sufficiently Efficient?

The decision authorising a dawn raid is typically very brief and rests on information submitted by an immunity applicant. Given the dynamics of the leniency programme, which rewards disclosure of as much information as possible at this early point in the investigation, such information will not have been subject to any independent verification or corroboration process. It will not have been supported or challenged by evidence from other parties and can therefore be considered at best as one-sided and at worse as unreliable, subjective, and potentially just plain wrong. Indeed, there is no possibility of *prior* judicial review of the actual substantive merits of a dawn-raid decision, either from the factual or the legal point of view.[25] A decision authorising a dawn raid may certainly be challenged before the General Court under Article 263 TFEU and an annulment would prevent the Commission from using the acquired evidence.[26] However, it is legitimate to query whether this control is sufficient in scope and effect.

In *Roquette Frères* the Court held that the review carried out by the EU Courts was limited to ensure that 'the investigation decision itself is in no way arbitrary, that is to say, that it has not been adopted in the absence of facts capable of justifying the investigation'.[27] In *Hoechst* and in *Dow* the Court held that the Commission is, in any case, required to specify the subject matter and purpose of the investigation.[28] However, the reality is that the Commission has never seen any of its dawn raid authorisation decisions even minimally criticised, let alone annulled, despite numerous rulings by the EU Courts. The courts have always rejected the claims put forward by applicants, who often argued that the statement of reasons of the inspection decision was insufficient, and this even in cases where the Commission had drafted the decision in very general terms[29] or when the scarce reasoning in

ECtHR, however, went on to observe that 'the right not to incriminate oneself . . . does not extend to the use in criminal proceedings of material which may be obtained from the accused through the use of compulsory powers but which has an existence independent of the will of the suspect'. Recently the ECtHR expressed clearly its broad take on the right to self-incrimination in the *JB* ruling (*JB v Switzerland*, ECHR 2001-III, § 66) at paras 66 ('the authorities were attempting to compel the applicant to submit documents which would have provided information as to his income with a view to the assessment of his taxes'), 68 ('the present case does not involve material of this nature which, like that considered in Saunders, has an existence independent of the person concerned and is not, therefore, obtained by means of coercion and in defiance of the will of that person') and 71 ('the Court considers that there has been a violation of the right under Art 6 § 1 of the Convention not to incriminate oneself').

[25] See Cases T-289/11 and T-290/11 *Deutsche Bahn and ors v Commission*, [2011] OJ C/238/22: 'Second plea: infringement of the fundamental right to an effective legal remedy by reason of the lack of possibility of prior judicial review of the inspection decision, both from the factual and the legal point of view' (the investigated conduct is not a cartel but a rebate system in the supply of electromotive power).

[26] Commission Decision of 7 October 1992, Case IV/33.791 – *CSM* [1992] OJ L/305/16, recital 18.

[27] See, eg Case C-94/00 *Roquette Frères and ors v Commission* [2002] ECR I-9011, para 55.

[28] Joined Cases 46/87 and 227/88 *Hoechst v Commission* [1989] ECR 2859, para 29; Case 85/87 *Dow Benelux v Commission* [1989] ECR 3137, para 40.

[29] Joined Cases 46/87 and 227/88 *Hoechst v Commission* [1989] ECR 2859, para 42 ('[a]lthough the statement of the reasons on which the contested decision is based is drawn up in very general terms which might well have been made more precise, and is therefore open to criticism in that respect, it

combination with the particular context of the case made it very difficult for the company to comprehend the actual scope of the investigation.[30]

The General Court is currently being confronted with cases where the applicant argues that the Commission has not been precise enough when describing the subject matter of an inspection thus creating the risk of a fishing expedition.[31] While it is true that some degree of control may be available at national level, the levels of judicial oversight by the national courts rarely go beyond examining whether the coercive measures in question are not arbitrary and are proportionate to the purpose of the investigation.[32] In particular, a national court may not demand the information and evidence in the Commission's file on which the latter's suspicions are based.[33] In addition, the national court may refuse to grant assistance only after giving the Commission the opportunity to rectify its decision.[34] Finally, the decision of the national court cannot be challenged before the General Court.[35]

Invariably endorsing dawn raid decisions does not give the Commission any incentive to pay more attention to the reasoning and material scope of such decisions. The clear perception among practitioners is that the Commission does not pay sufficient attention to such issues when crafting dawn raid decisions, which are the only elements available to their addressees in order to decide, within minutes, how best to co-operate with the inspectors without compromising their defence.[36]

The Commission's conduct during a dawn raid can only be reviewed if the company brings an action against the infringement decision. This review is arguably more complete,[37] yet it may well remain insufficient and unsatisfactory par-

none the less contains the essential indications'); Case 85/87 *Dow Benelux v Commission* [1989] ECR 3137, para 11. See also Case T-23/09 *CNOP and CCG v Commission*, judgment of 26 October 2010 nyr, para 41 ('[i]mposer une obligation de motivation plus lourde à la Commission à cet égard ne tiendrait pas dûment compte du caractère préliminaire de l'inspection').

[30] Cases T-339/04 *France Télécom v Commission* [2007] ECR II-00521, paras 57–58: '[t]he fact that that information was not mentioned in the contested decision could not have adversely affected the rights of the defence or prevented the applicant from assessing the scope of its duty to co-operate with the Commission during the inspection'; Case T-266/03 *Groupement des cartes bancaires v Commission* [2007] ECR II-83, paras 47 ff: 'quant au contexte dans lequel la décision attaquée s'inscrit, force est de constater que les différents éléments avancés par le requérant ne démontrent pas en quoi le contexte de la décision attaquée implique que la Commission a manqué à son obligation de motivation'.

[31] See Cases T-289/11 and T-290/11 *Deutsche Bahn and ors v Commission*, [2011] OJ C/238/22: '[t]hird plea: infringement of defence rights by reason of a disproportionately wide and non-specific subject-matter of the inspection ('fishing expedition')'.

[32] Case C-94/00 *Roquette Frères and ors v Commission*, [2002] ECR I-9011, paras 30–40. See also Regulation 1/2003, at Art 20(8), which codifies the *Roquette Frères* ruling.

[33] ibid, para 62.

[34] ibid, para 94.

[35] *France Télécom v Commission*, n 30 above, paras 51–52.

[36] See C-521/09 P *Elf Aquitaine* v *Commission*, judgment of 29 September 2011 nyr, paras 118–19, where the Court of Justice considers the appropriate reasoning of a dawn-raid decision as a right of defence.

[37] See Case T-59/99 *Ventouris Group Enterprises v Commission* [2003] ECR II-5257, para 161, where the General Court alluded to the right of the involved undertaking to ask for judicial review of the 'intrinsic lawfulness of the investigation as part of its . . . action for annulment of the final decision'.

ticularly as it would only take place once a decision on the merits has been reached.

These concerns are all the more relevant since the ECtHR partially invalidated a French court order authorising the searches on the premises of certain companies because the order could only be reviewed on points of law by the French Supreme Court, the Cour de cassation.[38] The ECtHR emphasised that parties must be able to rely on 'the certainty of effective judicial review within a reasonable time period'.

Access to the File

Companies involved in a cartel investigation can assess the evidence in possession of the Commission. Indeed, access to the file is one of the procedural guarantees intended to protect the principle of equality of arms and the rights of the defence. The Commission has taken considerable steps to ensure that it satisfies its obligations to grant parties to investigations appropriate access to the information contained in its investigation file: when the Statement of Objections ('SO') is issued in cartel cases, parties are provided with a CD-ROM that contains an electronic version of the Commission's file.[39] Further, there is a procedure by which the Hearing Officer can settle disputes between the parties, the information providers and the DG Competition over access to information contained in the Commission's file.[40]

However, the effectiveness of the 'access to file' procedure is undermined by a number of factors, namely the fact that access to the file is limited in time and not available to investigated companies before the issuance of the SO.[41] The situation is different at national level where several Member States (Spain, France and Italy), allow parties to have access to the file very early in the process and as many times as required.

This limitation is compounded by the fact that the parties are not given access to the replies to the SO of the other parties involved ('SO Replies'), despite settled case law requiring that the undertaking concerned must have been given the opportunity during the administrative procedure to make its views known on the

[38] *Compagnie des Gaz de Pétrole Primagaz v France* (21 December 2010) and *Société Canal Plus and ors v France* (21 December 2010).

[39] Access to the file is provided for in Art 27(1) and (2) of Regulation 1/2003 as well as in Art 15(1) of Commission Regulation (EC) No 773/2004 of 7 April 2004 relating to the conduct of proceedings by the Commission pursuant to Arts 81 and 82 of the EC Treaty (current Arts 101 and 102 TFEU), [2004] OJ L/123/18 (Implementing Regulation). See also Commission Notice on the rules for access to the Commission file in cases pursuant to Arts 81 and 82 of the EC Treaty (current Arts 101 and 102 TFEU), Arts 53, 54 and 57 of the EEA Agreement and Council Regulation (EC) No 139/2004, [2005] OJ C/325/7. See also Best Practices for Proceedings Concerning Arts 101 and 102 TFEU, n 13 above, s 3.1.2, paras 80 ff. Lastly, special rules govern access to corporate statements in cartel cases and settlement procedures: see Commission Notice on immunity from fines and reduction of fines in cartel cases, [2006] OJ C/298/17, paras 31–35; Commission Notice on the conduct of settlement procedures in view of the adoption of Decisions pursuant to Art 7 and Art 23 of Council Regulation (EC) No 1/2003 in cartel cases, [2008] OJ C/167/1, paras 35–40.

[40] Art 7 of the Terms of Reference of the Hearing Officer, n 22 above.

[41] Art 27(2) of Regulation 1/2003 and Arts 15 and 16 of the Implementing Regulation.

veracity and relevance of allegations made by the Commission in its decision.[42] It should not be for the Commission to decide which documents are of use to the defence;[43] the undertaking concerned should have the opportunity to examine all the documents in the investigation file.[44] SO Replies may include both incriminating and exculpatory evidence.[45]

Clearly, the failure to give access to inculpatory evidence breaches the rights of the defence if the Commission relied on that document to support its objections concerning the existence of an infringement.[46] Yet, in its decisions, the Commission often does not hesitate to quote SO Replies from other companies to rebut arguments put forward by a party contesting the existence of the cartel, its duration or its characteristics, as well as its participation.

In addition, where an exculpatory document has not been communicated, the undertaking concerned should only be required to establish that its non-disclosure was able to influence, to its disadvantage, the course of the proceedings and the content of the decision of the Commission.[47] With particular reference to SO Replies, the Court of Justice has specified that the undertaking concerned does not have to show that, had it had access to those replies, the Commission decision would have been different in content, but only that it would have been able to use the replies for its defence.[48] It is sufficient for the undertaking to show that it would have been able to put forward evidence which did not converge with the Commission's at that stage and would therefore have been able to have some influence on the Commission's assessment.[49] Access to the file is intended to enable the company concerned to *ensure a better defence*.[50]

In light of the above, the Commission should allow investigated companies to have access to SO Replies and to give them an opportunity to comment on such replies when they consider it necessary to their defence – as is customary practice

[42] See *Dresdner Bank and ors v Commission*, n 2 above, para 155, and the case law cited therein.

[43] See Case T-36/91 *ICI v Commission*, [1995] ECR II-1847, para 91.

[44] See Joined Cases C-204/00 P, C-205/00 P, C-211/00 P, C-213/00 P, C-217/00 P and C-219/00 P *Aalborg Portland and ors v Commission*, [2004] ECR I-123, para 68, and the case law cited therein. In particular, '[a] party will . . . be granted access to documents received after notification of the objections at later stages of the administrative procedure, where such documents may constitute new evidence – whether of an incriminating or of an exculpatory nature -, pertaining to the allegations concerning that party in the Commission's statement of objections. This is particularly the case where the Commission intends to rely on new evidence' (see Commission Notice on the rules for access to the Commission file, [2005] OJ C/325/7, para 27(2)).

[45] Case C-407/08 P *Knauf Gips v Commission*, [2010] ECR I-6375, para 22.

[46] See *Dresdner Bank and ors v Commission*, n 2 above, paras 157–58.

[47] *Aalborg Portland and ors v Commission*, [2004] ECR I-123, para 74, and the case law cited therein.

[48] See Cases C-109/10 *Solvay* v *Commission*, 25 October 2011 nyr, para 57

[49] Case T-24/07 *ThyssenKrupp Stainless v Commission*, [2009] ECR II-2309, para 274.

[50] The Court of Justice emphasises in its case-law concerning competition and anti-dumping proceedings that an infringement of the rights of defence must always be assumed where the undertaking concerned would have been *better able to ensure its defence* had there been no procedural error (C-194/99 P *Thyssen Stahl v Commission*, [2003] ECR I-10821, para 31; and Case C-141/08 P *Foshan Shunde Yongjian Housewares & Hardware v Council*, [2009] ECR I-9147, para 94). In addition, the jurisprudence of the ECtHR does not require a showing that the final outcome of the case would have been different in order to prove a breach of the rights of defence (*Monnell and Morris v UK*, 2 March 1987, 10 EHRR 205 (1988)).

in national proceedings.[51] This would avoid tedious litigation in Luxembourg, where companies are currently obliged to request the General Court to arrange for access to the file during the proceedings, an ex post exercise that has limitations in terms of ensuring effective judicial protection.

Role of the Hearing Officer

The oral hearing allows the parties to be heard in reply to the SO, and, where appropriate, to supplement the written evidence or to inform the Commission of other relevant matters. The fact that the hearing is not open to the general public and may even be held partially *in camera* guarantees that all attendees can express themselves freely and without constraint.[52]

However, certain characteristics of the hearing could be improved. For instance, the hearing offers no real opportunity for cross-examination of either the immunity applicant or the DG Competition's case team. There is no real debate on the merits between the case team and the parties (at most the former will have the possibility of raising relevant issues in answering the latter's questions). Also, a party that is not a leniency applicant has only very limited opportunity to engage in a dialogue with the leniency applicants. Cross-examination of witnesses is not possible.

Currently the Hearing Officer may make certain observations on the substance of part of the case. After the oral hearing, the Hearing Officer prepares a report to the Commissioner for Competition concerning procedural issues which may contain also

> observations on the further progress and impartiality of the proceedings. In so doing, the hearing officer shall seek to ensure in particular that, in the preparation of draft Commission decisions, due account is taken of all the relevant facts, whether favourable or unfavourable to the parties concerned, including the factual elements relevant to the gravity and duration of any infringement. Such observations may relate to, inter alia, the need for further information, the withdrawal of certain objections, or the formulation of further objections or suggestions for further investigative measures.[53]

While it is certain that the Hearing Officer can be a useful safeguard, the role remains predominantly reactive rather than proactive. Its capacity to push back the case team and the lower hierarchy is limited to highly exceptional cases, where investigation failures are blatant.

[51] See, eg decision of the Italian competition authority of 4 August 2011, Case no I729 – *Public Tender for Magnetic Resonance Equipment.*

[52] Best Practices for Proceedings Concerning Arts 101 and 102 TFEU, no 13 above, paras 92–94.

[53] See Art 14(2) of the Terms of Reference of the Hearing Officer, n 22 above; see also M Albers and J Jourdan 'The Role of Hearing Officers in EU Competition Proceedings: A Historical and Practical Perspective' (2011) 2 *JECLAP* 185. The text contained in the revised Terms of Reference of the Hearing Officer is broader than it used to be. It remains to be seen whether this will affect the depth of the Hearing Officer's observations on the substance of the case.

The Commission has so far been reluctant to give the Hearing Officer a clear role of checking and balancing the merits of the case. While the recently revised mandate strengthens the role of the Hearing Officer as the guardian of procedural rights,[54] it still does not allow for the effective scrutiny of the work of the case team. Such changes would not require any Copernican revolution of the current enforcement model but would greatly improve the current perception of the system in terms of due process and objectivity.

Another suggestion would be to make it compulsory for the Cabinet of the Competition Commissioner (and ideally also for other Commissioners) to be present at the hearing. As of today, one leaves the hearing room with the impression that the exercise is merely a benign waste of time as it is directed at the case team and its immediate hierarchy, whose views on the case are probably already well determined and whose capacity to reconsider the positions expressed in the SO is also extremely limited.

Duration of Cartel Proceedings

Another hurdle for any company involved in a cartel investigation is the length of time needed to reach a decision, which is rarely less than four years and often six or even seven years. These time spans are so significant as to be unfair, due to the lack of legal certainty that the investigated companies must face during such prolonged periods and other negative consequences including harm to reputation, significant loss of management time, attention and resources required to handle the defence, and the disclosing and provisioning obligations that listed companies have to meet during years of investigation.

Under Article 6(1) ECHR and Article 41 of the Charter, every person has the right to have his or her affairs handled impartially, fairly and within a reasonable time.[55] It is a general principle of EU law that the Commission must act within a reasonable time in handling the administrative procedures of its competence, including obviously those related to cartel investigations.[56] The excessive length of cartel proceedings can entail an annulment of the decision when there is proof that it adversely affected the ability of the undertakings concerned to defend themselves.[57]

While the reasonableness of a period cannot be assessed by reference to a precise maximum limit determined in the abstract but, rather, must be appraised in

[54] The Hearing Officer has new functions in the investigation phase, such as resolving issues regarding legal professional privilege, intervening when a company considers that it has not been informed of its procedural status or intervening in disputes about the extension of deadlines to reply to information requests. See Art 4 of the Terms of Reference of the Hearing Officer, n 22 above.

[55] *Vallée v France*, Series A no 289, (1991) 18 EHRR 549.

[56] *Cimenteries CBR and ors v Commission*, n 4 above, para 707.

[57] Joined Cases T-5/00 and T-6/00, *Nederlandse Federatieve Vereniging voor de Groothandel op Elektrotechnisch Gebied v Commission* [2003] ECR II-5761, para 74, as confirmed by Case C-105/04 P [2006] I-8725, paras 41–62.

the light of the specific circumstances of each case,[58] it is worth noting that EU Courts have considered as 'reasonable' extremely long administrative proceedings, namely between five and six years.[59] In the *Dutch Beer* cartel, the Commission reduced the fine on each undertaking involved by 100,000 euro, as it accepted the claim that the length of the administrative procedure, which had continued for more than seven years after the initial inspections were conducted, had been unreasonable.[60] In turn, the General Court found that the length of the administrative procedure infringed the principle that proceedings must be completed within a reasonable time period.[61]

In reaching decisions and making judgment calls on how to instruct a cartel investigation the Commission should take due account of the fact that as long as the procedure lasts, companies must continue to make accounting provision for a possible fine, pay legal advisors, commit company time and resources, and disclose the ongoing investigation to shareholders, insurers, and auditors. The lack of binding deadlines (with rules to stop the clock if need be) in cartel investigations by the Commission, in contrast with merger procedures, is very difficult to explain and understand. The fact that many national competition authorities have to comply with binding deadlines to instruct and decide their cases, and that they have consistently managed to adopt decisions, often within less than two years, is a clear indication of the usefulness and feasibility of introducing binding deadlines for the DG Competition when handling cartel investigations. Translation requirements should not be an acceptable explanation for such differences between national authorities and the Commission. Binding deadlines (eg 3 years) should not be difficult to implement and would significantly improve legal certainty and due process.

PROTECTION OF RIGHTS OF DEFENCE AND OTHER LEGITIMATE INTERESTS OF APPLICANTS DURING PROCEEDINGS BEFORE THE EU COURTS

As concerns judicial proceedings, the EU Courts' efforts to reduce the costs and time required to adjudicate cases should not come at the expense of the rights of defence of applicants.

[58] Joined Cases C-238/99 P, C-244/99 P, C-245/99 P, C-247/99 P, C-250/99 P to C-252/99 P and C-254/99 P *Limburgse Vinyl Maatschappij (LVM) and ors v Commission* [2002] ECR I-8375, para 192.

[59] The administrative procedure lasted approximately 68 months from the initial acts of the investigation to the adoption of the decision in '*Cement*' (*Cimenteries CBR and ors v Commission*, n 4 above, paras 706–11), and approximately 62 months in the '*PVC*' case (see Joined Cases T-305/94, T-306/94, T-307/94, T-313/94 to T-316/94, T-318/94, T-325/94, T-328/94, T-329/94 and T-335/94 *Limburgse Vinyl Maatschappij and ors v Commission*, [1999] ECR II-391, para 123). In both cases the duration of the proceedings was held to be 'reasonable' and, thus, not affecting the rights of defence of the parties.

[60] Commission Decision of 18 April 2007, Case COMP/B/37.766 – *Dutch Beer Market.*

[61] The Court also found that the flat-rate reduction given by the Commission did not take account of the amount of the fines and did not therefore constitute a reduction in the fine that was capable of adequately redressing the harm resulting from the excessive period taken. Consequently, the Court considered that in order to give the companies just satisfaction for the excessive duration of the procedure, the reduction should be increased to 5% of the fine. Case T-240/07 *Heineken and ors v Commission*, judgment of 16 June 2011 nyr, paras 429–34; Case T-235/07 *Bavaria v Commission*, judgment of 16 June 2011 nyr, paras 341–43 (appeal pending, see Case C-445/11).

Length of Written Submissions

The 'Practice Directions to Parties' limit the length of written submissions: the application and the defence should not exceed 50 pages (and 25 pages for the reply and the rejoinder).[62] This limit may be exceeded 'in cases involving particularly complex legal or factual issues'. Despite the fact that cartel cases are usually complex, the General Court regularly requires the applicant to abide by the 'indicative' page limitation. These limits apply – with some flexibility – to applications challenging cartel decisions, which often have more than 300 pages, excluding annexes.

Given the complexity of these decisions, limiting the applicants to 100 or 120 pages can seriously compromise their right to effective judicial protection,[63] which supposes the right to raise, and duly reason, all pleas that appear serious and appropriate. Indeed, the fundamental principle of effective judicial protection, enshrined in Article 47 of the Charter, prevails over the Practice Directions, which in any event are not binding.[64] The non-binding nature of the Practice Directions makes the insistence with which the General Court requires the parties to shorten submissions above 50 pages all the more surprising. But in practice, non-compliance is rarely an option as most counsel would rather avoid initiating proceedings by contradicting a specific request of the court.

Shifting parts of their main text to footnotes or to annexes in order to bring down the number of pages of an application cannot be beneficial to the Court, its judges and référendaires. If the justification and final goal of the General Court is to reduce the number of pages that have to be translated the applicant should be asked to provide a French translation of its briefs. But why should the General Court be more worried about the workload of its translation division than the Commission seems to be when it comes to its own decisions? After all, its cartel decisions are also translated, and not only into French, but also into all official languages for publication in the Official Journal.

The right to an impartial tribunal entails that a company is de facto but also de jure, in a position to present its arguments fully and without improper limitations.[65] It is submitted that capping the length of written submissions is unnecessary and can result in unfairness and a breach of the principle of equality of arms. In our view, there should be no maximum length of pleadings for complex cartel cases. The General Court in deciding on legal costs will always be able to act against excessively lengthy submissions.[66]

[62] Practice Directions to Parties, [2007] OJ L/232/7, as amended, para 10.

[63] Case T-279/02 *Degussa v Commission*, [2006] ECR II-897, para 421, and case law cited.

[64] Case C-113/09 P(R) *Ziegler v Commission*, [2010] ECR I-50, para 33 ('les instructions pratiques du Tribunal aux parties sont non pas juridiquement contraignantes, mais indicatives').

[65] The President of the General Court, Marc Jaeger, in an interview indicated that 'it is obvious that if the Commission takes a decision with 200 or 300 pages . . . the lawyers may legitimately feel the need to answer all the paras' (see *Mlex Magazine*, 'The View from the Bench', July–September 2011, 9).

[66] Rules of Procedure of the General Court, [1991] OJ L/136/1, as amended, Art 87(3) ('The General Court may order a party, even if successful, to pay costs which it considers that party to have unreasonably or vexatiously caused the opposite party to incur').

Limits on the Use of Annexes

The standard applicable to the admissibility and use of annexes is too onerous: there must be no new arguments in law in the annexes;[67] the main pleading must contain specific references to annexes.[68] A general reference in the annexes to all the arguments made during the administrative procedure is not admissible.[69] The nature of annexes is purely evidential and ancillary.[70] When combined with the strict application of the practice guidelines on the length of applications, these limits and conditions can come very close to denying an effective right to judicial protection.

A more flexible approach would be desirable. Indeed, the judges are often open to reading annexes in English (ie, not requiring a translation into French), which shows that the translation concern is not so serious.

Single Round of Written Submissions

Until very recently the normal practice of the EU Courts in most cases – and certainly in cartel cases – was to allow for a second round of briefs (reply and rejoinder) in which the parties could further discuss, clarify or nuance their arguments. However, in recent times this approach seems to have been revisited by the General Court,[71] making it more challenging for addressees of cartel decisions to make their case. The possibility of having a second round of briefs was no doubt helpful in alleviating the effects of the aforementioned cap on the length of briefs. However, if this second round is no longer available, the quality of the debate before the General Court may suffer.

Hearings at the General Court allow for a thorough discussion of issues of fact and law. However, doing away with the second round of written pleadings will have a negative impact on the hearing, in particular when it comes to evidence. The second round is not a mere repetition, but rather a focused set of clarifications, nuances and confirmations that allow the court and the parties to have a better understanding of the boundaries of the case, the main issues at stake and the detailed argumentation of each party. Such clarifications, responses and corrections cannot be properly addressed in the course of the oral procedure. Many arguments would require a verbatim reading of documents or case law. The time required would vastly exceed the duration of an oral submission.

[67] See T-201/04 *Microsoft v Commission*, [2007] ECR II-3601, paras 91–96.

[68] ibid, paras 97–99.

[69] See Case T-30/09 *Engelhorn v OHIM*, [2010] ECR II-3803, paras 18–19; Case T-87/05 *Energias de Portugal v Commission*, [2005] ECR II-3753, para 182.

[70] See T-151/05 *NVV and ors v Commission*, [2009] ECR II-1219, paras 61–63.

[71] In at least one recent cartel case (*Airfreight*), the General Court, having established that the case file was sufficiently comprehensive to enable the parties to elaborate their pleas and arguments in the course of the oral procedure, and in accordance with Art 47(1) of the Rules of Procedure, decided that a second exchange of pleadings was unnecessary. The General Court rejected the request for a submission of further documents to supplement the application for annulment and the defence under Art 47(1) of the Rules of Procedure and, in particular, to submit a reply to the Commission's defence.

In addition to the right to a fair trial (Article 6 ECHR and Article 47 Charter), the principle of equality of arms is also at stake. The Commission has two chances to develop its argument, firstly in its not-limited-in-length decisions adopted without any time constraint, and subsequently, in its defence. Applicants should be granted the possibility of rebutting all allegations against them in writing, including those raised by the Commission in its pleadings.[72] The EU Courts need to take into consideration 'all the information'[73] casting doubts about the correctness of the decision. Procedural economy cannot justify a limit on the applicants' right to use that information or otherwise defend themselves.

The seriousness of the problem is exacerbated by recent changes concerning the report for the hearing. Recent changes to the Practice Directions have removed the right of the parties to use the report for the hearing 'to check that their pleas and arguments have been properly understood' and to suggest amendments.[74] This means that the hearing is the only opportunity to correct any errors or misunderstandings.

CONCLUSION

This short contribution to the *Liber Amicorum* in honour of Judge Pernilla Lindh – a Judge who has always been preoccupied by issues relating to the rights of defence and due process – identifies a few areas where protection could be enhanced in proceedings before the Commission and subsequent appeals before the EU Courts in Luxembourg. Our suggestions for improvement would be relatively easy to implement.

The increased focus on fundamental rights due to the Charter, and the future accession of the EU to the ECHR, provides a genuine opportunity to reflect upon

[72] The principle of equality of arms is a corollary of the very concept of a fair hearing, see Case C-514/07 *Sweden v API and Commission*, judgment of 21 September 2010 nyr, para 88.

[73] See Case C-12/03 P *Commission v Tetra Laval*, [2005] ECR I-987, para 39: 'Not only must the Community Courts, inter alia, establish whether the evidence relied on [by the Commission] is factually accurate, reliable and consistent but also whether that evidence contains all the information which must be taken into account in order to assess a complex situation and whether it is capable of substantiating the conclusions drawn from it'. See also Case C-269/90 *Technische Universität München v Hauptzollamt München-Mitte*, [1991] ECR I-5469, para 14: '[W]here the Community institutions have such a power of appraisal, respect for the rights guaranteed by the Community legal order in administrative procedures is of even more fundamental importance. Those guarantees include, in particular, the duty of the competent institution to examine carefully and impartially all the relevant aspects of the individual case and the right of the person concerned to make his views known and to have an adequately reasoned decision. Only in this way can the Court verify whether the factual and legal elements upon which the exercise of the power of appraisal depends were present'.

[74] See the General Court Amendments to the Practice Directions of the Parties, [2011] OJ L/180/52, where the Court has removed a passage detailing that the hearing report 'provides an objective summary of the case' and 'is meant to enable the parties to check that their pleas and arguments have been properly understood and to facilitate study of the documents before the Court by the other Members of the bench hearing the case'. An accompanying paragraph was also deleted that provided a mechanism for the parties to identify 'factual errors' in the hearing report and propose amendments where the parties believe the hearing report 'does not correctly convey the essence of a party's argument'.

improvements which could easily be implemented without delay. The EU would be better positioned to counter the growing chorus of voices criticising the current enforcement model where the same entity investigates and decides. As for the EU Courts, the main change brought about by the Lisbon Treaty is the likelihood that their rulings may one day be challenged before the ECtHR in Strasbourg. Such prospect should also trigger a reflection as to the importance of making sure that any measure adopted to reduce the backlog of the General Court does not negatively affect the effective exercise of the rights of defence and, in particular, the principle of equality of arms. Cost and time efficiency should not come at the expense of due process and the right to a full and effective judicial review.

28

The Technische Glaswerke Ilmenau *Ruling: A Step Backwards for Transparency in EU Competition Cases?*

OLIVIER SPELTDOORN*

INTRODUCTION

IT WAS WITH great pleasure that I accepted the invitation to contribute to this *Liber Amicorum* for Pernilla Lindh, for whom I have a deep admiration and a lot of respect and affection. Among the four main topics proposed by the editorial board, I chose without hesitation that of transparency. First, this seemed to me to be an excellent way of honouring Pernilla Lindh considering that her home country – Sweden – is generally regarded as having the most open and transparent institutions in the world. Second, transparency is a very topical issue, which occupies a prominent place on the political agenda of the EU and is the subject of heated debate among its institutions, as is most clearly illustrated by the ongoing process recasting Regulation No 1049/2001.[1] Third, transparency is a

* Legal Secretary, General Court of the European Union. All the views expressed in this contribution are strictly personal. This contribution takes into account the law and the case law as they stand on 31 October 2011. The author would like to thank Emma-Jean Hinchy for her kind review of this contribution.

[1] Regulation (EC) No 1049/2001 of the European Parliament and the Council of 30 May 2001 regarding public access to European Parliament, Council and Commission documents, OJ 2001 L 145, p 43. On 30 April 2008, the Commission submitted a proposal for recasting that Regulation (COM(2008) 229 final). On 11 March 2009, the Parliament, considering that many of the changes put forward by the Commission represented a step backwards in terms of transparency, adopted a report containing substantive amendments to the proposal (PE T6-0114/2009) but postponed the vote on the legislative resolution accompanying the report. Thus, no position was formally adopted by the Parliament at the first reading. On the advice of its legal service, the Council rejected a number of the Parliament's amendments, taking the view that some were 'inadmissible' because they fell outside the scope of Art 255 of the EC Treaty, while others went beyond the object of the recasting proposal and could be included in future negotiations only if they were accepted by the Commission and incorporated into a modified proposal. The Parliament disagreed with that position (see Opinion of the legal service of the Council dated 24 February 2009, doc no 7791/09 of the Council dated 20 March 2009 and Opinion of the legal service of the Parliament dated 24 April 2009, accessible at www.statewatch.org/news/2011/mar/06eu-access-regulation-state-of-play.htm). The Commission took the view that it could not take into account the Parliament's amendments until they were adopted as a first reading position and the

domain in which the case law of the EU Courts has played – and still plays – a crucial role. In particular, it has, over a relatively short period of time,[2] shaped the right of public access to documents held by the EU institutions – generally towards more openness[3] – by specifying how requests for access should be dealt with by these institutions and by clarifying the scope of the exceptions to that right.

More precisely, I decided to deal with an issue relating to the above-mentioned access right, namely the use of Regulation No 1049/2001 in order to access the Commission's administrative file in EU competition proceedings.[4] Although very specific, this issue is of great importance in practice, as appears from the Commission's Report of 12 August 2011 on the Application of Regulation No 1049/2001 in 2010 which indicates that '[c]ompetition policy comes first on the list of domains of interest with 9.07% of initial applications'.[5] As will be set out in greater detail below, in each of the three main areas of EU competition law, that is, antitrust (Articles 101 and 102 TFEU), merger control, and State aid, access to the Commission's file – both by the parties involved in the proceedings and by third parties – is governed by specific, and rather restrictive, rules that may con-

latter refused to do so because of the Council's rejection of many of those amendments. Thus, the recasting process came to a stalemate. On 12 May 2010, the Committee on Civil Liberties, Justice and Home Affairs of the Parliament circulated an amended draft report on the recasting proposal (PE439.989). On 21 March 2011, the Commission put forward a new proposal, amending Regulation No 1049/2001 only with regard to the changes brought about by the entry into force of the Treaty of Lisbon (Art 15(3) TFEU extends the scope of Regulation No 1049/2001 to all institutions, bodies, offices, and agencies of the EU) (COM (2011)137 final). The Commission's recasting proposal has also been strongly criticised by the European Ombudsman, P Nikiforos Diamandouros, who stated, at a public hearing before the Parliament's Civil Liberties, Justice and Home Affairs Committee on 2 June 2008, that it 'would mean access to fewer, not more, documents [, which] raise[d] fundamental issues of principle about the EU's commitment to openness and transparency' (see www.ombudsman.europa.eu/resources/otherdocument.faces/en/3888/html.bookmark).

[2] At the time of writing, more than 130 cases on public access to documents held by the EU institutions have been dealt with by the EU Courts, the first being Case T-194/94 *Carvel and Guardian Newspapers v Council*, [1995] ECR II-2765.

[3] See, eg Joined Cases C-39/05 P and C-52/05 P *Sweden and Turco v Council* [2008] ECR I-4723, in which the ECJ stated that opinions of the legal services of the EU institutions relating to legislative processes are not, in principle, covered by the exception provided for in the second indent of Art 4(2) of Regulation No 1049/2001, and Case C-64/05 P *Sweden v Commission*, [2007] ECR I-11389, in which the ECJ ruled that Art 4(5) of Regulation No 1049/2001 could not be interpreted as conferring on the Member States a general and unconditional right to veto disclosure of documents originating from them and held by EU institutions. It should be pointed out that, besides the EU Courts, the European Ombudsman has also played a key role in the development of the right of public access to documents and, more generally, of the principle of transparency.

[4] The Commission Notice on the rules for access to the Commission file in cases pursuant to Articles [101 and 102 TFEU], Articles 53, 54 and 57 of the EEA Agreement and Council Regulation (EC) No 139/2004 (Notice on the Rules for Access to the File) indicates that '[t]he "Commission file" in a competition investigation . . . consists of all documents, which have been obtained, produced and/or assembled by the Commission Directorate General for Competition during the investigation' ([2005] OJ C325/7, para 8). In that Notice, as in Regulation No 1049/2001, the concept of 'document' is broadly defined such that it encompasses all forms of information support, irrespective of the storage medium as well as any electronic data storage device as may be or become available. It can be considered that these definitions are also valid in relation to access to the Commission's file in State aid proceedings.

[5] COM(2011) 492 final, point 4.3.

flict with those laid down by Regulation No 1049/2001.[6] The question of how to reconcile those different rules was at the heart of the case which gave rise to the judgment of the ECJ in the *Technische Glaswerke Ilmenau*[7] (*TGI*) case.

Before considering the above-mentioned issue, it should be pointed out that transparency involves much more than just the right of public access to documents. The concept of transparency, in the EU context, is both a very broad and a flexible concept and one which is not clearly circumscribed. As rightly observed by Professor Deirdre Curtin, '[g]enerally the term transparency is referred to in such a loose fashion that it can seem to resemble a "garbage-can" of different concepts and principles'.[8] In addition, transparency – which is today clearly recognised as a general principle of EU law[9] – is expected to fulfil a range of functions including strengthening the democratic nature of the institutions and the public's confidence in the administration,[10] bringing the EU closer to its citizens, stimulating a more informed and involved debate on EU policy matters,[11] enabling citizens to participate more closely in the decision-making process, guaranteeing the legitimacy of the administration, ensuring it is more effective and more accountable to the citizens,[12] and guaranteeing that the power and resources entrusted to political and public bodies are handled with care and never abused for personal gain.[13]

That said, the right of public access to documents is undoubtedly a key feature[14] of transparency, and this almost since the advent of the principle of transparency

[6] For previous articles on the same issue, see O Brouwer and D Mes, 'The Tide of Transparency has Reached Antitrust Shores: The Use of Regulation 1049/2001 in EU Antitrust (Related) Proceedings' in *Liber Amicorum in Honour of Bo Vesterdorf* (Brussels, Bruylant, 2007) 451; L Idot, 'Le règlement no 1049/2001 doit-il s'appliquer aux procédures concurrence? À propos des affaires Technische Glaswerke Ilmenau, Odile Jacob et Agrofert' (2010) *Europe*, Étude 11; G Muguet-Poullennec, 'Vers la fin de la transparence dans les procédures administratives?' (2010) 25 *Revue Lamy de la Concurrence: droit, économie, régulation* 51; G Goddin, 'Recent Judgments Regarding Transparency and Access to Documents in the Field of Competition Law: Where Does the Court of Justice of the EU Strike the Balance?' (2011) 1 *Journal of European Competition Law & Practice* 10.

[7] Case C-139/07 P *Commission v Technische Glaswerke Ilmenau*, [2010] ECR I-5885.

[8] D Curtin, 'Through the Looking Glass: The Myths of Transparency in the European Union', lecture given in 2004 at Durham European Law Institute, accessible at www.dur.ac.uk/deli/events/annuallecture/pastlectures.

[9] See, eg Joined Cases C-514/07 P, C-528/07 P and C-532/07 P *Sweden and ors v API and Commission* [2010] ECR I-8533, paras 81, 84, 95, 152, 156, 158. For a discussion of the question of whether transparency can be qualified as a general principle of EU law, see S Prechal and M de Leeuw, 'Transparency: A General Principle of EU Law?' in U Bernitz, J Nergelius and C Cardner (eds), *General Principles of European Community Law in a Process of Development* (Alphen aan den Rijn, Kluwer Law International, 2008) 201.

[10] Declaration No 17 on the right of access to information annexed to the Final Act of the Treaty on the EU, signed in Maastricht on 7 February 1992. See also *Sweden and Turco v Council*, n 3 above, paras 46, 59.

[11] Commission Communication on Public Access to the Institutions' Documents, COM(93) 193 final.

[12] Recital 2 of Regulation No 1049/2001. See also Case C-41/00 P *Interporc v Commission* [2003] ECR I-2125, para 39.

[13] Green Paper on European Transparency Initiative, COM(2006) 194 final.

[14] Other aspects of transparency include inter alia: the simplification of the EU legislation and the improvement of its quality and accessibility, the opening by the Council to the public of deliberations on legislative acts adopted by co-decision, the publication of the records and votes in the Council, the consultation of the public by the Commission before making proposals, including the use of white and green papers, the adoption, by the Commission, of a 'Code of good administrative behaviour', the disclosure of beneficiaries of EU funds and the regulation of lobbying activities.

at the EU level. To the best of my knowledge, the first formal reference to this principle in the EU context is found in Declaration No 17 on the right of access to information annexed to the Final Act of the Treaty on the EU, signed in Maastricht on 7 February 1992, which simply 'recommends' that the Commission submit a report on measures designed to improve 'the public access to the information available to the institutions'. In 1993, the Commission implemented that Declaration by focussing on access, not to information per se, but to documents.[15] This led to the adoption, on 6 December 1993, by the Council and the Commission of a Code of Conduct designed to set out the principles governing access to documents held by these institutions.[16] The Council, on 20 December 1993,[17] and the Commission, on 8 February 1994,[18] each adopted, on the basis of their respective rules of internal organisation, a decision implementing the access principles. They were followed, on 10 July 1997, by the Parliament.[19] The Amsterdam Treaty, signed a few months later,[20] formally enshrined in the EU legal order the right of public access to documents of the Parliament, the Council, and the Commission by introducing a new Article 255 in the EC Treaty (now Article 15 TFEU). With the Amsterdam Treaty, right of access to documents has become a genuine subjective right for individuals. In addition, it has since acquired the status of a fundamental right, as demonstrated by its incorporation into the Charter of Fundamental Rights of the EU.[21] In accordance with Article 255(2) of the EC Treaty, the Parliament and the Council adopted, on 30 May 2001,[22] after lengthy and complex inter-institutional negotiations, Regulation No 1049/2001. The purpose of this regulation was 'to give the fullest possible effect to the right of public access to documents and to lay down the general principles and limits on such access'.[23] The Lisbon Treaty, which entered into force on 1 December 2009,[24] has (formally)[25] extended the public right of access to documents held by all the EU

[15] See Commission Communication on Public Access to the Institutions' Documents, n 11 above; Commission Communication on Openness in the Community, COM(93) 258 final. In the latter communication, the Commission elaborated on the basic principles governing access to documents.

[16] Code of Conduct Concerning Public Access to Council and Commission Documents, [1993] OJ L340/41.

[17] Council Decision 93/731/EC of 20 December 1993 on Public Access to Council Documents, [1993] OJ L340/43.

[18] Commission Decision 94/90/ECSC, EC, Euratom of 8 February 1994 on Public Access to Commission Documents, [1994] OJ L46/58.

[19] European Parliament Decision 97/632/EC, ECSC, Euratom of 10 July 1997 on Public Access to European Parliament Documents, [1997] OJ L263/27.

[20] The Amsterdam Treaty was signed on 2 October 1997 and entered into force on 1 May 1999.

[21] Art 42 of the Charter.

[22] Regulation No 1049/2001 became applicable on 3 December 2001.

[23] Recital 4 of Regulation No 1049/2001.

[24] The Lisbon Treaty was signed on 13 December 2007.

[25] Shortly after Regulation No 1049/2001 entered into force, its applicability was extended to the EU agencies by virtue of a specific provision in each of their respective founding acts. In addition, the European Central Bank, the European Investment Bank, the European Court of Auditors, the European Economic and Social Committee, the Committee of the Regions, Europol, and Eurojust had already voluntarily adopted acts laying down rules that were identical, or similar, to those contained in Regulation No 1049/2001.

institutions, bodies, offices, and agencies.[26] Documents of the Court of Justice of the EU, of the European Central Bank, and of the European Investment Bank are now also subject to this right, but only to the extent that they relate to relevant organisation's administrative activities.

Below, I shall recall, first, the main characteristics and provisions of Regulation No 1049/2001 as well as the main principles laid down by the case law of the EU Courts in the field of public access to documents and, second, the rules applicable to access to the Commission's file in EU competition proceedings (Rules on Access to the File). Then, I shall present an overview of the case law of the EU Courts on the application of Regulation No 1049/2001 in the latter proceedings, with special emphasis on the *TGI* judgment. Lastly, I shall provide some thoughts on the possible future developments in the case law initiated by the *TGI* judgment.

REGULATION NO 1049/2001 AND THE MAIN PRINCIPLES DERIVING FROM THE CASE LAW ON PUBLIC ACCESS TO DOCUMENTS

Aims, Scope and Beneficiaries

Regulation No 1049/2001 purports to define the principles, conditions, and limitations – on grounds of public or private interest – governing the right of access to documents of the Parliament, the Council, and the Commission in such a way as to ensure the widest possible access to documents, to establish rules ensuring the easiest possible exercise of this right, and to promote good administrative practice by the institutions on access to documents.[27] It applies to all documents held by those institutions, that is to say, documents drawn up or received by them, and in their possession, in all areas of activity of the EU.[28] The concept of 'document' is defined very broadly as meaning

> any content whatever its medium (written on paper or stored in electronic form or as a sound, visual or audiovisual recording) concerning a matter relating to the policies, activities and decisions falling within the institution's sphere of responsibility.[29]

The right of access is granted to any citizen of the EU and any natural or legal person residing or having its registered office in a Member State.[30] The institutions '*may*' also confer that right, on the same terms, to citizens of third countries not residing in a Member State and to legal persons having their registered office in a third country.[31]

[26] Art 15(3) TFEU.
[27] Art 1 of Regulation No 1049/2001.
[28] Art 2(3) of Regulation No 1049/2001.
[29] Art 3(a) of Regulation No 1049/2001.
[30] Art 2(1) of Regulation No 1049/2001.
[31] Art 2(2) of Regulation No 1049/2001.

Procedure

Applications for access to documents must be made in writing, in any of the 23 official EU languages, and be sufficiently precise.[32] The applicant is not obliged to state reasons for his application.[33] Within 15 working days from registration of the application, the institution must either grant access to the document requested or reply stating the reasons for its total or partial refusal.[34] If access is refused, the applicant may, within 15 working days following receipt of the reply, make a confirmatory application asking the institution to reconsider its position.[35] The institution then has 15 working days within which to grant access to the document requested or to confirm its refusal. If the refusal is confirmed, the applicant can bring an action for annulment before the General Court or submit a complaint to the European Ombudsman.[36] The '15 working days' time limits imposed on the institution may be extended to 30 working days in exceptional cases, for example where access is requested to a very long document or to a very large number of documents.[37]

If the document requested originates from a third party, the institution is required to consult that party in order to assess whether an exception in Article 4(1) or (2) of Regulation No 1049/2001 applies, unless it is clear that the document must or must not be disclosed.[38] Among third parties, Member States are subject to special treatment in that they may request that the institution does not disclose documents originating from them without their prior agreement.[39] The ECJ has ruled, however, that this power does not confer on Member States a general and unconditional right of veto, such that they could, in a discretionary manner, oppose the disclosure of documents originating from them and held by an institution.[40]

Special rules apply to sensitive documents, that is, documents classified as top secret, secret or confidential which protect essential interests of the EU or of its Member States in the areas specified by Article 4(1)(a).[41]

[32] Art 6(1) of Regulation No 1049/2001. The institutions must ask the applicants to clarify their application if the latter is not sufficiently precise and assist them in doing so: see Art 6(2) of Regulation No 1049/2001.

[33] Art 6(1) of Regulation No 1049/2001.

[34] Art 7(1) of Regulation No 1049/2001. If the institution fails to reply within the prescribed time limit, the applicant is entitled to make a confirmatory application: see Art 7(4) of Regulation No 1049/2001.

[35] Art 7(2) of Regulation No 1049/2001.

[36] Art 8(1) of Regulation No 1049/2001. Failure by the institution to reply within the prescribed time limit is considered as a negative reply: see Art 8(3) of Regulation No 1049/2001.

[37] Arts 7(3) and 8(2) of Regulation No 1049/2001.

[38] Art 4(4) of Regulation No 1049/2001.

[39] Art 4(5) of Regulation No 1049/2001.

[40] *Sweden v Commission*, n 3 above, paras 58, 75.

[41] Art 9 of Regulation No 1049/2001.

Exceptions

The exceptions to the right of access are laid down in Article 4 of Regulation No 1049/2001. Since their earliest judgments in this area, which concerned the application of the 1993 code of conduct, the EU Courts have made it clear that the exceptions to the right of access should be interpreted and applied strictly, in order not to frustrate the principle of providing the public with the widest possible access to documents.[42]

Pursuant to Article 4(1)(a) and (b), an institution must refuse access to a document where its disclosure would undermine the protection of certain public (public security, defence and military matters, international relations, or the financial, monetary or economic policy of the EU or of a Member State) or private interests (the privacy and integrity of the individual). In accordance with Article 4(2), access to a document must also be refused where its disclosure would undermine the protection of the commercial interests of a natural or legal person (first indent), court proceedings and legal advice (second indent), or the purpose of inspections, investigations, and audits (third indent). Article 4(3) contains an exception to protect the decision-making process of the institutions, which applies only if disclosure would *seriously* undermine that process. That provision distinguishes between situations where an institution has taken or not taken a decision on the matter concerned. Thus, according to its first sub-paragraph, any document drawn up by an institution for its internal use or received by it which relates to a matter where it has not yet made a decision falls within the scope of the exception. Under the second sub-paragraph of that provision,[43] where such a decision has been taken, the exception covers only 'opinions for internal use as part of deliberations and preliminary consultations within the institution'. Unlike the exceptions contained in Article 4(1), which are absolute, those provided for in Article 4(2) and (3) are relative in that they are conditional upon there being no 'overriding public interest in disclosure'.

The exceptions only apply for the period during which protection is justified on the basis of the content of the document and (except in the case of documents covered by the exception relating to privacy or commercial interests and of sensitive documents) for a maximum period of 30 years.[44]

Finally, in accordance with Article 4(6) of Regulation No 1049/2001, if only parts of the requested document are covered by an exception, the remaining parts must be released. This duty to grant partial access was initially laid down – on the basis of proportionality considerations – by the General Court in its judgment of 19 July 1999 in *Hautala* v *Council*.[45]

[42] See, eg concerning the exceptions provided for in the 1993 Code of Conduct, Case T-105/95 *WWF UK v Commission* [1997] ECR II-313, para 56, and concerning the exceptions set out in Regulation No 1049/2001; Case T-84/03 *Turco v Council* [2004] ECR II-4061, para 60.

[43] See, for a very recent interpretation of the second sub-paragraph of Art 4(3) of Regulation No 1049/2001, Case C-506/08 P *Sweden v MyTravel and Commission*, judgment of 21 July 2011 nyr, paras 72–103.

[44] Art 4(7) of Regulation No 1049/2001.

[45] Case T-14/98 *Hautala v Council* [1999] ECR II-2489, paras 75–88, confirmed on appeal by the ECJ in Case C-353/99 P *Council v Hautala* [2001] ECR I-9565, paras 21–31.

Examination to be Undertaken by the Institution

The case law has gradually specified how applications for access to documents should be treated by the institutions. The approach to be followed is described below.

First, the institution concerned must assess whether the requested document comes within one of the exceptions set out in Article 4 of Regulation No 1049/2001.[46] For example, in its judgment in *Agrofert* v *Commission*,[47] the General Court considered the requested documents could be covered by the exception relating to the protection of commercial interests laid down in the first indent of Article 4(2), having found that they were likely to concern, inter alia, commercial strategies, turnover, market shares and business relations, and thus commercially sensitive information relating to parties to a merger, as well as the effects of this merger on the relevant markets and the potential efficiency gains. It should be noted that, in its assessment, the institution cannot simply rely on the title of the document concerned. Thus, in its judgment in *Sweden and Turco* v *Council*,[48] the ECJ stated that the fact that a document is entitled 'legal advice/opinion' does not mean that it automatically benefits from the protection of legal advice set out in the second indent of Article 4(2) of Regulation No 1049/2001. According to the ECJ, '[o]ver and above the way a document is described, it is for the institution to satisfy itself that that document does indeed concern such advice'.

Second, the institution must examine whether disclosure of the requested document could specifically and effectively[49] harm the interest protected by the exception upon which it is relying.[50] The mere fact that a document concerns an interest protected by an exception is indeed not, in itself, sufficient to justify application of that exception.[51] Moreover, the risk of harm must be reasonably foreseeable and not purely hypothetical.[52] Consequently, the examination must be carried out by the institution in a concrete manner.[53] In addition, the 'concrete examination' must be undertaken in respect of *each* document referred to in the request for access.[54] Only such a concrete, individual examination (as opposed to an abstract, general examination) can enable the institution to assess, on the one hand, the extent to which an exception is applicable and, on the other, the possibility of granting the applicant partial access in accordance with Article 4(6) of Regulation No 1049/2001.[55]

[46] *Sweden and Turco v Council*, n 3 above, paras 35, 38; Case T-111/07 *Agrofert v Commission*, judgment of 7 July 2010 not reported, para 53, appeal pending before the ECJ Case C-477/10 P *Commission v Agrofert*.

[47] ibid, para 54.

[48] *Sweden and Turco v Council*, n 3 above, para 39.

[49] In the case of the exception relating to the protection of the decision-making process, set out at Art 4(3) of Regulation No 1049/2001, the harm must also be serious.

[50] *Agrofert v Commission*, n 46 above, paras 53, 56, 58.

[51] Case T-20/99 *Denkavit Nederland v Commission* [2000] ECR II-3011, para 45.

[52] *Sweden and Turco v Council*, n 3 above, para 43.

[53] *Agrofert v Commission*, n 46 above, para 58.

[54] ibid, para 59.

[55] Case T-2/03 *Verein für Konsumenteninformation v Commission* [2005] ECR II-1121, para 75.

However, according to the General Court, a concrete, individual examination may not be necessary 'where, due to the particular circumstances of the individual case, it is obvious that access must be refused or, on the contrary, granted'.[56] Similarly, the ECJ, quickly followed by the General Court, ruled that it was possible for the institution to base its decision refusing access to a document on 'general presumptions which apply to certain categories of documents'.[57] In other words, the EU Courts consider that, in certain cases, there exists a general presumption that disclosure of documents in principle harms the interest protected by an exception, which allows the institution to reject the request for access without first making a concrete, individual examination of those documents. The applicant can, however, demonstrate that a given document is not covered by the presumption or, in the case of the relative exceptions laid down in Article 4(2) and (3) of Regulation No 1049/2001, that there is a higher public interest justifying disclosure.[58] The scope of those 'general presumptions' will be discussed in more detail below.

In 'exceptional cases' and subject to certain conditions, the institution is also entitled to refuse disclosure without carrying out a concrete, individual examination of the documents concerned where this would impose on it a particularly heavy administrative burden.[59]

Third, if the institution considers that one of the relative exceptions laid down in Article 4(2) and (3) of Regulation No 1049/2001 is applicable, it must also verify whether there is any overriding public interest justifying disclosure of the document concerned and, if this is the case, balance such interest against the particular interest to be protected by non-disclosure. The overriding public interest may coincide with the principles underlying Regulation No 1049/2001.[60] On the other hand, any overriding public interest must be of an 'objective and general ... nature' and, therefore, be distinct from 'individual or private interests', such as the possibility for the applicant to use the requested document in the context of proceedings brought against an institution.[61]

Finally, it should be recalled that the reasons for any decision of an institution

[56] ibid. See also Case T-237/05 *Éditions Odile Jacob v Commission*, [2010] ECR II-2245, para 45, appeal pending before the ECJ (Case C-404/10 P *Commission v Éditions Odile Jacob*); *Agrofert v Commission*, n 46 above, para 79.

[57] *Commission v Technische Glaswerke Ilmenau*, n 7 above, para 54; *Sweden and ors v API and Commission*, n 9 above, para 74; Joined Cases T-494/08 to T-500/08 and T-509/08 *Ryanair v Commission*, judgment of 10 December 2010 nyr, para 70.

[58] *Commission v Technische Glaswerke Ilmenau*, n 7 above, para 62; *Ryanair v Commission*, n 57 above, para 72.

[59] *Verein für Konsumenteninformation v Commission*, n 55 above, paras 94–115. This particular derogation will be discussed in more detail below. The EU Courts had previously recognised a similar derogation, based on the excessive administrative burden caused by a request, in their case law relating to the 1993 Code of Conduct: see, eg Case T-14/98 *Hautala v Council*, n 45 above, para 86, confirmed on appeal in Case C-353/99 P *Council v Hautala*, n 45 above; Case T-188/98 *Kuijer v Council* [2000] ECR II-1959, para 55.

[60] *Sweden and Turco v Council*, n 3 above, para 45–47, 67, 74; *Éditions Odile Jacob v Commission*, n 56 above, para 190.

[61] Joined Cases T-110/03, T-150/03 and T-405/03 *Sison v Council* [2005] ECR II-1429, para 55; Case T-403/05 *MyTravel v Commission* [2008] ECR II-2027, paras 65–68; *Éditions Odile Jacob v Commission*, n 56 above, paras 191–94.

taken on the basis of the exceptions set out in Article 4 of Regulation No 1049/2001 must be stated.

RULES APPLICABLE TO ACCESS TO THE COMMISSION'S FILE IN COMPETITION PROCEEDINGS

Antitrust and Merger Proceedings

In antitrust (Articles 101 and 102 TFEU) and merger proceedings, access to the Commission's file is regarded as a fundamental procedural safeguard intended to protect the rights of the defence and to ensure, in particular, that the right to be heard can be exercised effectively.[62] This access is provided for in Article 27(1) and (2) of Regulation No 1/2003[63] and Article 15(1) and (2) of Regulation No 773/2004,[64] as far as antitrust proceedings are concerned and in Article 18(1) and (3) of Regulation No 139/2004[65] and Article 17 of Regulation No 802//2004,[66] as far as merger proceedings are concerned.

The Notice on the Rules for Access to the File explains in more detail who is entitled to access to the file in those proceedings, which documents may be accessed, when access will take place, and which procedures for allowing access and for the treatment of confidential information apply.

Access to the file is granted only to the persons, undertakings or associations of undertakings to which the Commission has addressed a statement of objections[67] (ie, in merger proceedings, the notifying parties). Third parties do not enjoy this right of access[68] (see, however, the particular situation of complainants and 'other involved parties' set out below). All documents making up the file are accessible, with the exception of internal documents (including drafts, opinions, and memos

[62] See, eg Case C-199/99 P *Corus UK v Commission* [2003] ECR I-11177, paras 125–28; Case T-186/06 *Solvay v Commission*, judgment of 16 June 2011 nyr, para 213; Notice on the Rules for Access to the File, n 4 above, para 1.

[63] Council Regulation (EC) No 1/2003 of 16 December 2002 on the implementation of the rules on competition laid down in Articles [101 and 102 TFEU], [2003] OJ L1/1.

[64] Commission Regulation (EC) No 773/2004 of 7 April 2004 relating to the conduct of proceedings by the Commission pursuant to Articles [101 and 102 TFEU], [2004] OJ L123/18.

[65] Council Regulation (EC) No 139/2004 of 20 January 2004 on the control of concentrations between undertakings, [2004] OJ L24/1 (Merger Control Regulation).

[66] Commission Regulation (EC) No 802/2004 of 21 April 2004 implementing [the Merger Control Regulation], [2004] OJ L133/1.

[67] Art 15(1) of Regulation No 773/2004; Art 17(1) of Regulation No 802/2004; Notice on the Rules for Access to the File, para 3, 7.

[68] However, para 103 of the Commission Notice on best practices for the conduct of proceedings concerning Articles 101 and 102 TFEU, [2011] OJ C308/6, provides that the Commission may, 'in appropriate cases', give complainants and third parties which have 'a sufficient interest to be heard' a copy of the non-confidential version of the parties' written replies to the statement of objections (or specific excerpts thereof). Likewise, the DG Competition's Best Practices on the conduct of merger control proceedings provide that the Commission may in the interest of the investigation in appropriate cases provide third parties that have shown a 'sufficient interest in the procedure' (such as customers, suppliers, and competitors) with a non-confidential version of the statement of objections (para 36).

drawn up by the Commission's departments, correspondence between the Commission and other public authorities, and internal documents received from such authorities), business secrets of other undertakings and other confidential information (ie, information whose disclosure would significantly harm a person or undertaking and military secrets).[69] Statements made by an undertaking under the Commission Notice on immunity from fines and reduction of fines in cartel cases[70] as well as settlement submissions made under the Commission Notice on the conduct of settlement procedures[71] are accessible to the addressees of a statement of objections and to the addressees of a statement of objections who have not requested settlement, respectively, provided, however, that they commit not to make any copy and to use the information solely for the purposes mentioned below. On the other hand, in cases brought under Articles 101 and 102 TFEU, the replies to the statement of objections submitted by the other undertakings are, in principle, not accessible.[72]

Documents obtained through access to the file can only be used 'for the purposes of judicial or administrative proceedings for the application of Articles [101 and 102 TFEU]' or 'for the purposes of the relevant proceeding pursuant to [the Merger Regulation]'.[73]

In antitrust proceedings, access to the file is granted to the parties upon request and (normally) only once, following notification of the statement of objections.[74] In merger proceedings, the notifying parties are granted access to the file upon request at every stage of the procedure from the notification of the statement of objections up to the consultation of the Advisory Committee.[75]

The Notice on the Rules for Access to the File provides for a separate right of access to the file for complainants, in antitrust cases, and 'other involved parties' (ie, parties to the proposed concentration other than the notifying parties, such as the seller and the target undertaking), in merger cases. Thus, complainants who, pursuant to Article 7(1) of Regulation No 773/2004, have been informed of the Commission's intention to reject their complaint may request access to the docu-

[69] Art 27(2) of Regulation No 1/2003; Arts 15(2) and 16(1) of Regulation No 773/2004; Art 18(3) of Regulation No 139/2004; Art 17(3) of Regulation No 802/2004; Notice on the Rules for Access to the File, paras 10–20.

[70] Commission Notice on immunity from fines and reduction of fines in cartel cases, [2006] OJ C298/17, para 33.

[71] Commission Notice on the conduct of settlement procedures in view of the adoption of decisions pursuant to Art 7 and Art 23 of Council Regulation (EC) No 1/2003 in cartel cases, [2008] OJ C167/1, para 35.

[72] Notice on the Rules for Access to the File, para 27. See, however, Commission Notice, n 68 above, para 103, which provides that '[w]here required by the rights of defence, or where it may in the Commission's view help to further clarify factual and legal issues relevant for the case, the Commission may give parties a copy of the non-confidential version (or specific parts thereof) of other parties' written replies to the statement of objections'.

[73] Art 15(4) of Regulation No 773/2004; Art 17(4) of Regulation No 802/2004; Notice on the Rules for Access to the File, para 48.

[74] Notice on the Rules for Access to the File, para 27. Access will, however, be granted for documents received after notification of the statement of objections and which constitute new evidence.

[75] Notice on the Rules for Access to the File, para 28.

ments on which the Commission has based its provisional assessment.[76] The 'other involved parties' in merger proceedings can access the Commission's file if they request it 'in so far as this is necessary for the purposes of preparing their comments'.[77]

State Aid Proceedings

Regulation No 659/1999,[78] which governs the procedure for reviewing State aid, does not contain any explicit provision on access to the Commission's file. Article 20 of that regulation only provides for the right for 'interested parties', that is, the Member States, persons, undertakings or associations of undertakings whose interests might be affected by the granting of aid (in particular the beneficiary of the alleged aid, competing undertakings, and trade associations),[79] to submit comments to the Commission following a decision to initiate the formal investigation procedure, to inform the Commission of any alleged unlawful aid and any alleged misuse of aid, and to obtain a copy of the Commission's decisions. However, it results from Article 6(2) of Regulation No 659/1999 and from the principle of the respect for the rights of the defence that the Member State responsible for granting the alleged aid must be entitled to consult the documents contained in the Commission's administrative file. That provision states, indeed, that the comments received by the Commission following the initiation of the formal investigation procedure must be submitted to the Member State and that the latter must then be afforded the opportunity to reply to those comments within a prescribed time limit. The reason why other 'interested parties' do not enjoy a similar right to consult the Commission's file is that the procedures for reviewing State aid are exclusively procedures initiated with respect to the Member State responsible for granting the alleged aid.[80] Those other 'interested parties' are merely sources of information for the Commission, which suggests that the rights of the defence do not apply to them.

[76] Art 8 of Regulation No 773/2004; Notice on the Rules for Access to the File, paras 30–32. Pursuant to Art 6(1) of Regulation No 773/2004, the complainants are also entitled to receive a non-confidential version of the statement of objections.

[77] Art 17(2) of Regulation No 802/2004; Notice on the Rules for Access to the File, paras 33, 34.

[78] Council Regulation (EC) No 659/1999 of 22 March 1999 laying down detailed rules for the application of Article [88] of the EC Treaty [now Article 108 TFEU], [1999] OJ L83/1.

[79] Art 1(h) of Regulation No 659/1999.

[80] Joined Cases C-74/00 P and C-75/00 P *Falck and Acciaierie di Bolzano v Commission* [2002] ECR I-7869, para 81; Case T-109/01 *Fleuren Compost v Commission* [2004] ECR II-127, para 44. In particular, those procedures are not procedures initiated *against* the aid recipient.

BRIEF COMPARISON OF THE DIFFERENT ACCESS SYSTEMS AND POTENTIAL PROBLEMS

It is clear from the foregoing that the rules for access to documents laid down by Regulation No 1049/2001, on the one hand, and those for access to the Commission's administrative file in competition proceedings, on the other, differ in many significant ways and that the latter rules are far more restrictive. Amongst the most significant differences between the two access systems is that while Regulation No 1049/2001 grants the right to access documents to the general public[81] (without the applicant having to state reasons for his application), access to the Commission's file in competition proceedings is essentially limited to the parties concerned (to one degree or another) by the investigation. Under Regulation No 1049/2001, access to documents contained in a competition file may (normally) be refused only after a concrete and individual examination of those documents. Further, the refusal must (normally) be carefully reasoned with respect to each of those documents. On the other hand, under the Rules on Access to the File, in most cases, such access may be denied 'globally' and 'automatically', and by means of a brief statement of reasons. In addition, while there is no restriction on the use that may be made of documents obtained on the basis of Regulation No 1049/2001,[82] those obtained through access to the file can only be used for the purposes of judicial or administrative proceedings for the application of the EU competition rules at issue. Another major difference is that, in antitrust and merger proceedings, internal documents are automatically excluded from access, while under Regulation No 1049/2001 these documents are accessible subject to the exceptions set out in its Article 4 (which are construed narrowly). Finally, it should also be stressed that the Rules on Access to the File are much more restrictive in terms of timing. The reason for all these differences is that the two types of access system do not pursue the same objectives: while Regulation No 1049/2001 purports to bring greater transparency into the work of the EU institutions and to strengthen the democratic legitimacy of the EU, the Rules on Access to the File are exclusively designed to apply the principle of equality of arms and to enable the parties concerned by an investigation to exercise their rights of defence.

There is no doubt that documents contained in the Commission's administrative file in competition proceedings fall within the material scope of Regulation No 1049/2001, as the latter Regulation applies to 'all documents held by an institution . . . in all areas of activity of the [EU]'[83] and – unlike the 2008 Commission's

[81] The EU Courts have stated that the purpose of Regulation No 1049/2001 is 'to guarantee access for everyone to public documents and not only access for the requesting party to documents concerning him'. See *Sison v Council*, n 61 above, para 50; see also Case C-266/05 P *Sison v Council* [2007] ECR I-1233, paras 43, 44.

[82] But see Art 16 of Regulation No 1049/2001, which provides that '[t]his Regulation shall be without prejudice to any existing rules on copyright which may limit a third party's right to reproduce or exploit released documents'.

[83] *Sweden v MyTravel and Commission*, n 43 above, para 88.

proposal for recasting that Regulation[84] – does not contain any provision specifically excluding those documents (which relate to the exercise of the investigative powers of the EU institutions) from the general rules on the right of access to documents. It is equally clear that the specific rules relating to access to the file in competition cases do not constitute a *lex specialis* overriding the public access rules laid down by Regulation No 1049/2001 and, therefore, that the two types of rules apply in parallel. First, this may be inferred from the preparatory works to Regulation No 1049/2001. The provision that '[the Regulation] shall not apply where specific rules on access to documents exist', contained in the initial proposal[85] presented by the Commission, was not retained in the amended proposal[86] following, in particular, opposition from the Parliament. Second, this is the path that has been taken, thus far, by both the Commission and the EU Courts, as it appears from the analysis of the case law below.

In view of the differences mentioned above, it would be tempting for a person – either a party directly concerned by an investigation, a third party or someone from the general public – desiring access to documents contained in the Commission's file in a competition case to circumvent the very restrictive rules on access to file by availing himself of Regulation No 1049/2001. Some of the cases discussed below show that this is not merely a theoretical possibility. Thus, the *TGI* judgment arose from a request for access to documents in a State aid file made under Regulation No 1049/2001 by the beneficiary of the aid measures (declared incompatible with the internal market), namely, the German company TGI. A few months before, the Commission rejected TGI's request for access to the non-confidential part of the file. The request was made in TGI's observations submitted as part of the formal investigation procedure provided for in Article 88(2) EC (now Article 108(2) TFEU). Similarly, the *Verein für Konsumenteninformation* judgment[87] arose from a situation where the applicant, an Austrian consumers' association, requested access to documents contained in a cartel file on the basis of Regulation No 1049/2001. The association, being a third party in the cartel procedure at issue, would have been precluded from accessing the file under the antitrust rules. Likewise, the applicant in *Éditions Odile Jacob*[88] sought access, under the access to documents regulation, to a series of documents contained in a file concerning a merger control procedure (in

[84] See n 1 above. The proposed new Art 2(6) excludes from the right of access 'documents forming part of the administrative file of an investigation or of proceedings concerning an act of individual scope . . . until the investigation has been closed or the act has become definitive'. The right would be negated, even at a later stage, with respect to '[d]ocuments containing information gathered or obtained from natural or legal persons by an institution in the framework of such investigations'. That proposed new Art 2(6) was unsurprisingly rejected by the Parliament in its March 2009 report.

[85] Art 2(2), second sub-para, of the Proposal for a Regulation of the European Parliament and of the Council regarding public access to European Parliament, Council and Commission documents, [2000] OJ C177E/70. See also recital 8 in the preamble of the proposal, which states that '[t]he principles laid down by this Regulation are to be without prejudice to the specific rules applicable to access to documents, in particular those directly concerning persons with a specific interest'.

[86] Amended proposal for a Regulation of the European Parliament and of the Council regarding public access to European Parliament, Council and Commission documents, [2001] OJ C240E/165.

[87] *Verein für Konsumenteninformation v Commission*, n 55 above.

[88] *Éditions Odile Jacob v Commission*, n 56 above.

which it was a third party), including a number of internal Commission documents. On the basis of the merger control rules, access to the internal documents would automatically have been refused not only to third parties,[89] but also to the notifying parties and the 'other involved parties' without any need for a detailed statement of reasons. The case that gave rise to the judgment in *Agrofert*[90] involved an identical situation.

The possibility of accessing the Commission's file in competition proceedings on the basis of Regulation No 1049/2001 – which was clearly not conceived or designed for that purpose by the EU legislator – is likely to cause a series of problems.

Some of these problems are practical. In most cases, the competition file is extremely voluminous and a concrete examination by the Commission – within the tight deadlines provided for by that Regulation – of the content of each of the documents included in the file will necessarily entail extensive administrative work.[91] That work is all the more complex because of the various conflicting interests involved: the rights of the defence and other procedural rights of the parties concerned, the legitimate interest of those parties, of complainants or of third parties that certain information should be kept confidential, the general interest in identifying and sanctioning infringements to the EU competition rules. . . . More generally, the enforcement of EU competition rules could be adversely affected should the officials from the Commission's DG Competition be forced to devote too much time and effort dealing with applications for access to documents. However, such considerations alone do not usually constitute sufficient grounds for denying or restricting access to documents under Regulation No 1049/2001. As Advocate General Kokott correctly pointed out in her Opinion in *TGI*, '[p]rejudicial effects on [the] performance of the traditional principal tasks of the competent services cannot justify an across-the-board limit on the right of access'. None of the Commission's services is exempt from the 'new additional task' allocated to the institutions by Article 255 of the EC Treaty (now Article 15 TFEU), Article 42 of the Charter of Fundamental Rights, and Regulation No 1049/2001, which is 'to hand over requested documents to a citizen unless contrary to interests deserving of protection'. Furthermore, that Regulation contains provisions that could help to reduce – albeit only to a limited extent – the burden resulting from applications relating to a very large number of documents. Thus, the Commission could extend by 15 working days the time limit for deciding on the application[92] or invite the applicant to clarify its application, should the latter not be sufficiently precise.[93] In addition, pursuant to Article 6(3), the Commission could confer with the applicant informally, with a view to finding a 'fair solution'

[89] Not to mention that, by reason of its status as a third party, it would most likely not have been entitled to any access to the file.

[90] *Agrofert v Commission*, n 46 above.

[91] In the case that gave rise to the judgment in *Verein für Konsumenteninformation v Commission*, the cartel file to which access was requested under Regulation No 1049/2001 contained more than 47,000 pages, excluding internal Commission documents.

[92] Arts 7(3) and 8(2) of Regulation No 1049/2001.

[93] Art 6(2) of Regulation No 1049/2001.

(it being understood that, if such a solution cannot be reached, the Commission would still be obliged to carry out a concrete, individual examination). However, in *Verein für Konsumenteninformation*, the General Court, relying on the principle of proportionality, acknowledged that the institution is also entitled to refuse disclosure without carrying out a concrete, individual examination of the documents concerned where this would entail a particularly heavy administrative burden, thereby exceeding the limits of what may reasonably be required.[94] This derogation to the principle of a concrete, individual examination is permissible only in 'exceptional cases' and provided that the institution has genuinely investigated all other conceivable options and explained in detail in its decision the reasons for which those various options would also involve an unreasonable volume of work.

Other problems are of a substantive nature. The most obvious (and the most difficult to accept) is that, at least in theory, the general public might, by relying on Regulation No 1049/2001, benefit from more extensive rights than the parties directly concerned in a competition procedure. In addition, both in antitrust and in merger proceedings, the applicable regulations oblige the undertakings involved to reveal business secrets and other information of a very confidential nature to the Commission and confer on the latter extensive powers to request all necessary information and to conduct all necessary inspections.[95] Those obligations and powers of investigation are, however, counterbalanced by other provisions which are designed to safeguard the legitimate interests of the undertakings such that the information and documents they provide to the Commission are used only for the purposes of the investigation concerned and are not disclosed to third parties. Those provisions include Article 28 of Regulation No 1/2003 and Article 17 of Regulation No 139/2004, which implement the professional secrecy obligation set out in Article 339 TFEU and provide for a restriction on the use of information acquired during an investigation.[96] They also include the Rules on Access to the File, described above, which restrict the right of access to specified categories of parties and strictly limit

[94] *Verein für Konsumenteninformation v Commission*, n 55 above, paras 94–115. The EU Courts previously recognised a similar derogation, based on the excessive administrative burden caused by a request, in their case law relating to the 1993 Code of Conduct: see, eg Case T-14/98 *Hautala v Council*, n 45 above, para 86, confirmed by the ECJ in Case C-353/99 P *Council v Hautala*, n 45 above; Case T-188/98 *Kuijer v Council* [2000] ECR II-1959, para 55.

[95] See, eg Arts 18 to 21 of Regulation No 1/2003; Arts 4, 11 and 13 of Regulation No 139/2004; Art 4 of Regulation No 802/2004.

[96] The restriction on the use of information and the professional secrecy obligations are all the more important in this context because, according to the case law, they are not only intended to preserve business secrets and other commercial interests of the companies but also to guarantee their rights of defence: see Case C-67/91 *Asociación Española de Banca Privada and ors* [1992] ECR I-4785, paras 35–37; Joined Cases C-238/99 P, C-244/99 P, C-245/99 P, C-247/99 P, C-250/99 P to C-252/99 P and C-254/99 P *Limburgse Vinyl Maatschappij and ors v Commission* [2002] ECR I-8375, paras 298, 299. The restriction on the use of information provided for in Art 28(1) of Regulation No 1/2003 and in Art 17(1) of Regulation No 139/2004 could, however, be narrowly interpreted as simply meaning that the Commission may not use the information it has acquired in the context of specific proceedings as grounds or evidence for other proceedings against the undertakings concerned. That would imply that the Commission would not be precluded from using that information for other purposes, such as a disclosure in response to a request for access made pursuant to Regulation No 1049/2001.

the use they can make of the documents to which they have been granted access. A balance is thus ensured between the public interest in the application of the EU competition rules, on the one hand, and the legitimate interests of the undertakings, on the other. The fact that – at least in theory – any member of the general public could access the same documents by merely relying on Regulation No 1049/2001 and use them for any purpose of his own is difficult to reconcile with the obligation to respect professional secrecy and, in particular, the restriction on the use of information. It could, in fact, undermine the whole system of investigation and punishment of infringements of EU antitrust rules or of merger control rules.

Another potential problem is related to the fact that in antitrust proceedings (in particular in cartel cases), the effective application of EU competition law increasingly depends on the active co-operation of the undertakings under investigation. Thus, the leniency policy[97] operated by the Commission, whereby undertakings that voluntarily provide information and evidence about a cartel in which they participated might receive either total immunity from fines or a reduction of fines, is an essential tool for detecting and investigating cartels.[98] However, undertakings might be dissuaded from fully co-operating with the Commission in leniency procedures, or even from applying for leniency, which would put at risk the leniency policy and consequently render the detection, prosecution, and punishment of infringements in competition matters more difficult, if they fear that their statements could be disclosed to third parties under Regulation No 1049/2001. In particular, there is a risk that leniency statements could be relied on as incriminating evidence by the victims of the anti-competitive practices concerned in subsequent private damages actions before national courts, which actions are actively encouraged by the Commission.[99] In practice, it appears that Regulation No 1049/2001 is more and more often relied upon in order to access documents which are subsequently used to support damages actions.[100] The same problem arises with respect to submissions made in the context of settlement procedures.

[97] Commission Notice on Immunity from fines and reduction of fines in cartel cases, n 70 above.

[98] About 75% of cartel investigations are based on immunity applications: see Commission Staff Working Document (accompanying the Report from the Commission on Competition Policy 2009), SEC(2010) 666, para 100.

[99] See Commission White Paper on damages actions for breach of the [EU] antitrust rules, COM(2008) 165 final. It should be noted that, in its White Paper, the Commission suggests that 'adequate protection' against disclosure of corporate statements submitted by leniency applicants in private actions for damages should be ensured. This would avoid placing the leniency applicants in a less favourable situation than co-infringers that did not co-operate with the Commission. In Case C-360/09 *Pfleiderer*, judgment of 14 June 2011 nyr, the ECJ ruled that the provisions of EU law on cartels must be interpreted as not precluding a person who has been adversely affected by an infringement of EU competition law and is seeking to obtain damages from being granted access to documents relating to a leniency procedure which have been voluntarily submitted by the perpetrator of that infringement to a national competition authority pursuant to a national leniency programme. The ECJ has specified that it was, however, for the courts and tribunals of the Member States, on the basis of their national law, to determine the conditions under which such access might be permitted or refused by weighing the interests protected by EU law.

[100] In the case which led to the judgment in *Verein für Konsumenteninformation v Commission*, n 55 above, the applicant sought access to the cartel file concerned in order to substantiate a claim for damages which it had brought before the Austrian courts against one of the participants to the cartel.

More generally, disclosure to the general public of documents or information contained in the Commission's antitrust file prior to adoption of the decision concerned could compromise the independence of the decision-making process or infringe the principle of the presumption of innocence[101] (which applies to the procedures relating to infringements of competition rules that may result in the imposition of fines or periodic penalty payments). Similarly, in procedures for reviewing State aid, which often involve complex and sensitive discussions between the Commission and the Member State responsible for granting the aid, disclosure of parts of the file to third parties before a decision on that aid has been adopted could subject the Commission to undue external influence (for example, from the press and public opinion) and hence compromise the proper conduct of its investigations and/or its decision-making process. This is particularly the case for those procedures, which like proceedings for failure to fulfil obligations under Article 258 TFEU, call for genuine co-operation and mutual confidence.

The question then arises whether the scheme of exceptions provided for by Regulation No 1049/2001 is sufficient to resolve the above-mentioned problems (which are non-exhaustive). The exceptions invoked by the Commission to refuse access to documents contained in a competition file are usually those set out in Article 4(2) and (3) of that regulation. As will be discussed in the following section, the General Court has, until recently, interpreted these exceptions strictly, while the ECJ, in the *TGI* judgment, has ruled that, where procedures for reviewing State aid are concerned, the Commission is entitled to base its refusal to give access to documents contained in its file on a 'general presumption' that their disclosure would undermine protection of the objectives of investigation activities.

OVERVIEW OF THE CASE LAW OF THE EU COURTS

In *Verein für Konsumenteninformation* v *Commission*[102] the General Court ruled for the first time on the application of Regulation No 1049/2001 in EU competition proceedings. The case involved a decision by which the Commission rejected a request for access to a cartel file made by the Verein für Konsumenteninformation (VKI) under Regulation No 1049/2001. The Commission based its refusal primarily on the exception relating to the protection of the purpose of investigations, referred to in the third indent of Article 4(2). It stated, first, that the cartel decision at issue was the subject of a number of pending actions before the General Court and that, if that decision were annulled, the Commission might have to re-assess the case. It also maintained that allowing third parties access to docu-

Likewise, pending Case T-380/08 *Netherlands v Commission* concerns a request for access made by the Netherlands under Regulation No 1049/2001, to the full (confidential) version of a Commission's decision relating to a proceeding under Art 101 TFEU, with a view to preparing an action for damages against members of the cartel before the Dutch courts.

[101] See, to that effect, Case T-62/98 *Volkswagen v Commission* [2000] ECR II-2707, paras 279–82.

[102] *Verein für Konsumenteninformation v Commission*, n 55 above.

ments that were provided by the members of the cartel either on the basis of the Commission Notice on the non-imposition or reduction of fines in cartel cases,[103] or in connection with requests for information or investigations, would deter undertakings from co-operating with it. In addition, the Commission stated that a concrete examination of each of the documents comprising the cartel file, in order to assess whether partial access could be granted, did not take place because this would have entailed an excessive and disproportionate volume of work. Following an action for annulment brought by the VKI, the General Court annulled the Commission's decision refusing access to the file on the ground that the latter had failed to carry out a concrete, individual examination of the documents referred to in the request for access. First, the General Court pointed out that the Commission was obliged, *in principle*, to undertake such an examination.[104] It added that this might, however, not be necessary where, due to the particular circumstances of the individual case, it is obvious that access must be refused or, on the contrary, granted. This could be the case, inter alia, where certain documents are 'manifestly covered in their entirety by an exception . . . or, conversely, manifestly accessible in their entirety' or where they have already been the subject of such an examination 'in similar circumstances'.[105] In the circumstances, the General Court found that this derogation was not applicable. It was apparent from the contested decision that the exceptions relied on by the Commission did not necessarily cover the whole of the cartel file and that, even in the case of the documents to which they might have applied, they would only cover certain passages in those documents.[106] Secondly, the General Court, relying on the principle of proportionality, ruled that the institution was also entitled to refuse disclosure without carrying out a concrete, individual examination of the documents concerned in *exceptional cases*, where such an examination would entail a particularly heavy administrative burden.[107] The institution may however dispense with such an examination where it has genuinely studied all other possible options and provided a detailed explanation as to why these options would also involve an unreasonable volume of work.[108] In the case at issue, the General Court found that it was not apparent from the statement of reasons in the contested decision that the Commission had *specifically and exhaustively* considered the various options available to it.[109] Thus the judgment confirms that Regulation No 1049/2001 can be used by third parties to access the Commission's administrative file in antitrust proceedings, although the General Court did not expressly rule on the relationship between the regulation and the Rules on Access to the

[103] [1996] OJ C207/4.

[104] *Verein für Konsumenteninformation v Commission*, n 55 above, para 74.

[105] ibid, para 75.

[106] ibid, para 90.

[107] ibid, para 112. The burden of proof of demonstrating the unreasonableness of the task arising from the request for access rests on the institution.

[108] ibid, para 115.

[109] ibid, para 126.

File or on the merits of the exceptions relied upon by the Commission. It seems, however, that the General Court was sensitive to the potential problems for the Commission in such a situation, since it recognised the existence of two derogations to the principle of a concrete, individual examination.

The *TGI*[110] proceedings arose out of a privatisation process carried out in the mid-90s in the Land of Thuringia (Germany), by which TGI took over part of the glass production lines of a company owned by the Treuhandanstalt (a public law body responsible for the restructuring of undertakings of the former German Democratic Republic which subsequently became the Bundesanstalt für vereinigungsbedingte Sonderaufgaben, BvS). TGI was experiencing financial difficulties and the BvS agreed to reduce the purchase price of the production lines and the Land granted a loan to TGI. Germany notified those measures to the Commission, which decided to initiate two separate formal investigations. In March 2002, while the second investigation was still ongoing, TGI requested access under Regulation No 1049/2001 to, inter alia, all documents relating to the aid procedures concerning it. The Commission rejected that request on the ground that the disclosure of those documents could undermine the protection of the purpose of inspections and investigations within the meaning of the third indent of Article 4(2) of Regulation No 1049/2001. TGI brought a successful appeal against that decision before the General Court, which ruled that the Commission had failed to undertake a concrete, individual assessment of the content of the documents requested. The General Court considered that neither of the two derogations laid down in *Verein für Konsumenteninformation* was applicable here. First, it rejected the Commission's argument based on the fact that, in the context of current investigations into the compatibility of State aid with the single market, co-operation in good faith and mutual confidence between the Commission, the Member State, and the undertakings concerned is indispensable in order to enable the different 'parties' to express themselves freely. According to the General Court,

> so general an assessment, applying to the entire administrative file relating to the investigation procedures in respect of the aid granted to [TGI], does not demonstrate that there were special circumstances of the individual case permitting the conclusion that it was not necessary to undertake a concrete, individual examination of the documents which comprised it.

It pointed out, in particular, that 'it does not establish that those documents were manifestly covered in their entirety by an exception to the right of access'.[111] Second, the General Court found that the Commission did not rely, in the contested decision, in its pleadings, or at the hearing, on a surfeit of work connected to the examination of TGI's request for access. In that judgment, the General Court was again able to decide on the merits of the case without having to rule

[110] Case T-237/02 *Technische Glaswerke Ilmenau v Commission* [2006] ECR II-5131.

[111] ibid, para 89.

expressly on the relationship between Regulation No 1049/2001 and the specific Rules on Access to the File. This is a consequence of the manner in which the Commission itself presented its case: it was defending the position that Regulation No 1049/2001 was fully applicable in these circumstances, but that the exception in Article 4(2) allowed it to refuse access to the documents relating to current aid procedures.[112] As will be discussed below, on appeal, both the Commission and the ECJ followed a different approach, with more regard to the specificities of the State aid procedural rules.

In *MyTravel* v *Commission*,[113] it was not contested that the Commission had carried out a specific and individual examination of the documents requested (which were internal documents relating to a merger case), and, this time, the General Court ruled on the merits of the exceptions invoked. It should be noted at the outset that, in its judgment, the General Court interpreted strictly the right of access to documents. This was, however, unconnected to the fact that, in merger proceedings, internal documents are not accessible per se by virtue of Article 17(3) of Regulation No 802/2004. In fact, the Commission elected not to rely on an argument based on that provision in the contested decisions.[114] The proceedings arose out of the annulment by the General Court, in June 2002,[115] of a Commission decision prohibiting, under the Merger Regulation, the proposed acquisition, by Airtours plc (later renamed MyTravel Group plc), of all the shares in First Choice plc. Following that annulment, the Commission established a working group comprising officials of DG Competition and of the Legal Service to assess the implications of the judgment for merger control and other procedures and to consider whether it was appropriate to bring an appeal. In May 2005, Airtours requested access, under Regulation No 1049/2001, to the report of the working group (report), the documents relating to its preparation (working papers), and the documents relating to the Airtours/First Choice concentration on which the report was based or which were referred to in it (other internal documents).[116] By two separate decisions of September and October 2005, the Commission granted full or partial access to a number of the working papers and of the other internal documents but refused to furnish the report and the remaining documents. Airtours brought an action for annulment against these decisions

[112] ibid, paras 35–37.

[113] *MyTravel v Commission*, n 61 above.

[114] This suggests that the Commission itself does not consider that the Rules on Access to the File constitute a *lex specialis*. It should be noted that, at para 89 of the judgment, the General Court confirmed that it does not necessarily follow from the fact that an undertaking which is a party to a concentration does not enjoy a right of access to internal documents in the administrative file by virtue of Art 17(3) of Regulation No 802/2004 that any person, whoever it may be, will be precluded access to those documents on the basis of Regulation No 1049/2001.

[115] Case T-342/99 *Airtours v Commission* [2002] ECR II-2585.

[116] Airtours intended to use the specified documents to support an action for damages that it had brought in June 2003 seeking compensation for the loss it allegedly suffered by reason of the Commission's handling and assessment of the proposed acquisition; see Case T-212/03 *MyTravel v Commission* [2008] ECR II-1967.

before the General Court, which dismissed it as unfounded except as regards one of the working papers.[117]

First, the General Court concluded that the Commission had properly applied the exception concerning the protection of the decision-making process set out in the second sub-paragraph of Article 4(3) of Regulation No 1049/2001.[118] It held that the interest of the public in obtaining access to a document pursuant to the principle of transparency does not carry the same weight in the particular context of a document drawn up in an administrative procedure intended to apply the rules governing the control of concentrations or competition law, as is the case for a document relating to a procedure in which the EU institution acts in its capacity as legislator.[119] The General Court found that disclosure of the report would carry the risk not only that possibly critical opinions of Commission officials might be made public, but also that the content of the report (which is a preparatory document) could be compared with the final decision(s). Such a situation could seriously undermine the decision-making freedom of the Commission, whose Members must be completely independent in the performance of their duties. Moreover, in the future, the authors of a report of the kind at issue might be inclined to practise self-censorship and to refrain from putting forward any views that might involve the addressee of the report 'being exposed to risk', with the result that the Commission could no longer benefit from the frankly-expressed and complete views required of its officials.[120] Finally, if such reports were disclosed, the Commissioner responsible for competition would be inclined to refrain from requesting the written, and potentially critical, views of his advisers.[121] As regards the working papers, the General Court considered that, since they were drafted in order to prepare the report, the Commission was entitled to refuse disclosure for the same reasons as those invoked in relation to the report itself. With regard to the 'other internal documents', the General Court held essentially that the Commission correctly considered that the disclosure of those documents would reduce the ability of its services to express their point of view and would seriously undermine its decision-making process in the field of the control of concentrations.[122] It took the view that these preparatory documents might indeed indicate the opinions, the doubts or the changes of mind of the

[117] Refusal to disclose that working paper was solely based on the exception relating to the protection of the purpose of inspections, investigations, and audits. The General Court ruled that the Commission had not demonstrated to the requisite legal standard that the particular exception applied to that document. See *MyTravel v Commission*, n 61 above, paras 71–78.

[118] As explained above, Art 4(3) of Regulation No 1049/2001 draws a clear distinction by reference to whether a decision has or has not been taken. The exception laid down in the second sub-para of that provision can be relied upon 'even after the decision has been taken'. Such a situation existed in the present case since, at the time when Airtours made its request for access, the *Airtours/First Choice* decision had not only already been adopted but had also been annulled by the General Court, and the time limit for lodging an appeal had already expired. In addition, a number of recommendations contained in the report had already been implemented.

[119] ibid, para 49.

[120] ibid, paras 48–53.

[121] ibid, para 54.

[122] ibid, paras 94–100.

Commission services, which – at the end of the decision-making process in question – may no longer appear in the final versions of the decisions. It also referred to the risk of self-censorship mentioned in relation to the report. The General Court added that its analysis was not put in question by the mere fact that the merger proceedings in question had ended. It observed that the Commission had explained that disclosure of the documents at issue risked undermining its assessment of similar concentrations which might arise between the parties concerned or in the same sector, or of cases involving the concept of a collective dominant position. Finally, it held that the risk (in the present case) of the decision-making process being seriously undermined was reasonably foreseeable and not purely hypothetical: such documents could be used – even though they did not necessarily represent the Commission's definitive position – to influence the position of its services in the examination of similar cases involving the same sector of activities or the same economic concepts.

Second, the General Court ruled that the Commission had correctly applied the exception relating to the protection of legal advice laid down in the second indent of Article 4(2) of Regulation No 1049/2001 to refuse disclosure of some Legal Service notes replying to notes from the DG Competition. It found that disclosure of those notes would risk communicating to the public information on the state of internal discussions between DG Competition and the Legal Service on the lawfulness of the assessment of the compatibility of the *Airtours/First Choice* concentration with the common market and, further, would be liable to lead the Legal Service to display reticence and caution in the future in its drafting of such notes. Disclosure of the notes could result in the difficult position whereby the Legal Service might find itself required to defend a position before the EU Courts that was not the same as the position which it had argued for internally in its role as adviser to the Commission. This could have a considerable impact on both the freedom of the Legal Service to express its views and on its ability to defend the Commission's final position effectively before the EU Courts on an equal footing with the other representatives of the various parties to legal proceedings.[123]

The Kingdom of Sweden appealed the judgment to the ECJ, which partially set it aside and partially annulled the Commission's decisions.[124] With regard to the first exception relied on by the Commission, the ECJ stated that it followed from the wording of Article 4(3) of Regulation No 1049/2001 that, once the decision concerned by the documents requested had been adopted, the requirements for protecting the decision-making process were less acute. It recognised that the mere possibility of using the exception laid down in the second sub-paragraph of that provision to refuse access to documents containing opinions for internal use as part of deliberations and preliminary consultations within the institution concerned was not in any way affected by the fact that the decision has been adopted. That did not, however, mean, that

[123] ibid, paras 124–26.

[124] *Sweden v MyTravel and Commission*, n 43 above.

> the assessment which the institution concerned is called upon to make in order to establish whether or not the disclosure of one of those documents is likely seriously to undermine its decision-making process must not take account of the fact that the administrative procedure to which those documents relate has been closed.

According to the ECJ, indeed,

> [t]he reasons invoked by an institution and capable of justifying refusal of access to such a document of which communication has been requested before the closure of the administrative procedure might not be sufficient for refusing disclosure of the same document after the adoption of the decision, without that institution explaining the specific reasons why it considers that the closure of the procedure does not exclude the possibility that that refusal of access may remain justified having regard to the risk of a serious undermining of its decision-making process.[125]

The ECJ continued that, in the present case, the General Court wrongly omitted to verify whether the Commission had supplied such 'specific reasons'.[126] Thus, the considerations which led the General Court to conclude that access to the report and to the other internal documents could be refused were held to be insufficient by the ECJ.[127] It should be observed that those considerations were not regarded as being irrelevant per se. It cannot therefore be ruled out that they could justify a refusal to disclose internal documents contained in a competition file in the situation referred to in the first sub-paragraph of Article 4(3) of Regulation No 1049/2001, where the procedure to which the documents relate is still ongoing. With regard to the exception relating to the protection of legal advice set out in the second indent of Article 4(2) of that regulation, the ECJ held that the considerations adopted by the General Court were insufficient to support the conclusion that the Commission was correct to refuse access to the notes from the Legal Service. First, it rejected the argument that disclosure of such notes could lead to doubts as to the lawfulness of the final decision, pointing out that it is precisely openness in this regard that contributes to conferring greater legitimacy on the institutions in the eyes of European citizens and increasing their confidence by allowing divergences between various points of view to be openly debated.[128] Second, it found that the other considerations relied upon by the General Court were of a general and abstract nature.[129]

[125] ibid, paras 80–82.

[126] ibid, paras 89–98. At para 101, the ECJ recognised that, with respect to some of the 'other internal documents', the Commission had provided explanations as to why its refusal to disclose those documents remained justified even after the closure of the merger proceedings at issue. It considered, however, that the Commission's explanations were not in any way supported on the facts.

[127] ibid, para 100. Concerning the working papers, the ECJ accordingly found that the General Court was not justified to consider, solely on the basis of the fact that those documents had enabled the report to be produced, that their disclosure would have seriously undermined the decision-making process of the Commission.

[128] ibid, para 113. Thus, the ECJ took exactly the same view as in *Sweden and Turco v Council*, n 3 above, which concerned disclosure of an opinion of the Council's Legal Service relating to a legislative proposal.

[129] *Sweden v MyTravel and Commission*, n 43 above, paras 115–16.

The *Éditions Odile Jacob* v *Commission*[130] case involved a decision by which the Commission rejected a request for access to a large number of documents contained in a merger file made by Éditions Odile Jacob (Odile Jacob) under Regulation No 1049/2001. Odile Jacob intended to use the documents to support two actions it had brought before the General Court and which were pending at the time of the request, including an action seeking the annulment of the Commission decision of 7 January 2004 clearing, under the Merger Regulation, the proposed acquisition by Lagardère of control of certain assets of Vivendi Universal Publishing.[131] The Commission refused access to most of the documents requested. It considered that all those documents were covered by the exception laid down in the third indent of Article 4(2) of Regulation No 1049/2001, and that some were also covered by the exception set out in the first or second indent of the same provision or by that set out in the second sub-paragraph of Article 4(3). Odile Jacob brought an action for annulment against that decision before the General Court, which essentially held the action to be well founded except as it related to an opinion of the Legal Service. It is interesting to note that Lagardère, which intervened in support of the Commission in this case, claimed that the request for access should have been examined solely in the light of the specific rules relating to access to the file in merger cases pursuant to the maxim '*lex specialis derogat legi generali*'. Unfortunately, the General Court did not rule on the merits of that argument, since it was dismissed as inadmissible on the ground that it had not been raised by the main parties and did not support the form of order sought by the Commission.[132] As regards the exception relating to the protection of the purpose of inspections, investigations, and audits, the General Court first found that all the documents requested, including those which had been submitted at the informal 'pre-notification' stage, related to the investigation carried out by the Commission in the context of the examination of the notified concentration and, therefore, fell within the scope of that exception.[133] Second, the General Court held that the documents were, however, no longer covered by the exception because the investigation that led to the adoption of the merger decision was already closed when the contested decision was taken. It rejected the Commission's argument that, in the event of the annulment of that merger decision, the latter would have to adopt a new decision on the proposed acquisition and, accordingly, to re-open the investigation. To accept such an argument would indeed make access to those documents dependent on an 'uncertain, future and possibly distant event'.[134] Third, the General Court held that, in any event, it was not clear from the statement of reasons in the contested decision that the Commission undertook a concrete, individual assessment of the documents requested. The considerations set out in the decision were considered too

[130] *Éditions Odile Jacob v Commission*, n 56 above.
[131] Case T-279/04 *Éditions Odile Jacob v Commission*, judgment of 13 September 2010 nyr.
[132] *Éditions Odile Jacob v Commission*, n 56 above, paras 37–38.
[133] ibid, para 67.
[134] ibid, paras 70–77.

vague and general.[135] In that context, the General Court interpreted narrowly the 'restriction on the use of information' obligation provided for in Article 17(1) of the Merger Regulation, stating that that provision concerns 'the manner in which the Commission may use the information supplied and does not govern the access to documents guaranteed by Regulation No 1049/2001'.[136] With respect to the exception relating to the protection of commercial interests, the General Court recognised that the documents concerned were likely to contain sensitive information on the commercial strategies of the parties to the merger and, accordingly, to come within the scope of that exception.[137] However, as in the case of the first exception, it considered that it was not apparent from the contested decision that a concrete, individual assessment of those documents had been carried out.[138] As regards the exception concerning the protection of the decision-making process set out in the second sub-paragraph of Article 4(3) of Regulation No 1049/2001, the General Court found that the two internal notes concerned were preparatory documents drawn up before the final decision that were exchanged within the Commission to facilitate the drafting of the documents formalising the institution's position. Those notes thus came within the scope of the exception.[139] The General Court held, however, that the considerations put forward by the Commission to justify the application of that exception were insufficient, since they were general and abstract and not substantiated by detailed arguments based on the content of the notes in question.[140] Finally, with respect to the exception based on the protection of legal advice, the General Court recognised that the document concerned fell within its scope, since it was an opinion of the Legal Service as to the application of a specific provision of the Merger Regulation to the proposed acquisition.[141] It also recognised that the Commission had correctly applied that exception to refuse disclosure of the opinion.[142] In that regard, it relied on considerations similar to those which, in *MyTravel* v *Commission*, led it to conclude that access to some notes from the Legal Service could be refused. It also invoked the fact that the opinion at issue had been drawn up pursuant to the Commission's (purely) administrative functions.[143] In view of the position

[135] ibid, paras 78–88.

[136] ibid, para 89.

[137] ibid, para 113.

[138] ibid, paras 117–19, 123. It should be added that, with respect to both that exception and the one relating to the protection of the purpose of inspections, investigations, and audits, the General Court also considered that the first derogation to the principle of a concrete, individual examination laid down in *Verein für Konsumenteninformation v Commission* was not applicable. For example, it held that it cannot be accepted that, in the context of merger control, all the correspondence exchanged between the Commission and the undertakings concerned is manifestly covered by the exception relating to the protection of commercial interests.

[139] ibid, para 138.

[140] ibid, para 143.

[141] ibid, para 154.

[142] ibid, paras 189–94. The General Court also ruled that the fact that the requested document might enable Odile Jacob to better put forward its arguments in the context of the two parallel actions for annulment did not constitute an overriding public interest justifying disclosure of the Legal Service's opinion at issue.

[143] ibid, paras 158–61.

adopted by the ECJ with respect to the exception for protecting legal advice in its judgment in *Sweden* v *MyTravel and Commission*, it would not be surprising if that part of the General Court's judgment were annulled within the framework of the appeal, which is currently pending before the ECJ.[144] Thus, in its judgment in *Éditions Odile Jacob* v *Commission*, the General Court interpreted the exceptions strictly (except for the exception relating to the protection of legal advice).

The *Agrofert* v *Commission*[145] case displays many similarities to *Éditions Odile Jacob* v *Commission* discussed above. It also involved a decision by which the Commission rejected, on the basis of the same exceptions, a request for access to practically all the documents contained in a merger file made under Regulation No 1049/2001 by a third party to the merger (Agrofert). At the time of the request, the Commission had already adopted a decision on that merger,[146] which, unlike the merger decision concerned in *Éditions Odile Jacob* v *Commission*, was not challenged before the General Court. Following an action for annulment brought by Agrofert, the General Court annulled the Commission's refusal decision. In its judgment, the General Court followed, to a very large extent, the (strict) approach it had adopted in *Odile Jacob* v *Commission*. Thus, it first ascertained whether the requested documents came within the scope of the exceptions relied on by the Commission. Second, having answered that question in the affirmative, it assessed whether disclosure of the documents was likely 'specifically and effectively' to harm the interest protected by those exceptions. In that context, it insisted on the need for a concrete, individual examination of the documents requested and on the fact that this examination must be evident from the grounds of the decision. It considered, inter alia, that none of the Rules on Access to the File laid down by the Merger Regulation, the obligation of professional secrecy[147] or the protection of business secrets in any way relieved the Commission of the obligation to undertake such an examination, including with respect to the documents submitted by the notifying parties on a confidential basis during the first phase of the merger notification.[148] The General Court found that the Commission did not comply with these requirements in the present case. For example, with respect to the exception based on the protection of commercial interests, it held that the Commission' assertion that all documents submitted by the notifying parties for the purpose of merger control proceedings necessarily relate to commercially sensitive information was too vague and general.[149] As regards the exception relating

[144] Odile Jacob has lodged a cross-appeal seeking to have that part of the judgment annulled.

[145] *Agrofert v Commission*, n 46 above.

[146] Decision of 20 April 2005 authorising, pursuant to Art 6(1)(b) of the Merger Regulation, the planned acquisition of the Czech company Unipetrol by the Polish company Polski Koncern Naftowy Orlen (Case Comp/M.3543).

[147] Art 339 TFEU and Art 17(2) of the Merger Regulation. See *Agrofert v Commission*, n 46 above, paras 69–70.

[148] ibid, paras 77, 86.

[149] ibid, paras 63–64. Likewise, at paras 78–80, the General Court rejected the Commission's argument that the documents provided in the context of a merger should necessarily be regarded as being manifestly covered by the exception relating to the protection of commercial interests (which would have justified the application of the first derogation laid down in *Verein für Konsumenteninformation v Commission*).

to the protection of the purpose of investigations, the General Court held that it was not applicable in the present case, since there was no 'ongoing investigation concerning the merger in question at the date of the [contested] decision'.[150] Moreover, it rejected the Commission's argument that disclosure of documents provided by the parties involved in merger proceedings would 'undermine the climate of trust and mutual cooperation' as being too vague and general.[151] With respect to the exception based on the protection of legal advice, the General Court ruled that the Commission incorrectly relied on this exception to refuse access to a note and some e-mails from its Legal Service. It found that the Commission's reasoning – which merely pointed out the need to maintain the confidentiality of the documents concerned in order to obtain full and frank legal advice – was based on general and abstract considerations and hence insufficient.[152] It noted, in particular, that the merger decision was definitive at the date on which the request for access was made[153] and that there was no mention of any connected pending proceedings or proceedings concerning the same sector. Finally, as regards the exception relating to the protection of the decision-making process laid down in the second sub-paragraph of Article 4(3) of Regulation No 1049/2001, the General Court held, as in *Éditions Odile Jacob* v *Commission*, that the reasons invoked by the Commission to justify its application were insufficient and not supported by any evidence.[154]

In the cases discussed above, the EU Courts confirmed that Regulation No 1049/2001 can be used by any member of the general public to access documents (including purely internal and commercially sensitive documents, or even opinions from the Legal Service) contained in the Commission's file in antitrust, State aid or merger proceedings. Their reasoning appears to rely on the total independence of the general rules on public access to documents laid down in Regulation No 1049/2001 from the specific Rules on Access to the File, although they did not expressly rule on the relationship between those two sets of rules. Further, they took a broad approach towards the right of access to documents, first, by stressing that, in principle,[155] exceptions to that right can be applied only after a concrete, individual examination of the documents requested and, second, by interpreting those exceptions narrowly.[156]

In the *TGI* judgment, delivered at about the same time as *Éditions Odile Jacob* v *Commission* and *Agrofert* v *Commission* following an appeal lodged by the Commission against the *Technische Glaswerke Ilmenau* v *Commission* judgment,

[150] ibid, para 98.

[151] ibid, paras 100–03.

[152] ibid, paras 126–29.

[153] This perhaps explains why the General Court's position in respect to the exception at issue contrasts with the position adopted in *Éditions Odile Jacob v Commission*.

[154] ibid, paras 140–50.

[155] In none of those cases did the EU Courts apply one or other of the two derogations to the principle of a concrete, individual examination laid down in *Verein für Konsumenteninformation v Commission*.

[156] With the exception of *MyTravel v Commission*.

the ECJ adopted a different approach, which led it to annul that (last-cited) judgment and, ruling itself on the dispute, to reject the action for annulment brought by TGI against the Commission decision refusing to give it access to the documents relating to the aid procedures at issue. The ECJ seems to have been receptive to the Commission's position in highlighting (more than it did at first instance) the specificities of the State aid procedural rules and insisting on the need for a harmonious interpretation of the various applicable provisions.

In *TGI*, on appeal, the ECJ first recalled the case law holding that, in order to justify refusal of access to a document, it is not sufficient for the institution concerned to claim that the latter comes within one of the exceptions set out in Article 4 of Regulation No 1049/2001. The institution must also 'supply explanations as to how access to that document could specifically and effectively undermine the interest protected by [the] exception [concerned]'.[157] The ECJ stated immediately afterwards, with reference to paragraph 50 of its judgment in *Sweden and Turco* v *Council*,[158] that

> it is, in principle, open to the [EU] institution to base its decisions in that regard on general presumptions which apply to certain categories of documents, as considerations of a generally similar kind are likely to apply to requests for disclosure relating to documents of the same nature.[159]

It stated that, as far as procedures for reviewing State aid are concerned, such general presumptions may arise from Regulation No 659/1999 and from the case law on the right to consult documents contained in the Commission's administrative file. In that regard, it recalled that, in those procedures, 'interested parties' other than the Member State responsible for granting the aid do not enjoy such a right, but are only entitled to submit comments to the Commission following a decision to initiate the formal investigation procedure. The procedure for reviewing State aid being exclusively a procedure initiated with respect to that Member State, the other 'interested parties' cannot themselves claim a right to debate the issues with the Commission. According to the ECJ, if those parties were able to obtain access,

[157] *Commission v Technische Glaswerke Ilmenau*, n 7 above, para 53.

[158] *Sweden and Turco v Council*, n 3 above.

[159] *Commission v Technische Glaswerke Ilmenau*, n 7 above, para 54. The reference to para 50 of the judgment in *Sweden and Turco v Council* does not seem to be entirely convincing. First, in that judgment, the recognition of the existence of general presumptions was made in the context of legal considerations on the 'requirements to be satisfied by the statement of reasons' in the case of a refusal to disclose, and this after a presentation of the rules applicable to the examination to be undertaken by the institution when dealing with applications for access to documents. Second, at para 54 of the *TGI* judgment, the ECJ omits to mention the second sentence of the said para 50, which could in fact be interpreted as meaning that, even where the institution is able to justify its decision to refuse disclosure of a category of documents by relying on general considerations, it is still bound to ascertain specifically, for each of the documents falling within that category, whether that general consideration is actually applicable (see, in that regard, Muguet-Poullennec, n 6 above, 53). This is the approach that seems to have been taken by the General Court at paras 125–28 of its judgment in *Agrofert v Commission*. A reference to the first derogation laid down in *Verein für Konsumenteninformation v Commission* (ie, the derogation based on the 'particular circumstances of the individual case') could perhaps have been more persuasive.

on the basis of Regulation No 1049/2001, to the Commission's file, 'the system for the review of State aid would be called into question'. In that regard, it stated that

> [w]hatever the legal basis on which it is granted, access to the file enables the interested parties to obtain all the observations and documents submitted to the Commission, and, where, appropriate, adopt a position on those matters in their own observations, which is likely to modify the nature of [the review procedure opened in accordance with Article 108(2) TFEU].[160]

In other words, the ECJ was anxious to ensure that the *inter partes* procedure provided for by the latter provision is strictly limited to the Member State responsible for granting the aid. The ECJ concluded from all the foregoing considerations that, 'for the purposes of interpreting the exception laid down in Article 4(2), third indent, of Regulation No 1049/2001', the General Court should have taken account of the fact that, in State aid proceedings, 'interested parties' other than the Member State concerned do not have the right to consult the Commission's file and, therefore, ought to have acknowledged the existence of a general presumption that 'disclosure of documents in the administrative file in principle undermines protection of the objectives of investigation activities'.[161] Those interested parties do, however, have the possibility of demonstrating that 'a given document disclosure of which has been requested is not covered by that presumption, or that there is a higher public interest justifying the disclosure of the document concerned by virtue of Article 4(2) of Regulation No 1049/2001'.[162] Thus, in the *TGI* judgment, the ECJ did not construe the Rules on Access to the File in State aid cases as a *lex specialis* overriding the public access rules laid down by Regulation No1049/2001, but used them to interpret one of the exceptions provided for by that regulation. It should be noted that, in its judgment handed down on the same day in *Commission* v *Bavarian Lager*,[163] which raised the difficult issue of how to reconcile the EU rules on public access to documents with those on the protection of personal data set out in Regulation (EC) No 45/2001,[164] the ECJ took the same approach. Similarly, in *Sweden and Others* v *API and Commission*,[165] it interpreted the exception relating to the protection of court proceedings set out in the second indent of Article 4(2) of Regulation No 1049/2001 by taking account of the fact that neither the Statute of the Court of Justice nor the Rules of Procedure of the EU Courts provide for any third party rights of access to pleadings submitted.

In the *TGI* judgment, giving final judgment in the case, the ECJ held that, in view of the general presumption mentioned above, the Commission was correct to refuse access to all the documents requested by TGI on the basis of Regulation

[160] ibid, paras 55–59.

[161] ibid, para 61.

[162] ibid, para 62.

[163] Case C-28/08 P *Commission v Bavarian Lager* [2010] ECR I-6055.

[164] Regulation of the European Parliament and of the Council of 18 December 2000 on the protection of individuals with regard to the processing of personal data by the Community institutions and bodies and on the free movement of such data, OJ 2001 L 8, p 1.

[165] *Sweden and ors v API and Commission*, n 9 above, paras 96–102.

No 1049/2001, and 'could do so without first making a concrete, individual examination of those documents'.[166] Further, it found that no evidence was advanced in the course of that action which would be capable of rebutting that general presumption and that TGI did not state what higher public interest might justify the disclosure of the documents concerned. Consequently, the action brought by TGI was dismissed.[167]

In *Ryanair* v *Commission*,[168] delivered a few months later, the General Court aligned itself with the principles laid down by the ECJ in the *TGI* judgment. The case involved several decisions by which the Commission rejected requests for access to certain administrative files concerning State aid allegedly granted to Ryanair and made by the latter under Regulation No 1049/2001 while the administrative investigations were still ongoing. The Commission based its refusals, inter alia, on the exception relating to the protection of the purpose of investigations (ie, the third indent of Article 4(2) of that Regulation). The General Court dismissed the appeals brought by Ryanair against these decisions, reiterating the general presumption that disclosure of documents contained in the administrative file relating to a State aid procedure, in principle, undermines protection of the objectives of investigation activities. The General Court confirmed that the Commission was thus entitled to refuse access to all the documents without first making a concrete, individual examination of their content.[169] The General Court clarified that the general presumption can be rebutted but only if the applicant's confirmatory application (and not after the adoption of the refusal decision) identifies 'expressly and individually' the documents that he considers not to be covered by that presumption and he adduces sufficient evidence and arguments to that effect.[170] The Court's position is rather strict particularly because at the time that the applicant makes his confirmatory application he does not (normally) know the content of the documents requested. Accordingly, in practice, it could be difficult for an applicant to comply with these requirements and hence to rebut the presumption.

The judgment in *NLG* v *Commission*[171] adds little to the discussion, since the General Court mainly ruled on issues of reasoning. In these cases, the applicant, Navigazione Libera del Golfo (NLG), had requested access, under Regulation No 1049/2001, to the full text of a Commission decision authorising the grant of aid by Italy to certain shipping companies. NLG requested access, in particular, to analytical data, including detailed elements of the extra annual costs linked to the public service obligations of one of these companies with respect to passenger transport services on the Naples-Beverello/Capri line. By two separate decisions, the Commission rejected the request. In the first decision, it considered that

[166] *Commission v Technische Glaswerke Ilmenau*, n 7 above, para 67.
[167] ibid, paras 67, 68, 70–71.
[168] *Ryanair v Commission*, n 57 above.
[169] ibid, paras 70–71.
[170] ibid, paras 75–80.
[171] Joined Cases T-109/05 and T-444/05 *NLG v Commission*, judgment of 24 May 2011 nyr.

disclosure of the data concerned could undermine the commercial interests of the shipping companies (ie, the first indent of Article 4(2) of Regulation No 1049/2001). In the second decision, it based its refusal on the exception set out in Article 4(5) of Regulation No 1049/2001, claiming that the Italian authorities explicitly objected to disclosure. Following two actions for annulment brought by NLG, the General Court annulled the first decision in part and the second in its entirety. With respect to the first decision, it held, inter alia, that the Commission had correctly applied the exception relating to the protection of the commercial interests to refuse disclosure of part of the data concerned since they amounted to business secrets[172] (they would reveal some elements of the relevant costs). It should be noted that paragraphs 131 to 135 of the judgment could be understood to mean that – in other circumstances – the General Court would be ready to extend the general presumption from the *TGI* judgment to a situation where a refusal to allow access to documents contained in a State aid file is based on the exception set out in the first indent of Article 4(2) of Regulation No 1049/2001.

CONCLUSION

The question in the title of this contribution calls clearly for an affirmative answer. Although the general presumption recognised by the ECJ in the *TGI* judgment does not exclude all rights of public access to documents contained in the Commission's file in State aid proceedings, it obviously sets out more onerous conditions, and does so at the expense of the principle of transparency. First, once it is established that the documents covered by a request for access relate to a State aid investigation, the general presumption allows the Commission to reject that request without carrying out a concrete, individual examination of these documents. This is difficult to reconcile with the consistent case law according to which the risk of harm to the interest protected by the exception must be reasonably foreseeable and not purely hypothetical. More generally, it could be argued that such a solution (which may result in whole categories of documents being de facto automatically covered by one of the exceptions to the right of access), although it is justified both by the need to preserve the effectiveness of the State aid procedural rules and by practical reasons, goes against the spirit of Regulation No 1049/2001. Second, while it is true than the general presumption can be rebutted, the fact remains that, in practice, it is extremely difficult for an applicant to do so.

The *TGI* judgment leaves certain questions open. First, one may wonder whether the general presumption is confined to State aid matters or whether it will also be extended to other areas of EU competition law. In view of the very specific nature of the procedure for reviewing State aid, the former approach might be followed. However, I would be more inclined to see the second approach

[172] ibid, paras 141–42.

prevail. The reasoning followed by the ECJ in the *TGI* judgment could equally apply to antitrust and merger proceedings in which third party access to the file is also strictly limited. Further, it should be stressed that the ECJ's reasoning is based, inter alia, on the distinction between the administrative and the legislative activities of the institutions,[173] a wider access to documents being required in the latter case. The fact that the *TGI* general presumption could be applied to administrative procedures other than those for reviewing State aid is illustrated by the recent judgment in *LPN* v *Commission*,[174] where the General Court held that the Commission was entitled to rely on such presumptions to refuse to disclose documents contained in an infringement proceedings file.[175] The future decisions of the ECJ on the appeals brought against *Éditions Odile Jacob* v *Commission* and *Agrofert* v *Commission* as well as the future decisions of the General Court on some pending cases[176] should hopefully clarify the issue.

Second, neither the ECJ in the *TGI* judgment nor the General Court in *Ryanair* v *Commission* stated expressly whether the Commission is entitled to invoke the general presumption only where, at the time the request for access is made, the State aid investigation is still ongoing.[177] At first sight, this seems to be the case. To my mind, indeed, the main reason advanced by the ECJ in the *TGI* judgment to justify the general presumption – that is, the need to ensure that the *inter partes* procedure provided for by Article 108(2) TFEU is strictly limited to the Member State responsible for granting the aid – is no longer valid once the Commission has taken a final decision on the State aid measures concerned. However, it could be argued that the general presumption also applies if, at the time of the request for access, that decision is the subject of judicial proceedings before the General Court (action for annulment) or the ECJ (appeal). It cannot be excluded, indeed, that were the decision annulled the Commission might be obliged to re-open the administrative procedure. The fact that the General Court rejected a similar argument in *VKI* v *Commission* and in *Éditions Odile Jacob* v *Commission* is probably not decisive in that regard, because those judgments predate *TGI*. Further, that argument might find some support in paragraph 77 of *Sweden* v *MyTravel and Commission*, where the ECJ, in order to assess the relevance (for the application of the exception relating to the protection of the decision-making process) of the

[173] *Commission v Technische Glaswerke Ilmenau*, n 7 above, para 60 where the ECJ stated: 'Moreover, it is important to note that, in contrast with cases where the Community institutions act in the capacity of a legislature, in which wider access to documents should be authorised pursuant to recital 6 of Regulation No 1419/2001 . . ., documents relating to procedures for reviewing State aid . . ., fall within the framework of administrative functions specifically allocated to the said institutions by Article [108 TFEU]'.

[174] Case T-29/08 *LPN v Commission*, judgment of 9 September 2011 nyr, paras 123–29.

[175] It could, however, be argued that the extension of the general presumptions system to infringement proceedings is justified by the fact that these proceedings display some similarities to procedures for reviewing State aid.

[176] Case T-344/08 *EnBW Energie Baden-Württemberg v Commission*, Case T-380/08 *Netherlands v Commission*; Case T-437/08 *CDC Hydrogene Peroxide v Commission*.

[177] In both cases, it was not necessary to rule on that issue or, more generally, on the temporal scope of the exception relating to the protection of the purpose of inspections, investigations, and audits, since the administrative investigations were still ongoing.

fact that the documents requested related to 'an administrative procedure that has already been closed', drew a clear distinction between the situation where the final (competition) decision concerned is no longer subject to any appeal proceedings[178] and the facts at issue in *TGI*. Finally, it should be borne in mind that the exception set out in the third indent of Article 4(2) of Regulation No 1049/2001 'is designed not to protect investigations as such but the purpose of those investigations'.[179] The application of that exception is therefore not limited to a specific investigation. Again, the future decisions of the ECJ on the appeals brought against *Éditions Odile Jacob* v *Commission* and *Agrofert* v *Commission* should clarify the issue of the temporal scope of the exception.

Third, one may wonder whether a similar general presumption could also be invoked where the refusal to disclose documents contained in an administrative file[180] is based on exceptions other than that relating to the protection of the purpose of inspections, investigations, and audits, and, in particular, on the exception for the protection of commercial interests. In *NLG* v *Commission*, the Commission, in reply to a written question from the Court on the consequences to be inferred from the *TGI* judgment, appears to have proposed an analogous solution and, as mentioned above, the General Court does not appear to have rejected it as a matter of principle. A general presumption to the effect that the disclosure of documents would undermine the protection of commercial interests could perhaps be justified where access is requested to a merger file.

[178] See n 118 above.

[179] Case T-194/04 *Bavarian Lager v Commission* [2007] ECR II-4523, para 149.

[180] In *Sweden and ors v API and Commission*, n 9 above, para 94, the ECJ stated with respect to judicial (and not administrative) activities, that there is 'a general presumption that disclosure of the pleadings lodged by one of the institutions in court proceedings would undermine the protection of those proceedings, for the purposes of the second indent of Article 4(2) of Regulation No 1049/2001, while those proceedings remain pending'.

29

Transparency – An Everlasting Challenge for the European Union

VIRPI TIILI*

PRELIMINARY REMARKS

I WOULD LIKE to start with an anecdote. I believe it was in 1996 when my dear friend and colleague Judge Pernilla Lindh and I were having a general discussion on transparency, which at the time was a rather novel legal issue in the European Union (EU). I remember very well the following remark made by Judge Lindh: 'You can't annul a Commission's refusal to give access to certain documents only because you are Nordic'. Of course she was right.

The interest in transparency and especially access to documents increased thanks to the accession of Sweden and Finland to the EU in the beginning of 1995. It was also at this time that, due to the Swedish accession to the EU, Judge Lindh was nominated the first Swedish judge to the General Court – known at that time as the Court of First Instance of the European Communities. A general right of public access to documents was for a long time an unknown subject in the Community legal order. The rule seemed to be secrecy or confidentiality: each institution could decide by itself whether it wanted to grant access to a document requested; institutions could even, with relative ease, decide that all documents were secret, except those which had already been released to the public. It was a long way indeed to achieve the objective of giving a right of access to all citizens of the EU.[1] Transparency was improved only after increased pressure for the democratisation of the EU decision-making, following the 'no' vote in the Danish referendum on the Maastricht Treaty. The situation has been described as follows:

> Perhaps the penny began to drop after the first Danish referendum on Maastricht, followed by the narrow squeak in the French referendum. There was a panic that people

* Former Judge of the General Court of the European Union.

[1] H Ragnemalm, 'Démocratie et Transparence: sur le Droit Général d'Accès des Citoyens de l'Union Européenne aux Documents Détenus par les Institutions Communautaires' in Giuffrè (ed), *Scritti in onore di Giuseppe Federico Mancini* (Rome, Giuffrè, 1998) 819, 821.

might be becoming disaffected with the European dream. Leaders started thinking about how to bring the EU institutions 'closer to the citizens'.[2]

The history and development of transparency and public access to documents in the EU Treaties and legislation extend from the Maastricht Treaty in 1992 to the Lisbon Treaty in 2009.[3] It has been a long journey and, fortunately, the EU transparency regime is still evolving.

The first step towards including transparency in EU legislation was the incorporation of Declaration No 17 into the Maastricht Treaty in 1992[4] which states that '[t]he Conference considers that transparency of the decision-making process strengthens the democratic nature of the institutions and the public's confidence in the administration'. The following year, on 6 December 1993, the Council and the Commission approved a Code of Conduct concerning public access to Council and Commission Documents,[5] designed to establish the principles governing access to the documents held by them. Only one year later, the first case dealing with access to documents of the institutions was brought before the General Court.[6]

1995 was also the year when the Office of the European Ombudsman, established by the Maastricht Treaty, started to function. The Office of the Ombudsman has made an important contribution to promoting transparency and public access to documents.[7] As Jacob Söderman, the first European Ombudsman, a Finn, has stated: 'As European Ombudsman, I have a particular responsibility in relation to transparency'.[8]

A major development for transparency in the EU took place with the entry into force of the Treaty of Amsterdam on 1 May 1999 and the introduction of Article 255 which explicitly recognised that EU citizens and natural and legal persons residing in the EU have the right of access to European Parliament, Council and Commission documents – such right being subject, however, to general prin-

[2] V Deckmyn and I Thomson (eds), *Openness and Transparency in the European Union* (Maastricht, European Institute of Public Administration, 1998) 57.

[3] Since the entry into force of the Lisbon Treaty on 1 December 2009, Art 255 TEC is now Art 15 TFEU.

[4] Declaration on the Right of Access to Information, [1992] OJ C191/101.

[5] [1993] OJ L340/41.

[6] Case T-194/94 *Carvel and Guardian Newspaper v Council* [1995] ECR II-02765. In this case the Council had refused Mr John Carvel, European Affairs Editor of The Guardian newspaper, access to documents relating to the Council's deliberations. The General Court found that the Council did not balance the interest of citizens gaining access to its documents against its own interest in maintaining the confidentiality of its deliberations when the Council considered that its Rules of Procedure did not allow the disclosure. In this first access to documents case decided before the adoption of Regulation No 1049/2001, under the Code of Conduct ([1993] OJ L340/41), the General Court annulled the contested decision.

[7] See about the Ombusdman's activities in this field, I Harden, 'The European Ombudsman's Efforts to Increase Openness' in V Deckmyn (ed), *Increasing Transparency in the European Union* (Maastricht, European Institute of Public Administration, 2002). See also J Heliskoski and P Leino, 'Darkness at the Break of Noon: The Case Law on Regulation No 1049/2001 on Access to Documents' (2006) 43 *CML Rev* 735, 779.

[8] J Söderman, 'The Role and Impact of the European Ombudsman in Access to Documentation and the Transparency of Decision-making' in Deckmyn and Thomson, *Openness and Transparency in the European Union*, n 2 above, 75.

ciples, limits and provisions to be determined and elaborated by such institutions. A new milestone in the development of public access to documents was reached by Regulation (EC) No 1049/2001 of the European Parliament and of the Council of 30 May 2001 regarding public access to European Parliament, Council and Commission documents (Regulation No 1049/2001).[9] This Regulation defined the principles, conditions and limits to the right of access to documents held by the three institutions, codified the existing case law from the General Court and the ECJ and thus provided a stronger legal basis to public access to documents. The Regulation, in force since 3 December 2001,[10] has been criticised for not protecting efficiently enough the right to access to documents.[11]

Transparency in the EU is a very broad theme; much has been written about the topic during the last 15 years and the case law of the Union Courts on the subject is quite voluminous with some 150 judgments.[12] This article will, thus, focus on one specific aspect, that is, the exception laid down in Article 4(1)(b) of Regulation No 1049/2001. According to this provision, the institutions shall refuse access to a document where disclosure would undermine the protection of privacy and the integrity of the individual, in particular in accordance with Community legislation regarding the protection of personal data.[13]

ACCESS TO DOCUMENTS AND EXCEPTIONS

Regulation No 1049/2001 is designed to ensure the greatest possible transparency of the decision-making process of public authorities and the information on which they base their decisions. The Regulation aims at facilitating, as far as possible, the exercise of the right of access to documents and the promotion of good administrative practices.[14]

The beneficiaries and scope of Regulation No 1049/2001 can be summarised as follows: the right of access to documents belongs to all citizens of the EU and to any natural or legal person residing, or having its registered office, in a Member

[9] [2001] OJ L145/43.

[10] See especially for the pre-Regulation regime in case law, C Naômé, 'The Case Law of the Court of Justice and the Court of First Instance of the European Communities on Transparency: From Carvel to Hautala II (1995–2001)' in Deckmyn, *Increasing Transparency in the European Union?*, n 7 above, 147–98; Heliskoski and Leino, n 7 above, 735–81.

[11] See, eg ME De Leeuw, 'The Regulation on Public Access to European Parliament, Council and Commission Documents in the European Union: Are Citizens Better Off?' (2003) 28 *EL Rev* 324.

[12] Judge Lindh has acted as a judge in a number of important transparency rulings of the General Court, see, eg Case T-174/95 *Svenska Journalistförbundet v Council* [1998] ECR II-2289; Case T-105/95 *WWF UK v Commission* [1997] ECR II-313; Case T-204/99 *Mattila v Council and Commission* [2001] ECR II-2265; Case T-83/96 *van der Wal v Commission* [1998] ECR II-545.

[13] All opinions presented in this article are strictly personal ones. I also want to thank Senior Counsel Inga Korpinen, associate lawyer Ms Mari Antila and my former référendaire, Market Court Judge Nina Korjus for their valuable remarks and our fruitful discussions when writing this article.

[14] According to recital 4 of Regulation No 1049/2001, '[t]he purpose of this Regulation is to give the fullest possible effect to the right of public access to documents and to lay down the general principles and limits on such access in accordance with Article 255(2) of the EC Treaty'.

State. The Regulation applies to all documents held by EU institutions covered by the Regulation, that is, the European Parliament, the Council and the Commission. In this context, it must be borne in mind that the Regulation applies not only to documents created by these EU institutions but also to other documents held by them, including documents drawn up or received by them, in all areas of activity of the EU. There is no obligation to state reasons for an application to have access to a document held by an EU institution.[15]

Access to documents constitutes the main rule and a decision to refuse access is valid only if it is based on one of the exceptions laid down in Article 4 of Regulation No 1049/2001. The Regulation proceeds from the premise that while all documents of the institutions should be accessible to the public, certain public and private interests should be protected by way of exceptions. Where necessary to safeguard their ability to carry out their tasks, the EU institutions should be entitled to protect their internal consultations and deliberations. According to Article 4 of the Regulation, the institutions shall refuse access to a document, for example, where disclosure would undermine the protection of the public interest as regards public security, defence and military matters and international relations (Article 4(1)(a)), privacy and the integrity of the individual (Article 4(1)(b)), commercial interests, court proceedings and legal advice, the purpose of inspections, investigations and audits (Article 4(2)) or the institution's decision-making process (Article 4(3)). Any exceptions must be construed and applied restrictively so as not to defeat the general principle enshrined in the Regulation.

RELATIONSHIP BETWEEN ACCESS TO DOCUMENTS AND PROTECTION OF PERSONAL DATA

According to Article 4(1)(b) of Regulation No 1049/2001, the institutions shall refuse access to a document where disclosure would undermine the protection of privacy and the integrity of the individual – in particular in accordance with Community legislation regarding the protection of personal data. This exception raises the question of possible conflict between the protection of two fundamental rights of equal value: public access to documents and protection of personal data.

Protection of personal data as a fundamental right means that everyone has the right to respect for his private and family life, home and communication. This fundamental right consists of the right to the protection of personal data concerning him or her, the right that such personal data should be processed on the basis of the consent of the person concerned and that the person should also have the right of access to the data collected on him or her.[16]

[15] Art 6(1).

[16] The Charter of Fundamental Rights of the European Union, proclaimed in Nice on 7 December 2000, [2000] OJ C364/1, Arts 7 and 8. See also Art 8 of the European Convention for the Protection of Human Rights and Fundamental Freedoms, signed in Rome on 4 November 1950 (ECHR).

How has this potential conflict between these two fundamental rights been solved in secondary EU legislation, that is, Regulation No 1049/2001 and Regulation No 45/2001?[17] The problem is that these Regulations governing access to documents and protection of personal data do not explicitly indicate which principle should prevail. In the recitals of the said Regulations there is only a kind of cross-reference to the respective principles. According to recital 15 of Regulation No 45/2001

> Access to documents, including conditions for access to documents containing personal data, is governed by the rules adopted on the basis of Article 255 of the EC Treaty the scope of which includes Titles V and VI of the Treaty on European Union.

On the other hand, protection of personal data is explicitly mentioned in Recital 11 of Regulation No 1049/2001 stating that:

> In principle, all documents of the institutions should be accessible to the public. . . . In assessing the exceptions, the institutions should take account of the principles in Community legislation concerning the protection of personal data, in all areas of Union activities.

As to the relationship between the right of access to documents and the protection of personal data, it should be noted that, while a person requesting access to documents is not required to justify the request and does not have to demonstrate any interest in having access to the documents requested under Article 6(1) of Regulation No 1049/2001, Article 8(b) of Regulation No 45/2001 requires that the recipient of personal data establishes the necessity of having the data transferred. Moreover, according to Article 18 of Regulation No 45/2001, the data subject has the right to object to the processing of data concerning him or her, subject to only a few exceptions – for example, cases where the processing of data is necessary for compliance with a legal obligation to which the controller[18] is subject. In the absence of a clear legal obligation to disclose personal data to the public, in fact, the data protection rules seem to make it quite difficult to disclose personal data for reasons of transparency, at least without the consent of the data subject. The central question remains whether the data protection rules should be applied strictly, leaving the institutions no means to disclose the information without the consent of the data subject, or whether these rules should be applied in a more flexible manner making the disclosure possible for the sake of transparency.

[17] Regulation (EC) No 45/2001 of the European Parliament and of the Council of 18 December 2000 on the protection of individuals with regard to the processing of personal data by Community institutions and bodies and on the free movement of such data, [2001] OJ L8/1.

[18] According to Art 2(d) of Regulation No 45/2001 '"controller" shall mean the Community institution or body, the Directorate-General, the unit or any other organisational entity which alone or jointly with other determines the purposes and means of processing of personal data; where purposes and means of processing are determined by a specific Community act, the controller or the specific criteria for its nomination may be designated by such Community act'.

DATA PROTECTION AND ACCESS TO DOCUMENTS IN CASE LAW: *BAVARIAN LAGER*

In the *Bavarian Lager* cases, the EU courts and the Advocate General were confronted with the relationship between access to documents and protection of data in the application of Article 4(1)(b) of Regulation No 1049/2001.[19] All three gave a partly different solution and reasoning to this problem. The *Bavarian Lager* cases have lately been some of the most discussed decisions concerning access to documents. The Bavarian Lager Company probably could not have guessed, when lodging its first application in 1997,[20] how significantly the decisions of the General Court would affect the discussion about transparency in the EU.

The facts in the *Bavarian Lager* case are not straightforward: in 1993, the Bavarian Lager Company, an importer of German beer to the United Kingdom, triggered an investigation of a UK law that blocked foreign beer providers from supplying the domestic market. Following its investigation, the Commission brought proceedings against the UK for failure to fulfil its obligations. In 1996, a meeting took place that included officials from the Commission and the UK, and lobbyists from a brewery association. Bavarian Lager was not allowed to attend the meeting.

A year later, the Commission closed its proceedings after the UK changed its legislation. Bavarian Lager asked the Commission for the full minutes of the 1996 meeting. In 2004, the Commission finally blanked out the names of five participants, arguing that Bavarian Lager had not established either an express and legitimate purpose or any need for such disclosure, as was allegedly required by Regulation No 45/2001 on the protection of personal data, and that, therefore, the exception concerning the protection of private life applied.

Action before the General Court

Bavarian Lager brought an action for annulment of the Commission's decision to the General Court. The General Court found that the list of participants in the minutes contained personal data, since the persons who had taken part in that meeting could be identified. However, the mere fact that a document contains such data does not necessarily mean that the privacy or integrity of the person concerned is affected, even though professional activities are not in principle excluded from the concept of 'private life'.

According to the General Court, it was decisive for the application of Article 4(1)(b) regarding the names of the participants to the 11 October 1996 meeting to examine whether public access to the five names in question was capable of actu-

[19] Case T-194/04 *Bavarian Lager v Commission* [2007] ECR II-4523; Case C-28/08 P *Commission v Bavarian Lager* [2010] ECR I-6055.

[20] Case T-309/97 *Bavarian Lager v Commission* [1999] ECR II-3217.

ally and specifically undermining the protection of the privacy and integrity of the persons concerned.[21] The General Court stated that the participants could be identified by the list of meeting participants appearing in the minutes. The list classified the participants by reference to the bodies in the name and on behalf of whom they were present, described by their title, the initial of their forename, their surname and where relevant, the service, department or association to which they belonged within those bodies.[22]

The General Court held that in this concrete case, disclosure of names of representatives of a collective body was not capable of actually and specifically affecting the protection of the privacy and integrity of the persons concerned. In this interpretation the General Court gave major importance to Article 8 ECHR as interpreted by the European Court of Human Rights (ECtHR).[23] The mere presence of the name of the person concerned in the list of participants at a meeting, under the heading of the body which that person represented, did not have that effect, and the protection of the privacy and integrity of the persons concerned was not compromised. Since the exception relating to the protection of privacy and integrity did not apply, the objection of those persons could not prevent disclosure. Moreover, Bavarian Lager did not have to prove any need for disclosure of the names for the purposes of Article 8(b) of Regulation No 45/2001.[24]

According to the General Court, if the disclosure of personal data (here the names of the five meeting participants) falls outside the scope of the privacy exception, Article 4(1)(b) does not apply even if the personal data falls within the scope of data protection laid down in Regulation No 45/2001.[25] In its judgment, the General Court found that Article 4(1)(b) hinders the application of data protection rules when communication of data would not undermine protection of the privacy and the integrity of the individual concerned. This has been seen as a narrow interpretation of the exception in Article 4(1)(b) as covering only privacy and not data protection.[26]

Some in the media portrayed the judgment as a victory for campaigners who wanted to bring into the light the thousands of lobbyists in Brussels seeking to shape EU public policy[27] and who wanted to improve transparency in EU decision-making[28]. Others lamented that the judgment could discourage whistle-blowers from coming forward with information about anti-competitive behaviour, if the Commission is unable to guarantee confidentiality and protection from undue harm or damage.[29]

[21] *Bavarian Lager*, n 19 above, para 120.

[22] ibid, paras 121, 122.

[23] ibid, paras 114, 115, 118, 119.

[24] Opinion of AG Sharpston in *Bavarian Lager*, n 19 above, para 138.

[25] See further H Kranenborg, 'Access to Documents and Data Protection in the European Union: On the Public Nature of Personal Data' (2008) 45 *CML Rev* 1079.

[26] D Adamski, 'How Wide is "the Widest Possible"? Judicial Interpretation of the Exceptions to the Right of Access to Official Documents Revisited' (2009) 46 *CML Rev* 521, 528, 529.

[27] Reuters UK, 8 November 2007.

[28] EU Observer, 9 November 2007; Bloomberg USA, 8 November 2007.

[29] Global Competition Review Online, 9 November 2007 (www.globalcompetitionreview.com).

Appeal by the Commission and the Opinion of the Advocate General

The Commission brought an appeal against the *Bavarian Lager* judgment. It criticised first the General Court's statement that Article 8(b) (need to demonstrate necessity of the transfer) of Regulation No 45/2001 on protection of personal data may not apply in the case of personal data in documents held by an institution falling under Regulation No 1049/2001.[30] According to the Commission, no provision of either Regulation requires or permits this provision to be disabled in order to permit a norm under the Regulation on public access to documents to have effect. The General Court therefore, in the Commission's view, erred in law in interpreting Article 4(1)(b) of Regulation No 1049/2001 so as require a provision of Community law to be set aside. Secondly, according to the Commission, the General Court erred in law when adopting a restrictive interpretation of the exception in Article 4(1)(b) and in limiting the scope of the said exception to cases where there is a clear risk of undermining the protection of the right of privacy and integrity of the individual and excluding at the same time Community legislation on data protection from its scope in a case where access was requested to personal data contained in a document.

Both the Advocate General and the Court of Justice concurred that the General Court had erred in law in its interpretation of Article 4(1)(b) of Regulation No 1049/2001 but they otherwise diverged in their interpretation of the relationship between the two Regulations.

Advocate General Sharpston pointed out first that the General Court erred in holding that the disclosure to third parties of the names of those present at the October 1996 meeting did not amount to a potential interference with private life. The Advocate General underlined that the interpretation of the concept of 'interference' adopted by the ECtHR is very broad. Simply put, the names identify the persons. In principle, therefore, their disclosure – even in the context of business relations – constitutes a potential interference of that kind.[31] Secondly, the Advocate General thought that the General Court failed to apply the test for justification 'of interference in private life in accordance with the criteria laid down in Article 8(2) ECHR'.[32]

Third, the Advocate General stated that the General Court failed to pay sufficient attention to the second limb of Article 4(1)(b), under which regard must be had to Community legislation on protection of personal data. This error caused the General Court to reach a result that wholly sacrificed the fundamental right to data protection in the interests of transparency. In reality, however, the inference to be drawn from a proper reading of the two Regulations is that no such conflict need exist.[33]

[30] *Bavarian Lager*, n 19 above, paras 107, 108.

[31] Opinion of AG Sharpston in *Bavarian Lager*, n 19 above, paras 153, 155, 185.

[32] ibid, paras 154 and 185; para 154: '. . . namely that the measure must be in accordance with the law, the measure must be necessary in a democratic society and it must be proportionate to the aims pursued . . .'.

[33] ibid, para 184.

In this perspective Advocate General Sharpston presented an interesting and creative interpretation of the relationship between the two Regulations in question based on the scope of Regulation No 45/2001 as defined in its Article 3(1) and (2).[34] According to the Advocate General, within Regulation No 45/2001, Article 3(2) should *not* be read as subordinate or ancillary to Article 3(1). They simply correspond to different aspects of defining the 'scope' of the measure. Article 3(2) deals with *what* is regulated (automatic and semi-automatic data processing and non-automatic processing of data from, or destined for inclusion in, databases (or, as the Regulation describes them, 'filing systems')). Article 3(1) of the Regulation deals with *when* it is regulated (that is, when the data controller is engaged in various categories of activity). *Together*, the answers to these two questions determine the scope of Regulation No 45/2001.[35]

In addition, Advocate General Sharpston divided documents which include personal data into two distinct subcategories.[36] The first group consists of documents which contain incidental mention of personal data, where the privacy purpose of compiling the data has little to do with personal data as such, for example, a record of a meeting. A request for such a document has to be regarded simply as a request for public documents and should be handled under Regulation No 1049/2001.[37] But it will also be necessary to apply the Article 8 ECHR test in order to assess whether access to the full unexpurgated document should be refused because unrestricted disclosure would violate the data subjects' privacy.[38] In the second subcategory are documents which essentially contain a large quantity of personal data, for instance, a list of persons and their characteristics. An application for such a document, even if it has been submitted under Regulation No 1049/2001, constitutes in reality a 'disguised' request for disclosure of personal data, because the document's content reveals that de facto access to personal data is what is sought.[39] This document forms storage of personal data. By virtue of Article 3(2) of Regulation No 45/2001 the documents in this second subcategory fall under this Regulation.[40]

As to the application of the two Regulations, the main points in the final outcome of the Opinion of the Advocate General can be summarised as follows:[41]

> The document requested, the full text of the minutes of the October 1996 meeting, unquestionably concerned with 'the policies, activities and decisions' of a Community

[34] Art 3(1) reads: 'This Regulation shall apply to the processing of personal data by all Community institutions and bodies insofar as such processing is carried out in the exercise of activities all or part of which fall within the scope of Community law'. Art 3(2) reads: 'This Regulation shall apply to the processing of personal data wholly or partly by automatic means, and to the processing otherwise than by automatic means of personal data which form part of a filing system or are intended to form part of a filing system'.

[35] Opinion of AG Sharpston in *Bavarian Lager*, n 19 above, paras 108–17, 150, 170.

[36] ibid, paras 159–61.

[37] ibid, para 161.

[38] ibid, para 164.

[39] ibid, para 160.

[40] ibid, para 161.

[41] ibid, paras 188–90.

institution and contained incidental mention of personal data in the form of the names of those attending the meeting, as minutes usually do.

Bavarian Lager's request was not a disguised request for personal data, but a request for an ordinary official document.

Because the request did not involve 'the processing of personal data wholly or partly by automatic means' or 'the processing otherwise than by automatic means of personal data which form part of a filing system or are intended to form part of a filing system', it did not fall within the scope of Article 3(2) of Regulation No 45/2001. Thus the request had to be handled solely and exclusively on the basis of Regulation No 1049/2001.

Judgment of the Court of Justice

The last word in this long-lasting dispute was finally pronounced by the Grand Chamber of the ECJ in June 2010.[42] The core of the ECJ's reasoning can be found in paragraphs 61–65 of the ruling:

> 61. According to Article 1(1) of Regulation No 45/2001, the purpose of that Regulation is to 'protect the fundamental rights and freedoms of natural persons, and in particular their right to privacy with respect to the processing of personal data'. That provision does not allow cases of processing of personal data to be separated into two categories, namely a category in which that treatment is examined solely on the basis of Article 8 of the ECHR and the case-law of the European Court of Human Rights relating to that article and another category in which that processing is subject to the provisions of Regulation No 45/2001.
>
> 62. It is clear from the first sentence of recital 15 of Regulation No 45/2001 that the Union legislature has pointed to the need to apply Article 6 EU and, by that means, Article 8 of the ECHR, '[w]here such processing is carried out by Community institutions or bodies in the exercise of activities falling outside the scope of this Regulation, in particular those laid down in Titles V and VI of the [EU Treaty in its version prior to the Treaty of Lisbon]'. By contrast, such a reference was not found necessary for processing carried out in the exercise of activities within the scope of that Regulation, given that, in such cases, it is clearly Regulation No 45/2001 itself which applies.
>
> 63. It follows that, where a request based on Regulation No 1049/2001 seeks to obtain access to documents including personal data, the provisions of Regulation No 45/2001 become applicable in their entirety, including Articles 8 and 18 thereof.
>
> 64. By not taking account of the reference in Article 4(1)(b) of Regulation No 1049/2001 to the legislation of the Union concerning the protection of personal data and thus to Regulation No 45/2001, the General Court dismissed at the outset, in paragraph 107 of the judgment under appeal, the application of Article 8(b) of Regulation No 45/2001, and, in paragraph 109 of the judgment under appeal, the application of Article 18 of Regulation No 45/2001. And yet those articles constitute essential provisions of the system of protection established by Regulation No 45/2001.

[42] *Bavarian Lager*, n 19 above, paras 188–90.

> 65. Consequently, the particular and restrictive interpretation which the General Court gave to Article 4(1)(b) of Regulation No 1049/2001 does not correspond to the equilibrium which the Union legislature intended to establish between the two Regulations in question.

According to the ECJ, the Commission had rightly decided that the list of participants to the October meeting contained personal data and that in requiring, for persons who had not given their express consent, that Bavarian Lager establishes the necessity of having those personal data transferred, the Commission complied with Article 8(b) of Regulation No 45/2001.[43] With these considerations the ECJ decided to set aside the judgment of the General Court in so far as it annulled the contested decision of the Commission.[44]

The judgment of the ECJ has been seen as giving quite strong protection for personal data and unnecessarily restricting access to documents.[45] The ruling concerns a very large number of administrative documents held by the EU institutions: all documents which include a reference, by name or otherwise, to an individual even in his professional capacity, who has not given his consent to the disclosure. Of course, in general the administration can make public an expurgated version of the documents, where for instance the names are blanked out. Nevertheless such a version might not be very useful for the applicant.[46]

THE WAY FORWARD – COMMISSION PROPOSALS OF 2008 AND 2011

Despite the rather rapid development of the transparency regulations, access to documents in the EU has not been, and is still not, an easy question to tackle. We all know that the traditions and interests of Member States diverge more than what might be suggested by the seemingly resemblant letter of their respective statutory instruments.[47]

This is reflected in the interest – or lack thereof – that Member States have shown in intervening in access to document litigation. Not surprisingly, Sweden often intervenes in support of the applicant. Denmark, Finland and the Netherlands are also quite active. On the other side, France, the United Kingdom and Germany have

[43] ibid, paras 77, 78.

[44] ibid, para 81.

[45] According to Leino: 'If the ruling of General Court was challenged because it relied heavily on Regulation No 1049/2001 – on the basis of which the application had, after all, been made – the ruling of the Court of Justice does not have seem to have paid much attention to this Regulation or to the Treaty provisions guaranteeing openness in the activities of the Union. As it seems that for the applicant the five names were of considerable interest, the Court's argument that the Commission had 'sufficiently complied with its duty of openness' seems odd. It is not the amount of information – however trivial – to which access is granted that counts, but granting access to the information that the applicant is interested in gaining'. P Leino, 'Just a Little Sunshine in the Rain: The 2010 Case Law of the European Court of Justice on Access to Documents' (2011) 48 *CML Rev* 1215, 1238.

[46] See also for instance Opinion of the EDPS, OJ 2009, para 48 in the context of Commission Proposal 2008; Leino n 45 above, 1239.

[47] Kranenborg, n 25 above, 1079, 1102–05.

quite often supported the institution denying access. For example, in the *Bavarian Lager* case the Council and the United Kingdom intervened in support of the Commission, whereas Finland, Sweden and Denmark intervened in support of Bavarian Lager.[48] This goes along with the two tendencies among the Member States, some of which have in principle 'open' administration, while others are traditionally considered to have a more 'closed' administration.[49]

On 30 April 2008 the Commission made a proposal for a new Regulation of the European Parliament and of the Council regarding public access to European Parliament, Council and Commission documents.[50] In addition, the Commission made, on 21 March 2011, another proposal for a Regulation amending Regulation No 1049/2001, with the view of taking account of the extension of the institutional scope of the right of access in Article 15(3) TFEU. This provision introduced by the Treaty of Lisbon extends the public right to access to documents of all Union institutions, bodies, offices and agencies with the limitation that only the administrative documents of the Court of Justice, the European Central Bank and the European Investment Bank fall within the scope of public right of access.[51]

As to the 2008 Proposal, the Commission proposes to delete the current Article 4(1)(b) containing the exception related to privacy and integrity of the individual, instead of which the Commission proposes a new provision, Article 4(5), according to which:

> Names, titles and functions of public office holders, civil servants and interest representatives in relation with their professional activities shall be disclosed unless, given the particular circumstances, disclosure would adversely affect the persons concerned. Other personal data shall be disclosed in accordance with the conditions regarding lawful processing of such data laid down in EC legislation on the protection of individuals with regard to the processing of personal data.[52]

The Commission claims in its explanatory memorandum that the proposed amendments also aim to take into account the General Court's *Bavarian Lager* judgment. According to the Commission, Article 4(1)(b) is reformulated in order to clarify the relationship between the Regulation on Public Access to Documents and the Regulation on Protection of Personal Data. However, both the European Data Protection Supervisor (EDPS) and the Committee for Constitutional Law of

[48] As to the interventions, see also other recent landmark cases: Case C-139/07 P *Commission v Technische Glaswerke Ilmenau* [2010] ECR I-5885; Joined Cases C-514/07, C-528/07 and C-532/07 *Sweden v Commission* [2010] ECR I-8533; C-506/08 P *Sweden and MyTravel v Commission*, judgment of 21 July 2011 nyr.

[49] A Tournepiche, 'Vers de nouveaux champs d'application pour la transparence administrative en droit communautaire. Réflexion sur le Livre vert "Initiative européenne en matière de transparence"' (2007) 43 *Cahiers de Droit Européen* 625.

[50] Commission, 'Proposal for a Regulation of the European Parliament and of the Council regarding public access European Parliament, Council and Commission documents', COM(2008) 229 final.

[51] Commission, 'Proposal for a Regulation of the European Parliament and of the Council amending Regulation (EC) No 1049/2001 regarding public access to European Parliament, Council and Commission documents', COM(2011) 137 final.

[52] COM(2008) 229 final 4.

the Parliament of Finland have stated in their opinions that the proposal does not reflect the General Court's ruling.[53]

The Commission's 2008 proposal covers, as such, the factual situation in the *Bavarian Lager* case – that is – a request to access to the names, titles or functions of lobbyists. But the personal data that shall be disclosed is determined narrowly. As for all the other personal data, the Regulation on Protection of Personal Data should apply with the need to justify and demonstrate an interest in having access to the document requested. By doing so, the proposal deletes any reference to the harm to 'the privacy and the integrity' of the individual as a necessary threshold to justify a refusal to access to documents containing personal data. In fact, it shifts the focus from the Regulation on Access to Documents to the Regulation on Protection of Personal Data. Consequently, it jeopardises the principle that the Regulation on Access to Documents is the general norm governing access to documents in the EU.[54] Though the Commission's 2008 Proposal has been heavily criticised by a number of authors, Member States and the EDPS, after the ECJ's ruling in *Bavarian Lager* several among them have concluded that the Commission's Proposal is, after all, more favourable to transparency than the ECJ's judgment.[55]

Taking into account the divergent opinions of different Member States and the discussion of the European Parliament it does not seem very likely, at the time of writing, that the Commission will be able to make any progress with the 2008 Proposal in the near future. Given the multitude of economic and other serious problems the EU is facing today, it is unlikely that the transparency Regulation will be the centre of the focus of Europe.

[53] Opinion of the European Data Protection Supervisor on the Proposal for a Regulation of the European Parliament and of the Council regarding public access to European Parliament, Council and Commission documents, of 30 June 2008 (OJ C2/7), para 44; Committee Report PeVL 22/2008 vp of 16 October 2008 of the Committee for Constitutional Law of the Finnish Parliament.

[54] See, eg I Harden, 'The Revision of Regulation 1049/2001 on Public Access to Documents' (2009) 15 *European Public Law* 239, 249; Leino, n 45 above, 1239–41.

[55] See, for instance Leino, n 45 above, 1240.

Index

[illegible]

[illegible]